D1315164

RHCSA™/RHCE® Red Hat® Linux Certification Study Guide, Sixth Edition

Exams (EX200 & EX300)

Michael Jang

McGraw Hill

New York   Chicago   San Francisco   Lisbon   London   Madrid
Mexico City   Milan   New Delhi   San Juan   Seoul   Singapore   Sydney   Toronto

The McGraw·Hill Companies

Cataloging-in-Publication Data is on file with the Library of Congress.

McGraw-Hill books are available at special quantity discounts to use as premiums and sales promotions, or for use in corporate training programs. To contact a representative, please e-mail us at bulksales@mcgraw-hill.com.

RHCSA™/RHCE® Red Hat® Linux Certification Study Guide (Exams EX200 & EX300), Sixth Edition

1234567890 DOC DOC 10987654321

ISBN: Book p/n 978-0-07-176566-4 and CD p/n 978-0-07-176568-8
of set 978-0-07-176565-7

MHID: Book p/n 0-07-176566-2 and CD p/n 0-07-176568-9
of set 0-07-176565-4

Sponsoring Editor Timothy Green	**Technical Editor** Elizabeth Zinkann	**Production Supervisor** Jim Kussow
Editorial Supervisor Patty Mon	**Copy Editor** Robert Campbell	**Composition** Eurodesign-Peter Hancik
Project Editor LeeAnn Pickrell	**Proofreader** Susie Elkind	**Illustration** Eurodesign-Peter Hancik
Acquisitions Coordinator Stephanie Evans	**Indexer** Rebecca Plunkett	**Art Director, Cover** Jeff Weeks

For the young widows and widowers,
may they find the courage to face their fears,
to navigate their way through the pain,
and to find hope for a brighter future.

ABOUT THE CONTRIBUTORS

Author

Michael Jang (RHCE, LPIC-2, UCP, LCP, Linux+, MCP) is currently a full-time writer, specializing in operating systems and networks. His experience with computers goes back to the days of jumbled punch cards. He has written other books on Linux certification, including *LPIC-1 in Depth, Mike Meyers' Linux+ Certification Passport*, and *Sair GNU/Linux Installation and Configuration Exam Cram*. His other Linux books include *Linux Annoyances for Geeks, Linux Patch Management*, and *Mastering Fedora Core Linux 5*. He has also written or contributed to books on Microsoft operating systems, including *MCSE Guide to Microsoft Windows 98* and *Mastering Windows XP Professional, Second Edition*.

Technical Editor

Elizabeth Zinkann is a logical Linux catalyst, a freelance technical editor, and an independent computer consultant. She was a contributing editor and review columnist for *Sys Admin Magazine* for ten years. As an editor, some of her projects have included *Mastering Fedora Core Linux 5, LPIC-1 in Depth, Linux Patch Management*, and *Linux All-in-One Desk Reference for Dummies, Fourth Edition*. In a former life, she also programmed communications features, including ISDN at AT&T Network Systems.

CONTENTS AT A GLANCE

CONTENTS

ACKNOWLEDGMENTS

I personally would like to thank the following people:

- **Nancy E. Cropley, R.N. (d. 2002):** It's now been nearly ten years since you've left this world, but I continue to hold your spirit in my heart, and I hope you can still see the joy of the world through my eyes. You are my hero, even today. I hope you can see how happy I am with Donna, but I will always miss you.

  As a political activist, you fought for what you believed in: social justice, peace, and universal health care. You were never afraid to go to jail to support your beliefs. Your example is helping me find a backbone for life.

  As a nurse for the homeless, you helped so many who are less fortunate. You worked tirelessly in the clinics, in the shelters, and on the streets. Your efforts eased the pain of so many people. And you saved lives.

  As an Internet entrepreneur, you showed me how to be happy pursuing a life working from home. You made it possible for me to have the freedom to be, instead of getting stuck in the corporate world.

  Nancy, you were my partner, my lover, my soul mate. You helped me find joy in this world. I take your lessons with me. I thank you for everything you've done.

- **My wife Donna:** With hope and love, you make my life worth living. With your love and support, my life is now better than ever.
- All the incredibly hard-working folks at McGraw-Hill: Stephanie Evans, Tim Green, LeeAnn Pickrell, Robert Campbell, Susie Elkind, and Rebecca Plunkett for their help in launching a great series and being solid team players.

PREFACE

Linux is thriving. Red Hat is at the forefront of the Linux revolution. And Red Hat Certified System Administrators (RHCSA) and Engineers (RHCE) are making it happen.

Even in the current economic recovery, business, education, and governments are cost conscious. They want control of their operating systems. Linux—even Red Hat Enterprise Linux—saves money. The open-source nature of Linux allows users to control and customize their operating systems. While there is a price associated with Red Hat Enterprise Linux (RHEL), the cost includes updates and support. Now with KVM, it's possible to set up a cluster of virtual, independent installations of RHEL (and other operating systems) on a single physical computer. Many companies are already converting rooms full of physical systems into closets of just a few systems, each configured with banks of virtual machines. As an RHCSA and an RHCE, you can join in that revolution.

While there's a cost associated with a supported version of RHEL, you don't need to pay for such support. As I describe shortly, there are trial and student subscriptions that you can use, along with freely available "rebuilds" of RHEL that are built on the same source code.

A "rebuild" is software that is built by a third party from the same source code as the original "build." On the other hand, a "clone" is built from different source code.

Security is another reason to move toward Linux. The U.S. National Security Agency has developed its own version of the Linux kernel to provide context-based security in a system known as Security-Enhanced Linux (SELinux). RHEL has made SELinux a key part of a layered security strategy.

The RHCSA and RHCE exams are difficult. Available historical data suggests that less than 50 percent of first-time candidates pass the RHCE exam. But do not be intimidated. While there are no guarantees, this book can help you prepare for and pass the RHCSA and RHCE exams. And these same skills can help you in your career as a Linux administrator. Just remember, this book is not intended to be a substitute for the Red Hat prep courses that I describe shortly.

To study for this exam, you should have a network of at least three Linux computers. Since the RHCSA focuses on virtual machines, you're encouraged to use KVM-based systems for two of the computers. After configuring a service, especially a network service, it can be helpful to check your work from another computer.

Getting Red Hat Enterprise Linux

The Red Hat exams are based on your knowledge of *Red Hat* Enterprise Linux. But here's a significant change. The RHCSA objectives specify a number of points associated with virtual machines. The default RHEL 6 solution uses the Kernel-based Virtual Machine (KVM). Red Hat supports KVM as a host only on physical systems with 64-bit CPUs. Therefore, to study for the KVM-related objectives for the RHCSA, you'll need physical hardware that can handle a 64-bit version of RHEL 6. (However, 64-bit systems may not be absolutely required; 32-bit versions of KVM based on the same Red Hat source code are available from Scientific Linux, described later.)

And you should expect to install two or more virtual machines on that 64-bit physical system. Virtual hosts work better on systems with multiple CPUs or systems with multicore CPUs. So to avoid hardware that slows your studies, you'll want a 64-bit physical system with at least 2GB and preferably 4GB of RAM. (I prepared this book on a 64-bit system with 8GB of RAM.) If you're using a laptop system, read the information from https://bugzilla.redhat.com/show_bug.cgi?id=667485. If the listed bug has not been resolved by the time you read this, the useful lifetime of your hard drive may depend on it. As Red Hat Network updates are not explicitly listed as a requirement in the Red Hat Exam Prep guide, a "trial" subscription or a rebuild distribution is sufficient for these purposes. If you want a full subscription, which can help you test features associated with the Red Hat Network, the price depends on the hardware and the desired level of technical support. I've emphasized *Red Hat* solely to focus on distributions that use Red Hat source code, including the "rebuilds" described in this section (and more).

With Red Hat Enterprise Linux 6, Red Hat has modified its offerings into three categories:

■ RHEL Server includes varying levels of support, which themselves fall into three basic categories:

   ■ Regular 32- and 64-bit systems based on AMD and Intel CPUs; the cost varies with the number of CPU sockets and supported virtual guests.

- IBM POWER Systems; the cost varies with the number of CPU sockets.
- IBM System z.
- RHEL Desktop includes varying levels of support suitable for workstations.
- RHEL Add-Ons are available in areas such as High Availability, Resilient Storage, Load Balancing, and more.

I prepared this book with the help of RHEL 6 server. It appears that RHEL 6 workstation also has the server packages required for the RHCSA and/or the RHCE exams. While RHEL is released under open-source licenses, that applies just to the source code. Access to the binary packages requires the purchase of a subscription. And that can be expensive.

One of the advantages of an enterprise-level operating system is stability. When an enterprise upgrades to RHEL 6, it counts on the ability to revise its configuration just once. Security updates and bug fixes should then be automatic. To that end, Red Hat takes every possible measure to avoid forcing enterprises to revamp their systems just for a point release such as RHEL 6.1. If an enterprise had to revise its configuration files for any major service for any point release, the costs associated with Red Hat's enterprise-level operating systems would also rise.

For the same reasons, point releases do not affect the Red Hat exam objectives. While RHEL 6.1 improves the performance of the operating system, incorporates bug fixes, and collects security updates, it has not changed any of the defaults of any of the configuration files described in the book.

When RHEL 6.2, RHEL 6.3, and so on, are released in future months, I expect a similar result. Otherwise, Red Hat would likely lose customers, as enterprises would encounter unplanned costs to update their systems. I've monitored RHEL releases closely for nearly a decade. I've seen no evidence of a change to the exam objectives based just on a point release. If in doubt, monitor the content of the exam objectives listed at www.redhat.com/certification/rhcsa/objectives/ and www.redhat.com/certification/rhce/objectives/.

If you're just studying for the exams, trial subscriptions are available from the appropriate product page; for example, a link to "Free Evaluation Software" is available at www.redhat.com/rhel/server. An account on the Red Hat Network (RHN) is required. "Personal" e-mail addresses (such as those associated with certain search engines) are not accepted for RHN accounts. While trial subscriptions only support updates for 30 days, updates can also be tested using the mirror repositories associated with rebuild distributions. And you can download the same operating system (for the trial period) from the same sources as paying Red Hat users.

If you're a student or a member of an educational institution with a .edu e-mail address, academic subscriptions are available. As of this writing, the cost of an academic subscription to RHEL Server ($60) is a significant discount over the least expensive standard RHEL Server subscription ($349).

But if you don't have an .edu or business e-mail address, you don't have to pay for a full or a trial subscription to prepare for the RHCE exam. There are several projects dedicated to "rebuilds" of Red Hat Enterprise Linux. The source code for almost all RHEL RPM packages is released under the Linux General Public License (GPL) or related open-source licenses. This gives anyone the right to build Red Hat Enterprise Linux from the Red Hat released source code.

The source code is released in Source RPM package format, which means the RPM packages can be built using the **rpmbuild** commands described in Chapter 12. The developers behind rebuild distributions have all revised the source code to remove Red Hat trademarks. Some, like Scientific Linux 6, are freely available; others, like Oracle Linux, require registration and compliance with certain criteria such as U.S. export control laws.

You can select and download the rebuild that most closely meets your needs. I have tried several of the rebuilds, including those developed by Scientific Linux and Community Enterprise Linux (CentOS). As this book is going to print, Microsoft has announced support on its virtual machine software for CentOS.

The rebuilds of RHEL are freely available; however, you should have a high-speed Internet connection. While these rebuilds do make slight modifications to RHEL source code (primarily to remove or replace Red Hat trademarks), I have not seen any difference that would impair your ability to study for the Red Hat exams.

- **Scientific Linux** Formerly known as Fermi Linux, it includes a lot of intellectual firepower associated with the Fermi National Accelerator Lab as well as CERN, the lab associated with Tim Berners-Lee, the person most commonly credited with the invention of the World Wide Web.

- **Community Enterprise Linux** The Community Enterprise Operating System (CentOS) rebuild developed by the group at www.centos.org appears solid to me. This group probably has the largest community among the rebuilds. Some messages from CentOS developers suggest that CentOS-6 should be released by the time this book is available in print.

For the exams based on Red Hat Enterprise Linux 6, avoid Fedora Linux. Even though RHEL 6 is based loosely on Fedora 12, Fedora 13, and even Fedora 14, there are sufficient differences in the look and feel of all three releases that may prove confusing for the purpose of an exam. And I definitely recommend that you not use other distributions, as the Red Hat exams are based on Red Hat Enterprise Linux. In many cases, the changes that would be standard on a different Linux release would lead to trouble on RHEL 6.

For Instructors and More

I encourage everyone to read this guide for instructors. This book is organized to help you prepare coursework for, or study for, one exam at a time.

Perhaps the biggest change in this book is designed to help the instructor. Since the RHCSA and RHCE are two entirely separate exams, I've reorganized this book to reflect those changes. If you're studying just for the RHCSA, read Chapters 1 through 9. If you're studying just for the RHCE, read Chapter 1 and Chapters 10 through 17. The same changes will help you as a certification candidate as well, so you know what skills to gain for each exam.

Many, perhaps most, candidates have trouble finishing the tasks associated with the RHCSA and RHCE exams in the time allotted. One way to save time during these exams is to keep things simple. While it's important to read over the questions carefully, it's also important not to overdo things. For example, there's no need to configure virtual servers for the RHCSA exam. As suggested by one RHCE-related objective, it's normally sufficient to "configure the service for basic operation."

Every chapter includes at least 12 "fill-in-the-blank" questions. While there are no multiple-choice or file-in-the-blank questions on Red Hat exams, such questions can still help measure student mastery of chapter material. And the fill-in-the-blank format puts a premium on the practical experience required on the exam.

In the same fashion, for the RHCE exam, unless directed to do otherwise, keep everything as simple as possible. Don't include that production list of suspect IP addresses in your firewall for the exam. Configure a firewall that allows access to just the services specified. Simple firewalls are faster to set up, and many security experts suggest that simple firewalls are safer.

As several services are covered in both the RHCSA and RHCE objectives, several services are covered in multiple chapters. For example, the RHCSA objective on the HTTP and FTP services are covered in Chapter 1. The RHCE objectives related to the same services are addressed in Chapters 14 and 16, respectively.

Chapter 1 is dedicated to helping you set up a system to study for both exams. It also describes the experience associated with both exams in some detail. While it also addresses the RHCSA objective associated with the configuration of an FTP server and an HTTP server, it provides instructions on how to configure files from the RHEL 6 DVD as an installation server. With a few tips described in Chapter 7, you'll also be able to set up this installation server as a **yum**-based repository for the server services associated with the RHCE.

If you're studying for the RHCE exam, you may want to refer to some RHCSA chapters. In fact, the RHCE chapters assume that you've set up KVM-based virtual machines based on the instructions described in Chapter 2, as well as the networked repository configured in Chapter 1, Lab 2.

Before an Exam

There is no way to cram for a Red Hat exam. But as athletes warm up before a race, you can "warm up" before a Red Hat exam. Reread each of the objectives associated with the target exam. Review the "Scenario & Solution" tables available toward the end of most chapters. Reflect on the software that has to be installed, the files that need to be configured, and the key commands that you might have trouble remembering otherwise.

Remember, the Red Hat RHCSA and RHCE exams are designed to test candidate qualifications as Linux systems administrators and engineers. If you pass either of these exams, it's not because you've memorized a canned set of answers—it's because you have a set of Linux administrative skills and know how to use them under pressure, whether it be during an exam or in a real-world situation.

In This Book

Some of the key components of this book can be found only on the CD. Starting in Chapter 2 (Lab 2), the lab questions can be found on the CD, in a format that allows you to read the questions on a test system. The lab answers are still found at the end of each chapter. If you mount the CD on a Linux system on the /media directory, you'll find the labs in the /media/Chapter2, /media/Chapter3, /media/Chapter4 directories, and so on. The CD also includes the content of the book in electronic format. It's available in PDF files, in the same chapter directories as the labs. The PDFs do not include the labs in electronic format.

The Glossary is available only on the CD. Assuming the same mount directory, you'll find the Glossary in the /media/Glossary directory. For more information on the contents of the CD, along with how to install Adobe Reader for Linux, see Appendix F.

The RHCSA and the RHCE are separate exams. If you're studying for both exams, this book can help you remember the differences. For example, you'll find coverage of the RHCSA objectives on the Secure Shell (SSH) as a client in Chapter 2. In contrast, the RHCE objectives related to SSH as a server are covered in Chapter 11.

While this book is organized to serve as an in-depth review for the RHCSA and RHCE exams for both experienced Linux and Unix professionals, it is not intended as a substitute for Red Hat courses, or more important, real-world experience. Nevertheless, each chapter covers a major aspect of the exam, with an emphasis on the "why" as well as the "how to" of working with and supporting RHEL as a systems administrator or engineer. As the actual RHCSA and RHCE objectives (www.redhat.com/certification/rhcsa/objectives and www.redhat.com/certification/rhce/objectives) change with every release of RHEL (and even sometimes between releases), refer to the noted URL for the latest information.

Red Hat says it's important to have real-world experience to pass their exams, and they're right! However, for the RHCSA and RHCE exams, they do focus on a specific set of Linux administrative skills, as depicted in the respective objectives. This book is intended to help you take advantage of the skills you already have—and more important, to brush up in those areas where you may have a bit less experience.

This book includes relevant information from Red Hat Enterprise Linux 6 (RHEL 6). There are significant changes from Red Hat Enterprise Linux 5. Several key differences between RHEL 5 and RHEL 6 include

- Better support for "large-scale, centrally managed enterprise deployments"
- Default support for KVM-based virtual machines, with a focus on performance, scalability, and security
- Improved power management
- The ext4 filesystem, which is now the default and supports files of up to 16TB
- Easier-to-configure SELinux

There are many more key features; those that I believe are relevant to the RHCSA and RHCE exams, as defined by the publicly available course outlines and the Exam Prep guide, are also included in this book.

While it's a risky practice in service, it is fastest to administer RHEL during the exam by logging in to the root user account. The command prompt and **PATH** assume use of that account. When logged in to the root account, you'll see a command line prompt similar to

```
[root@server1 root]#
```

As the length of this prompt would lead to a number of broken and wrapped code lines throughout this book, I've normally abbreviated the root account prompt as

```
#
```

Be careful. The hash mark (#) is also used as a comment character in Linux scripts and programs; for example, here is an excerpt from /etc/inittab:

```
# Default runlevel. The runlevels used are:
```

When logged in as a regular user, you will see a slightly different prompt; for user michael, it would typically look like the following:

```
[michael@server1 michael]$
```

Similarly, I've abbreviated this as

```
$
```

There are a number of command lines and blocks of code interspersed throughout the chapters. Commands embedded within regular text, such as **ls -l**, are shown in bold. User entries, and some variables in regular text, are also shown in bold.

Sometimes commands exceed the available length of a line. Take this example:

```
# virt-install -n outsider1.example.org -r 768 --disk
path=/var/lib/libvirt/images/outsider1.example.org.img -l
ftp://192.168.122.1/pub/inst -x "ks=ftp://192.168.122.1/pub/ks1.
cfg"
```

Unless this command is carefully formatted, line breaks might appear in unfortunate places, such as between the two dashes in front of the **--disk** switch. One way to address this is with the backslash (\ ), which "escapes" the meaning of the carriage return that follows. (The backslash can also "escape" the meaning of a space, making it easier to work with multiple-word filenames.) So, while the following command appears as if it is on four different lines, the backslashes mean that Linux reads it as one single command:

```
# virt-install -n outsider1.example.org -r 768 --disk \
path=/var/lib/libvirt/images/outsider1.example.org.img \
-l ftp://192.168.122.1/pub/inst \
-x "ks=ftp://192.168.122.1/pub/ks1.cfg"
```

Sometimes the differences are subtle. Sometimes, you'll need to actually type in a command or a response to a question at a command line. In that case, you'll see an instruction such as type **y**. Alternatively, some menus require a keypress; for instance, you may be asked to press P to access a password prompt. In that case, the letter *p* is not added to the screen when you press that letter. In addition, the A, despite its appearances, is in lowercase. In contrast, A is the uppercase version of that letter.

One area where some publishers have trouble is with the double-dash. Some publishing programs change the double-dash to an "em dash." But that can be a problem. The double-dash is common in many Linux commands. For example, the following command lists all packages currently installed on the local system:

```
# rpm --query --all
```

When I ran this command on my RHEL 6 system, it listed 1300 packages.

In contrast, the following command lists all files in all packages on the local system:

```
# rpm --query -all
```

When I ran this command on my RHEL 6 system, it listed 133,000 files, a rather different result. So pay attention to the dashes, and rest assured that the team who produced this book took care to make sure that double-dashes are shown as is!

Exam Readiness Checklist

At the end of the introduction, you will find an Exam Readiness Checklist. These tables have been constructed to allow you to cross-reference the official exam objectives with the objectives as they are presented and covered in this book. The checklist also allows you to gauge your level of expertise on each objective at the outset of your studies. This should allow you to check your progress and make sure you spend the time you need on more difficult or unfamiliar sections. References have been provided for the objective exactly as the vendor presents it, the section of the study guide that covers that objective, and a chapter and page reference.

In Every Chapter

For this series, we've created a set of chapter components that calls your attention to important items, reinforce important points, and provide helpful exam-taking hints. Take a look at what you'll find in every chapter:

- ■ Every chapter begins with the **Certification Objectives**—the skills you need to master in order to pass the section on the exam associated with the chapter topic. The Objective headings identify the objectives within the chapter, so you'll always know an objective when you see it.

■ **Exam Watch** notes call attention to information about, and potential pitfalls in, the exam. These helpful hints are written by authors who have taken the exams and received their certification—who better to tell you what to worry about? They know what you're about to go through!

■ **Practice Exercises** are interspersed throughout the chapters. These are step-by-step exercises that allow you to get the hands-on experience you need in order to pass the exams. They help you master skills that are likely to be an area of focus on the exam. Don't just read through the exercises; they are hands-on practice that you should be comfortable completing. Learning by doing is an effective way to increase your competency with a product. Remember, the Red Hat exams are entirely "hands-on"; there are no multiple-choice questions on these exams.

■ **On the Job** notes describe the issues that come up most often in real-world settings. They provide a valuable perspective on certification- and product-related topics. They point out common mistakes and address questions that have arisen from on-the-job discussions and experience.

■ **Inside the Exam** sidebars highlight some of the most common and confusing problems that students encounter when taking a live exam. Designed to anticipate what the exam will emphasize, they will help ensure you know what you need to know to pass the exam. You can get a leg up on how to respond to those difficult-to-understand labs by focusing extra attention on these sidebars.

■ **Scenario & Solution** sections lay out potential problems and solutions in a quick-to-read format.

■ The **Certification Summary** is a succinct review of the chapter and a restatement of salient skills regarding the exam.

✓■ The **Two-Minute Drill** at the end of every chapter is a checklist of the main points of the chapter. It can be used for last-minute review.

Q&A ■ The **Self Test** offers "fill in the blank" questions designed to help test the practical knowledge associated with the certification exams. The answers to these questions, as well as explanations of the answers, can be found at the end of each chapter. By taking the Self Test after completing each chapter, you'll reinforce what you've learned from that chapter. This book does not include multiple-choice questions, as Red Hat does not include any such questions on its exams.

■ The **Lab Questions** at the end of the Self Test section offer a unique and challenging question format that requires the reader to understand multiple chapter concepts to answer correctly. These questions are more complex and more comprehensive than the other questions, as they test your ability to take all the knowledge you have gained from reading the chapter and apply it to complicated, real-world situations. Starting with Chapter 2, Lab 2, all lab questions are available only on the CD, consistent with the electronic format associated with the Red Hat exams. Remember, the Red Hat exams contain *only* lab-type questions. If you can answer these questions, you have proven that you know the subject!

Additional Resources

Some readers will want to go further. Perhaps the best way to do so is with Red Hat documentation. Much of what I learned about RHEL 6 comes from the documents available at http://docs.redhat.com/docs/en-US/Red_Hat_Enterprise_Linux/. For our purposes, perhaps these are the most important of these guides:

■ **Installation Guide**   As the Red Hat exams are given on preconfigured systems, the Installation Guide is somewhat less important. But it includes key information on Kickstart.

■ **Deployment Guide**   The Deployment Guide is perhaps the most important with respect to Red Hat recommendations on how services can be configured for basic operation.

■ **Security-Enhanced Linux**   The Security Enhanced Linux guide details the options that that can help further secure your systems.

Some Pointers

Once you've finished reading this book, set aside some time to do a thorough review. You might want to return to the book several times and make use of all the methods it offers for reviewing the material:

■ *Reread all the Exam Watch notes*. Remember that these notes are written by authors who have taken the exam and passed. They know what you should expect—and what you should be on the lookout for.

■ *Review all the Scenario & Solution sections* for quick problem solving.

■ *Retake the Self Tests*. Focus on the labs, as there are no multiple-choice (or even "fill in the blank") questions on the Red Hat exams. I've included "fill in the blank" questions just to test your mastery of the practical material in each chapter.

■ *Complete the exercises*. Did you do the exercises when you read through each chapter? If not, do them! These exercises are designed to cover exam topics, and there's no better way to get to know this material than by practicing. Be sure you understand why you are performing each step in each exercise. If there is something you are not clear on, reread that section in the chapter.

The Red Hat Exam Challenge

This section covers the reasons for pursuing industry-recognized certification, explains the importance of your RHCSA or RHCE certification, and prepares you for taking the actual examination. It gives you a few pointers on how to prepare, what to expect, and what to do on exam day.

This book covers every published exam objective at the time of this writing. For the latest objectives, see www.redhat.com/certification/rhcsa/objectives/ and www.redhat.com/certification/rhce/objectives/. Red Hat has also published a syllabus for its prep courses for these exams, described shortly. While the published exam objectives are accurate, the prep course syllabi provide additional information. Each Red Hat prep course provides an excellent grounding in systems administration, network administration, security, and more. To that end, this book also includes coverage based on the public syllabi of Red Hat courses RH124, RH134, and RH254, described later.

Nevertheless, this book is not intended to be a substitute for any Red Hat course.

Leaping Ahead of the Competition!

Red Hat's RHCSA and RHCE certification exams are hands-on exams. As such, they are respected throughout the industry as a sign of genuine practical knowledge. If you pass, you will be head and shoulders above the candidate who has passed only a "standard" multiple-choice certification exam.

Red Hat has offered its hands-on exams since 1999. They've evolved over the years. As detailed in Chapter 1, the RHCSA is a 2.5-hour exam, and the RHCE is now a 2.0-hour exam. The requirements are detailed in the Exam Readiness Checklist later in this introduction. While the passing score for these exams is not currently published, it was at one time 70 percent for the relevant Red Hat exams on RHEL 5. Published third-party reports suggest that passing score has not changed.

Why a Hands-On Exam?

Most certifications today are based on multiple-choice exams. These types of exams are relatively inexpensive to set up and easy to proctor. Unfortunately, many people without real-world skills are good at taking multiple-choice exams. In some cases, the answers to these multiple-choice exams are already available online. This results in problems on the job with "certified" engineers who have an image as "paper tigers" and do not have any real-world skills.

In response, Red Hat wanted to develop a certification program that matters. In our opinion, they have succeeded with the RHCSA, the RHCE, and their other advanced certifications.

Linux administrators sometimes have to install Linux on a computer or virtual machine. In fact, the RHCSA includes several objectives on this subject. Depending on the configuration, they may need to install Linux from a central source through a network. Installing Linux is not enough to make it useful. Administrators need to know how to configure Linux: add users, install and configure services, create firewalls, and more.

---

exam

ⓦatch   *The RHCSA and RHCE exams are Red Hat exams. Knowledge of Unix or a Linux distribution such as Ubuntu is certainly helpful, as well as experience with services like Apache, SMB, NFS, DNS, iptables, and SSH. But it is important to* *know how to set up, configure, install, and debug these services under Red Hat Enterprise Linux (or rebuild distributions that use the same source code, such as Scientific Linux, CentOS, or Oracle Linux).*

Prepare for the RHCSA and RHCE Exams

With the release of RHEL 6, Red Hat has introduced the RHCSA as a replacement for the RHCT. The topics associated with the RHCSA are now independent of the RHCE. Yes, there is some overlap. For example, SELinux is covered on both exams. But the coverage is different. The RHCSA and RHCE certifications are based on separate exams.

The RHCSA is now the entry-level Red Hat certification. While you can take the RHCE exam first, Red Hat won't award you an RHCE unless you've also passed the RHCSA exam. Some candidates take both exams on the same day. As discussed in Chapter 1, Red Hat has also publicly stated that their exams are now "presented electronically." This book will include (most) labs and sample exams in electronic format on the CD that accompanies this book.

Work with Red Hat Enterprise Linux. Install it on a computer that you don't need for any other purpose. Configure the services described in this book. Find different ways to secure each of these services. Test the results from systems both inside and outside a network.

As you read this book, you'll have the opportunity to install RHEL several times. If you have more than one computer, you'll be able to install RHEL over a network. Then you can work with the different network services. Test out each service as you configure it, preferably from another computer on your network. Testing your work becomes especially important when verifying the security features that are required on an exam, or in a production network.

Red Hat Certification Program

Red Hat offers several courses that can help you prepare for the RHCSA and RHCE. Most of these courses are four or five days long. In some cases, the courses are offered electronically.

These aren't the only Red Hat courses available; there are a number of others related to the Red Hat Certified Architect (RHCA), Red Hat Certified Virtualization Administrator (RHCVA), Red Hat Certified Datacenter Specialist (RHCDS), and Red Hat Certified Security Specialist (RHCSS) certifications. But study this first; the RHCSA and RHCE are prerequisites for all Red Hat certifications but the RHCVA.

Should You Take an RHCSA/RHCE Course?

This book is *not* intended as a substitute for any particular Red Hat RHCSA or RHCE prep course. However, the topics in this book are based in part on the topics listed in the course outlines provided at www.redhat.com/courses. By design, these topics may help Linux users qualify as real-world administrators and can also be used as such. Just remember, Red Hat can change these topics and course outlines at any time, so monitor www.redhat.com for the latest updates. Table 1 describes those courses associated with the RHCSA and RHCE exams.

TABLE I	Red Hat RHCSA/RHCE-Related Courses

Course	Description
RH124	System Administration I: Core system administration skills
RH134	System Administration II: Command line skills for Linux administrators (RH135 without the RHCSA exam)
RH135	System Administration II with the RHCSA exam
RH199	RHCSA rapid-track course for experienced administrators
RH200	RH199 + RHCSA exam
EX200	Just the RHCSA exam
RH254	System Administration III: Advanced security and server skills
RH255	System Administration III with the RHCE exam
RH299	Red Hat rapid-track course for experienced administrators
RH300	RH299 + RHCSA and RHCE exams
EX300	The RHCE exam

The courses given by Red Hat are excellent. The Red Hat instructors who teach these courses are highly skilled. If you have the skills, it is the best way to prepare for the RHCSA and RHCE exams. If you feel the need for classroom instruction, read this book, and then take the appropriate course.

If you're not sure you're ready for the course or book, read Chapter 1. It includes a rapid overview of the requirements associated with the Red Hat RHCSA and RHCE certifications. If you find the material in Chapter 1 to be overwhelming, consider one of the books noted near the start of the chapter, or one of the other lower-level Red Hat courses. In addition, Chapter 1 includes a lab that prompts you to examine the requirements of the Linux Professional Institute for its level 1 certification (LPIC-1). Linux geeks like yourself who are ready to study for the Red Hat exams often take the LPIC-1 exams first.

Alternatively, you may already be familiar with the material in this book. You may have the breadth and depth of knowledge required to pass the RHCSA and RHCE exams. In that case, use this book as a refresher to help you focus on the skills and techniques needed to pass both exams.

Signing Up for the RHCSA/RHCE Course and/or Exam

Red Hat provides convenient web-based registration systems for the courses and test. To sign up for any of the Red Hat courses or exams, navigate to www.redhat.com, click the link for Training | Courses, and select the desired course or exam. As shown back in Table 1, exams may be taken as their own independent course. For example, the RHCSA and RHCE exams are associated with courses EX200 and EX300, respectively. Exams may also be taken as part of an online or instructor-led course. Alternatively, contact Red Hat Enrollment Central at training@redhat.com or (866) 626-2994.

Discounts may be available for candidates who have been previously certified as an RHCT or RHCE. Current discounts are shown at https://www.redhat.com /training/specials/. Remember to present any "offer code" before paying for the desired exam.

Before signing up, read current Red Hat policies, available at www.redhat.com /training/policy/. Be aware, Red Hat has sometimes canceled exams for low attendance.

Final Preparations

The Red Hat exams are grueling. Once you have the skills, the most important thing that you can take to the exam is a clear head. If you're tired or frantic, you may miss the easy solutions that are often available. Get the sleep you need the night before the exam. Eat a good breakfast. Bring snacks that can keep your mind in top condition.

The RHCSA exam is two and a half hours long. The RHCE exam is two hours long. In many cases, Red Hat makes it possible for candidates to take both exams in the same day. While it's a terrific convenience for those who have to travel to Red Hat exam facilities (in over 40 cities just in North America), taking the two exams in the same day is like running two world-class marathons. This is an advanced book, not designed for beginners to Unix or Linux. The former "prerequisite skills" have been incorporated in the body of the RHCSA requirements. Accordingly, I've only covered the tools associated with these prerequisites briefly—mostly in Chapters 1 and 3. If you need more information on these prerequisite skills, Red Hat offers other courses (see www.redhat.com/apps/training/); alternatively, read the reference books I've cited in Chapter 1.

INSIDE THE EXAM

The RHCSA and RHCE certifications are associated with two separate exams. However, the RHCE topics generally require skills more advanced than the RHCSA. As they are separate exams, I've cited the associated objectives separately. Watch for updates at www .redhat.com/certification/rhcsa/objectives/ and www.redhat.com/certification/rhce/objectives/.

The RHCSA Exam

TABLE 2	RHCSA Objective Exam Readiness Checklist

RHCSA Exam Readiness Checklist

Certification Objective	Study Guide Coverage	Ch #	Pg #
Category: Understand and Use Essential Tools			
Access a shell prompt and issue commands with correct syntax	Shells, Standard Command Line Tools	3	139, 143
Use **grep** and regular expressions to analyze text streams and file	The Management of Text Files	3	152
Use input/output redirection	Shells	3	139
Access remote systems using SSH	Administration with the Secure Shell	2	112
Access remote systems using VNC	Configure Access with VNC	9	517
Log in and switch users in multi-user runlevels	User and Shell Configuration	8	488
Archive, compress, unpack, and uncompress files using **tar**, **star**, **gzip**, and **bzip2**	Elementary System Administration Commands	9	527
Create and edit text files	The Management of Text Files	3	152
Create, delete, copy and move files and directories	Standard Command Line Tools	3	143
Create hard and soft links	Standard Command Line Tools	3	143
List, set, and change ugo/rwx permissions	Basic File Permissions	4	204
Locate, read, and use system documentation including **man**, **info**, and files in /usr/share/doc	Local Online Documentation	3	163
Category: Operate Running Systems			
Boot, reboot, and shut down a system normally	Bootloaders and GRUB, Between GRUB and Login	5	268, 285
Boot systems into different runlevels manually	Bootloaders and GRUB	5	268
Use single user mode to gain access to a system	Bootloaders and GRUB	5	268
Identify CPU/Memory intensive processes, adjust process priority with **renice**, and **kill** processes	Elementary System Administration Commands	9	527
Locate and interpret system log files	Local Log File Analysis	9	548
Access a virtual machine's console	Configure a Virtual Machine on KVM	2	82

RHCSA Exam Readiness Checklist

Certification Objective	Study Guide Coverage	Ch #	Pg #
Start and stop virtual machines	Configure a Virtual Machine on KVM	2	82
Start, stop, and check the status of network services	A Networking Primer	3	168
Category: Create and Configure File Systems			
Create, mount, unmount, and use ext2, ext3, and ext4 file systems	Volume management and partitions, Filesystem Formats, Filesystem Management	6	333, 351, 381
Mount, unmount, and use LUKS-encrypted filesystems	Volume Encryption with the Linux Unified Key Setup	6	375
Mount and unmount CIFS and NFS network filesystems	Filesystem Management	6	381
Configure systems to mount ext4, LUKS-encrypted and network filesystems automatically	Filesystem Management	6	381
Extend existing unencrypted ext4-formatted logical volumes	Logical Volume Management (LVM)	6	361
Configure and set-GID directories for collaboration	Special Groups	8	500
Create and manage Access Control Lists (ACLs)	Access Control Lists and More	4	212
Diagnose and correct file permission problems	Basic File Permissions	4	204
Category: Deploy, Configure, and Maintain Systems			
Configure networking and hostname resolution statically or dynamically	Network Configuration and Troubleshooting	3	177
Schedule tasks using **cron**	Automate System Administration: **cron** and **at**	9	539
Configure systems to boot into a specific runlevel automatically	Between GRUB and Login	5	285
Install Red Hat Enterprise Linux automatically using Kickstart	Automated Installation Options	2	96
Configure a physical machine to host virtual guests	Configure KVM for Red Hat	2	70
Install Red Hat Enterprise Linux systems as virtual guests	Configure a Virtual Machine on KVM	2	82
Configure systems to launch virtual machines at boot	Configure a Virtual Machine on KVM	2	82

RHCSA Exam Readiness Checklist

Certification Objective	Study Guide Coverage	Ch #	Pg #
Configure network services to start automatically at boot	Control by Runlevel	5	294
Configure a system to run a default configuration HTTP server	Configure Default File Sharing Services	1	51
Configure a system to run a default configuration FTP server	Configure Default File Sharing Services	1	51
Install and update software packages from Red Hat Network, a remote repository, or from the local filesystem	The Red Hat Package Manager, Dependencies and the **yum** Command, More Package Management Tools	7	411, 424, 447
Update the kernel package appropriately to ensure a bootable system	The Red Hat Package Manager	7	411
Modify the system bootloader	Bootloaders and GRUB	5	268
Category: Manage Users and Groups			
Create, delete, and modify local user accounts	User Account Management	8	467
Change passwords and adjust password aging for local user accounts	User Account Management	8	467
Create, delete, and modify local groups and group memberships	User Account Management	8	467
Configure a system to use an existing LDAP directory service for user and group information	Users and Network Authentication	8	493
Category: Manage Security			
Configure firewall settings using **system-config-firewall** or **iptables**	Basic Firewall Control	4	221
Set enforcing and permissive modes for SELinux	A Security-Enhanced Linux Primer	4	235
List and identify SELinux file and process context	A Security-Enhanced Linux Primer	4	235
Restore default file contexts	A Security-Enhanced Linux Primer	4	235
Use boolean settings to modify system SELinux settings	A Security-Enhanced Linux Primer	4	235
Diagnose and address routine SELinux policy violations	A Security-Enhanced Linux Primer	4	235

TABLE 3	RHCE Exam Readiness Objective Checklist

RHCE Exam Readiness Checklist

Certification Objective	Study Guide Coverage	Ch #	Pg #
Category: System Configuration and Management			
Route IP traffic and create static routes	Special Network Options	12	704
Use iptables to implement packet filtering and configure network address translation (NAT)	Firewalls and Network Address Translation	10	573
Use /proc/sys and sysctl to modify and set kernel run-time parameters	Kernel Run-time Parameters	12	689
Configure system to authenticate using Kerberos	Special Network Options	12	704
Build a simple RPM that packages a single file	Create an RPM Package	12	692
Configure a system as an iSCSI initiator that persistently mounts an iSCSI target	Special Network Options	12	704
Produce and deliver reports on utilization (processor, memory, disk, and network)	Set Up System Utilization Reports	17	944
Use shell scripting to automate system maintenance tasks	Automate System Maintenance	12	683
Configure a system to log to a remote system	Configure a System Logging Server	17	949
Configure a system to accept logging from a remote system	Configure a System Logging Server	17	949
Category: Network Services (The following five objectives apply to all network services)			
Install the packages need to provide the service	All RHCE chapters	10–17	563-966
Configure SELinux to support the service	Security-Enhanced Linux, other chapters for each service	10–17	637, 681-966
Configure the service to start when the system is booted	A Security and Configuration Checklist	11	663
Configure the service for basic operation	All RHCE chapters	10–17	563-966
Configure host-based and user-based security for the service	All RHCE chapters	10–17	566-966
Subcategory: HTTP/HTTPS			
Configure a virtual host	Regular and Secure Virtual Hosts	14	801

RHCE Exam Readiness Checklist

Certification Objective	Study Guide Coverage	Ch #	Pg #
Configure private directories	Specialized Apache Directories	14	794
Deploy a basic CGI application	Deploy a Basic CGI Application	14	815
Configure group-managed content	Specialized Apache Directories	14	794
Subcategory: DNS (Candidates are not expected to configure master or slave name servers)			
Configure a caching-only nameserver	Minimal DNS Server Configurations	17	935
Configure a caching-only nameserver to forward DNS queries	Minimal DNS Server Configurations	17	935
Subcategory: FTP			
Configure anonymous-only download	The Very Secure FTP Server	16	908
Subcategory: NFS			
Provide network shares to specific clients	The Network File System (NFS) Server	16	885
Provide network shares suitable to group collaboration	The Network File System (NFS) Server	16	885
Subcategory: SMB			
Provide network shares to specific clients	Samba Services, Samba Troubleshooting	15	833, 869
Provide network shares suitable to group collaboration	Samba Services, Samba Troubleshooting	15	833, 869
Subcategory: SMTP			
Configure a mail transfer agent (MTA) to accept inbound email from other systems	The Configuration of Postfix, The Other SMTP Service: sendmail	13	736, 747
Configure an MTA to forward (relay) email through a smart host	The Configuration of Postfix, The Other SMTP Service: sendmail	13	736, 747
Subcategory: SSH			
Configure key-based authentication	The Secure Shell Server	11	648
Configure additional options described in documentation	The Secure Shell Server	11	648
Subcategory: NTP			
Synchronize time using other NTP peers	The Network Time Server Service	17	953

1

Prepare for Red Hat Hands-on Certifications

T he Red Hat exams are an advanced challenge. While this book covers the Red Hat Certified System Administrator (RHCSA) exam, it provides the foundation for those who want to earn the Red Hat Certified Engineer (RHCE) certification. Red Hat offers several courses to help prepare for these exams, as described in the front matter and in this chapter.

The focus of this chapter is installation, to create a common version of Red Hat Enterprise Linux (RHEL) as a test bed for future chapters. It assumes and describes hardware required to implement Red Hat's default virtual machine (VM) solution, the Kernel-based Virtual Machine (KVM). As rebuild distributions such as the Community Enterprise Operating System (CentOS) and Scientific Linux are essentially identical to RHEL, you should be able to use those solutions too. Just about the only difference between a rebuild and RHEL is the trademarks and the access to repositories, which will be described in Chapter 7.

Those of you familiar with earlier versions of the Red Hat requirements may note the recent changes to the Red Hat exams. Red Hat no longer gives a RHCT exam. It has now been replaced with the RHCSA. While the RHCSA is in many ways similar to the RHCT, there are significant differences. Most RHCSA objectives were covered on the former RHCT exam. However, the RHCSA is certainly not easier than the RHCT; it is just now a prerequisite to the RHCE. The RHCSA also includes a number of requirements that were formerly part of the RHCE objectives.

Nevertheless, Red Hat suggests that candidates for the RHCSA will have one to three years of experience with the bash shell, user administration, system monitoring, basic networking, software updates, and more. Details are described in the introduction to this book.

If you're new to Linux or Unix, this book may not be enough for you. It's not possible to provide sufficient detail, at least in a way that can be understood by newcomers to Linux and other Unix-based operating systems. If after reading this book, you find gaps in your knowledge, please refer to one of the following guides:

■ *Linux Administration: A Beginner's Guide,* by Wale Soyinka (McGraw-Hill, 2008), provides a detailed step-by-step guide to this operating system.

- *Security Strategies in Linux Platforms and Applications,* by Michael Jang (Jones & Bartlett, 2010), gives you a detailed look at how you can secure your Linux system and networks in every possible way.
- *LPIC-1 in Depth,* by Michael Jang (Course Technology PTR, 2009), covers the certification many Linux professionals qualify for prior to working on the RHCSA and RHCE.

Before installing Red Hat Enterprise Linux (RHEL), you need the right hardware. You'll need to have a physical system with a 64-bit CPU capable of hardware virtualization. Details are discussed in the chapter. As such, while the RHCSA and RHCE exams are by and large not hardware exams, some basic hardware knowledge is a fundamental requirement for any Linux administrator. As for the operating system itself, you can purchase a subscription to RHEL, or you can use one of the "rebuild" distributions where the distribution is built by third parties from source code publicly released by Red Hat.

If you're experienced with other Unix-type operating systems such as Solaris, AIX, or HP-UX, prepare to leave some defaults at the door. There are even significant differences between the Ubuntu and Red Hat distributions. When Red Hat developed its Linux distribution, the company made some choices that are not consistent with standard Unix practices. When I took Red Hat's RH300 course, some students with these backgrounds had difficulties with the course and the RHCE exam.

For the purpose of this book, I'll be running most commands as the Linux administrative user, root. Logging in as the root user is normally discouraged unless you're administering a computer. However, since the RHCSA and RHCE exams test your administrative skills, it's appropriate to run commands in this book as the root user. But you'll also need to know how to set up regular users with partial or full administrative privileges.

INSIDE THE EXAM

A Virtual Host

The RHCSA assumes that you know how to "configure a physical machine to host virtual guests." In other words, you need to be able to prepare a system to house VMs where other instances of RHEL (or even other operating systems such as Microsoft Windows) can be installed.

As this is RHEL, this is based on the Red Hat default VM system, KVM. As appropriate rebuild distributions such as CentOS and Scientific Linux use the same source code, they also use KVM. In this chapter, not only will you install RHEL, but also you will install those packages that support KVM.

Default File Sharing Configuration Services

RHCSAs are expected to know how to "Configure a system to run a default configuration HTTP server" and "Configure a system to run a default configuration FTP server." The default Red Hat solutions for these services are the Apache Web server and the very secure FTP (vsFTP) server. While these services can be complex, the steps required to set up these

servers to share files are fairly simple. In fact, no changes are required to the default configuration files for these services. Some of the related steps described in this chapter depend on skills presented in future chapters.

The original release of the RHCSA objectives was worded slightly differently: "Deploy file sharing services with HTTP/FTP." I believe this provides a significant clue to Red Hat's intent with these objectives. To that end, you'll examine how to set up these services as file servers, based on their default configurations.

Using Other Versions of Red Hat

For the purpose of this chapter, you can install RHEL 6 using a paid subscription or from a demonstration DVD. You can also use one of the rebuild distributions. However, while RHEL 6 is based in part on the work done on the Fedora Linux distribution, it's based in part on both the Fedora 12 and 13 releases. So it's possible if you use Fedora 12 or 13, the configuration files may in some cases be quite different from RHEL 6. Later versions of Fedora are likely to have features not found in RHEL 6.

CERTIFICATION OBJECTIVE 1.01

The RHCSA and RHCE Exams

Red Hat first started giving certification exams in 1999. Since that time, their exams have evolved. The former RHCT was a complete subset of the RHCE. Today, the RHCSA now covers topics separate from but closely related to the RHCE.

In addition, Red Hat has focused the exams more on hands-on configuration. Multiple choice questions were removed from the exam in 2003. More recently, in 2009, they simplified the exam by removing the requirement to install Linux on a "bare-metal" system. (However, the changes implemented in 2011 suggest that you need to know how to install Linux over a network on a VM.) In addition, there is no longer a separate troubleshooting portion of the exam. For more information, see www.redhat.com/certification/faq.

exam
Watch

Red Hat provides "pre-assessment" tests for Red Hat RHCSA and RHCE Exam Prep courses. They correspond to the RH134 and RH254 courses, respectively. These tests are available through the Red Hat web pages for each course. Red Hat requires contact information before providing those preassessment tests.

The Exam Experience

Red Hat's certification tests are hands-on exams. As such, they are respected throughout the industry as a sign of genuine practical knowledge. When you pass a Red Hat exam, you will stand head and shoulders above the candidate who has passed only a "standard" multiple-choice certification exam.

When time starts, you'll be faced with a live system. You'll be given actual configuration problems associated with the items listed in the exam objectives for each certification, shown at www.redhat.com/certification/rhcsa/objectives/ and www.redhat.com/certification/rhce/objectives/. Naturally, this book is dedicated to helping you gain the skills described on those web pages.

While you won't have Internet access during the exam, you will have access to online documentation such as man and info pages as well as documentation in the /usr/share/doc/ directories, assuming appropriate packages are installed.

In addition, Red Hat provides the exam in electronic format. While the basic instructions may be in a local language such as English, the RHCSA and RHCE exams are available in 12 different languages: English, Simplified Chinese, Traditional Chinese, Dutch, French, Italian, Japanese, Korean, Portuguese, Russian, Spanish, and Turkish. If one of these alternatives is desired, you should contact Red Hat training to be sure, at training@redhat.com or 1-866-626-2994.

Red Hat also has prep courses for both exams. The outline for those courses are available from www.redhat.com. While this book is not intended as a substitute for such courses, they are consistent with the outline of those courses. This book covers the objectives associated with each of these exams.

---

exam

✪atch *This book's coverage of the items listed in the RHCSA and RHCE exam objectives can be found in the front matter for this book, in Table 2, page xlviii.*

The RHCSA Exam

The RHCSA exam allows you to demonstrate your ability to configure live physical and virtual systems for networking, security, custom filesystems, package updates, user management, and more. In essence, the RHCSA exam covers those skills required to configure and administer a Linux workstation in the enterprise.

The RHCSA exam lasts two and a half hours. When you sit down to take the exam, you'll have tasks to perform on a live RHEL system. Any changes that are made must survive a reboot. When you've completed the given tasks, the person grading the exam will see if the system is configured to meet the requirements. For example, if you're told to "create, delete, and modify local user accounts," it doesn't matter if the associated configuration file has been modified with the vi editor or the graphical User Manager tool. As long as you don't cheat, it's the results that matter.

The RHCE Exam

The RHCE exam tests your ability to configure live physical and virtual servers to configure network services such as Apache, vsFTP, the Network File System (NFS), Samba, the Postfix e-mail service, remote logging, and more. It also tests your ability to handle complex configuration options associated with Security Enhanced Linux (SELinux), firewalls, networking, and more. In essence, if you pass the RHCE exam, hiring managers will know that you're qualified to help manage their enterprises of Linux systems.

The RHCE exam also lasts two hours. When you sit down to take the exam, you'll be given tasks to perform on a live RHEL system. As with the RHCSA, any changes that are made must survive a reboot. In any case, it doesn't matter if you've configured the associated configuration file with the nano editor or a GUI tool. As long as you don't cheat, it's the results that matter.

The topics in the Red Hat preparation courses in a few areas go beyond those listed in the Red Hat Exam Prep guide. While such topics are not currently part of the exam, they may be included in future versions of the Red Hat exams.

If You're Studying "Just" for the RHCSA Exam

Red Hat has been known to make minor changes to the requirements on occasion. Future changes may be based on topics covered in the Red Hat RHCSA Rapid Track course, RH199/RH200. So if you're not planning to take the RHCSA within the next few months, watch the outline for that course. It may in effect be a preview of where Red Hat wants to take the RHCSA exam in the future.

Evolving Requirements

Changes happen to the requirements for the Red Hat exams. You can see that in the differences between the RHCT and the RHCSA. You can see that in the changes to the exam format, where bare-metal installations are no longer required. In fact, that change happened over two years into the life of RHEL 5. Changes happened in the first month after RHEL 6 was released. So when you're preparing for the RHCSA or RHCE exams, watch the associated exam objectives carefully. In addition, Red Hat announced the removal of separate troubleshooting problems from the exams through the WordPress blog publishing site, at http://redhatcertification.wordpress.com/.

CERTIFICATION OBJECTIVE I.02

Basic Hardware Requirements

Now it's time to explore in detail the hardware that Red Hat Enterprise Linux can handle. While some manufacturers now include their own Linux hardware drivers, most Linux hardware support comes from third parties, starting with the work of volunteers. Fortunately, there is a vast community of Linux users, many of whom produce drivers for Linux and distribute them freely on the Internet. If a certain piece of hardware is popular, you can be certain that Linux support for that piece of hardware will pop up somewhere on the Internet and will be incorporated into various Linux distributions, including Red Hat Enterprise Linux.

Hardware Compatibility

If you only have 32-bit systems available, be prepared to spend some money. KVM is the default VM solution for RHEL 6. Red Hat has configured it to operate only on 64-bit systems. Fortunately, most PCs and servers sold today are 64-bit systems. Even the lowly Intel i3 CPU can handle 64-bit operating systems. There are even 64-bit versions of the Intel Atom CPU common on netbook systems. Similar comparisons can be made for CPUs from Advanced Micro Devices.

Be careful when purchasing a new computer to use with Linux. Though Linux has come a long way the last few years, and you should have little problem installing it on most modern servers or PCs, you shouldn't assume Linux will install or run flawlessly on *any* computer, especially if the system in question is a state-of-the-art laptop computer. (And you do need 64-bit-capable hardware to prepare for the Red Hat exams.) Laptops are often designed with proprietary configurations that work with Linux only after some reverse engineering. For example, when I installed RHEL 6 on a brand-name business laptop built in 2010, I had to do a bit of extra work to make the wireless adapter work with RHEL 6.

The architecture of a server or PC defines the components that it uses as well as the way that they are connected. In other words, the architecture describes much more than just the CPU. It includes standards for other hardware such as the hard drive, the network card, the keyboard, the graphics adapter, and more. All software is written for a specific computer architecture.

Even when a manufacturer creates a device for a CPU platform, it may not work with Linux. Therefore, it's important to know the basic architecture of a computer. But strictly speaking, if you want hardware compatible with and supported by Red Hat, consult the hardware compatibility list at http://hardware.redhat.com/hcl/.

---

exam
watch

While it is important to know how Linux interacts with your hardware, the Red Hat exams are not hardware exams. With the possible exception of the Internet Small Computer Systems Interface (iSCSI) targets in the RHCE objectives, no part of the exam

objectives directly addresses hardware. However, to practice for the exams, you do need to install RHEL 6. And to configure a system for KVM, which requires hardware-assisted virtualization, you need a system with 64-bit CPUs and related hardware.

Architectures

While RHEL 6 has been built for a variety of architectures, you can focus on the Intel/AMD 64-bit or x86_64 architecture for the RHCSA and RHCE exams. As of this writing, these exams are offered only on computers with such CPUs, so you need not worry about special architecture-specific issues such as specialty bootloaders or 64-bit module directories. Nevertheless, customized Red Hat distributions are available for a variety of platforms.

You can install RHEL 6 on systems with a wide variety of CPUs. But remember, to test a system for the required KVM virtualization solution, you'll need a 64-bit system. Red Hat supports four basic different CPU architectures:

- x86 (32-bit)
- Intel/AMD64 (x86_64)
- IBM Power Architecture (64-bit)
- IBM System Z Architecture

There's one significant omission from this list. Red Hat no longer builds RHEL 6 for the Intel Itanium CPU. To identify the architecture of a system, run the following command:

```
# uname -p
```

If you're planning to configure VMs on RHEL 6, be sure to choose an architecture that supports hardware-assisted virtualization, along with Basic Input/Output System (BIOS) or Universal Extensible Firmware Interface (UEFI) menu options that allow you to activate hardware-assisted virtualization. A configuration that supports hardware-assisted virtualization will have either the **vmx** (Intel) or **svm** (AMD) flags in the /proc/cpuinfo file.

Be aware, RHEL 6 installations on 32-bit systems with UEFI menus are not supported.

on the Job

If you're not sure about a system, see if you can try it out at the "store" with one of the "Live CD" distributions. If allowed by store personnel, boot the system from that Live CD (or DVD). Once booted, you should be able to access the /proc/cpuinfo file from the command line. You may need to tinker a bit with the BIOS or UEFI menus. A system configured to support hardware-assisted virtualization will have the vmx or svm flags in that file, even when read from a Live CD distribution.

RAM Requirements

While it's possible to run RHEL 6 on less, the RAM memory requirements are driven by the needs of the Red Hat installer. For basic Intel/AMD-based 32- and 64-bit architectures, Red Hat officially requires 512MB of RAM and recommends at least 1GB of RAM per system. However, I've installed RHEL 6 on VMs with considerably less RAM. On a VM where the GUI wasn't installed, I didn't even need 200MB of RAM.

Of course, actual memory requirements depend on the load from every program that may be run simultaneously on a system. That can also include the memory requirements of any VMs that you might run on a physical RHEL 6 system. There is no practical maximum RAM, as theoretically, you could run 128TB (that's 128,000GB) of RAM on RHEL 6. But that's just theory. The maximum RAM supported by Red Hat on RHEL 6 is 16GB on 32-bit systems and 2TB on 64-bit systems.

on the Job

If you're setting up Linux as a server, RAM requirements increase with the number of users who may need to log in simultaneously. The same may be true if you're running several different VMs on a single system. However, administrators typically "overbook" RAM on VMs configured with different functionality.

Hard Drive Options

Before a computer can load Linux, the BIOS or UEFI has to recognize the active primary partition on the hard drive. This partition should include the Linux boot files. The BIOS or UEFI can then set up and initialize that hard drive, and then load Linux boot files from that active primary partition. You should know the following about hard drives and Linux:

- The number of drives that can be installed on modern computers has increased. With port multipliers, it's relatively easy to configure 16 Serial Advanced Technology Attachment (SATA) drives on a system (assuming you can fit all of those drives).

  Older PCs could handle only four Parallel Advanced Technology Attachment (PATA) drives.

- Depending on the SCSI (Small Computer Systems Interface) hardware available, you can attach up to 31 different SCSI hard drives.

- While you can install as many PATA, SATA, or SCSI drives as the hardware can handle, the Linux boot files from the /boot directory works only on one of the first two hard drives. If Linux is installed on a later drive, you'll need other boot media that are recognized by the BIOS / UEFI, such as a USB (Universal Serial Bus) or CD/DVD. (Red Hat no longer creates an image for a boot floppy.)

- RHEL 6 doesn't even have to be installed on a local drive. During the installation process, the specialized storage devices option supports the use of Storage Area Networks (SANs), Direct Access Storage Devices (DASDs), hardware RAID (Redundant Array of Independent Disk) devices, and more.

Networking

As Linux was originally designed as a clone of Unix, it retains the advantages of Unix as a network operating system. However, not every network component works with Linux. A number of manufacturers of wireless network devices have not built Linux drivers. In most such cases, Linux developers have been working furiously to develop appropriate drivers, and to get those drivers incorporated into the major distributions, including RHEL.

Virtual Machine Options

As virtualization makes it relatively easy to set up a large number of systems, it can help you configure a large number of systems, each dedicated to a specific service. To that end, virtualization can be divided into five different categories, as described in the aforementioned book: *Security Strategies in Linux Platforms and Applications.*

- **Application-level** Systems like Wine Is Not an Emulator (WINE) support the installation of a single application. In this case, WINE allows an application designed for Microsoft Windows to be installed on Linux. Loosely, that is one example of an application configured in a VM.
- **Platform-level VMs** Applications such as VMware Player and Virtualbox are open-source edition examples of platform-level VMs that emulate a complete computer system for the installation of a separate operating system.
- **Paravirtualization** While it's functionally similar to a platform-level VM, it works with fewer resources and usually requires a specialized kernel such as Xen.
- **Hardware-assisted virtualization** A hardware interface where VMs have access to the hardware features of a CPU, such as those described earlier with **vmx** or **svm** flags in the /proc/cpuinfo file.
- **Bare-metal virtualization** Some VM systems include a minimal operating system dedicated to VM operation. Two examples of bare-metal virtualization systems are VMware ESX and Citrix XenServer.

The KVM solution configured with RHEL 6 is known as a hypervisor, a VM monitor that supports the running of multiple operating systems concurrently on the same CPU. KVM replaces the previous default, Xen.

KVM has replaced Xen in many open-source distributions. XenSource is owned by Citrix, which started working with Microsoft after RHEL 5 was released.

CERTIFICATION OBJECTIVE 1.03

Get Red Hat Enterprise Linux

The RHCSA and RHCE exams are based on your knowledge of RHEL. When you take the RHCSA and/or the RHCE exams, it will be on a "standard" 64-bit computer. To get an official copy of RHEL, you'll need a subscription. In some cases, trial subscriptions are available. However, if you don't need the same "look and feel" of RHEL to prepare for an exam, third-party rebuilds are available. As such "rebuilds" use the same source code as RHEL, except for the trademarks and the connection to the Red Hat Network, they're essentially functionally identical to RHEL.

Once you either purchase a subscription or get approved for an evaluation copy, you'll be able to download RHEL 6 from the Red Hat Network (RHN) at https://rhn.redhat.com/. Downloads are available for the operating system in a format appropriate for a DVD. There's also a download available for a network boot CD. You'll even be able to download files with the source code for associated packages. These downloads are in ISO format, with a .iso extension. Such files can be burned to appropriate media, using standard tools such as K3b, Brasero, or even corresponding tools on Microsoft systems. Alternatively, you can set up a VM where the virtual CD/DVD drive hardware points directly to the ISO file, as discussed in Chapter 2. Unless you purchase an actual boxed subscription, the burning or other use of these ISO files is your responsibility.

Be aware, some of the installation options described in this part of the chapter have been subdivided into different sections. For example, the ways you can configure partitions using Red Hat's Disk Druid tool are spread across multiple sections.

An ISO file is an image file that can be burned to CD/DVD media. The actual acronym is irrelevant, as it is based on a political compromise.

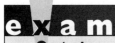

e x a m

ⓦatch   *While it is important to*   *a part of the objectives for the RHCSA or*
know how to get RHEL, that skill is not   *RHCE exam.*

Purchase a Subscription

Different subscriptions are available for the desktop and the server. While the RHCSA is focused on workstations, it also does require the configuration of HTTP and FTP servers. Of course, the RHCE also requires the configuration of a variety of server services. So most readers will need a server subscription.

A variety of server subscriptions are available, depending on the number of CPU sockets and virtual guests. A system associated with a regular RHEL subscription is limited to two CPU sockets and one virtual guest. Each socket can have a multicore CPU. Significant discounts for academic users are available.

Get an Evaluation Copy

Red Hat currently offers a 30-day unsupported evaluation option for RHEL. Red Hat requires some personal information from such users. Once approved by Red Hat, you'll get instructions on how to download the distribution. For more information, see www.redhat.com/rhel/details/eval. The 30-day limit is simply a limit on access between your system and the Red Hat Network. The operating system continues to work, but without updates. No support is given.

Third-Party Rebuilds

You don't have to pay for operating system support to prepare for Red Hat exams. You don't have to live with a limited test subscription. To comply with the Linux General Public License (GPL), Red Hat releases the source code for just about every RHEL package at ftp.redhat.com. However, the GPL only requires that Red Hat release the source code. Red Hat's understanding is that it does not have to release the binary packages compiled from that source code.

on the
ⓙob

The description of the GPL and trademark law in this book is not a legal opinion and is not intended as legal advice.

Under trademark law, Red Hat can prevent others from releasing software with its trademarks, such as its red fedora symbol. Nevertheless, the GPL gives anyone the right to compile that source code. If they make changes, all they need to do is release their changes under the same license. And several "third parties" have taken this opportunity to remove the trademarks from the released source code, and compiled that software into their own rebuilds, functionally equivalent to RHEL.

The source code is released in Source RPM package format, which means the RPM packages can be built using the **rpm** commands described in Chapter 7. However, the building of a distribution, even from source code, is a tricky process. But once complete, the rebuild has the same functionality as RHEL. It is true, rebuild distributions don't have a connection to and can't get updates from the Red Hat Network. However, the Red Hat Network is not part of the Red Hat Exam Prep guide. And the developers behind rebuild distributions also use the source code associated with new RHEL packages to keep their repositories up to date. Two options for rebuild distributions include:

- **Community Enterprise Operating System (CentOS)**   The rebuild known as CentOS includes a number of experienced developers who have been working with RHEL source code since the release of RHEL 3 back in 2002. For more information, see www.centos.org.

- **Scientific Linux**   This distribution is developed and supported by experts from the U.S. Government's Fermilab and the European Organization for Nuclear Research, known by its French acronym, CERN. The people associated with these labs are among the smartest scientists around. For more information, see www.scientificlinux.org.

A number of the figures in this book are based on "snapshots" from a distribution that uses RHEL 6 source code, known as Scientific Linux. It was developed by two organizations with some of the smartest scientific minds in the world at Fermilab and CERN.

Check the Download

For downloads from the RHN, Red Hat provides checksums based on both the Message Digest 5 (MD5) and the 256-bit Secure Hash Algorithm (SHA256). You can check these ISO files to the given checksum numbers with the **md5sum** and

sha256sum commands. For example, the following commands calculate those checksums for the initial RHEL 6 DVD:

```
# md5sum rhel-server-6.0-x86_64-dvd.iso
# sha256sum rhel-server-6.0-x86_64-dvd.iso
```

While it's a good sign when a downloaded DVD passes these tests, such a result is not a guarantee that such DVDs are free of errors.

CERTIFICATION OBJECTIVE 1.04

Installation Requirements

According to the Red Hat certification blog, Red Hat now provides "pre-installed systems" for their exams. So you won't start from scratch, at least for the host physical system. But you'll still need to set up practice systems. The RHCSA objectives suggest that you need to do so with a network installation. On a pre-installed system, given the other requirements, that suggests that you need to know how to set up network installations on KVM-based VMs.

The installation requirements described in this section are suited to the creation of an environment for practice labs. That environment may also work as a baseline for other RHEL systems. On many real networks, new virtual systems are created or cloned from that baseline. Those new systems are then dedicated for a single service.

If you're creating a physical host for test VMs, make sure to have enough room available for the host physical system and the guest VMs. This section suggests that you create three VMs for test purposes. You should consider including a fourth VM as a backup, in case one of the VMs suffers a catastrophic failure due to a mistake or malfunction. For such purposes, 80GB of free space on a physical system would be sufficient. With some careful planning, you may be able to live with a smaller amount of free space and just two VMs. For more information how to configure RHEL 6 on a VM, see Chapter 2.

on the job

Since Linux filesystems are efficient, they can be filled to near capacity with minimal defragmentation issues. If you're configuring VMs on Microsoft-formatted partitions, considerable additional free space is required due to volume fragmentation.

You Won't Start from Scratch

Before installing RHEL 6, it may be helpful to review what is known about the latest RHCSA and RHCE exams. As described in the Red Hat blog announcement at http://redhatcertification.wordpress.com/, Red Hat now provides:

■ Pre-installed systems
■ Questions presented "electronically"

In other words, when seated for an exam, you'll see an installed copy of RHEL 6 on the test system, with questions in some electronic format. No public information is available on the format of the questions. This book will assume the most basic format for Red Hat exam questions, text files available in the root administrative user's home directory, /root.

The Advantages of Network Installation

Network installation means you don't have to use a full DVD on every system when installing RHEL 6. It means that every system is installed from the same set of installation packages. Network installations are faster than those from physical DVDs.

Network installations become especially powerful when combined with Kickstart files and the Pre-boot eXecution Environment (PXE). In that configuration, all you need to do to install RHEL 6 is boot a system, point the remote installer to the appropriate Kickstart file, and voila! After a few minutes, you'll have a complete RHEL 6 system.

Red Hat and Virtual Machines

The objectives associated with the RHCSA suggest that you need to know how to "configure a physical machine to host virtual guests." It also suggests that you need to know how to perform a number of tasks with VMs, and "install Red Hat Enterprise Linux automatically using Kickstart." That's consistent with the use of Kickstart files to set up RHEL 6 on a KVM-based VM.

One of the advantages of a VM is how it supports the use of an ISO file on a virtual CD/DVD drive. Files accessed from that virtual drive are not slowed by the mechanical speed of physical CD/DVD media. And as such access may not be slowed by network traffic, virtual CD/DVD drives may be as fast as network access from a host system.

Virtual and Physical Systems

Virtual systems can't stand alone. They require some connection to a physical system. Even "bare-metal" virtualization solutions such as VMware ESX and Citrix XenSource were built from or otherwise rely on specialized versions of the Linux kernel, which acts as the operating system on the physical host.

However, it's possible to install a substantial number of virtual systems on a single physical system. If those systems are dedicated to different services, they'll load the physical system at different times. Such loads makes it possible to "overbook" the RAM and other resources of the physical system.

For our purposes, there is no real difference whether the installation is performed on a physical or a virtual system. The software functions in the same way. As long as IP forwarding is enabled on the physical host system, networking on the virtual system works in the same way as well.

A Pre-installed Environment for Practice Labs

The baseline RHEL 6 system configured in this chapter is relatively simple. It starts with a 12GB virtual disk. Part of that disk will be organized as shown in Table 1-1. They will be configured as regular partitions. The remaining space on the hard drive will be left empty, for potential configuration during the exam as logical volumes.

Two additional virtual disks of 1GB each are included to facilitate the post-installation configuration of a logical volume. The 12GB hard disk and 8GB partition are arbitrary sizes that provide plenty of room for RHEL 6 software. If space is limited on your system, you might go as low as 8GB for a hard disk, as long as swap space is also appropriately limited. Swap space in Linux is used as an extension of local RAM, especially when that resource runs short.

The baseline minimum installation of RHEL 6 does not include a GUI. While it is fairly easy to install the package groups associated with the GUI after installation is complete, that process requires the installation of several hundred MB of packages. And that takes time. Since Red Hat provides a pre-installed system for the exam

TABLE 1-1	Location	Size
Model Partitions	/boot	500MB
	/	8GB
	/home	1024MB
	Swap	1024MB

to reduce the time required for the exam, it is reasonable to suggest that the system provided by Red Hat includes the GUI. And the default GUI for Red Hat systems is the GNOME Desktop Environment.

GNOME is an acronym within an acronym. It stands for the GNU Network Object Model Environment. GNU is itself a recursive acronym, as it stands for GNU's Not Unix. Linux is filled with similar recursive acronyms, such as PHP: Hypertext Preprocessor (PHP).

The amount of RAM to allocate is more complex, especially on a VM. For the purpose of this book, I've configured VMs with 768MB of RAM to comfortably enable GUI-based illustrations of the RHEL installation process. If text-mode installations are acceptable, you can run a RHEL 6 GUI in 512MB, or possibly even less RAM. As different VMs rarely use the same RAM simultaneously, it's possible to "overbook" RAM; for example, it may be possible to set up three VMs, with 1GB of RAM each, on a physical host system with less than 3GB of physical RAM. Some RAM on the VMs will remain unused, available to the physical host system.

System Roles

Ideally, you can set up several systems, each dedicated to different roles. A network with a dedicated DNS (Domain Name Service) server, a dedicated DHCP (Dynamic Host Configuration Protocol) server, a dedicated Samba file sharing server, and so on, is more secure. In that situation, a security breach in one system does not affect any other services.

However, that's not practical, especially during the Red Hat exams. Table 1-2 lists the roles appropriate for each of the three systems described in Lab 1.

TABLE 1-2	Roles for Test Systems
System	**Roles**
server1	Workstation and servers to be configured throughout the book, configured as server1.example.com on the 192.168.122.0/24 network. This book assumes a fixed IP address of 192.168.122.50.
tester1	Secure shell server that supports remote access, configured as tester1.example.com on the 192.168.122.0/24 network. May include servers for client testing, such as the Domain Name Service (DNS). This book assumes a fixed IP address of 192.168.122.150.
outsider1	Workstation on a third IP address, configured as outsider1.example.org. Some services should not be accessible from that workstation. This book assumes a fixed IP address of 192.168.100.100.

There's also another implicit fourth system in this network—the physical host for the virtual machines. When multiple networks are configured, that host will have virtual network adapters that connect to each network. For this book, I've set up a system named maui.example.com. The following excerpts from the **ifconfig** command display the virbr0 and virbr1 adapters, with connections to both networks:

```
virbr0 Link encap:Ethernet  HWaddr 9E:56:D5:F3:75:51
       inet addr:192.168.122.1 Bcast:192.168.122.255 Mask:255.255.255.0
virbr1 Link encap:Ethernet  HWaddr 86:23:B8:B8:04:70
       inet addr:192.168.101.1 Bcast:192.168.101.255 Mask:255.255.255.0
```

Of course, you can change the names and IP addresses associated with each of these systems. They are just the defaults to be used in this book. The server1. example.com system is the designated exam system, which will be used for exercises that address actual Red Hat exam requirements. For convenience, I've also set up some RHCE services on the physical host system.

The tester1 system can be used to verify the configuration on the server1 system. For example, if you've configured two virtual web sites with different names, you should be able to access both web sites from the tester1 system. The Red Hat exams assume that you may connect a system as a client to servers such as Samba and LDAP. They also assume that a DNS server is configured with appropriate hostnames and IP addresses. While the configuration of some servers such as Kerberos is beyond the scope of the RHCSA/RHCE exams, they may be used during the exams by the other systems as clients.

Finally, the outsider1 system is essentially a random system from an external network such as the Internet. Appropriate security settings mean that some services on the server1 machine won't be accessible to outsider1.

As suggested earlier, it would be best to have a fourth virtual system available, in case of a failure in one of the three virtual systems described. Before following these recommendations, read Chapter 2. This chapter is focused on the configuration of a physical host system.

CERTIFICATION OBJECTIVE 1.05

Installation Options

Even most beginning Linux users can install RHEL 6 from a CD/DVD. While this section addresses some of the options associated with installation, it is focused on the creation of that baseline system that can be used to set up other custom RHEL 6 systems.

In addition, the installation process is an opportunity to learn more about RHEL 6, not only boot media, but the logical volumes that can be configured after installation is complete. But as pre-installed physical systems are now the norm for Red Hat exams, detailed discussion of logical volumes have been consolidated in Chapter 6.

The steps described in this section assume a connection to the FTP server with RHEL 6 installation files created and configured in Lab 2. The steps are modestly different if you're installing RHEL 6 directly from a full DVD.

Boot Media

When installing RHEL 6, the simplest option is to boot it from the RHEL 6 DVD. While rebuild distributions may offer CDs, Red Hat only offers RHEL 6 on DVD. It also offers boot media in ISO format. From those media, there's no fuss about a separate boot disk, no worry about network connections. But in some organizations, you may not want to distribute the RHEL 6 DVD to everyone. In some cases, there is no CD/DVD drive. In essence, there are four methods available to start the RHEL 6 installation process:

- Boot from an RHEL 6 DVD.
- Boot from a network RHEL boot CD.
- Boot from a USB key.
- Boot from a Kickstart server using a PXE network boot card.

The last three options generally assume that you're going to install RHEL over a network. The installation and boot media are available from the Red Hat Network for users with a subscription. It should also be available from servers associated with rebuild distributions.

Some Red Hat documentation suggests that the network boot CD doesn't work on 64-bit systems with UEFI. For me, that was not true. It worked fine on both my UEFI-based laptop and server. For more information, see Red Hat Bugzilla item 661135. Nevertheless, if you need to create a boot USB key, find the efidisk.img file in the images/ subdirectory of the RHEL 6 DVD. You can then write that image to a USB key. If that key is located on device /dev/sdd, you'd write that image with the following command:

```
# dd if=efidisk.img of=/dev/sdd
```

Be careful—if /dev/sdd is a drive with data, these commands will overwrite all data on that drive.

Know how to create the right boot disk for your system. If you have a problem, the installation boot CD or USB key can also serve as a rescue disk. At the boot prompt, the Rescue Installed System *option will eventually bring you to a rescue mode that can mount appropriate volumes and recover specific files or directories.*

CD/DVD or Boot USB Starts Installation

Now you can boot a target system from the network boot CD, the installation DVD, or the installation USB key. After a few files are opened and decompressed, an RHEL installation screen should appear with at least the following four options:

- Install or upgrade an existing system
- Install system with basic video driver
- Rescue installed system
- Boot from local drive

The first option should work for most users. If there is trouble with the graphics after the first option, try rebooting the system and work with the second option, which specifies a standard Video Electronics Standard Association (VESA) adapter associated with older Super Video Graphics Association (SVGA) monitors.

There are two modes associated with the Red Hat installation program, also known as Anaconda: text mode and graphical mode. While the minimum supported requirement is 512MB of RAM, you may be able to install graphically in a bit less. But if you have more than enough RAM and prefer text-mode installation, return to the RHEL installation screen. Highlight the Install Or Upgrade An Existing System option and press the TAB key. When you do, the following options are revealed on that screen, on one line:

```
> vmlinuz initrd=initrd.img
```

To force installation in text mode, add the word **text** to the end of this line.

o n t h e
ob

While Red Hat published information suggests that a minimum of 512MB of RAM for a graphical installation, my experiments on KVM suggest that the minimum for a GUI installation on a VM is 652MB.

Basic Installation Steps

The basic RHEL installation is straightforward and should already be well understood by any Red Hat certification candidate. Most of the steps are described here for reference; it's useful to remember this process as you work on advanced configuration situations such as the Kickstart files described in Chapter 2.

The order of these steps vary depending on whether they're run directly from the CD/DVD or over a network. Variations occur depending on whether there's a previous version of Linux and Linux-formatted partitions on the local system. For this section, the following assumptions are made:

- Network installation based on the RHEL 6 network boot disk
- At least 652MB of RAM
- An available FTP server with the installation files, such as the one configured in Lab 2.
- RHEL 6 as the only operating system on the local computer

However, dual-boot situations are acceptable. In fact, I've written this book on an Intel I7 laptop system in a triple-boot configuration where RHEL 6 co-exists with Windows 7 and Ubuntu 10.04. If you're installing the system on a dedicated physical computer or a VM, the basic steps are the same. As a physical host is required for VMs, I assume you'll be first installing RHEL 6 on a physical system.

The most efficient, and thus (in my opinion) the most likely, way to install Red Hat Enterprise Linux is via a text or graphical installation from a remote server. For that purpose, Lab 2 configures an FTP server with the RHEL 6 installation files. Alternatively, it's possible to set up those installation files on an HTTP server such as the Apache Web server, as discussed later in this chapter.

The sequence of steps for the installation process varies, depending on whether you're installing from the DVD or the network installation CD, as well as whether you're installing in text or graphical mode. It also may vary if you're using a rebuild distribution of RHEL 6. In fact, these instructions are something of a hybrid between two different types of installations, depending on what you do in Step 2. In fact, the developers behind rebuild distributions have modified the installation steps (slightly) as well. What you see will likely differ from the steps shown here. So be flexible when reading these instructions.

1. Boot your computer from the RHEL DVD, the RHEL network boot CD, or a boot USB key. This procedure assumes you're using the network boot CD. Five options are normally shown:

   - Install Or Upgrade An Existing System
   - Install System With Basic Video Driver
   - Rescue Installed System
   - Boot From Local Drive
   - Memory Test

2. Figure 1-1 illustrates the options from the Scientific Linux rebuild. The options are the same as from a genuine RHEL 6 DVD. For installation, only the first two options matter. Try the first option. If there's trouble with the graphics part way through the installation, restart the system and try the second option listed.

   If you're booting from the first RHEL 6 installation DVD, and want to be sure to review the options shown in Step 4, press tab, add a space and the word **askmethod** to the command line that appears, and then press enter. However, that first brings up the text-mode versions of the Choose A Language And Keyboard Type screens described in Steps 9 and 10. In addition, that would skip the Disc Found screen described in the next step.

3. The system responds with a Disc Found screen. The first steps of the network installation process starts in text mode (which is actually a low-resolution graphical mode), even if sufficient RAM is available. Choices are not "clickable." In this mode, use the TAB key to switch between options, and the SPACE or ENTER key to select or deselect an option.

4. If you like, you can use the Disc Found screen to test the integrity of the media. While it's good if the disc passes this test, it does not provide a guarantee that such media are free of errors. If you choose to test, be aware that the media is ejected after the test is complete. Accept the test or skip it and proceed to Step 4.

The Installation
Boot Screen

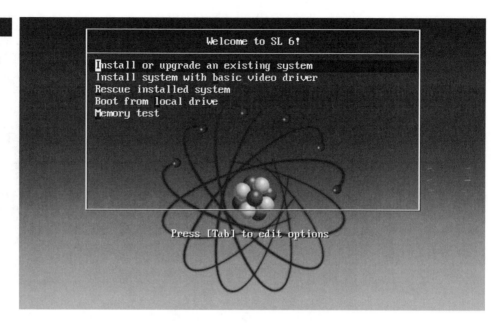

```
                        Welcome to SL 6!

Install or upgrade an existing system
Install system with basic video driver
Rescue installed system
Boot from local drive
Memory test




                Press [Tab] to edit options
```

If you test the integrity of an ISO file used for CD/DVD media in a KVM-based VM, the system will "eject" that file without changing the status of the media in the VM. You'll have to disconnect and then restore the media in the KVM Detail screen, as discussed in Chapter 2.

5. Choose your installation method. Four options are shown in Figure 1-2.

The options are straightforward:

■ Local CD/DVD can be used if the CD/DVD (or equivalent ISO file) is loaded.

■ Hard Drive assumes the RHEL 6 ISO file is available on a local hard drive partition. If you select this option, the program prompts you to specify the volume and directory with that file.

■ NFS Directory assumes the installation files are available from a shared NFS directory.

■ URL, short for Uniform Resource Locator, works with installation files stored on both an Apache Web server and an FTP server.

To point to the FTP server configured in Lab 2, select URL and click OK.

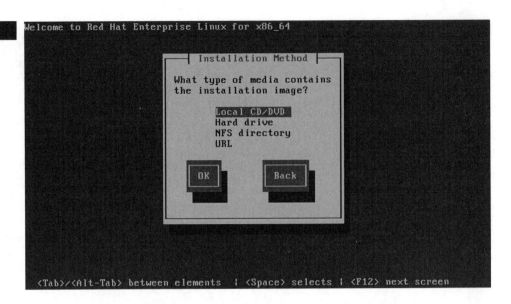

FIGURE 1-2

Select an
Installation
Method.

6. In the Configure TCP/IP screen, shown in Figure 1-3, choose how you want IP addressing configured. Your options are to enable support as a DHCP client for IPv4 and/or IPv6 addresses. (If the network DHCP server, such as a home router, does not support IPv6, enabling this option with DHCP slows the installation process.) As fixed IPv4 addresses will be needed for the test systems, select Manual Configuration, at least for IPv4 addresses. Fixed IPv4 addresses will be set up for all three systems from Table 1-2. In any case, KVM currently only supports IPv4.

7. Specify an IPv4 address for the system, the gateway, and the name server. If you're not sure what to do, this is an excellent time to plan a network as described in Lab 1. If you've configured a system on a VM, the gateway address is probably something like 192.168.122.1 or 192.168.100.1, on the same subnet as the IP address. For the purpose of this book, I've designated an IPv4 address for the server1.example.com system of 192.168.122.50. The name server, another name for the DNS server, is typically located on the same IP address as the gateway. Alternatively, for a physical system on a home network, the appropriate IP address for both the gateway and the name server is the IP address of the home router.

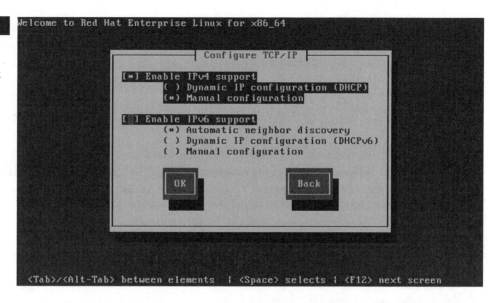

FIGURE 1-3

Configure the type of network addressing.

```
Welcome to Red Hat Enterprise Linux for x86_64
                    ┤ Configure TCP/IP ├
       [*] Enable IPv4 support
           ( ) Dynamic IP configuration (DHCP)
           (*) Manual configuration

       [ ] Enable IPv6 support
           (*) Automatic neighbor discovery
           ( ) Dynamic IP configuration (DHCPv6)
           ( ) Manual configuration

              OK                    Back


<Tab>/<Alt-Tab> between elements  | <Space> selects | <F12> next screen
```

8. Direct your computer to the remote FTP server. As shown in Figure 1-4, you can enter the hostname or IP address of the FTP server, as well as the shared directory.

FIGURE 1-4

Enter the URL of the installation server.

```
Welcome to Red Hat Enterprise Linux for x86_64
                    ┤ URL Setup ├
             Please enter the URL containing the Red
             Hat Enterprise Linux installation image on
             your server.
   ftp://192.168.122.1/pub/inst_____

   [ ] Enable HTTP proxy

   Proxy URL    _____
   Username     _____

   Password     _____

              OK                    Back


<Tab>/<Alt-Tab> between elements  | <Space> selects | <F12> next screen
```

9. If a proper connection is made, and the files are available, you'll see the first installation screen. Assuming sufficient RAM, it's a graphical screen. Click Next to continue.

10. Select a language to use during the installation process, as shown in Figure 1-5. English is the default; over 50 options are available.

11. Select a keyboard type; the default depends on the language selected.

on the **!** **Ʊob**

If you encounter problems, examine the messages in the third, fourth, and fifth consoles; to do so, press ALT-F3, ALT-F4, or ALT-F5. A command line is available by pressing ALT-F2. To return to the GUI screen, press CTRL-ALT-F6. If in text-mode installation, you can return to that screen by pressing ALT-F1.

FIGURE 1-5   Select a language for installation.

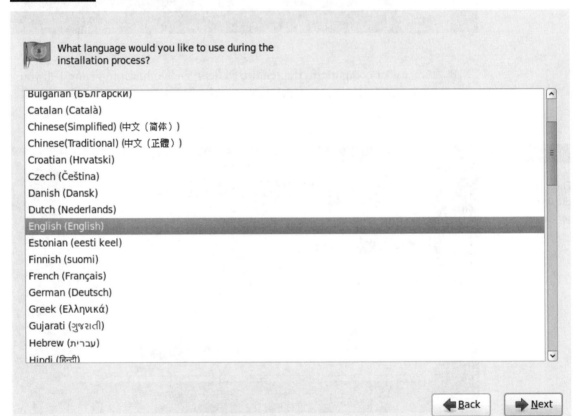

12. The next screen relates to local or specialized storage devices. If you have one or more "regular" local hard drives (SATA, PATA, or a virtual hard drive on a KVM system), select Basic Storage Devices, and click Next.

13. If there are new hard disks being applied to the system, you'll be asked to confirm changes to those disks.

14. If there's a previous version of RHEL (or a similar recognized Linux operating system) installed, you may see a Fresh Installation option. If it appears, select it. Otherwise, Anaconda skips to the next step.

15. You're now asked to give a hostname for the local system, such as server1. example.com. Click Configure Network to open the Network Connections tool described in Chapter 5. In some cases, the network settings configured in Step 6 may not be reflected in this tool. Make appropriate changes and click Next to continue.

16. Now you'll see a world map, where you can select the time zone of the local system. The System Clock Uses UTC option is a reference to the local hardware clock and the atomic realization of Greenwich Mean Time. (UTC is a non–English language acronym also based on a political compromise.) While incompatible with Microsoft Windows, the UTC option supports changes for daylight saving time. Make appropriate changes and click Next to continue.

17. The next step is to enter the password for the root administrative user, twice. Do so and click Next to continue.

18. The next step, shown in Figure 1-6, determines how space on configured hard disks, local and remote, is used. The options are fairly well explained in the figure. To summarize:

    ■ **Use All Space**   Removes all partitions on all configured devices, including those created by non-Linux operating systems.

    ■ **Replace Existing Linux System(s)**   Removes all Linux-formatted partitions, including those created for other Linux distributions such as Fedora and Ubuntu Linux.

    ■ **Shrink Current System**   Takes account of unused space on available existing partitions, shrinks those partitions, allowing that free space to be used for the new installation.

    ■ **Use Free Space**   Uses existing free space for the new installation.

    ■ **Create Custom Layout**   Supports custom configuration using Disk Druid, the Red Hat disk partitioning tool, during the installation process.

■ **Encrypt System** Supports encryption of the partitions created during the process. You'll learn to encrypt and manage an existing partition in Chapter 6.

■ **Review And Modify Partitioning Layout** Starts the Disk Druid utility described in the next section.

For the purpose of this installation, select Create Custom Layout. Note how that blanks out the deselection of the Encrypt System and the selection of the Review And Modify Partitioning Layout options. Click Next to continue.

19. If there's more than one hard drive installed, you'll have to select those drives on which RHEL 6 will be installed. One example is shown in Figure 1-7. Per the baseline discussion earlier in this chapter, choose the 12GB drive. The actual size will be shown in MB and will vary by a few percent. That variance is irrelevant on the Red Hat exams.

20. In this case, select the 12GB drive by clicking the arrow pointing right. You should now see that 12GB drive in the right-hand column, listed in the

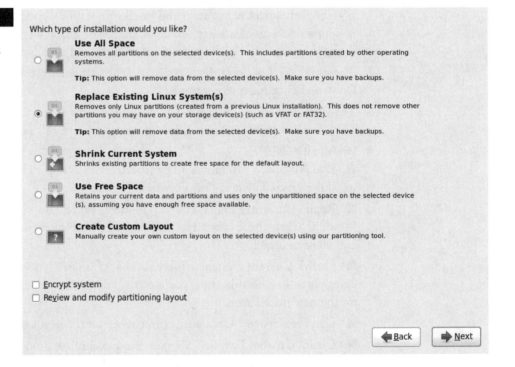

FIGURE 1-6

Partition layout options

Which type of installation would you like?

Use All Space
Removes all partitions on the selected device(s). This includes partitions created by other operating systems.

Tip: This option will remove data from the selected device(s). Make sure you have backups.

Replace Existing Linux System(s)
Removes only Linux partitions (created from a previous Linux installation). This does not remove other partitions you may have on your storage device(s) (such as VFAT or FAT32).

Tip: This option will remove data from the selected device(s). Make sure you have backups.

Shrink Current System
Shrinks existing partitions to create free space for the default layout.

Use Free Space
Retains your current data and partitions and uses only the unpartitioned space on the selected device(s), assuming you have enough free space available.

Create Custom Layout
Manually create your own custom layout on the selected device(s) using our partitioning tool.

☐ Encrypt system
☐ Review and modify partitioning layout

◀ Back ➡ Next

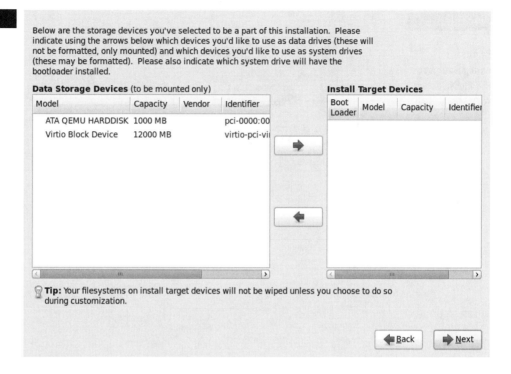

FIGURE 1-7

Select from available local hard drives.

Install Target Devices box. Click Next to continue. You'll see the Please Select A Device screen shown in Figure 1-8, the main Disk Druid screen. Detailed discussion of this utility continues in the next section.

The Installation Perspective on Partitions

Although it's possible to create more, RHEL will recognize only up to 16 partitions on any individual SATA, SCSI, PATA, or virtual hard drive. Once a partition is created, you can configure Linux to mount a directory directly on that partition. Alternatively, that partition can be designated as a RAID device or as part of a logical volume.

To define a partition, you may need some background on naming conventions, the configuration of different filesystems, uses of swap space, logical volumes, and RAID arrays. This is just an overview. Detailed information is available in Chapter 6, including tasks that may be required during the Red Hat exams, and on real systems.

Partition
configuration at
the Please Select
A Device screen.

Naming Conventions

Linux has a simple naming standard for disk partitions: three letters followed by a
number. The first letter identifies the type of drive (*s* is for PATA, SATA, or SCSI;
and *v* is for virtual disks on KVM-based VMs). The second letter is *d* for disk, and
the third letter represents the relative position of that disk, starting with *a*. For
example, the first SATA drive is *sda*, followed by *sdb*, *sdc*, and *sdd*.

The number that follows is based on the relative position of the primary,
extended, or logical partition. Primary partitions can contain the boot files for an
operating system. Hard drives can also be configured with one extended partition,
which can then contain a number of logical partitions.

Hard disks are limited to four primary partitions. When four partitions are not
enough, an extended partition can be substituted for the last primary partition. That
extended partition can then be subdivided into logical partitions. So when planning
a partition layout, make sure that extended partition is big enough.

Each partition is associated with a Linux device file. At least that is straightforward; for example, the device filename associated with the first logical partition on the first SATA drive is /dev/sda5.

A volume is a generic name for a formatted segment of space that can be used to contain data. Volumes can be partitions, RAID arrays, or those logical volumes associated with Logical Volume Management (LVM).

A filesystem is the way a volume is formatted to allow it to store files. For example, Red Hat uses the fourth extended filesystem (ext4) as the default format for its volumes. The standard way to access data in Linux is to first mount that filesystem onto a directory. For example, when the /dev/sda1 partition is formatted to the ext4 filesystem, it can then be mounted on a directory such as /boot. It is common to say something like, "The /dev/sda1 filesystem is mounted on the /boot directory." For more information, see Chapter 6.

Separate Filesystem Volumes

Normally, you should create several volumes for RHEL 6. Even in the default configuration, RHEL is configured with at least three volumes, for a top-level root directory (/), a /boot directory, and Linux swap space. Additional volumes may be suitable for directories such as /home, /opt, /tmp, and /var. They're also suitable for any custom directories such as for web sites, dedicated groups of users, and more. While it's important to configure the /boot directory on a regular partition, other directories can readily be configured on logical volumes or RAID arrays.

Dividing the space from available hard drives in this manner keeps system, application, and user files isolated from each other. This helps protect the disk space used by the Linux kernel and various applications. Files cannot grow across volumes. For example, an application such as a web server that uses huge amounts of disk space can't crowd out space needed by the Linux kernel. Another advantage is that if a bad spot develops on the hard drive, the risk to your data is reduced, as is recovery time. Stability is improved.

While there are many advantages to creating more volumes, it isn't always the best solution. When hard drive space is limited, the number of partitions should be kept to a minimum. For example, if you have a 4GB hard drive and want to install 3000MB of packages, a dedicated /var or even a /home volume could lead to situations where disk space runs out far too quickly.

Linux Swap Space

Linux swap space is normally configured either on a dedicated partition or a logical volume. Such space is used to extend the amount of effective RAM on a system, as virtual memory for currently running programs. But you can't just buy extra RAM and eliminate swap space. Linux moves infrequently used programs and data to swap space even if you have gigabytes of RAM. As such, RAID arrays of swap space make little sense, as why would anyone back up fragments of data from RAM?

The way Red Hat assigns default swap space is based on the amount of RAM on a system and the space available in local hard drives. For systems of up to 2GB, the default swap space size is twice the amount of installed RAM. Above 2GB, it's the amount of RAM + 2GB. But those are not "hard and fast" rules. Workstations with several GB of RAM frequently use very little swap space. On my home server, I have 8GB of RAM and 4GB of swap space. That swap space is rarely used, but it may be used more frequently on systems that aren't rebooted for months at a time or have heavy demand from certain services. In any case, the default installation configures swap space not in a dedicated partition, but as a logical volume.

Basic Information on Logical Volumes

The creation of a logical volume from a partition requires the following steps. Details on these concepts as well as the actual commands required to execute these steps are described in Chapter 6. Some of these steps are run automatically if you create a logical volume during the installation process.

- The partition needs to be labeled as a logical volume.
- The labeled partition can then be initialized as a physical volume.
- One or more physical volumes can be combined as a volume group.
- A volume group can be subdivided into logical volumes.
- A logical volume can then be formatted to a Linux filesystem or as swap space.
- The formatted logical volume can be mounted on a directory or as swap space.

Basic Information on RAID Arrays

RAID was an explicit requirement on the RHCT/RHCE exams up to the release of RHEL 6. As it is no longer found in either the RHCSA/RHCE objectives or the outlines of the prep courses for these certifications, you can relax a bit on that topic.

In any case, the RAID configured on RHEL 6 is software RAID. The acronym, Redundant Array of Independent Disks, is somewhat misleading, as software RAID is usually based on independent partitions. Redundancy comes from the use of partitions from different physical hard drives.

Partition Creation Exercises

Now return to the installation process. If you followed the steps described so far in this chapter and the system has sufficient RAM, you should see the Disk Druid Please Select A Device screen shown in Figure 1-8.

At this screen, you have the opportunity to configure partitions, logical volumes, and RAID arrays.

1. Configure standard partitions as described earlier in Table 1-1. Larger partitions are acceptable if you have the space. They would be necessary if you're creating the physical host system that will contain the VMs. The Create button supports the creation of standard partitions, logical volumes, and RAID arrays, as shown in Figure 1-9. Select Standard Partition and click Create to continue.

2. You should now see the Add Partition window shown in Figure 1-10. It supports a number of choices:

■ Allowable drives. For the purpose of this installation, limit the partitions to be configured to the virtual hard drive, labeled as the Virtio Block Device.

■ The Mount Point, which is the directory (such as /boot) whose files will be stored on the partition. You can type in the mount point; alternatively, it's a drop-down text box that provides options for typical mount point directories.

■ The File System Type; the default ext4 filesystem is sufficient. Click the box; options for other formats, along with configuration as a physical volume, RAID array component, or swap space, are also available.

■ The Size of the partition in MB; in this case, the partitions to be configured for this baseline system are defined in Table 1-1.

Now it's time for some exercises. First, examine how you can create and configure partitions during the installation process. You'll also look at how to allocate a filesystem to a partition or a logical volume.

FIGURE 1-10

Add a partition.

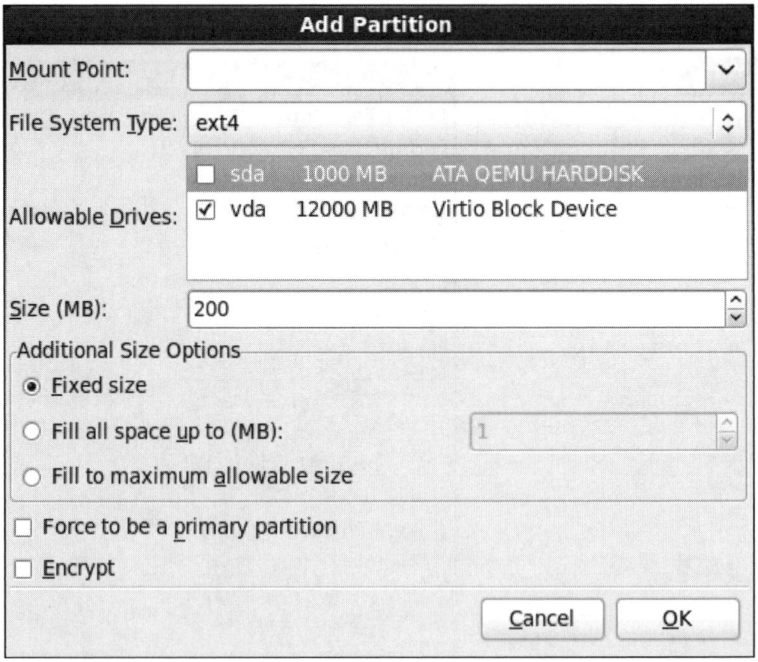

EXERCISE 1-1

Partitioning During Installation

This exercise is based on an in-process installation of RHEL 6. Mistakes are easy to recover from on VMs, as it's fairly easy to restart the installation process. This exercise starts with the Please Select A Device screen shown in Figure 1-8 and continues with the windows shown in Figures 1-9 and 1-10. In addition, it assumes sufficient RAM to work with the graphical installation.

1. Start creating a custom layout. If you're starting with blank hard disks, no partitions will be configured. Delete configured partitions if no space is available.

2. Try to create a regular partition. Click Create to open the Create Storage window. Select Standard Partition and click Create to open the Add Partition window shown in Figure 1-10. Set up an appropriate mount point, such as /home/user. Click the File System Type drop-down text box and review the available formats. If more than one allowable drive is available, make sure an appropriate drive is selected.

3. Retain the default ext4 File System Type, and click OK to continue.

4. Create one additional partition, using the steps just described. For the purpose of this exercise, the default 200MB is good enough, assuming sufficient free space is available.

5. Now click Create again, select LVM Physical Volume (LVM), and click Create. Note how it opens the Add Partition window with the Physical Volume (LVM) File System Type. If more than one allowable drive is available, make sure an appropriate drive is selected. Click OK.

6. Repeat the preceding step to create a second LVM partition. If more than one allowable drive is available, make sure to select a drive different from that chosen in Step 5.

7. Click Create. You should now be able to select LVM Volume Group. Do so and click Create.

8. In the Make LVM Volume Group window, click the Physical Extent drop-down text box. Review the available Physical Extents, which are units associated with volume groups. Typically, no changes are needed.

9. Make sure all available Physical Volumes To Use are active.

10. Click Add; this opens the Make Logical Volume window.

11. Enter an appropriate mount point such as /home/volume. The Logical Volume Name shown is just the default; you can use any legal filename for your logical volume. Set a size that does *not* use all available space. Click OK.

12. Review the result in the Make LVM Volume Group window. Click OK and review the result in the original partition window.

13. Now it's time for some clean-up. Click Cancel to return to the main partitioning window. Click Reset to restore the original Disk Druid configuration before the start of the exercise.

Now that the exercise is complete, the partition configuration should reflect at least the minimums shown in Table 1-1. One version is shown in Figure 1-11. If a mistake is made, highlight a partition and click Edit. The Edit Partition window that appears includes the same options shown. Different partitions and modest variations in size are not relevant on the Red Hat exams.

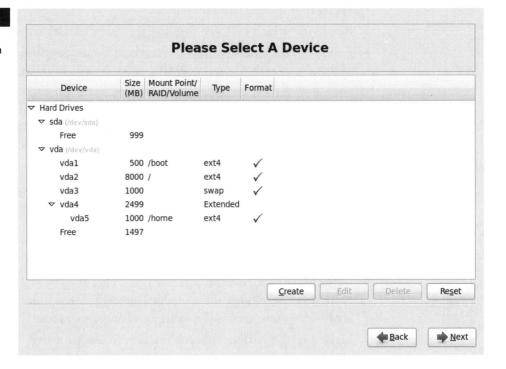

FIGURE 1-11

Sample partition configuration

To complete this part of the process, click Next. If you see a Format Warnings window, there may be existing data on the partitions that have been created. This is your last chance to cancel before proceeding. Assuming you're satisfied, click Format to continue, and in the next window, click Write Changes To Disk.

Configure the Bootloader

The standard Linux bootloader is GRUB, the GRand Unified Bootloader. While RHEL 6 uses a slightly older version of GRUB, version 0.97, it's a "tried and true" bootloader. The settings shown in Figure 1-12 are reasonable defaults for a dual-boot configuration. On a VM, the screen will be simpler. In most cases, no changes are required.

on the **Job**

The terms "boot loader" and "bootloader" are interchangeable. Both are frequently found in Red Hat documentation.

FIGURE 1-12

Configure the bootloader.

☑ Install boot loader on /dev/sda. [Change device]

☐ Use a boot loader password [Change password]

Boot loader operating system list

Default	Label	Device	
○	Other	/dev/sda1	[Add]
◉	Exam Prep System	/dev/sda8	[Edit]
			[Delete]

[← Back] [→ Next]

watch *The Linux Loader (LILO) hasn't been supported by Red Hat for nearly a decade. In addition, while* *GRUB 2.0 is available, it is also not supported for RHEL 6, at least as of the initial release.*

- The Install Boot Loader On /dev/sda option would install the bootloader on the master boot record of the noted hard drive. Unless another bootloader is installed, that is appropriate.

- The Use A Boot Loader Password can help secure the system. As you'll see in Chapter 5, without a bootloader password, anyone with access to the boot menu can access Linux with full administrative privileges just by booting into runlevel 1.

- The Boot Loader Operating System List specifies a list of detected operating systems. While you might see a second entry for an operating system such as Microsoft Windows in real life, RHEL 6 should be the only operating system installed here for the Red Hat exams.

While it's possible to add an entry from this menu for other operating systems, it won't work for other Linux installations on the same system. For that purpose, it's more effective to modify the GRUB bootloader configuration file directly after installation is complete.

While you may choose to set up a bootloader password, the defaults should be acceptable on any system where RHEL 6 is the only operating system installed on the local machine. Make any appropriate changes and click Next to continue.

Wow, Look at All That Software!

There are over 2500 packages available just from the RHEL 6 installation DVD. That number does not include a number of packages available only through the Red Hat Network. With so many packages, it's important to organize them into groups. After configuring the GRUB bootloader, you'll see the options shown in Figure 1-13, which allows you to configure the local system to a desired functionality. The selection depends on your objective. If you're installing on a physical system to set up KVM-based virtualization, select Virtual Host. If you're setting up virtual guests

FIGURE 1-13

Functional
installation
options

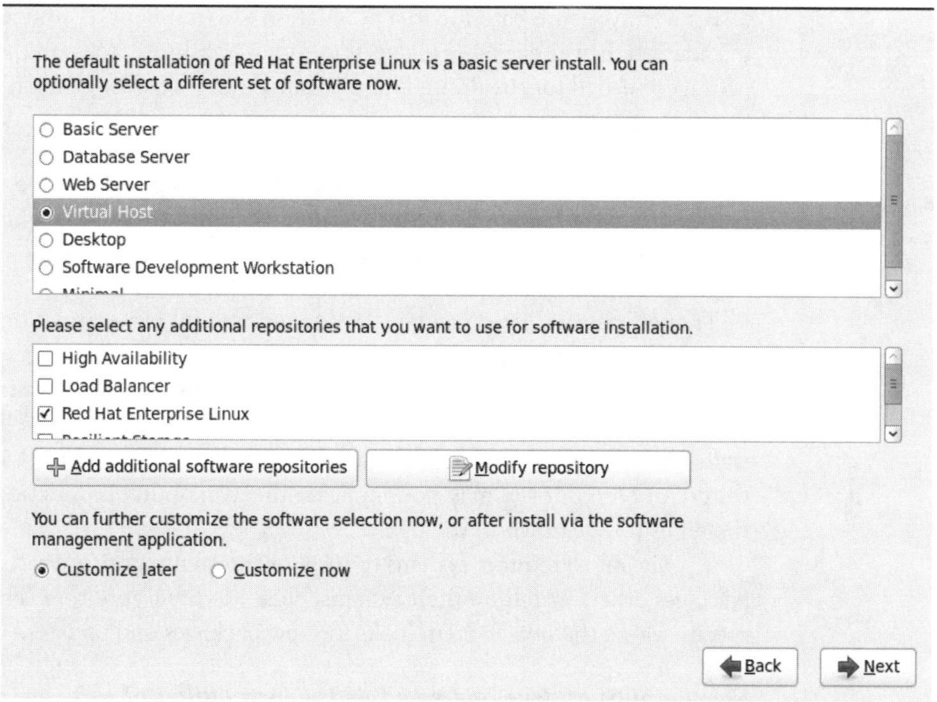

The default installation of Red Hat Enterprise Linux is a basic server install. You can
optionally select a different set of software now.

○ Basic Server
○ Database Server
○ Web Server
◉ Virtual Host
○ Desktop
○ Software Development Workstation
○ Minimal

Please select any additional repositories that you want to use for software installation.

☐ High Availability
☐ Load Balancer
☑ Red Hat Enterprise Linux

＋ Add additional software repositories   📄 Modify repository

You can further customize the software selection now, or after install via the software
management application.

◉ Customize later   ○ Customize now

← Back   → Next

(or other dedicated servers), select Basic Server. During a Red Hat exam, you'll be
installing most additional software after basic operating system installation is
complete. Other options are listed in Table 1-3. Depending on the rebuild
distribution, the options may vary significantly.

TABLE 1-3   Installation Software Categories

Category	Description
Basic Server	Installs basic packages for Red Hat as a server
Database Server	Includes MySQL and PostgreSQL database packages
Web Server	Sets up a system with the Apache Web server
Virtual Host	Configures a system with the KVM VM system
Desktop	Includes desktop productivity software
Software Development Workstation	Adds tools to modify and compile software
Minimal	Includes a minimal list of packages for the operating system

For a truly secure baseline in a production environment, consider the minimal installation. Fewer packages means fewer vulnerabilities. You can then add just the packages needed for the desired functionality. Any software that isn't installed can't be exploited by a cracker.

In the world of Linux, the term "hacker" refers to good people who want to create better software. The term "cracker" refers to people who want to break into other systems with evil intent.

The repositories listed can be useful for additional server functionality. As suggested by their names, the unselected repositories shown in Figure 1-13 support the installation of software in a number of categories, including storage clusters, systems that require high availability, and systems that balance the load for high-traffic services. As these are Red Hat repositories, maintained by Red Hat, some third-party repositories may not duplicate the availability or functionality of some of the repositories shown in the figure.

If you want to redirect systems to local or internal repositories, to control the packages others install on their systems, click Modify Repository. That allows you to specify where the local system looks for new packages and updates.

Some groups of developers enable the installation of software not supported by Red Hat. Two examples can be found at http://atrpms.net and http://rpmrepo.org.

For the purpose of this chapter, retain the default Red Hat Enterprise Linux repository (or the defaults for a rebuild distribution such as CentOS/Scientific Linux). Make sure to select Customize Now; otherwise, you won't be able to follow along with the next section. Click Next to continue.

Baseline Packages

In this section, you'll get a basic overview of what's available during the RHEL 6 installation process. During the exams, you may refer to one of these package groups with the Red Hat Add/Remove Software tool. You can also find a list of available package groups with the **yum grouplist** command. More information is available in Chapter 7.

Red Hat package groups are organized logically; for example, packages associated with a specific language can be found in the Languages package group. It's important to choose only the package groups you need. Fewer installed packages means more room for personal files, as well as the log files needed to monitor systems.

Package Groups

This section includes the briefest possible overview of each of the package groups available during the RHEL installation process. As you can see from Figure 1-14, there are high-level groups in the left-hand pane, such as Desktops, and regular package groups in the right-hand pane, such as the X Window System. The details of the RPMs associated with each package group are stored in an XML file. To review that file, go to the RHEL installation DVD and read the compressed *-comps-rhel6-Server.xml.gz file in the /repodata directory.

For an example of the details within a package group, select Desktop and click Optional Packages. This opens the Packages In Desktop window shown in Figure 1-15. Compare this list to the aforementioned XML file. Mandatory packages aren't shown in the associated window, as their installation is required for the package group. As

---

FIGURE 1-14

Red Hat
Enterprise Linux
package groups

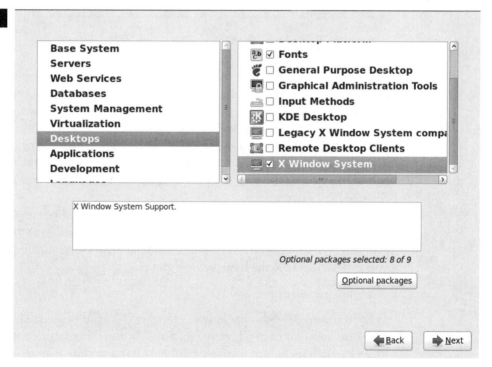

FIGURE 1-15

Red Hat
Enterprise Linux
Desktop package
group details

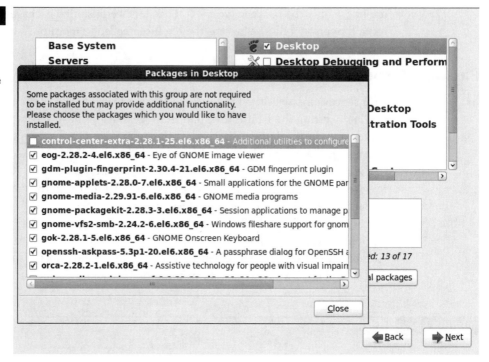

the XML labels suggest, default packages are selected by default; optional packages are not selected.

Take some time studying this screen. Examine the packages within each package group. You'll learn about the kinds of packages that are installed by default. If you don't add them during the installation process, it isn't the end of the world. You can still add them with the **rpm** and **yum** commands or the Add/Remove Packages tool described in Chapter 7.

If the XML file is too confusing, just make a note of the name of a package group. From that name, you can find a list of associated packages after installation is complete. For example, the following command identifies mandatory, default, and optional packages for the **base** package group:

```
$ yum groupinfo base
```

For the purpose of this book, I've created two different baseline installations. One baseline is suited as a host system for VMs; the other is suited to be installed in a VM. Both include a relatively minimal GUI installation, as most Linux administrators appreciate the convenience of multiple open command line consoles, side by side. To that end, I selected the following package groups during the installation process.

- **Desktops – Desktop**   Includes the basic GNOME Desktop Environment.
- **Desktops – Fonts**   Installs fonts that improve system readability in the GUI.
- **Desktops – X Window System**   Adds the server packages associated with the GUI.
- **Applications – Internet Browser**   Includes the Firefox Web browser.

The package groups fall into different categories; for example, to select the X Window System package group, I first highlighted the Desktops category in the left-hand pane. I could then select the X Window System package group in the right-hand pane.

In addition, for the physical host system configured for KVM-based VMs, I made sure the Virtualization package groups were included. They should be automatically included if you selected the Virtual Host system category earlier in the installation process.

Once desired packages are selected, click Next. Anaconda then proceeds to the installation process. When the process is complete, you'll see a final screen that confirms the installation, along with an option to reboot the system.

on the *ob*

On the system used to write this book, I also installed the OpenOffice.org suite and The GIMP (The GNU Image Manipulation Program).

On Reboot

When installation is complete, you'll see a final message to that effect, with an option to reboot the system. If you've installed RHEL 6 on a physical system, don't forget to eject or remove the boot disk and/or the installation DVD.

For RHEL 6 installed in a KVM-based VM, you'll need to change the boot device. If it isn't already open, click Applications | System Tools | Virtual Machine Manager. Enter the root administrative password if prompted, and double-click on the desired VM. Then change the boot device with the following steps:

1. In the window associated with the VM, click View | Details.
2. In the window that appears, shown in Figure 1-16, click Boot Options.

FIGURE 1-16	

Boot devices
in the Virtual
Machine Manager

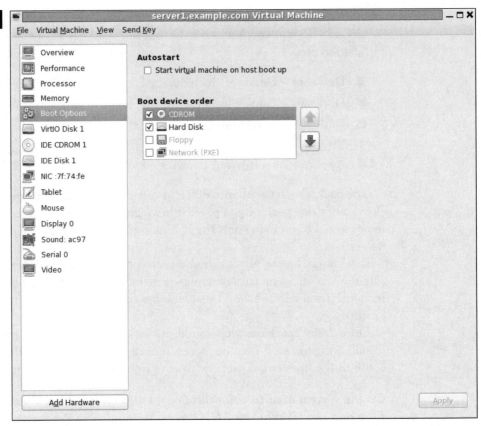

3. If the default boot device is set to CDROM, you should be able to change it
   to Hard Disk (or vice versa) using the arrow buttons. Once your selections
   are complete, click Apply. Be aware, the changes aren't implemented until
   the next time the KVM VM is powered on.

4. Click View | Console. If you haven't already done so, click Reboot to com-
   plete the RHEL 6 installation process.

5. Click Virtual Machine | Shut Down | Force Off. Confirm if prompted.

6. Click Virtual Machine | Run. The system should then boot normally into
   the newly installed system.

on the job

*As of this writing, the Virtual Machine | Shut Down | Reboot and Virtual
Machine | Shut Down | Shut Down menu options do not work.*

In most installations, RHEL 6 will start the first boot process discussed later in this chapter.

CERTIFICATION OBJECTIVE 1.06

System Setup Options

Baseline configurations are important. Once configured, you can clone that baseline to set up as many systems as needed. On a real network, a good baseline can be used to create systems dedicated to specific services. To enable remote access, it will have a Secure Shell (SSH) server, configured with a regular user.

For the boot process, RHEL 6 includes an implementation of the Upstart system, which replaces the Unix-based SysVInit system. It determines the consoles, services, and displays, as well as the runlevel that starts when a system is booted. Some systems use remote authentication, configured to connect to remote servers for username and password verification. While these systems are covered in other chapters, enough information is provided in this section to set up a baseline system.

The First Boot Process

But first, there's the process that starts the first time most RHEL 6 systems are booted after installation. And that's the first boot process. While there's a functionally similar text-mode version of the process, the default installation described earlier in this chapter leads to the GUI version of the process. The steps described in this section are based on an installation of the actual RHEL 6; the steps associated with a rebuild distribution will vary.

1. It starts with a welcome screen. Click Forward to continue.

2. The first boot process continues with a license agreement, which varies depending on whether this is RHEL 6 or a rebuild distribution. (Scientific Linux 6 doesn't even include this step.) If you refuse the license agreement, you're prompted to shut down and remove RHEL 6 from the local system. If you can accept this agreement, select Yes and click Forward to continue.

3. You're prompted to connect the system to the RHN. The illustration includes the window that appears if you click Why Should I Connect To RHN.

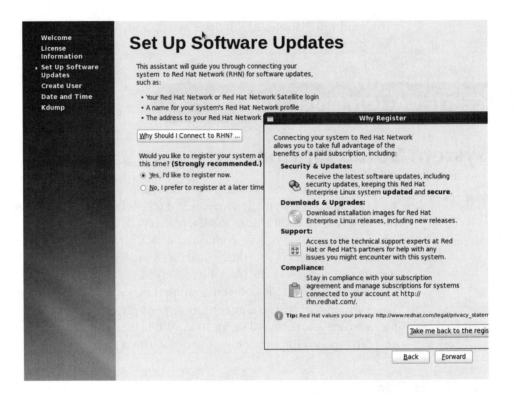

4. To register, you'll need a RHN account, with an available subscription. As that is not required in the RHCSA/RHCE objectives, select No and click Forward to continue.

5. You're prompted with the reasons shown in the illustration for registering. To avoid registering at this time, click No Thanks, I'll Connect Later to continue. You can register on the RHN later with the **rhn_register** command.

6. You're prompted with a window that the local system is not set up for software updates. As you'll perform this task in Chapter 7, click Forward to continue.

7. While not required for installation, the next step allows you to create a regular user for the system. While you can also connect to a remote database of users, a regular local user is required in this step. If you click Advanced, it opens the Red Hat User Manager, which can help customize user details,

as discussed in Chapter 8. Set up at least a local user, and click Forward to continue.

8. Now you can set up a date and time for the local system. The date and time that appears reflects that configured in the local hardware. If you select the Synchronize Date And Time Over The Network option, the window changes to show available NTP servers, based on the options associated with the Date/Time Properties tool briefly described in Chapter 5 and covered in detail in Chapter 17. Make desired changes and click Forward to continue.

9. Unless you're working with a system with a lot of memory, a message about "Insufficient memory to configure kdump" appears. That system collects data associated with kernel crashes. Click OK or make appropriate changes, and click Finish.

If you haven't installed GUI options such as the GNOME Desktop Environment and the X Window System, you'll see the text-mode alternative to the First Boot tool, as shown in Figure 1-17. Even if the noted GUI options are configured, you can start the equivalent of that tool with the **setup** command.

It includes six tools. The functionality associated with each of these tools is discussed in several different chapters.

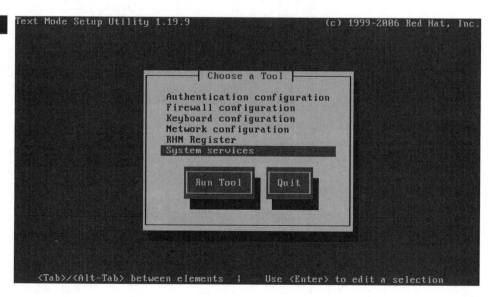

FIGURE 1-17

The Text-Mode Setup Tool

Default Security Settings

When RHEL 6 is installed, there are default settings associated with SELinux and **iptables**-based firewalls. As this section just summarizes default settings, it does not include much detail. For more information on these security options, see Chapters 4, 10, and others.

First, SELinux is enabled in enforcing mode by default. You can confirm the setting with the **sestatus** command, which should lead to the following output:

```
SELinux status:                 enabled
SELinuxfs mount:                /selinux
Current mode:                   enforcing
Mode from config file:          enforcing
Policy version:                 24
Policy from config file:        targeted
```

You'll learn more about SELinux and the RHCSA exam in Chapter 4. If you go for the RHCE, you'll also learn to configure SELinux in Chapters 10 and on to support a wide variety of services.

If you want detailed information about the current **iptables** command, examine the /etc/sysconfig/iptables file. That file is used by the iptables service, courtesy of the **/etc/init.d/iptables** script. The following line from that file allows traffic sent through port 22 access from the outside.

```
-A INPUT -m state --state NEW -m tcp -p tcp --dport 22 -j ACCEPT
```

Port 22 is the default port for the Secure Shell (SSH) service, which supports remote administration of the local system. If there's a good network connection, you'll be able to connect remotely to this system. If the local IP address is 192.168.122.50, you can connect remotely to user michael's account with the following command:

```
# ssh michael@192.168.122.50
```

The SSH server can be configured to enhance security even further. For more information, see Chapter 11.

Special Setup Options for Virtual Machines

On a KVM-based virtual host, you may notice additional firewall rules. For example, in the /etc/sysconfig/iptables file of the virtual host on my system, I see the following additional rule, which accepts traffic over a physical bridged network device.

```
-I FORWARD -m physdev --physdev-is-bridged -j ACCEPT
```

It works for IPv4 networking with the help of active IP forwarding in the dynamic file, /proc/sys/net/ipv4/ip_forward. It's a binary file; if it's set to 1, IPv4 forwarding is active. To set it on a permanent basis, open the /etc/sysctl.conf file, and make sure the following directive is set to 1:

```
net.ipv4.ip_forward=1
```

To implement the changes immediately on the local system, run the following command:

```
# sysctl -p
```

This information is also covered briefly in Chapter 5 in the context of network configuration. A detailed discussion of the related /proc filesystem is a RHCE topic covered in Chapter 12.

CERTIFICATION OBJECTIVE 1.07

Configure Default File Sharing Services

One of the requirements of the RHCSA guide is to "Configure a system to run a default configuration HTTP server," as well as "Configure a system to run a default configuration FTP server." Let's interpret those statements. The default HTTP server on RHEL 6 is the Apache Web server. The corresponding default FTP server is vsFTP.

While detailed configuration of these services is the province of the RHCE, these systems include basic functionality in their default installations. You'll confirm the operation of the default installation. Next, you'll take this process one step further, to set up these services to share files, specifically the files copied from the installation DVD.

The configuration of these services for file sharing is fairly simple. No changes are required to the main configuration files. Assuming SELinux is enabled (as it should be during the exams), the basic steps are:

- Copy the contents of the RHEL 6 installation DVD to the appropriate directory.
- Make sure the contents of the noted directory are configured with the right SELinux contexts.
- Configure the noted service to point to the specified directory, and to start when the system is booted.

Naturally, the steps vary by service. The details described in this chapter are rudimentary and may not be good enough if the related commands and services are new to you. For more information on the **mount** command, see Chapter 6. For more information on SELinux, see Chapter 4. For more information on the Apache Web and vsFTP services, see Chapters 14 and 16, respectively.

Mount and Copy the Installation DVD

You may already know that the **mount** command is used to connect a device such as a partition or a DVD drive to a specified directory. For example, the following command mounts the standard DVD drive onto the /media directory:

```
# mount /dev/dvd /media
```

RHEL 6 includes a number of similar device files in the /dev directory. With the **ls -l** command, you can confirm that these files are all linked to the /dev/sr0 device file:

```
# ls -l /dev/dvd
# ls -l /dev/dvdrw
# ls -l /dev/cdrom
```

If the DVD is properly configured, it should automatically find the appropriate filesystem format from the /etc/filesystems file. In this case, it's shown in the file as iso9660, which is the ISO standard for CD and DVD formats. It is reasonable to expect that the DVD is properly configured. If there's a problem, you'd see the following error message from the noted **mount** command:

```
mount: you must specify the filesystem type
```

The most likely cause is an error either in the ISO file or in the way that file was burned to the physical media. Speaking of the ISO file, it's easy to mount it directly on a directory, without wasting a physical DVD. The following command would work on the RHEL 6 DVD:

```
# mount -o loop rhel-server-6.0-x86_64-dvd.iso /media
```

The next step is to copy the contents of the DVD to the directory that's shared with the file server of your choice, FTP or HTTP. Generically, the following command makes sure to copy files in archive (**-a**) mode, recursively (**-r**). The dot makes sure to include hidden files. The files are copied to the noted directory:

```
# cp -ar /media/. /path/to/dir
```

The directory that should be used depends on the server. Of course, servers can be configured to use directories in other than default locations.

Set Up a Default Configuration Apache Server

The Red Hat implementation of the Apache Web server uses the /var/www/html directory for HTML files. Subdirectories that you create are suitable for file sharing. It works with the default Apache configuration, as installed from Red Hat packages. Nevertheless, you'll have to make sure port 80 is open in any existing firewall.

The steps required to configure Apache as a RHEL installation server are similar to those required to configure vsFTP. In Exercise 1-2, you'll take the steps required to configure Apache as an installation server. But first, you need to make sure Apache is installed with the following command:

```
# yum install httpd
```

If the command is successful, you can find the main Apache configuration file, httpd.conf, in the /etc/httpd/conf/ directory, as well as the main data directory in /var/www/html. But remember, don't touch that configuration file! To make sure the default installation works, first start the Apache service with the following command:

```
# /etc/init.d/httpd start
```

Next, use a browser on the system where Apache is installed and navigate to the localhost IP address with the following URL: http://127.0.0.1/. An example from the Scientific Linux rebuild of RHEL 6 is shown in Figure 1-18.

FIGURE 1-18

Proof of a
working default
Apache server

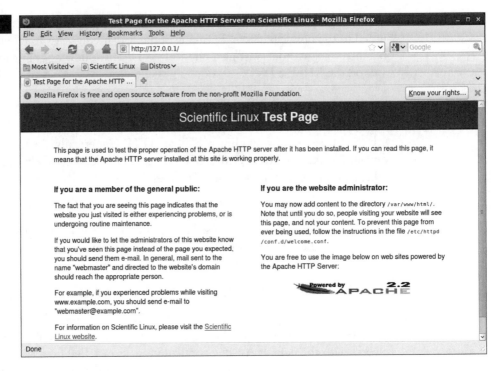

If port 80 is open in an existing local firewall, this page should be accessible from remote systems as well. In addition, you'll need to make sure Apache starts automatically the next time RHEL 6 is booted. One way to do so is with the following command:

```
# chkconfig httpd on
```

For more information on how services like Apache are controlled during the boot process, see Chapter 11. While that is an RHCE chapter, the **chkconfig** command shown here is simple.

EXERCISE 1-2

Configure Apache as an Installation Server

In this exercise, you'll install and configure the Apache Web server as a file server, suited for RHEL 6 installations. You'll need a copy of the RHEL 6 DVD, or the associated downloaded file in ISO format. In this exercise, you'll take the steps needed to create an appropriate directory, copy the installation files, set an appropriate SELinux context, open port 80 in any existing firewall, and restart the Apache service. These are basic steps; detailed Apache configuration is discussed in Chapter 14.

1. Mount the RHEL 6 DVD on an empty directory. You might use one of the following two commands. While the first mounts an actual physical DVD, the second mounts the ISO file:

```
# mount /dev/dvd /media
# mount -o loop rhel-server-6.0-x86_64-dvd.iso /media
```

2. Create an appropriate directory for the installation files. Since the standard directory for Apache Web server files is /var/www/html, it's simplest to create a subdirectory there with the following command:

```
# mkdir /var/www/html/inst
```

3. Copy the files from the mounted DVD to the new directory:

```
# cp -ar /media/. /var/www/html/inst/
```

4. Make sure the files have the right SELinux context with the **chcon** command. The **-R** applies the changes recursively through the copied installation files. The **--reference=/var/www/html** switch applies the default SELinux context from that directory.

```
# chcon -R --reference=/var/www/html/ /var/www/html/inst
```

5. Open port 80 associated with the Apache Web server; it's fairly easy to do with the utility that you can start with the **system-config-firewall** command. If that's too complex, just run the following command to disable the firewall on the current system. You'll learn to configure firewalls in more detail in Chapters 4 and 10.

```
# iptables -F
```

6. Make sure the Apache Web server is running with the following command:

```
# /etc/init.d/httpd restart
```

The Apache Web server should now be ready for use as a file server, sharing the installation files from the RHEL 6 DVD. To confirm, point your browser to the IP address for the server and to the inst/ subdirectory. If that IP address is 192.168.0.200, you'd navigate to:

```
http://192.168.0.200/inst
```

If successful, you'll see a page of clickable and downloadable files as shown here:

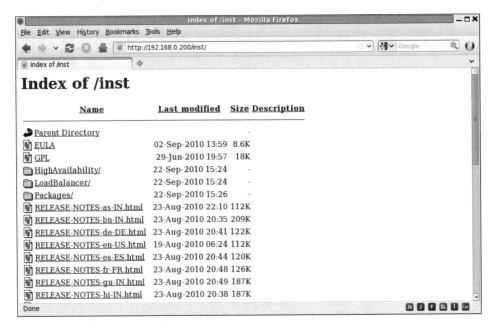

Share Copied Files via FTP Server

The Red Hat implementation of the vsFTP server includes the /var/ftp/pub directory for published files. For the purpose of the installation files, you can create the /var/ftp/pub/inst directory. To make the system compatible with SELinux, you'll then change the security contexts of each of those files with one command. When you then start or restart the vsFTP server, it will be ready for use as an installation server.

The process is documented in Lab 2. Assuming an appropriate connection to remote repositories using the RHN or from a rebuild distribution, you can make sure the latest version of the vsFTP server is installed with the following command:

```
# yum install vsftpd
```

If successful, you can find the main vsFTP configuration file, vsftpd.conf, in the /etc/vsftpd directory, as well as the main data directory in /var/ftp/pub. Just don't touch that configuration file, as the requirements point to a default configuration server. Just make sure to start the vsFTP service with the following command:

```
# /etc/init.d/vsftpd start
```

As web browsers can access FTP servers, you can confirm the default FTP server configuration on the local system by navigating to ftp://127.0.0.1/. The default result in the Firefox Web browser is shown in Figure 1-19. The pub/ directory shown is actually the /var/ftp/pub directory.

Note the security associated with the vsFTP server. Click the Up To Higher Level Directory hyperlink. The current directory does not change. Users who connect to this FTP server are unable to see, much less download, files from anything above the

FIGURE 1-19	
Access to the default FTP server	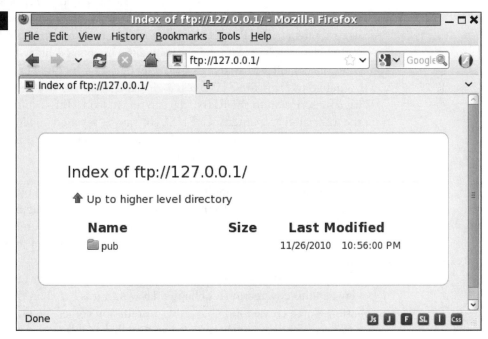

/var/ftp directory. This is a security concept known as a chroot jail. It's often used on other systems such as the Domain Name Service (DNS) server to increase security on the host system.

If port 21 is open in the local firewall, this FTP server should also be accessible from remote systems. In addition, you'll need to make sure the vsFTP server starts automatically the next time RHEL 6 is booted. One way to do so is with the following command:

```
# chkconfig vsftpd on
```

The *d* at the end of vsFTP refers to its daemon. For more information on how services like vsFTP are controlled during the boot process, see Chapter 11. While that is an RHCE chapter, it should not be hard to remember this one **chkconfig** command.

CERTIFICATION SUMMARY

The RHCSA and RHCE exams are not for beginners. This chapter helps you install a basic RHEL system, with the packages and settings suitable for the remainder of this book. Both exams are practical, hands-on exams. When you sit for either exam, you'll be faced with a live RHEL system with a series of problems to solve and systems to configure. The RHCSA covers core system administration skills.

The Red Hat exams now implicitly assume the use of a 64-bit system. Red Hat configures the default VM system, KVM, only in the 64-bit build of RHEL 6. And you're required to configure RHEL 6 as a virtual host for the RHCSA.

With a subscription to the RHN, you can download RHEL installation ISO files from the associated account. Since RHEL software is released under open-source licenses, third parties such as CentOS and Scientific Linux have used that source code without Red Hat trademarks. You can also use such rebuild distributions to study for the RHCSA and RHCE exams.

It will be helpful to create multiple installations of RHEL 6 to practice the skills you'll learn in later chapters. To that end, I recommend the configuration of three systems. While many users don't have three spare physical computers to dedicate to their studies, VMs make it possible to set up these systems on a single physical computer.

As the installation of RHEL 6 is relatively easy even for newer Linux users, not every detail is covered in this chapter. However, it is based on the network installation source created in Lab 2. After installation comes the First Boot process, which varies depending on whether you've installed a GUI.

✓ ## TWO-MINUTE DRILL

Here are some of the key points from the certification objectives in Chapter 1.

The RHCSA and RHCE Exams

❑ The RHCSA is a separate exam from the RHCE.

❑ Red Hat exams are all "hands-on"; there are no multiple-choice questions.

❑ If you're studying for the RHCSA, focus on Chapters 1–9. If you're studying for the RHCE, while you're responsible for the information in the entire book, focus on Chapters 1 and 10–17.

Basic Hardware Requirements

❑ While RHEL 6 can be installed on a variety of architectures, you'll need hardware that can handle the 64-bit version with hardware-assisted virtualization for the Red Hat exams.

❑ Red Hat supports RHEL 6 installations on systems with at least 512MB of RAM. Less is possible, especially on systems without a GUI. More is required for a GUI installation within KVM.

❑ RHEL 6 can be installed on local or a variety of network hard drives.

Get Red Hat Enterprise Linux

❑ The Red Hat exams use Red Hat Enterprise Linux.

❑ Subscriptions and test copies of RHEL 6 are available.

❑ Since Red Hat releases the source code for RHEL 6, third parties are free to "rebuild" the distribution from the Red Hat source code (except for the trademarks).

❑ Third-party rebuilds of RHEL 6 are functionally identical, except for access to the Red Hat Network.

❑ Reputable third-party rebuilds are available from CentOS and Scientific Linux.

Installation Requirements

❑ Red Hat has stated that exams are presented on "pre-installed systems" with questions presented "electronically."

❑ The RHCSA requires the configuration of a physical machine as a virtual host.

❑ The native RHEL 6 VM solution is KVM.

❑ It's useful to set up multiple VMs to simulate network communications.

Installation Options

❑ You can start the installation process from a variety of boot media.

❑ RHEL 6 can be installed from DVD, from a local drive, from an NFS directory, from an Apache web server, or from an FTP server.

❑ RHEL 6 should be configured on separate volumes for at least the top-level root directory (/), the /boot directory, and Linux swap space.

❑ RHEL 6 includes installation package groups in a number of categories.

System Setup Options

❑ The first post-installation step is the First Boot process.

❑ SELinux and **iptables**-based firewalls are enabled by default.

Configure Default File Sharing Services

❑ The RHCSA exam includes requirements to deploy HTTP and FTP servers in their default configurations.

❑ The default services associated with the HTTP/FTP protocols are the Apache Web server and the vsFTP server.

❑ One way to deploy a default HTTP or FTP server is to configure it with the installation files from the RHEL DVD.

SELF TEST

The following questions will help you measure your understanding of the material presented in this chapter. As there are no multiple-choice questions on the Red Hat exams, there are no multiple-choice questions in this book. These questions exclusively test your understanding of the chapter. While the topics in this chapter are "prerequisites," it is okay if you have another way of performing a task. Getting results, not memorizing trivia, is what counts on the Red Hat exams.

The RHCSA and RHCE Exams

1. How many multiple-choice questions are there on the RHCE exam? And on the RHCSA exam?

   _____

Basic Hardware Requirements

2. Assuming Intel-based PC hardware, what's the default virtualization technology for RHEL 6?

   _____

3. How many bits are required of a CPU that can be used to configure KVM on RHEL 6?

   _____

Get Red Hat Enterprise Linux

4. Name one third-party distribution based on RHEL 6 source code.

   _____

Installation Requirements

5. How much time is allocated for installation during the RHCSA and RHCE exams?

   _____

Installation Options

6. Name two different options for installation media that will boot the RHEL 6 installation program.

   _____

   _____

7. Name three types of volumes that can be configured and formatted during the RHEL 6 installation process to store data.

_____

_____

_____

8. Say you've mounted the RHEL 6 DVD on the /media directory. There's an XML file on that DVD with a database of packages and package groups. In what directory can you find that XML file?

_____

System Setup Options

9. What command starts the same menu as the text-mode First Boot process?

_____

10. What service is allowed through the default firewall?

_____

Configure Default File Sharing Services

11. What is the standard directory for file sharing for the RHEL 6 implementation of the vsFTP server?

_____

12. What is the standard directory for HTML files on the Apache Web server?

_____

LAB QUESTIONS

The first lab is fairly elementary, designed to get you thinking in terms of networks and networking. The second lab should help you configure an installation server. The third lab suggests that you look at the requirements associated with the Linux Professional Institute, for a different perspective on system administration.

Lab 1

In this lab, you'll plan the systems required for a Red Hat network. You have three computers configured with RHEL 6. Two of these computers are to be configured on one domain, example.com. These computers will have hostnames server1 and tester1. The third computer is to be configured on a second domain, example.org, with a hostname of outsider1.

One of the computers in the example.com domain, server1, may be configured with two network cards. Alternatively, if these systems are configured as guests on a KVM virtual host, IP Forwarding will make it possible for these systems to communicate, even though they're set up on different networks. The focus will be on IPv4 addressing.

■ Systems on the example.com domain will be configured on the 192.168.122.0/24 network.

■ Systems on the example.org domain will be configured on the 192.168.100.0/24 network.

Ideally, you should set up the server1.example.com system as a workstation and a server. The basic instructions described in this chapter should suffice, as it will be up to you to install and configure required services after installation is complete. It will be the primary system you use for practice. You'll install RHEL 6 on this system in Chapter 2, and you'll clone it for different chapters as well as the sample exams at the end of this book.

The tester1.example.com system will be a system that allows remote access only from the SSH service. In some cases, server services not necessarily required for certification may be configured on the outsider1.example.org network. That will allow you to test clients that are required for certification.

Lab 2

This lab assumes you've downloaded the DVD-based ISO for RHEL 6 or a rebuild such as CentOS or Scientific Linux. The DVD-based ISO is important, as it will serve two purposes. It will be the installation repository used earlier in this chapter as well as the package repository to be configured in Chapter 7. This lab simply includes those commands required to configure the noted files on the vsFTP server.

While the Red Hat exams are given on a pre-installed system, the associated requirements do suggest that you need to know how to install systems over a network, and configure Kickstart installations. And as you don't have Internet access during the exam, you won't have access to the Red Hat Network or any other Internet repository.

1. Create a directory for your installation files. With the following command, create the /var/ftp/pub/inst directory. (If you get an error message, vsFTP may not be properly installed.)

```
# mkdir /var/ftp/pub/inst
```

2. Insert the RHEL 6 installation DVD into its drive. If not automatically mounted, do so with a command such as **mount /dev/cdrom /media**. (If all you have are the ISO files, say in the Downloads/ subdirectory, substitute **mount -ro loop Downloads/rhel*.iso /media**.)

3. Copy the required files from the RHEL 6 installation DVD. Use the **cp -ar /source/. /var/ftp/ pub/inst** command, where *source* is the mount directory (such as /media/). Don't forget the dot (.); it makes sure to copy hidden files, including the .discinfo file.

4. Make sure there's nothing blocking access to your vsFTP server. Use a tool like the Firewall configuration tool to open up port 21 on the local system. For more information on firewalls and SELinux, see Chapter 4.

5. If SELinux is enabled on the local system, run the following command to apply appropriate SELinux contexts to the files on the new directory:

   ```
   # chcon -R -t public_content_t /var/ftp/
   ```

6. Now activate the FTP server with the following command:

   ```
   # service vsftpd restart
   ```

7. Test the result. On a remote system, you should be able to use the **lftp** command to connect to the local FTP server, using its IP address. Once connected, you'll be able to find the installation files in the pub/inst/ subdirectory.

Lab 3

The Red Hat exams are an advanced challenge. In this lab, you'll examine the Red Hat exam prerequisites from a slightly different perspective. If you're uncertain about your readiness for this exam, the Linux Professional Institute has Level 1 exams that test basic skills in more detail. In addition, they cover a number of related commands which I believe are implied prerequisites for the Red Hat certifications.

To that end, examine the detailed objectives associated with the noted exams 101 and 102. Links to those objectives are available from www.lpi.org. If you're comfortable with most of the files, terms, and utilities listed in the objectives for those exams, you're ready to start your studies for the Red Hat exams.

SELF TEST ANSWERS

The RHCSA and RHCE Exams

1. There are no multiple choice questions on any Red Hat exams. It's been nearly a decade since the Red Hat exams had a multiple-choice component. The Red Hat exams are entirely "hands-on" experiences.

Basic Hardware Requirements

2. The default virtualization technology for RHEL 6 is KVM. While there are many excellent virtualization technologies available, KVM is the default option supported by Red Hat on RHEL 6.

3. 64. To configure KVM on RHEL 6, you need a system with one or more 64-bit CPUs.

Get Red Hat Enterprise Linux

4. There are several different distributions available built on RHEL 6 source code. Two options are Oracle Linux and Scientific Linux. There may be additional correct answers.

Installation Requirements

5. There is no correct answer to this question. While the Red Hat exams are now presented on pre-installed systems, it's possible that you'll have to install RHEL 6 on a VM within an existing RHEL 6 installation.

Installation Options

6. Options for installation boot media for RHEL 6 include a CD, a DVD, and a USB stick. Red Hat no longer creates boot media in a floppy format.

7. You can configure and format regular partitions, RAID arrays, and logical volumes during the installation process to store data.

8. You can find the specified XML file under the noted conditions in the /media/repodata directory.

System Setup Options

9. The command is **setup**, which requires root administrative privileges.

10. The default RHEL 6 firewall allows access to the Secure Shell service, SSH for short.

Configure Default File Sharing Services

11. The standard directory for file sharing for the RHEL 6 implementation of the vsFTP server is /var/ftp/pub.

12. The standard directory for HTML files for the RHEL 6 implementation of the Apache Web server is /var/www/html.

LAB ANSWERS

Lab 1

When configuring a network connected to the Internet, you'll want to allow access to some systems and deny them to others. To that end, this lab provides a framework for the systems you'll want to set up to study for the RHCSA/RHCE exams.

As the RHCSA is in many ways an exercise in configuring a workstation, it may seem less important to set up a network to study for that exam. However, there are server elements to that exam, such as the configuration of FTP and HTTP file servers, so networks can't be neglected for the RHCSA.

With the development of VMs, the cost of hardware should be less of a handicap even for home users who are studying for the Red Hat exams. However, the RHCSA requires the configuration of VMs. And the default Red Hat solution, KVM, can only be configured for RHEL 6 on 64-bit systems.

While dynamic IPv4 addresses are used for most workstations, static IPv4 addresses are more appropriate in many cases, such as for DNS and e-mail servers. Clients are easier to configure when the IP address of such servers are known. So it's appropriate to set up static IPv4 addresses for such systems.

Three systems is a suggested minimum, as the rules associated with firewalls are typically not applied to a local system. The second system is a remote client that should have access to local server services. The third system is a remote client that should not have such access. All of these systems can be configured on VMs.

Of course, "real-life" networks are much more complex. And you're welcome to set up a network with more systems.

In Chapter 2, when you install RHEL 6 systems on KVM-based virtual machines, you'll want to clone that system to support configuration from a baseline. And, in fact, that's what happens in many enterprises. VMs makes it practical to dedicate one or more RHEL 6 systems to a specific service, such as the Apache Web server.

Lab 2

During the Red Hat exams, you won't have access to the Internet. However, many installations and updates require Internet access to get to those files associated with installation and updates.

When you configure the files from the RHEL 6 installation DVD on a remote system, you're configuring an effective substitute for the purpose of installation of additional packages. In addition, those files support network installation, which is still a RHCSA requirement.

The steps described are associated with the configuration of the vsFTP server, protected by SELinux. Do not fear SELinux. As suggested by the steps in this lab, the configuration of the vsFTP server is fairly simple. While the use of SELinux may seem intimidating to the RHCSA candidate, it is a requirement. The commands described in this lab show how you can live with SELinux on a vsFTP server. Chapter 4 will explain how you can make live with SELinux work for you in a number of other situations.

Lab 3

This lab may seem odd, as it references the requirements for a different Linux certification. However, many Linux administrators take the exams of the Linux Professional Institute (LPI) seriously. LPI creates excellent certifications. Many Linux administrators study for and pass the LPIC Level 1 exams. Passing the LPIC 101 and 102 exams provides an excellent foundation for the RHCSA and RHCE exams.

If you feel the need to get more of a grounding in Linux, refer to some of the books described at the beginning of this chapter.

The Red Hat exams are an advanced challenge. Some of the requirements for the RHCSA and RHCE exams may seem intimidating. It's okay if some of them seem beyond your capabilities at the moment, as that is the purpose of this book. However, if you're uncomfortable with basic command line tools such as **ls**, **cd**, and **cp**, you might need more of a grounding in Linux first. But many candidates are successfully able to fill in the gaps in their knowledge with some self-study and practice.

2

Virtual Machines and Automated Installations

Even though installation is specified as a requirement in the RHCSA objectives, Red Hat has also stated that their exams are now given on pre-installed systems. In other words, you won't have to install RHEL 6 on a bare-metal system during the exams. However, the management of virtual machines (VMs) and Kickstart installations are also required RHCSA skills. In other words, you need to be prepared to install RHEL 6 on a VM over a network, manually, and with the help of Kickstart.

Chapter 1 covered the basics of the installation process. It assumed that you could also set up virtualization during the installation process. But it's possible that you'll need to install and configure KVM after installation is complete. Of course, this assumes you're working on a system with a physical 64-bit CPU.

Kickstart is the Red Hat system for automated installations. It works from a text file that provides answers to the RHEL 6 installation program. With those answers, the RHEL 6 installation program can work automatically, without further intervention.

Once installation is complete on the systems used for test, study, and service, you'll want to be able to administer them remotely. Not only is an understanding of SSH connections an RHCSA requirement, but also it's an excellent skill in the real world. The references to menu options in this book are based on the GNOME desktop environment. If you're using a different desktop environment, like KDE, the steps are somewhat different.

CERTIFICATION OBJECTIVE 2.01

Configure KVM for Red Hat

In Chapter 1, you configured a physical 64-bit RHEL 6 system with the packages required to set up VMs. If all else fails, that configuration can help you set up multiple installations of RHEL 6. But if you're faced with a RHEL installation without the needed packages, what do you do?

With the right packages, you can set up KVM modules, get access to VM configuration commands, and set up detailed configuration for a group of VMs. Some of the commands described in this section are in a way previews of future chapters. For example, the tools associated with updates are covered in Chapter 7. But first, it's important to discuss why anyone would want to use a VM, when physical hardware is so much more tangible.

INSIDE THE EXAM

Manage Virtual Machines

The RHCSA objectives suggest that you need to know how to

- Access a virtual machine's console
- Start and stop virtual machines
- Configure systems to launch virtual machines at boot
- Install Red Hat Enterprise Linux systems as virtual guests

It's reasonably safe to assume the VMs in question are based on Red Hat's default VM solution, KVM. While in Chapter 1, you installed that solution during the installation process on a 64-bit system, you may also need to install the associated packages on a live system during an exam. In addition, there is a Virtual Machine Manager graphical console used by Red Hat to manage such VMs. Of course, that Virtual Machine Manager is a front end to command line tools that can also be used to install a system. Such tools can also be used to configure that system to be started automatically during the boot process.

While the Red Hat exam blog noted in Chapter 1 suggests that you'll take an exam on a "pre-installed" system, that doesn't preclude installations on VMs. So in this chapter, you'll learn how to set up an installation of RHEL 6 on KVM.

Kickstart Installations

The RHCSA objectives state that you need to know how to

- Install Red Hat Enterprise Linux automatically using Kickstart

To that end, every RHEL installation includes a sample Kickstart file, based on the given installation. In this chapter, you'll learn how to use that file to automate the installation process. It's a bit trickier than it sounds, as the sample Kickstart file must be modified first, beyond unique settings for different systems. But once configured, you'll be able to set up as many installations of RHEL as you need using that baseline Kickstart file.

Access Remote Systems

The RHCSA objectives state that you need to know how to

- Access remote systems using SSH and VNC

If systems administrators had to be in physical contact with every system they have to administer, half of their lives would be spent en route from system to system. With tools such as the Secure Shell (SSH) and Virtual Network Computing (VNC), administrators have the ability to do their work remotely. While this chapter focuses on the uses of SSH, Chapter 9 focuses on the configuration of VNC. While SSH is automatically installed in a standard configuration in RHEL 6, custom configuration options such as passphrases are the province of the RHCE exam.

I probably should warn you that production systems should not be used as an exam testbed KVM-based virtual hosts. However, I'm writing this book on one such RHEL 6 system.

Why Virtual Machines

It seems like everyone wants to get into the VM game. And they should. Enterprises had once dedicated different physical systems for every service. Actually, to ensure reliability, they may have dedicated two or more systems for each of those services. Sure, it's possible to configure multiple services on a single system. In fact, you might do so on the Red Hat exams. But in enterprises that are concerned about security, systems are frequently dedicated to individual services, to reduce the risk if one system or service is compromised.

With appropriately configured systems, each service can be configured on its own dedicated VM. You might find ten VMs all installed on a single physical host system. As different services typically use RAM and CPU cycles at different times, it's often reasonable to "overbook" the RAM and CPU on the local physical system. For example, on a system with 8GB of RAM, it's often reasonable to allocate 1GB each to ten VMs configured on that system.

In practice, an administrator might replace ten physical machines on an older network with two physical systems. Each of the ten VMs would be installed twice, once on each physical system. Of course, those two physical systems require some powerful hardware. But the savings otherwise are immense, not only in overall hardware costs, but also in facilities, energy consumption, and more.

If You Have to Install KVM

If you have to install any sort of software on RHEL 6, the Add/Remove Software tool can be a great help. Log in to the GUI as a regular user. To open it from the GUI, click System | Administration | Add/Remove Software. As long as there's an appropriate connection to repositories such as the RHN or those associated with third parties, it'll take a few moments to search. In the left-hand pane, click the arrow next to Virtualization. The four virtualization package groups should appear. Click the Virtualization package group, and the first package in that group to see a screen similar to that shown in Figure 2-1.

The list may be a bit too comprehensive; in Figure 2-1, you might note two different versions of the qemu-kvm package. Generally, only the latest version of the package

FIGURE 2-1   Add/Remove Software Tool

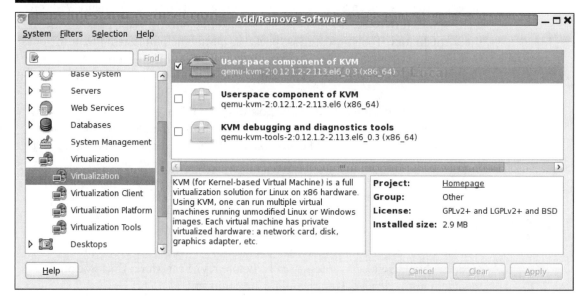

is required. All you need to do to install KVM packages is select appropriate packages from the Virtualization, Virtualization Client, and Virtualization Platform package groups. If you don't remember the list shown in Table 2-1, just install the latest version of all virtualization packages.

TABLE 2-1	**Package**	**Description**
	qemu-kvm	The main KVM package
Packages Associated with Virtualization	python-virtinst	Command line tools and libraries for creating VMs
	virt-manager	GUI VM administration tool
	virt-top	Command for VM statistics
	virt-viewer	GUI connection to configured VMs
	libvirt	C language toolkit with the libvirtd service
	libvirt-client	C language toolkit for VM clients

That's just seven packages! Of course, in most configurations, they'll pull in other packages as dependencies. But that's all you really need to configure VMs on a physical RHEL 6 system with a 64-bit CPU. While none of these packages are in the Virtualization Tools group, those packages may be helpful in real life. It includes tools that can help read and manage the VM disk images. If you choose to convert images from Xen or from some formats of VMware, the virt-v2v package is what you need.

Installation with the Add/Remove Software tool is fairly simple. Just select (or deselect) desired packages and click Apply. If there are dependent packages that also require installation, you'll be prompted with the full list of those packages. Of course, from the command line interface, you can install these packages with the **yum install** *packagename* command.

The Right KVM Modules

In most cases, installation of the right packages is good enough. Appropriate modules should be loaded automatically. Before KVM can work, the associated modules must be loaded. Run the following command:

```
# lsmod | grep kvm
```

If KVM modules are properly loaded, you'll see one of the following two sets of modules:

```
kvm_intel        45578    4
kvm             291875    1 kvm_intel
```

or

```
kvm_amd          35678    4
kvm             261575    1 kvm_amd
```

As the module names suggest, the output depends on the CPU manufacturer. If you don't get this output, first make sure the hardware is suitable. And as suggested in Chapter 1, make sure the svm or vmx flag is listed in the contents of the /proc/cpuinfo file. Otherwise, additional configuration may be required in the system BIOS or UEFI menu. Some menus include specific options for hardware virtualization, which should be enabled.

If one of the noted flags exists in the /proc/cpuinfo file, the next step is to try loading the applicable modules. The simplest method is with the **modprobe** command. The following command should also load the dependent module, whether it be kvm_intel or kvm_amd:

```
# modprobe kvm
```

Configure the Virtual Machine Manager

The Virtual Machine Manager is part of the virt-manager package. And you can start it in a GUI with the command of the same name. Alternatively in the GNOME desktop, click Applications | System Tools | Virtual Machine Manager. It opens the Virtual Machine Manager window shown in Figure 2-2.

In some cases, two hypervisors, also known as virtual machine monitors, are shown on the localhost system. These hypervisors work with QEMU as processor emulators within the virtual machines. QEMU is also known by its former acronym, the quick emulator. If a usermode emulator appears, it is appropriate if you want to run 32-bit applications on a 64-bit system. But that's inefficient. In most cases, you'll want to create and manage VMs in the localhost (QEMU) regular mode.

__As of the RHEL 6 release, the QEMU usermode emulator is subject to bug 634876 at https://bugzilla.redhat.com. The issue was addressed with an update to the virt-manager package.__

FIGURE 2-2	
Virtual Machine Manager	

Connections to Hypervisors

If desired, the KVM-based VMs can be configured and administered remotely. All you need to do is connect to the remote hypervisor. To do so, click File | Add Connection. It opens an Add Connection window that allows you to select:

■ A hypervisor, normally KVM or Xen. (Xen was the default hypervisor on RHEL 5, but is not supported for RHEL 6.)

■ A connection, which may be local, or remote using a connection such as SSH.

Remote connections can be given with the hostname or IP address of the remote system.

Configuration by Hypervisor

Each hypervisor can be configured in some detail. Right-click the localhost (QEMU) hypervisor and select Details in the pop-up menu that appears. It opens a details window named after the host of the local system, as shown in Figure 2-3.

As shown, the Overview tab lists the basics of the VM configuration, as discussed in Table 2-2.

FIGURE 2-3

VM Host Details

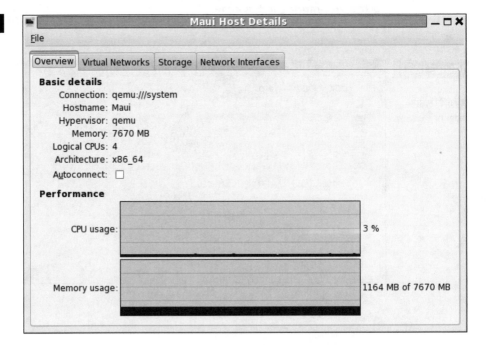

TABLE 2-2	VM Host Details

Setting	Description
Connection	Universal Resource Identifier (URI) for the hypervisor
Hostname	Hostname for the VM host
Hypervisor	QEMU is used by KVM
Memory	Available RAM from the physical system for VMs
Logical CPUs	Available CPU cores; "4" indicates four CPUs or a quad-core system
Architecture	CPU architecture
Autoconnect	Whether to automatically connect to the hypervisor during the boot process

For the next section, stay in the host details window for the current hypervisor.

Virtual Networks on a Hypervisor

Now you'll examine the networks configured for VMs within the Virtual Machine Manager. In the host details window for the current hypervisor, click the Virtual Networks tab. The default virtual network shown in Figure 2-4 illustrates the standard network for VMs created with this hypervisor.

FIGURE 2-4	

VM Host Details

You'll note the given network is configured to start automatically when the VM is booted. So if there's an appropriate virtual network card configured on the VM, along with a client command associated with the Dynamic Host Configuration Protocol (DHCP), it's automatically given an IP address from the noted range. As noted in the figure, assigned addresses are configured to forward information using Network Address Translation (NAT).

With the buttons in the lower-left part of the screen, you can add a new virtual network, start and stop an existing virtual network, and delete that network. In Exercise 2-1, you'll create a second virtual network. For the next section, stay in the host details window for the current hypervisor.

EXERCISE 2-1

Create a Second Virtual Network

In this exercise, you'll create a second virtual network on the standard KVM hypervisor in the GUI Virtual Machine Manager. This exercise requires a RHEL 6 system configured, is based on an in-process installation of RHEL 6, and assumes the Virtual Machine Manager as discussed early in this chapter.

1. Right-click the standard localhost (QEMU) hypervisor. In the pop-up menu that appears, select Details.

2. In the Host Details window that appears with the name of the local system, select the Virtual Networks tab.

3. Click the plus sign in the lower-left corner of the Virtual Networks tab to open the Create A New Virtual Network Wizard.

4. Read the instructions, which you will follow in coming steps. Click Forward to continue.

5. Assign a name for the new virtual network. For the purpose of this book, enter the name **outsider**. Click Forward to continue.

6. If not already input, type in the **192.168.100.0/24** network address in the Network text box. The system automatically calculates appropriate entries for other network information, as shown in the illustration. Click Forward to continue.

on the
Job

Take care to avoid IP address conflicts with existing hardware on the local network, such as with routers and wireless access points. For example, at least one cable "modem" uses IP address 192.168.100.1 for maintenance. In that case, the noted 192.168.100.0/24 network would make that cable "modem" inaccessible. If you have such hardware, do change the network address shown in the illustration.

7. Now you can select the range of IP addresses within the configured network that can be assigned by a DHCP client. Per Chapter 1, Table 1-2, you'll configure a static IP address for the outsider1.example.org system on this network. As long as the noted 192.168.100.100 IP address is outside the range of DHCP-assignable IP addresses, no changes are required. Make any needed changes and click Forward to continue.

8. Now you'll want a system that forwards network communication to the physical network, if only because that's how systems on this network communicate with systems on different virtual networks, possibly on different virtual hosts. The destination can be Any Physical Device, in NAT mode, to help hide these systems from remote hosts. Unless you want to limit routing from VMs to a specific physical network card, the defaults under Forwarding To Physical

Network should work. The options are covered later in this chapter, in the discussion of the Network Interfaces tab. Make appropriate selections and click Forward to continue.

9. Review the summary of what's been configured. If satisfied, click Finish. The outsider network will now be available for use by new VM systems and network cards.

Virtual Storage on a Hypervisor

Now you'll examine the virtual storage configured for VMs within the Virtual Machine Manager. In the host details window for the current hypervisor, click the Storage tab. The default filesystem directory shown in Figure 2-5 configures the /var/lib/libvirt/images directory for virtual images. Such images are essentially huge files of reserved space used as hard drives for VMs.

Those huge files can easily overwhelm many systems. One way to get control over such files is to dedicate a partition or logical volume to that /var/lib/libvirt/images directory.

As I had already dedicated the largest amount of free space to a partition dedicated to my /home directory, I chose to create dedicated storage in that area. To that end, I created a /home/michael/KVM directory to contain my VM files used for virtual hard drives.

The following commands would create the appropriate directory as a regular user, log in as the root user, set appropriate SELinux contexts, remove the /var/lib/libvirt/images directory, and re-create that directory as a link to the appropriate user directory:

```
$ mkdir /home/michael/KVM
$ su - root
# chcon -R --reference /var/lib/libvirt/images /home/michael/KVM
# rmdir /var/lib/libvirt/images
# ln -s /home/michael/KVM /var/lib/libvirt/images
```

One advantage of this setup is that it retains the default SELinux settings for the /var/lib/libvirt/images directory, as defined in the file_contexts file in the /etc/selinux/targeted/contexts/files directory. In other words, this configuration survives a relabel of SELinux, as defined in Chapter 11.

Virtual Network Interfaces on a Hypervisor

Now you'll examine the virtual network interfaces configured for VMs within the Virtual Machine Manager. In the host details window for the current hypervisor, click the Network Interfaces tab. The network interface devices shown in Figure 2-6 specify the physical devices to which KVM-based VMs can connect.

If the local system connects via the standard first Ethernet network card, the defaults with device eth0 should be sufficient. A properly configured VM should have access to external networks, given the firewall and IP forwarding configuration options described in Chapter 1. However, Figure 2-6 specifies one added interface, wlan0. That's a typical wireless network interface device file.

In the same fashion as with the Virtual Network and Storage tabs, you can add another network interface by clicking the plus sign in the lower-left corner of the Network Interfaces tab. It opens a Configure Network Interfaces window that can help you configure one of four different types of network interfaces:

- **Bridge**   Binds a physical and a virtual interface; typically associated with Xen.
- **Bond**   Connects two or more network interfaces as if they were a single interface.

FIGURE 2-6

VM network cards

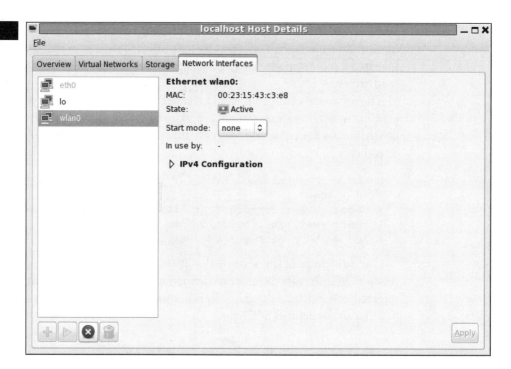

- ■ **Ethernet** Sets up a virtual interface as a bridge.
- ■ **VLAN** Connects a real or a virtual network interface to the VM system.

CERTIFICATION OBJECTIVE 2.02

Configure a Virtual Machine on KVM

The process for configuring a VM on KVM is straightforward, especially from the Virtual Machine Manager. In essence, all you have to do is right-click the desired hypervisor, click New, and follow the prompts that appear. But as it's important to understand the process in detail, you'll read about the process, step-by-step. New VMs can be configured not only from the GUI, but also from the command line interface. As with other Linux services, the resulting VMs are configured in text files.

Configure a Virtual Machine on KVM

To follow along with this section, open the Virtual Machine Manager in the GUI. Another way to do so is from a GUI-based command line. Run the **virt-manager** command. It should open the Virtual Machine Manager a touch more quickly than the GUI menu command. Right-click the localhost (QEMU) hypervisor and click Connect in the pop-up menu that appears. If prompted, enter the root administrative password. With the following steps, you'll set up the VM associated with the server1.example.com system discussed in Chapter 1. Now to set up a new VM, take the following steps:

1. Right-click the localhost (QEMU) hypervisor. In the pop-up menu that appears, click New to open the New VM window shown in Figure 2-7.

2. Type in a name for the new VM; to match the discussion in the remainder of this book, you should name this VM **server1.example.com**.

3. Now select whether the installation media is available on Local Install Media (ISO Image Or CDROM) or from a Network Installation server. That server may be associated with the HTTP, NFS, or FTP protocol. Select Local Install

FIGURE 2-7

Create a New VM.

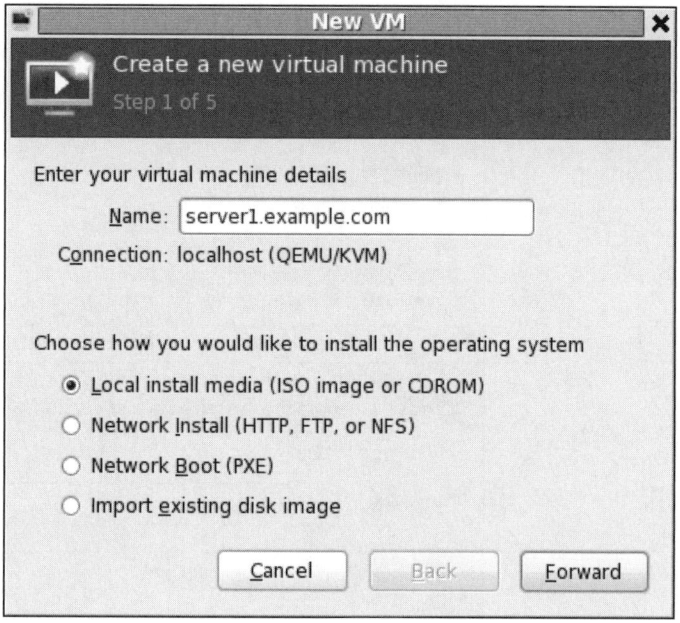

New VM

Create a new virtual machine
Step 1 of 5

Enter your virtual machine details
Name: server1.example.com
Connection: localhost (QEMU/KVM)

Choose how you would like to install the operating system
◉ Local install media (ISO image or CDROM)
○ Network Install (HTTP, FTP, or NFS)
○ Network Boot (PXE)
○ Import existing disk image

[Cancel] [Back] [Forward]

Media and click Forward to continue. (In Lab 1, you'll rerun this process with the Network Install option.)

4. If the media is available in a local CD/DVD drive, an option for such will be selectable, as shown in Figure 2-8. But in this case, select Use ISO Image and click Browse to navigate to the location of the RHEL 6 DVD or Network Boot ISO image. In addition, you'll need to use the OS Type and Version drop-down text boxes to select an operating system type and distribution, as shown.

5. Choose the amount or RAM memory and number of CPUs to allocate to the VM. Be aware of the minimums described earlier in this chapter and Chapter 1 for RHEL 6. As shown in Figure 2-9, in smaller print, you'll see information about available RAM and CPUs. Make appropriate selections and click Forward to continue.

6. Now you'll set up the hard drives for the VM, in the screen shown in Figure 2-10. While it's possible to set it up in dedicated physical volumes, the standard is to set up big files as virtual hard drives. While the default location for such files is the /var/lib/libvirt/images/ directory, it can be changed, as

New VM
Create a new virtual machine
Step 2 of 5

Locate your install media

○ Use CDROM or DVD

  No media detected (/dev/sr0)

● Use ISO image:

  /home/michael/KVM/rhel-server-6.0-x86_6 ∨ | Browse...

Choose an operating system type and version

OS type: Linux

Version: Red Hat Enterprise Linux 6

Cancel · Back · Forward

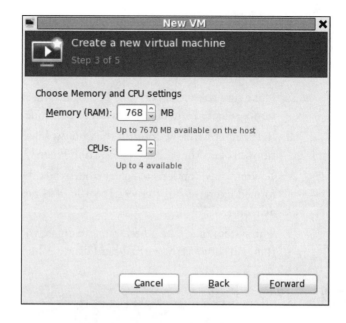

discussed earlier in this chapter. On an exam, it's likely that you'll have more than sufficient room in the /var/lib/libvirt/images directory. The Select Managed Or Other Existing Storage option supports the creation of a virtual hard drive in a different pre-configured storage pool.

7. Make sure the virtual drive is 12GB and the Allocate Entire Disk Now option is selected and click Forward to continue.

8. In the next window, confirm the options selected so far. Click Advanced Options to open the selections shown in Figure 2-11.

   You may have options to select from available virtual networks. If you performed Exercise 2-1, the 192.168.100.0/24 network address option should be available.

9. The system may take a little time to create the VM, including the huge file that will serve as the virtual hard drive. When complete, the Virtual Machine

Manager should automatically start the system from the RHEL 6 installation DVD in a VNC window.

10. If the new system doesn't start automatically, that VM should be listed in the Virtual Machine Manager shown back in Figure 2-2. You should then be able to highlight the new VM (in this case, named server1.example.org), and click Open.

11. You should now be able to proceed with the installation of RHEL 6 in the VM as discussed in Chapter 1.

    If you choose to check the integrity of the DVD during the installation process within the VM, the installation program "ejects" that DVD. KVM does not recognize that "eject." In that case, you'd have to click View | Details, select the IDE CDROM1 option, click Disconnect, and then click Connect. In the Choose Media window that appears, select the appropriate file with the DVD ISO image or CD-ROM for physical media.

12. Be aware, when selecting software, this system is a virtual guest, not a virtual host configured in Chapter 1. There is no need to add any virtualization packages to the installation. A basic server for the host systems on a VM is sufficient, with the Desktop, Fonts, X Window System, and Internet Browser package groups added on.

13. When the installation is complete, click Reboot. If the system tries to boot from the DVD drive again, you'll need to change the boot order between the DVD and the hard drive. If the system boots directly from the hard drive, you're done!

14. If the system tries to reboot from the DVD, you would need to shut down the system. To do so, click Virtual Machine | Shut Down | Force Off. (The Shut Down | Shut Down option does not work at this time.)

15. If this is the first time you've run that command sequence, the Virtual Machine Manager prompts for confirmation. Click Yes.

16. Now click View | Details.

17. In the left-hand pane, select Boot Options, as shown in Figure 2-12.

18. One way to change the boot order is to highlight CDROM, and then click the down arrow button. Click Apply, or the changes won't be recorded.

19. Now click View | Console and then Virtual Machine | Run. The system should now boot normally into the First Boot process discussed in Chapter 1.

FIGURE 2-12

Boot Options in
the VM

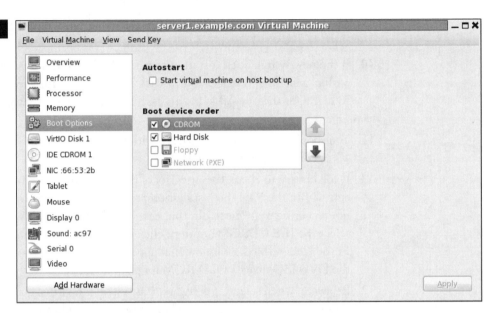

FIGURE 2-12

Boot Options in
the VM

**The steps discussed in this
section describe how to meet the RHCSA
objective to "access a virtual machine's
console." It also suggests one method that
you can use to "start and stop virtual
machines."**

One more reason for the use of VMs is
the ease with which additional virtual hard
drives can be added. The process varies by
VM solution. For the RHEL 6 default Virtual
Machine Manager with KVM solution, you can
do so from the machine window by clicking
View | Details. You'll see an Add Hardware
option in this screen.

EXERCISE 2-2

Add Virtual Hard Drives

In this exercise, you'll create an additional virtual hard drive on a KVM-based VM.
It assumes there's an existing KVM VM for that purpose, along with the use of the
GUI Virtual Machine Manager. Of course, given that it's KVM, it assumes that the
local physical system supports hardware virtualization.

1. Open the Virtual Machine Manager. From the command line in a GUI, run the **virt-manager** command.

2. Highlight the regular localhost (QEMU) hypervisor. If it isn't already connected, right-click it and select Connect from the pop-up menu that appears. This step may happen automatically.

3. If prompted, enter the root administrative password and click Authenticate.

4. Right-click an existing VM, and click Open in the pop-up menu that appears.

5. Click View | Details. In the bottom-left corner of the window that opens, click Add Hardware.

6. In the Add New Virtual Hardware window that appears, select Storage from the drop-down menu, and click Forward to continue.

7. In the Storage window that appears, shown in the illustration, set up a 1.0GB drive, select Allocate Entire Disk Now, select IDE Device Type, in default Cache Mode. (You can also select a SCSI, USB, or Virtual (Virtio) Disk.) Make desired choices and click Forward to continue.

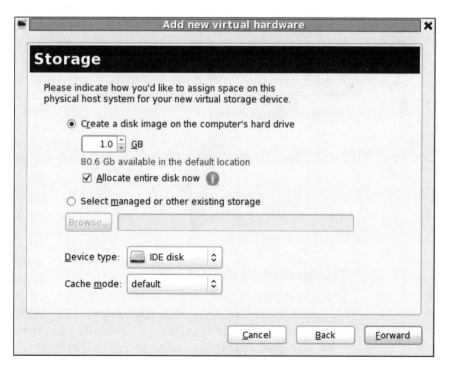

8. You'll see a confirmation of selected settings. If satisfied, click Finish to create the new virtual hard drive.

9. Repeat previous steps to create a second 1GB hard drive. To learn more about KVM, it would be useful to set up something different, such as a SCSI disk. However, that's not required.

10. The next time you boot this system, run the **fdisk -l** command from the root account. It should confirm appropriate information about the configured hard drive devices.

KVM Configuration Files

KVM-based VMs are normally configured in two different directories: /etc/libvirt and /var/lib/libvirt. When a KVM VM is configured, it is set up in files in XML format in the /etc/libvirt/qemu directory. For example, Figure 2-13 shows a relevant excerpt of the configuration file for the main VM I used to help prepare this book (server1.example.com.xml).

Important parameters for the VM are labeled. For example, the amount of memory is shown in KB, two virtual CPUs are allocated, KVM is the emulator, the disk can be found in the server1.example.com.img file in the /var/lib/libvirt/images directory, and so on.

While you can edit this configuration file directly, changes aren't implemented until the **libvirtd** script in the /etc/init.d directory is restarted with a command like **/etc/init.d/libvirtd restart**.

Control Virtual Machines from the Command Line

Of course, command line tools can be used to create, clone, convert, and install VMs on RHEL 6. The key commands to that end are **virt-install**, **virsh**, and **virt-clone**. The **virsh** command is an especially useful way to address two different RHCSA objectives.

The virt-install Command

You can perform the same steps as was done earlier in this chapter using the Virtual Machine Manager. All you need is the **virt-install --prompt** command. The command automatically prompts for the required information described earlier. Look at the command and prompts shown in Figure 2-14.

FIGURE 2-13

The Configuration
file for a KVM
Virtual Machine

```
<domain type='kvm'>
  <name>server1.example.com</name>
  <uuid>d60a8c0a-d795-c0fc-893f-174ac0f37f6e</uuid>
  <memory>786432</memory>
  <currentMemory>786432</currentMemory>
  <vcpu>2</vcpu>
  <os>
    <type arch='x86_64' machine='rhel6.0.0'>hvm</type>
    <boot dev='hd'/>
    <boot dev='cdrom'/>
  </os>
  <features>
    <acpi/>
    <apic/>
    <pae/>
  </features>
  <clock offset='utc'/>
  <on_poweroff>destroy</on_poweroff>
  <on_reboot>restart</on_reboot>
  <on_crash>restart</on_crash>
  <devices>
    <emulator>/usr/libexec/qemu-kvm</emulator>
    <disk type='file' device='disk'>
      <driver name='qemu' type='raw' cache='none'/>
      <source file='/var/lib/libvirt/images/server1.example.com.img'/>
      <target dev='vda' bus='virtio'/>
      <address type='pci' domain='0x0000' bus='0x00' slot='0x05' function='0x0'/>
    </disk>
    <disk type='file' device='cdrom'>
      <driver name='qemu' type='raw'/>
      <source file='/var/lib/libvirt/images/rhel-server-6.0-x86_64-boot.iso'/>
      <target dev='hdc' bus='ide'/>
      <readonly/>
      <address type='drive' controller='0' bus='1' unit='0'/>
"/etc/libvirt/qemu/server1.example.com.xml" 80L, 2844C
```

FIGURE 2-14

Configure a VM
with the
virt-install
command.

```
[root@Maui ~]# virt-install --prompt
What is the name of your virtual machine? tester1.example.com
 How much RAM should be allocated (in megabytes)? 768
 What would you like to use as the disk (file path)? /home/michael/KVM/tester1.example
.com.img
 How large would you like the disk (/home/michael/KVM/tester1.example.com.img) to be (
in gigabytes)? 12
 What is the install CD-ROM/ISO or URL? ftp://192.168.122.1/pub/inst


Starting install...
Retrieving file .treeinfo...                            | 3.3 kB    00:00 ...
Retrieving file vmlinuz...                              | 7.2 MB    00:00 ...
Retrieving file initrd.img...                           |  57 MB    00:00 ...
Allocating 'tester1.example.com.img'                    |  12 GB    00:00
Creating domain...                                      |   0 B     00:00
Domain installation still in progress. You can reconnect to
the console to complete the installation process.
```

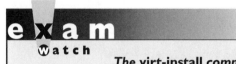

@atch

The virt-install command is one method to address the RHCSA objective "Install Red Hat Enterprise Linux systems as virtual guests."

For many, that's simpler than configuring the GUI Virtual Machine Manager. The Creating Domain message at the end of Figure 2-14 starts a VNC window with a graphical view of the given installation program.

If you make a mistake with the **virt-install** command, you can abort the process by pressing CTRL-C. But be aware that newly created VM is still running. And there's now a configuration file and virtual disk for that VM. If you try to rerun the **virt-install** command with the same name for the VM, an error message will appear. Thus, if you want to use the same name for the VM, take the following steps:

1. Stop the VM just created. If it's the tester1.example.com system shown in Figure 2-14, you can do so with the following command:

   ```
   # virsh destroy tester1.example.com
   ```

2. Delete the associated XML configuration file in the /etc/libvirt/qemu directory. For the given system name, that file would be tester1.example.com.xml.

3. If desired, you may also want to delete the virtual disk file, normally created in the /var/lib/libvirt/images directory. However, this is not necessary if the file is of an acceptable size, as it is reusable. For the given system name, that file would be tester1.example.com.img.

4. With the following command, restart the VM daemon, to erase the tester1.example.com system from RAM:

   ```
   # /etc/init.d/libvirtd restart
   ```

5. Now you'll be able to run the **virt-install** command again with the same name for the VM.

The virt-install Command and Kickstart

For Kickstart installations described later in this chapter, the **virt-install --prompt** command can't be used to cite a Kickstart configuration file. For that purpose, you'll need to understand some of the key switches associated with the **virt-install** command, as shown in Table 2-3.

For example, the following **virt-install** command would install a system named outsider1.example.org automatically from a Kickstart file named ks1.cfg

TABLE 2-3	Switch	Description
	-n (--name)	Sets the name for the VM
Command Switches for virt-install	-r (--ram)	Configures the amount of RAM in MB
	--disk	Defines the virtual disk; often used with **path=/var/lib/libvirt/ images/*virt*.img**
	-l (--location)	Specifies the directory or URL with the installation files (equivalent to **--location**)
	-x (--extra-args=)	Includes extra data, such as the URL of a Kickstart file

from the FTP server on the noted IP address, with 768MB of RAM, and an outsider1.example.org.img virtual disk.

```
# virt-install -n outsider1.example.org -r 768 --disk \
path=/var/lib/libvirt/images/outsider1.example.org.img \
-l ftp://192.168.122.1/pub/inst \
-x "ks=ftp://192.168.122.1/pub/ks1.cfg"
```

If you run the **virt-install** command with a Kickstart file customized from a previous KVM-based installation, it may fail. A standard KVM-based installation configures the first virtual disk on device /dev/vda. In contrast, the **virt-install** command assumes that the first virtual disk in question is device /dev/sda. The Kickstart file described later in this chapter would need to be customized for this difference.

The noted file contains a number of switches. Most of the switches shown are described in the examples listed in the man page for the **virt-install** command. The exception is the **-x**, another name for the **--extra-args=** switch. You may note additional switches, which are helpful but are not required for RHEL 6 installation. However, they are required to look for the given Kickstart file. So remember the format for the extra arguments, with the quotes, which may also be expressed as:

```
--extra-args="ks=ftp://192.168.122.1/pub/ks1.cfg"
```

The virsh Command

The **virsh** command starts a front end to existing KVM VMs. When run alone, it moves from a regular command line to the following prompt:

```
virsh #
```

From that prompt, run the **help** command. It includes access to a number of commands, some of which are listed in Table 2-4. Not all of those commands shown in the output to the **help** command are active for KVM. Those **virsh** commands that are usable can also be run directly from the bash shell prompt; for example, the **virsh list --all** command lists all configured VMs, whether or not they're currently running. In the context of KVM, the name of each VM is a domain, which is used by different **virsh** commands.

Take a look at the output to the **virsh --list all** command on my system:

```
Id Name                          State
----------------------------------
 - server1.example.com  shut off
 - tester1.example.com  shut off
```

With the right **virsh** commands, you can meet two RHCSA objectives. First, the following command starts the noted server1.example.com system:

```
# virsh start server1.example.com
```

Unfortunately, the **virsh shutdown** command does not work as of this writing. So to actually stop a VM from the command line, you'd have to run a somewhat more severe command:

```
# virsh destroy server1.example.com
```

The **virsh destroy** command switch is functionally equivalent to disconnecting the power cord on a physical system. As that can lead to different problems, it's best to stop a VM by running the **poweroff** command from within the VM.

on the

Ob

While the shutdown command works in Kickstart configuration files, to shut down a system from the command line, the functional command is poweroff.

TABLE 2-4	virsh Command	Description
Commands at the virsh Prompt	autostart <domain>	Start a domain during the host system boot process
	capabilities	Lists abilities of the local hypervisor
	edit <domain>	Edits the XML configuration file for the domain
	list --all	List all domains
	start <domain>	Boot the given domain
	shutdown <domain>	Gracefully shut down the given domain

*To start and stop a VM, you can run the **virsh start** vmname and **virsh destroy** vmname **commands, where** vmname **is the name of the VM, as shown in the output to the virsh list --all command.***

Even on the most protected systems, power failures happen. Kernel updates still require a system reboot. In those cases, it's helpful to automate the start of VMs on a virtual host during the boot process.

In addition, the **virsh** command is the most straightforward way to make sure a VM is started the next time a system is booted. For example, the following command boots the noted tester1.example.com system during the boot process of the host system.

```
# virsh autostart tester1.example.com
```

Once the boot process is complete for both the host and the VM, you'll be able to use commands like **ssh** to connect to that VM system normally. However, from the virtual host GUI, you'll still have to start the Virtual Machine Manager and connect to the associated hypervisor to actually connect to the virtual console for that tester1.example.com system.

The command creates a soft linked file in the /etc/libvirt/qemu/autostart directory. To reverse the process, either run the following command:

```
# virsh autostart --disable tester1.example.com
```

or delete the soft linked file named after the target VM from that directory.

*To configure a VM to start automatically when a system is booted, you can run the **virsh autostart** vmname command, where vmname **is the name of the VM, as shown in the output to the virsh list --all command.***

The virt-clone Command

The **virt-clone --prompt** command can be used to clone an existing VM. Before starting the process, make sure the system to be cloned is shut down. It's straightforward; one example where a tester1.example.com system is created from a server1.example.com system is shown in Figure 2-15.

Once the process is complete, not only will you find the noted hard drive images in the specified directories, but also you'll find a new XML configuration file for that VM in the /etc/libvirt/qemu directory.

```
[root@Maui ~]# virt-clone --prompt
What is the name of the original virtual machine? server1.example.com
  What is the name for the cloned virtual machine? tester1.example.com
   What would you like to use as the cloned disk (file path) for '/var/lib/libvirt/image
s/server1.example.com.img'? /var/lib/libvirt/images/tester1.example.com.img
   What would you like to use as the cloned disk (file path) for '/var/lib/libvirt/image
s/server1.example.com-1.img'? /var/lib/libvirt/images/tester1.example.com-1.img
   What would you like to use as the cloned disk (file path) for '/var/lib/libvirt/image
s/server1.example.com-2.img'? /var/lib/libvirt/images/tester1.example.com-2.img
Allocating 'tester1.example.com.img'                      |   12 GB      01:23
Allocating 'tester1.example.com-1.img'                    |  1.0 GB      00:01
Allocating 'tester1.example.com-2.img'                    |  1.0 GB      00:01

Clone 'tester1.example.com' created successfully.
[root@Maui ~]# █
```

The first time you boot a cloned machine, it may be best to boot it into runlevel 1.
As described in Chapter 5, runlevel 1 does not start most services, including
networking. In that case, you'll be able to modify any fixed networking settings, such
as the hostname and IP address before starting that cloned machine on a production
network. In addition, you'll want to make sure to change the hardware address for
the related network card, to avoid conflicts with the original network card.

While that process may not be difficult for one or two VMs, imagine setting up
a few dozen VMs, each later configured for different services. That situation would
be helped by more automation. To that end, Red Hat provides a system known as
Kickstart.

CERTIFICATION OBJECTIVE 2.03

Automated Installation Options

Kickstart is Red Hat's solution for an automated installation of Red Hat. Think of
each of the steps performed during the installation process as questions. With
Kickstart, each of those questions can be answered automatically with one text file.
With Kickstart, you can set up identical systems very quickly. To that end, Kickstart
files are useful for quick deployment and distribution of Linux systems.

In addition, the installation process is an opportunity to learn more about
RHEL 6, not only boot media, but the partitions and logical volumes that can be

configured after installation is complete. With the advent of VMs, it isn't difficult to set up an automated installation on a new VM with the help of Kickstart.

The steps described in this section assume a connection to the FTP server with RHEL 6 installation files created and configured in Chapter 1, Lab 2.

Kickstart Concepts

One of the problems with a Kickstart-based installation is that it does not include the custom settings created after the basic installation was complete. While it's possible to include those settings based on post-installation scripts, that's beyond the scope of the RHCSA exam.

There are two methods for creating the required Kickstart configuration file:

- Start with the anaconda-ks.cfg file from the root user's home directory, /root.
- Use the graphical Kickstart Configurator, accessible via the **system-config-kickstart** command.

e x a m
ⓦ **a t c h**
While it's a good idea to monitor https://bugzilla.redhat.com for bugs related to key components, it may be especially important with respect to Kickstart. For example, bug 624536 suggests that NFS-based Kickstart installs are problematic. While that has been superseded by bug 602455, the issue remains.

The first option lets you use the Kickstart template file created for the local system by Anaconda, anaconda-ks.cfg in the /root directory. The second option, the Kickstart Configurator, is discussed in detail later in this chapter.

It's relatively easy to customize the anaconda-ks.cfg file for different systems. Shortly, you'll see how to customize that file as needed for different hard disk sizes, host-names, IP addresses, and more.

Set Up Local Access to Kickstart

Once the Kickstart file is configured, you can set it up on local media such as a USB key, a CD, a spare partition, or even a floppy drive. (Don't laugh; many VM systems, including KVM, make it easy to use virtual floppy drives.) To do so, follow these basic steps:

1. Configure and edit the anaconda-ks.cfg file as desired. I'll describe this process in more detail shortly.

2. Mount the desired local media. You may need to run a command like **fdisk -l** as the root user to identify the appropriate device file. If the drive doesn't mount automatically, you can then mount the drive with a command such as **mount /dev/sdb /mnt**.

3. Copy the Kickstart file to ks.cfg on the mounted local media. (Other names are okay; ks.cfg is just the most common filename for this purpose in Red Hat documentation.)

4. Make sure the ks.cfg file has at least read permissions for all users. If SELinux is active on the local system, the contexts should normally match that of other files in the same directory. For more information, see Chapter 4.

Be aware, a Kickstart configuration file on an FTP server may be a security risk. It's almost like the DNA of a system. If a cracker gets a hold of that file, he could use that to set up a copy of your systems, to see how to break into and compromise your data. As that file normally contains a root administrative password, you should change that password as soon as that system is booted for the first time.

on the **job**

Be careful with the Kickstart configuration file. Unless direct root logins are disabled, the file includes the root administrative password. Even if that password is encrypted, a cracker with the right tools and a copy of that Kickstart configuration file can decrypt that password faster than you might expect.

5. You should now be ready to use the Kickstart media on a different system. You'll get to try this again shortly in an exercise.

6. Now try to access the Kickstart file on the local media. Boot the RHEL 6 installation CD/DVD. When the first menu appears, highlight Install Or Upgrade An Existing System and press TAB. Commands to Anaconda should appear, similar to the following. A cursor should appear at the end of that line.

```
vmlinuz initrd=initrd.img
```

7. Add information for the location of the Kickstart file to the end of the line. For example, the following addition locates that file on the first partition of the second hard drive, which may be a USB drive.

```
ks=hd:sdb1:/ks.cfg
```

Alternatively, if the kickstart file is on the boot CD, try adding the following command:

```
ks=cdrom:/ks.cfg
```

Alternatively, if the kickstart file is on the first floppy drive, enter the following:

```
ks=hd:fd0:/ks.cfg
```

There may be some trial and error with this method. Yes, device files are assigned in sequence (sda, sdb, sdc, and so on). However, unless you boot Linux with the given storage media, there is no certainty about which device file is assigned to a specific drive.

Set Up Network Access to Kickstart

The process of setting up a Kickstart file from local media can be time consuming, especially if you have to go from system to system to load that file. In many cases, it's more efficient to set up the Kickstart file on a network server. One logical location is the same network server used for the installation files. For example, based on the FTP server created in Chapter 1, Lab 2, assume there's a ks.cfg file in the FTP server's /var/ftp/pub directory. Furthermore, the SELinux contexts should match that of that directory, which can be confirmed with the following commands:

```
# ls -Zd /var/ftp/pub
# ls -Z /var/ftp/pub
```

Once an appropriate ks.cfg file is in the /var/ftp/pub directory, you can access it by adding the following directive to the end of the **vmlinuz initrd=initrd.img** line described earlier in Step 6:

```
ks=ftp://192.168.122.1/pub/ks.cfg
```

Similar options are possible for a Kickstart file on an NFS and an HTTP server, as follows:

```
ks=nfs:192.168.122.1/ks.cfg
ks=http://192.168.122.1/ks.cfg
```

However, you should not use NFS for sharing Kickstart files until the aforementioned bug 602455 has been addressed.

If there's an operational DNS server on the local network, you can substitute the hostname or fully qualified domain name of the target server for the IP address.

Red Hat is working to ease the process of creating a Kickstart-based installation server. For more information, see the Cobbler project at https:// fedorahosted.org/cobbler/.

Sample Kickstart File

I've based this section on the anaconda-ks.cfg file created when I installed RHEL 6 on a KVM-based VM. I've added a number of comments. While you're welcome to use it as a sample file, be sure to customize it for your hardware and network. This section just scratches the surface on what you can do with a Kickstart file; your version of this file may vary.

exam watch

Unlike what's available for many other Red Hat packages, available Kickstart documentation within an installed RHEL 6 system is somewhat sparse. In other words, you can't really rely on man pages or files in the /usr/share/doc directory for help during an exam. If you're uncertain about specific commands to include in the Kickstart file, the Kickstart Configurator described later in this chapter can help.

While most of the options are self-explanatory, I've interspersed my explanation of each command within the file. This file illustrates just a small portion of available commands. For more information on each command (and options) in this file, read the latest RHEL 6 Installation Guide, which is available online at http://docs.redhat .com/docs/en-US.

Follow these ground rules and guidelines when setting up a Kickstart file:

- In general, retain the order of the directives. However, some variation is allowable depending on whether the installation is from local media or over a network.
- You do not need to use all the options.
- If you leave out a required option, the user will be prompted for the answer.
- Don't be afraid to make a change; for example, partition-related directives are commented out by default.
- Line wrapping in the file is acceptable.

on the job

If you leave out an option, the installation process will stop at that point. This is an easy way to see if a Kickstart file is properly configured. But as some Kickstart options change the partitions on a hard drive, even tests can be dangerous. So it's best to test a Kickstart file on a test system, or even better, an experimental VM.

The following is the code from one of my anaconda-ks.cfg files. The first two lines are comments that tell me that this file was created during the installation process for RHEL 6:

```
# Kickstart file automatically generated by anaconda.
#version=RHEL6
```

The first command is simple; it starts the installation process. It defaults to the first available local media; in this case, the first RHEL installation DVD/CD or USB key.

```
install
```

The next step is to specify the source of the installation files. To use RHEL 6 DVDs, enter **cdrom**. To install from an NFS server, specify the URI as follows. If there's a reliable DNS server for the local network, you can substitute the hostname for the IP address.

```
nfs --server=192.168.122.1 --dir=/inst
```

You can also configure a connection to an FTP or HTTP server by substituting one of the commands shown here. The directories I specify are based on the FTP and HTTP installation servers created in Chapter 1:

```
url --url http://192.168.122.1/inst
```

or

```
url --url ftp://192.168.122.1/pub/inst
```

If the ISO file that represents the RHEL 6 DVD exists on a local hard drive partition, you can specify that as well. For example, the following directive points to ISO CDs or DVDs on the /dev/sda10 partition:

```
harddrive --partition=/dev/sda10 --dir=/home/michael/
```

The **lang** command specifies the language to use during the installation process. It matters if the installation stops due to a missing command in this file. The **keyboard** command is self-explanatory, as it specifies the keyboard to configure on this computer.

```
lang en_US.UTF-8
keyboard us
```

The required **network** command is simplest if there's a DHCP server for the local network: **network --device eth0 --bootproto dhcp**. In contrast, the following line configures static IP address information, with the noted network mask (**--netmask**), gateway address (**--gateway**), DNS server (**--nameserver**), and computer name (**--hostname**).

```
network --device eth0 --bootproto static --ip 192.168.122.150 --netmask
255.255.255.0 --gateway 192.168.122.1 --nameserver 192.168.122.1 --hostname
tester1.example.com
```

Please note that all options for the **network** command *must* be on *one* line. Line wrapping, if the options exceed the space in a text editor, is acceptable. If you're setting up this file for a different system, don't forget to change the IP address and hostname information accordingly. Be aware, if you did not configure networking during the installation process, it won't be written to the subject anaconda-ks. cfg file. Given the complexity of the network directive, you could either use the Kickstart Configurator to help set up that directive, or configure networking after installation is complete.

As the password for the root user is part of the RHEL 6 installation process, the Kickstart configuration file can specify that password in encrypted format. While encryption is not required, it can at least delay a cracker who might break into a system after installation is complete. Since the associated cryptographic hash function is the same as is used for the /etc/shadow file, you can copy the desired password from that file.

```
rootpw --iscrypted $6$5UrLfXTk$CsCW0nQytrUuvycuLT317/
```

As for security, the **firewall** directive suggests that it's enabled. When coupled with **--service=ssh**, it specifies the service port number that's allowed through the firewall, based on how it's defined in the /etc/services file.

```
firewall --service=ssh
```

Next, the **authconfig** command sets up the Shadow Password Suite (**--enableshadow**), the SHA 512 bit encryption algorithm for password encryption (**--passalgo=sha512**), and authentication with any existing fingerprint reader. A password encrypted to the SHA512 algorithm starts with a **$6**, like the root administrative password just shown.

```
authconfig --enableshadow --passalgo=sha512
--enablefingerprint
```

The **selinux** directive can be set to **--enforcing**, **--permissive**, or **--disabled**.

```
selinux --enforcing
```

The **timezone** command is associated with a long list of time zones. They're documented in the tzdata package. For a full list, run the **rpm -ql tzdata** command. By default, Red Hat sets the hardware clock to the equivalent of Greenwich Mean Time with the **--utc** switch. That setting supports automated changes for daylight saving time. The following setting can be found as a subdirectory and file in the /usr/share/zoneinfo directory.

```
timezone America/Los_Angeles
```

The default bootloader is GRUB. It should normally be installed on the Master Boot Record (MBR) of a hard drive. You can include a **--driveorder** switch to specify the drive with the bootloader and an **--append** switch to specify commands for the kernel. While the given **crashkernel=auto** option should automatically select available memory upon a crash, early reports on RHEL 6 suggest that you may need to replace it with a specific memory location such as **crashkernel=128M@16M**.

```
bootloader --location=mbr --driveorder=vda
--append="crashkernel=auto rhgb quiet"
```

As suggested by the comments that follow, it's first important to clear some existing sets of partitions. First, the **clearpart --drives=vda --all --initlabel** directive clears all volumes on the vda virtual hard drive. If it hasn't been used before, **--initlabel** initializes that drive. Of course, before such a command takes effect, any existing comment character (#) must be removed. The **ignoredisk** directive that follows specifies volumes only on the noted vda drive. Of course, this works only if there is a specified virtual drive on the target VM. (It's possible to specify PATA or SCSI drives on such VMs, which would conflict with these directives.)

```
# The following is the partition information you requested
# Note that any partitions you deleted are not expressed
# here so unless you clear all partitions first, this is
# not guaranteed to work
clearpart --drives=vda --all --initlabel
ignoredisk --only-use=vda
```

If you're planning to use this Kickstart file with the **virt-install** command described earlier, you'll need to substitute the sda device for vda, as the **virt-install** command does not recognize that virtual hard drive device file.

Changes are required in the partition (**part**) directives that follow. They should specify the directory, filesystem format (**--fstype**), and **--size** in MB.

```
part /boot --fstype=ext4 --size=500
part / --fstype=ext4 --size=8000
part swap --size=1000
part /home --fstype=ext4 --size=1000
```

Be aware, your version of an anaconda-ks.cfg file may include an **--onpart** directive that specifies partition device files such as /dev/vda1. That would lead to an error unless the noted partitions already exist. So if you see those **--onpart** directives, it's simplest to delete them. Otherwise, you'd have to create those partitions before starting the installation process, and that can be tricky.

While other partition options are available with respect to setting up RAID arrays and logical volumes, the implicit focus of the Red Hat exams is to set up such volumes after installation is complete. If you want to try out other options such as logical volumes, create your own Kickstart file. It's best if you set it up from a different VM installation. Just be aware, the Kickstart file that appears configures Physical Volumes (PVs), Volume Groups (VGs), and Logical Volumes (LVs) in that order (and the order is important), similar to that shown here:

```
#part pv.KKb1QT-Sm1q-TNoC-L4Ww --grow --size=1

#volgroup vg_minimalrhel6 --pesize=4096 pv.KKb1QT-Sm1q-TNoC-L4Ww
#logvol / --fstype=ext4 --name=lv_root --vgname=vg_minimalrhel6 --size=51200

#logvol swap --name=lv_swap --vgname=vg_minimalrhel6 --size=1504
```

The alphanumeric that starts with the KK is an abbreviated Universally Unique Identifier (UUID). For more information on how LVs are configured, see Chapter 8.

The default version of the Kickstart file may contain a **repo** directive. It would point to the FTP network installation source from Chapter 1, Lab 2, and should be deleted from or commented out of the Kickstart file as follows:

```
#repo --name="Red Hat Enterprise Linux"
--baseurl=ftp://192.168.122.1/pub/ --cost=100
```

To make sure the system actually completes the installation process, this is the place to include a directive such as **reboot**, **shutdown**, **halt**, or **poweroff**. I personally prefer the **shutdown** directive; if you want to avoid the First Boot process described earlier, you can also include the **firstboot --disabled** directive. As there's no way to set up a Kickstart file with answers to the First Boot prompts, that **--disabled** directive helps automate the Kickstart process.

```
shutdown
firstboot --disabled
```

If you're reusing an existing KVM-based VM, it may be necessary to shut off the system to change the boot media from the CD/DVD to the hard drive. So instead, you may prefer to substitute the following directive:

```
shutdown
```

What follows is a list of package groups that are installed through this Kickstart configuration file. These names correspond to the names that you can find in the *-comps-rhel6-Server.xml file in the RHEL 6 DVD /repodata directory described in Chapter 1. Since the list is long, the following is just excerpts of package groups (which start with the @) and package names:

```
%packages
@ base
@ console-internet
...
nss-pam-ldapd
perl-DBD-SQLite
%end
```

After the package groups are installed, you can specify post-installation commands after the following directive. For example, you could set up custom configuration files. But the %post directive and anything that follows is not required.

```
%post
```

EXERCISE 2-3

Create and Use a Sample Kickstart File

In this exercise, you will use the anaconda-ks.cfg file to duplicate the installation from one computer to another with identical hardware. This exercise installs all the exact same packages with the same partition configuration on the second computer. This exercise even configures the SELinux context for that Kickstart file.

As the objective is to install the same packages as the current installation, no changes are required to packages or package groups from the default anaconda-ks.cfg file in the /root directory. This assumes access to a network installation source such as that created in Chapter 1 Lab 2.

The steps in this exercise assume sufficient space and resources for at least two different KVM-based VMs, as discussed in Chapter 1.

1. Review the /root/anaconda-ks.cfg file. Copy it to ks.cfg.

2. If there's an existing **network** directive in the file, modify it to point to an IP address of 192.168.122.150, with a hostname of tester1.example.com. If a system with that hostname and IP address already exists, use a different hostname and IP address on the same network. It is okay if such a directive doesn't already exist; networking can be configured after installation is complete, using the techniques discussed in Chapter 3.

3. Make sure the directives associated with drives and partitions in ks.cfg file are active, as they're commented out by default in the /root/anaconda-ks.cfg file. Pay attention to the **clearpart** directive; it should normally be set to **--all** to erase all partitions and **--initlabel** to initialize newly created disks. If there's more than one hard drive on the system, the **--drives=vda** switch can focus on the first virtual drive on a KVM-based VM.

4. Review the location of the installation server, associated with the **url** or **nfs** directives. This lab assumes it's an FTP server accessible on IP address 192.168.122.1, in the pub/inst/ subdirectory. If it's a different IP address and directory, substitute accordingly.

5. Make sure the following directives are included just before the **%post** directive at the end of the file:

```
shutdown
firstboot --disabled
```

6. Copy the ks.cfg file to the base directory of the installation server; if it's the vsFTP server, that directory is /var/ftp/pub. Make sure that file is readable to all users. One method is with the following command:

```
# chmod +r /var/ftp/pub/ks.cfg
```

7. Assuming that base directory is /var/ftp/pub, modify the SELinux context of that file with the following command:

```
# chcon --reference /var/ftp/pub /var/ftp/pub/ks.cfg
```

8. Make sure any existing firewalls do not block the communication port associated with the installation server. For detailed information, see Chapter 4. The simplest, though insecure way to do so is with the following command:

```
# iptables -F
```

9. Prepare the second computer so that it has sufficient hard drive space. That second computer can be a KVM-based VM on a local host. Boot that second computer into the RHEL 6 DVD.

10. At the Red Hat Installation menu, highlight the first option and press TAB. It will display the startup directives toward the bottom of the screen. At the end of that line, add the following directive:

```
ks=ftp://192.168.122.1/pub/ks.cfg
```

If the Kickstart file is on a different server or on local media, substitute accordingly.

You should now see the system installation creating the same basic setup as the first system. If the installation process stops before rebooting, then there's some problem with the Kickstart file, most likely a case of insufficient information.

The Kickstart Configurator

Even users who prefer to work at the command line can learn from the Red Hat GUI tool known as the Kickstart Configurator. It includes most (but not all) of the basic options associated with setting up a Kickstart configuration file. You can install it with the following command:

```
# yum install system-config-kickstart
```

As a GUI tool associated with the installation process, this command typically includes a number of dependencies. When I installed it on my system, this one command found 27 dependencies, meaning that command installed a total of 28 packages.

Those of you sensitive to properly written English may object to the term "Kickstart Configurator." But it is the name given by Red Hat to the noted GUI configuration tool.

Now that you understand the basics of what goes into a Kickstart file, it's time to solidify your understanding through the graphical Kickstart Configurator. It can help you learn more about how to configure the Kickstart file. Once the right packages are installed, it can be opened from a GUI command line with the **system-config-kickstart** command. To start it with the default configuration for the local system, cite the anaconda-ks.cfg file as follows:

```
# system-config-kickstart /root/anaconda-ks.cfg
```

It should open the Kickstart Configurator shown in Figure 2-16. (Of course, it's probably a good idea to back up the anaconda-ks.cfg file first.)

Before starting the Kickstart Configurator, it's best to make sure there's an active connection to a remote RHEL 6 repository through the RHN. Alternatively, you can also connect the local system to the installation source created in Chapter 1, Lab 2 using the techniques described in Chapter 7.

The Kickstart
Configurator

The screen shown in Figure 2-16 illustrates a number of basic installation steps. If you've already installed RHEL, all of these steps should look familiar.

A number of other options appear in the left-hand pane, each associated with different Kickstart commands. To learn more about Kickstart, experiment with some of these settings. Use the File | Save command to save these settings with the filename of your choice, which you can then review in a text editor. Alternatively, you can choose File | Preview to see the effect of different settings on the Kickstart file.

The following sections provide a brief overview of each option shown in the left-hand pane. A detailed understanding of the Kickstart Configurator can also help you understand the installation process.

Basic Configuration

In the Basic Configuration screen, you can assign settings for the following components:

■ **Default Language**   Specifies the default language for the installation and operating system.

■ **Keyboard**   Sets the default keyboard; normally associated with language.

- **Time Zone**   Supports computers in which the hardware clock is set to the atomic realization of UTC, which is essentially the same as Greenwich Mean Time.

- **Root Password**   Specifies the password for the root administrative user; may be encrypted.

- **Target Architecture**   Can help customize a Kickstart file for different systems.

- **Reboot System After Installation**   Adds the **reboot** command to the end of the kickstart file.

- **Perform System Installation In Text Mode**   Supports automated installation in text mode. Once automated, the installation mode should not matter.

- **Perform Installation In Interactive Mode**   Allows review of the steps associated with a Kickstart installation.

Installation Method

The Installation Method options are straightforward. You're either installing Linux for the first time or upgrading a previous installation. The installation method, and your entries, are based on the location of the installation files. For example, if you select an NFS installation method, the Kickstart Configurator prompts you for the name or IP address of the NFS server and the shared directory with the RHEL installation files.

You can set up the Kickstart file to install RHEL from a CD/DVD, a local hard drive partition, or one of the standard network servers: NFS, HTTP, or FTP.

Boot Loader Options

The next section lists boot loader options. The default boot loader is GRUB, which supports encrypted passwords for an additional level of security during the boot process.

Linux boot loaders are normally installed on the MBR. If you're dual-booting Linux and Microsoft Windows with GRUB, you *can* set up the Windows boot loader (or an alternate boot loader such as Partition Magic or System Commander) to point to GRUB on the first sector of the Linux partition with the /boot directory.

Partition Information

The Partition Information options determine how this installation configures the hard disks on the affected computers. While it supports the configuration of standard and RAID partitions, it does not yet support the configuration of LVM groups. The Clear Master Boot Record option allows you to wipe the MBR from an older hard disk that might have a problem there; it includes the **zerombr yes** command in the Kickstart file.

on the **job**

***Don't use the zerombr yes** option if you want to keep an alternate bootloader on the MBR such as Partition Magic or the Windows 7 Bootmgr.*

You can remove partitions depending on whether they've been created to a Linux filesystem. If you're using a new hard drive, it's important to Initialize the Disk Label as well. Click the Add command; it opens the Partition Options dialog box.

Network Configuration

The Network Configuration section enables you to set up IP addressing on the network cards on a target computer. You can customize static IP addressing for a specific computer, or configure the use of a DHCP server. Just click Add Network Device and explore the Network Device Information window.

Authentication

The Authentication section lets you set up two forms of security for user passwords: Shadow Passwords, which encrypts user passwords in the /etc/shadow file, and the encryption hash for those passwords. This section also allows you to set up authentication information for various protocols:

- **NIS**   Network Information Service to connect to a login authentication database on a network with Unix and Linux computers.
- **LDAP**   In this context, the Lightweight Directory Assistance Protocol is an alternative login authentication database.
- **Kerberos 5**   The MIT system for strong cryptography to authenticate users on a network.
- **Hesiod**   Associated with Kerberos 5.
- **SMB**   Samba (CIFS) connects to a Microsoft Windows–style network for login authentication.

■ **Name Switch Cache** Associated with NIS for looking up passwords and groups.

Firewall Configuration

The Firewall Configuration section allows you to configure a default firewall for the subject computer. On most systems, you'll want to keep the number of trusted services to a minimum. However, in a situation like the Red Hat exams, you may be asked to set up a multitude of services on a single system, which would require the configuration of a multitude of trusted services on a firewall.

In this section, you can also configure basic SELinux settings. The Active and Disabled options are straightforward; the Warn option corresponds to a Permissive implementation of SELinux. For more information, see Chapter 4.

Display Configuration

The Display Configuration section supports the installation of a basic Linux GUI. The actual installation depends on those packages and package groups selected in the next section. While there is a lot of debate on the superiority of GUI- or text-based administrative tools, text-based tools are more stable. For this reason (and more), many Linux administrators don't even install a GUI. However, if you're installing Linux on a series of workstations, as might be done with a series of Kickstart file, it's likely that most of the users won't be administrators.

In addition, you can disable or enable the Setup Agent, also known as the First Boot process. For a completely automated installation, the Setup Agent should be disabled.

Package Selection

The Package Selection section allows you to choose the package groups that are installed through this Kickstart file. You should recognize it as the custom installation screens shown during the installation process.

As noted earlier, the associated screens are blank if there's no current connection to a remote repository such as updates from the RHN or the installation server described earlier.

Installation Scripts

You can add pre-installation and post-installation scripts to the Kickstart file. Post-installation scripts are more common, and they can help configure other parts of a Linux operating system in a common way. For example, if you wanted to install a directory with employee benefits information, you could add a post-installation script that adds the appropriate **cp** commands to copy files from a network server.

CERTIFICATION OBJECTIVE 2.04

Administration with the Secure Shell

Red Hat Enterprise Linux installs the Secure Shell (SSH) packages by default. The RHCSA requirement with respect to SSH is simple; you need to know how to use it to access remote systems. Therefore, in this section, you'll examine how to use the **ssh** command to access remote systems as a client.

As suggested earlier, the stage is already set by the default installation of SSH on standard installations of RHEL 6. While firewalls are enabled by default, the standard RHEL 6 firewall leaves port 22 open for SSH access. Related configuration files are stored in the /etc/ssh directory. Detailed server configuration is part of the RHCE requirements. Related client commands are **scp** and **sftp**, also covered in this section.

The Secure Shell daemon is secure because it encrypts messages. In other words, users who are listening on a network can't read the messages that are sent between SSH clients and servers. And that's important on a public network like the Internet. RHEL incorporates SSH version 2, which includes a key exchange algorithm, which is the enhancement relative to SSH version 1. If you're studying for the RHCE objectives on SSH, read Chapter 11.

Configure an SSH Client

The main SSH client configuration file is /etc/ssh/ssh_config. Individual users can have custom SSH client configurations in their ~/.ssh/config files. There are four directives included by default. First, the **Host *** directive applies the other directives to all connections.

```
Host *
```

This is followed by a directive that supports authentication using the Generic Security Services Application Programming Interface for client/server authentication:

```
GSSAPIAuthentication yes
```

This next directive supports remote access to GUI tools. X11 is a legacy reference to the X Window System server used on Linux.

```
ForwardX11Trusted yes
```

The next directives allow the client to set several environmental variables. The details are normally trivial between two Red Hat Enterprise Linux systems.

```
SendEnv LANG LC_CTYPE LC_NUMERIC LC_TIME LC_COLLATE LC_MONETARY LC_MESSAGES
SendEnv LC_PAPER LC_NAME LC_ADDRESS LC_TELEPHONE LC_MEASUREMENT
SendEnv LC_IDENTIFICATION LC_ALL
```

This sets the stage for command line access of remote systems.

Command Line Access

This section is based on standard access with the **ssh** command. To access a remote system, you need the username and password on that remote system. By default, direct ssh-based access to the root account is enabled. For example, the following command accesses that account on the noted server1 system:

```
$ ssh root@server1.example.com
```

The following command works in the same way:

```
$ ssh -l root server1.example.com
```

Without the username, the **ssh** command assumes that you're logging in remotely as the username on the local system. For example, if I were to run the following command from my user michael account:

```
$ ssh server1.example.com
```

The **ssh** command assumes that I'm trying to log in to the server1.example. com system as user michael. The first time the command is run between systems, it presents something similar to the following message:

```
$ ssh server1.example.com
The authenticity of host 'server1.example.com (192.168.122.50)'
can't be established.
RSA key fingerprint is b9:8a:c8:cd:c3:02:87:b3:1c:a9:a7:ed:d8:9c
:28:b8.
Are you sure you want to continue connecting (yes/no)? yes

Warning: Permanently added 'server1.example.com,192.168.122.50'
```

```
(RSA) to the list of known hosts.
michael@server1.example.com's password:
```

One of the flaws of this type of **ssh** command is how it sends the password over the network. More secure access is possible using passphrase-based access to 1024-bit (and higher) private/public keypairs. But that more secure option is the province of the RHCE exam, discussed in Chapter 11. When the connection is made, a copy of the remote key fingerprint is appended to the user's ~/.ssh/known_hosts file. The RSA is a reference to the public encryption key from the remote system; the acronym is based on the last names of its developers, Rivest, Shamir, and Adelman. The public key is given to remote systems; the private key is kept on the local system to match authorized remote requests.

Once connected via **ssh**, you can do anything on the remote system that's supported by your user privileges on that remote system. For example, you can even shut down the remote system gracefully with the **poweroff** command. After executing that command, you'll typically have a couple of seconds to exit out of the remote system with the **exit** command.

More SSH Command Line Tools

If you prefer to access the remote system with an FTP-like client, the **sftp** command is for you. While the **-l** switch doesn't work with that command, it still can be used to log in to the account of any user on the remote system. While regular FTP communication proceeds in clear text, communication with the **sftp** command can be used to transfer files in encrypted format.

Alternatively, if you just want to copy over an encrypted connection, the **scp** command can help. For example, I created some of the screenshots for this book on the test VMs configured in Chapters 1 and 2. To transmit that screenshot to my laptop system, I used a command similar to the following, which copied the F02-20. tif file from the local directory to the remote system with the noted hostname, in the /home/michael/RHbook/Chapter2 directory.

```
# scp F02-20.tif michael@server1:/home/michael/RHbook/Chapter2/
```

Unless a passphrase-based connection has been established (as discussed in Chapter 11), the command prompts for the password of the user michael on the system named server1. Once the password is confirmed, the **scp** command copies the F02-20.tif file in encrypted format to the noted directory on the remote system named server1.

Graphical Secure Shell Access

The **ssh** command can be used to transmit GUI tools over a network. As strange as it sounds, it works if the local system works as a GUI server while you call remote GUI client applications from remote systems.

By default, both the SSH server and client configuration files are set up to support X11 communication over a network. All you need to do is connect to the remote system with the **-X** switch. For example, you could use the command sequence shown in Figure 2-17 to administer users on the remote system.

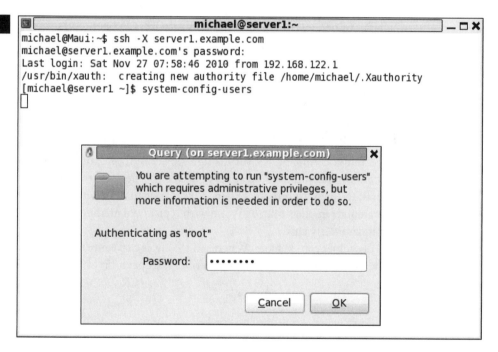

```
michael@Maui:~$ ssh -X server1.example.com
michael@server1.example.com's password:
Last login: Sat Nov 27 07:58:46 2010 from 192.168.122.1
/usr/bin/xauth:  creating new authority file /home/michael/.Xauthority
[michael@server1 ~]$ system-config-users
```

Query (on server1.example.com)

You are attempting to run "system-config-users"
which requires administrative privileges, but
more information is needed in order to do so.

Authenticating as "root"

Password: ....

Cancel   OK

CERTIFICATION OBJECTIVE 2.05

Consider Adding These Command Line Tools

You may want to consider adding several command line tools to help administer various Linux systems. These tools will be used later in this book to make sure various servers are actually operational. While it's best to test services like Postfix with actual e-mail clients like Evolution and Thunderbird, command tools like **telnet**, **nmap**, and **mutt** can be used to check these services remotely, from a command line interface. For exam purposes, you can use these tools to test, diagnose, and solve system issues in the time that it would take to download a complex tool like Evolution. While the **ssh** command can help access GUI tools remotely, communication with such tools can be time consuming.

For administrative purposes, tools of interest include the following:

- **telnet** and **nmap** to verify remote access to open ports.
- **mutt** as an e-mail client to verify the functionality of an e-mail server.
- **elinks** as a web browser to make sure web services are accessible.
- Use **lftp** to access FTP servers with command completion.

Checking Ports with telnet

The **telnet** command is a surprisingly powerful tool. Anyone who is aware of the security implications of clear text clients may hesitate to use **telnet**. People who use **telnet** to log in to remote servers do transmit their usernames, passwords, and other commands in clear text. Anyone with a protocol analyzer such as Ethereal can read that data fairly easily.

But **telnet** can do more. When run locally, it can verify the operation of a service. For example, the following command verifies the operation of vsFTP on the local system:

```
$ telnet localhost 21
Trying 127.0.0.1...
Connected to localhost.
Escape character is '^]'.
220 (vsFTPd 2.2.2)
```

The "Escape character" is the CTRL key and the right square bracket (]) pressed simultaneously. Pressing this command combination from the noted screen brings up the **telnet>** prompt. From there, you can exit with the **quit** command.

```
^]
telnet> quit
```

In most cases, you don't even need to execute the Escape character to quit; just type in the **QUIT** command.

If vsFTP were not running or had been configured to communicate on a port other than 21, you'd get the following response:

```
Trying 127.0.0.1...
telnet: connect to address 127.0.0.1: Connection refused
```

If there's no firewall, you'd get the same result from a remote system. If a firewall is blocking communications over port 21, however, you'd get a message similar to the following:

```
telnet: connect to address 192.168.122.50: No route to host
```

Some services such as the Postfix e-mail server are by default configured to accept connections only from the local system. In that case, with or without a firewall, you'd get the "connection refused" message when trying to connect from a remote system.

Checking Ports with nmap

The **nmap** command is a powerful port scanning tool. As such, the web site of the **nmap** developers states that "when used improperly, **nmap** can (in rare cases) get you sued, fired, expelled, jailed, or banned by your ISP." Nevertheless, it is included in the standard RHEL 6 repositories. As such, it is supported by Red Hat for legal use. It's a quick way to get a view of the services that are open locally, and remotely. For example, the **nmap localhost** command shown in Figure 2-18 detects and reveals those services that are running on the local system.

But in contrast, when the port scanner is run from a remote system, it looks like only one port is open. That shows the effect of the firewall on the server.

```
Starting Nmap 5.21 ( http://nmap.org ) at 2010-11-29 09:52 PST
Nmap scan report for server1.example.com (192.168.122.50)
Host is up (0.00027s latency).
Not shown: 999 filtered ports
PORT    STATE SERVICE
22/tcp open  ssh
```

FIGURE 2-18

Apply a port
scanner locally.

```
[root@server1 ~]# nmap localhost

Starting Nmap 5.21 ( http://nmap.org ) at 2010-11-29 09:47 PST
mass_dns: warning: Unable to determine any DNS servers. Reverse DNS is disabled.
  Try using --system-dns or specify valid servers with --dns-servers
Nmap scan report for localhost (127.0.0.1)
Host is up (0.0000070s latency).
Hostname localhost resolves to 2 IPs. Only scanned 127.0.0.1
Not shown: 997 closed ports
PORT     STATE SERVICE
22/tcp   open  ssh
25/tcp   open  smtp
111/tcp  open  rpcbind

Nmap done: 1 IP address (1 host up) scanned in 0.07 seconds
[root@server1 ~]# ▮
```

Configure an E-Mail Client

The configuration process for a GUI e-mail client should be trivial for any candidate for Red Hat certification. However, the same may not necessarily be true for command line clients, and they're useful for testing the functionality standard e-mail server services such as Postfix and sendmail. For example, once a server is configured for Post Office Protocol (POP) e-mail, even e-mail that is delivered using the near ubiquitous version 3 (POP3), it can be checked with the following command:

```
# mutt -f pop://username@host
```

Since GUI e-mail clients should be trivial for readers, the remainder of this section is focused on the use of command line e-mail clients.

Command Line Mail

One way to test a local mail system is with the built-in command line **mail** utility. It provides a simple text-based interface. The system keeps each user's mail in /var/mail directory files associated with each username. Users who read messages with the **mail** utility can also reply, forward, or delete associated messages.

You can certainly use any of the other mail readers, such as mutt, or the e-mail managers associated with different GUI web browsers to test your system. Other mail readers store messages in different directories. For example, the **pine** utility would create and store messages for user mj in the /home/mj/mail directory. Mail readers like **mutt**, **mail**, and **pine** can be used to send messages if a Simple Mail Transfer Protocol (SMTP) server is active for the local system.

There are two basic methods for using **mail**. First, you can enter the subject and then the text of the message. When done, press CTRL-D and then enter another addressee in the Cc: line, if desired. When you press ENTER, the message is sent and the **mail** utility stops and returns to the command line.

```
$ mail Michael
Subject: Test Message
Sent and received
Cc: mjang@example.com
$
```

Alternatively, you can redirect a file as the text of an e-mail to another user. For example, the following command sends a copy of /etc/hosts to the root user, with the Subject name of "hosts file":

```
$ mail -s 'hosts file' < /etc/hosts root@localhost
```

Reading Mail Messages

By default, the **mail** system doesn't open for a user unless there is actual e-mail in the appropriate file. Once the mail system is open, the user will see a list of new and already read messages. If you've opened the **mail** system for an account, you can enter the number of the message and press ENTER. If you press ENTER with no argument, the mail utility assumes you want to read the next unread message. To delete a mail message, use the **d** command after reading the message, or use **d#** to delete the message numbered #.

Alternatively, mail messages can be read from the user-specified file in the local /var/mail directory. Files in this directory are named for the associated username.

The Use of Text and Graphical Browsers

Linux includes a variety of graphical browsers. Access of regular and secure web sites is available through their associated protocols, the Hypertext Transfer Protocol (HTTP), and its secure cousin, Hypertext Transfer Protocol, Secure (HTTPS). The use of graphical browsers should be trivial for any serious user of Linux.

You may not always have access to the GUI, especially when working from a remote system. In any case, text-based browsers work more quickly. The standard text-based browser for Red Hat is elinks. Once the package is installed, you can use it from the command line to open the web site of your choice. For example. Figure 2-19 illustrates the result of the **elinks http://www.mheducation.com** command.

To exit from elinks, press the ESC key to access the menu bar, and then press F | X and accept the prompt to exit from the browser.

If you configure a web server, the easiest way to make sure it works is with a simple text home page. No HTML coding is required. For example, I could add the following text to home.html:

```
This is my home page
```

I could then run the **elinks home.html** command to view this text in the elinks browser. If you've set up an Apache file server on the /var/www/html/inst directory as discussed in Chapter 1, you can also use **elinks** to review the files copied to that server with the following command:

```
$ elinks http://192.168.122.1/inst
```

FIGURE 2-19	
The elinks browser	

The elinks browser

Using lftp to Access URLs

The original FTP client software was a basic command line, text-oriented client application that offered a simple but efficient interface. Most web browsers offer a graphical interface and can also be used as an FTP client.

Any FTP client allows you to view the directory tree and files. Using **ftp** as a client is easy. You could use the **ftp** command to connect to a server such as ftp.redhat.com with the following command:

```
# ftp ftp.redhat.com
```

But that client asks for a username and password. You could enter username anonymous and a random password to access the Red Hat FTP server. But if you accidentally enter a real username and password, that data is sent in clear text, available to anyone who happens to be using the right network analyzer applications on the network. Strangely enough, the **ftp** command client is not installed on standard RHEL 6 installations.

That's one reason why **lftp** is better. It automatically attempts an anonymous login, without prompting for a username or password. It also supports command completion, which can especially help you access files and directories with longer names.

Sure, there are risks with most FTP clients, as they transmit data in clear text. But as long as usage of this command is limited to public servers with anonymous access, the risk is minimal. After all, if you use **lftp** to download Linux packages from public servers, it's not like you're putting any private information at risk. To be sure, there are other security risks with such clients, but Red Hat developers are constantly working to keep that client up to date.

If the risks are acceptable, the **lftp** command can be used to log in to an FTP server where usernames and passwords are enabled. Those of you studying for the RHCE will set up that kind of very secure FTP (vsFTP) server in. User michael could log in to such a server with the following command:

```
$ lftp ftp.example.org -u michael
```

The **lftp** client can handle a number of different commands, as shown in Figure 2-20. Some of these commands are described in Table 2-5.

FIGURE 2-20

Commands in lftp

```
[root@Maui ~]# lftp ftp.redhat.com
lftp ftp.redhat.com:~> help
    !<shell-command>                 (commands)
    alias [<name> [<value>]]         bookmark [SUBCMD]
    cache [SUBCMD]                   cat [-b] <files>
    cd <rdir>                        chmod [OPTS] mode file...
    close [-a]                       [re]cls [opts] [path/][pattern]
    debug [<level>|off] [-o <file>]  du [options] <dirs>
    exit [<code>|bg]                 get [OPTS] <rfile> [-o <lfile>]
    glob [OPTS] <cmd> <args>         help [<cmd>]
    history -w file|-r file|-c|-l [cnt]  jobs [-v]
    kill all|<job_no>                lcd <ldir>
    lftp [OPTS] <site>               ls [<args>]
    mget [OPTS] <files>              mirror [OPTS] [remote [local]]
    mkdir [-p] <dirs>                module name [args]
    more <files>                     mput [OPTS] <files>
    mrm <files>                      mv <file1> <file2>
    [re]nlist [<args>]               open [OPTS] <site>
    pget [OPTS] <rfile> [-o <lfile>] put [OPTS] <lfile> [-o <rfile>]
    pwd [-p]                         queue [OPTS] [<cmd>]
    quote <cmd>                      repeat [OPTS] [delay] [command]
    rm [-r] [-f] <files>             rmdir [-f] <dirs>
    scache [<session_no>]            set [OPT] [<var> [<val>]]
    site <site_cmd>                  source <file>
    torrent [-0 <dir>] <file>        user <user|URL> [<pass>]
    version                          wait [<jobno>]
    zcat <files>                     zmore <files>
lftp ftp.redhat.com:~> ▮
```

Almost all commands from the FTP prompt are run at the remote host, similar to a Telnet session. You can run regular shell commands from that prompt; just start the command with an exclamation point (!).

This is only a subset of the commands available through **lftp**. If you don't remember something, the command **help cmd** yields a brief description of the command itself.

CERTIFICATION SUMMARY

Given the importance of virtualization in today's computing environment, it's no surprise that Red Hat has made KVM part of the requirements associated with the RHCSA. Assuming a valid connection to appropriate repositories, installation of KVM-related packages is fairly easy. You may need to use a command like **modprobe kvm** to make sure appropriate modules are loaded. The Virtual Machine

TABLE 2-5	Command	Description
	cd	Changes the current working directory at the remote host
Standard lftp Client Commands	ls	Lists files at the remote host
	get	Retrieves one file from the remote host
	mget	Retrieves many files from the remote host with wildcards or full filenames
	put	Uploads one file from your computer to the remote host
	mput	Uploads a group of files to the remote host
	pwd	Lists the current working directory on the remote host
	quit	Ends the FTP session
	!ls	Lists files on your host computer in the current directory
	lcd	Changes the local host directory for upload/download
	!pwd	Lists the current working directory on local host computer

Manager can then be used to set up VMs using KVM on an RHEL 6 system. You can also use commands like **virt-install**, **virt-clone**, and **virsh** to install, clone, and manage those VMs.

You can automate your entire installation with Kickstart. Every RHEL system has a Kickstart template file in the /root directory, which you can modify and use to install RHEL on other systems automatically. Alternatively, you can use the GUI Kickstart Configurator to create an appropriate Kickstart file.

With all of these systems, remote access is a must. The SSH command can help set up remote encrypted communications between Linux systems. The RHCSA requires that you know how to use an SSH client. The **ssh** command can be used to log in to remote systems; the **ssh -X** command can even be used to access remote GUI applications. The **scp** copy command can copy files remotely over that encrypted connection.

When reviewing and troubleshooting RHEL services, it can be helpful to have some command line tools at your disposal. The **telnet** command can connect to remote services on selected ports. The **nmap** command can be used as a port scanner. The **mutt** command can check the functionality of an e-mail server. The **elinks** command can be used as a command line browser. Finally, the **lftp** command is an excellent FTP client that supports command completion.

TWO-MINUTE DRILL

The following are some of the key points from the certification objectives in Chapter 2.

Configure KVM for Red Hat

- ❑ Packages required for KVM are part of the Virtualization package groups.
- ❑ KVM-based VMs can be configured with the Virtual Machine Manager.
- ❑ The modules required for KVM include kvm and kvm_intel or kvm_amd.

Configure a Virtual Machine on KVM

- ❑ The default storage directory for KVM-based VMs is /var/lib/libvirt/images.
- ❑ VM configuration files are stored in various /etc/libvirt subdirectories.
- ❑ VM consoles are accessible with the Virtual Machine Manager, which you can start in the GUI with the **virt-manager** command.
- ❑ VMs can be installed, cloned, and configured with the **virt-install**, **virt-clone**, and **virsh** commands.
- ❑ The **virsh list --all** command lists all configured VMs.
- ❑ The **virsh autostart *vmname*** command configures the VM named *vmname* to start automatically when the host system is booted.
- ❑ The **virsh start *vmname*** command starts the boot process for the VM named *vmname*.
- ❑ The **virsh destroy *vmname*** command in effect cuts power to the VM named *vmname*.

Automated Installation Options

❏ Installation of a system is documented in the /root/anaconda-ks.cfg Kickstart text file.

❏ The Kickstart file can be modified directly, or with the Kickstart Configurator tool.

❏ Kickstart files can be called from local media or network servers.

Administration with the Secure Shell

❏ SSH is installed by default on RHEL 6. It's even accessible through default firewalls.

❏ The **ssh** command can be used to access remote systems securely. It can even enable access to remote GUI utilities.

❏ Related commands include **sftp** and **scp**.

Consider Adding These Command Line Tools

❏ Administrators may sometimes only have the command line to verify access to servers.

❏ The **telnet** and **nmap** commands can be used to verify remote access to open ports.

❏ The **mutt** e-mail client can be used to verify the functionality of an e-mail server.

❏ The **elinks** console web browser can verify the working of a web server.

❏ The **lftp** client can be used to verify access to FTP servers with the benefits of command completion.

SELF TEST

The following questions will help measure your understanding of the material presented in this chapter. As no multiple-choice questions appear on the Red Hat exams, no multiple-choice questions appear in this book. These questions exclusively test your understanding of the chapter. Getting results, not memorizing trivia, is what counts on the Red Hat exams. There may be more than one answer to many of these questions.

Configure KVM for Red Hat

1. Name one kernel module associated with KVM.

   _____

2. What is the name of the tool that can configure KVM-based VMs in the GUI?

   _____

Configure a Virtual Machine on KVM

3. What command starts the Virtual Machine Manager in the GUI?

   _____

4. In what directory are default virtual disks stored by the Virtual Machine Manager?

   _____

5. What command can be used to create a new VM?

   _____

Automated Installation Options

6. What command starts the GUI-based Kickstart configuration tool?

   _____

7. What's the name of the file in the /root directory that documents how RHEL was installed?

   _____

8. What directive in the Kickstart configuration file is related to networking?

   _____

9. If the installation FTP server is located at ftp://server1.example.com/pub/inst, what directive in the Kickstart configuration file points to that server?

    _____

10. What directive in the Kickstart configuration file would shut down a system after installation is complete?

    _____

Administration with the Secure Shell

11. What **ssh** command switch is used to specify a different user for remote logins?

    _____

12. What **ssh** command switch enables access to remote GUI utilities?

    _____

Consider Adding These Command Line Tools

13. What command would you use to see if a server is running on port 25 on a system with IP address 192.168.122.1?

    _____

14. What command can be used to verify active and available services on a remote system with IP address 192.168.122.1?

    _____

LAB QUESTIONS

Several of these labs involve installation exercises. You should do these exercises on test machines only. The instructions in some of these labs delete all of the data on a system. However, even though it's required for the RHCSA exam, some readers may not have hardware that supports KVM. Options to KVM include VM solutions such as VMware, available from www.vmware.com or Virtualbox, open source edition, available from www.virtualbox.org.

Red Hat presents its exams electronically. For that reason, most of the labs in this and future chapters are available from the CD that accompanies the book, in the Chapter2/ subdirectory. In case you haven't yet set up RHEL 6 on a system, the first lab is presented here in the book.

Lab I

In this lab, you will install RHEL to create a basic server, on a KVM-based VM. You will need sufficient room for one hard disk of at least 12GB (with sufficient space for 11GB of data plus a swap partition, assuming at least 512MB of RAM). If you want to run the GUI installation program, you'll need at least 652MB of RAM. You'll also need room for an additional two virtual hard drives of 1GB each (14GB total).

The steps in this lab assume an installation on a KVM-based VM. To start the process, open a GUI and run the **virt-manager** command. If it doesn't happen automatically, right-click the Localhost (QEMU) option and click Connect in the pop-up menu that appears. Enter the root administrative password if prompted to do so. Once connected, you can then right-click the same option and then click New. That starts the wizard that helps configure a VM.

If you're configuring the actual VMs to be used in future chapters, this will be the server1.example.com system discussed in Chapter 1.

Ideally, there will be sufficient space on this system for at least four different virtual systems of the given size. That includes the three systems specified in Chapter 1, plus one spare. In other words, a logical volume or partition with 60GB of free space would be (barely) sufficient.

The steps described in this lab are general. By this time, you should have some experience with the installation of RHEL 6. In any case, exact steps vary with the type of installation and the boot media.

1. Start with the first RHEL 6 network boot CD. At the welcome screen, select Install Or Upgrade An Existing System. (If you use the RHEL 6 DVD, press TAB. Add **askmethod** after the initrd=initrd.img directive.)

2. Based on the steps discussed in Chapter 1, start the installation process for RHEL 6.

3. When prompted, set up the local system on a network configured on the KVM VM. The default is the 192.168.122.0/24 network; for the server1.example.com system, this will be on IP address 192.168.122.50.

4. At the appropriate step, point the system to the FTP-based installation server created in Chapter 1. If you followed the directions in that chapter, the server will be on ftp://192.168.122.1/pub/inst.

5. When prompted to enter a hostname, enter **server1.example.com**. In the same screen, there will be a Configure Network button. Enter the IPv4 network information for the system in the window that appears.

6. Select custom partitioning at the appropriate step.

7. Create the first partition of about 500MB of disk space, formatted to the ext4 filesystem, and assign it to the /boot directory.

8. Create the next partition with 1GB of disk space (or more, if space is available), reserved for swap space.

9. Create a third partition with about 8GB disk space, formatted to the ext4 filesystem, and assign it to the top-level root directory, /.

10. Create another partition with about 1GB of disk space, and assign it to the /home directory.

11. Continue with the installation process, using your best judgment.

12. Choose to customize the package groups to be installed. Include a GUI, the X Window server. Installation of virtualization packages within a VM is not required.

13. Finish the installation normally.

14. Reboot when prompted and log in as the root user. Run the **poweroff** command when you're ready to finish this lab.

SELF TEST ANSWERS

Configure KVM for Red Hat

1. Three kernel modules are associated with KVM: kvm, kvm_intel, and kvm_amd.

2. The tool that can configure KVM-based VMs in the GUI is the Virtual Machine Manager.

Configure a Virtual Machine on KVM

3. The command that starts the Virtual Machine Manager in the GUI is **virt-manager**. Since menus are not always available, the Applications | System Tools | Virtual Machine Manager click sequence is not an acceptable answer.

4. The directory with default virtual disks for the Virtual Machine Manager is /var/lib/libvirt/ images.

5. The command that can be used to create a new VM is **virt-install**.

Automated Installation Options

6. The command that starts the GUI-based Kickstart configuration tool is **system-config-kickstart**.

7. The name of the Kickstart file in the /root directory that documents how RHEL was installed is anaconda-ks.cfg.

8. The directive in the Kickstart configuration file related to networking is **network**.

9. The directive that points to the given FTP installation server is **url --url ftp://server1.example .com/pub/inst**.

10. The directive in the Kickstart configuration that would shut down a system after installation is complete is **shutdown**.

Administration with the Secure Shell

11. The **ssh** command switch that is used to specify a different user for remote logins is **-l**.

12. The **ssh** command switch that enables access to remote GUI utilities is **-X**. The **-Y** switch is also an acceptable answer.

Consider Adding These Command Line Tools

13. The command that you would use to see if a server is running on port 25 on a system with IP address 192.168.122.1 is **telnet 192.168.122.1 25**.

14. The command that can be used to verify active and available services on a remote system with IP address 192.168.122.1 is **nmap 192.168.122.1**.

LAB ANSWERS

Lab 1

While there is nothing truly difficult about this lab, it should increase your confidence with VMs based on KVM. Once complete, you should be able to log in to the VM as the root administrative user, and run the following checks on the system:

1. Check mounted directories, along with the space available. The following commands should confirm those directories that are mounted, along with the free space available on the associated volumes.

```
# mount
# df -m
```

2. Assuming you have a good connection to the Internet and a subscription to the Red Hat Network, make sure the system is up to date. If you're using a rebuild distribution, access to their public repositories is acceptable. In either case, run the following command to make sure the local system is up to date:

```
# yum update
```

This lab confirms your ability to "Install Red Hat Enterprise Linux system as virtual guests."

Lab 2

Remember, this and all future labs in this book can be found on the CD that comes with this book. Labs 2 through 8 can be found in the Chapter2/ subdirectory of that CD.

One of the issues with system cloning is how it includes the hardware address of any network cards. Such conflicts can lead to problems on a network. So not only would you have to change the IP address, but you'll also need to assign a unique hardware address to the given network card. Because of such issues, KVM normally sets up a different network card for a cloned system. For example, if the original system had an eth0 network card with one hardware address, the cloned system would have an eth1 network card with a different hardware address.

If this seems like too much trouble, feel free to delete the cloned system. After all, there is no reference to VM cloning in the RHCSA requirements. However, it may be helpful to have a different backup system. And that's an excellent opportunity to practice the skills gained in Lab 4 with Kickstart installations.

Lab 3

The purpose of this lab is to show you the command line method for configuring a KVM-based VM. If you haven't yet set up the four different VMs suggested in Chapter 1 (three VMs and a backup), this is an excellent opportunity to do so. One way to do so is with the **virt-install** command and the **--prompt** switch. That command prompts for the following information:

- Allocated RAM, which should be at least 512MB (652MB for a GUI-based installation).
- The path to the virtual disk file, which should be the same as that virtual disk created in Lab 2.
- The size of the virtual disk file, if that file doesn't already exist.
- The URL for the FTP installation server created in Chapter 1, Lab 2. Alternatively, you could use the HTTP installation server also discussed in Chapter 1.

You can now complete this installation normally or run a variation of that installation in Lab 5.

Lab 4

If you're not experienced with Kickstart configuration, some trial and error may be required. But it's best to run into problems now, and not during a Red Hat exam or on the job. If you're able to set up a Kickstart file that can be used to install a system without intervention, you're ready to address this challenge on the RHCSA exam.

One common problem relates to virtual disks that have just been created. They must be initialized first; that's the purpose of the **--initlabel** switch to the **clearpart** directive.

Lab 5

If you've recently run a Kickstart installation for the first time, it's best to do it again. If you practice now, it means you'll be able to set up a Kickstart installation faster during an exam. And that's just the beginning. Imagine the confidence that you'll have if your boss needs a couple of dozen VMs with the same software and volumes. Assuming the only differences are hostname and network settings, you'll be able to accomplish this task fairly quickly.

If you can set up a Kickstart installation from the command line with the **virt-install** command, it'll be a lot easier to set it up on a remote virtual host. You'll be able to configure new systems from remote locations, increasing your value in the workplace.

If you haven't yet set up the four VMs suggested in Chapter 1 (three as test systems, one as a backup), this is your opportunity to do so.

To use a Kickstart file with **virt-install**, you'll need to use regular command switches. Since you're not allowed to bring this book into an exam, try to perform this lab without referring to the main body of this chapter. You'll be able to refer to the man page for the **virt-install** command for all of the important switches except the **-x** or **--extra-args=** needed to call the URL for the Kickstart file.

Be sure to put the **ks=** directive along with the URL of the Kickstart file within quotes. Success is the installation of a new system.

Lab 6

This lab is designed to increase your understanding of the use of the **ssh** command as a client. The encryption performed should be transparent, and will not affect any commands used through a SSH connection to administer remote systems.

Lab 7

This lab is somewhat critical with respect to several different RHCSA objectives. Once you under-stand the process, the actual tasks are deceptively simple. After completing this lab, you should have confidence in your abilities to

- Start and stop virtual machines
- Configure systems to launch virtual machines at boot

The lab also suggests one method for remotely accessing the console of a VM.

Lab 8

This lab is designed to increase your familiarity with two important network troubleshooting tools, **telnet** and **nmap**. Network administrators with some Linux experience may prefer other tools. If you're familiar with other tools such as **nc**, great. It's the results that matter.

3

Fundamental Command Line Skills

T he Red Hat exams are an advanced challenge. This chapter covers RHCSA requirements that were formerly listed as prerequisites for the now-obsolete RHCT certification. Many of these requirements specify basic command line tools associated with entry-level certifications such as those offered by the Linux Professional Institute.

As such command line skills are no longer listed as prerequisites, they have been combined with networking configuration objectives, something you can set up with some of these command line tools.

As most candidates for the RHCSA exam should already be familiar with these command line tools, this chapter covers the related topics in a minimum of detail. If after reading this chapter, you feel the need for more guidance about these topics, other excellent beginning Linux books described in Chapter 1 can help.

Linux gurus should recognize that I've "oversimplified" a number of explanations, to keep this chapter as short as possible. But as most IT professionals are specialists, you may feel a bit uncertain about a few topics in this chapter. That is okay. In fact, it's natural that many experienced Linux administrators don't frequently use every command. Many candidates are successfully able to fill in the gaps in their knowledge with some self-study and practice.

INSIDE THE EXAM

Shells

The related RHCSA exam objective is pretty generic:

■ Access a shell prompt and issue commands with correct syntax; use pipelines and I/O redirection

The default shell for Linux is bash, the "Bourne-Again shell." In fact, the original release of the RHCSA objectives specified the use of bash. However, many Linux gurus use one of the many other shells available.

Whatever shell you select, you need to know how to get to a shell prompt and run regular commands from that prompt. Some basic commands are described in some of the other objectives. It's fairly easy to open a shell prompt from a console and within the GUI.

Pipelines and Redirection

Data into and out of a shell are often thought of in Linux as streams of information. One basic Linux skill is the ability to redirect those streams. As described in the RHCSA requirements, that's the ability to

■ Use input/output redirection (>, >>, |, 2>, etc.)

The operators in parentheses can redirect the streams from command output, command error, data files, and more.

File and Directory Management

So when you get to a command line, what's next? That's the province of file and directory management. With related commands, you can navigate around the Linux directory tree as well as perform all of the tasks suggested in the related objectives:

■ Create/delete/copy/move files and directories

■ Create hard and soft links

The Analysis of Text Output

Most Linux configuration files are text files. As such, it's important to understand and analyze the flow of text as it is sent through the shell. To that end, tools like the **grep** command can help focus on needed information. In that way, you'll examine how to meet the following objective:

■ Use **grep** and regular expressions to analyze text output

The Variety of Local Documentation

While Internet access is not available during the Red Hat exams, that's okay. Google is not your only friend. Linux has some excellent documentation installed with most packages. Command manuals are also available. The following objective is straightforward, as it describes the commands and directory associated with most Linux online documentation.

■ Locate, read, and use system documentation using **man**, **info**, and files in /usr/share/doc

The objectives include an interesting modifier to that objective:

■ Note: Red Hat may use applications during the exam that are not included in Red Hat Enterprise Linux for the purpose of evaluating candidate's abilities to meet this objective.

Most Linux developers follow the basic parameters just described for system documentation. Does Red Hat's "note" mean they'll "hide" some key information in a man page or a file in the /usr/share/doc directory? The wording suggests you need to be prepared for such a scenario.

The Use of Text Editors

To configure Linux, you need to know how to edit text files. And for those newer to Linux, that requires a different paradigm. While word processors like OpenOffice.org Writer and Microsoft Word can save files in text format, a mistake with a key configuration file can render a Linux system unbootable. So you need to know how to handle the following objective:

■ Create and edit text files

The Management of Network Services

While there are excellent GUI tools to help manage network services, mistakes are too easy to make with such tools. Command line tools can help you understand and manage network services directly or through associated configuration files. The associated objective is

■ Start, stop, and check the status of network services

Of course, this objective requires a basic understanding of IP networking.

The Configuration of Networking and Name Resolution

Name resolution depends on databases of hostnames or fully qualified domain names (FQDN) such as server1.example.com and IP addresses like 192.168.122.50. Name resolution depends on the local hostname, the local /etc/hosts database of hostnames and IP addresses, and available databases of Domain Name Service (DNS) servers as well. That is an interpretation of the following RHCSA objective:

■ Configure networking and hostname resolution statically or dynamically

When the RHCSA was first released, this was depicted as two objectives. While these objectives are no longer officially in effect, they do provide more information on what it means to configure networking and hostname resolution:

■ Manage network devices: understand basic IP networking/routing, configure IP addresses/default route statically or dynamically

■ Manage name resolution: set local hostname, configure /etc/hosts, configure to use existing DNS server

While network troubleshooting is no longer a part of the entry-level Red Hat exam, the way you address problems with respect to network configuration and hostname resolution can help you better understand how networks operate.

CERTIFICATION OBJECTIVE 3.01

Shells

A *shell* is a user interface. It is also used as a command line interpreter. In Linux, the shell is the interpreter that allows you to interact with Linux using various commands. With the right file permissions, you can set up commands in scripts to run as needed, even in the middle of the night. Linux shells can process commands in various sequences, depending on how you manage the input and output of each command. The way commands are interpreted is in part determined by variables and parameters associated with each shell.

The default shell in Linux is bash, also known as the Bourne-Again Shell. The focus of commands in this book is based on how they're used in bash. However, a number of other shells are available that are popular with many users. As long as the appropriate RPMs are installed, users can start any of these shells. If desired, you can change the default shell for individual users in the /etc/passwd file.

Other Shells

As four shells are included with RHEL 6, users have their choice in command line interpreters. While bash is the default, long-time Linux and Unix users may prefer something else:

- **bash** The default Bourne-Again shell, based on the command line interpreter originally developed by Stephen Bourne.
- **dash** A simpler shell with fewer features than bash, but faster.
- **tcsh** An enhanced version of the Unix C shell.
- **zsh** A sophisticated shell, similar to the Korn shell.

These shells are configured in the /bin directory. If a user prefers one of these options as their default shell, it's easy to change. The most direct method is to change the default shell in the /etc/passwd file. For example, the line that applies to my regular account is

```
michael:x:1000:1000:Michael Jang:/home/michael:/bin/bash
```

For example, to change the default to the dash shell, change /bin/bash to /bin/dash.

e x a m

ⓦ a t c h

Even though it should be trivial for most Linux users, a part of one RHCSA objective is to "access a shell prompt." You should now know how to set up access to different shell prompts.

Terminal Consoles

By default, six command line consoles are available on RHEL systems. They're defined by the start-ttys.conf file in the /etc/init directory. Take a look at that file. You'll see that consoles are defined for runlevels 2, 3, 4, and 5. Active consoles are defined as device files /dev/tty1 through /dev/tty6. When a GUI is configured, it takes /dev/tty1. It's possible to configure more virtual consoles, limited by those allowed for the root administrative user in the /etc/securetty file.

Normally, to change between consoles, press ALT and the function key associated with the console. For example, the ALT-F2 key combination moves to the second console. However, in the RHEL GUI, the ALT-F2 key combination is used to start the Run Application tool; therefore, you'll need to press CTRL-ALT-F2 to move to that second virtual console.

At a text console login, you'd see the following prompt, which depends a bit on the release of RHEL, the version number of the kernel, and the system hostname:

```
Red Hat Enterprise Linux release 6.0 (Santiago)
Kernel 2.6.32-71.el6.x86_64 on x86_64

server1 login:
```

The graphical login, which requires the installation of the GNOME Display Manager (GDM), is more intuitive, as shown in Figure 3-1.

GUI Shell Interfaces

Once logged in to the GUI, access to the bash shell is easy. If you're in the default GNOME desktop environment, click Applications | System Tools | Terminal. Traditionally, administrators have worked from the console. But in many cases, working the command line from the GUI can be helpful, especially with the consoles that can be placed side by side. A right-click on a GUI terminal screen supports opening of additional terminals in different windows or in tabs. It also supports copy and paste as needed.

The screenshots of the command line taken for this book are based on the GUI-based command line, in part because dark text on a white screen is easier to read.

FIGURE 3-1

A first GUI login
console

Differences Between Regular and Administrative Users

What you can do at the command line depends on the privileges associated with the
login account. Two basic prompts are available. The following is an example of what
you might see when logged in as a regular user:

```
[michael@server1 ~]$
```

Note how it includes the username, the hostname of the local system, the current
directory, and a $ prompt. The $ prompt is the standard for regular users. As noted in
the introduction to the book, examples of commands run from a regular user account
just show the following:

```
$
```

In contrast, take a look at a prompt for the root administrative user on the
same system. It should look familiar. Except for the name of the account, the only
consistent difference is the prompt.

```
[root@server1 ~]#
```

So examples of commands run from the root administrative account just show the following:

```
#
```

Besides ownership and permissions, other differences between regular and administrative accounts are discussed in Chapter 8.

Text Streams and Command Redirection

Linux uses three basic data streams. Data goes in, data comes out, and errors are sent in a different direction. These streams are known as standard input (stdin), standard output (stdout), and standard error (stderr). Normally, input comes from the keyboard and goes out to the screen, while errors are sent to a buffer. Error messages are also sent to the display (as text stream 2). In the following example, *filename* is stdin to the **cat** command:

```
# cat filename
```

When you run **cat *filename*,** the contents of that file are sent to the screen as standard output.

You can redirect each of these streams to or from a file. For example, if you have a program named database and a datafile with a lot of data, the contents of that datafile can be sent to the database program with a left redirection arrow (**<**). As shown here, datafile is taken as standard input:

```
# database < datafile
```

Standard input can come from the left side of a command as well. For example, if you need to scroll through the boot messages, you can combine the **dmesg** and **less** commands with a pipe:

```
# dmesg | less
```

The output from **dmesg** is redirected as standard input to **less**, which then allows you to scroll through that output as if it were a separate file.

Standard output is just as easy to redirect. For example, the following command uses the right redirection arrow (**>**) to send the standard output of the **ls** command to the file named filelist.

```
# ls > filelist
```

e x a m

🐾 **a t c h** *Command redirection symbols like >, >>, 2>, and | are associated with the "input/output redirection" objective in the RHCSA exam objectives.*

You can add standard output to the end of an existing file with a double redirection arrow with a command such as **ls >> filelist**.

If you believe that a particular program is generating errors, redirect the error stream from it with a command like the following:

```
# program 2> err-list
```

CERTIFICATION OBJECTIVE 3.02

Standard Command Line Tools

While newer Linux users may prefer to use the GUI, the most efficient way to administer Linux is from the command line interface. While excellent GUI tools are available, the look and feel of those tools varies widely by distribution. In contrast, if you know the standard command line tools, you'll be able to find your way around every Linux distribution.

Two basic groups of commands are used to manage Linux files. One group helps you get around Linux files and directories. The other group actually does something creative with the files. Remember, in any Linux file operation, you can take advantage of the HISTORY (this is capitalized because it's a standard environment variable) of previous commands, as well as the characteristics of command completion, which allow you to use the TAB key almost as a wildcard to complete a command or a filename, or give you the options available in terms of the absolute path.

Almost all Linux commands include switches, options that allow you to do more. Few are covered in this chapter. If you're less familiar with any of these commands, use their man pages. Study the switches. Try them out! Only with practice, practice, and more practice can you really understand the power behind some of these commands.

e x a m

🐾 **a t c h** *This section covers only the most basic of commands available in Linux. It describes only a few capabilities of each command. Nevertheless, it allows you to "issue commands with correct syntax," as described in the RHCSA objectives.*

File and Directory Concepts

As noted previously, everything in Linux can be reduced to a file. Directories are special types of files that serve as containers for other files. To navigate and find important files, you need some basic concepts to tell you where you are and how to move from directory to directory. The command is **pwd**, a variable that always leads to a user's home directory is the tilde (~), and the concept that describes where you are in the Linux directory tree is the path. Closely related are the directories searched when a command is typed in, which is based on the environment variable known as the PATH. Once these concepts are understood, you can navigate between directories with the **cd** command.

pwd

At the command line interface, the current directory may be either in the top-level root (/) directory, or a subdirectory. The **pwd** command identifies the current directory. Try it out. It'll give you a directory name relative to the top-level root directory (/). With this information in hand, you can move to a different directory if needed. Incidentally, **pwd** is short for print working directory (which has nothing to do with modern printers, but respects the days when output was printed on a teletype). For example, when I run that command in my home directory, I get the following output:

```
/home/michael
```

The Tilde (~)

Upon a standard login, every Linux user is taken to a home directory. The tilde (~) can be used to represent the home directory of any currently active user. For example, when user john logs in, he's taken to his home directory, /home/john. In contrast, the home directory of the root administrative user is /root.

Thus, the effect of the **cd ~** command depends on your username. For example, if you've logged in as user mj, the **cd ~** command navigates to the /home/mj directory. If you've logged in as the root user, this command navigates to the /root directory. You can list the contents of your home directory from anywhere in the directory tree with the **ls ~** command. The **cd** and **ls** commands are described shortly. When I log in as the root administrative user and run the **ls** command, I see:

```
anaconda-ks.cfg  install.log  install.log.syslog
```

Incidentally, these files describe what happened during the installation process, the packages that were installed, and the users and groups added to the local system. The anaconda-ks.cfg command is important for automated Kickstart installations, as described in Chapter 2.

Directory Paths

There are two path concepts you need to know when working with Linux directories: absolute paths and relative paths. An absolute path describes the complete directory structure in terms of the top-level directory, root (/). A relative path is based on the current directory. Relative paths do not include the slash in front.

The difference between an absolute path and a relative one is important. Especially when creating a script, absolute paths are essential. Otherwise, scripts executed from other directories may lead to unintended consequences. For example, say you're in the top-level root directory, and you have backed up the /home directory using the relative path. If you happen to be in the /home directory when restoring that backup, the files for user michael would be restored to the /home/home/michael directory.

In contrast, if the /home directory was backed up using the absolute path, the current directory doesn't matter when restoring these files. That backup will be restored to the correct directories.

Environment PATHs

Strictly speaking, when running a command, you should cite the full path to that command. For example, since the **ls** command is in the /bin directory, users should actually run the **/bin/ls** command to list files in the current directory.

With the benefit of the PATH, an environment variable, that's not required. The bash shell automatically searches through the directories listed in a user's PATH for the command that user just typed at the command line. Environment variables are constant from console to console.

To determine the PATH for the current user account, run the **echo $PATH** command. You should see a series of directories in the output. The differences between the PATH for a regular user and one for a root user have narrowed in RHEL 6:

```
$ echo $PATH
/usr/local/bin:/usr/bin:/bin:/usr/local/sbin:/usr/sbin:/sbin
```

```
# echo $PATH
/usr/local/sbin:/usr/local/bin:/sbin:/bin:/usr/sbin:/usr/bin:/root/bin
```

Today, the directories in the PATH for regular and the root administrative users are essentially the same. But the differences matter, as the directories are searched in order. For example, the **system-config-keyboard** command is available from both the /usr/bin and /usr/sbin directories. As you can see from the default PATH for regular and root users, the version that is run varies because of the differences in the PATH.

The PATH is determined globally by current settings in the /etc/profile file. You might notice differences between the PATH as configured for User ID (UID) 0 and all other users. UID 0 corresponds to the root administrative user.

The PATH for individual users can be customized with an appropriate entry in that user's home directory, in the hidden file named .profile.

cd

It's easy to change directories in Linux. Just use **cd** and cite the absolute path of the desired directory. If you use the relative path, just remember that the destination depends on the present working directory.

By default, the **cd** command by itself navigates to your home directory. The tilde is not required for that command.

File Lists and ls

Now that you've reviewed those commands that can navigate from one directory to another, it's time to see what files exist in a directory. And that's the province of the **ls** command.

The Linux **ls** command, with the right switches, can be quite powerful. The right kind of **ls** can tell you everything about a file, such as creation date, last access date, and size. It can help you organize the listing of files in just about any desired order. Important variations on this command include **ls -a** to reveal hidden files, **ls -l** for long listings, **ls -t** for a time-based list, and **ls -i** for inode numbers. You can combine switches; I often use the **ls -ltr** command to display the most recently changed files last. The **-d** switch, when combined with others, can give you more information on the current directory.

One important feature that returns SELinux contexts is the **ls -Z** command. Take a look at the output in Figure 3-2. The system_u, object_r, var_t, and s0 output demonstrates the current SELinux contexts of the noted files. During the RHCSA exam (and RHCE as well), you'll be expected to configure a system with SELinux enabled. Starting with Chapter 4, this book covers how SELinux can be configured for every service that's installed.

```
[root@server1 ~]# \ls -Z /var/
drwxr-xr-x. root root system_u:object_r:acct_data_t:s0 account
drwxr-xr-x. root root system_u:object_r:var_t:s0         cache
drwxr-xr-x. root root system_u:object_r:var_t:s0         crash
drwxr-xr-x. root root system_u:object_r:cvs_data_t:s0   cvs
drwxr-xr-x. root root system_u:object_r:var_t:s0         db
drwxr-xr-x. root root system_u:object_r:var_t:s0         empty
drwxr-xr-x. root root system_u:object_r:games_data_t:s0 games
drwxrwx--T. root gdm  system_u:object_r:xserver_log_t:s0 gdm
drwxr-xr-x. root root system_u:object_r:var_lib_t:s0    lib
drwxr-xr-x. root root system_u:object_r:var_t:s0         local
drwxrwxr-x. root lock system_u:object_r:var_lock_t:s0   lock
drwxr-xr-x. root root system_u:object_r:var_log_t:s0    log
lrwxrwxrwx. root root system_u:object_r:mail_spool_t:s0 mail -> spool/mail
drwxr-xr-x. root root system_u:object_r:var_t:s0         nis
drwxr-xr-x. root root system_u:object_r:var_t:s0         opt
drwxr-xr-x. root root system_u:object_r:var_t:s0         preserve
drwxr-xr-x. root root system_u:object_r:var_t:s0         report
drwxr-xr-x. root root system_u:object_r:var_run_t:s0    run
drwxr-xr-x. root root system_u:object_r:var_spool_t:s0  spool
drwxrwxrwt. root root system_u:object_r:tmp_t:s0         tmp
drwxr-xr-x. root root system_u:object_r:var_yp_t:s0     yp
[root@server1 ~]# █
```

File Creation Commands

Two commands are used to create new files: **touch** and **cp**. Alternatively, you can let
a text editor such as vi create a new file. Of course, while the **ln**, **mv**, and **rm**
commands don't create files, they do manage them in related ways.

touch

Perhaps the simplest way to create a new file is with the **touch** command. For
example, the **touch abc** command creates an empty file named abc in the local
directory. The **touch** command is also used to change the last access date of a file.
For example, try the following three commands:

```
# ls -l /etc/passwd
# touch /etc/passwd
# ls -l /etc/passwd
```

Note the date and time associated with the output of each **ls -l** command. The
change is associated with the current date and time, which is associated with the
date command.

cp

The **cp** (copy) command allows you to take the contents of one file and place a copy with the same or different name in the directory of your choice. For example, the **cp** *file1 file2* command takes the contents of *file1* and saves the contents in *file2*. One of the dangers of **cp** is that it can easily overwrite files in different directories, without prompting you to make sure that's what you really wanted to do.

The **cp** command, with the **-r** switch, supports recursive changes. For example, the following command copies all subdirectories of the noted directory, along with associated files:

```
# cp -ar /usr/share/doc/. /doc/
```

mv

While you can't rename a file in Linux, you can move it. The **mv** command essentially puts a different label on a file. For example, the **mv** *file1 file2* command changes the name of *file1* to *file2*. Unless you're moving the file to a different partition, everything about the file, including the inode number, remains the same. The **mv** command works with directories too.

ln

Linked files allow users to edit the same file from different directories. When linked files are devices, they may represent more common names, such as /dev/dvd. Linked files can be hard or soft.

Hard links include a copy of the file. As long as the hard link is made within the same partition, the inode numbers are identical. You could delete a hard-linked file in one directory, and it would still exist in the other directory. For example, the following command creates a hard link from the actual Samba configuration file to smb.conf in the local directory:

```
# ln /etc/samba/smb.conf smb.conf
```

On the other hand, a soft link serves as a redirect; when you open a file created with a soft link, the link redirects you to the original file. If you delete the original file, the file is lost. While the soft link is still there, it has nowhere to go. The following command is an example of how you can create a soft linked file:

```
# ln -s /etc/samba/smb.conf smb.conf
```

rm

The **rm** command is somewhat dangerous. At the Linux command line, there is no trash bin. So if you delete a file with the **rm** command, it's at best difficult to recover that file.

The **rm** command is powerful. For example, when I downloaded the source files for the Linux kernel, it included several thousand files in the /root/rpmbuild/BUILD/ kernel-2.6.32-71.1.el6 directory. As it's not practical to delete those files one by one, the **rm** command includes some powerful switches. The following command removes all of those files in one command:

```
# rm -rf /root/rpmbuild/BUILD/kernel-2.6.32-71.1.el6
```

The **-r** switch works recursively, and the **-f** switch overrides any safety precautions, such as shown in the output to the **alias** command for the root administrative user. It's still quite a dangerous command, as a simple typing mistake that puts a space between the first forward slash and the directory name, as shown here:

```
# rm -rf / root/rpmbuild/BUILD/kernel-2.6.32-71.1.el6
```

would first delete every file starting with the top-level root directory, before looking for the root/rpmbuild/BUILD/kernel-2.6.32-71.1.el6 subdirectory.

Directory Creation and Deletion

The **mkdir** and **rmdir** commands are used to create and delete directories. The ways these commands are used depend on the already-discussed concepts of absolute and relative paths. For example, the following command creates the test subdirectory to the current directory. If you're currently in the /home/michael directory, the full path would be /home/michael/test.

```
# mkdir test
```

Alternatively, the following command creates the /test directory:

```
# mkdir /test
```

If desired, the following command creates a series of directories:

```
# mkdir -p /test1/test2/test3
```

That command is equivalent to the following commands:

```
# mkdir /test1
# mkdir /test1/test2
# mkdir /test1/test2/test3
```

Conversely, the **rmdir** command deletes a directory only if it's empty. If you're cleaning up after the previous **mkdir** commands, the **-p** switch is useful there as well. The following command deletes the noted directory and subdirectories, as long as all of the directories are otherwise empty:

```
# rmdir -p /test1/test2/test3
```

alias

The **alias** command can be used to simplify a few commands. For the root administrative user, the default aliases provides a bit of safety. To see the aliases for the current user, run the **alias** command. The following output is the default Red Hat aliases for the root user:

```
alias cp='cp -i'
alias l.='ls -d .* --color=auto'
alias ll='ls -l --color=auto'
alias ls='ls --color=auto'
alias mv='mv -i'
alias rm='rm -i'
alias which='alias | /usr/bin/which --tty-only --read-alias
--show-dot --show-tilde'
```

Some of these aliases help protect key files from mistakes. The **-i** switch prompts the user for confirmation before a file is deleted or overwritten with the **cp**, **mv**, or **rm** command. Just be aware, the **-f** switch supersedes the **-i** for the noted commands.

As suggested by the technical editor, some administrators set a different alias for the rm command: alias rm='mv -t ~/.Trash'. Files in that directory are like a standard trashbin. The default trash directory for the GNOME desktop can be found in each user's .local/share/Trash/files/ subdirectory.

Wildcards

Sometimes you may not know the exact name of the file or the exact search term. That is when a wildcard is handy, especially with the commands described throughout the book. Three basic wildcards are shown in Table 3-1.

Wildcards are sometimes known in the Linux world as globbing.

File Searches

Most users who study Linux for a while become familiar with key files. For example, named.conf is the key configuration file for the standard DNS (Domain Name Service) servers, based on the Berkeley Internet Name Domain (BIND). But not many people remember that the sample named.conf file, with all kinds of useful configuration hints, can be found in the /usr/share/doc/bind-*/sample/etc directory.

To that end, there are two basic commands for file searches: **find** and **locate**.

find

The **find** command searches through directories and subdirectories for a desired file. For example, if you wanted to find the directory with the named.conf DNS sample configuration file, you could use the following command, which would start the search in the root directory:

```
# find / -name named.conf
```

TABLE 3-1	Wildcard	Description
Wildcards in the Shell	*	Any number of alphanumeric characters (or no characters at all). For example, the **ls ab*** command would return the following filenames, assuming they exist in the current directory: ab, abc, abcd.
	?	One single alphanumeric character: For example, the **ls ab?** command would return the following filenames, assuming they exist in the current directory: abc, abd, abe.
	[]	A range of options. For example, the **ls ab[123]** command would return the following filenames, assuming they exist in the current directory: ab1, ab2, ab3. Alternatively, the **ls ab[X-Z]** command would return the following filenames, assuming they exist in the current directory: abX, abY, abZ.

But the speed of that search depends on the memory and processing power available on the local system. With the advent of virtual machines, that processing power may be relatively small. Alternatively, if you know that this file is located in the /usr subdirectory tree, you could start in that directory with the following command:

```
# find /usr -name named.conf
```

That command should now find the desired file more quickly.

locate

If this is all too time consuming, RHEL allows you to set up a database of installed files and directories. Searches with the **locate** command are almost instantaneous. And **locate** searches don't require the full filename. The drawback is that the **locate** command database is normally updated only once each day, as documented in the **/etc/cron.daily/mlocate.cron** script.

As daily jobs are run only once every 24 hours, that's not good enough, especially during a 2.0 hour exam. Fortunately, the noted script can be executed directly from the command line interface, by the root administrative user. Just type in the full path to the file as if it were a command:

```
# /etc/cron.daily/mlocate.cron
```

CERTIFICATION OBJECTIVE 3.03

The Management of Text Files

Linux and Unix are managed through a series of text files. Linux administrators do not normally use graphical editors to manage these configuration files. Editors such as WordPerfect, OpenOffice.org Writer, and yes, even Microsoft Word normally either save files in a binary format or add tags. Unless text files are preserved in their original format, without tags, changes that are made can render a Linux system unbootable.

Linux commands have been set up to manage text files as streams of data. You've seen tools such as redirection arrows and pipes. But that data can be overwhelming without tools that can sort through that data. But even before files are edited, it's important to know how to read these files at the command line interface.

Commands to Read Text Streams

Previously, you reviewed commands like **cd**, **ls**, and **pwd** that can help you get around Linux files. With commands like **find** and **locate**, you reviewed how to identify the location of desired files.

Now it's time to start reading, copying, and moving the files around. Most Linux configuration files are text files. Linux editors are text editors. Linux commands are designed to read text files. To identify the types of files in the current directory, try the **file *** command.

cat

The most basic command for reading files is **cat**. The **cat** *filename* command scrolls the text within the *filename* file. It also works with multiple filenames; it concatenates the filenames that you might list as one continuous output to your screen. You can redirect the output to the filename of your choice, as described in the section "Text Streams and Command Redirection."

less and more

Larger files demand a command that can help you scroll through the file text at your leisure. Linux has two of these commands: **more** and **less**. With the **more** *filename* command, you can scroll through the text of a file, from start to finish, one screen at a time. With the **less** *filename* command, you can scroll in both directions through the same text with the PAGE UP and PAGE DOWN keys. Both commands support vi-style searches.

As the **less** and **more** commands do not change files, they're an excellent way to scroll through and search for items in a large text file such as an error log. For example, to search through the basic /var/log/messages file, run the following command:

```
# less /var/log/messages
```

You'll then be able to scroll up and down the log file for important information. You can then use the forward slash and question mark to search through the file. For example, once you've run the command just shown, you'll be taken to a screen similar to that shown in Figure 3-3.

```
Nov 29 08:15:02 server1 kernel: imklog 4.6.2, log source = /proc/kmsg started.
Nov 29 08:15:02 server1 rsyslogd: [origin software="rsyslogd" swVersion="4.6.2"
x-pid="1132" x-info="http://www.rsyslog.com"] (re)start
Nov 29 09:43:01 server1 NetworkManager[1219]: <error> [1291052581.244599] [nm-ma
nager.c:1312] user_proxy_init(): could not init user settings proxy: (3) Could n
ot get owner of name 'org.freedesktop.NetworkManagerUserSettings': no such name
Nov 29 09:43:04 server1 NetworkManager[1219]: <error> [1291052584.455664] [nm-ma
nager.c:1312] user_proxy_init(): could not init user settings proxy: (3) Could n
ot get owner of name 'org.freedesktop.NetworkManagerUserSettings': no such name
Nov 29 09:44:33 server1 kernel: ata2.00: exception Emask 0x0 SAct 0x0 SErr 0x0 a
ction 0x6
Nov 29 09:44:33 server1 kernel: sr 1:0:0:0: CDB: Test Unit Ready: 00 00 00 00 00
 00
Nov 29 09:44:33 server1 kernel: ata2.00: cmd a0/00:00:00:00:00/00:00:00:00:00/a0
 tag 0
Nov 29 09:44:33 server1 kernel:          res 01/60:00:00:00:00/00:00:00:00:00/a0
Emask 0x3 (HSM violation)
Nov 29 09:44:33 server1 kernel: ata2.00: status: { ERR }
Nov 29 09:44:33 server1 kernel: ata2: soft resetting link
Nov 29 09:44:33 server1 kernel: ata2.00: configured for MWDMA2
Nov 29 09:44:33 server1 kernel: ata2: EH complete
Nov 29 19:05:56 server1 NetworkManager[1219]: <error> [1291086356.880466] [nm-ma
nager.c:1312] user_proxy_init(): could not init user settings proxy: (3) Could n
/var/log/messages
```

For example, to search forward in the file for the term "IPv4 tunneling," type the following in the pager:

```
/IPv4 tunneling
```

To search in the reverse direction, substitute a **?** for the **/**.

The **less** command has one more feature unavailable to commands like **more** and **cat**; it can read text files compressed in Gzip format, normally shown with the .gz extension. For example, the man pages associated with many standard commands that are run in the shell can be found in the /usr/share/man/man1 directory. All of the files in this directory are compressed in .gz format. Nevertheless, the **less** command can read those files, without uncompressing them.

And that points to the operation of the **man** command. In other words, these two commands are functionally equivalent:

```
# man cat
# less /usr/share/man/man1/cat.1.gz
```

head and tail

The **head** and **tail** commands are separate commands that work in essentially the same way. By default, the **head** *filename* command looks at the first 10 lines of a file; the **tail** *filename* command looks at the last 10 lines of a file. You can specify the number of lines shown with the **-nxy** switch. Just remember to avoid the space when specifying the number of lines; for example, the **tail -n15 /etc/passwd** command lists the last 15 lines of the /etc/passwd file.

The **tail** command can be especially useful for problems in progress. For example, if there's an ongoing problem, the following command monitors the noted file for login attempts:

```
# tail -f /var/log/secure
```

Commands to Process Text Streams

A text stream is the movement of data. For example, the **cat** *filename* command streams the data from the *filename* file to the screen. When these files get large, it's convenient to have commands that can filter and otherwise process these streams of text.

To that end, Linux includes simple commands to help you search, check, or sort the contents of a file. And there are special files that contain others; some of these container files are known colloquially as "tarballs."

on the **Job**

Tarballs are a common way to distribute Linux packages. They are normally distributed in a compressed format, with a .tar.gz or .tgz file extension, consolidated as a package in a single file.

sort

You can sort the contents of a file in a number of ways. By default, the **sort** command sorts the contents in alphabetical order depending on the first letter in each line. For example, the **sort /etc/passwd** command would sort all users (including those associated with specific services and such) by username.

grep and egrep

The **grep** command uses a search term to look through a file. It returns the full line that contains the search term. For example, **grep 'Michael Jang' /etc/passwd** looks for the name of this author in the /etc/passwd file.

The **egrep** command is more forgiving; it allows you to use some unusual characters in your search, including +, ?, |, (, and). While it's possible to set up **grep** to search for these characters with the help of the backslash, the command can be awkward.

diff

One useful option to find the difference between files is the **diff** command. If you've just used a tool such as the Network Connections tool described later in this chapter, it'll modify a file such as ifcfg-eth0 in the /etc/sysconfig/network-scripts directory.

If you've backed up that ifcfg-eth0 file, the **diff** command can identify the differences between the two files. For example, the following command identifies the differences between the ifcfg-eth0 file in the /root and the /etc/sysconfig/network-scripts directories:

```
# diff /root/ifcfg-eth0 /etc/sysconfig/network-scripts/ifcfg-eth0
```

So if you've backed up the ifcfg-eth0 file to the /root directory, the command shown can help identify changes made by configuration tools.

wc

The **wc** command, short for word count, can return the number of lines, words, and characters in a file. The **wc** options are straightforward; for example, **wc -w** *filename* returns the number of words in that file.

sed

The **sed** command, short for stream editor, allows you to search for and change specified words or even text streams in a file. For example, the following command changes the first instance of the word "Windows" with "Linux" in each line of the file opsys, and writes the result to the file newopsys:

```
# sed 's/Windows/Linux' opsys > newopsys
```

However, this may not be enough. If there's more than one instance of "Windows" in a line in the opsys file, it does not change the second instance of that word. But you can fix this by adding a "global" suffix:

```
# sed 's/Windows/Linux/g' opsys > newopsys
```

The following example would make sure that all Samba shares configured with the **writable = yes** directive are reversed:

```
# sed 's/writable = yes/writable = no/g' /etc/samba/smb.conf > ~/smb.conf
```

Of course, you should then review the results in the /root/smb.conf file before overwriting the original /etc/samba/smb.conf file.

awk

The **awk** command, named for its developers (Aho, Weinberger, and Kernighan), is more of a database manipulation utility. It can identify lines with a keyword, and read out the text from a specified column in that line. A common example is with the /etc/passwd file. For example, the following command will read out the username of every user with a listing of "mike":

```
# awk '/mike/ {print $1}' /etc/passwd
```

Edit Text Files at the Console

The original version of the RHCSA objectives specified the use of the vim editor. Strictly speaking, it doesn't matter what text editor you use to edit text files. However, I believe that you need to know how to use the vim editor, and apparently some at Red Hat agree. The vim editor is short for vi, improved. When installed, you can also start the vim editor with the **vi** command. Hereafter, I refer to that text editor as vi.

I believe every administrator needs at least a basic knowledge of vi. While emacs may be more popular and flexible, vi may help you save a broken system. If you ever have to restore a critical configuration file using emergency boot media, vi may be the only editor that you'll have available.

While RHEL 6 also includes access to the more intuitive nano editor, a knowledge of vi commands can help you identify key sections of man pages and other text files more quickly. While RHEL rescue media supports more console-based editors, I describe vi here simply because it's the editor I know best.

You should know how to use the two basic modes of vi: command and insert. When you use vi to open a file, it opens in command mode. Some of the commands start insert mode. Opening a file is easy: just use the **vi** *filename* command. By default, this starts vi in command mode. An example of vi with the /etc/nsswitch.conf file is shown in Figure 3-4.

The following is only the briefest of introductions to the vi editor. For more information, there are a number of books available, as well as an extensive manual formatted as a HOWTO available from the Linux Documentation Project at www. tldp.org. Alternatively, a tutorial is available through the **vimtutor** command.

vi Command Mode

In command mode, you can do everything to a text file except edit it. The options in command mode are broad and varied, and they are the subject of a number of book-length texts. In summary, options in vi command mode fall into seven categories:

- **Open** To open a file in the vi editor from the command line interface, run the **vi** *filename* command.

- **Search** For a forward search, start with a backslash (/), followed by the search term. Remember, Linux is case sensitive, so if you're searching for

FIGURE 3-4

The vi editor with
/etc/nsswitch.conf

```
passwd:      files
shadow:      files
group:       files

#hosts:      db files nisplus nis dns
hosts:       files dns

# Example - obey only what nisplus tells us...
#services:   nisplus [NOTFOUND=return] files
#networks:   nisplus [NOTFOUND=return] files
#protocols:  nisplus [NOTFOUND=return] files
#rpc:        nisplus [NOTFOUND=return] files
#ethers:     nisplus [NOTFOUND=return] files
#netmasks:   nisplus [NOTFOUND=return] files
█
bootparams: nisplus [NOTFOUND=return] files

ethers:      files
netmasks:    files
networks:    files
protocols:   files
rpc:         files
```

"Michael" in /etc/passwd, use the **/Michael** (not **/michael**) command. For a reverse search, start with a question mark (?).

■ **Write**   To save your changes, use the **w** command. You can combine commands; for example, **:wq** writes the file and exits vi.

■ **Close**   To leave vi, use the **:q** command.

■ **Abandon**   If you want to abandon any changes, use the **:q!** command.

■ **Edit**   You can use a number of commands to edit files through vi, such as **x**, which deletes the currently highlighted character, **dw**, which deletes the currently highlighted word, and **dd**, which deletes the current line. Remember, **p** places text from a buffer, and **U** restores text from a previous change.

■ **Insert**   A number of commands allow you to start insert mode, including **i** to start inserting text at the current position of the editor, and **o** to open up a new line immediately below the current position of the cursor.

Basic Text Editing

In modern Linux systems, editing files with vi is easy. Just use the normal navigation keys (arrow keys, PAGE UP, and PAGE DOWN), and then one of the basic commands such as **i** or **o** to start vi's insert mode, and type your changes directly into the file. When you're finished with insert mode, press the ESC key to return to command mode. You can then save your changes, or abandon them and exit vi.

on the
()ob

There are several specialized variations on the **vi** *command. Three are* **vipw, vigw,** *and* **visudo,** *which edit* **/etc/passwd, /etc/group,** *and* **/etc/sudoers,** *respectively. The* **vipw -s** *and* **vigr -s** *commands edit the* **/etc/shadow** *and* **/etc/ gshadow** *files.*

EXERCISE 3-1

Using vi to Create a New User

In this exercise, you'll create a new user by editing the /etc/passwd file with the vi text editor. While there are other ways to create new Linux users, this exercise helps you verify your skills with vi and at the command line interface.

1. Open a Linux command line interface. Log in as the root user, and type the **vipw** command. This command uses the vi editor to open /etc/passwd.

2. Navigate to the end of the file. As you should already know, there are several ways to do this in command mode, including the DOWN ARROW key, the PAGE DOWN key, the **G** command, or even the K key.

3. Identify a line associated with a regular user. If you've just created a new user, it should be the last line in the file, with numbers of 500 and above. If a regular user does not yet exist, identify the first line, which should be associated with the root administrative user, with the number 0 in the third and fourth column.

4. Make one copy of this line. If you're already comfortable with vi, you should know that you can copy an entire line to the buffer with the **yy** command. This "yanks" the line into buffer. You can then restore or put that line as many times as desired with the **p** command.

5. Change the username, user ID, group ID, user comment, and home directory for the new user. For detailed information on each entry, see Chapter 8. For example, in the following illustration, this corresponds to tweedle, 501, 501, Tweedle Dee, and /home/tweedle. Make sure the username also corresponds to the home directory.

```
dbus:x:81:81:System message bus:/:/sbin/nologin
avahi-autoipd:x:170:170:Avahi IPv4LL Stack:/var/lib/avahi-autoipd:/sbin/nologin
vcsa:x:69:69:virtual console memory owner:/dev:/sbin/nologin
rpc:x:32:32:Rpcbind Daemon:/var/cache/rpcbind:/sbin/nologin
rtkit:x:499:499:RealtimeKit:/proc:/sbin/nologin
abrt:x:498:498::/etc/abrt:/sbin/nologin
nscd:x:28:28:NSCD Daemon:/:/sbin/nologin
haldaemon:x:68:68:HAL daemon:/:/sbin/nologin
nslcd:x:65:55:LDAP Client User:/:/sbin/nologin
saslauth:x:497:495:"Saslauthd user":/var/empty/saslauth:/sbin/nologin
postfix:x:89:89::/var/spool/postfix:/sbin/nologin
avahi:x:70:70:Avahi mDNS/DNS-SD Stack:/var/run/avahi-daemon:/sbin/nologin
ntp:x:38:38::/etc/ntp:/sbin/nologin
rpcuser:x:29:29:RPC Service User:/var/lib/nfs:/sbin/nologin
nfsnobody:x:65534:65534:Anonymous NFS User:/var/lib/nfs:/sbin/nologin
pulse:x:496:494:PulseAudio System Daemon:/var/run/pulse:/sbin/nologin
gdm:x:42:42::/var/lib/gdm:/sbin/nologin
sshd:x:74:74:Privilege-separated SSH:/var/empty/sshd:/sbin/nologin
tcpdump:x:72:72::/:/sbin/nologin
oprofile:x:16:16:Special user account to be used by OProfile:/home/oprofile:/sbin/nologin
michael:x:500:500:Michael Jang:/home/michael:/bin/bash
tweedle:x:501:501:Tweedle Dee:/home/tweedle:/bin/bash
```

6. Return to command mode by pressing the ESC key. Save the file with the **:w** command, and then exit with the **:q** command. (You can combine the two

commands in vi; the next time you make a change and want to save and exit, run the **:wq** command.)

7. You should see the following message:

```
You have modified /etc/passwd.
You may need to modify /etc/shadow for consistency.
Please use the command 'vipw -s' to do so.
```

That message can be ignored, as the next step adds appropriate information to the /etc/shadow file. However, you don't need to modify /etc/shadow directly.

8. As the root user, run the **passwd *newuser*** command. Assign the password of your choice to the new user. For this example, the new user is tweedle.

9. The process is not yet complete; every user needs a group. To that end, run the **vigr** command. Repeat the earlier steps that copied an appropriate line from near the end of the file. Note that group names and group ID numbers normally are identical to their usernames and user ID numbers.

10. All you need to change for the new entry is the group name and group ID number. Based on the information shown the previous illustration, that would be a group name of tweedle and a group number of 501.

11. Repeat the aforementioned **:wq** command to close vi and save the change. Actually, you'll get a message that suggests that the file is read only. You'd have to run the **:wq!** in this case to write to this "read only" file, overriding current settings.

12. Pay attention to the following message:

```
You have modified /etc/group.
You may need to modify /etc/gshadow for consistency.
Please use the command 'vigr -s' to do so.
```

13. As suggested, run the **vigr -s** command to open the /etc/gshadow file. You'll note that there's less information in this file. Once a copy is made of an appropriate line, all you'll need to do is change the group name.

14. Repeat the aforementioned **:wq!** command to close vi and save the change.

15. Additional steps are required to properly set up the new user, related to that user's home directory and standard files from the /etc/skel directory. For more information, see Chapter 8.

If You Don't Like vi

By default, when you run commands like **edquota** and **crontab**, associated quota and cron job configuration files are opened in the vi editor. If you absolutely hate vi, the default editor can be changed with the following command:

```
# export EDITOR=/bin/nano
```

To change the default editor for all users, add the preceding line to the /etc/ environment configuration file. You don't absolutely have to use the vi editor to change /etc/environment; instead, the following appends the noted command to the end of the /etc/environment file:

```
# echo 'export EDITOR=/bin/nano' >> /etc/environment
```

As the nano editor is fairly intuitive, as shown in Figure 3-5, instructions will not be provided in this book. The full manual is available from www.nano-editor.org/ dist/v2.1/nano.html.

Similar changes can be made if you prefer a different editor such as emacs, pico, or joe.

FIGURE 3-5

The nano editor with /etc/ nsswitch.conf

```
GNU nano 2.0.9              File: /etc/nsswitch.conf

#
# /etc/nsswitch.conf
#
# An example Name Service Switch config file. This file should be
# sorted with the most-used services at the beginning.
#
# The entry '[NOTFOUND=return]' means that the search for an
# entry should stop if the search in the previous entry turned
# up nothing. Note that if the search failed due to some other reason
# (like no NIS server responding) then the search continues with the
# next entry.
#
# Valid entries include:
#
#       nisplus                 Use NIS+ (NIS version 3)
#       nis                     Use NIS (NIS version 2), also called YP
#       dns                     Use DNS (Domain Name Service)
#       files                   Use the local files
#       db                      Use the local database (.db) files
                              [ Read 63 lines ]
^G Get Help  ^O WriteOut  ^R Read File ^Y Prev Page ^K Cut Text   ^C Cur Pos
^X Exit      ^J Justify   ^W Where Is  ^V Next Page ^U UnCut Text ^T To Spell
```

Edit Text Files in the GUI

No question, the Red Hat exams have become more friendly toward the GUI. The gedit text editor was even included for a short time in the RHCSA objectives. More traditional Linux administrators may have been horrified. (The gedit editor has since been deleted from the objectives.)

The gedit text editor is not installed by default. Fortunately, installation is easy with the **yum install gedit** command. Once installed, you can start it by clicking Applications | Accessories | gedit Text Editor. As it is an intuitive GUI text editor, its use is trivial. Don't obsess about editors; they are just tools on exams and in real life.

However, if you're editing configuration files on remote systems, it's possible that you won't have access to gedit on that system, especially if the GUI hasn't been installed there. Of course, you can install the GUI on any Red Hat system. But many administrators set up VMs without the GUI to save space and reduce security risks.

CERTIFICATION OBJECTIVE 3.04

Local Online Documentation

While there's no Internet access allowed during Red Hat exams, there is a lot of help available online, already installed on an RHEL 6 system. It starts with the man pages, which document the options and settings associated with most commands and many configuration files. It continues with the info documents. While fewer commands and files have such documents, when available, they do provide even more information.

exam

watch *When Red Hat says that it "may use applications during the exam that are not included in Red Hat Enterprise Linux for the purpose of evaluating* *candidate's abilities" with respect to documentation, I would not be shocked to find important exam information in the /usr/share/doc directory.*

Many packages include extensive documentation in the /usr/share/doc directory. Just apply the **ls** command to that directory. Every subdirectory there includes information about the capabilities of each associated package. Of course, there's more.

When You Need Help

The first thing I do when I need help with a command is to run it by itself. If more information is required, the command prompts with a request for more information, including a variety of options. As an example, look at the output to the following command:

```
$ yum
```

If that approach doesn't work, generally some amount of help is available with the **-h** or the **--help** switches. Sometimes a mistake leads to some hints; the output to following command suggests legal switches to the **cd** command:

```
$ cd -h
bash: cd: -h: invalid option
cd: usage: cd [-L|-P] [dir]
```

FIGURE 3-6		
Help with Process Management		

```
-A all processes                      -C by command name
-N negate selection                   -G by real group ID (supports names)
-a all w/ tty except session leaders  -U by real user ID (supports names)
-d all except session leaders         -g by session OR by effective group name
-e all processes                      -p by process ID
T  all processes on this terminal     -s processes in the sessions given
a  all w/ tty, including other users  -t by tty
g  OBSOLETE -- DO NOT USE             -u by effective user ID (supports names)
r  only running processes             U  processes for specified users
x  processes w/o controlling ttys     t  by tty
********** output format **********    *********** long options ***********
-o,o user-defined  -f full            --Group --User --pid --cols --ppid
-j,j job control    s  signal         --group --user --sid --rows --info
-O,O preloaded -o   v  virtual memory --cumulative --format --deselect
-l,l long           u  user-oriented  --sort --tty --forest --version
-F   extra full     X  registers      --heading --no-heading --context
                    ********* misc options *********
-V,V  show version      L  list format codes  f  ASCII art forest
-m,m,-L,-T,H  threads   S  children in sum    -y change -l format
-M,Z  security data     c  true command name  -c scheduling class
-w,w  wide output       n  numeric WCHAN,UID  -H process hierarchy
michael@Maui:~$ ls bookRHCE6/Chapter3/
56503.doc  Ch3Lab3         ch3.zip      F03-01.tif  F03-03.tif  fifthedition
Backup     Ch3Lab3testfile F03-01.png  F03-02.tif  F03-04.tif
michael@Maui:~$ █
```

Sometimes the **-h** switch is more helpful; take a look at the output to the **fdisk -h** command. But the **-h** switch doesn't always work; sometimes the **--help** switch is more helpful. Look at Figure 3-6 as an example, which displays the output to the **ps --help** command.

A Variety of man Pages

Few people can remember every switch to every command. That's one reason why command documentation is so important. Most Linux commands are documented in a format known as the man page. If you run the **man** command by itself, RHEL returns the following message:

```
What manual page do you want?
```

For example, say you need to set up a physical volume but have forgotten the switches associated with the **lvexpand** command. To browse the man page for that command, run **man lvexpand**. As with many other commands, there's an EXAMPLES section, like that shown in Figure 3-7. If you've run the **lvexpand** command before, that section may help jog your memory.

FIGURE 3-7

Examples from
the lvexpand man
page

```
-r, --resizefs
        Resize  underlying  filesystem  together with the logical volume
        using fsadm(8).

Examples
        "lvextend -L +54 /dev/vg01/lvol10 /dev/sdk3" tries to extend  the  size
        of  that  logical volume by 54MB on physical volume /dev/sdk3.  This is
        only possible if /dev/sdk3 is a member of volume group vg01 and  there
        are enough free physical extents in it.

        "lvextend  /dev/vg01/lvol01 /dev/sdk3" tries to extend the size of that
        logical volume by  the  amount  of  free  space on  physical  volume
        /dev/sdk3.   This is equivalent to specifying "-l +100%PVS" on the com-
        mand line.

        "lvextend -L+16M vg01/lvol01 /dev/sda:8-9 /dev/sdb:8-9"
        tries to extend a logical volume "vg01/lvol01" by 16MB  using  physical
        extents /dev/sda:8-9 and /dev/sdb:8-9 for allocation of extents.

SEE ALSO
        fsadm(8),   lvm(8),  lvcreate(8),  lvconvert(8),  lvreduce(8),  lvresize(8),
        lvchange(8)

:
```

Such man pages are available for most configuration files and commands. However, there may be more. So what if you're not sure about the name of the man page? In that case, the **whatis** and **apropos** commands can help. For example, to find the man pages with "nfs" in the title, run the following command:

```
# whatis nfs
```

If you want to find the man pages with nfs in the description, the following command can identify related commands.

```
# apropos nfs
```

However, if you've just installed a service such as Samba, associated with the Linux implementation of Microsoft networking, commands like **whatis smb.conf** and **apropos smbpasswd** probably won't provide any information. These commands work from a database in the /var/cache/man directory. You can update that database with the makewhatis.cron job in the /etc/cron.daily directory. Since that script is already executable, the following command updates the database of man pages:

```
# /etc/cron.daily/makewhatis.cron
```

If you encounter a situation, such as during a Red Hat exam, where the associated man page is not installed, there are at least three possible reasons. The associated functional software package may not be installed. The RPM package named man-pages may also not be installed. In some cases, there is a package specifically dedicated to documentation that must be installed separately. For example, there's a system-config-users-doc package that includes GUI-based documentation for the User Manager configuration tool. There's a separate httpd-manual package installed separately from the Apache Web server.

In some cases, there are multiple man pages available. Take a look at the following output to the **whatis smbpasswd** command:

```
smbpasswd              (5)  - The Samba encrypted password file
smbpasswd              (8)  - change a user's SMB password
```

The numbers (5) and (8) are associated with different sections of man pages. If you're interested in details, they're shown in the output to the **man man** command. The man page shown by default is the command. In this case, if you want the man page for the encrypted password file, run the following command:

```
$ man 5 smbpasswd
```

To exit from a man page, press **q**.

The info Manuals

The list of available info manuals is somewhat limited. For a full list, run the **ls /usr/share/info** command. When an info manual is not available, a request defaults to the associated man page.

To learn more about the bash shell, run the **info bash** command. As shown in Figure 3-8, info manuals are organized into sections. To access a section, move the cursor to the asterisked entry and press ENTER.

To exit from an info page, press **q**.

Detailed Documentation in /usr/share/doc

The list of documentation available in the /usr/share/doc directory seems impressive. But the quality of the documentation depends on the work of its developers. The subdirectories include the name and version number of the installed package. Some of these subdirectories include just one file, normally named COPYING, which specifies the license under which the given software was released. For example, most of the system-config-* packages include a copy of the GNU GPL in the COPYING file in the associated /usr/share/doc directory.

FIGURE 3-8	

A sample info manual

```
* Menu:

* Introduction::              An introduction to the shell.
* Definitions::               Some definitions used in the rest of this    S
                              manual.
* Basic Shell Features::      The shell "building blocks".
* Shell Builtin Commands::    Commands that are a part of the shell.
* Shell Variables::           Variables used or set by Bash.
* Bash Features::             Features found only in Bash.
* Job Control::               What job control is and how Bash allows you
                              to use it.
* Command Line Editing::      Chapter describing the command line
                              editing features.
* Using History Interactively:: Command History Expansion
* Installing Bash::           How to build and install Bash on your system.
* Reporting Bugs::            How to report bugs in Bash.
* Major Differences From The Bourne Shell::    A terse list of the differences
                                               between Bash and historical
                                               versions of /bin/sh.
* GNU Free Documentation License::    Copying and sharing this documentation.
* Indexes::                   Various indexes for this manual.

--zz-Info: (bash.info.gz)Top, 44 lines --Bot-----------------------------------
```

Sometimes, the documentation directory includes useful examples. For example, the sudo-*/ subdirectory includes sample configuration files and directives for administrative control, which can be helpful when configuring administrators with different privileges.

Sometimes the documentation includes entire manuals in HTML format. For an example, take a look at the rsyslog-*/ subdirectory, which includes an entire online manual for the logging daemon server discussed in Chapters 9 and 17.

CERTIFICATION OBJECTIVE 3.05

A Networking Primer

TCP/IP is a series of protocols organized in layers, known as a protocol suite. It was developed for Unix and eventually adopted as the standard for communication on the Internet. With IP addresses, it can help you organize a network. There are a number of TCP/IP tools and configurations that can help you manage a network.

As with the previous sections in this chapter, the statements here are oversimplifications. So if you find this section overwhelming and/or incomplete, read the references cited in Chapter 1. Linux is built for networking, and there is no practical way to pass either any Red Hat exam unless you understand networking in some detail.

While the focus of current networks is still on IP version 4 addressing, some organizations have mandated a move toward IP version 6 (IPv6) networks. Even though the Internet has run out of new public IPv4 addresses, hardware that supports the routing of IPv6 networks is still somewhat rare. Hopefully, that will change during the life of this book.

IP Version 4 Numbers and Address Classes

Every computer that communicates on a network needs its own IP address. Some addresses are assigned permanently to a particular computer; these are known as *static* addresses. Others are leased from a DHCP server for a limited amount of time; these are also known as *dynamic* IP addresses.

IPv4 addresses are organized into five different classes, as shown in Table 3-2. The academics among you may note that this table differs slightly from the official addresses in each IPv4 class as specified in RFC 1518 from the Internet Engineering

Task Force (www.ietf.org). The *assignable* address range includes those IP addresses that can be assigned to a specific computer on a network.

In addition, there are a number of private IP addresses that are not to be assigned to any computer that is directly connected to the Internet. They are associated with network addresses 10.0.0.0, 172.168.0.0, and 192.168.0.0 through 192.168.255.0.

Basic IP Version 6 Addressing

Network experts have been predicting the demise of IPv4 for years. It is true, there aren't enough IPv4 addresses for the Internet. However, with the help of private IP address blocks, users on enterprise-level networks don't need that many public IP addresses.

Nevertheless, there will be a time where IPv6 addresses are the norm. First, to compare, IPv4 addresses have 32 bits and are set up in octets in dotted decimal notation. IPv6 addresses have 128 bits and are set up in hexadecimal notation, also known as base 16. In other words, the "numbers" in an IPv6 address may include the following:

```
0, 1, 2, 3, 4, 5, 6, 7, 8, 9, a, b, c, d, e, f
```

An IPv6 address is normally organized in eight groups of four hexadecimal numbers each, and it may look like 4abe:03e2:c132:69fa:0000:0000:c0b8:2148. The current IPv6 address of the local system is shown in the output to the **ifconfig** command.

With 128 bits, IPv6 addresses can be divided into a number of categories. First, there are three relevant address formats.

■ **Unicast**   A unicast address is associated with a single network adapter. Routable unicast addresses include a 48-bit network prefix, a 16-bit subnet

TABLE 3-2	Class	Assignable Address Range	Note
IP Address Classes	A	1.1.1.1–126.255.255.254	Allows networks of up to 16 million computers
	B	128.0.0.1–191.255.255.254	Allows networks of up to 65,000 computers
	C	192.0.0.1–223.255.255.254	Allows networks of up to 254 computers
	D	224.0.0.1–239.255.255.254	Reserved for multicasts
	E	240.0.0.1–255.255.255.254	Reserved for experimental use

identifier, and a 64-bit interface identifier associated with a network adapter hardware address. Link-local unicast addresses include a 10-bit prefix, 54 zeros, and the same 64-bit interface identifier. Link-local unicast addresses are not routable.

■ **Multicast** A multicast address is used to send a message to multiple network adapters simultaneously. The organization of a multicast address varies.

■ **Anycast** An anycast address is used to send a message to one of several optional network adapters. It's useful for systems with multiple backups, such as a group of Web servers. Anycast addresses have the same basic organization as a unicast address.

With that diversity of address formats, IPv4-style broadcast addresses aren't used. Instead, IPv6 addressing uses multicast addressing for the purpose. IPv6 addresses are also organized in a number of different ranges, as described in Table 3-3. The default IPv6 address is sometimes also listed as ::/128.

How to Define a Network with IP Addresses

Three key IP addresses define a network: the network address, the broadcast address, and the subnet mask. The network address is always the first IP address in a range; the broadcast address is always the last address in the same range. The subnet mask helps your computer define the difference between the two addresses. You can assign IP addresses between the network and broadcast addresses (not including these addresses) to any computer on the network.

on the **job** *A subnet mask is also known as a network mask or netmask. An example of an IPv4 netmask is 255.255.255.0. An example of an IPv6 netmask is /64.*

TABLE 3-3	Address	Description
IP Address Classes	::1	Loopback address
	::	Default address
	::ffff:0000:0000	IPv4 mapped IPv6 addresses in the last 8 zeros
	fe80::	Link-local addresses; no routing between networks
	fec0::	Site-local addresses, for a single network
	ff::	Multicast addresses
	2000::	Global unicast addressees are routable

As an example, let's define the range of addresses for a private network. Start with the private network address 192.168.122.0. Use the standard subnet mask for a class C network, 255.255.255.0. Based on these two addresses, the broadcast address is 192.168.122.255, and the range of IP addresses that you can assign on that particular network is 192.168.122.1 through 192.168.122.254. That subnet mask is also defined by the number of associated bits, 24. In other words, the given network can be represented by 192.168.122.0/24. That's also known as Classless Inter-Domain Routing (CIDR) notation.

IPv6 networks use a similar concept for netmasks, which are always expressed in CIDR notation. For example, even point-to-point networks have a netmask of /64. That allows 64 bits to be used for the 48-bit hardware address. Remaining addresses can be allocated to specific network cards.

The standard IPv6 network has a 48-bit netmask. That supports the configuration of 16 bit subnets. The remaining 64 bits are still used in part for network cards, as described previously for point-to-point networks.

Related to networking and netmasks is the concept of the gateway. It's an IP address that defines the junction between the local network and an external network. While that gateway IP address is part of the local network, it's attached to a system or a router with an IP address on a different network such as the public Internet. The gateway IP address is normally configured in the routing table for the local system, as defined by the **route** or **netstat -r** command described in the following section.

If this is confusing to you in any way, please refer to the IP Sub-Networking Mini-HOWTO and the Linux IPv6 HOWTO of the Linux Documentation Project at www.tldp.org.

Tools, Commands, and Gateways

There are a substantial number of tools available to manage the TCP/IP protocol suite on your Linux computer. Four of the more important network management commands are **ping, ifconfig, arp, netstat -r**, and **route**. There's also an IPv6-specific version of the **ping** command, **ping6**. The **dhclient** command is frequently used to automate the configuration that can be done with some of these commands.

But these are just the commands. In the next section, you'll examine the Red Hat files that determine the commands that are called upon to configure networks automatically during the boot process. Such commands are governed by the main network configuration service script, /etc/init.d/network. They can also be manually called with commands such as **ifup** and **ifdown**.

ping and ping6

The **ping** command allows you to test connectivity. It can be applied locally, within a network, and across networks on the Internet. For the purpose of this section, assume your IP address is 192.168.122.50, and the gateway address on the local network is 192.168.122.1. If you're having problems connecting to a network, try the following **ping** commands in order. The first step is to test the integrity of TCP/IP on your computer:

```
# ping 127.0.0.1
```

Normally, **ping** works continuously on Linux; you'll need to press CTRL-C to stop this command. If you need to verify a proper connection to a LAN, **ping** the IP address of the local network card:

```
# ping 192.168.122.50
```

If that works, **ping** the address of another computer on your network. Then start tracing the route to the Internet. **ping** the address for the network gateway, in this case, 192.168.122.1. If possible, **ping** the address of the network's connection to the Internet, which would be on the other side of the gateway. It may be the public IP address of the LAN on the Internet. And finally, **ping** the address of a computer that you know is *active* on the Internet.

You can substitute hostnames such as www.google.com for an IP address. If the hostname doesn't work, there is likely a problem with the database of hostnames and IP addresses, more commonly known as a Domain Name Service (DNS), Berkeley Internet Name Domain (BIND), or nameserver. It could also indicate a problem with the /etc/hosts configuration file.

In contrast, the **ping6** command works in almost the same way. The exception on Red Hat systems is that you need to specify the network adapter. For example, the following command pings the noted IPv6 network through the virtual virbr0 adapter:

```
# ping6 -I virbr0 fe80::5652:ff:fe39:24d8
```

If you've configured global IPv6 addresses and have set up routing to the Internet, Google has a test IPv6 URL at ipv6.google.com.

Review Current Network Adapters with ifconfig

The **ifconfig** command can display the current state of active network adapters. It also can be used to assign network addresses and more. Run the **ifconfig** command by itself to review the active network adapters on the local system. If there seems to be a missing network adapter, try the **ifconfig -a** command, which displays the current configuration of all network adapters, whether or not they're currently active.

The **ifconfig eth0** command shown here reflects the current configuration of the first Ethernet network adapter:

```
# ifconfig eth0
eth0      Link encap:Ethernet  HWaddr 00:50:56:40:1E:6A
          inet addr:192.168.122.50  Bcast:192.168.122.255  Mask:255.255.255.0
          inet6 addr: fe80::2e0:4cff:fee3:d106/64 Scope:Link
          UP BROADCAST RUNNING MULTICAST  MTU:1500  Metric:1
          RX packets:11253 errors:0 dropped:0 overruns:0 frame:0
          TX packets:1304 errors:0 dropped:0 overruns:0 carrier:0
          collisions:0 txqueuelen:1000
          RX bytes:2092656 (1.9 Mb)  TX bytes:161329 (157.5 Kb)
```

Configure a Network Adapter with ifconfig

You can also use **ifconfig** to assign IP address information as well. For example, the following command assigns the noted IP address and network mask to the eth0 network adapter:

```
# ifconfig eth0 192.168.122.150 netmask 255.255.255.0
```

The first parameter, **eth0**, tells you which interface is being configured. The next argument, **192.168.122.150**, specifies the new IP address being assigned to this interface. To make sure the change worked, run the **ifconfig eth0** command again to view its current settings.

With the right switch, the **ifconfig** command can modify a number of other settings for a selected network adapter. Some of these switches are shown in Table 3-4.

Activate and Deactivate Network Adapters

It's possible to use the **ifconfig** command to activate and deactivate network adapters. For example, the following commands deactivate and reactivate the first Ethernet adapter:

```
# ifconfig eth0 down
# ifconfig eth0 up
```

TABLE 3-4	Parameter	Description
ifconfig Switches	up	Activates the specified adapter.
	down	Deactivates the specified adapter.
	netmask *address*	Assigns the *address* subnet mask.
	broadcast *address*	Assigns the *address* as the broadcast address. Rarely required, since the default broadcast address is standard for most current networks.
	metric N	Allows you to set a metric value of N for the routing table associated with the network adapter.
	mtu N	Sets the maximum transmission unit as N, in bytes.
	-arp	Deactivates the Address Resolution Protocol (ARP), which collects network adapter hardware addresses.
	promisc	Activates promiscuous mode. This allows the network adapter to read all packets to all hosts on the LAN. Can be used to analyze the network for problems or to try to decipher messages between other users.
	-promisc	Deactivates promiscuous mode.

However, a couple of more intuitive scripts are designed to control network adapters: **ifup** and **ifdown**. Unlike the **ifconfig** command, they call appropriate configuration files and scripts in the /etc/sysconfig/network-scripts directory, for details on how a network adapter is to be activated and deactivated.

For example, the **ifup eth0** command brings up the first Ethernet network adapter based on the ifcfg-eth0 configuration file and the ifcfg-eth script in the /etc/sysconfig/network-scripts directory. If you've configured the network adapter with the Network Connections tool described later in this chapter, the filename in the /etc/sysconfig/network-scripts directory may be something like ifcfg-System_eth0.

arp as a Diagnostic Tool

The ARP protocol associates the hardware address of a network adapter with an IP address. The **arp** command displays a table of hardware and IP addresses on the local computer. The **arp** command can help detect problems such as duplicate addresses on the network. Such problems may happen with improperly cloned systems. If needed, the **arp** command can be used to set or modify hardware routing tables. As hardware addresses are not routable, an arp table should be limited to the local network. Here's a sample **arp** command, showing all **arp** entries in the local database:

```
# arp
Address              HWtype  HWaddress            Flags Mask        Iface
192.168.122.150      ether   52:A5:CB:54:52:A2    C                 eth0
192.168.100.100      ether   00:A0:C5:E2:49:02    C                 eth0
192.168.122.1        ether   00:0E:2E:6D:9E:67    C                 eth0
```

If the ARP table is empty, no recent connections exist to other systems on the local network. The Address column lists known IP addresses on the LAN. The HWtype column shows the hardware type of the adapter, while the HWaddress column shows the hardware address of the adapter.

Routing Tables with netstat -r and route

The **netstat** command is versatile; it can help you see the channels available for network connections, interface statistics, and more. One important version of this command, **netstat -r**, displays routing tables that can tell you if the system knows where to send a message. It's functionally equivalent to the **route** command. When run on a system, it's frequently run with the **-n** switch, to display addresses in numeric format.

The routing table for the local system normally includes a reference to the local gateway address, coupled with the default route. For example, look at the following output to the **route -n** command:

```
Kernel IP routing table
Destination    Gateway       Genmask        Flags Metric Ref Use Iface
192.168.122.0  0.0.0.0       255.255.255.0  U     0      0   0   eth0
0.0.0.0        192.168.122.1 0.0.0.0        UG    0      0   0   eth0
```

The **netstat -nr** command should display the same table. For this routing table, the gateway IP address is 192.168.122.1. It's the gateway to the destination IP address of 0.0.0.0, which is the default IP address. In other words, network transmission to anything other than the 192.168.122.0 network is sent to the gateway address. The system at the gateway address, usually a router, is responsible for forwarding that message to an external network.

If the destination is on the LAN, no gateway is required, so an asterisk (or 0.0.0.0) is shown in this column. The Genmask column lists the network mask. Networks look for a route appropriate to the destination IP address. The IP address is compared against the destination networks, in order. When the IP address is found to be part of one of these networks, it's sent in that direction. If there is a gateway address, it's sent to the computer with that gateway. The Flags column describes how this is done. Flag descriptions are listed in Table 3-5.

TABLE 3-5	Flag	Description
The netstat Flag Indicates the Route	G	The route uses a gateway.
	U	The network adapter, listed in the Iface column, is up.
	H	Only a single host can be reached via this route.
	D	This entry was created by an ICMP redirect message.
	M	This entry was modified by an ICMP redirect message.

In contrast, while an IPv6 routing table is more complex, the principles are the same. In other words, the IPv6 gateway address is associated with the default IPv6 route, symbolized by the ::/128 address. The same **route** and **netstat** commands can be used for IPv6 routing tables, when coupled with the **-A inet6** switch.

Dynamically Configure IP Addresses with dhclient

While the name of the command has changed from time to time, the functionality has remained the same. Ever since Dynamic Host Configuration Protocol (DHCP) servers were created to ration IPv4 addresses, commands have been needed by clients to call upon the services of that server. At this time, the key command is **dhclient**. When used with the device name of a network card, it calls upon a DHCP server for an IP address and more. In fact, a command like the following may call on that DHCP server for a number of parameters.

```
# dhclient eth0
```

Generally, the network options that are configured through a DHCP server include the IP address, the network mask, the gateway address for access to external networks, and the IP address of any DNS servers for that network.

In other words, the **dhclient eth0** command not only assigns IP address information in the way done with the **ifconfig** command described earlier, but also it sets up the default route for the routing table shown with the **route -n** command. In addition, it adds the IP address of the DNS server to the /etc/resolv.conf configuration file.

CERTIFICATION OBJECTIVE 3.06

Network Configuration and Troubleshooting

Now that you've reviewed the basics of IP addressing and associated commands, it's time to look at the associated configuration files. These configuration files determine whether networking is started during the boot process. If started, these files also determine whether addresses and routes are configured statically as documented, or dynamically with the help of commands like **dhclient**.

Basic network configuration only confirms that systems can communicate through their IP addresses. But that is not enough. Whether you're pointing to systems such as server1.example.com or URLs such as www.mheducation.com, network configuration is not enough if the hostname (or FQDN) configuration is not working.

on the job

The most common cause of network problems is physical. This section assumes you've checked all network connections. On a VM, that means making sure the virtual network card wasn't accidentally deleted on the VM or on the physical host.

Network Configuration Files

If there's trouble with a network configuration, one thing to check is the current status of the network. To do so, run the following command:

```
# /etc/init.d/network status
```

The command should list configured and active devices. If a key device such as eth0 is not listed as active, that explains why the network seems to be down. Key configuration files start with /etc/sysconfig/network. They continue with files in the /etc/sysconfig/network-scripts directory.

Sometimes mistakes happen. If you've deactivated an adapter or just lost a wireless connection, one simple solution may be to restart networking. The following command restarts networking with current configuration files.

```
# /etc/init.d/network restart
```

If a simple restart of networking services doesn't work, then it's time to get into the files.

Services such as networking may be configured to start during the boot process, as discussed in Chapter 5.

/etc/sysconfig/network

If you run the **ifconfig** command and see no output, that means all network devices are currently inactive. If you run the **ifconfig -a** command and don't see an **UP** in the output to any configured network device, that confirms the inactivity. The first thing to check in that case is the contents of the /etc/sysconfig/network configuration file. It's a pretty simple file. In general, you should see something similar to the following in that file:

```
NETWORKING=yes
HOSTNAME=server1.example.com
```

If **NETWORKING=no**, then the /etc/init.d/network script doesn't activate any network devices. The one other issue that may prevent networking from starting is the status of the script. Run the **chkconfig --list network** command. The output should look like:

```
network         0:off   1:off   2:on    3:on    4:on    5:on    6:off
```

If the settings next to runlevels 3 and 5 are off, that's a problem. To make sure a service is active in appropriate runlevels, run the **chkconfig network on** command. For more information on **chkconfig**, see Chapter 5.

If IPv6 networking is active on a system, you'll see the following directive in the file:

```
NETWORKING_IPV6=yes
```

One other network-related directive that may appear is **GATEWAY**, if it's the same IP address for all network devices. Otherwise, that configuration is supported either by the **dhclient** command or set up in the IP address information for a specific network device, in the /etc/sysconfig/network-scripts directory.

/etc/sysconfig/network-scripts/ifcfg-lo

Speaking of the /etc/sysconfig/network-scripts directory, perhaps the foundation of networking is the loopback address. That information is configured in the ifcfg-lo file in that directory. The contents of the file can help you understand how files in that directory are used for network devices. By default, you should see the following entries in that file, starting with the name of the loopback device:

```
DEVICE=lo
```

It's followed by the IP address (**IPADDR**), network mask (**NETMASK**), the network IP address (**NETWORK**), along with the corresponding broadcast address (**BROADCAST**).

```
IPADDR=127.0.0.1
NETMASK=255.0.0.0
NETWORK=127.0.0.0
BROADCAST=127.255.255.255
```

The next entries specify whether the device is activated during the boot process, and the common name of the device.

```
ONBOOT=yes
NAME=loopback
```

/etc/sysconfig/network-scripts/ifcfg-eth0

What you see in the ifcfg-eth0 file depends on how that first Ethernet network adapter was configured. For example, look at the situation where networking was configured only for the purposes of installation. If you did not configure networking when configuring the hostname during the GUI installation process, networking will not be configured on the system. In that case, the ifcfg-eth0 file would contain the following directives, starting with the name of the device, along with the hardware address:

```
DEVICE="eth0"
HWADDR="F0:DE:F3:06:C6:DB"
```

By default, RHEL 6 uses a service known as the Network Manager. If a network card is controlled by that service, the following directive would be set to yes:

```
NM_CONTROLLED="yes"
```

The Network Manager is a service; to make sure it's running, execute the **/etc/init.d/NetworkManager start** command. Of course, if networking were not configured during the installation process, there's no reason for it to be activated during the boot process:

```
ONBOOT="no"
```

The alternative to the Network Manager service is to configure it directly. For that purpose, the configuration file shown in Figure 3-9 provides a guide.

FIGURE 3-9

A static
configuration
not controlled
by Network
Manager

```
DEVICE="eth0"
BOOTPROTO="static"
DNS1="192.168.122.1"
GATEWAY="192.168.122.1"
HWADDR="52:54:00:5A:97:F6"
IPADDR="192.168.122.50"
NETMASK="255.255.255.0"
NM_CONTROLLED="yes"
ONBOOT="yes"
~
~
~
~
```

Of course, if you prefer to use a DHCP server, that static network address
information would be omitted, and the following directive would be changed:

```
BOOTPROTO=dhcp
```

Shortly, you'll see how to use Network Manager's Network Connections tool to
modify the configuration of a network device. But first, for a different perspective,
review Figure 3-10, which illustrates the configuration for a wireless network card on
my RHEL 6 laptop system.

FIGURE 3-10

A wireless
network
configuration

```
ESSID=wifi1
MODE=Managed
KEY_MGMT=WPA-PSK
TYPE=Wireless
BOOTPROTO=none
DEFROUTE=yes
IPV4_FAILURE_FATAL=yes
IPV6INIT=no
NAME=wifi1
UUID=b44e0567-d13a-4af1-b30a-38745f99ee91
ONBOOT=yes
IPADDR=192.168.0.200
PREFIX=24
GATEWAY=192.168.0.1
DNS1=192.168.0.1
LAST_CONNECT=1290340839
DEVICE=wlan0
USERCTL=no
~
~
~
~
~
```

Other /etc/sysconfig/network-scripts Files

Most of the files in the /etc/sysconfig/network-scripts directory are actually scripts. In other words, they are executable files based on a series of text commands. Most of those scripts are based on the **ifup** and **ifdown** commands, customized for network device type. If there's a special route to be configured, the configuration settings get their own special file in this directory, with a name like route-eth0. That special route would specify the gateway to a remote network address / network mask pair. One example based on the systems described in Chapter 1 might include the following directives:

```
ADDRESS0=192.168.100.100
NETMASK0=255.255.255.0
GATEWAY0=192.168.122.1
```

Network Configuration Tools

Red Hat includes two tools that can be used to configure network devices in RHEL 6. The first is the console network configuration tool. You can start it from the command line with the **system-config-network** command. The second is the Network Connections tool that you can start from a GUI command line with the **nm-connection-editor** command.

The Network Manager also includes another tool to display the current status of network devices. The output is somewhat similar to the output to the **ifconfig** command.

The Console Network Configuration Tool

As suggested by the name, you can start this tool from a command line console. Just run the **system-config-network** command. With a console tool, you'd need to press TAB to switch between options, and the spacebar or the ENTER key to select the highlighted option. Since this tool is not the Network Manager, you'll have to deactivate the associated device to put the configuration customized with this tool into effect. Exercise 3-2 illustrates this process.

Press TAB until Quit is highlighted and press ENTER. For now, make a backup of the ifcfg-eth0 file from the /etc/sysconfig/network-scripts directory. Based on the **diff** command, Figure 3-11 compares the contents of an eth0 card that uses the DHCP protocol, as configured during the installation process, with a card that uses static IP addressing, configured with the system-config-network tool.

The directives shown in Figure 3-11 are described in Table 3-6.

| **FIGURE 3-11** | ```
[root@Maui ~]# diff ifcfg-eth0 /etc/sysconfig/network-scripts/ifcfg-eth0
1,4c1,17
< DEVICE="eth0"
< HWADDR="F0:DE:F1:06:C6:DC"
< NM_CONTROLLED="yes"
< ONBOOT="no"
---
> DEVICE=eth0
> NM_CONTROLLED=yes
> ONBOOT=no
> BOOTPROTO=none
> NETMASK=255.255.255.0
> TYPE=Ethernet
> IPV6INIT=no
> USERCTL=no
> HWADDR=f0:de:f1:06:c6:dc
> DEFROUTE=yes
> PEERROUTES=yes
> IPV4_FAILURE_FATAL=yes
> NAME="System eth0"
> UUID=5fb06bd0-0bb0-7ffb-45f1-d6edd65f3e03
> IPADDR=192.168.122.60
> GATEWAY=192.168.122.1
> DNS1=192.168.122.1
[root@Maui ~]#
``` |

The differences
between static
and dynamic
network
configuration

TABLE 3-6	Network Configuration Directives in the /etc/sysconfig/network-scripts Directory

Directive	Description
DEVICE	Network device; eth0 is the first Ethernet network card
HWADDR	Hardware address for the network card
NM_CONTROLLED	Binary directive (yes or no) that specifies whether the card is controlled by the NetworkManager service
ONBOOT	Binary directive that specifies whether the network device is started during the boot process
BOOTPROTO	May be set to none for static configuration, DHCP to acquire IP addresses from a DHCP server
NETMASK	Network mask based on a static IP address configuration
TYPE	Network type, typically Ethernet
IPV6INIT	Binary directive that specifies the use of IPv6 addressing
USERCTL	Binary directive for user control of devices
```

TABLE 3-6	Network Configuration Directives in the /etc/sysconfig/network-scripts Directory (*continued*)

Directive	Description
DEFROUTE	Binary directive for using the default route, defined by route -n
PEERROUTES	Binary directive allowing the use of defined routes
IPV4_FAILURE_ FATAL	Binary directive supporting network failure if there's an error
NAME	Name of the Ethernet device; if present, the device becomes the value, such as System_eth0
UUID	Universal Unique Identifier for the device
IPADDR	Static IP address
GATEWAY	IP address of the default gateway

EXERCISE 3-2

Configure a Network Card

In this exercise, you'll configure the first Ethernet network card with the console-based Network Configuration tool. All you need is a command line interface. It doesn't matter whether the command line is in the GUI. If you're not logged in as the root user, you'll be prompted for the root administrative password. To configure a network card, take the following steps:

1. Back up a copy of the current configuration file for the first Ethernet card. Normally, it's ifcfg-eth0 in the /etc/sysconfig/network-scripts directory. For other cards, such as eth1, substitute accordingly. (Hint: use the **cp** and not the **mv** command.)

2. Run the **system-config-network** command.

3. In the Select Action menu that appears, Device Configuration should be highlighted. If necessary, press the TAB key until it is. Then press ENTER.

4. In the Select A Device screen that appears, the first Ethernet network card should be highlighted. When it is, press ENTER.

5. In the Network Configuration window shown in here, the Use DHCP option may be selected. If so, highlight it and press the SPACEBAR to deselect it.

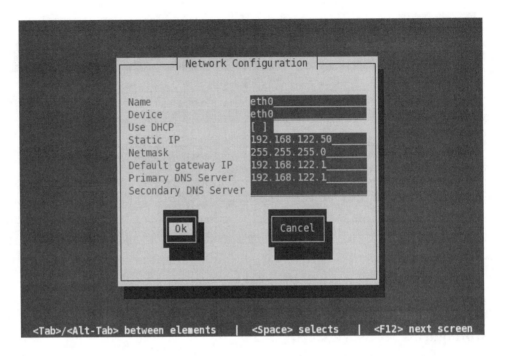

6. Enter the IP address information for the system. The settings shown in the window are based on the settings described in Chapter 1 for the server1. example.com system. When complete, highlight OK and press ENTER.

7. You're taken back to the Select A Device screen. Make sure Save is highlighted and press ENTER.

8. You're taken back to the Select Action screen. Make sure Save&Quit is highlighted and press ENTER.

9. Deactivate and then reactivate the first Ethernet card with the **ifdown eth0** and **ifup eth0** commands, and check the result with the **ifconfig eth0** and **route -n** commands. The configuration of the network card and the associated routing table should reflect the new configuration.

10. To restore the original configuration, restore the ifcfg-eth0 file to the /etc/sysconfig/network-scripts directory and restart the network with the **/etc/init.d/network restart** command.

The Network Manager Network Connections Tool

Now you'll work with the new default network management tool for RHEL 6, the Network Connections tool. With the number of users on multiple network connections, the Network Manager is designed to make that switching between say a wireless and an Ethernet connection as seamless as possible. But that's something more applicable to portable systems, as opposed to servers. For our purposes, all you need to know is how to configure a network card with that tool.

It's not really new, as it's been in use on the Fedora Linux test bed for several years. It only runs in the GUI. To start it, you can run the **nm-connection-editor** command or click System | Preferences | Network Connections. It opens the Network Connections tool shown in Figure 3-12.

As you can see from the figure, the tool lists the detected first Ethernet network card, even though it hasn't been used before. The other tabs support the configuration of other types of network connections, including wireless, mobile broadband cards such as those used to connect to 3G and 4G networks, virtual private network (VPN) connections, and Digital Subscriber Line (DSL) connections. On a regular server, the focus is on reliable connections, and that is still based on a standard wired Ethernet device.

FIGURE 3-12

The Network Manager Network Connections tool

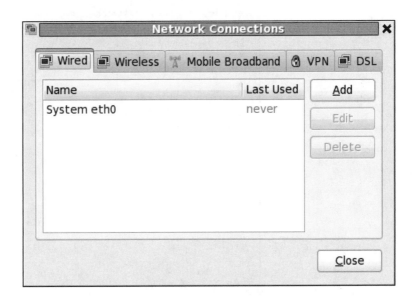

Highlight the first Ethernet device (eth0) and click Edit. It'll open the Editing System window shown in Figure 3-13. Note how the window includes the name of the Ethernet device and the hostname of the system. That means I've accessed the window remotely, with the ssh -X command described in Chapter 2. (If access is local, the hostname won't be shown.)

Click the IPv4 settings tab. Unless previously configured, it assumes that network card will receive configuration settings from a DHCP server.

Click the Method drop-down text box. While it supports the configuration of a network card in several different ways, the only one of interest in this case is Manual. Select that option, and the Addresses section of the window should no longer be blanked out. Now add the IP address information for the system. Based on the server1.example.com system described in Chapter 1, the appropriate options include the following:

- ■ **IP Address** 192.168.122.50

FIGURE 3-13

Editing an Ethernet connection in the Network Settings tool

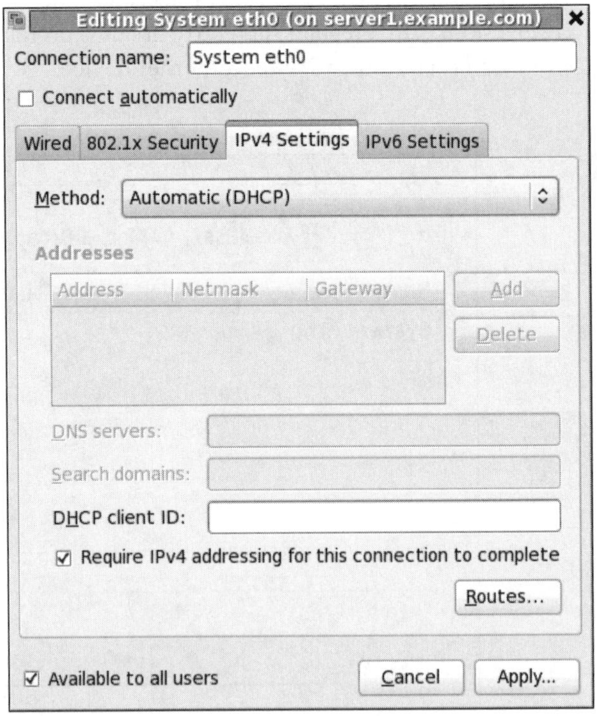

■ **Network Mask**   255.255.255.0 (24 in CIDR notation is an acceptable equivalent in this field)

■ **Gateway Address**   192.168.122.1

■ **DNS Server**   192.168.122.1

■ **Search Domains**   No entry required

■ **Require IPv4 Addressing For This Connection To Complete**   Supports IPv4 addressing

■ **Available To All Users**   If deselected, access is disabled for all users

If properly entered, the configuration associated with the first Ethernet card is entitled with the Connection Name listed in Figure 3-13. For that configuration, the settings are saved in the ifcfg-System_eth0 file in the /etc/sysconfig/network-scripts directory.

Hostname Configuration Files

RHEL 6 includes at least four hostname configuration files of interest: /etc/sysconfig/network, /etc/nsswitch.conf, /etc/hosts, and /etc/resolv.conf. These four files, taken together, contain the local hostname, the local database of hostnames and IP addresses, the IP address of a DNS server, and the order in which these databases are considered.

/etc/nsswitch.conf

The /etc/nsswitch.conf includes database search entries for everything from authentication to name services. As the name server switch file, it includes the following entry, which determines what database is searched first.

```
hosts: files dns
```

When a system gets a request to search for a hostname such as outsider1.example.org, the preceding directive means the /etc/hosts file is searched first. If that name is not found in /etc/hosts, the next step is to search available configured DNS servers, normally using that configured in the /etc/resolv.conf file.

A few older software components use the /etc/host.conf file for this purpose. The entries in this file are simple, as they support searches of multiple entries in

/etc/hosts, along with a search starting with that file, followed by a DNS server configured with the Berkeley Internet Name Domain (BIND) software.

```
multi on
order hosts,bind
```

/etc/hosts

The /etc/hosts file is a static database of hostnames/FQDN and IP addresses. It's suitable for small, relatively static networks. However, it can be a pain for networks where there are frequent changes. Every time a system is added or removed, you'll have to change this file—not only on the local system, but also on every other system on that network.

It's well suited to the local network systems created in Chapter 1. A simple version of the file might include the following entries:

```
192.168.122.50 server1.example.com
192.168.122.150 tester1.example.com
192.168.100.100 outsider1.example.org
127.0.0.1localhost.localdomain localhost
::1server1.example.com server1 localhost6.localdomain6 localhost6
```

Due to the IPv6 localhost entries, you can't just copy this file to all three test systems. However, it's not hard to replace an entry like server1 with tester1 in a local /etc/hosts file. In some cases, you may want to set up multiple entries for an IP address. For example, the following entries could be added to specify the IP addresses for Web and FTP servers:

```
192.168.122.50 www.example.com
192.168.122.150 ftp.example.com
```

/etc/resolv.conf

The standard file for documenting the location of DNS servers is still /etc/resolv.conf. Typically, it'll have one or two entries, similar to the following:

```
search example.com
nameserver 192.168.122.1
```

The **search** directive appends the example.com domain name to searches for simple hostnames. The **nameserver** directive specifies the IP address of the configured DNS server. If in doubt about whether the DNS server is operational, run the following command:

```
# dig @192.168.122.1 mheducation.com
```

If needed, substitute the IP address associated with the **nameserver** directive in your /etc/resolv.conf file.

Hostname Configuration Options

During the boot process, the network service looks to the /etc/sysconfig/network file to define the value of the local hostname. It's okay if that hostname is set as a FQDN like tester1.example.com. As suggested earlier, it's a simple file, where the hostname may be documented with a directive like the following:

```
HOSTNAME=tester1.example.com
```

Of course, you can change the value of the hostname with the **hostname** *newname* command. However, as such changes aren't reflected in the /etc/hosts file or any DNS server, such changes may not be very helpful.

The Network Manager Applet

The Network Manager also includes an applet to help users manage configured network connections. For example, on my personal system, I've configured one Ethernet and one wireless connection. When I left-click the network applet, it reveals available and active connections as shown in Figure 3-14. Note the available connections on wired and wireless networks. I can select different connections as desired. The actual icon associated with the applet varies, depending on whether there's a current active connection. The applet is in the upper-right area of the GNOME Desktop screen, near the date and time, on the top panel. (To help protect the privacy of my neighbors, the names of the wireless networks shown in Figure 3-14 have been partially obscured.)

If you right-click the Network Manager applet, it brings up a menu with configuration options. The options are for our purposes self-explanatory and trivial.

One Network
Manager applet
menu

Wired Network
disconnected
—————————————— Available ——————————————
System eth0
Wireless Networks
kat   🔒📶
Disconnect
—————————————— Available ——————————————
h   🔒📶
my   🔒📶
q   🔒📶
T   🔒📶
—————————————————————————————————————
<u>V</u>PN Connections   >
—————————————————————————————————————
<u>C</u>onnect to Hidden Wireless Network...
Create <u>N</u>ew Wireless Network...

SCENARIO & SOLUTION

Networking is down.	Check physical connections. Run **ifconfig** to check active connections. Run the **/etc/init.d/network status** command. Review the /etc/sysconfig/network file
Unable to access remote systems.	Use the **ping** command to test access to local, and then remote IP addresses.
Current network settings lead to conflicts.	Check network device configuration in /etc/sysconfig/network-scripts files. Review settings with the Network Connections tool.
Network settings not consistent.	Check network device configuration in /etc/sysconfig/network-scripts files. Review settings with the Network Connections tool. The scenario suggests a desire for a static network configuration, so review accordingly.
Hostname is not recognized.	Review /etc/sysconfig/network, run the hostname command, review /etc/hosts for consistency.
Remote hostnames not recognized.	Review /etc/hosts. Check /etc/resolv.conf for an appropriate DNS server IP address. Run the **dig** command to test the DNS server.

CERTIFICATION SUMMARY

The focus of this chapter is two-fold. It covered the basic command line tools formerly associated with Red Hat exam prerequisites. As those objectives have been incorporated into the main body of the RHCSA, they have been combined with network configuration, to allow you to practice these command line tools.

The command line starts with a shell, an interpreter that allows you to interact with the operating system using various commands. While no shell is specified in the objectives, the default shell in most Linux distributions, including RHEL 6, is bash. You can start a command line prompt at one of the default consoles, or at a terminal in the GUI. At the bash prompt, you can manage the files and directories through which Linux is configured and organized. As Linux configuration files are by and large in text format, they can be set up as databases to be searched and modified with a variety of commands. Linux text files can be processed as streams of data that can be interpreted and processed. To edit a text file, you need a text editor such as vim and gedit.

Documentation online within Linux is extensive. It starts with command switches such as **-h** and **--help** that provide hints on what goes with a command. It continues with man and info pages. Many packages include extensive documentation files in the /usr/share/info directory. In many, perhaps most, cases, you do not need Internet access to find the hints needed.

Linux is inherently a network operating system. Network devices such as eth0 can be configured with both IPv4 and IPv6 addressees. Network review and configuration commands include **ifconfig**, **ifup**, **ifdown**, and **dhclient**. Additional related commands include **arp**, **route**, **netstat**, and **ping**. Associated configuration files start with /etc/sysconfig/network. Individual devices are configured in the /etc/sysconfig/network-scripts directory. Network devices can also be configured with the **system-config-network** command at the console and the Network Manager Network Connections tool.

✓ TWO-MINUTE DRILL

Here are some of the key points from the certification objectives in Chapter 3.

Shells

- ❏ The default Linux shell is bash.
- ❏ Six command line consoles are available by default; if the GUI is installed, it takes over the first console.
- ❏ You can open multiple command line terminals in the GUI.
- ❏ Shells work with three data streams: stdin, stdout, and stderr. To that end, command redirection means streams of data can be managed with operators such as >, >>, <, |, and 2>.

Standard Command Line Tools

- ❏ Everything in Linux can be reduced to a file.
- ❏ Commands like **pwd** and **cd** can help navigate directories.
- ❏ Concepts like directory paths, the PATH, and the tilde (~) can help you understand and use commands at the shell.
- ❏ Basic commands allow you to find needed files and read file contents. These commands include **ls**, **find**, and **locate**.
- ❏ File creation (and deletion) commands include **touch**, **cp**, **ln**, **mv**, and **rm**; corresponding directory creation and deletion commands are **mkdir** and **rmdir**.
- ❏ Commands can be customized with the **alias** command.

The Management of Text Files

- ❏ Linux is managed through a series of text configuration files.
- ❏ Text files can be read as streams of data with commands like **cat**, **less**, **more**, **head**, and **tail**.

❏ New files can be created, copied, moved, linked, and deleted with the **touch**, **cp**, **mv**, **ln**, and **rm** commands. Commands can be customized with the alias command.

❏ File filters such as the **sort**, **grep**, **egrep**, **wc**, **sed**, and **awk** commands support the processing of text streams.

❏ Understanding text-editors is a critical skill. An earlier version of the RHCSA objectives specified the use of vim and gedit.

Local Online Documentation

❏ If you need a hint for a command, try it by itself; alternatively, try the **-h** or **--help** switches.

❏ Command man pages often include examples; **whatis** and **apropos** can search for man pages on different topics.

❏ If an info manual is available for a command or file, you'll find it in the /usr/share/info directory.

❏ Many packages include extensive documentation and examples in the /usr/share/doc directory.

A Networking Primer

❏ IPv4 addresses have 32 bits. There are five classes of IPv4 addresses, and three different sets of private IPv4 addresses suitable for setting up TCP/IP on a LAN.

❏ IPv6 addresses have 128 bits, and can be unicast, multicast, or anycast. Unicast addresses can be limited to local networks, or routable.

❏ Tools such as **ping**, **ping6**, **arp**, **ifconfig**, and **netstat** can help you diagnose problems on that LAN.

❏ Name resolution configuration files such as /etc/resolv.conf determine how a system finds the right IP address; that file may be configured from a DHCP server with the **dhclient** command.

Network Configuration and Troubleshooting

❏ Linux networking starts with the /etc/init.d/network script and the /etc/sysconfig/network configuration file.

❏ Individual network devices are configured in the /etc/sysconfig/network-scripts directory.

❏ Network configuration tools include the console-based **system-config-network** command and the Network Manager Network Connections tool.

❏ Hostname configuration files include /etc/nsswitch.conf, /etc/hosts, and /etc/resolv.conf.

SELF TEST

The following questions will help you measure your understanding of the material presented in this chapter. As there are no multiple-choice questions on the Red Hat exams, there are no multiple-choice questions in this book. These questions exclusively test your understanding of the chapter. Getting results, not memorizing trivia, is what counts on the Red Hat exams.

Shells

1. What is the name of the default Linux shell?

_____

2. From the GUI, what key combination moves to virtual console 3?

_____

Standard Command Line Tools

3. What single command creates the /abc/def/ghi/jkl series of directories?

_____

4. What symbol represents the home directory of the current user?

_____

The Management of Text Files

5. What command lists the last ten lines of the /var/log/messages file?

_____

6. What command returns lines with the term Linux from the /var/log/dmesg file?

_____

Local Online Documentation

7. What command searches the database of man pages for manuals that reference the passwd command and configuration file?

_____

8. If there are man pages for the hypothetical abcde command and file, in sections 5 and 8, type in the command that is sure to call up the man pages from section 5?

_____

A Networking Primer

9. In IPv4 addressing, with a network address of 192.168.100.0 and a broadcast address of 192.168.100.255, what is the range of assignable IP addresses?

_____

10. Given the addresses described in question 9, what command assigns IPv4 address 192.168.100.100 to network device eth0?

_____

Network Configuration and Troubleshooting

11. What is the full path to the configuration file with the hostname of the local system?

_____

12. What is the full path to the configuration file associated with the first Ethernet adapter for the local system?

_____

LAB QUESTIONS

Several of these labs involve configuration exercises. You should do these exercises on test machines only. It's assumed that you're running these exercises on virtual machines such as KVM.

Red Hat presents its exams electronically. For that reason, most of the labs in this and future chapters are available from the CD that accompanies the book, in the Chapter3/ subdirectory. In case you haven't yet set up RHEL 6 on a system, refer to Chapter 1 for installation instructions.

The answers for each lab follows the Self Test answers for the fill-in-the-blank questions.

SELF TEST ANSWERS

Shells

1. The default Linux shell is bash, also known as the Bourne-Again shell.

2. From the GUI, the key combination moves to virtual console 3 is CTRL-ALT-F3.

Standard Command Line Tools

3. The single command that creates the /abc/def/ghi/jkl series of directories is **mkdir -p /abc/def/ghi/jkl**.

4. The symbol that represents the home directory of the current user is the tilde (~).

The Management of Text Files

5. The command that lists the last ten lines of the /var/log/messages file is **tail -n10 /var/log/messages**.

6. The command that returns lines with the term Linux from the /var/log/dmesg file is **grep Linux /var/log/dmesg**. Other variations are acceptable, such as **cat /var/log/dmesg | grep Linux.**

Local Online Documentation

7. The command that searches the database of man pages for manuals that reference the passwd command and configuration file is **whatis passwd**. The **apropos** and **man -k** commands go further, as they list man pages with the text "passwd" in the command or the description.

8. The command that calls up the man page from section 5 for the hypothetical **abcde** command and file is **man 5 abcde**.

A Networking Primer

9. The range of assignable IP addresses in the noted IPv4 network is 192.168.100.1 through 192.168.100.254.

10. Given the addresses described in question 9, the command that assigns IPv4 address 192.168.100.100 to network device eth0 is **ifconfig eth0 192.168.100.100**.

Network Configuration and Troubleshooting

11. The full path to the configuration file with the hostname of the local system is /etc/hosts.

12. The full path to the configuration file associated with the first Ethernet adapter for the local system is /etc/sysconfig/network-scripts/ifcfg-eth0. If you're used to configuring network cards with the Network Connections tool, ifcfg-System_eth0 is also acceptable.

LAB ANSWERS

Lab 1

This lab tested the situation where networking was deactivated with the most innocuous of settings, the NETWORKING directive in the /etc/sysconfig/network file. When set to no, that setting deactivates networking on a system. Nothing else is changed; the IP address information for specific network cards is still correct. Sure, you could still activate networking through other means, but unless **NETWORKING=yes** in the noted file, such changes would not survive a reboot.

The script used in this lab saved the original copy of /etc/sysconfig/network in the /root/backup directory. Now that the lab is complete, you may restore that file to its original location. Be aware, the immutable flag has been applied to the copied file; to delete it from the /root/backup directory, you'd first have to remove the immutable flag with the **chattr -i** command.

Lab 2

This lab set up an invalid IP address configuration for the first Ethernet adapter, eth0. The standard for the systems configured in Chapter 1 is based on the 192.168.122.0/24 network. The configuration file in the /etc/sysconfig/network-scripts directory may go by slightly different names, depending on how that adapter was configured. The original file from that directory was moved to the /root/backup directory. If your efforts in re-creating that configuration file fail, restore the original configuration file from that /root/backup directory.

Be aware, the immutable flag has been applied to the copied file; to delete it from the /root/backup directory, you'd first have to remove the immutable flag with the **chattr -i** command. In fact, before Lab 3 works, you'll have to run the following command:

```
# chattr -i /root/backup/*
```

Lab 3

This lab deactivates the first Ethernet device on the system, and works if that device has the default eth0 device file name. It should also work if you've run the Network Manager Network Connections tool without changing too many defaults, as the Ch3Lab3 script also deactivates the System_eth0 device file.

Lab 4

This lab replaced the /etc/resolv.conf file. If the local network already uses a DNS server on the 192.168.1.111 IP address, this lab should not cause any problems. The original version of that file was moved to the /root/backup directory. If your efforts in re-creating that configuration file fail, restore the original configuration file from that backup directory.

Lab 5

In this lab, you'll set up the /etc/hosts file on each of the systems described in Chapter 1. Except for the local system settings added by the Network Manager, the data in /etc/hosts on all three systems may be identical. Specifically, that file should include the following entries:

```
192.168.122.50   server1 server1.example.com
192.168.122.150  tester1 tester1.example.com
192.168.100.100  outsider1 outsider1.example.org
```

It doesn't matter that the systems are on different IP networks. As long as there's a routing path between systems, this data in each /etc/hosts file will work. And duplication with data inserted by the Network Manager is not a problem, as long as the data is consistent. In fact, it's possible to set up multiple names for an IP address; for example, if I set up a web server on the 192.168.122.50 system, I could add the following entry to /etc/hosts.

```
192.168.122.50   www.example.com
```

Lab 6

The first four lines were from the original configuration of an eth0 network card. While the values associated with the DEVICE, HWADDR, NM_CONTROLLED, and ONBOOT directives have not changed, the format provided by the RHEL 6 installation is different.

Lab 7

If you've used the Network Connections tool, there may be an ifcfg-System_eth0 file in place of the ifcfg-eth0 file. The system-config-network tool can still handle that file. Just be sure to substitute accordingly. Be sure to learn the settings associated with directives such as USERCTL, BOOTPROTO, and DNS1.

4

RHCSA-Level Security Options

L inux security starts with a concept known as "discretionary access controls." They include the permissions and ownership associated with files and directories. Default permissions on new files depend on the umask. Permissions can go further with specialized bits. Linux discretionary access controls can be configured on a more fine-grained basis with the help of access control lists (ACLs). Those ACLs support permissions given to specific users, overriding standard ownership and permissions.

Also in the realm of security is the firewall. In this chapter, you'll examine the default firewall, how it works with the **iptables** command, and how it can also be configured with Red Hat firewall configuration tools. What you create can be further protected with a different kind of security known as "mandatory access control." The RHEL 6 implementation of such is known as Security-Enhanced Linux (SELinux). Red Hat expects you to work with SELinux enabled on their exams. To that end, you'll examine how to set enforcing modes, change file contexts, use boolean settings, and diagnose SELinux policy violations.

If you're starting with the default installation created during the installation process, you may need to install additional packages during this chapter. If a network installation is available, take the name of the package and apply the **yum install** command to it. For example, to review the GUI-based firewall configuration tool, you'll need to install it with the following command:

```
# yum install system-config-firewall
```

For more information on the process, see Chapter 7.

INSIDE THE EXAM

Basic File Permissions

Security in Linux starts with the permissions given to files. As everything in Linux can be defined as a file, it's an excellent start. In any case, the related objective, once understood, is fairly straightforward:

■ List, set, and change standard ugo/rwx permissions

Standard permissions for Linux files are defined for users, groups, and others, which leads to the *ugo*. Those permissions are read, write, and execute, which defines the *rwx*.

Such permissions are defined as discretionary access control, to contrast with the mandatory access control system known as SELinux, also discussed in this chapter.

Access Control Lists

ACLs can be configured to override basic file permissions. For example, with ACLs, you can set up a file in your home directory that can be read by a limited number of other users and groups. The related RHCSA objective is:

- Create and manage Access Control Lists (ACLs)

Firewall Control

As configured in Linux, a firewall can block traffic on all but a few network ports. It also can be used to regulate traffic in a number of other ways, but that is the province of the RHCE exam. The related RHCSA objective is:

- Configure firewall settings using system-config-firewall or iptables

Security-Enhanced Linux

There's no way around it. On the Red Hat exams, you're expected to work with SELinux. It's not clear whether you can even pass the Red Hat exams unless at least some services are configured with SELinux in mind. To help exam candidates understand

what's needed, Red Hat has broken down SELinux-related objectives. The first objective is fundamental to SELinux, as it relates to the three modes available for SELinux on a system (enforcing/permissive/disabled):

- Set enforcing/permissive modes for SELinux

The next objective requires that you understand the SELinux contexts defined for different files and processes. While the associated commands are straightforward, the available contexts are as broad as the number of services available on Linux:

- List and identify SELinux file and process contexts

As you experiment with different SELinux contexts, mistakes happen. You may not remember the default contexts associated with important directories. But with the right commands, you don't have to remember everything, as suggested by the following objective, it's relatively easy to restore the default:

- Restore default file contexts

Finally, the last objective may seem complex. But the boolean settings associated with SELinux have descriptive names. Excellent tools are available to further clarify those boolean contexts that are available. In essence, this means to run a certain service under SELinux, all you need to do is turn on one (or more) switches:

- Use boolean settings to modify system SELinux settings

CERTIFICATION OBJECTIVE 4.01

Basic File Permissions

The basic security of a Linux computer is based on file permissions. Default file permissions are set through the **umask** shell variable. Super user permissions can be configured to give all users and/or groups access to specific files. These are known as the super user ID (SUID) and super group ID (SGID) special permission bits. Ownership is based on the default user and group IDs of the person who created a file. The management of permissions and ownership involves commands such as **chmod**, **chown**, and **chgrp**. Before exploring these commands, it's important to understand the permissions and ownership associated with a file.

File Permissions and Ownership

Linux file permissions and ownership are straightforward. As suggested by the related objective, they're read, write, and execute, classified by the user, the group, and all other users. Consider the following output from **ls -l /sbin/fdisk**:

```
-rwxr-xr-x.  1 root  root 103432 Aug 13 01:23  /sbin/fdisk
```

The permissions are shown on the left side of the listing. Ten characters are shown. The first character determines whether it's a regular or a special file. The remaining nine characters are grouped in threes, applicable to the file owner (user), the group owner, and everyone else on that Linux system. The letters are straightforward: r = read, w = write, x = execute. These permissions are described in Table 4-1.

TABLE 4-1	Position	Description
	1	Type of file; - = regular file, d = directory, b = device, l = linked file
Description of File Permissions	234	Permissions granted to the owner of the file
	567	Permissions granted to the group owner of the file
	890	Permissions granted to all other users on the Linux system

It's common for the user and group owners of a file to have the same name. In this case, the root user is a member of the root group. But they don't have to have the same name. For example, directories designed for collaboration between users may be owned by a special group. As discussed in Chapter 8, that involves groups with several regular users as members.

There's a relatively new element with permissions. It's subtle. Notice the dot after the last x in the output to the **ls -l /sbin/fdisk** command? It specifies control by SELinux. If you've configured ACL permissions on a file, that dot is replaced by a plus sign (+). But that symbol doesn't override SELinux control.

You need to consider another type of permission: the special bit. Not only are these the SUID and SGID bits, but also another special permission known as the sticky bit. An example of the SUID bit is associated with the **passwd** command, in the /usr/bin directory. The **ls -l** command on that file leads to the following output:

```
-rwsr-xr-x. 1 root root 31768 Jan 28 2010 /usr/bin/passwd
```

The **s** in the execute bit for the user owner of the file is the SUID bit. It means the file can be executed by other users with the authority of the file owner, the root administrative user. But that doesn't mean that any user can change other user's passwords. Access to the **passwd** command is further regulated by Pluggable Authentication Modules (PAM) described in Chapter 10, an RHCE skill.

An example of the SGID bit can be found with the **ssh-agent** command, also in the /usr/bin directory. It has the SGID bit to properly store passphrases discussed in Chapter 11, which supports the most secure connections between SSH client and server. The **ls -l** command on that file displays the following output:

```
-rwxr-sr-x. 1 root nobody 112000 Aug 12 07:04 /usr/bin/ssh-agent
```

The **s** in the execute bit for the group owner of the file (group nobody) is the SGID bit.

Finally, an example of the sticky bit can be found in the permissions of the /tmp directory. It means users can copy their files to that directory, while retaining ownership of those files (which is the "sticky"). The **ls -ld** command on that directory shows the following output:

```
drwxrwxrwt. 22 root root 4096 Dec 15 17:15 /tmp/
```

The **t** in the execute bit for other users is the sticky bit.

The Loophole in Write Permissions

It's easy to remove write permissions from a file. For example, if you wanted to make the license.txt file "read-only," the following command removes write permissions from that file:

```
$ chmod a-w license.txt
```

But the user that owns the file can still make changes. It won't work in GUI text editors such as gedit. It won't even work in the nano text editor. However, if a change is made in the vi text editor, the user who owns that file can override a lack of write permissions with the bang character, which looks like an exclamation point (!). In other words, while in the vi editor, the user who owns the file can run the following command to override the lack of write permissions:

```
!w
```

Basic User and Group Concepts

Linux, like Unix, is configured with users and groups. Everyone who uses Linux is set up with a username, even if it's just "guest." There's even a standard user named "nobody". Take a look at /etc/passwd. One version of this file is shown in Figure 4-1.

FIGURE 4-1

The /etc/passwd file

```
games:x:12:100:games:/usr/games:/sbin/nologin
gopher:x:13:30:gopher:/var/gopher:/sbin/nologin
ftp:x:14:50:FTP User:/var/ftp:/sbin/nologin
nobody:x:99:99:Nobody:/:/sbin/nologin
dbus:x:81:81:System message bus:/:/sbin/nologin
rpc:x:32:32:Rpcbind Daemon:/var/cache/rpcbind:/sbin/nologin
avahi-autoipd:x:170:170:Avahi IPv4LL Stack:/var/lib/avahi-autoipd:/sbin/nologin
nscd:x:28:28:NSCD Daemon:/:/sbin/nologin
vcsa:x:69:69:virtual console memory owner:/dev:/sbin/nologin
rtkit:x:499:499:RealtimeKit:/proc:/sbin/nologin
abrt:x:498:498::/etc/abrt:/sbin/nologin
saslauth:x:497:495:"Saslauthd user":/var/empty/saslauth:/sbin/nologin
postfix:x:89:89::/var/spool/postfix:/sbin/nologin
rpcuser:x:29:29:RPC Service User:/var/lib/nfs:/sbin/nologin
nfsnobody:x:65534:65534:Anonymous NFS User:/var/lib/nfs:/sbin/nologin
haldaemon:x:68:68:HAL daemon:/:/sbin/nologin
nslcd:x:65:55:LDAP Client User:/:/sbin/nologin
avahi:x:70:70:Avahi mDNS/DNS-SD Stack:/var/run/avahi-daemon:/sbin/nologin
ntp:x:38:38::/etc/ntp:/sbin/nologin
pulse:x:496:494:PulseAudio System Daemon:/var/run/pulse:/sbin/nologin
gdm:x:42:42::/var/lib/gdm:/sbin/nologin
qemu:x:107:107:qemu user:/:/sbin/nologin
sshd:x:74:74:Privilege-separated SSH:/var/empty/sshd:/sbin/nologin
tcpdump:x:72:72::/:/sbin/nologin
oprofile:x:16:16:Special user account to be used by OProfile:/home/oprofile:/sbin/nologin
examprep:x:500:500::/home/examprep:/bin/bash
michael:x:501:501:Michael Jang:/home/michael:/bin/bash
```

As shown, all kinds of usernames are listed in the /etc/passwd file. Even a number of Linux services such as mail, news, ftp, and apache have their own usernames. In any case, the /etc/passwd file follows a specific format, described in more detail in Chapter 8. For now, note that the only regular users shown in this file are examprep and michael, their user IDs (UID) and group IDs (GID) are 500 and 501, and their home directories match their usernames. The next user gets UID and GID 502, and so on.

This matching of UIDs and GIDs is based on the Red Hat user private group scheme. Now run the **ls -l /home** command. The output should be similar to the following.

```
drwx------. 4 examprep examprep  4096 Dec 15 16:12 examprep
drwx------. 4 michael michael    4096 Dec 16 14:00 michael
```

Pay attention to the permissions. Based on the rwx/ugo concepts described earlier in this chapter, only the named user owner has access to the files in their home directories.

The umask

The way **umask** works in Red Hat Enterprise Linux may be surprising, especially if you're coming from a different Unix-style environment. You cannot configure **umask** to allow the automatic creation of new files automatically with executable permissions. This promotes security: if fewer files have executable permissions, fewer files are available for a cracker to use to run programs to break through your system.

on the job

In the world of Linux, a hacker *is a good person who simply wants to create better software. A* cracker *is someone who wants to break into your system for malicious purposes. In the world of computer security, these terms may be translated to "white-hat hacker" and "black-hat hacker," respectively.*

Every time you create a new file, the default permissions are based on the value of **umask**. In the past, the value of **umask** canceled out the value of numeric permissions on a file. For example, if the value of **umask** is 000, the default permissions for any file created by that user were once 777 − 000 = 777, which corresponds to read, write, and execute permissions for all users. They're now 666, as regular new files can no longer get executable permissions. Directories, on the other hand, require executable permissions so that any file contained therein can be read.

When you type the **umask** command, the command returns a four-number output such as 0245. As of this writing, the first number in the **umask** output is always 0 and is not used. In the future, this first number may be usable to allow for new files that automatically include the SUID or SGID bits.

Also, no matter what the value of **umask**, new files in Red Hat Enterprise Linux can no longer be automatically created with executable permissions. In other words, a **umask** value of 0454 leads to identical permissions on new files as a **umask** value of 0545. You need to use commands such as **chmod** to set executable permissions on a specific file.

The Default umask

With that in mind, the default **umask** is driven by the /etc/bashrc file, specifically the following stanza, which drives a value for **umask** depending on the value of the UID:

```
if [ $UID -gt 199 ] && [ "'id -gn'" = "'id -un'" ]; then
    umask 002
else
    umask 022
fi
```

In other words, the **umask** for user accounts with UIDs of 200 and above is 002. In contrast, the **umask** for UIDs below 200 is 022. In RHEL 6, service users such as adm, postfix, and apache have lower UIDs; this affects primarily the permissions of the log files created for such services. Of course, the root administrative user has the lowest UID of 0. By default, files created for such users have 644 permissions; directories created for such users have 755 permissions.

In contrast, regular users have a UID of 500 and above. Files created by such users normally have 664 permissions. Directories created by such users normally have 775 permissions.

Commands to Change Permissions and Ownership

Key commands that can help you manage the permissions and ownership of a file are **chmod**, **chown**, and **chgrp**. In the following subsections, you'll examine how to use those commands to change permissions along with the user and group that owns a specific file, or even a series of files.

One tip that can help you change the permissions on a series of files is the **-R** switch. It is the recursive switch for all three of these commands. In other words, if you specify the **-R** switch with any of the noted commands on a directory, it applies the changes recursively. The changes are applied to all files in that directory, including all subdirectories. Recursion means that the changes are also applied to files in each subdirectory, and so on.

The chmod Command

The **chmod** command uses the numeric value of permissions associated with the owner, group, and others. In Linux, permissions are assigned the following numeric values: $r = 4$, $w = 2$, and $x = 1$. For example, if you were crazy enough to want to give read, write, and execute permissions on **fdisk** to all users, you could run the **chmod 777 /sbin/fdisk** command. The **chown** and **chgrp** commands adjust the user and group owners associated with the cited file.

The **chmod** command is flexible. You don't always have to use numbers. For example, the following command sets execute permissions for the user owner of the Ch3Lab1 file:

```
# chmod u+x Ch3Lab1
```

Note how the **u** and the **x** follow the ugo/rwx format specified in the associated RHCSA objective. To interpret, this command adds (with the plus sign) for the user owner of the file (with the **u**) execute permissions (with the **x**).

These symbols can be combined. For example, the following command disables write permissions for the group owner and all other users on the local file named special:

```
# chmod go-w special
```

While you can use all three user types in the **chmod** command, it's not necessary. As described in the labs in Chapter 3, the following command makes the noted file executable by all users:

```
# chmod +x Ch3Lab2
```

For the SUID, SGID, and sticky bits, some special options are available. If you choose to use numeric bits, those special bits are assigned numeric values as well, where SUID=4, SGID=2, and sticky bit=1. For example, the following command configures the SUID bit. It includes rwx permissions for the user owner, rx permission for the group owner, and r permissions for other users, on the file named testfile:

```
# chmod 4764 testfile
```

If you'd rather use the ugo/rwx format, the following command activates the SGID bit for the local testscript file:

```
# chmod g+s testscript
```

And the following command turns on the sticky bit for the /test directory:

```
# chmod o+t /test
```

While the **chmod** command described in this section assumes changes are made by the root administrative user, that's not always required. The user owner of a file is allowed to change the permissions associated with that file.

The chown Command

The **chown** command can be used to modify the user that owns a file. For example, take a look at the ownership for the first figure that I created for this chapter, based on the **ls -l** command:

```
-rw-r--r--. 1 michael examprep 855502 Oct 25 14:07 F04-01.tif
```

The user owner of this file is michael; the group owner of this file is examprep. The **chown** command shown changes the user owner to user elizabeth:

```
# chown elizabeth F04-01.tif
```

You can do more with **chown**; for example, the following command changes both the user and group owner of the noted file to user donna and group supervisors, assuming that user and group already exists.

```
# chown donna.supervisors F04-01.tif
```

The chgrp Command

You can change the group owner of a file with the **chgrp** command. For example, the following command changes the group owner of the noted F04-01.tif directory to the group named project (assuming it exists):

```
# chgrp project F04-01.tif
```

Special File Attributes

Just beyond regular rwx/ugo permissions are file attributes. Such attributes can help you control what anyone can do with different files. While the **lsattr** command lists current file attributes, the **chattr** command can help you change those attributes. For example, the following command protects /etc/fstab from accidental deletion, even by the root administrative user:

```
# chattr +i /etc/fstab
```

With that attribute, if you try to delete that file as the root administrative user, you'll get the following response:

```
# rm /etc/fstab
rm: remove regular file `/etc/fstab'? y
rm: cannot remove `/etc/fstab': Operation not permitted
```

The **lsattr** command shows how the previous **chattr +i** command added the immutable attribute to /etc/fstab:

```
# lsattr /etc/fstab
----i--------e- /etc/fstab
```

Of course, the root administrative user can unset that attribute with the following command. Nevertheless, the initial refusal to delete the file should at least give pause to that administrator before changes are made:

```
# chattr -i /etc/fstab
```

Several key attributes are described in Table 4-2. Other attributes, such as **c** (compressed), **s** (secure deletion), and **u** (undeletable) don't work for files stored in the ext2, ext3, and ext4 filesystems. The extent format attribute is associated with ext4 systems.

TABLE 4-2	Attribute	Description
File Attributes	append only (**a**)	Prevents deletion, but allows appending to a file—for example, if you've run **chattr +a tester**, **cat /etc/fstab >> tester** would add the contents of /etc/fstab to the end of the tester file.
	no dump (**d**)	Disallows backups of the configured file with the **dump** command.
	extent format (**e**)	Set with the ext4 filesystem; an attribute that can't be removed.
	immutable (**i**)	Prevents deletion or any other kind of change to a file.
	indexed (**I**)	Set on directories for indexing with hashed trees; an attribute that can't be removed.

CERTIFICATION OBJECTIVE 4.02

Access Control Lists and More

There was a time where users had read access to the files of all other users. But by default, users have permissions only in their own directories. With ACLs, you can give selected users read, write, and execute permissions to selected files in your home directory. It provides a second level of discretionary access control, a method that supports overriding of standard ugo/rwx permissions.

Strictly speaking, regular ugo/rwx permissions are the first level of discretionary access control. In other words, ACLs start with the ownership and permissions described earlier in this chapter. You'll see how that's displayed with ACL commands shortly.

To configure ACLs, you'll need to configure the appropriate filesystem with the **acl** option. Next, you'll need to set up execute permissions on the associated directories. Only then can you configure ACLs with desired permissions for appropriate users.

Now that RHEL 6 uses the Network File System (NFS) version 4, these ACLs can be shared over a network.

Every File Already Has an ACL

As suggested by the title, every file already is configured with an access control list. Assuming the acl package is installed, you should have access to the **getfacl** command, which displays the current ACLs of a file. For example, the following command displays the current ACLs for the anaconda-ks.cfg file in the /root directory:

```
# file: anaconda-ks.cfg
# owner: root
# group: root
user::rw-
group::---
other::---
```

Run the **ls -l /root/anaconda-ks.cfg** command. You should recognize every element of the ACLs shown here in the output. The ACLs that you'll add shortly are over and above those shown here. But first, you'll need to make a filesystem friendly to that second level of ACLs.

Make a Filesystem ACL Friendly

Before a file or directory can be configured with ACLs, you need to mount the associated filesystem with the same attribute. If you're just testing a system for ACL, you can remount an existing partition appropriately. For example, if /home is mounted on /dev/sda3, I can remount it with ACL using the following command:

```
# mount -o remount -o acl /dev/sda3 /home
```

To make sure this is the way /home is mounted on the next reboot, edit /etc/fstab. Based on the previous command, the associated line might read as follows:

```
/dev/sda3      /home      ext3      defaults,acl      1,2
```

In most cases on RHEL 6, you'll see **UUID=***somelargehexidecimalnumber* in place of the device file. Once the change is made to /etc/fstab, you can activate it with the following command:

```
# mount -o remount /home
```

To confirm that the /home directory is mounted with the acl option, run the **mount** command alone, without switches or options. You should see acl in the output similar to what's shown here:

```
/dev/sda3 on /home type ext4 (rw,acl)
```

Now you can start working with ACL commands to set secondary access controls on desired files and directories.

Manage ACLs on a File

Now with a properly mounted filesystem and appropriate permissions, you can manage ACLs on a system. To review default ACLs, run the **getfacl** *filename* command. For this example, I've created a text file named TheAnswers in the /home/examprep directory. The following is the output from the getfacl **/home/examprep/TheAnswers** command:

```
# file home/examprep/TheAnswers
# owner: examprep
# group: proctors
user::rw-
group::r--
other::---
```

Note that the TheAnswers file is owned by user examprep and group proctors. That user owner has read and write permissions; that group owner has read permissions to that file. In other words, while the examprep user can change the Answers file, user members of the proctors group can read the TheAnswers file.

Now if you were the examprep or the root user on this system, you could assign ACLs for the file named TheAnswers for myself (user michael) with the **setfacl** command. For example, the following command gives me read permissions to that file:

```
# setfacl -m u:michael:rwx /home/examprep/TheAnswers
```

This command modifies the ACLs for the noted file, modifying (**-m**) the ACLs for user michael, giving that user read, write, and execute permissions to that file. To confirm, run the **getfacl** command on that file, as shown in Figure 4-2.

But when I try to access that file from my user account, it doesn't work. Actually, if I try to access the file with the vi text editor, it suggests that /home/examprep/TheAnswers is a new file. Then it refuses to save any changes I might make to that file.

Before files from the /home/examprep directory are accessible, the administrative user will need to either change the permissions or the ACL settings associated with that directory. Before we get to modifying discretionary access controls on a directory, let's explore some different setfacl commands.

Despite the name, the **setfacl** command can be used to remove such ACL privileges with the **-x** switch. For example, the following command deletes the previously configured rwx privileges for user michael:

```
# setfacl -x u:michael /home/examprep/TheAnswers
```

FIGURE 4-2	
The ACLs of a file	

```
[root@Maui ~]# getfacl /home/examprep/TheAnswers
getfacl: Removing leading '/' from absolute path names
# file: home/examprep/TheAnswers
# owner: examprep
# group: examprep
user::rw-
user:michael:rwx
group::r--
mask::rwx
other::r--

[root@Maui ~]# █
```

In addition, the **setfacl** command can be used with groups; for example, if the teachers group exists, the following command would give read privileges to users who are members of that group:

```
# setfacl -m g:teachers:r-- /home/examprep/TheAnswers
```

If you want to see how ACLs work, don't remove the ACL privileges on the TheAnswers file, at least not yet. Alternatively, if you want to start over, the following command, with the **-b** switch, removes all ACL entries on the noted file.

```
# setfacl -b /home/examprep/TheAnswers
```

Some of the switches available for the **setfacl** command are shown in Table 4-3:

One slightly dangerous option relates to other users. For example, the following command:

```
# setfacl -m o:rwx /home/examprep/TheAnswers
```

allows other users read, write, and execute permissions for the TheAnswers file. It does so by changing the primary permissions for the file, as shown in the output to the **ls -l /home/examprep/TheAnswers** command. The **-b** and the **-x** switches don't remove such changes; you'd have to use one of the following commands:

```
# setfacl -m o:--- /home/examprep/TheAnswers
```

```
# chmod o-rwx /home/examprep/TheAnswers
```

TABLE 4-3	Switch	Description
Description of File Permissions	-b (--remove-all)	Removes all ACL entries; retains standard ugo/rwx permissions
	-k	Deletes default ACL entries
	-m	Modifies the ACL of a file, normally with a specific user (u) or group (g)
	-n (--mask)	Omits the mask in recalculating permissions
	-R	Applies changes recursively
	-x	Removes a specific ACL entry

Configure a Directory for ACLs

There are two ways to set up a directory for ACLs. First, you could set the regular execute bit for all other users. One way to do so on the noted directory is with the following command:

```
# chmod 701 /home/examprep
```

It is a minimal way to provide access to files in a directory. Users other than examprep and root can't list the files in that directory. They have to know that the file TheAnswers actually exists to access that file.

However, with the execute bit set for other users, any user can access files in the /home/examprep directory for which he has permission. That should raise a security flag. Any user? Even though the file is hidden, do you ever want to give real privileges to anything to all users? Sure, ACLs have been set for only the TheAnswers file in that /home/examprep directory, but that's one layer of security that you've taken down voluntarily.

The right approach is to apply the **setfacl** command to the /home/examprep directory. The safest way to set up sharing is to set ACL execute permissions just for the user michael account on the noted directory, with the following command:

```
# setfacl -m u:michael:x /home/examprep
```

As the examprep user is the owner of the /home/examprep directory, that user can also run the noted **setfacl** command.

Sometimes, you may want to apply such ACLs to all files in a directory. In that case, the **-R** switch can be used to apply changes recursively; for example, the following command allows user michael to have read and execute permissions on all files in the /home/examprep directory as well as any subdirectories that may exist:

```
# setfacl -R -m u:michael:r-x /home/examprep
```

There are two methods available to unset these options. First, you could apply the **-x** switch to the previous command, omitting the permission settings:

```
# setfacl -R -x u:michael /home/examprep
```

Alternatively, you could use the **-b** switch; however, that would erase the ACLs configured for all users on the noted directory (and with the **-R** switch, applicable subdirectories):

```
# setfacl -R -b /home/examprep
```

Special Restrictions with ACLs

ACLs can also be used to limit permissions to specific users. For example, some RHEL 6 installations include a standard guest user for the GUI, xguest. For such systems, you may want to use ACLs to limit access to certain files or directories. For example, the following **setfacl** command can be used to limit access to the /etc/passwd file:

```
# setfacl -m u:xguest:--- /etc/passwd
```

While the /etc/passwd file does not normally include any passwords, it does include usernames. That's often a starting point for many crackers; malicious users with password cracking programs can then focus their efforts on standard users with known weaknesses. Without an xguest user, this command leads to a slightly confusing error message. If desired, you can test this by installing the xguest package, or by substituting a different username.

Of course, such actions can be applied recursively; if you don't want to allow user xguest access to any files in the /etc directory tree, the following command applies the aforementioned changes recursively:

```
# setfacl -R -m u:xguest:--- /etc
```

To test the result, try the **getfacl** command on a file somewhere down the /etc directory tree. For example, the **getfacl /etc/httpd/conf/httpd.conf** command examines the ACLs associated with the primary configuration file for the Apache web server. Note the difference between regular users and the xguest user in the following output:

```
# file: etc/httpd/conf/httpd.conf
# owner: root
# group: root
user::rw-
user:xguest:---
group::r--
mask::r--
other::r--
```

The user owner has read and write permissions. All other regular users have read permissions. But the xguest user has no permissions to do anything with the noted file.

As with individual files, the changes to the ACLs for the xguest user can be canceled with the **-x** switch. For example, the following command cancels ACL settings for that user recursively:

```
# setfacl -R -x u:xguest /etc
```

However, with ACLs, you can't deny access for a user to his home directory.

ACLs and Masks

The mask associated with an ACL limits the permissions available on a file. The mask shown in Figure 4-2 is rwx, which means there are no limits. If it were set to r, then the only permissions that could be granted with a command like **setfacl** is read. To change the mask on the TheAnswers file to read-only, run the following command:

```
# setfacl -m mask:r-- /home/examprep/TheAnswers
```

Now review the result with the **getfacl /home/examprep/TheAnswers** command. Pay attention to the entry for a specific user. Based on the ACL privileges given to user michael earlier, you'll see a difference with Figure 4-2:

```
user:michael:rwx    #effective:r--
```

In other words, with a mask of **r--**, you can try to provide other users with all the privileges in the world. But all that can be set with that mask is read privileges.

EXERCISE 4-1

Use ACLs to Deny a User

In this exercise, you'll set up ACLs to deny access to the loopback configuration file to a regular user. That is the ifcfg-lo file in the /etc/sysconfig/network-scripts directory. This exercise assumes that you've configured a regular user. As I've configured user michael on my systems, that is the regular user listed in this exercise. Substitute accordingly. To deny such access, take the following steps:

1. Back up a copy of the current configuration file for the loopback device. It's the ifcfg-lo file in the /etc/sysconfig/network-scripts directory. (Hint: use the **cp** and not the **mv** command.)

2. Execute the **setfacl -m u:michael:--- /etc/sysconfig/network-scripts/ifcfg-lo** command.

3. Review the results. Run the **getfacl** command on both copies of the file, in the /etc/sysconfig/network-scripts and the backup directories. What are the differences?

4. Log in as the target user. From the root administrative account, one method to do so is with the **su - michael** command.

5. Try to read the **/etc/sysconfig/network-scripts/ifcfg-lo** file in the vi text editor or even with the **cat** command. What happens?

6. Repeat the preceding step with the file in the backup directory. What happens?

7. Now run the **cp** command from the backup of the ifcfg-lo file, and overwrite the current version in the /etc/sysconfig/network-scripts file. (Don't use the **mv** command for this purpose.) You may need to return as the root user to do so.

8. Try the **getfacl /etc/sysconfig/network-scripts/ifcfg-lo** command again. Are you surprised at the result?

9. There are two ways to restore the original ACL configuration for the ifcfg-lo file. First apply the **setfacl -b** command on the file. Did that work? Confirm with the **getfacl** command. If any other related commands have been applied, it may or may not have worked.

10. The only certain way to restore the original ACL of a file is to restore the backup, by first deleting the changed file in the /etc/sysconfig/network-scripts directory, and then by copying the file from the backup directory.

11. However, if you run Step 10, you may also need to restore the SELinux contexts of the file with the command

```
restorecon -F /etc/sysconfig/network-scripts/ifcfg-lo
```

More information on the **restorecon** command is available later in this chapter.

NFS Shares and ACLs

While there's no evidence that the Red Hat exams will cover NFS-based ACLs, it is a feature that Linux administrators should know. As such, the description in this section just provides examples and is far from complete. One more complete description is available from IBM at www.ibm.com/developerworks/aix/library /au-filesys_NFSv4ACL/index.html.

Frequently, the /home directory is taken from a shared NFS directory. In fact, NFS-based ACLs are more fine-grained than standard ACLs. This feature was introduced with NFS version 4, the standard for RHEL 6. To that end, the **nfs4_getfacl** command can display the ACLs associated with files on a shared directory. Based on the ACLs previously given, Figure 4-3 shows the output to the **nfs4_getfacl** command.

The output is in the following format:

```
type:flags:principal:permissions
```

where the settings are delineated by the colon. Briefly, the two types shown either allow (**A**) or deny (**D**) the noted principal (a user or group) the specified permissions. No flags are shown in Figure 4-3, which can provide relatively fine-grained control. The principal may be a regular user or group, in lowercase. It may also be a generic user such as the file OWNER, the GROUP that owns the file, or other users, as specified by EVERYONE. The permissions as shown in Table 4-4, are more fine-grained. The effect varies depending on whether the object is a file or a directory.

The configuration of NFS as a client is covered in Chapter 6, with other local and network filesystems. The configuration of an NFS server is an RHCE objective covered in Chapter 16.

FIGURE 4-3	
| NFS version 4 ACLs | ```
[michael@server1 ~]$ nfs4_getfacl /test/examprep/
A::OWNER@:rwaDxtTcCy
A::michael@localdomain:xtcy
A::GROUP@:tcy
A::EVERYONE@:tcy
[michael@server1 ~]$ nfs4_getfacl /test/examprep/TheAnswers
D::OWNER@:x
A::OWNER@:rwatTcCy
A::michael@localdomain:rwaxtcy
A::GROUP@:rwatcy
A::EVERYONE@:tcy
[michael@server1 ~]$ █
``` |
```

TABLE 4-4	Permission	Description
Description of NFSv4 ACL Permissions	r	Read file or list directory
	w	Write to a file or create a new file in a directory
	a	Append data to a file or create a subdirectory
	x	Execute a script or change a directory
	d	Delete the file or directory
	D	Delete the subdirectory
	t	Read the attributes of the file or directory
	T	Write the attributes of the file or directory
	c	Read the ACLs of the file or directory
	C	Write the ACLs of the file or directory
	y	Synchronize the file or directory

CERTIFICATION OBJECTIVE 4.03

Basic Firewall Control

Traditionally, firewalls were configured only between LANs and outside networks such as the Internet. But as security threats increase, there's an increasing need for firewalls on every system. RHEL 6 includes firewalls in every default configuration.

The best firewalls come in layers. They include packet filters with commands such as **iptables**. They include TCP Wrappers to control traffic to and from TCP-based services. They include controls from individual services. Arguably, they also include mandatory access control tools such as SELinux. While SELinux is covered in part later in this chapter, tools like TCP Wrappers and firewalls from individual services are covered in the RHCE portion of this book.

Before you send a message over a network, the message is broken down into smaller units called *packets*. Administrative information, including the type of data, the source address, and destination address, is added to each packet. The packets are reassembled when they reach the destination computer. A firewall examines these administrative fields in each packet to determine whether to allow the packet to pass.

e x a m

ⓦ a t c h

RHEL 6 also includes a firewall command for IPv6 networks, ip6tables. The associated commands are almost identical. Unlike iptables, the ip6tables command is not listed in the Red Hat objectives.

There are RHCSA and RHCE requirements related to the **iptables** command. For the RHCSA, you need to understand how to configure a firewall to either block or allow network communication through one or more ports. For the RHCE, you need to know how to use the iptables command to filter packets based on elements such as source and destination IP addresses.

Standard Ports

Linux communicates over a network, primarily using the TCP/IP protocol suite. Different protocols use certain ports and protocols by default, as defined in the /etc/services file. It may be useful to know some of these ports by heart, such as those described in Table 4-5. Be aware, some of these ports may communicate using one or more of the following protocols: the Transmission Control Protocol (TCP), the User Datagram Protocol (UDP), and the Internet Control Message Protocol (ICMP). Such communications are listed in the /etc/services file. For example, as noted in the following excerpts from the /etc/services file, communications to FTP servers may proceed using both TCP and UDP protocols.

on the

ⓞ o b

Strictly speaking, "transport level" protocols other than TCP, UDP, and ICMP may be specified with the iptables command. For example, the Encapsulating Security Payload (ESP) and the Authentication Header (AH) protocols are used with the Internet Protocol Security (IPsec) suite.

```
ftp     21/tcp
ftp     21/udp
```

However, you'll see shortly that the Red Hat firewall configuration tools open only TCP communications for FTP services, and the default vsFTP server configured in Chapter 1 works fine under such circumstances.

Port	Description
21	FTP
22	Secure Shell (SSH)
23	Telnet
25	Simple Mail Transfer Protocol (SMTP), e.g., Postfix, sendmail
53	Domain Name Service servers
80	Hypertext Transfer Protocol (HTTP)
88	Kerberos
110	Post Office Protocol, version 3 (POP3)
139	Network Basic Input/Output System (NetBIOS) session service
143	Internet Mail Access Protocol (IMAP)
443	HTTP, secure (HTTPS)

TABLE 4-5

Common
TCP/IP Ports

A Focus on iptables

The philosophy behind **iptables** is based on "chains." These are sets of rules applied to each network packet, chained together. Each rule does two things: it specifies the conditions a packet must meet to match the rule, and it specifies the action if the packet matches.

The **iptables** command uses the following basic format:

```
iptables -t tabletype <action direction> <packet pattern> -j <what to do>
```

Now analyze this command, step by step. First is the *-t tabletype* switch. There are two basic *tabletype* options for **iptables**:

- **filter**   Sets a rule for filtering packets.
- **nat**   Configures Network Address Translation, also known as masquerading, discussed later in this chapter.

The default is **filter**; if you don't specify a *-t tabletype,* the **iptables** command assumes that the command is applied as a packet filter rule.

Next is the *<action direction>*. There are four basic actions associated with **iptables** rules:

- **-A (--append)**   Appends a rule to the end of a chain.

- **-D (--delete)** Deletes a rule from a chain. Specify the rule by the number or the packet pattern.
- **-L (--list)** Lists the currently configured rules in the chain.
- **-F (--flush)** Flushes all of the rules in the current **iptables** chain.

If you're appending to (**-A**) or deleting from (**-D**) a chain, you'll want to apply it to network data traveling in one of three directions:

- **INPUT** All incoming packets are checked against the rules in this chain.
- **OUTPUT** All outgoing packets are checked against the rules in this chain.
- **FORWARD** All packets being sent to another computer are checked against the rules in this chain.

Typically, each of these directions is the name of a chain.

Next, you need to configure a **<*packet pattern*>**. All **iptables** firewalls check every packet against this pattern. The simplest pattern is by IP address:

- **-s *ip_address*** All packets are checked for a specific source IP address.
- **-d *ip_address*** All packets are checked for a specific destination IP address.

Packet patterns can be more complex. In TCP/IP, packets are transported using the TCP, UDP, or ICMP protocol. You can specify the protocol with the **-p** switch, followed by the destination port (**--dport**). For example, the **-p tcp --dport 80** extension affects users outside your network who are trying to use an HTTP connection.

Once the **iptables** command finds a packet pattern match, it needs to know what to do with that packet, which leads to the last part of the command, **-j <*what to do*>**. There are three basic options:

- **DROP** The packet is dropped. No message is sent to the requesting computer.
- **REJECT** The packet is dropped. An error message is sent to the requesting computer.
- **ACCEPT** The packet is allowed to proceed as specified with the **-A** action: **INPUT**, **OUTPUT**, or **FORWARD**.

Take a look at some examples of how you can use **iptables** commands to configure a firewall. The first step is always to see what is currently configured, with the following command:

```
# iptables -L
```

If **iptables** is properly configured, it should return chain rules in three different categories: **INPUT**, **FORWARD**, and **OUTPUT**. More examples are described in Chapter 10.

Keep That Firewall in Operation

Linux firewalls based on the **iptables** command are based on the service of the same name. To review current rules, run the **iptables -L** command. Suppose all you see is the following blank list of rules:

```
Chain INPUT (policy ACCEPT)
target     prot opt source              destination

Chain FORWARD (policy ACCEPT)
target     prot opt source              destination

Chain OUTPUT (policy ACCEPT)
target     prot opt source              destination
```

The **iptables** service may not be running. Make sure to start it, and to make sure firewalls are running after the next reboot, run the following commands:

```
# /etc/init.d/iptables start
# chkconfig iptables on
```

The rules used by a Red Hat firewall are based on the /etc/sysconfig/iptables file, described in the next section.

The Default RHEL 6 Firewall

The current RHEL 6 firewall is shown in the output to the **iptables -L** command. The output on the default server1.example.com system is shown in Figure 4-4.

Firewall rules are divided into three categories, based on the direction of the data. INPUT rules are applied to data packets destined for the local system. FORWARD rules limit data going through the local system to another system. OUTPUT rules may limit data that goes out from the local system.

| **FIGURE 4-4**<br><br>Default RHEL 6<br>firewall rules | ```
[root@server1 ~]# iptables -L
Chain INPUT (policy ACCEPT)
target     prot opt source          destination
ACCEPT     all  --  anywhere        anywhere          state RELATED,ESTABLISHED
ACCEPT     icmp --  anywhere        anywhere
ACCEPT     all  --  anywhere        anywhere
ACCEPT     tcp  --  anywhere        anywhere          state NEW tcp dpt:ssh
REJECT     all  --  anywhere        anywhere          reject-with icmp-host-prohibited

Chain FORWARD (policy ACCEPT)
target     prot opt source          destination
REJECT     all  --  anywhere        anywhere          reject-with icmp-host-prohibited

Chain OUTPUT (policy ACCEPT)
target     prot opt source          destination
[root@server1 ~]# █
``` |

Six columns of information are shown in Figure 4-4, which correspond to various **iptables** command options. The firewall shown is based on the following rules listed in the /etc/sysconfig/iptables file. The first line specifies that the rules to follow are filtering rules. Alternative rules support Network Address Translation (NAT) or mangling; NAT is discussed in Chapter 10.

```
*filter
```

Next, network traffic that is directed to the local system, intended to be forwarded, and is sent out, is normally accepted by default with the ACCEPT option.

```
:INPUT ACCEPT [0:0]
:FORWARD ACCEPT [0:0]
:OUTPUT ACCEPT [0:0]
```

Some security professionals, including the U.S. National Security Agency, suggest that the ACCEPT should be changed to DROP for at least the INPUT and FORWARD lines. If you accept this recommendation, packets that aren't explicitly accepted by other rules are automatically dropped. However, that level of security may be covered in Red Hat's Enterprise Security Network Services course (RHS333), which is open to those who have already passed the RHCE exam. The [0:0] are byte and packet counts, which each start at 0.

The lines that follow are all applied to the **iptables** command. Every switch and option listed in this file should be available on the associated man page.

The next line keeps current network communications going. The ESTABLISHED option continues to accept packets on current network connections. The RELATED
```

option accepts packets for follow-on network connections, such as for FTP data transfers.

```
-A INPUT -m state --state ESTABLISHED,RELATED -j ACCEPT
```

The next connection accepts packets associated with ICMP, most commonly associated with the **ping** command. When a packet is rejected, the associated message also uses the ICMP protocol.

```
-A INPUT -p icmp -j ACCEPT
```

That may raise a warning flag, as the "ping of death" is one common attack. You could block or limit responses to the **ping** command using some of the filtering discussed in Chapter 10.

The following line adds (**-A**) a rule to an INPUT chain, associated with the network interface (**-i**) known as the loopback adapter (lo). Any data processed through that device jumps (**-j**) to acceptance.

```
-A INPUT -i lo -j ACCEPT
```

The next line is the only one that directly accepts new regular network data, using the TCP protocol, over anything but the loopback adapter. It looks for a match (**-m**) for a NEW connection state (**state --state**), for matching TCP packets, using the TCP protocol (**-p tcp**), sent to a destination port (**--dport**) of 22. Network packets that meet all of these criteria are accepted (**-j ACCEPT**). Once the connection is established, the first regular rule described in this chapter continues to accept packets on that established connection.

```
-A INPUT -m state --state NEW -m tcp -p tcp --dport 22 -j ACCEPT
```

The last two rules reject all other packets, with an **icmp-host-prohibited** message sent to the originating system.

```
-A INPUT -j REJECT --reject-with icmp-host-prohibited
-A FORWARD -j REJECT --reject-with icmp-host-prohibited
```

The COMMIT ends the list of rules.

```
COMMIT
```

As this is the section associated with the RHCSA exam, a more detailed discussion can be found in Chapter 10 for the RHCE exam. At this level, you need to know how to manage these firewalls with the standard configuration tools provided.

The Firewall Configuration Tools

You can automate the process of configuring a firewall. For that purpose, RHEL includes both console and GUI versions of the Firewall Configuration tool. In this case, both tools are just filled with about the same number of features. While the look and feel of the two tools are different, the basic capabilities with respect to configuring access for trusted services are the same.

If you want to experiment with the Firewall Configuration tools, it's a good practice to first back up the associated configuration file, /etc/sysconfig/iptables. If mistakes are made, restore the original version of the file and run the following command:

```
# /etc/init.d/iptables restart
```

To learn about the changes that are made, compare the resulting /etc/sysconfig /iptables file with the backup. Any differences will be based on what you do in the Firewall Configuration tool.

Trusted Services for Firewall Configuration Tools

Whichever tool is selected, both support easy configuration of a firewall to allow access to a variety of servers described in Table 4-6.

When comparing Table 4-6 to Table 4-5, you might note that while both TCP and UDP protocols are frequently reserved on a port for a specific service, frequently only one of these protocols is used by the actual service.

The Console Firewall Configuration Tool

You can start the console firewall configuration tool with the **system-config-firewall-tui** command; the result is shown in Figure 4-5. As shown in the figure, firewalls are enabled by default; the option can be deselected.

TABLE 4-6	Service	Description
Common TCP/IP Ports	Amanda Backup Client	A client associated with the Advanced Maryland Automatic Network Disk Archiver (AMANDA), associated with UDP port 10080
	Bacula	An open-source network backup server; associated with TCP ports 9101, 9102, and 9103
	Bacula client	Client for the Bacula server; associated with TCP port 9102
	DNS	Domain Name Service (DNS) server; associated with port 53, using both TCP and UDP protocols
	FTP	File Transfer Protocol (FTP) server, associated with TCP port 21
	IMAP over SSL	IMAP over the Secure Sockets Layer (SSL) normally uses TCP port 993
	IPsec	Associated with UDP port 500 for the Internet Security Association and Key Management Protocol (ISAKMP), along with the ESP and AH transport-level protocols
	Mail (SMTP)	Simple Mail Transport Protocol server, such as sendmail or Postfix, using TCP port 25
	Multicast DNS (mDNS)	Associated with UDP port 5353 to support the Linux implementation of zero configuration networking (zeroconf), known as Avahi
	NFS4	NFS version 4 uses TCP port 2049, among others
	Network Printing Client	The standard print client uses UDP port 631, based on the Internet Print Protocol (IPP)
	Network Printing Server	The standard print server client uses TCP and UDP ports 631, based on the Internet Print Protocol (IPP)
	OpenVPN	The open-source Virtual Private Network system, which uses UDP port 1194
	POP-3 over SSL	POP-3 over the Secure Sockets Layer (SSL) normally uses TCP port 995
	RADIUS	The Remote Authentication Dial In User Service (RADIUS) protocol uses UDP ports 1812 and 1813
	Red Hat Cluster Suite	The Red Hat suite for multiple systems uses TCP ports 11111 and 21064, along with UDP ports 5404 and 5405

TABLE 4-6	Service	Description
Common TCP/IP Ports (*continued*)	Samba	The Linux protocol for communication on Microsoft networks uses TCP ports 139 and 445, along with UDP ports 137 and 138
	Samba Client	The Linux protocol for client communication on Microsoft networks uses UDP ports 137 and 138
	Secure WWW (HTTPS)	Communications to a secure web server uses TCP port 443
	SSH	The SSH server uses TCP port 22
	TFTP	Communications with the Trivial File Transfer Protocol (TFTP) server requires TCP port 69
	TFTP Client	Strangely enough, no open port is required for a TFTP client; all communications proceed over the open TCP port 69 through the TFTP server
	Virtual Machine Management	Remote access to KVM-based VMs use TCP port 16509
	Virtual Machine Management (TLS)	Remote access to KVM-based VMs use TCP port 16509 and can be configured with Transport Layer Security (TLS)
	WWW (HTTP)	The well-known web server uses TCP port 80

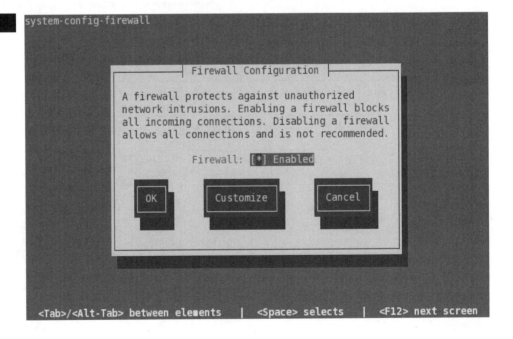

FIGURE 4-5

The Console Firewall Configuration tool

Press the TAB key as needed to highlight the Customize option and press ENTER to continue. Review the list of trusted services; while the order varies slightly, they match the list shown in Table 4-6. If you've configured one of these services on the local system, you'll want to activate the option to set them as trusted services. Scroll down until you see SSH. It should be enabled by default. Make appropriate selections and select Forward to continue.

In the Other Ports window, highlight Add and press ENTER to open the Port and Protocol screen shown in Figure 4-6. The entries in that figure demonstrate how you might open up ports 10000 through 10010 under the TCP protocol in a firewall. Make any desired changes and select OK or abort by selecting Cancel.

Back in the Other Ports window, you can configure additional ports. If desired, you can click Forward to enter the Trusted Interfaces window, and then configure Masquerading, Port Forwarding, and ICMP filtering, but those details are more closely associated with the RHCE exam objectives discussed in Chapter 10.

Instead, select Close and press ENTER to return to the screen shown in Figure 4-5. You can repeat the Customize process again, select Cancel to disable the changes, or select OK to implement them. Before implementing changes, you're given a warning as shown in Figure 4-7.

FIGURE 4-6	

Configure other ports for the firewall.

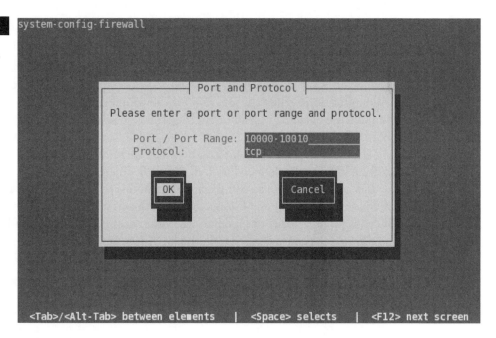

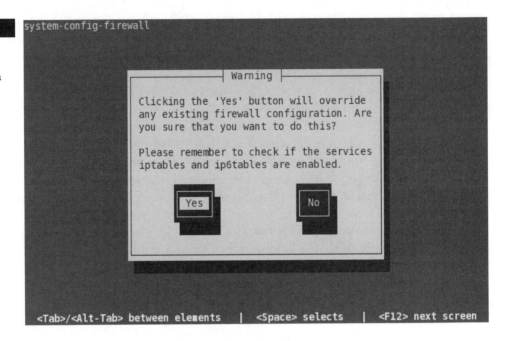

FIGURE 4-7

Before
implementing a
new firewall

The GUI Firewall Configuration Tool

If the system-config-firewall package is installed, you can start the GUI Firewall Configuration tool in a GUI-based command line with the **system-config-firewall** command. Alternatively, in the GNOME Desktop Environment, click System | Administration | Firewall. The result is shown in Figure 4-8. As shown in the figure, firewalls are enabled by default, but they can be disabled by pressing the Disable button.

The GUI Firewall Configuration tool has the same list of services as the corresponding console-based tool, in a slightly different order.

If desired, you can also configure custom access ports; click Other Ports and click Add to open the Port and Protocol window shown in Figure 4-9. Note how the window prompts for ports based on the contents of the /etc/services file.

As with the console-based tool, the other features of the GUI Firewall Configuration tool are more closely associated with the RHCE exam. For more information, see Chapter 10.

FIGURE 4-8

The GUI Firewall Configuration tool

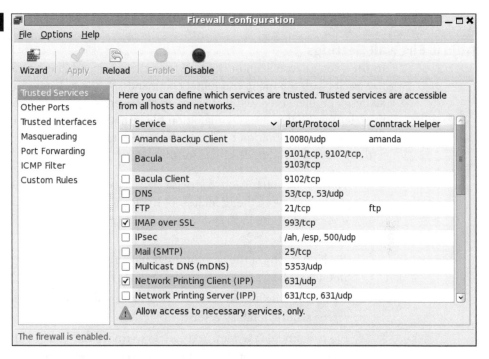

FIGURE 4-9

Adding custom ports in the GUI Firewall Configuration tool

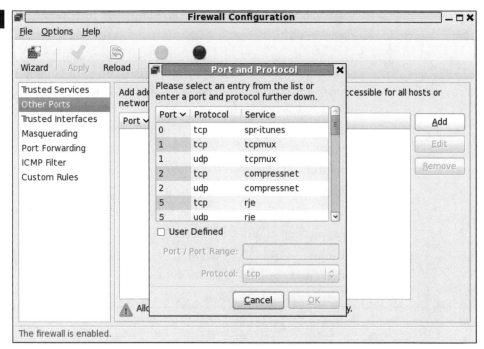

EXERCISE 4-2

Adjust Firewall Settings

In this exercise, you'll adjust firewalls from the command line interface and review the results with the **nmap** and **telnet** commands. While it does not matter how you address a problem on a Red Hat exam, in this exercise, you'll see what happens when the /etc/sysconfig/iptables configuration file is modified. Of course, it's possible to use the Firewall Configuration tool to perform the same tasks. This assumes a system with the default firewall described in this chapter.

1. Review the current active services on the local system with the **nmap localhost** command. Note the IP address of the local system with the **ifconfig eth0** command. If the local system is server1.example.com, that IP address should be 192.168.122.50.

2. Back up a copy of the current firewall configuration file, /etc/sysconfig /iptables. Make sure to use the **cp** and not the **mv** command.

3. Make sure the firewall is currently operational with the command **/etc/sysconfig/iptables restart**.

4. Go to a different system. You can do so from a different virtual machine, or you can access it remotely with the **ssh** command. If the tester1.example.com system is running, you can log into that system with the **ssh 192.168.122.150** command.

5. Use the **nmap** command to review what is seen through the firewall; for the noted server1.example.com system, the right command would be **nmap 192.168.122.50**; if the IP address found from Step 1 is different, substitute accordingly.

6. Return to the original system. Open the /etc/sysconfig/iptables file in a text editor.

7. Substitute 25 for 22 in the file, and save the changes.

8. Restart the firewall as was done in Step 3.

9. Navigate back to the tester1.example.com system as was done in Step 4.

10. Repeat Step 5. What do you see?

11. Return to the original system. If desired, restore the iptables file from backup, and restart the firewall as was done in Step 3.

CERTIFICATION OBJECTIVE 4.04

A Security-Enhanced Linux Primer

Security-Enhanced Linux (SELinux) was developed by the U.S. National Security Agency to provide a level of mandatory access control. It goes beyond the discretionary access control associated with file permissions and ACLs. In essence, SELinux limits the damage if there is a security breach. For example, if the system account associated with an FTP service is compromised, SELinux makes it more difficult to use that account to compromise other services.

Basic Features of SELinux

SELinux assigns different contexts to each file, known as *subjects*, *objects*, and *actions*. In the SELinux world, a subject is a process, such as a command in action, or an application such as the Apache web server in operation. An object is a file. An action is what may be done by the subject to the object.

For example, the Apache web server process can take objects such as web pages and display them for the clients of the world to see. That action is normally allowed in the RHEL 6 implementation of SELinux, as long as the object files have appropriate SELinux contexts.

The contexts associated with SELinux are fine-grained. In other words, if a cracker breaks in and takes over your web server, SELinux contexts prevent that cracker from using that breach to break into other services.

To see the context of a particular file, run the **ls -Z** command. As an example, review what this command does in Figure 4-10, as it displays security contexts in my /root directory.

As noted at the beginning of this chapter, four objectives relate to SELinux on the RHCSA exam. You'll explore how to meet these objectives in the following sections.

SELinux Status

As suggested in the RHCSA objectives, you need to know how to "Set enforcing /permissive modes for SELinux." There are three available modes for SELinux: **enforcing**, **permissive**, and **disabled**. The **enforcing** and **disabled** modes are

```
[root@server1 ~]# ls -Z
-rw-------. root root system_u:object_r:admin_home_t:s0 anaconda-ks.cfg
drwxr-xr-x. root root unconfined_u:object_r:admin_home_t:s0 backup
-rwxr--r--. root root unconfined_u:object_r:admin_home_t:s0 Ch3Lab2
-rw-r--r--. root root unconfined_u:object_r:admin_home_t:s0 Ch3Lab2testfile
-rwxr--r--. root root unconfined_u:object_r:admin_home_t:s0 Ch3Lab3
-rw-r--r--. root root unconfined_u:object_r:admin_home_t:s0 Ch3Lab3testfile
-rwxr--r--. root root unconfined_u:object_r:admin_home_t:s0 Ch3Lab4
-rw-r--r--. root root unconfined_u:object_r:admin_home_t:s0 Ch3Lab4testfile
drwxr-xr-x. root root unconfined_u:object_r:admin_home_t:s0 Desktop
drwxr-xr-x. root root unconfined_u:object_r:admin_home_t:s0 Documents
drwxr-xr-x. root root unconfined_u:object_r:admin_home_t:s0 Downloads
-rw-r--r--. root root unconfined_u:object_r:admin_home_t:s0 hosts
-rw-r--r--. root root unconfined_u:object_r:admin_home_t:s0 ifcfg-eth0
-rw-r--r--. root root unconfined_u:object_r:admin_home_t:s0 ifcfg-System_eth0
-rw-r--r--. root root system_u:object_r:admin_home_t:s0 install.log
-rw-r--r--. root root system_u:object_r:admin_home_t:s0 install.log.syslog
-rw-------. root root unconfined_u:object_r:admin_home_t:s0 ks.cfg
drwxr-xr-x. root root unconfined_u:object_r:admin_home_t:s0 Music
drwxr-xr-x. root root unconfined_u:object_r:admin_home_t:s0 Pictures
drwxr-xr-x. root root unconfined_u:object_r:admin_home_t:s0 Public
-rw-r--r--. root root system_u:object_r:net_conf_t:s0  route-System_eth0
drwxr-xr-x. root root unconfined_u:object_r:admin_home_t:s0 Templates
drwxr-xr-x. root root unconfined_u:object_r:admin_home_t:s0 Videos
[root@server1 ~]#
```

self-explanatory. SELinux in **permissive** mode means that any SELinux rules that are
violated are logged, but the violation does not stop any action.

If you want to change the basic status of SELinux, change the **SELINUX** directive.
The next time you reboot, the changes are applied to the system.

If SELinux is configured in **enforcing** mode, it protects systems in one of two
ways: in **targeted** mode or in **mls** mode. The default is **targeted**, which allows you to
customize what is protected by SELinux in a fine-grained manner. In contrast, MLS
goes a step further, using the Bell-La Padula model developed for the Department of
Defense. That model, as suggested in the /etc/selinux/targeted/setrans.conf file,
supports layers of security between levels c0 and c3. While the c3 level is listed as
"Top Secret," the range of available levels goes all the way up to c1023. Such
fine-grained levels of secrecy have yet to be fully developed. If you want to explore
MLS, install the selinux-policy-mls RPM.

	Directive	Description
TABLE 4-7 Standard Directives in /etc /sysconfig/selinux	SELINUX	Basic SELinux status; may be set to **enforcing, permissive,** or **disabled.**
	SELINUXTYPE	Specifies the level of protection; set to **targeted** by default, where protection is limited to daemons. The alternative is **mls,** which is associated with Multi-Level Security (MLS).

watch

If you have to configure SELinux during an exam, it's no longer possible to do so during the installation process. SELinux is by default implemented in enforcing and targeted modes. If you have to configure SELinux and then reboot, the process of applying SELinux policies can take several minutes. You won't be able to log in or do anything else during your exam. So plan ahead!

on the job

*If you just want to experiment with SELinux, configure it in permissive mode. It'll log any violations without stopping anything. It's easy to set up with the SELinux Management tool, or you can set **SELINUX=permissive** in /etc/sysconfig/selinux. If the auditd service is running, violations are logged in the audit.log file in the /var/log/audit directory. Just remember, it's likely that Red Hat wants candidates to configure SELinux in enforcing mode during their exams.*

SELinux Configuration at the Command Line

While SELinux is still under active development, it has become much more useful with the release of RHEL 6. Nevertheless, given the fear associated with SELinux, it may be more efficient to use the SELinux Administration tool to configure SELinux settings. And it's much improved from the GUI SELinux functionality that was part of the Security Level Configuration tool. You can even set SELinux contexts for individual directories.

To that end, the following sections show how you can configure and manage SELinux from the command line interface. However, as it's easier to demonstrate the full capabilities of SELinux using GUI tools, a detailed discussion of such capabilities will follow later in this chapter.

Configure Basic SELinux Settings

There are some essential commands that can be used to review and configure basic SELinux settings. To see the current status of SELinux, run the **getenforce** command; it returns one of three self-explanatory options: **enforcing**, **permissive**, or **disabled**. The **sestatus** command provides more information, with output similar to the following.

```
SELinux status:              enabled
SELinuxfs mount:             /selinux
Current mode:                enforcing
Mode from config file:       enforcing
Policy version:              24
Policy from config file:     targeted
```

You can change the current SELinux status with the **setenforce** command; the options are straightforward:

```
# setenforce enforcing
# setenforce permissive
```

This changes the /selinux/enforce boolean. As booleans, you could substitute 1 and 0, respectively, for **enforcing** and **permissive**. However, changes to detailed SELinux booleans require different commands.

Alternatively, if SELinux is disabled for some reason, the output would be:

```
SELinux status:      disabled
```

In that case, the **setenforce** command will not work. Instead, you'll have to set **SELINUX=enforcing** in the /etc/sysconfig/selinux file. And that requires a "relabel," where SELinux labels are applied to each file on the local system. That can take valuable time.

If SELinux is disabled, it may take a few minutes to reboot a system after setting SELinux in enforcing mode. However, the process is much less time-consuming than it was for RHEL 5.

Configure Regular Users for SELinux

One change from RHEL 5 is the SELinux status of regular default users. To review the status of current users, run the **semanage login -l** command. Based on the default installation of RHEL 6, it leads to the following output:

```
__default__      unconfined_u      s0-s0:c0.c1023
root             unconfined_u      s0-s0:c0.c1023
system_u         system_u          s0-s0:c0.c1023
```

In other words, regular "default" users have the same SELinux privileges of the root administrative user. To confirm, run the **id -Z** command as a regular user. Without changes, it leads to the following output, which suggests that user is not confined by any SELinux settings.

```
unconfined_u:unconfined_r:unconfined_t:s0-s0:c0.c1023
```

While it may not be an exam requirement, regular users should be confined by SELinux. When user accounts are compromised, and they will be compromised, you want any damage that might be caused limited by SELinux rules. The following example confines adds (**-a**) regular user michael, specifying (**-s**) the user_u role for confinement:

```
# semanage login -a -s user_u michael
```

The user_u role should not have the ability to run the **su** or **sudo** commands described in Chapter 8. If desired, you can reverse the process with the **semanage -d michael** command. As user roles are still a work in progress, you should focus on the available user roles listed in the latest Red Hat documentation, as shown in Table 4-8.

One other commonly seen "user" role is system_u, which typically does not apply to regular users. It is a common user seen in the output to the **ls -Z** command for system and configuration files.

When a user role is changed, they don't take effect until the next login. For example, if I were to change the role for user michael to user_u in a GUI-based command line, the change would not take effect until I logged out and logged back in to the GUI. When I tried it on my system, I was no longer able to start any administrative configuration tools, and I did not have access to the **sudo** and **su** commands.

On some networks, you may want to change the role of future users to user_u. If you don't want regular users tinkering with administrative tools, you could make that change for future default users with the following command:

```
# semanage login -m -S targeted -s "user_u" -r s0 __default__
```

This command modifies (**-m**) the targeted policy store (**-S**), with SELinux user (**-s**) user_u, with the MLS s0 range (**-r**) for the default user. The "__default__" includes two underscore characters on each side of the word. As long as user_u is in

TABLE 4-8	User Role	Features
Options for SELinux User Roles	guest_u	No GUI, no networking, no access to the **su** or **sudo** commands
	xguest_u	GUI, networking only via the Firefox web browser
	user_u	GUI and networking available
	staff_u	GUI, networking, and the **sudo** command available
	unconfined_u	Full system access

effect for the default SELinux user, regular users won't have access to use administrative tools or commands like **su** and **sudo**. The following command reverses the process:

```
# semanage login -m -S targeted -s "unconfined_u" \
-r s0-s0:c0.c1023 __default__
```

The full MLS range is required (s0-s0:c0.c1023), as the unconfined_u user is not normally limited by MLS restrictions.

ⓦatch *MLS mode adds complexity to SELinux. Targeted mode with appropriate booleans and file contexts normally provides more than adequate security.*

Manage SELinux Boolean Settings

Most SELinux settings are boolean—in other words, they're activated and deactivated by setting them to 1 or 0. Once set, the booleans are stored in the /selinux/booleans directory. One simple example is user_ping, which is normally set to 1, which allows users to run the **ping** command. Many of these SELinux settings are associated with specific RHCE services and will be covered in the second half of this book.

These settings can be read with the **getsebool** and modified with the **setsebool** commands. For example, the following output from the **getsebool allow_user_exec_content** command confirms that SELinux allows users to execute scripts either in their home directories or from the /tmp directory:

```
allow_user_exec_content --> on
```

This default applies to SELinux user_u users. In other words, with this boolean, such users can create and execute scripts in the noted directories. That boolean can be disabled either temporarily, or in a way that survives a reboot. One method for doing so is with the **setsebool** command. For example, the following command disables the noted boolean until the system is rebooted:

```
# setsebool allow_user_exec_content off
```

You can choose to substitute **=0** for **off** in the command. As this is a boolean setting, the effect is the same; the flag is switched off. However, the **-P** is required to make the change to the boolean setting survive a system reboot. Be aware, the changes don't take effect until the next time the affected user actually logs into the associated system.

A full list of available booleans is available in the output to the **getsebool -a** command.

For more information on each boolean, run the **semanage boolean -l** command. While the output includes descriptions of all available booleans, it is a database that can be searched with the help of the **grep** command.

List and Identify SELinux File Contexts

If you've enabled SELinux, the **ls -Z** command lists current SELinux file contexts, as shown earlier in Figure 4-10. As an example, take the relevant output for the anaconda-ks.cfg file from the /root directory:

```
-rw-------. root root system_u:object_r:admin_home_t:s0 anaconda-ks.cfg
```

The output includes the regular ugo/rwx ownership and permission data. It also specifies four elements of SELinux security: the user, role, type, and MLS level for the noted file. Generally, the SELinux user associated with a file is system_u or unconfined_u, and this generally does not affect access. In most cases, files are associated with an object_r, an object role for the file. It's certainly possible that future versions of SELinux will include more fine-grained options for the user and role.

The key file context is the type; in this case, admin_home_t. When you configured FTP and HTTP servers in Chapter 1, you changed the type of the configured directory and the files therein to match the default type of shared files from those services with the **chcon** command.

For example, to configure a nonstandard directory for an FTP server, make sure the context matches the default FTP directory. Consider the following command:

```
# ls -Z /var/ftp/
drwxr-xr-x  root root system_u:object_r:public_content_t pub
```

The contexts are the system user (**system_u**) and system objects (**object_r**), for type sharing with the public (**public_content_t**). If you create another directory for FTP service, you'll need to assign the same security contexts to that directory. For example, if you create an /ftp directory as the root user and run the **ls -Zd /ftp** command, you'll see the contexts associated with the /ftp directory as shown:

```
drwxr-xr-x. root  root  unconfined_u:object_r:root_t  ftp
```

To change the context, use the **chcon** command. If there are subdirectories, you'll want to make sure changes are made recursively with the **-R** switch. In this case, to change the user and type contexts to match /var/ftp, run the following command:

```
# chcon -R -u system_u -t public_content_t /ftp
```

If you want to support uploads to your FTP server, you'll have to assign a different type context, specifically **public_content_rw_t**. That corresponds to the following command:

```
# chcon -R -u system_u -t public_content_rw_t /ftp
```

But wait, in Chapter 1, you used a different variation on the **chcon** command. To use that lesson, the following command uses user, role, and context from the /var/ftp directory, and applies the changes recursively:

```
# chcon -R --reference-/var/ftp /ftp
```

Restore SELinux File Contexts

Default contexts are configured in /etc/selinux/targeted/contexts/files/file_contexts. If you make a mistake and want to restore the original SELinux settings for a file, the **restorecon** command restores those settings based on the file_contexts configuration file. However, the defaults in a directory may vary. For example, the following command (with the **-F** switch forcing changes) leads to a different set of contexts for the /ftp directory:

```
# restorecon -F /ftp
# ls -Zd /ftp
drwxr-xr-x.  root  root  system_u:object_r:default_t  ftp
```

You may notice that the user context is different from when the /ftp directory was created. That's due to the first line in the aforementioned file_contexts file, which applies the noted contexts:

```
/.*     system_u:object_r:default_t:s0
```

The file_contexts file is important for another reason. Any files and subdirectories created in listed directories inherit the file contexts associated with each directory. In other words, if you create a /srv/ftp directory, it inherits the var_t file context associated with that directory.

Identify SELinux Process Contexts

As discussed in Chapter 9, the **ps** command lists currently running processes. In a SELinux system, there are contexts for each running process. To see those contexts for all processes currently in operation, run the **ps -eZ** command, which lists every

(**-e**) process SELinux context (**-Z**). Figure 4-11 includes a varied excerpt from the output of that command on my system.

While the user and role don't change often, the process type varies widely, frequently matching the purpose of the running process. For example, from the top of the figure, you can see how the Hardware Authentication Layer Daemon (hald) is matched by the hald_t SELinux type. You should be able to identify how at least some of the other SELinux types match the associated service.

In other words, while there is a large variety of SELinux types, they're consistent with the running process.

Diagnose and Address SELinux Policy Violations

If there's a problem, SELinux is running in enforcing mode, and you're sure there are no problems with the target service or application, don't disable SELinux! Red Hat has made it easier to manage and troubleshoot. According to Red Hat, the top three causes of SELinux-related problems are: labeling, context, and boolean settings. As the first two relate to those contexts shown in the output to the **ls -Z** command, they are closely related.

FIGURE 4-11

SELinux security
contexts
of different
processes

```
system_u:system_r:hald_t:s0        2018 ?          00:00:00 hald-addon-acpi
system_u:system_r:automount_t:s0 2038 ?          00:00:00 automount
system_u:system_r:sshd_t:s0-s0:c0.c1023 2056 ? 00:00:00 sshd
system_u:system_r:ftpd_t:s0-s0:c0.c1023 2067 ? 00:00:00 vsftpd
system_u:system_r:postfix_master_t:s0 2143 ?    00:00:00 master
system_u:system_r:postfix_qmgr_t:s0 2150 ?      00:00:00 qmgr
system_u:system_r:ksmtuned_t:s0    2159 ?        00:00:00 ksmtuned
system_u:system_r:crond_t:s0-s0:c0.c1023 2168 ? 00:00:00 crond
system_u:system_r:crond_t:s0-s0:c0.c1023 2179 ? 00:00:00 atd
system_u:system_r:virtd_t:s0-s0:c0.c1023 2190 ? 00:00:00 libvirtd
system_u:system_r:initrc_t:s0      2208 ?        00:00:00 rhnsd
system_u:system_r:xdm_t:s0-s0:c0.c1023 2227 ?   00:00:00 gdm-binary
system_u:system_r:local_login_t:s0-s0:c0.c1023 2247 ? 00:00:00 login
system_u:system_r:getty_t:s0       2262 tty4     00:00:00 mingetty
system_u:system_r:getty_t:s0       2266 tty5     00:00:00 mingetty
system_u:system_r:getty_t:s0       2270 tty6     00:00:00 mingetty
system_u:system_r:dnsmasq_t:s0-s0:c0.c1023 2292 ? 00:00:00 dnsmasq
system_u:system_r:dnsmasq_t:s0-s0:c0.c1023 2325 ? 00:00:00 dnsmasq
system_u:system_r:svirt_t:s0:c458,c877 2414 ?   00:22:57 qemu-kvm
system_u:system_r:kernel_t:s0      2417 ?        00:00:00 kvm-pit-wq
system_u:system_r:consolekit_t:s0-s0:c0.c1023 2496 ? 00:00:00 console-kit-dae
system_u:system_r:devicekit_power_t:s0-s0:c0.c1023 2572 ? 00:00:02 devkit-power-da
system_u:system_r:policykit_t:s0-s0:c0.c1023 2612 ? 00:00:01 polkitd
:
```

SELinux Audits

Problems with SELinux should be documented in the associated log file, audit.log in the /var/log/audit directory. The file may be confusing, especially the first time you read it. A number of tools are available to help decipher this log.

First, the audit search (**ausearch**) command can help filter for specific types of problems. For example, the following command lists all SELinux events associated with the use of the **sudo** command:

```
# ausearch -m avc -c sudo
```

Such events are known as Access Vector Cache (**-m avc**) messages; the **-c** allows you to specify the name commonly used in the log, such as httpd or su. If you've experimented with the user_u SELinux user described earlier in this chapter, there should be several related messages available from the audit.log file.

Even for most administrators, the output is still a lot of gobblygook. However, it should include identifying information such as the audited user ID (shown as auid), which can help you identify the offending user. Perhaps the user needs such access, perhaps that user's account has been compromised. In any case, the alert may cause you to pay more attention to that account.

In contrast, the **sealeart -a /var/log/audit/audit.log** command may provide more clarity. An excerpt is shown in Figure 4-12.

SELinux Label and Context Issues

Considering Figure 4-12 and the SELinux concepts described so far, you might wonder if the user in question is allowed to run the **sudo** command. If the problem were in the /etc/sudoers file covered in Chapter 8, the SELinux alert message might not even appear. So you should pay attention to the source and target contexts. As they match, the file context is not the issue.

By process of elimination, that points to the user context described earlier as the problem. The UID of the user in question should be listed later in the file, under "Raw Audit Messages". If the user in question requires access to the **sudo** command, you should change the context of that user with the **semanage login** command described earlier. Otherwise, the user might just be experimenting with Linux. Any access to the **sudo** command will be documented in the /var/log/secure log file. So if that user actually gets by the SELinux-based limits on the use of the **sudo** command, it'll be documented in that file.

FIGURE 4-12	Summary:
	SELinux is preventing /usr/bin/sudo "setuid" access .
One SELinux alert	Detailed Description:

SELinux denied access requested by sudo. It is not expected that this access is required by sudo and this access may signal an intrusion attempt. It is also possible that the specific version or configuration of the application is causing it to require additional access.

Allowing Access:

You can generate a local policy module to allow this access - see FAQ (http://docs.fedoraproject.org/selinux-faq-fc5/#id2961385) Please file a bug report.

Additional Information:

```
Source Context              user_u:user_r:user_t:s0
Target Context              user_u:user_r:user_t:s0
Target Objects              None [ capability ]
Source                      sudo
Source Path                 /usr/bin/sudo
Port                        <Unknown>
Host                        <Unknown>
Source RPM Packages         sudo-1.7.2p2-9.el6
Target RPM Packages
Policy RPM                  selinux-policy-3.7.19-54.el6_0.3
Selinux Enabled             True
Policy Type                 targeted
Enforcing Mode              Enforcing
Plugin Name                 catchall
Host Name                   Maui
Platform                    Linux Maui 2.6.32-71.7.1.el6.x86_64 #1 SMP Wed Oct
                            27 03:44:59 EDT 2010 x86_64 x86_64
Alert Count                 13
First Seen                  Tue Dec 21 20:52:00 2010
Last Seen                   Wed Dec 22 09:03:57 2010
Local ID                    02a40edf-9dfb-40f7-9841-56a143286f86
:█
```

SELinux Boolean Issues

After deactivating the allow_user_exec_content boolean described earlier, I created a simple script named script1 for a user governed by the user_u label. After making that script executable, I tried running it with the **/home/examprep/script1** command. Even though that user had ownership of the file, with executable permissions set, that attempt led to the following message:

```
-bash: /home/examprep/script1: Permission denied
```

That led to the log excerpt shown in Figure 4-13. Note the Fix Command section; it explicitly cites the command required to address the problem. As an administrator, you need to decide whether such users should be given the ability to execute their own scripts. If so, then the noted command would address the problem.

The GUI SELinux Management Tool

If you've taken the time to learn SELinux from the command line, this section should be just a review. For many users, the easiest way to change SELinux settings is with the SELinux Administration tool, which you can start with the **system-config-selinux** command. As shown in Figure 4-14, it starts with a basic view of the status of SELinux on the local system, reflecting some of the information shown in the output to the **sestatus** command.

ⓦ a t c h   *To install the GUI SELinux Management tool, run the yum install policycoreutils-gui command. In this case, there is no system-config-selinux package.*

FIGURE 4-13

A SELinux alert and a solution

```
Summary:

SELinux is preventing /bin/bash "execute" access on script1.

Detailed Description:

SELinux denied access requested by bash. The current boolean settings do not
allow this access. If you have not setup bash to require this access this may
signal an intrusion attempt. If you do intend this access you need to change the
booleans on this system to allow the access.

Allowing Access:

Confined processes can be configured to run requiring different access, SELinux
provides booleans to allow you to turn on/off access as needed. The boolean
allow_user_exec_content is set incorrectly.
Boolean Description:
allow_user_exec_content


Fix Command:

# setsebool -P allow_user_exec_content 1
:█
```

FIGURE 4-14

SELinux
Status in the
Administration
tool

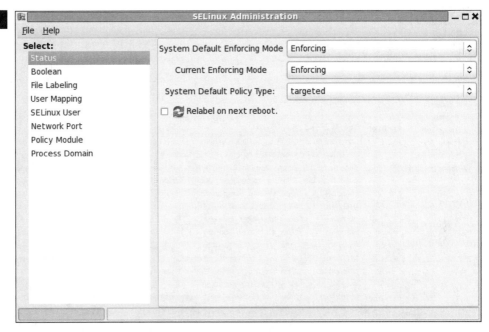

The SELinux Management tool is much more capable than the previous utility that was part of the Security Level Configuration tool. As you can see, there are options for Default and Current Enforcing Modes, which you can set to Enforcing, Permissive, or Disabled. While the focus of SELinux is on a Targeted policy, MLS is also available. Generally, you don't need to activate the Relabel On Next Reboot option unless you've changed the default policy type.

There are a number of categories shown in the left pane of the SELinux Management Tool window described in the following sections. In the RHCE half of this book, you'll revisit this tool with more of a focus on Boolean settings in the second half of this book.

SELinux Boolean Settings

In the SELinux Administration tool, click Boolean in the left-hand pane. Scroll through available modules. As you can see, SELinux policy can be modified in a number of different categories, some related to administrative functions, others to specific services. A select number of these options are shown in Figure 4-15. Any changes you make are reflected in boolean variables in the /selinux/booleans

FIGURE 4-15   Booleans in the SELinux Management tool

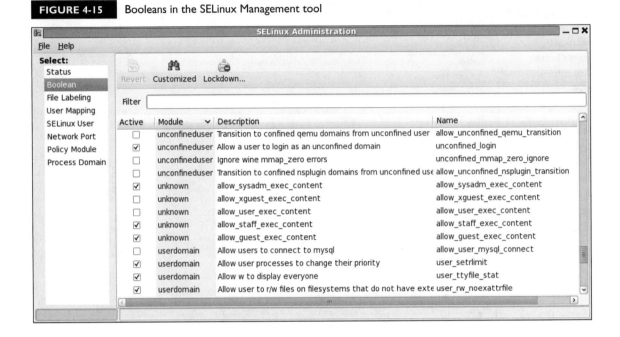

directory. Module categories of interest for the RHCSA exam include cron, init, mount, qemu, and that catch-all category: unknown. As the list is relatively short, the associated booleans are listed in Table 4-9. The booleans appear in the order shown in the SELinux Management tool.

File Labeling

You can change the default labels associated with files, some of which are described earlier in this chapter (and in other chapters discussing SELinux contexts). Some of the options are shown in Figure 4-16. Any changes to this screen are written to the file_contexts.local file in the /etc/selinux/targeted/contexts/files directory.

User Mapping

The User Mapping section allows you to go beyond the defaults for regular and administrative users. The display here illustrates the current output to the **semanage login -l** command. If you don't remember the intricacies of the **semanage** command, it may be easier to use this screen to map existing users to different maps. Click Add to open the Add User Mapping window shown in Figure 4-17. That figure also

Boolean	Description
fcron_crond	Supports fcron rules for job scheduling
cron_can_relabel	Allows cron jobs to change the SELinux file context label
allow_daemons_use_tty	Lets service daemons use terminals as needed
allow_daemons_dump_core	Supports writing of core files to the top-level root directory
init_upstart	Allows supplanting of SysVInit with upstart
allow_mount_anyfile	Permits the use of the **mount** command on any file
qemu_use_nfs	Supports the use of NFS filesystems for virtual machines
qemu_use_usb	Supports the use of USB devices for virtual machines
qemu_full_network	Supports networking for virtual machines
qemu_use_cifs	Supports the use of CIFS (Common Internet File System) filesystems for virtual machines
qemu_use_comm	Supports a connection for virtual machines to serial and parallel ports
allow_sysadm_exec_content	Allows sysadm_u users the right to execute scripts
allow_xguest_exec_content	Allows xguest_u users the right to execute scripts
allow_user_exec_content	Allows user_u users the right to execute scripts
allow_staff_exec_content	Allows staff_u users the right to execute scripts
allow_guest_exec_content	Allows guest_u users the right to execute scripts

TABLE 4-9

Selected SELinux Boolean Options

illustrates how you might reclassify a user named michael as a SELinux user_u user type.

SELinux User

The SELinux User section allows you to specify and modify default roles for standard users, such as regular users (user_u), system users (system_u), unconfined users (unconfined_u), and the administrative root user.

Network Port

The Network Port section associates standard ports with services.

FIGURE 4-16 File types in the SELinux Management tool

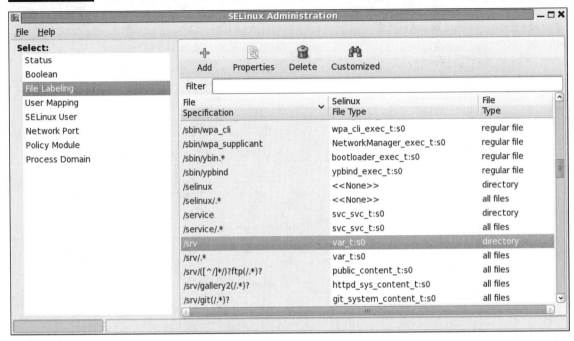

FIGURE 4-17

Map a user in the SELinux Management tool.

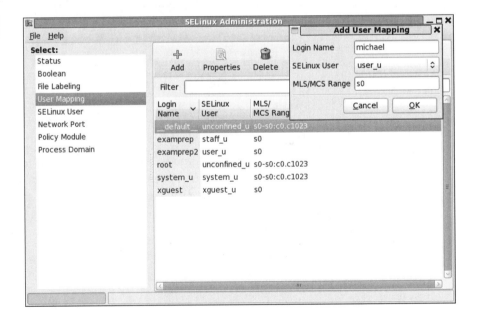

Policy Module

The Policy Module section specifies the SELinux policy version number applied to each module.

Process Domain

The Process Domain allows you to change the status of SELinux to Permissive or Enforcing mode.

The SELinux Troubleshoot Browser

RHEL 6 includes the SELinux Troubleshoot Browser shown in Figure 4-18. It provides tips and advice on any problems that you may encounter, in a language

FIGURE 4-18

Security alerts with the SELinux Troubleshoot Browser

more Linux administrators can understand, often including commands that you can run and that will address the subject problem.

To start the Browser from the GNOME desktop, click Applications | System Tools | SELinux Troubleshooter or run **sealert -b** from a GUI-based command line. The command is available from the setroubleshoot-server package.

EXERCISE 4-3

Test an SELinux User Type

In this exercise, you'll configure a user with the staff_u SELinux user type and test the results. You'll need a GUI, and at least one regular user other than the root administrative user.

1. If necessary, create a regular user. Even if you already have a regular user, a second regular user for the purpose of this exercise may reduce risks. Users can always be deleted, as discussed in Chapter 8. To that end, the **useradd user1** and **passwd user1** commands create a user named user1 with a password.

2. Review the SELinux types of current users with the **semanage login -l** command.

3. Configure the desired user as a staff_u user with the **semanage login -a -s staff_u user1** command. Substitute as desired for user1.

4. If you're completely logged in to the GUI, log out. Click System | Log Out, and click Log Out in the window that appears.

5. Log into the GUI with the newly revised staff_u account, user1 (or whatever else you may have configured in Step 3). If you don't already see a GUI login screen, press ALT-F1 or ALT-F7.

6. Try various administrative commands. Do you have access to the **su** command? What of **sudo**? What administrative tools discussed so far in this book are accessible? Is there a difference whether that tool is started from the GUI command line or from the GUI menu?

7. Log out of the new staff_u account, and log back into the regular account,

8. Delete the new user from the staff_u list; if that's user1, you can do so with the **semanage login -d user1** command.

9. Confirm the restored configuration with the **semanage login -l** command.

SCENARIO & SOLUTION

A file can't be read, written to, or executed.	Review current ownership and permissions with the **ls -l** command. Apply ownership changes with the **chown** and **chgrp** commands. Apply permission changes with the **chmod** command.
Access to a secure file required for a single user.	Configure ACLs for the appropriate filesystem and then apply the **setfacl** command to provide access.
The SSH service is not accessible on a server.	Assuming the SSH service is running (a RHCE requirement), make sure the firewall supports SSH access with the **iptables -L** command or the system-config-firewall tool.
Enforcing mode is not set for SELinux.	Set enforcing mode with the **setenforce enforcing** command.
Need to restore SELinux default file contexts on a directory.	Apply the **restorecon -F** command to the target directory.
Unexpected failure when SELinux is set in enforcing mode.	Use the **sealert -a /var/log/audit/audit.log** command or the SELinux Troubleshooter to find more information about the failure; sometimes a suggested solution is included.
Need to change SELinux options for a user.	Apply the **setsebool -P** command to the appropriate boolean setting.

CERTIFICATION SUMMARY

This chapter focuses on the basics of RHCSA-level security. On any Linux system, security starts with the ownership and permissions associated with a file. Ownership may be divided into users, groups, and others. Permissions may be divided into read, write, and execute, in a scheme known as discretionary access controls. Default file permissions are based on the value of **umask** for a user. Permissions may be extended with the SUID, SGID, and sticky bits.

ACLs can add another dimension to discretionary access controls. When configured on a mounted volume, ACLs can be configured to supersede basic ugo/rwx permissions. ACLs can be included in NFSv4 shared directories.

Firewalls can prevent communication on all but desired ports. Standard ports for most services are defined in the /etc/services file. However, some services may not use all of the protocols defined in that file. The default RHEL 6 firewall supports access only to a local SSH server.

SELinux provides another layer of protection, using mandatory access control. With a variety of available SELinux users, objects, file types, and MLS ranges, SELinux controls can help ensure that a breach in one service doesn't lead to trouble with other services.

TWO-MINUTE DRILL

Here are some of the key points from the certification objectives in Chapter 4.

Basic File Permissions

❑ Standard Linux file permissions are read, write, and execute, which may vary for the user owner, the group owner, and other users.

❑ Special permissions include the SUID, SGID, and sticky bits.

❑ Default user permissions are based on the value of the **umask**.

❑ Ownership and permissions can be changed with the **chown**, **chgrp**, and **chmod** commands.

❑ Special file attributes can be listed with the **lsattr** and modified by the **chattr** command.

Access Control Lists and More

❑ ACLs can be listed and modified on filesystems mounted with the **acl** option.

❑ Every file already has ACLs based on standard ownership and permissions.

❑ You can configure ACLs on a file to supersede standard ownership and permissions for specified users and groups on selected files. Actual ACLs may depend on the mask.

❑ Custom ACLs on a file are not enough; selected users and groups also need access to the directories that contain such files.

❑ Just as custom ACLs can support special access for selected users, it can also deny access to other selected users.

❑ ACLs can be configured on shared NFS directories.

Basic Firewall Control

❑ Standard Linux firewalls are based on the **iptables** command, with options stored in /etc/sysconfig/iptables.

❑ Standard Linux firewalls assume the use of some of the ports and protocols listed in /etc/services.

❏ The default RHEL 6 firewall supports remote access to the local SSH server.

❏ RHEL 6 firewalls can be configured with the GUI Firewall Configuration tool, or the console based tool accessible with the **system-config-firewall-tui** command.

A Security-Enhanced Linux Primer

❏ SELinux may be configured in enforcing, permissive, or disabled mode, with targeted or MLS policies, with the help of the setenforce command.

❏ User options for SELinux can be set with the **semanage login** command.

❏ SELinux files are defined by user roles, objects, file types, and MLS levels.

❏ SELinux booleans can be managed with the **setsebool** command; permanent changes require the **-P** switch.

❏ SELinux contexts can be changed with the **chcon** command, and restored to defaults with the **restorecon** command.

❏ The **sealert** command and the SELinux Troubleshoot Browser can be used to interpret problems documented in the audit.log file in the /var/log/audit directory.

SELF TEST

The following questions will help you measure your understanding of the material presented in this chapter. As no multiple-choice questions appear on the Red Hat exams, no multiple-choice questions appear in this book. These questions exclusively test your understanding of the chapter. Getting results, not memorizing trivia, is what counts on the Red Hat exams. There may be more than one right answer to many of these questions.

Basic File Permissions

1. What command configures read and write permissions on the file named question1 in the local directory, with no permissions for any other user?

    _____

2. What single command changes the user owner to professor and group owner to assistants for the local file named question2?

    _____

3. What command would change the attributes of a file named question3 to allow you to only append to that file?

    _____

Access Control Lists and More

4. What command would add ACLs to the mount of the /dev/sda2 partition on the /home directory? Assume the filesystem is already mounted.

    _____

5. What command reads current ACLs for the local file named question5? Assume that file is on a filesystem mounted with ACLs.

    _____

6. What single command gives members of the group named managers read access to the project6 file in the /home/project directory? Assume the managers group already has read and execute access to the directory.

    _____

7. What command prevents members of the group named temps from having any access to the secret7 file in the /home/project directory?

_____

Basic Firewall Control

8. What TCP/IP port number is associated with the FTP service?

_____

9. Name the full path to the file with RHEL 6 firewall configuration rules based on the **iptables** command.

_____

A Security-Enhanced Linux Primer

10. What command configures SELinux in enforcing mode?

_____

11. What command lists the SELinux status of current users?

_____

12. What directory includes boolean settings for SELinux?

_____

LAB QUESTIONS

Several of these labs involve configuration exercises. You should do these exercises on test machines only. It's assumed that you're running these exercises on virtual machines such as KVM, and they're not used for production.

Red Hat presents its exams electronically. For that reason, most of the labs in this and future chapters are available from the CD that accompanies the book, in the Chapter4/ subdirectory. In case you haven't yet set up RHEL 6 on a system, refer to Chapter 1 for installation instructions.

The answers for each lab follows the self test answers for the fill-in-the-blank questions.

SELF TEST ANSWERS

Basic File Permissions

1. The command that configures read and write permissions on the file named question1 in the local directory, with no permissions for any other user is:

```
# chmod 600 question1
```

2. The single command that changes the user owner to professor and group owner to assistants for the noted file is:

```
# chown professor.assistants question2
```

It's acceptable to substitute a colon (:) for the dot (.).

3. The command that change the attributes of a file named question3 to allow you to only append to that file is:

```
# chattr +a question3
```

Access Control Lists and More

4. The command that adds ACLs to the mount of the /dev/sda2 partition on the /home directory is:

```
# mount -o remount,acl /dev/sda2 /home
```

Since you don't know whether the filesystem is configured in /etc/fstab, you need the device a nd directory for the command.

5. The command that reads current ACLs for the local file named question5 is:

```
# getfacl question5
```

6. The single command gives that members of the group named managers read access to the project6 file in the /home/project directory is:

```
# setacl -m g:managers:r /home/project/project6
```

7. The command that prevents members of the group named temps from having any access to the secret7 file in the /home/project directory is:

```
# setacl -m g:temps:--- /home/project/secret7
```

Basic Firewall Control

8. The TCP/IP port number associated with the FTP service is 21.

9. The full path to the file with RHEL 6 firewall configuration rules is /etc/sysconfig/iptables.

A Security-Enhanced Linux Primer

10. The command that configures SELinux in enforcing mode is:

```
# setenforce enforcing
```

11. The command that lists the SELinux status of current users is:

```
# semanage login -l
```

12. The directory that includes boolean settings for SELinux is:

```
/selinux/booleans
```

LAB ANSWERS

Lab 1

In some ways, Lab 1 could have been split into two different labs. It's designed to let you practice configuring those permissions required to set up executable scripts for user owners and other users. Success with the script is straightforward; if it's executed, you'll find a file named filelist, with a list of files, in the local directory.

It's also designed to help you understand the effect of the SUID bit of /usr/bin/passwd, a compiled executable.

Lab 2

Lab 2 is essentially an extension of Lab 1, in that ACLs are another approach to making a script, owned by the root administrative user, executable by a single regular user. You can check for success in the same way; if the script is properly executed by the ACL configured regular user, you'll find a file named filelist in the local directory.

Lab 3

The configuration of ACLs on the /root administrative directory is a bad security practice. However, it is an excellent way to illustrate the capabilities of ACLs on a system, how it can allow access by selected regular users to the inner sanctums of the root administrative account. Because of the risks, just be sure to disable the ACLs when the lab is complete. If the selected user is michael, one method is with the following command:

```
# setfacl -b u:michael /root
```

If you've configured ACLs on files within the /root directory, be sure to disable those as well. Of course, in standard Linux configurations, the /root directory is mounted on the same volume as the top-level root directory (/). During the lab, you should have mounted that top-level root directory with the acl option. That should be confirmed in the output to the **mount** command. Given the risks, you should restore the original configuration with the following command:

```
# mount -o remount /
```

Lab 4

This lab is designed to raise awareness of the time and effort required to disable and re-enable SELinux in enforcing mode. If you switch between disabled and permissive mode, the time and effort required should be about the same. While it may not seem to take that much time, if you have to reconfigure SELinux in enforcing mode, it might seem to take "forever" as nothing else can be done while the system is being rebooted and relabeled.

Lab 5

Standard users in RHEL 6 run as unconfined_u SELinux user types. As such, there are few limits on their user accounts. If instructions on an exam or from a corporate policy require certain limits on regular users, you may want to set up the __default__ user with the SELinux user_u user type. Alternatively, if you're told to set up specific users to a limited type, such as xguest_u or staff_u, multiple **semanage login** commands may be appropriate.

Lab 6

After testing a user as a guest_u user, most administrators will want regular users to have more privileges.

Lab 7

Users configured with the guest_u SELinux user type are not normally allowed to execute scripts even in their own home directories. That can change with the allow_guest_exec_content boolean described in the lab. Success in this lab is based on a simple comparison; whether a script can be executed with and without the active boolean.

While the easiest way to restore the original configuration is with the GUI SELinux management tool, you should also know how to use commands like the following, which disables a custom SELinux user type for user michael:

```
# semanage login -d michael
```

Lab 8

Success in this lab can be measured first with the **ls -Zd** command. When applied to both the /ftp and the /var/ftp/pub directories, it should lead to the same list of SELinux roles, objects, types, and MLS options for each directory.

This lab also contains a solvable mystery. Why is it that the SELinux contexts of a newly created directory differ from those where the contexts have been restored with the **restorecon** command.

The basic reason is the difference between regular unconfined_u SELinux user types and the options listed in the file_contexts file in the /etc/selinux/targeted/contexts/files directory. You'll learn how to modify default file contexts in Chapter 11.

Lab 9

Everyone will experiment with SELinux in different ways. So the results of this lab are up to you. The objective is to analyze a current relevant log file and process it at the command line. Try to identify the problems associated with each alert. While you may not be able to address many SELinux issues, at least until the second half of this book, you should be able to identify the problems or at least the users and/or commands associated with each alert. If you don't have enough of a log, two related files are available in the Chapter4/ directory of the CD.

5

The Boot Process

T his chapter is focused on what happens from the moment a system is powered up to the time a login prompt is available. Those are the fundamentals of the boot process. When RHEL 6 is properly installed, the BIOS/UEFI points to a specific media device. Assuming it's a local hard drive, the master boot record (MBR) of that device points to the GRUB bootloader. Once an option to boot RHEL 6 is selected in GRUB, the associated commands point to and initialize the Linux kernel, which then starts **init**, the first Linux process. The **init** process then initializes the system and moves into appropriate runlevels. When Linux boots into a specific runlevel, it starts a series of services, including the client associated with the Network Time Protocol (NTP). You can customize this process.

INSIDE THE EXAM

Understanding the Boot Process

Objectives related to the boot process have been consolidated into the RHCSA exam. Perhaps the most basic skill related to the boot process is an understanding of the commands that start and stop the boot process, such as **shutdown** and **reboot**:

■ Boot, reboot, and shut down a system normally

Of course, that starts with the way a system is powered up. In this chapter, you'll review the standard Linux runlevels. From the standard RHEL 6 boot menu, you need to know how to:

■ Boot systems into different runlevels manually

Closely related to this objective is this one:

■ Use single-user mode to gain access to a system

If you are already familiar with single-user mode, you should understand that "access" in single user mode is password-free access to the root administrative account. An early release of the RHCSA objectives included the following phrase: "for which the root password is not known."

Also closely related is this objective, focused on the configuration file associated with different runlevels:

■ Configure systems to boot into a specific runlevel automatically

As Linux is a network operating system, and as most users can't do much without networking, it's important to know how to

■ Configure network services to start automatically at boot

With the focus on the boot process, you'll also learn how to

■ Modify the system bootloader

Closely related to these objectives, and part of the boot process, are objectives related to how filesystems are mounted, covered in Chapter 6.

CERTIFICATION OBJECTIVE 5.01

The BIOS and the UEFI

While not officially a Red Hat exam prerequisite or requirement, a basic understanding of the BIOS and the UEFI is a fundamental skill for all serious computer users. The UEFI has replaced the BIOS on many modern systems and can do so much more. But as the UEFI supports changes to boot media in similar ways, the functionality for our purposes is the same.

Because of the variety of BIOS/UEFI software available, this discussion is general. It's not possible to provide any sort of step-by-step instructions for modifying the wide array of available BIOS/UEFI menus. In any case, such instructions are not directly relevant either to the administration of Linux or to any of the Red Hat exams. However, these skills can help you boot from different Linux installation media, access default virtualization settings, and more.

Basic System Configuration

When a computer is powered up, the first thing that starts is the BIOS/UEFI. Based on settings stored in stable, read-only memory, the BIOS/UEFI system performs a series of diagnostics to detect and connect the CPU and key controllers. This is known as the Power On Self Test (POST). If you hear beeps during this process, there may be a hardware problem such as an improperly connected hard drive controller. The BIOS/UEFI system then looks for attached devices such as the graphics card. After the graphics hardware is detected, you may see a screen similar to Figure 5-1, which displays other hardware as detected, tested, and verified.

If your system has an UEFI menu, it may include a Trusted Platform Module (TPM). While it's built to enhance security on a system, it has caused controversy within the open-source community, due to privacy issues. Many open-source professionals are working to minimize any such problems through the Open Trusted Computing (OpenTC) group of the European Union. RHEL 6 takes advantage of TPM hardware features to enhance system security.

Once complete, the BIOS/UEFI passes control to the MBR of the boot device, normally the first hard drive. The first stage of the GRUB bootloader is normally copied to the MBR. It serves as a pointer to the other information from the GRUB menu. At that point, you should see a bootloader screen.

FIGURE 5-1

The BIOS
Initialization menu

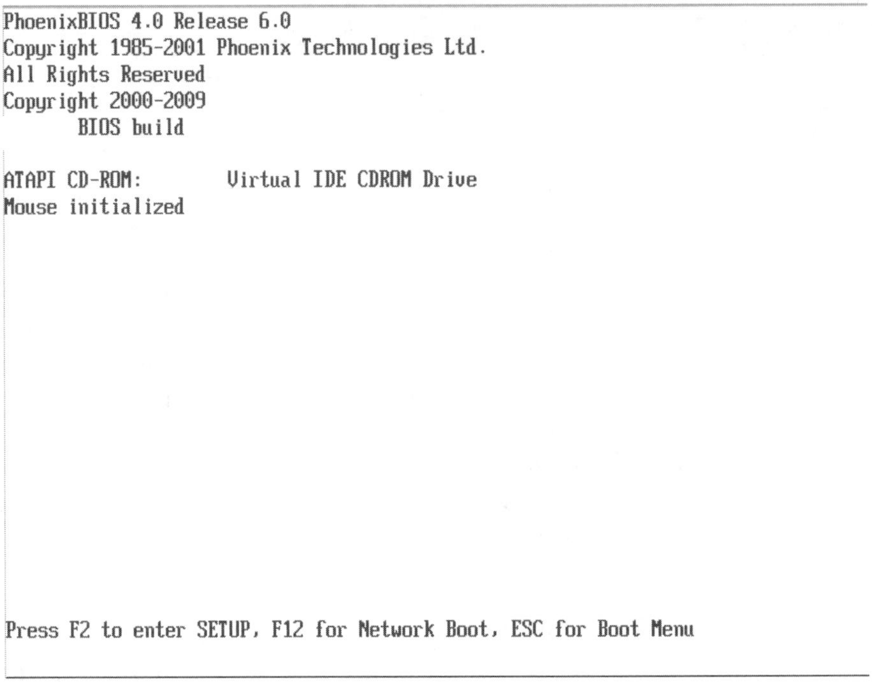

```
PhoenixBIOS 4.0 Release 6.0
Copyright 1985-2001 Phoenix Technologies Ltd.
All Rights Reserved
Copyright 2000-2009
        BIOS build

ATAPI CD-ROM:        Virtual IDE CDROM Drive
Mouse initialized




Press F2 to enter SETUP, F12 for Network Boot, ESC for Boot Menu
```

Startup Menus

Generally, the only reason to go into the BIOS/UEFI menu during the Red Hat exams is to boot from different media, such as a CD, floppy, or USB key. In many cases, you can bypass this process. Return to Figure 5-1. The options for this particular system are shown in the bottom of the screen. In this case, pressing F2 enters SETUP, the BIOS menu; pressing F12 boots directly from a network device; and pressing ESC starts a boot menu. The actual keys vary by system.

In many cases, all you see after POST is a blank screen. The BIOS/UEFI is often configured in this way. In that case, you'll need to do some guessing based on your experience on how to reveal the screen shown in Figure 5-1 and access the boot or BIOS menu.

In many cases, boot menus are directly accessible by pressing a key such as ESC, DEL, F1, F2, or F12. Such boot menus may have entries similar to:

```
    Boot Menu
1. Removable Devices
2. Hard Drive
```

```
3. CD-ROM Drive
4. USB Drive
5. Built-In LAN
```

From that or similar menus, you should be able to select the desired boot device using the arrow and ENTER keys. If that doesn't work, you'll have to use the BIOS /UEFI menu to boot from the desired drive.

Access to Linux Bootloaders

As noted in Chapter 2, the default bootloader is GRUB, and the first part of it (known as stage 1) is installed in the MBR of the default drive. Normally, the BIOS should automatically start the bootloader, with a message similar to:

```
Booting Red Hat Enterprise Linux Server (2.6.32-71.el6) in 5
seconds...
```

Alternatively, if you press a key before those five seconds are complete, GRUB will present a menu similar to that shown in Figure 5-2.

If the system includes more than one Linux kernel, or more than one operating system, there may be multiple choices available, which you can highlight with the UP ARROW and DOWN ARROW keys. To boot Linux from the highlighted option, press ENTER.

| **FIGURE 5-2** | `GNU GRUB  version 0.97  (637K lower / 785388K upper memory)` |

The GRUB menu

```
 Red Hat Enterprise Linux (2.6.32-71.el6.x86_64)




 




 




 

```

```
Use the ↑ and ↓ keys to select which entry is highlighted.
Press enter to boot the selected OS, 'e' to edit the
commands before booting, 'a' to modify the kernel arguments
before booting, or 'c' for a command-line.
```

On old PCs (pre-21st century), some BIOSes can't find your bootloader unless it's located within the first 1024 cylinders of the hard disk. For that reason, the partition where the /boot directory is configured is normally the first available primary partition.

On systems with multiple hard drives, there is one more caveat. On PATA (Primary Advanced Technology Attachment) hard drives, the /boot directory must be on a hard drive attached to the primary PATA controller. If local drives are all SCSI (Small Computer Systems Interface) hard drives, the /boot directory must be located on a hard drive with SCSI ID 0 or ID 1. For systems with a mix of hard drives, the /boot directory must be located on either the first IDE drive or a SCSI drive with ID 0.

CERTIFICATION OBJECTIVE 5.02

Bootloaders and GRUB

The standard bootloader associated with Red Hat Enterprise Linux (RHEL) is GRUB, the GRand Unified Bootloader. Red Hat has not supported LILO, the Linux Loader, for years. As suggested by the Red Hat exam requirements, for the RHCSA exam, you need to know how to use the GRUB menu to boot into different runlevels, and diagnose and correct boot failures arising from bootloader errors. RHEL 6 uses the traditional version of GRUB, 0.97. The associated configuration file is relatively easy to understand and customize, as you'll see later in this chapter. Some Linux distributions such as Ubuntu have moved to GRUB 2.0. While the look and feel of the GRUB 2.0 menu is similar to what's seen on RHEL 6, the steps required to configure that bootloader are quite different.

on the job

If you want to take full advantage of the security features associated with TPM, consider TrustedGRUB as a bootloader. TrustedGRUB can become part of the "chain of trust" from the TPM through RHEL 6, verifying the integrity of the local operating system. For more information, see http://sourceforge .net/projects/trustedgrub/.

GRUB, the GRand Unified Bootloader

Red Hat has implemented GRUB as the only bootloader for its Linux distributions. It's normally configured to boot into a default kernel, presumably one associated with RHEL 6. The selected GRUB option finds the kernel in the /boot directory and finds the GRUB menu, which will look similar to Figure 5-2. You can use the GRUB menu to boot any operating system detected during the Linux installation process, or any other operating system added to appropriate configuration files.

GRUB is flexible. Not only can it be edited through its configuration file, but also it can be edited directly from the GRUB menu. If GRUB is password-protected, press P. You should now see the options shown in Figure 5-2. In that menu, you can press E to temporarily edit the file, press A to just add a directive to the end of the kernel command line, or press C to open a GRUB command prompt. This section is focused on booting into different runlevels.

Boot into Different Runlevels

To pass a parameter to the kernel through GRUB, press A at the first GRUB menu. This allows you to append the command sent to the kernel. You might then see a single line of commands similar to the following:

```
grub append> ro root=UUID=somelonghexadecimalnumber
rd_NO_LUKS rd_NO_LVM rd_NO_MD rd_NO_DM LANG=en_US.UTF-8
SYSFONT=latarcyrheb-sun16 KEYBOARDTYPE=pc KEYTABLE=us
crashkernel=auto rhgb quiet
```

Yeah, that's a lot of stuff that will be explained shortly. What matters for the RHCSA is that you can add more commands to the end of this line. For example, if you add the number **1** to the end of this line, Linux starts in single-user mode.

From single-user mode, type **exit** and the system will go into multiuser mode. If you have made changes or repairs to any partitions, the next step is to reboot the computer with the **reboot** command. At some point, changes made during a Red Hat exam should be tested with a reboot.

The concept of the runlevel is detailed later in this chapter. For now, all you need to know is that when RHEL 6 is configured to boot into a GUI, it's configured to boot into runlevel 5 by default. That runlevel can be changed by appending a runlevel to the end of the kernel command line.

If you encounter a problem with a system booting into the GUI, the first thing to try is to add a **3** at the end of the kernel command line. If successful, it will boot RHEL 6 into text mode, with a command line console-based login.

If you need direct access into the root administrative account, add a **1** to the end of the kernel command line. That boots into runlevel 1, which automatically logs in to the account of the root administrative user. As that supports full root administrative privileges, including changes to the root administrative password, it's important to password-protect the GRUB menu, as discussed shortly.

In rare cases, some systems are so troubled, they don't boot into runlevel 1. In that case, two other runlevels are available:

- **single** Does everything but run the scripts listed in the /etc/rc1.d directory.
- **init=/bin/sh** Does not load init-related files; mounts only the top-level root directory (/) in read-only mode.

The runlevel option known as **emergency** is no longer recognized in RHEL.

Now you should understand how to boot into different runlevels during the boot process. As defined in the Red Hat Exam Prep guide, this is explicitly described as an RHCSA requirement:

Boot systems into different runlevels manually.

EXERCISE 5-1

Boot into a Different Runlevel

One key skill is knowing how to boot into a different runlevel. This exercise assumes you've configured RHEL 6 per Chapter 2, which sets the default runlevel as 5. Check your /etc/inittab file. If the current system reflects the defaults, it should read as follows:

```
id:5:initdefault:
```

Change this directive if needed and reboot your system. Now you can start the exercise.

1. When you see the following message, make sure to press any key to access the GRUB menu:

```
Press any key to enter the menu
```

2. If the menu is password-protected, you'll have to press P to access the password prompt. Then you can enter the GRUB password. Next, you can press A to access the kernel command line.

3. At the end of the kernel command line, type a space followed by the runlevel of your choice. First, delete the **rhgb quiet**, enter **2**, and press B to boot this kernel.

4. Watch the boot messages. What kind of login screen do you see?

5. Log in to this system. You can use any existing user account.

6. Run the **reboot** command to restart this system.

7. Repeat Steps 1 through 3, but boot this system into runlevel **1**.

8. Watch the boot messages. What kind of login screen do you see? Do you have to log in at all?

9. Repeat Steps 1 through 3, but boot this system into runlevel **s**.

10. Watch the boot messages. What kind of login screen do you see? Do you have to log in at all?

11. Run the **reboot** command to restart this system.

12. Repeat Steps 1 through 3, but boot this system into runlevel **init=/bin/sh**.

13. Watch the boot messages. What kind of login screen do you see?

14. Run the **halt** command to stop this system.

Modify the System Bootloader

The RHCSA specifically requires that you need to know how to "modify the system bootloader." That means you need to know the GRUB configuration file in detail. It's available in the /boot/grub/grub.conf file. The following is a detailed analysis of a typical version of that configuration file. Some of the details, especially as related to the **kernel** command, are not necessary.

```
# grub.conf generated by anaconda
#
# Note that you do not have to rerun grub after making changes
to this file
# NOTICE:  You have a /boot partition. This means that
#          all kernel and initrd paths are relative to /boot/,
eg.
#          root (hd0,0)
#          kernel /vmlinuz-version ro root=/dev/vda2
#          initrd /initrd-[generic-]version.img
# boot=/dev/vda
```

As you can see, even the comments are significant. The first line suggests that this file was created by Anaconda, the RHEL installation program. The next line notes that you don't have to rerun the **grub** command; in other words, configuration changes do not have to be written to the MBR. If you've previously configured GRUB (as is the default during the RHEL 6 installation process), there's already a pointer in the MBR that reads the current version of the GRUB configuration file.

The commented "NOTICE" in the configuration file appears when there's a separate partition for the /boot directory. The last commented line indicates the hard drive with the MBR—in this case, /dev/vda.

```
default=0
```

GRUB configuration options are organized in stanzas. The **default=0** may be slightly confusing, as it points to the first available stanza. A **default=1** would point to a second stanza; a **default=2** would point to a third stanza, and so on, if included in the configuration file.

```
timeout=5
```

In other words, if nothing is done in the five seconds specified by the **timeout=5** directive, GRUB automatically runs the commands in the first stanza.

```
splashimage=(hd0,0)/grub/splash.xpm.gz
```

The **splashimage** is the screen presented with the GRUB menu. Strangely enough, it's a black screen.

```
hiddenmenu
```

The **hiddenmenu** option does not display the menu automatically; instead, it displays the "Booting Red Hat Enterprise Linux" message described earlier. The directives that follow are the first stanza; additional stanzas are commonly shown for different versions of the kernel or even different operating systems such as Microsoft Windows.

```
title Red Hat Enterprise Linux (2.6.32-71.el6.x86_64)
```

The **title** directive displays the option shown in the GRUB menu.

```
    root (hd0,0)
```

Now this is really weird—there are two definitions for the word **root** in this file. First, the /boot directory in the GRUB configuration file is associated with root, in this case, **root(hd0,0)**.

```
root=UUID=somelonghexadecimalnumber
```

The UUID is an acronym for the universally unique identifier. It's a 128-bit number, expressed in hexadecimal (base 16) format. It's a unique number generated for each volume configured on RHEL 6. While you could use the **LABEL** directive from RHEL 5 or even the device file associated with the top-level root directory (/) volume, the UUID is the new default standard for RHEL 6 in the GRUB configuration file as well as the /etc/fstab file as discussed in Chapter 6.

The **root(hd0,0)** directive uses numbers starting with 0. In other words, this directive points to the first partition on the first hard drive. The /boot directory is mounted on this partition. If it were the fifth partition on the first hard drive, for example, this directive would read *root(hd0,4)*.

The **timeout=5** directive specifies the time, in seconds, before GRUB automatically boots the default operating system. The **splashimage** directive locates the graphical GRUB screen. In this case, you can find it on the first partition of the first hard drive, in the /grub/splash.xpm.gz file. It happens to configure a black background. As **(hd0,0)** has been previously defined as the /boot directory, you can find the splash screen file in /boot/grub/splash.xpm.gz. The **hiddenmenu** directive means that the GRUB options are hidden, with the message shown here:

```
Booting Red Hat Enterprise Linux Server (2.6.32-71.el6.x86_64) in 5 seconds...
```

Each of the next two stanzas has a title normally associated with the operating system, such as:

```
title Red Hat Enterprise Linux Server (2.6.32-71.el6.x86_64)
```

This is a standard, based on the currently installed kernel. If multiple kernels are installed, you'll probably see more than one stanza. Both would boot RHEL 6, using a different kernel.

The next three lines specify the location of the /boot directory, the kernel, and the initial RAM disk, respectively. The **kernel** line may have a number of directives; it is actually one line in the actual GRUB configuration file.

```
root (hd0,0)
     kernel /vmlinuz-2.6.32-71.el6.x86_64 ro root=UUID=21754e41-bd5d-4faa-8c0d-
33c2e70950 rd_NO_LUKS rd_NO_LVM rd_NO_MD rd_NO_DM LANG=en_US.UTF-8
SYSFONT=latarcyrheb-sun16 KEYBOARDTYPE=pc KEYTABLE=us crashkernel=auto rhgb quiet
initrd /initrd-2.6.32-55.el6.i686.img
```

In this case, the /boot directory, as described earlier, is on the first partition of the first hard drive, as specified by **root (hd0,0)**. The kernel is specified by the vmlinuz-2.6.32-71.el6.x86_64 file, in the /boot directory. It's opened as read only (**ro**) to protect it from any accidental writes from the initial RAM disk; the actual top-level root directory is associated with the noted Universally Unique Identifier (UUID).

The **rd_NO_LUKS** disables detection of volumes encrypted to the Linux Unified Key Setup (LUKS) system. If a top-level root directory partition is encrypted, the system would be unbootable. The **rd_NO_LVM** disables detection of volumes configured with the Logical Volume Manager (LVM). The **rd_NO_MD** and **rd_NO_DM** options disable detection of the software version of Redundant Array of Independent Disks (RAID) devices. Except for RAID, which is not part of the Red Hat exams, these specialty systems are covered in Chapter 6.

The directives that follow specify language, font, and keyboard directives during the boot process, when the Initial RAM disk is loaded. These directives are **LANG=en_US.UTF-8 SYSFONT=latarcyrheb-sun16 KEYBOARDTYPE=pc KEYTABLE=us**.

As suggested in the discussion on the Kickstart process in Chapter 2, in some cases you may need to change **crashkernel=auto** to **crashkernel=128M**. Finally, at the end of the line, the **rhgb quiet** directive hides the boot messages by default.

In most configurations, all that's absolutely needed is the following line:

```
kernel /vmlinuz-2.6.32-71.el6.x86_64 ro root=/dev/vda2
```

The initial RAM disk file (initrd-2.6.32-71.el6.x86_64.img) creates a temporary filesystem during the boot process. It includes kernel modules and user space programs needed to mount actual filesystems and run the first initialization programs.

The final three lines are trivial with respect to the Red Hat exams; however, many users see them when they configure their computers in a dual boot with Microsoft Windows. In most cases, you'll actually see the first line as:

```
title Other
```

On my laptop, I've modified it to specify the actual operating system on the other partition.

```
title Windows 7
```

With the following directive, GRUB points to the partition with Microsoft Windows 7, the second partition on the first hard drive:

```
rootnoverify (hd0,1)
```

This is different from the aforementioned **root (hd0,0)** directive, as **rootnoverify** does not attempt to mount the noted partition in a Linux fashion.

Finally, the **chainloader +1** directive points to the first sector of the noted partition, where Microsoft Windows 7 continues the boot process:

```
chainloader +1
```

More Options

Administrators can do more than just use GRUB to boot into a different runlevel. For example, if Linux does not recognize all of the RAM on the local system, try adding **mem=*xyz*M** (where *xyz*M represents the amount of memory on the local computer) at the end of the line. Alternatively, some problems related to graphics cards can be addressed by the **vga** directive; for example, the **vga=791** directive sets up a 16-bit 1024 × 768 screen.

A huge number of options are available, in a kernel-parameters.txt file. On RHEL 6, it's available from the kernel-doc package.

GRUB Security and Password Protection

If you've configured GRUB password protection during the RHEL installation process, you'll see a line similar to the following in the GRUB configuration file:

```
password --md5 $1$hfBhb8zA$sYrw4B1VzrrpPHpDtyhb.
```

This directive specifies a password hash, encrypted to the Message-Digest 5 algorithm. When it's included in the first GRUB commands, before the commands associated with individual kernels, it protects the GRUB menu. That can keep a cracker from breaking into this system and gaining access to the root administrative account.

If you want to create an MD5 password for this file, run the **grub-md5-crypt** command. You'll be prompted for a password that is converted to an MD5 hash. You can then copy this hash to the GRUB configuration file. If the **password** directive is included before a stanza, it password-protects the entire menu. Users won't be able to edit the GRUB menu unless they know the password. If the **password** directive is placed within a stanza, it prompts for the password before the option is selected.

On RHEL 6, a GRUB menu that's not password-protected may allow a user access to the root administrative account. To put it mildly, that's a serious security risk. Sure, access to the given system can be protected by other means. But password protection for the GRUB menu can at least ensure that anyone who gets access to that menu can't just boot into runlevel 1 (or any other runlevel) at will.

Anyone with access to a system CD/DVD drive can use the RHEL 6 installation DVD or network CD to start rescue mode. That also provides password-free access to the root administrative account. To prevent such security breaches, you may want to password-protect the BIOS/UEFI menu to prevent access or changes to the boot menu described earlier. Some systems may even include physical locks on the CD/DVD drive and even USB ports to prevent such unauthorized access to the root administrative account.

How to Update GRUB

If you've previously installed a different bootloader to the MBR, such as Microsoft's NTLDR or BOOTMGR, or TeraByte's BootIt Next Generation, just run the **grub-install** command. If it doesn't automatically write the GRUB pointer to the MBR, or multiple hard drives are available, you may need to include the hard drive device such as /dev/sdb. It's also possible to set up GRUB on a portable drive; just specify the device with the command.

When the GRUB configuration file is changed, no additional commands are required. The pointer from the MBR automatically reads the current version of the /boot/grub/grub.conf file.

Effects of GRUB Errors

An error in the GRUB configuration file can result in an unbootable system. For example, identifying the wrong volume as the root partition (/) can lead to a kernel panic. Other configuration errors in /boot/grub/grub.conf can also cause a kernel panic during the boot process.

Now that you've analyzed the GRUB configuration file, you can probably visualize some of the effects of errors in this file. If some of the filenames or partitions are wrong, GRUB won't be able to find critical files such as the Linux kernel.

First, if the **root (hdx,y)** directive does not point to the /boot directory, you'll see one of three possible error messages, described in Table 5-1.

If the GRUB configuration file is completely missing, you'll see a prompt similar to this:

```
grub>
```

It's possible to get to a grub> prompt from within Linux with the grub command. However, that option does not include command completion features; and some commands provide different information when Linux is running.

TABLE 5-1	Message	Description
GRUB Error Messages	Error 15: File not found	The partition was mounted; the kernel was not found on that partition. Cause: **root (hdx,y)** directive does not point to the partition with the /boot directory.
	Error 17: Cannot mount selected partition	The partition is not formatted to a filesystem with files. Cause: the **root (hdx,y)** directive points to a partition formatted to a system such as Linux swap.
	Error 22: No such partition	There is no partition specified by the **root (hdx,y)** directive.

The GRUB Command Line

If you see a GRUB command line, you may feel lost. To see a list of available commands, press the TAB key at the **grub>** prompt.

Some trial and error may be required. You should be able to find all detected hard drives on a standard PC from the BIOS/UEFI menus (SCSI drives can be a different story). You can use the **find** command to identify the partition with the GRUB configuration file.

By default, the /boot directory is mounted on a separate partition. For example, to find grub.conf on this particular system, start with the following command:

```
grub> find /grub/grub.conf
```

GRUB should return the partition with the /boot directory. In this case, it's the first partition on the first hard drive:

```
(hd0,0)
```

There's one more way to identify the partition with the /boot directory. Just run **root** at the **grub>** command line:

```
grub> root
(hd0,0): Filesystem type is ext2fs, partition type 0x83
```

Next, use that information to identify configured partitions:

```
grub> find (hd0,0)/grub/grub.conf
```

If the file is not on the noted partition, you'll see an "Error 15: File not found" error message. For the standard server1.example.com installation, the output includes the partitions with Linux-formatted drives:

```
(hd0,0)
(hd0,1)
(hd0,4)
```

We know that the /boot directory is on (hd0,0). While many administrators configure the /boot directory earlier in a drive sequence, it's not required. To confirm the location of grub.conf, run the **cat** command as follows to display the contents of the GRUB configuration file:

```
grub> cat (hd0,0)/grub/grub.conf
```

Now you can use these commands from the GRUB configuration file to boot Linux from the **grub>** command line. If the top-level root directory is normally mounted on a partition, you may even confirm the contents of the /etc/fstab file with a command like the following:

```
grub> cat (hd0,1)/etc/fstab
```

Command completion works from the GRUB command line. For example, if you don't remember the name of the Kernel file, type **kernel /** and then press the TAB key to review the available files in the /boot directory.

EXERCISE 5-2

Using the GRUB Command Line

In this exercise, you'll use the printout of the GRUB configuration file from Exercise 5-1 to boot RHEL 6 manually. Look at the printout and identify the desired commands in the stanza. Now follow these steps:

1. Boot the system. When you see the following line at the top of the screen, press any key to access the GRUB menu:

   ```
   Press any key to enter the menu
   ```

2. If the GRUB configuration file is password-protected, you'll have to press P to access a password prompt.

3. Press C for a GRUB-based command line interface. You should see the **grub>** prompt.

4. Type in the commands listed in the selected stanza. Start by issuing the first **root** directive. If the command is successful, you should see output similar to:

   ```
   Filesystem type is ext2fs, partition type 0x83
   ```

   Other filesystems such as XFS lead to a slightly different result.

5. Enter the second command from your selected GRUB configuration file stanza, which specifies the kernel and root directory partition. Yes, this is a long line; however, you can use command completion (press the TAB key) to make it faster. In addition, the only important parts of the line are the kernel file, the "read-only" status, and the location of the top-level root directory, in other words:

   ```
   kernel /vmlinuz-2.6.32-71.el6.x86_64 ro root=/dev/vda2
   ```

If successful, you'll see the following message (the setup and size numbers may vary):

```
[Linux-bzImage, setup=0x1e00, size=0x16eb71]
```

6. Enter the third command from the stanza, which specifies the initial RAM disk command and file location. If successful, you'll see the following message (the numbers may vary):

```
[Linux-initrd @ 0x16544000, 0x19b6c7 bytes]
```

7. Now enter the **boot** command. If successful, Linux should now boot the selected kernel and initial RAM disk just as if you selected that option from the GRUB configuration menu.

Create Your Own GRUB Configuration File

If you need to rebuild the GRUB configuration file from scratch, a sample configuration file is available in the documentation associated with the GRUB package. As suggested in Chapter 3, that documentation is available in the /usr/share/doc directory. As the installed version of the grub package is 0.97, the directory with GRUB documentation is /usr/share/doc/grub-0.97.

In that directory, you'll find a menu.lst file. That file is used as the GRUB bootloader configuration file on some other Linux distributions. In fact, on RHEL 6, in the /boot/grub directory, the menu.lst file is soft-linked to the grub.conf file.

In that file, you can find the following commands, associated with the default RHEL 6 version of the configuration file, with comments:

```
# Boot automatically after 30 secs.
timeout = 30
# By default, boot the first entry
default = 0
```

In addition, there's a stanza associated with Linux:

```
# For booting GNU/Linux
title   GNU/Linux
root (hd1,0)
kernel /vmlinuz root=/dev/hdb1
#initrd /initrd.img
```

Of course, that stanza would need changes. The words after the **title** directive could be anything you want. The **root (hd1,0)** directive would have to be changed to the actual partition with the /boot directory, unless that directory is already configured on the first partition of the second hard drive. The *vmlinuz* would have to be changed to the full name of the file associated with the desired Linux kernel. You need to add a **ro** to make sure the kernel is initially loaded in read-only mode for the initial RAM disk. The */dev/hdb1* in that line would have to be changed to the device of the partition or volume where the top-level root directory is located.

There was a time when no Initial RAM disk file was required during the boot process. That is no longer true. Thus, the **initrd** directive line would have to be uncommented (by removing the # in front of the line), with the *initrd.img* filename changed to the name of the actual Initial RAM disk file in the /boot directory.

Of course, if the GRUB configuration file is missing and you weren't able to boot the system to even read this menu.lst file, you might need to resort to an option known as rescue mode.

An Option to Booting from GRUB: Rescue Mode

The troubleshooting objectives associated with the 2007 version of the RHCE exam prep guide suggest that you needed to be able to recover from a complete boot failure, such as if the GRUB configuration file were corrupt or missing. To that end, you might need to rebuild that GRUB configuration file from scratch. In other words, if you've tried to boot directly from the **grub>** prompt described earlier and failed, you might need to resort to the option known as rescue mode. That required access to the installation DVD, or the network boot disk.

The RHCSA and RHCE objectives no longer include a requirement associated with rescue mode. However, as the rescue of unbootable systems is part of the curriculum for Red Hat's RH254 course, it may be included in future versions of one of these exams.

To that end, boot from one of those media options. When you see the installation screen with the following options:

```
Install or upgrade an existing system
Install system with basic video driver
Rescue installed system
Boot from local drive
Memory test
```

Select the Rescue Installed System option and press ENTER. Rescue mode installs a stable minimal version of the RHEL 6 operating system on the local machine. It's in essence a console version of the "Live DVD" media available on other Linux distributions such as Knoppix, Ubuntu, and yes, even the Scientific Linux rebuild distribution. But none of those distributions will be available during a Red Hat exam. If you don't have access to a CD or DVD during an exam, that should mean that there's at least one method other than rescue mode for addressing a problem. However, practice from rescue mode can help you learn an intricate component such as GRUB.

on the
()ob

For RHEL 6, it's best to use RHEL 6 rescue media. Such media uses a kernel compiled by Red Hat, customized for supported software. Nevertheless, options such as Knoppix are excellent.

To that end, even unbootable systems can be started in the rescue environment. It is functionally nearly the same prompt as was available from the installation DVD in previous versions of RHEL. To get that boot prompt from the boot screen with the options just listed, press the ESC key at that screen.

The first couple of steps should be easily recognizable for anyone who has installed RHEL 6. Specifically, you're prompted to enter a language and keyboard type standard for the installation process. New for RHEL 6 is the step shown in Figure 5-3. It illustrates where the rescue image can be located. If the Red Hat installation DVD or network boot disk is installed, you can select Local CD/DVD. Alternatively, you can select a local or network location for an installation server as described in Chapter 1.

If you select a network location, the next step prompts for network configuration, just as was done during the network installation process described in Chapter 1. If you select a local location, the next step asks if you want to set up networking on the local system. Unless access to a remote installation server such as that set up in Chapter 1 is needed, that's generally not required.

FIGURE 5-3

Options for the
rescue image

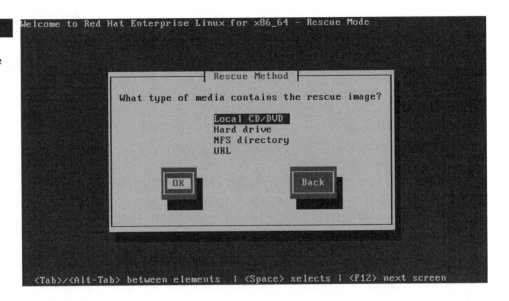

FIGURE 5-4

Options for
the rescue
environment

If the rescue environment detects more than one local Linux system, you may be prompted for the volume device of the desired top-level root directory. Some trial and error may be required at that point. As it's highly unlikely that there will be more than one RHEL system on the same drive for an exam, no further explanation will be provided. In most cases, the next step will be the choice shown in Figure 5-4.

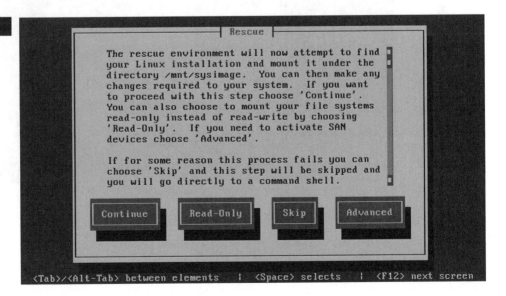

Generally, you'll choose Continue at this point. If you need to connect a network storage device, choose Advanced. Related devices such as iSCSI are described in Chapter 11. The Read-Only option mounts detected volumes in read-only mode. The Skip option moves straight to a command line interface.

The Continue option, as suggested in Figure 5-5, mounts all detected volumes as subdirectories of the /mnt/sysimage directory. After confirmation, you're given choices shown in Figure 5-6. The First Aid Kit quickstart menu includes diagnostics that may help recover some configuration files. But it is not included in the objectives for either exam. For now, just select Start Shell and press ENTER.

From the shell prompt, enter **chroot /mnt/sysimage** command. Since the regular top-level root directory for the system is mounted on the /mnt/sysimage directory, the **chroot** command mounts that filesystem as if the system were booted from a properly configured GRUB bootloader.

FIGURE 5-5

Rescue environment options for mounting

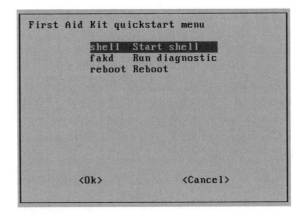

FIGURE 5-6

The First Aid Kit

CERTIFICATION OBJECTIVE 5.03

Between GRUB and Login

This section provides a basic overview of the boot process that occurs after the GRUB bootloader finds the kernel. Understanding what happens here can help you diagnose a wide variety of boot problems. The messages associated with the kernel provide a step-by-step view of the process.

The loading of Linux depends on a temporary filesystem, known as the initial RAM disk. Once the boot process is complete, control is given to init, known as the first process. Most Linux distributions, including RHEL 6, are converting from the old Unix init system, known as SysVinit to a system known as Upstart. This section will describe the contents of Upstart files in detail, through the configuration of terminals and login screens.

Also in the realm of the boot process are the commands that allow you to reboot and shut down a system normally.

Kernels and the Initial RAM Disk

Just a few messages after you select a kernel from the GRUB configuration menu, Linux hands over boot responsibilities to the kernel, with the help of a construct known as the initial RAM disk. It's actually a file system, as suggested by its filename in the /boot directory, initramfs.

That temporary filesystem is uncompressed within RAM. That filesystem is used to load information from key files such as the actual filesystems to be mounted from the /etc/fstab configuration file. It also loads init, as the first process.

To learn more, disable the **quiet** directive for the desired kernel in the GRUB configuration file. (Don't forget to restore it later.) Then you can watch as the messages pass quickly through the screen. Alternatively, you can reviews these messages in the /var/log/dmesg file or by running the **dmesg** command.

What you see depends on the hardware and configuration of the local system. Key messages include:

- The version of the kernel
- SELinux status, if active. By default, SELinux first starts in permissive mode, until the configured policy (enforcing) is loaded near the end of the boot process.
- Amount of recognized RAM (which does not necessarily match the actual amount of installed RAM)
- CPUs
- Kernel command line, specifying the logical volume or root filesystem label
- Freeing of memory associated with the initial RAM disk (initramfs)
- Hard drives and partitions (as defined by their device filenames, such as /dev /sda or /dev/vda1)
- Active filesystems
- Swap partitions

This file is filled with potential clues. If the system is loading the wrong kernel, you'll see evidence of that here. If Linux isn't using a partition that you've configured, you'll also see it here (indirectly). If SELinux isn't loading properly, you'll see it in messages toward the end of the file.

The First Process, Runlevels, and Services

The Linux kernel continues the boot process by calling the first process, **init**. The **init** process in turn runs /etc/rc.d/rc.sysinit, which performs a number of tasks, including network configuration, SELinux status, keyboard maps, system clock, partition mounts, and hostnames. It also loads the modules described in the previous section. It does even more: the default version of this file contains nearly 700 lines.

Through RHEL 5, **init** then used parameters configured in the /etc/inittab file. But that has changed. The /etc/inittab file now normally contains one line, which specifies the default runlevel.

```
id:5:initdefault:
```

As suggested by the comments at the start of /etc/inittab, there are seven available runlevels, 0 through 6. (There are actually a few other runlevels that may be used.) Linux services are organized by runlevel. Each runlevel is associated with a level of functionality. For example, in runlevel 1, only one user is allowed to connect to that Linux system. X11 mode, also known as runlevel 5, starts Linux into a GUI login screen, if appropriate packages are installed. As other Linux distributions define runlevels differently, the Red Hat definitions are shown in Table 5-2.

Runlevels are controlled by scripts, organized in runlevel-based directories. While the default runlevel is defined in /etc/inittab, you can override the default during the boot process from the GRUB menu.

One boot option described earlier in this chapter included the **single** command added to the end of the **kernel** directive during the boot process. It's different from the single-user mode associated with runlevel 1. As you'll see later in this chapter, there are scripts executed at each numbered runlevel.

TABLE 5-2	Runlevel	Description
Red Hat Runlevels	0	Halt
	1	Single-user mode, for maintenance and repair
	2	Multiuser, with some network services
	3	Multiuser, with networking
	4	Normally unused (but available)
	5	X11, defaults to a GUI login screen; logins bring the user to a GUI desktop, with networking
	6	Reboot (never set **initdefault** in /etc/inittab to this value)

In fact, each runlevel may be associated with a substantial number of scripts. Each script can start or stop Linux services such as printing (**cupsd**), scheduling (**crond**), the Apache web server (**httpd**), the Samba file server (**smbd**), and more. The starting and stopping of the right scripts becomes part of the boot process.

The default runlevel is specified in /etc/inittab by the **initdefault** directive. If that directive is set to 0, the system will shut down when Linux tries to boot. Likewise, if **initdefault** is set to **6**, Linux will enter a continuous reboot cycle.

Switch Between Runlevels

Now that you've examined the different runlevels available on RHEL 6, it's time to explore how to switch between runlevels. First, establish the current runlevel with the following command:

```
# runlevel
```

After a system is booted, the output that appears is normally something like:

```
N 5
```

That output refers to no previous runlevel (N), followed by the current runlevel (5). Now you can move to a different runlevel with the **init** or **telinit** command. While they're different commands, they're the same for our purposes. For example, the following command moves the system to runlevel 3:

```
# init 3
```

After that command is complete, rerun the runlevel command. The output confirms the result:

```
5 3
```

Now try something else. Since runlevel 0 is known as halt, what do you think happens when the following command is executed?

```
# telnint 0
```

Reboot and Shut Down a System Normally

RHEL 6 makes it easy to boot a system. Just power it up, and you're on your way. In contrast, you actually need to run a command to reboot or shut down a system. Both are straightforward. As just suggested in the previous section, the following commands are one way to shut down and reboot a system, respectively:

```
# init 0
# init 6
```

As with many things in Linux, there is more than one way to shut down and reboot a system. In fact, the commands associated with those very actions serve the purpose:

```
# shutdown
# reboot
```

Upstart Replaces SysVInit

As Upstart is designed as a "drop-in" replacement for the older SysVInit system, in one way, not much has changed. But the way these first files are organized has changed greatly. As you might expect, the Upstart system is associated with the upstart package. To see the files installed with that package, run the following command:

```
# rpm -ql upstart
```

Review this list of files. It starts with a connection to the ConsoleKit, which (among other things) tracks user interaction with administrative tools. It continues with a message bus connection to the files in the /etc/init directory, as defined by the init-system-dbus.conf file. It then includes those runlevel control commands that you should be familiar with, as shown in Table 5-3.

TABLE 5-3	Command	Description
Runlevel Control Commands	halt	Moves to runlevel 0, which shuts down the system
	init	Manages the current runlevel (different from the **init** daemon)
	initctl	Controls the **init** daemon
	poweroff	Moves to runlevel 0, which shuts down the system
	runlevel	Lists current and previous runlevel
	telinit	Manages the current runlevel

on the **Job**

Those of you familiar with the latest Ubuntu releases should recognize the Upstart system. Be aware, the RHEL 6 implementation of Upstart is quite different.

Upstart Configuration Files

The way the first process starts others during the boot process depends on various Upstart configuration files. As with many other services, it starts with the init file in the /etc/sysconfig directory. It continues with various files in the /etc/init directory. Many of the filenames in that directory are descriptive, such as control-alt-delete. conf. Once Upstart configuration is complete, the boot process continues with runlevel controls, as discussed later in this chapter.

Basic /etc/sysconfig/init Configuration

The parameters in the /etc/sysconfig/init file specify how the system looks and feels during the boot process. The directives in the default version of the file are described in Table 5-4.

TABLE 5-4		

Directives in
/etc/sysconfig/init

Directive	Description
BOOTUP	Supports a **color** or **verbose** display
RES_COL	Specifies column for status labels, such as [**OK**]
MOVE_TO_COL	Sets the column to where the cursor moves
SETCOLOR_SUCCESS	Specifies the color for a successful command
SETCOLOR_FAILURE	Specifies the color for a failed command
SETCOLOR_WARNING	Specifies the color for a warning message
SETCOLOR_RESET	Specifies the reset color
LOGLEVEL	Notes the initial log level, modified later by **rsyslog** daemon
PROMPT	Supports interactive startup
AUTOSWAP	Works with automatic swap device detection; not required
ACTIVE_CONSOLES	Sets standard command line consoles
SINGLE	Defines the login shell for single-user mode

/etc/init/control-alt-delete.conf

The control-alt-delete.conf file is straightforward, with two commands. First the following command listens for the combination of the noted keys:

```
start on control-alt-delete
```

The line that follows starts with an **exec**, which executes the command that follows. The **shutdown -r now** command reboots the local system immediately. While there is no warning, it does send the message noted in quotes:

```
exec /sbin/shutdown -r now "Control-Alt-Delete pressed"
```

If you prefer a delay before a reboot, substitute a number for the **now** switch. The number will be a time delay in the reboot process, in minutes.

/etc/init/init-system-dbus.conf

The comments at the start of the file describe its purpose: to connect the init process to the dbus server. In addition, it serves as the bridge between init and the configuration options in the other configuration files in the /etc/init directory. In other words, the following **kill** command listens for the dbus message bus and connects it to the process with a process identifier (PID) of 1.

```
exec /bin/kill -USR1 1
```

Plymouth files in /etc/init

Plymouth is the drop-in replacement for the Red Hat Graphical Boot (RHGB) system. While the **rhgb** directive is still used in the standard GRUB configuration file, RHGB-related packages are not used in RHEL 6. The **rhgb** directive now starts Plymouth splash screens. Three related files are normally stored in the /etc/init directory, which relate to what happens when the GUI stops:

- **plymouth-shutdown.conf** runs Plymouth splash screens as the system transitions from runlevel 5 to another runlevel.
- **splash-manager.conf** includes an appropriate message in the Plymouth splash screens when the system moves to runlevels 0 (halt) or 6 (reboot).
- **quit-plymouth.conf** quits the Plymouth service at the end of the boot process.

Readahead Files in /etc/init

The readahead system moves information from key files during the boot process into RAM, speeding access when needed. The files that are collected are in part defined in the /etc/sysconfig/readahead file. Three related files are normally stored in the /etc/init directory, which relate to what happens during the boot process:

- **readahead-collector.conf** uses the settings in /etc/sysconfig/readahead.
- **readahead-disable-services.conf** disables those services that can be trouble for readahead services; the only one disabled by default is the **audit** daemon associated with SELinux.
- **readahead.conf** actually starts the readahead process, assuming sufficient RAM is available.

Terminal Files in /etc/init

Linux systems can have serial and graphical-based terminals. They're configured, at least initially, by several files in the /etc/init directory. The prefdm.conf file is configured in runlevel 5 and is set up with the **respawn** command. In other words, if an X server crashes, say with the CTRL-ALT-BACKSPACE key combination, the **respawn** command restarts the GUI-based login screen, as defined in the /etc/X11/prefdm file. Four related files are normally stored in the /etc/init directory, which drive where and how terminals are started during the boot process.

- **prefdm.conf** starts and maintains the noted GUI login screen in runlevel 5.
- **start-ttys.conf** starts all terminals. Note how the X_TTY environment variable starts the GUI in the first virtual terminal. Pay attention to the **ACTIVE_CONSOLES** directive in the /etc/sysconfig/init file. Which one determines what virtual terminals get started?
- **tty.conf** refers to a "getty," which is another name for the standard command line terminal. Note how it is disabled in runlevels 0, 1, and 6, which corresponds to the halt, single-user, and reboot runlevels.
- **serial.conf** is used when there's a remote connection over a serial port.

Resource Control

In Linux, resource control relates to runlevels. Different scripts may be run in different runlevels; for example, if the default runlevel is 3, one of these files makes sure that the scripts in the /etc/rc3.d directory are executed during the boot process.

Four related files are normally stored in the /etc/init directory, based on the default runlevel defined in /etc/inittab:

- **rcS.conf** runs the /etc/rc.d/rc.sysinit script only during the boot process.
- **rcS-sulogin.conf** starts the use of a terminal in single-user mode, and then moves to the standard runlevel.
- **rc.conf** executes the scripts in the runlevel; it can be defined in /etc/inittab or the **init/telinit** commands. The executed scripts are in the /etc/rcn.d/ directory, where *n* is the runlevel.

Terminals and Login Screens

The login terminals in Linux are virtual consoles. Most Linux systems, including RHEL 6, are configured with six standard command line virtual consoles. These consoles are numbered from 1 to 6. When configured with a GUI and a login manager, other Linux distributions include a seventh virtual console, with a graphical login screen. That's one place where RHEL 6 is a bit different, as in most cases, it substitutes the graphical login screen for the first virtual console. That applies just for the graphical login screen. If you start the GUI with the **startx** command, the GUI is run in the seventh virtual console.

What does that all mean? In Linux, you can switch between virtual consoles with an ALT-function key combination. For example, ALT-F2 brings you to the second virtual console. You can switch between adjacent virtual consoles by pressing ALT-RIGHT ARROW or ALT-LEFT ARROW. For example, to move from virtual console 2 to virtual console 3, press ALT-RIGHT ARROW. If you're in a GUI virtual console, add the CTRL key. So in RHEL 6, if the GUI is installed and you're in the first virtual console, you'd have to press CTRL-ALT-F2 to get to the second virtual console.

When you log in to a regular virtual console, Linux returns a command line shell. The default shell is defined in the /etc/passwd file described in Chapter 6. When you log in to a GUI virtual console, Linux returns the configured GUI desktop. For more information on the Linux GUI, see Chapter 8.

Through RHEL 5, virtual consoles were configured in /etc/inittab. Now that Upstart has replaced SysVinit, virtual consoles are configured in files in /etc/sysconfig /init and the /etc/init directory, as described earlier in this chapter.

Virtual consoles really bring the multiuser capabilities of Linux to life. At work (or during a Red Hat exam), you might review a man page on one console, compile a program in another, and edit a configuration file in a third virtual console. Other users who are connected through a network can do the same thing at the same time.

CERTIFICATION OBJECTIVE 5.04

Control by Runlevel

Despite the aforementioned move from SysVinit to Upstart, Linux is still focused on the runlevel. The management of services is customized by runlevel. As Upstart includes the same functional commands as SysVinit, you can still control the current runlevel with commands like **init** and **telinit**.

Linux is highly customizable. So it makes sense that the services that start in each runlevel can be customized. Of course, even the scripts themselves can be customized, if you wish to go so far. While GUI tools are available to help customize scripts, it is generally a lot faster to customize them from the command line interface.

Functionality by Runlevel

As described earlier, the basic functionality of each runlevel is listed in the /etc/inittab file, as listed in Table 5-2. But those are just general descriptions. Actual functionality is determined by the scripts run at each runlevel. And that's highly customizable. For example, while runlevel 4 is normally not used in RHEL 6, there's nothing preventing you from setting up a custom group of services in that runlevel. Per the /etc/init/rc.conf file, the following command is executed during the boot process:

```
exec /etc/rc.d/rc $RUNLEVEL
```

Take a look at that file, rc in the /etc/rc.d directory. With the following command, it looks for a directory associated with the runlevel:

```
[ -d /etc/rc$runlevel.d ] || exit 0
```

In other words, if the default runlevel is 3, it looks to see if the /etc/rc3.d directory exists. It should exist on any standard RHEL 6 system. Take a quick look at the files in that directory. One sample is shown in Figure 5-7.

Take a look at the scripts in other runlevels. Run the following commands:

```
# ls /etc/rc0.d
# ls /etc/rc1.d
# ls /etc/rc2.d
# ls /etc/rc3.d
# ls /etc/rc4.d
# ls /etc/rc5.d
# ls /etc/rc6.d
```

FIGURE 5-7

Scripts in
runlevel 3

```
[root@server1 init]# \ls /etc/rc3.d/
K01certmonger   K80lldpad          S11auditd          S26haldaemon
K01smartd       K80sssd            S12rsyslog         S26udev-post
K02oddjobd      K84wpa_supplicant  S13cpuspeed        S28autofs
K10psacct       K86cgred           S13irqbalance      S50bluetooth
K10saslauthd    K87multipathd      S13iscsi           S55sshd
K15httpd        K87restorecond     S13rpcbind         S80postfix
K35vncserver    K88nslcd           S15mdmonitor       S82abrtd
K50dnsmasq      K89rdisc           S20kdump           S90crond
K50netconsole   S00microcode_ctl   S22messagebus      S95atd
K60nfs          S01sysstat         S23NetworkManager  S97libvirtd
K69rpcsvcgssd   S02lvm2-monitor    S24avahi-daemon    S97rhnsd
K73ypbind       S05cgconfig        S24nfslock         S98libvirt-guests
K74nscd         S07iscsid          S24rpcgssd         S99firstboot
K74ntpd         S08ip6tables       S24rpcidmapd       S99local
K75ntpdate      S08iptables        S25netfs
K80fcoe         S10network         S26acpid
[root@server1 init]#
```

Do you notice any patterns? What are the filenames of the scripts that are started in runlevels 0 and 6? You should discover script filenames that match the documented functionality of that runlevel, such as S01halt and S01reboot.

Now return to the /etc/rc.d/rc file. Slightly later in the file, you can find a loop that starts with the following command:

```
for i in /etc/rc$runlevel.d/K* ; do
```

That command takes the scripts that start with a *K*, in numeric order. In other words, based on Figure 5-7, the K01certmonger script is run first, and the K89rdisc script is run last. Now run the **ls -l** command on the /etc/rc3.d directory. You'll see links to scripts of the same name (without the *K* and the number) in the /etc/init.d directory.

Now examine the next stanza in the /etc/rc.d/rc file. You'll see a loop that starts with the following command:

```
for i in /etc/rc$runlevel.d/S* ; do
```

Based on the files shown in Figure 5-7, the S01sysstat script is run first, and the S99local script is run last. As suggested by the other commands in the stanza, those scripts are started, using their links to the actual scripts in the /etc/init.d directory.

Now it's time to take a look at the innards of runlevel scripts, as many of them can do more than just start and stop a service.

The Innards of Runlevel Scripts

Runlevel scripts are executed whenever a system moves to a different runlevel. So the scripts associated with the default runlevel are executed during the boot process. Appropriate scripts are also executed when you change runlevels; for example, when you run the **init 3** command, Linux executes the scripts in the /etc/rc3.d directory.

But administrators like yourself can control Linux scripts directly. As noted earlier, scripts in directories such as /etc/rc3.d are linked to the actual scripts in the /etc/init.d directory. Take some time to look at these scripts. As an example, scan the /etc/init.d/sshd script. The second active line pulls in configuration options from the /etc/sysconfig/sshd file. Much of the rest of the script describes actions associated with command options, as summarized by the **echo** directive. Exit the script and run the following command:

```
# /etc/init.d/sshd
```

It should return the following output, straight from the **echo** directive:

```
Usage: /etc/init.d/sshd {start|stop|restart|reload|force-reload|condrestart|try-
restart|status}
```

In other words, the following command stops the Secure Shell (SSH) service:

```
# /etc/init.d/sshd stop
```

Alternatively, the service command can be used with the noted options; for example, the following command reloads the SSH configuration file without stopping or starting the service:

```
# service sshd reload
```

The options shown from the SSH service are described in Table 5-5.

Service Configuration from the Command Line

It's generally fastest to control services at the command line. The **chkconfig** command gives you a simple way to maintain different runlevels within the /etc/rc.d directory structure. First, try the **chkconfig --list** command. As shown in Figure 5-8, you'll see the whole list of services in the /etc/init.d directory, along with their normal status in all seven runlevels.

But the **chkconfig** command can do more. With that command, you can add, remove, and change services; list startup information; and check the state of a

TABLE 5-5	Command	Description
Service Control Commands	start	Starts the service if it's currently not running
	stop	Stops the service if it is currently running
	restart	Stops and then restarts the service
	reload	If the service is currently running, it loads the current version of the configuration file(s) with any changes. The service is not stopped, users who have previously connected are not kicked off
	force-reload	Restarts a service if it's already running; otherwise, makes sure the new service is started with the latest version of a configuration file
	condrestart	Stops and then restarts the service, only if it is already running
	try-restart	Same as condrestart
	status	Lists the current operational status of the service

particular service. For example, the following command checks the runlevels where the Postfix service is set to start:

```
# chkconfig --list postfix
postfix 0:off 1:off 2:on 3:on 4:on 5:on 6:off
```

FIGURE 5-8

Service status by runlevel

```
nslcd          0:off  1:off  2:off  3:off  4:off  5:off  6:off
ntpd           0:off  1:off  2:off  3:off  4:off  5:off  6:off
ntpdate        0:off  1:off  2:off  3:off  4:off  5:off  6:off
oddjobd        0:off  1:off  2:off  3:off  4:off  5:off  6:off
postfix        0:off  1:off  2:on   3:on   4:on   5:on   6:off
psacct         0:off  1:off  2:off  3:off  4:off  5:off  6:off
rdisc          0:off  1:off  2:off  3:off  4:off  5:off  6:off
restorecond    0:off  1:off  2:off  3:off  4:off  5:off  6:off
rhnsd          0:off  1:off  2:on   3:on   4:on   5:on   6:off
rpcbind        0:off  1:off  2:on   3:on   4:on   5:on   6:off
rpcgssd        0:off  1:off  2:off  3:on   4:on   5:on   6:off
rpcidmapd      0:off  1:off  2:off  3:on   4:on   5:on   6:off
rpcsvcgssd     0:off  1:off  2:off  3:off  4:off  5:off  6:off
rsyslog        0:off  1:off  2:on   3:on   4:on   5:on   6:off
saslauthd      0:off  1:off  2:off  3:off  4:off  5:off  6:off
smartd         0:off  1:off  2:off  3:off  4:off  5:off  6:off
sshd           0:off  1:off  2:on   3:on   4:on   5:on   6:off
sssd           0:off  1:off  2:off  3:off  4:off  5:off  6:off
sysstat        0:off  1:on   2:on   3:on   4:on   5:on   6:off
udev-post      0:off  1:on   2:on   3:on   4:on   5:on   6:off
vncserver      0:off  1:off  2:off  3:off  4:off  5:off  6:off
wpa_supplicant 0:off  1:off  2:off  3:off  4:off  5:off  6:off
ypbind         0:off  1:off  2:off  3:off  4:off  5:off  6:off
[michael@server1 ~]$
```

This indicates that the Postfix e-mail server is configured to start in runlevels 2, 3, 4, and 5. If you want to make sure the Postfix service does not start in runlevel 4, execute the following command:

```
# chkconfig --level 4 postfix off
```

Run the **chkconfig --list postfix** command again to confirm the change. Now Postfix is configured to run only on runlevels 2, 3, and 5. To turn it back on for runlevel 4, run the same command, substituting **on** for **off**. With **chkconfig**, you can also add or delete services with the **--add** and **--del** switches. Installing a service sets up the appropriate links within the /etc/rc.d directory hierarchy. Uninstalling that service removes the associated links from the same hierarchy.

The commands need not even be that complex. If you leave out the runlevel, the following commands automatically deactivate the Postfix service in all runlevels and then activate it in runlevels 2, 3, 4, and 5:

```
# chkconfig postfix off
# chkconfig postfix on
```

The Text Console Service Configuration Tool

If you're managing a substantial number of services, the command line might not be quite so efficient. You don't need a GUI, just the **ntsysv** tool, which can be started with the command of the same name. However, it's a bit tricky; by default, it only changes the status of selected services in the current runlevel.

But you can do more. For example, to activate several services in runlevels 2, 3, 4, and 5, start **ntsysv** with the following command (don't forget the double-dash):

```
# ntsysv --level 2345
```

For this section, I've started **ntsysv** with the noted command and disabled the bluetooth service, as shown in Figure 5-9.

Once changes are complete, you can check the result with the following command:

```
# chkconfig --list bluetooth
bluetooth 0:off 1:off 2:off 3:off 4:off 5:off 6:off
```

You should also be able to confirm the changes in appropriate runlevel directories. For example, before the bluetooth service was deactivated, the following file was available for runlevel 3:

```
S50bluetooth
```

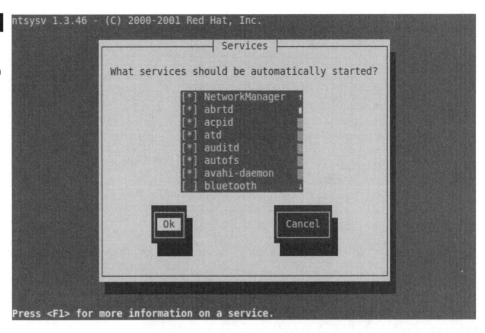

FIGURE 5-9

Service
management with
ntsysv

After the noted changes were made, the S50bluetooth file was replaced with the
following:

```
K83bluetooth
```

The GUI Service Configuration Tool

The Service Configuration tool shown in Figure 5-10 allows you to select the
services that are to be activated in runlevels 2 through 5. One way to start it is from
a command line in the GUI with the **system-config-services** command. The options
are fairly self-explanatory. Click Customize for a list of runlevels affected by any
changes made through this tool.

FIGURE 5-10

The Service
Configuration
tool

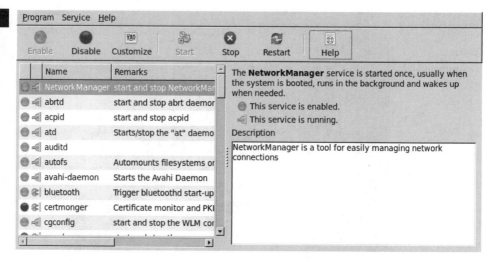

CERTIFICATION OBJECTIVE 5.05

Network Configuration

Network configuration is a key element in the administration of RHEL 6 and the Red Hat exams. Red Hat sets up a number of key configuration files in the /etc/sysconfig directory. Other configuration files such as /etc/resolv.conf and even /etc/hosts are also important. You can configure them with a text editor or different configuration tools.

But before making any permanent changes to configuration files, such changes should be tested with configuration commands. And Linux includes a number of commands that can help configure temporary changes to the network configuration of a system.

It's important to learn the configuration files in the /etc/sysconfig/network-scripts, /etc/sysconfig, and /etc directories. These are crucial to the network configuration of RHEL 6. If you have a network problem, a permanent solution probably involves changing files in one of these directories.

Network Configuration Commands

From the command line, you can reconfigure the network in a number of ways. The **ifup** and **ifdown** commands can activate and deactivate network devices. The **ifconfig** command supports detailed changes to individual network devices. The **route** command supports review of and changes to routing tables.

ifup/ifdown

You can activate or deactivate the adapter of your choice with the **ifup** and **ifdown** commands. For example, either of the following commands will activate the eth0 network adapter. The eth0 device is the standard for the first Ethernet adapter on a system.

```
ifup ifcfg-eth0
ifup eth0
```

As might be expected, you can reverse the process by substituting the **ifdown** command. Each installed network adapter has a corresponding ifcfg-* file in the /etc/sysconfig/network-scripts directory. When the **ifup** command is used, it starts the given network adapter based on its configuration file in that directory.

ifconfig

The **ifconfig** command is powerful in the area of network configuration. By itself, it lists all currently active network adapters. It can also be used to configure and display network devices. One sample output is shown in Figure 5-11.

The output shown reflects a typical configuration on most systems, with a loopback and a real network adapter, as labeled by their device filenames, lo and eth0, respectively. The loopback adapter supports network tests when a real network connection is not available.

Some systems have a number of network adapters. For example, my home server has two Ethernet cards, a loopback adapter, a virtual bridge to KVM virtual machines, and two virtual bridges to VMware virtual machines. That's six network adapters. But that may not be everything; the **ifconfig** command lists only active adapters by default. To see the full list, run the **ifconfig -a** command.

It may help to isolate a specific adapter; for example, the following command isolates settings associated with the first Ethernet adapter:

```
# ifconfig eth0
```

FIGURE 5-11

The ifconfig
command

```
[root@server1 ~]# ifconfig
eth0      Link encap:Ethernet  HWaddr 52:54:00:55:D0:A2
          inet addr:192.168.122.50  Bcast:192.168.122.255  Mask:255.255.255.0
          inet6 addr: fe80::5054:ff:fe55:d0a2/64 Scope:Link
          UP BROADCAST RUNNING MULTICAST  MTU:1500  Metric:1
          RX packets:16895 errors:0 dropped:0 overruns:0 frame:0
          TX packets:15364 errors:0 dropped:0 overruns:0 carrier:0
          collisions:0 txqueuelen:1000
          RX bytes:5725595 (5.4 MiB)  TX bytes:6162800 (5.8 MiB)

lo        Link encap:Local Loopback
          inet addr:127.0.0.1  Mask:255.0.0.0
          inet6 addr: ::1/128 Scope:Host
          UP LOOPBACK RUNNING  MTU:16436  Metric:1
          RX packets:15889 errors:0 dropped:0 overruns:0 frame:0
          TX packets:15889 errors:0 dropped:0 overruns:0 carrier:0
          collisions:0 txqueuelen:0
          RX bytes:9089760 (8.6 MiB)  TX bytes:9089760 (8.6 MiB)

[root@server1 ~]#
```

The **ifconfig** command can also be used to configure network interfaces. For example, you can assign a new IP address for eth0 with the following command:

```
# ifconfig eth0 192.168.122.250
```

The first parameter, **eth0**, tells you which interface is being configured. The next argument, **192.168.122.250**, indicates the new IP address being assigned to this interface. To make sure the change worked, issue the **ifconfig** command again (with the name of the adapter device) to view its current settings.

With the right switch, the **ifconfig** command can modify a number of other settings for your network adapter. Some of these switches are shown in Table 5-6.

Of course, you'll want to make sure the changes survive a reboot, whether it be for the exam or for a server that you want to administer remotely. That depends on appropriate changes to configuration files in the /etc/sysconfig/network-scripts directory, described shortly. And any changes made with the ifconfig command are, by definition, temporary.

TABLE 5-6	Switch	Description
Command Switches for ifconfig	up	Activates the specified adapter.
	down	Deactivates the specified adapter.
	netmask *address*	Assigns the *address* subnet mask.
	broadcast *address*	Assigns the *address* as the broadcast address. Rarely required, since the default broadcast address is standard for most current networks.
	metric **N**	Allows you to set a metric value of *N* for the routing table associated with the network adapter.
	mtu **N**	Sets the maximum transmission unit as *N*, in bytes.
	-arp	Deactivates the Address Resolution Protocol, which collects network adapter hardware addresses.
	promisc	Activates promiscuous mode. This allows the network adapter to read all packets to all hosts on the LAN. Can be used to analyze the network for problems or to try to decipher messages between other users.
	-promisc	Deactivates promiscuous mode.

Routing Tables with route or netstat -r

The **netstat** command is used to display a plethora of network connectivity information. The most commonly used option, **netstat -r**, is used to display local routing tables. Here's a sample **netstat -nr** output:

```
# netstat -nr
Kernel routing table
Destination    Gateway       Genmask        Flags MSS Window  irtt Iface
192.168.122.0  0.0.0.0       255.255.255.0  U     40  0          0 eth0
0.0.0.0        192.168.122.1 0.0.0.0        UG    40  0          0 eth0
```

Did you notice the use of the **-n** flag? **-n** tells **netstat** to display addresses as IP addresses, instead of as hostnames. This makes it a little easier to see what's going on. One equivalent option is the **route -n** command.

The Destination column lists networks by their IP addresses. The *default* destination is associated with all other IP addresses. The Gateway column indicates gateway addresses. If the destination is on the LAN, no gateway is required, so 0.0.0.0 is shown in this column. The Genmask column lists the network mask. Networks look for a route appropriate to the destination IP address. The IP address is compared against the destination networks, in order. When the IP address is found to be part of one of these networks, it's sent in that direction. If there is a gateway address, it's sent to the computer with that gateway. If you know IPv4 addresses, you should remember that 0.0.0.0 is the default IP address. In other words, all data that isn't going to the 192.168.122.0 network is sent through that network's gateway IPv4 address, 192.168.122.1.

The **netstat** and **route** commands do have different purposes. For example, the **route** command can also add routes. For systems with only one network adapter, the following command adds a default route over the aforementioned network gateway IP address. If desired, you can substitute **0.0.0.0** for **default**.

```
# route add default gw 192.168.122.1
```

Of course, you may want to set up a route to a specific network through a specific device. The following command sets up a route to the noted network/subnet mask combination through the second Ethernet device:

```
# route add -net 192.168.100.0 netmask 255.255.255.0 dev eth1
```

The **netstat** command can do more. With the right combination of switches, it can help identify open services on the local system. One command I like to use to assess potential vulnerabilities of a Linux system is:

```
# netstat -atunp
```

where the **netstat** command listens for all (**-a**) network connections, using both the TCP (**-t**) and UDP (**-u**) protocols, in numeric (**-n**) format, with the PID and program associated with each line. Figure 5-12 illustrates the output on the baseline server.

In the middle of the output, note the Foreign Address of 192.168.122.1:48092. The 48092 port number is just the return communications port. The corresponding Local Address of 192.168.122.50:22 specifies a port number 22 for a connection from the system at 192.168.122.1. Near the top of the file, there's a second entry with the same PID that identifies the associated SSH daemon (sshd) connection. Other lines in this output identify other open services, which may or may not be blocked by firewalls and more, as discussed in Chapters 4 and 10.

FIGURE 5-12	Output from the netstat -atunp command

```
[root@server1 ~]# netstat -atunp
Active Internet connections (servers and established)
Proto Recv-Q Send-Q Local Address           Foreign Address         State       PID/Program name
tcp        0      0 0.0.0.0:44742           0.0.0.0:*               LISTEN      1320/rpc.statd
tcp        0      0 0.0.0.0:111             0.0.0.0:*               LISTEN      1212/rpcbind
tcp        0      0 0.0.0.0:22              0.0.0.0:*               LISTEN      15993/sshd
tcp        0      0 127.0.0.1:25            0.0.0.0:*               LISTEN      1574/master
tcp        0      0 127.0.0.1:6010          0.0.0.0:*               LISTEN      16304/0
tcp        0      0 192.168.122.50:22       192.168.122.1:48092     ESTABLISHED 16304/0
tcp        0      0 :::44907                :::*                    LISTEN      1320/rpc.statd
tcp        0      0 :::111                  :::*                    LISTEN      1212/rpcbind
tcp        0      0 :::22                   :::*                    LISTEN      15993/sshd
tcp        0      0 ::1:6010                :::*                    LISTEN      16304/0
udp        0      0 0.0.0.0:648             0.0.0.0:*                           1320/rpc.statd
udp        0      0 0.0.0.0:42020           0.0.0.0:*                           1320/rpc.statd
udp        0      0 0.0.0.0:963             0.0.0.0:*                           1212/rpcbind
udp        0      0 0.0.0.0:5353            0.0.0.0:*                           1291/avahi-daemon:
udp        0      0 0.0.0.0:111             0.0.0.0:*                           1212/rpcbind
udp        0      0 0.0.0.0:33915           0.0.0.0:*                           1291/avahi-daemon:
udp        0      0 :::963                  :::*                                1212/rpcbind
udp        0      0 :::60636                :::*                                1320/rpc.statd
udp        0      0 :::111                  :::*                                1212/rpcbind
[root@server1 ~]#
```

arp as a Diagnostic Tool

The Address Resolution Protocol associates the hardware address of a network adapter with an IP address. The **arp** command displays a table of hardware and IP addresses on the local computer. With **arp**, you can detect problems such as duplicate addresses on the network, or you can manually add **arp** entries as required. Here's a sample **arp** command, showing all **arp** entries in the local database:

```
# arp
Address              HWtype  HWaddress            Flags Mask         Iface
192.168.0.121        ether   52:A5:CB:54:52:A2    C                  eth0
192.168.0.113        ether   00:A0:C5:E2:49:02    C                  eth0
```

If the **arp** table is empty, there are no recent connections to other computers on the local network. The Address column lists known IP addresses, usually on the LAN. The HWtype column shows the hardware type of the adapter, while the HWaddress column shows the hardware address of the adapter.

The **arp** command can help you with duplicate IP addresses, which can stop a network completely. To remove the offending machine's **arp** entry from your **arp** table, use the **-d** option:

```
# arp -d bugsy
```

This removes all **arp** information for the host bugsy. To add an **arp** entry, use the **-s** option:

```
# arp -s bugsy 00:00:c0:cf:a1:33
```

This entry will add the host bugsy with the given hardware address to the **arp** table. Hardware addresses are required; IP addresses won't work in this case.

Dynamic Host Configuration Protocol (DHCP) Clients

If the local system is set up as a Dynamic Host Configuration Protocol (DHCP) client, it should be noted as such in the associated configuration file for the network card, described shortly. Even if a system is configured with static IP address information, it can be reconfigured with the appropriate DHCP client, the **dhclient** command.

Of course, if other systems depend on a definitive static IP address, the use of the **dhclient** command can cause trouble. For example, other systems may not be able to find key servers on that system.

Network Configuration Files

The network configuration file that provides the foundation for RHEL 6 networking is /etc/sysconfig/network. It can contain up to six directives, as described in Table 5-7. If a directive from that table does not appear in the /etc/sysconfig/network file, the directive does not apply. For example, if you don't see the **GATEWAYDEV** directive, there's probably only one network card on the local system.

TABLE 5-7	Directive	Description
/etc/sysconfig /network Directives	NETWORKING	Can be yes or no, to configure or not configure networking.
	NETWORKING_IPV6	Can be yes or no, to configure networking under IPv6.
	NISDOMAIN	Should be set to the name of the NIS domain, if the local system is connected to an NIS network.
	HOSTNAME	Sets the hostname of the local computer. If you don't see this directive, it may be set by a DHCP server.
	GATEWAY	Sets the IP address for the gateway for your network. If you don't see this directive, it may be set by a DHCP server.
	GATEWAYDEV	Sets the network device, such as eth0, that this computer uses to reach a gateway. There's no need for this directive if there's only one network card.

In most cases, /etc/sysconfig/network contains at least two directives:

```
NETWORKING=yes
HOSTNAME=yourhostname
```

There is no requirement for the other directives shown in Table 5-7, including an NIS domain, for IPv6 networking, and a gateway address. Some of these directives, including the **HOSTNAME**, may be set by the DHCP server.

The /etc/sysconfig/network-scripts Files

The /etc/sysconfig/network-scripts directory is where Red Hat Enterprise Linux stores and retrieves networking information. With available Red Hat configuration tools, you don't have to touch these files, but it's good to know they're there. A few representative files are shown in Table 5-8.

Some of the commands in /etc/sysconfig/network-scripts may be hard-linked to files in the /etc/sysconfig/networking/devices and /etc/sysconfig/networking/ profiles/default directories.

TABLE 5-8	File in /etc/sysconfig/network-scripts	Description
/etc/sysconfig /network-scripts Files	ifcfg-lo	Configures the loopback device, a virtual device that confirms proper installation of TCP/IP.
	ifcfg-*	Each installed network adapter, such as eth0, gets its own ifcfg-* script. For example, eth0 is given file ifcfg-eth0. If the NetworkManager is used, it may be ifcfg-System_eth0. This file includes the IP address information required to identify this network adapter on a network.
	network-functions	This script contains functions used by other network scripts to bring network interfaces up and down.
	ifup-* and ifdown-*	These scripts activate and deactivate their assigned protocols. For example, **ifup-ppp** brings up a PPP device, usually a telephone modem.

Now take a look at an ifcfg-eth0 file. Based on the static network configuration defined in Chapter 2, the associated directives are:

```
DEVICE="eth0"
BOOTPROTO="static"
BROADCAST="192.168.122.255"
DNS1="192.168.122.1"
GATEWAY="192.168.122.1"
HWADDR="52:54:00:55:D0:A2"
IPADDR="192.168.122.50"
NETMASK="255.255.255.0"
NM_CONTROLLED="yes"
ONBOOT="yes"
```

Most of these directives are straightforward, as they define the device as the first Ethernet network card (eth0), with static networking, using a defined IP address for broadcast, a DNS server, the network gateway, the network card, and the network mask. Note that the hardware address of the network card shown here matches the hardware address defined in Figure 5-11. Yes, this eth0 network card is enabled during the Linux boot process.

One directive shown is extra cryptic: **NM_CONTROLLED**. That directive specifies whether the card can be configured and controlled with the Red Hat Network Manager. It's a terrific convenience for desktop users with multiple network connections, but it's less important for servers with single stable physical network connections.

Red Hat Configuration Tools

As with many other Red Hat configuration tools, there's a console and a graphical tool available. The console tool, naturally, can be run from text consoles. To open it, run the **system-config-network-tui** command. It's the same tool accessible from the **setup** command at the console; in either case, it starts an easily configurable Network Configuration tool shown in Figure 5-13.

With RHEL 6, the NetworkManager service replaces the Network Administration Tool. Not only does that mean the GUI configuration tool has changed, it also means the GUI tool is not installed by default. To use the GUI NetworkManager configuration tool, you may need to first install the associated package with the following command:

```
# yum install NetworkManager-gnome
```

FIGURE 5-13

The Console
Network
Configuration
tool

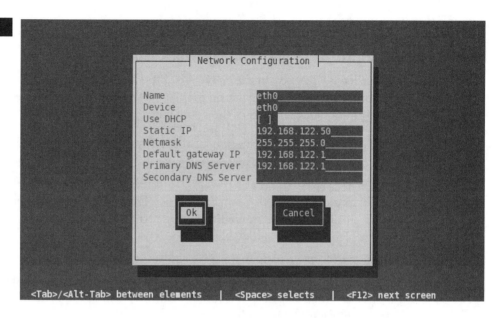

You can then start the GUI Network Connections tool shown in Figure 5-14 with the following command:

```
# nm-connection-editor
```

FIGURE 5-14

Network
Connections tool

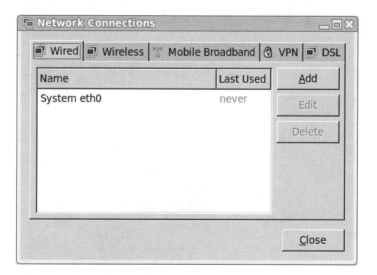

EXERCISE 5-3

Modify Network Interfaces with the Network Connections Tool

This exercise depends on the active use of the NetworkManager service and the accompanying GUI configuration tool. You'll see what's added to the key configuration file, courtesy of the noted tool.

1. Back up the configuration for the network card to be changed. If it's the first Ethernet card, back up the ifcfg-eth0 file from the /etc/sysconfig/network-scripts directory. Make sure a copy of the file exists in both directories.

2. Start the Network Connections tool. From a GUI terminal, press ALT-F2, and enter **nm-connection-editor** in the text box that appears. This opens the Network Connections tool.

3. Select the Wired tab if it isn't already active.

4. Select the adapter that you want to modify, and then click Edit. If it is an Ethernet adapter, you'll see an Editing System window similar to the one shown in the next illustration.

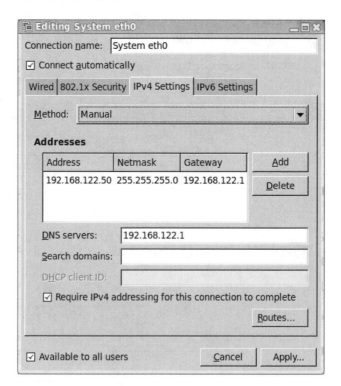

5. Select the IPv4 Settings tab. Highlight the current IP address, and then click Delete to remove the current IP address information. Click Add. Set an IP address to **192.168.1.11** and the network mask (Subnet Mask) to **255.255.255.0**. (If needed, substitute a different IP address to isolate this system from the local network.)

6. Click Apply. If prompted, enter the root administrative password. Back in the Network Connections tool window, click Close.

7. At the command prompt, run **ifconfig** from a command line interface to check the IP address settings of the target network card. Did anything happen?

8. Review the contents of the revised network configuration file. If it's the first Ethernet card, the filename includes the terms ifcfg and eth0 in the /etc/sysconfig/network-scripts directory. Are the changes reflected there? If the filename had changed, then it's likely that you forgot to save a copy of the ifcfg-eth0 file in the noted directory.

9. Run the **ifdown eth0** and **ifup eth0** commands to apply the changes from the new version of the ifcfg-eth0 file.

10. Rerun the **ifconfig** command to make sure it worked.

11. Compare the original and new versions of the configuration file. You could open them up in matching terminals, or apply the **diff** command.

12. What are the differences? Besides the different IP address information, what else was added by the Network Connections tool? The additional directives should be straightforward. Note how the Network Connections tool added a UUID to uniquely identify the configuration.

13. Restore the original version of the configuration file for the associated network card; if it's the first Ethernet card, it's ifcfg-eth0. If you forgot to save the ifcfg-eth0 file in the noted directory, it might now be named ifcfg-System_eth0.

---

e**x**a m

ⓦ a t c h *If you want to use the Network Connections tool during the exam, make sure you know the tool inside-out. Make sure you know how to install* *it. Experiment with the available options. Make some changes, and check the effect on the files I've described.*

Configure Name Resolution

The final piece in network configuration is typically name resolution. In other words, does the local system have the information required to translate domain names such as mcgraw-hill.com to IP addresses such as 198.45.24.143?

Name resolution was easy when Unix was first being developed. When the predecessor to the Internet was first put into use, the worldwide computer network had four hosts, one computer at each of four different universities. It was easy to set up a static file with a list of each of their names and corresponding addresses. That file has evolved into what is known in Linux as /etc/hosts.

But now the Internet is more complex. While you could try to set up a database of every domain name and IP address on the Internet in the /etc/hosts file, that would take almost forever. That's why most users set up connections to DNS, Domain Name Service, servers. On RHEL 6, that's still documented in the /etc/resolv.conf configuration file. On the baseline system created in Chapter 2, that file contains two lines:

```
search example.com
nameserver 192.168.122.1
```

The first line appends the example.com domain to given hostnames; for example, if you were to run the **ping** command on the server1 system, it would actually search for the server1.example.com system. The second line specifies the IP address associated with the local DNS server. As an RHCE, you need to know how to configure a caching-only DNS server; that subject is covered in Chapter 17. DNS server configuration is not an RHCSA requirement.

On smaller networks, some administrators set up an /etc/hosts file as a database for the name of each system and IP address on the local network. If desired, administrators could even set up a few IP addresses of domains on the Internet. For the systems described in earlier chapters, an appropriate /etc/hosts file might contain the following directives:

```
192.168.122.50 server1.example.com
192.168.122.150 tester1.example.com
192.168.100.100 outsider1.example.org
```

But if you've configured a connection to a DNS server and systems in /etc/hosts, what's searched first? The search order is specified by one line in the /etc/nsswitch. conf configuration file, which searches for hostnames first in local files (/etc/hosts) followed by any accessible DNS servers.

```
hosts:   files dns
```

EXERCISE 5-4

Revise Network Interfaces on a Cloned System

Now that you know something of networking on a RHEL system, you're ready to modify the network interfaces on a cloned system. Since cloned systems originally have the same network interfaces as the original, they should be changed before they're connected to a local network. Otherwise, there will be two systems on the same network, declaring their ownership of the same IP addresses. And that would be trouble for both systems.

These instructions assume that you want to set up the cloned system as the outsider1.example.org system described in Chapter 1, with an IP address of 192.168.100.100, on the 192.168.100.0/24 network. If an outsider1.example.org system already exists, you can substitute a different system name on a different IP address. (Some home network devices such as cable modems are configured on the 192.168.100.0 network. In that case, you may need to use a different network address.)

If you've set up a cloned system on a virtual machine such as KVM, the first steps involve deleting the current network card and creating a new network card. As this book is modeled on KVM-based virtual machines, the steps are based on that system. While not tested, the same principles should help you reconfigure networking on a cloned system on a different type of virtual machine such as KVM.

1. Open the Virtual Machine Manager with the **virt-manager** command.

2. Connect to the system with the target virtual machines, normally **localhost (QEMU)**.

3. Click Edit | Host Details, and click the Virtual Networks tab.

4. Select Add (which may be a plus sign). Follow the prompts to create the new virtual network, including the IP address range given. Call this the **outside** network (or another name of your choice). Do not delete the current default network; both networks are required. Traffic between the two networks can be routed through the physical host system.

5. Configure the system to forward information to the physical network, using Network Address Translation (NAT). The result should look like the illustration.

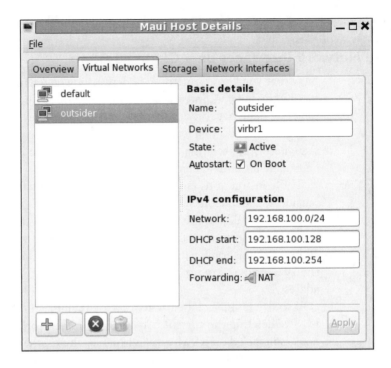

6. Return to the main Virtual Machine Manager window. Select the cloned system. Click View | Details.

7. Select the current network device and click Remove.

8. Click Add Hardware, select the Network hardware type, select the outside network, and create the new network card.

9. Click View | Console. Boot the cloned system into runlevel 1, which should not start networking.

10. Edit the /etc/sysconfig/network file. Be sure to make a change to the **HOSTNAME** directive, in this case, to outsider1.example.org.

11. Examine the /etc/sysconfig/network-scripts/ifcfg-eth0 file. Don't make any changes yet. Since you've changed network cards, the system will detect it and use the next available network device.

12. Move to runlevel 3 with a command like **telinit 3**. Unless you've made some unusual changes, that should start networking.

13. Run the **ifconfig -a** command. It'll display the detected Ethernet device, along with its hardware address. The detected Ethernet device will be different from eth0, perhaps eth1. You'll need both pieces of information, along with the desired IP address information described earlier.

14. Open the /etc/sysconfig/network-scripts/ifcfg-eth0 file. Make appropriate changes to the **DEVICE**, the various IP addresses, and the **HWADDR** directives.

15. Apply the **cp** or **mv** commands to the ifcfg-eth0 file. The new name should reflect the new Ethernet device, such as ifcfg-eth1 for the eth1 device.

16. Copy the resulting file to the /etc/sysconfig/networking/devices and /etc /sysconfig/networking/profiles/default directories.

17. Restart networking with the **/etc/sysconfig/network restart** command.

18. Verify the network device and routing table have the right settings with the **ifconfig** and **route -n** commands.

Assuming IP Forwarding has been enabled on the physical host system, and there are no blocks such as firewall rules, the virtual machines should now all be able to communicate with outside networks. In Chapter 10, you'll explore how to set appropriate IP forwarding rules based on **iptables** commands documented in the /etc/sysconfig/iptables file. For more information on firewalls and IP Forwarding, see Chapters 4 and 10, respectively. If you're studying only for the RHCSA exam, open the /etc/sysctl.conf file, make sure to set **net.ipv4.ip_forward=1** and run the **sysctl -p** command.

CERTIFICATION OBJECTIVE 5.06

Time Synchronization

The configuration of a Network Time Protocol (NTP) client is straightforward. While it's no longer part of the RHCSA objectives, it's still part of one of the prep courses for the RHCSA, RH124. It would be easy for Red Hat to include this topic as part of future RHCSA objectives. Therefore, this section provides a minimal overview of the client files and the associated GUI configuration tool.

There are good reasons to keep different systems running on the same clock. Otherwise, one system that may take web orders may miss the lack of inventory from a second system that manages a warehouse database, or even see out-of-date production figures from a third system associated with a manufacturing assembly line.

An NTP Client

Every system, real or virtual, starts with a hardware clock. The time on that clock may depend on the power in a battery; over time, batteries lose power and many hardware clocks end up losing time. The installation process on RHEL 6 normally sets the hardware clock to UTC, which is essentially identical to Greenwich Mean Time (GMT). Linux bases time changes such as Daylight Saving Time on the use of UTC.

Every RHEL 6 system includes a time zone configured in the /etc/sysconfig/clock file. The contents are simple; a typical system may include the following line:

```
ZONE="America/Los Angeles"
```

The default NTP configuration file, /etc/ntp.conf, is set up to connect to standard Red Hat servers that are part of the NTP pool project. Collectively, any errors from these servers relative to actual time is minimized.

```
server 0.rhel.pool.ntp.org
server 1.rhel.pool.ntp.org
server 2.rhel.pool.ntp.org
```

Users of rebuild distributions such as CentOS will see different Universal Resource Identifiers (URIs), such as 0.centos.pool.ntp.org.

Date/Time Properties

With the Date/Time Properties configuration tool, you can set the date, time, time zone, and NTP server for the local system. To start it in the GUI, run the **system-config-date** command. This opens the Date/Time Properties window shown in Figure 5-15.

You should recognize the URIs for the NTP servers as the pool servers previously discussed. In other words, the Date/Time Properties tool is a front end for editing the /etc/ntp.conf file. The advanced option to Speed Up Initial Synchronization minimizes the time lag effect of polling multiple NTP servers. The Use Local Time

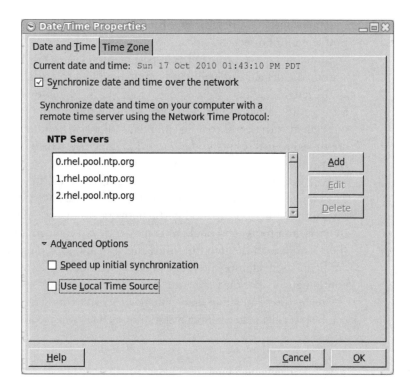

FIGURE 5-15

Date/Time
Properties tool

Source directive uses the local system as its own server. The Time Zone tab supports changes to the local time zone, handy for users who travel.

CERTIFICATION SUMMARY

This chapter covered the basic boot process of an RHEL system. It starts with the hardware POST and continues with the BIOS or UEFI systems. Once it finds boot media, it moves to the first stage of the GRUB bootloader. The GRUB menu allows you to select and customize the kernel to be booted. GRUB can be secured, as it supports booting into different runlevels, including a runlevel which supports root-level access without a user password.

Once you've selected an option from GRUB, it hands control to the kernel. It starts with a temporary filesystem known as the Initial RAM disk. Once essential drivers and filesystems are loaded, you can find out more about what happens through /var/log/dmesg and the drivers it loads. It hands control to the First Process, also known as **init**, as configured through the newer Upstart system with related files in the /etc/init directory.

Linux services are controlled in part by runlevel. While RHEL 6 uses the Upstart system, the default runlevel is still configured in /etc/inittab, and the service scripts in the /etc/rcn.d directories, where n represents the runlevel, determine which services are started and stopped. The status of those scripts in each runlevel can be configured with the **chkconfig** command (along with other tools). Runlevel scripts are linked to real scripts in the /etc/init.d directory, which can be used to start, stop, restart, reload, even status a service, and more.

For most users, network configuration is also an important part of the boot process. Most related configuration files can be found in the /etc/sysconfig/network-scripts directory. While you can modify the network configuration with the **ifup**, **ifdown**, **ifconfig**, and **route**, and **dhclient** commands, you can detail the current status of the network with the **ifconfig**, **route**, **netstat**, and **arp** commands. If you prefer to configure with administrative tools, RHEL 6 includes Network Manager and system-config-network packages.

You may need to set up local systems as NTP clients. The Date/Time Properties tool can help configure key configuration files such as /etc/sysconfig/ntp and /etc/ntp.conf.

✓ TWO-MINUTE DRILL

Here are some of the key points from the certification objectives in Chapter 5.

The BIOS and the UEFI

❑ While not strictly a part of the exam, it's important to know the basics of the BIOS and the UEFI.

❑ You can change the boot sequence from the BIOS/UEFI menu.

❑ Once the BIOS/UEFI detects a designated boot drive(s), it hands control to GRUB via the master boot record (MBR) of the appropriate drive.

Bootloaders and GRUB

❑ RHEL 6 uses the traditional version of GRUB, version 0.97.

❑ The GRUB configuration file is organized in stanzas.

❑ From the GRUB menu, you can boot into a runlevel other than the default. You can even boot into a runlevel that provides root administrative access without an account password.

❑ The GRUB menu, along with individual options, can be password-protected.

❑ The GRUB configuration file specifies a kernel, a root directory volume, and an initial RAM disk for each operating system.

❑ If the GRUB configuration file is missing, you may be able to boot from the grub> prompt with information on the /boot directory partition, the Linux kernel file, the top-level root directory, and the Initial RAM disk file.

Between GRUB and Login

❑ You can analyze boot messages through /var/log/dmesg or the **dmesg** command.

❑ There are six different runlevels available; the default is configured in /etc/inittab.

❑ Upstart has replaced SysVInit, with configuration files in the /etc/init directory.

❑ Once the kernel boots, it hands control to init, also known as the First Process.

❑ Different services are started based on the default or chosen runlevel.

Control by Runlevel

❑ The default runlevel configured in /etc/inittab runs scripts in the associated /etc/rcn.d directory, where *n* is the runlevel.

❑ Runlevel scripts in the /etc/rcn.d directories are links to actual scripts in the /etc/init.d directory.

❑ You can use runlevel scripts in the /etc/init.d directory to control a service with the start, stop, restart, reload, and other commands.

❑ The services that start in each runlevel can be controlled with the **chkconfig** command, as well as the tools associated with the **ntsysv** and **system-config-services** commands.

Network Configuration

❑ Important network configuration commands include **ifup**, **ifdown**, **ifconfig**, **route**, **netstat**, and **arp**.

❑ Key network configuration files are located primarily in the /etc, /etc/sysconfig, and /etc/sysconfig/network-scripts directories.

❑ You can edit the network configuration files directly, or configure network connections with the tools available through the **system-config-network-tui** or **nm-connection-editor** commands.

❑ Name resolution depends on appropriate settings in the /etc/resolv.conf, /etc/hosts, and /etc/nsswitch.conf files.

Time Synchronization

❑ The NTP service can help keep systems in sync with servers configured in the /etc/ntp.conf file.

❑ NTP clients can be configured with the Date/Time Configuration tool.

SELF TEST

The following questions will help measure your understanding of the material presented in this chapter. As no multiple-choice questions appear on the Red Hat exams, no multiple-choice questions appear in this book. These questions exclusively test your understanding of the chapter. It is okay if you have another way of performing a task. Getting results, not memorizing trivia, is what counts on the Red Hat exams. There may be more than one answer for many of these questions.

The BIOS and the UEFI

1. On what part of the boot hard drive is the first stage of the GRUB bootloader typically located?

   _____

Bootloaders and GRUB

2. When you see the GRUB configuration menu, what command would you use to modify the kernel arguments? Assume that GRUB is not password-protected.

   _____

3. What command would you enter at the **kernel** command line to boot into single-user mode?

   _____

4. If you see the **root(hd0,1)** directive in the GRUB configuration file, on what partition is the /boot directory? Assume the GRUB configuration file is properly configured.

   _____

Between GRUB and Login

5. What temporary file system is loaded directly from the GRUB menu?

   _____

6. What one-word command can you use to read the kernel initialization messages?

   _____

7. In what directory can you find the configuration files associated with the first process?

   _____

8. What is the name of the system that controls splash screens, configured in the /etc/init directory?

   _____

Control by Runlevel

9. In what directory can you find the scripts that control services? (Hint: scripts in specific runlevels are linked to the actual scripts in this directory.)

_____

10. Name three actions that can be typically run from scripts in the directory associated with question 9.

_____

_____

_____

Network Configuration

11. What command lists all network devices currently available on the local system, including those that are not active?

_____

12. What command lists the current routing table of the local system?

_____

Time Synchronization

13. What command starts the GUI-based configuration tool for time synchronization?

_____

LAB QUESTIONS

Several of these labs involve installation exercises. You should do these exercises on test machines only. The second Lab of Chapter 1 sets up KVM for this purpose. However, some readers may not have hardware that supports KVM. Options to KVM include virtual machine solutions such as VMware, available from www.vmware.com, or Virtualbox, open-source edition, available from www.virtualbox.org.

Red Hat presents its exams electronically. For that reason, most of the labs in this and future chapters are available from the CD that accompanies the book, in the Chapter5/ subdirectory. It's available in .doc, .html, and .txt formats, in the filename starting with 56505-labs. In case you haven't yet set up RHEL 6 on a system, refer to the first lab of Chapter 2 for installation instructions. The answers for each lab follows the Self Test answers for the fill-in-the-blank questions.

SELF TEST ANSWERS

The BIOS and the UEFI

1. For the BIOS/UEFI to hand control over to Linux, it needs to identify the Master Boot Record (MBR) of the boot hard drive.

Bootloaders and GRUB

2. From the GRUB menu, the command that modifies kernel arguments is **a**.
3. To boot into single-user mode from the GRUB **kernel** command line, you'd enter the **1** command; while not identical, **single** is also acceptable.
4. The **root (hd0,1)** directive documents the /boot directory on the second partition on the first hard drive.

Between GRUB and Login

5. The temporary filesystem loaded from the GRUB menu is the initial RAM disk filesystem, also known by its filename, initramfs.
6. The one-word command that you can use to read the kernel initialization messages is **dmesg**.
7. The configuration files associated with the first process are located in the /etc/init directory.
8. The name of the system that controls splash screens on RHEL 6 is Plymouth.

Control by Runlevel

9. Scripts that control services are located in the /etc/init.d directory. The /etc/rc.d/init.d directory is also an acceptable answer. While there are scripts that qualify in other directories, /etc/init.d is the location for the great majority of such scripts.
10. Typical actions that can be run from scripts in the /etc/init.d directory include **start, stop, restart, reload**, and more. Any of the actions listed near the end of a file in that /etc/init.d directory is an acceptable answer.

Network Configuration

11. The **ifconfig -a** command lists all detected network devices, active and inactive.

12. The route command lists the current routing table of the local system. Other acceptable answers include **route -n**, **netstat -r**, and **netstat -rn**.

Time Synchronization

13. The **system-config-date** command starts the Date/Time Configuration tool.

LAB ANSWERS

Yes, there are many Linux systems that run for years at a time without a reboot. But reboots are sometimes required, such as when newer kernels are installed. So when configuring a Linux system, make sure any changes survive a reboot. Otherwise, your supervisor may not believe that you ever did the work. On a Red Hat exam, you won't get credit unless changes survive a reboot.

Lab 1

If successful, this lab will show you how to change the default runlevel, along with the relative importance of the options in the GRUB bootloader. Normally, it's best to back up a file before making changes. However, the RHEL 6 version of the /etc/inittab file is pretty simple, as it contains only one line of significance:

```
id:5:initdefault:
```

This assumes the default runlevel is 5; if there's a different default runlevel for your system, substitute accordingly.

Lab 2

This lab should make a point: it's far too easy in the default configuration of RHEL 6 to get access to the root administrative account.

If you had to back up the /etc/shadow file and were successful with this lab, you should not have to restore that file from backup. The **passwd** commands executed during this lab should have restored the intended password for the root administrative user. One way to meet the requirements of this lab is with the following steps:

1. Power up the local system. During the boot process, when you see the following message (the operating system name and version number may vary), press a key.

```
Booting Red Hat Enterprise Linux Server (2.6.32-71.el6.x86_64) in 5 seconds....
```

2. Edit the default option. If the GRUB bootloader is already password-protected, press P and enter the password at the given prompt.

3. Press A to edit the **kernel** command line. You should see a line with a cursor similar to this:

```
< rhgb quiet
```

4. Add a 1 to the end of the kernel command line, as follows, and press ENTER.

```
< rhgb quiet 1
```

When the system boots, you should see entries similar to the following, including a command line prompt:

```
Telling INIT to go to single user mode.
[root@tester1 /]#
```

5. Try the **passwd** command. It should immediately prompt you for a new password. Go ahead and enter a password, confirming the new password when prompted.

In some configurations, the **passwd** command may not work in single-user mode. In that case, you'll have to edit the /etc/shadow file. Back it up first, perhaps to the /root directory. The first line in that file should look similar to this:

```
root:$6a24fdsaj..a432:14972:0:99999:7
```

In this case, delete the contents of the second column (between the first and second colons). If you're editing /etc/shadow in the vi editor, you'll have to save and exit with the **:wq!** command.

6. Test the result. Reboot the system, or run the **init 3** command.

7. Open a text login console. Log in as the root administrative user with the new root password. If you had to delete the password column in /etc/shadow, the system will log you in as the root administrative user without a password. In that case, you'll immediately want to set a root administrative password with the following command:

```
# passwd
```

Lab 3

In Lab 2, you should have seen how easy it is for a user with access to the GRUB menu to access the root administrative account, without the password. Now you should understand the importance of password protection of the GRUB menu. Successful completion of this lab should be easy to confirm. Reboot the system, and press a key in the five seconds before the default option is booted to get to the GRUB menu. In that menu, you should see the **'p' to enter a password to unlock the next set of features** message. One way to meet the requirements of this lab is with the following steps:

1. Power up the local system. During the boot process, when you see the following message (the operating system name and version number may vary), press a key.

```
Booting Red Hat Enterprise Linux Server (2.6.32-71.el6.x86_64) in 5 seconds....
```

2. If the GRUB bootloader is already password-protected, you'll see the following message:

   ```
   Press enter to boot the selected OS or 'p' to enter a password to unlock
   the next set of features.
   ```

   In the default RHEL 6 installation, the GRUB bootloader is not password-protected. The following steps assume that you're working with such a system.

3. Select a kernel and press ENTER to boot RHEL 6.

4. While it's possible on some systems to copy a hashed password from a text console, it is more convenient to do so from the GUI. To that end, log in to the GUI as the root administrative user.

5. Open two command line consoles in the GUI. One method is to click Applications | System Tools | Terminal, and repeat.

6. Open the GRUB configuration file in a text editor. While there are links from other files, the actual location is /boot/grub/grub.conf.

7. At the second command line interface, run the **grub-md5-crypt** command. Enter a password when prompted and repeat when prompted to confirm. The typed-in password won't be shown. The encrypted password starts with the $1. (In this case, the password is an encrypted hash of the word *redhat*.)

   ```
   # grub-md5-crypt
   Password:
   Retype password:
   $1$KdqKv/$T1L0luzEOU2zFJFm8UpCv0
   ```

8. In the GRUB configuration file, open a line before the first **title** directive. Type in the following:

   ```
   password --md5
   ```

9. Copy the password from the first command line console, and append it to the line in the GRUB configuration file; it should read as follows:

   ```
   password --md5 $1$KdqKv/$T1L0luzEOU2zFJFm8UpCv0
   ```

10. Save the changes to the GRUB configuration file. Reboot the system, and repeat Steps 1 and 2. You should now see the password prompt suggested in Step 2. The GRUB menu is now password protected.

While it's easy to delete the **password** directive from the GRUB configuration file, as configured in this lab, I suggest that you keep that directive. In fact, you should add it to all systems, at least those which may be accessed by other users.

Lab 4

After completing this lab, two stanzas should exist in the /boot/grub/grub.conf configuration file. They might appear similar to Figure 5-16. The only difference between the two stanzas is the **title** directive, the **password** directive, and the number **1** at the end of the **kernel** command.

To really test the result, reboot the system, select the Single-User Mode option, and then enter an incorrect password when prompted. What happens?

If desired, you can now remove the second stanza from the GRUB configuration file, /boot/grub /grub.conf. Alternatively, you can restore grub.conf from the backup location.

FIGURE 5-16

Sample GRUB configuration file with Single-User Mode stanza

```
grub.conf generated by anaconda
#
# Note that you do not have to rerun grub after making changes to this file
# NOTICE:  You have a /boot partition.  This means that
#          all kernel and initrd paths are relative to /boot/, eg.
#          root (hd0,0)
#          kernel /vmlinuz-version ro root=/dev/vda2
#          initrd /initrd-[generic-]version.img
#boot=/dev/vda
default=0
timeout=5
splashimage=(hd0,0)/grub/splash.xpm.gz
hiddenmenu
password --md5 $1$A.CLv/$.jw8JKlyQkknUM3siBf981
title Red Hat Enterprise Linux (2.6.32-71.el6.x86_64)
        root (hd0,0)
        kernel /vmlinuz-2.6.32-71.el6.x86_64 ro root=UUID=ffe37c21-53ab-46ab-b9d
f-4b856046e18f rd_NO_LUKS rd_NO_LVM rd_NO_MD rd_NO_DM LANG=en_US.UTF-8 SYSFONT=l
atarcyrheb-sun16 KEYBOARDTYPE=pc KEYTABLE=us crashkernel=auto rhgb quiet
        initrd /initramfs-2.6.32-71.el6.x86_64.img
title Single User Mode
        password --md5 $1$A.CLv/$.jw8JKlyQkknUM3siBf981
        root (hd0,0)
        kernel /vmlinuz-2.6.32-71.el6.x86_64 ro root=UUID=ffe37c21-53ab-46ab-b9d
f-4b856046e18f rd_NO_LUKS rd_NO_LVM rd_NO_MD rd_NO_DM LANG=en_US.UTF-8 SYSFONT=l
atarcyrheb-sun16 KEYBOARDTYPE=pc KEYTABLE=us crashkernel=auto rhgb quiet 1
        initrd /initramfs-2.6.32-71.el6.x86_64.img
```

Lab 5

The script executed in this lab moved the grub.conf configuration file to the /root/backup directory. If you understand GRUB well, you should have been able to boot the system from the grub> prompt.

Otherwise, you can recover the grub.conf file by booting into the rescue mode described in this Chapter. From the rescue mode command line prompt, you should be able to restore the original configuration with the following commands:

```
# chroot /mnt/sysimage
# cp /root/backup/grub.conf /boot/grub/
```

If that doesn't work, review Figure 5-16 for clues on what to put in the file. The UUID shown in the figure is almost definitely not the UUID for partition where your top-level root directory is mounted.

Alternatively, review the menu.lst file in the /usr/share/doc/grub-0.97 directory. If you absolutely need to include the UUID number for the volume, it's available in the default version of the /etc/fstab file. If you can't find it there, and the top-level root directory is mounted on partition /dev/vda2, you can find the appropriate UUID number with the following command:

```
# dumpe2fs /dev/vda2 | grep UUID
```

Lab 6

When you've completed this lab, you'll understand the relative importance of files in the /etc/sysconfig directory, even relative to the files in the /etc/init directory. The results may be a bit surprising, as init is the first process.

It's possible to configure up to 12 virtual terminals, which matches the number of function keys available on most keyboards. If you want to set up 12 virtual terminals (and that would be an interesting problem for the RHCSA exam), look at the /etc/securetty file and related man pages with the **man -k securetty** command. One way to accomplish the tasks in this lab is with the following steps:

1. Open the /etc/init/start-ttys.conf file. Change the following directive to limit the active consoles to terminals 1 and 2:

```
env ACTIVE_CONSOLES=/dev/tty[1-6]
```

2. To test the result, move to runlevel 1 and then move to runlevel 3. (Hint: you can use the **init** or **telint** commands for that purpose.)

3. What happens? Can you still log into terminals 3, 4, 5, and 6?

4. Now edit the /etc/sysconfig/init file. Note the ACTIVE_CONSOLES directive. Use it to limit the active consoles to terminals 1 and 2.

5. Rerun Step 3. Did the changes to the /etc/sysconfig/init file do the trick?

6. Next, comment out the applicable directive in the /etc/sysconfig/init file, and then rerun Step 3. What consoles are still active?

7. What can you conclude about the importance of the /etc/sysconfig/init and the files in the /etc/init directory?

8. When complete, just remember to restore the original versions of the /etc/sysconfig/init and /etc/init/start-ttys.conf files.

Lab 7

This lab is straightforward; it substituted a /etc/sysconfig/network file with the **NETWORKING=no** directive. After the **ifdown eth0** command is run, when the /etc/init.d/network script is restarted, it reads this file and does not activate networking.

6

Linux Filesystem Administration

L inux installation is easy, at least for anyone serious about Red Hat certification. Most administrators have to maintain existing systems. Critical skills related to filesystems include adding new partitions, creating logical volumes, setting up volume encryption, and more. In many cases, you'll want to make sure these filesystems are mounted automatically during the boot process, and that requires a detailed knowledge of the /etc/fstab configuration file.

Some filesystems, such as those available from unreliable network connections, should be mounted only on a temporary basis; that is the province of the automounter.

INSIDE THE EXAM

Some of the RHCSA objectives listed in this chapter overlap and may be in part covered in multiple sections. The objectives all relate in some way to filesystem management and should be considered as a whole in this chapter.

Partition Management

As in the real world, it is the results that matter. It doesn't matter whether you use Disk Druid, **fdisk**, or **parted** to create partitions. You can create new partitions at the command line or use GUI front ends to these tools such as the Disk Utility. Make sure that appropriate partitions meet the requirements of the exam. Just remember Disk Druid is available only during the installation process.

The current RHCSA objectives include the following related requirements:

■ Add new partitions, logical volumes, filesystems, and swap areas to a system non-destructively

■ List, create, delete, and set partition type for primary, extended, and logical partitions

Logical Volumes

Partitions are essential components of logical volumes. Related RHCSA objectives describe some of the skills required. For example, the following objective suggests that you need to know the process starting with the physical volume:

■ Create and remove physical volumes, assign physical volumes to volume groups, create and delete logical volumes

Of course, a logical volume isn't fulfilling its full potential unless you can increase its size, as suggested by the following objective:

■ Extend existing unencrypted ext4-formatted logical volumes

Storage Encryption

RHEL 6 includes the Linux Unified Key Setup (LUKS) system for encrypting formatted partitions and volumes. When properly configured, LUKS makes it more difficult for a cracker to decipher critical data. To that end, the relevant RHCSA requirements include:

■ Mount, unmount, and use LUKS-encrypted file systems

■ Create and configure LUKS-encrypted partitions and logical volumes to

prompt for password and mount a decrypted file system at boot

■ Configure systems to mount ext4, LUKS-encrypted, and network file systems automatically

Filesystem Management

Partitions and logical volumes must be formatted before they're ready to store files. To that end, you need to know how to meet the following RHCSA objectives:

■ Create, mount, unmount, and use ext2, ext3 and ext4 file systems

■ Mount and unmount CIFS and NFS network file systems

■ Configure systems to mount file systems at boot by Universally Unique ID (UUID) or label

---

CERTIFICATION OBJECTIVE 6.01

Storage Management and Partitions

While it's easier to create partitions, logical volumes, and RAID arrays during the installation process, not every administrator has that privilege. While this section is focused on the management of regular partitions, the techniques described in this section are also used to create the partition-based components of both logical volumes and RAID arrays. Once configured, a partition, a logical volume, and a RAID array can each be referred to generically as a volume.

In Linux, two tools still predominate for administrators who need to create and manage partitions: **fdisk** and **parted**. While these tools are primarily applied to local hard disks, they're frequently also used for other media such as drives attached over a network.

on the **job**

For both **fdisk** *and* **parted,** *partitions configured as logical volumes are given an LVM label, short for Logical Volume Management.*

Current System State

Before using the **fdisk** or **parted** utilities to create or modify a partition, it's important to check currently available free space along with mounted filesystems. That process is made easy with the **df** and **mount** commands. The following example illustrates how the **df** command displays the total, used, and available free space on all currently mounted filesystems.

on the **job**

The terms filesystem and file system are interchangeable. Both are used in official Linux documentation.

Note the numbers under the 1k-blocks column. In this case (except for the temporary filesystem, tmpfs, and the mounted DVD), they add up to about 10GB of allocated space. If the hard drive is larger, unallocated space may be used for another partition. Partitions can be combined with others to configure additional space in logical volumes and RAID arrays. And that can be useful when you need to expand the space available to appropriate directories, such as /home, /tmp, and /var.

```
[root@server1 ~]# df
Filesystem 1k-blocks       Used Available Use% Mounted on
/dev/vda2
                8063408  2158968   5494840  29% /
tmpfs            384576        0    384576   0% /dev/shm
/dev/vda1        495844    32140    438104   7% /boot
/dev/vda5       1007896    17716    938980   2% /home
/dev/sr0        2381288  2381288         0 100% /media
```

The second command, **mount**, lists the way each filesystem is formatted. In this case, examine the partition represented by device /dev/vda5 mounted with the ext4 file type on the /home directory. It separates the directories of regular users in a dedicated partition. For the following example, I've set up the data shown from the **mount** command in columns for clarity; what you actually see from the RHEL command line is less organized.

```
[root@server1 root]# mount
/dev/vda2 on / type ext4                                         (rw)
proc       on /proc type proc                                    (rw)
sysfs      on /sys type sysfs                                    (rw)
devpts     on /dev/pts type devpts
(rw,gid=5,mode=620)
tmpfs      on /dev/shm type tmpfs                                (rw)
/dev/vda1 on /boot type ext4                                     (rw)
/dev/vda5 on /home type ext4                                     (rw)
none       on /proc/sys/fs/binfmt_misc type binfmt_misc (rw)
/tmp on /tmp type none                                    (rw,bind)
/var/tmp on /var/tmp type none                            (rw,bind)
/home on /home type none                                  (rw,bind)
sunrpc     on /var/lib/nfs/rpc_pipefs type rpc_pipefs  (rw)
/dev/sr0  on /media type iso9660                            (ro)
```

The fdisk Utility

The **fdisk** utility is a near-universal tool available for a variety of computer operating systems. A capable version of **fdisk** is available on Macintosh OSes. A less capable version of **fdisk** is even available on older versions of Microsoft Windows. There are many commands within **fdisk**, more in expert mode, but you need to know only the few discussed here.

Though you can modify the physical disk partition layout using many programs, this section explores the Linux implementation of **fdisk**. In contrast, the Microsoft version is based on its heritage as the Disk Operating System (DOS) and works only on Microsoft partitions.

Start fdisk: Help and More

The following screen output lists commands that show how to start the **fdisk** program, how to get help, and how to quit the program. The /dev/vda drive is associated with the first virtual drive on a KVM-based virtual machine. As other systems may be configured with different hard drive device files, you may need to check the output from the **df** and **mount** commands for clues.

When you start **fdisk**, it now includes the following warning:

```
WARNING: DOS-compatible mode is deprecated. It's strongly recommended to
         switch off the mode (command 'c') and change display units to
         sectors (command 'u').
```

There's no requirement to make these changes. If you do, be prepared to make these changes again the next time fdisk is open.

However, such changes can help avoid annoying error messages. And the results are more precise, as sectors more closely match desired partition sizes. On production systems, it's unlikely that you're going to add or modify partitions on a daily basis. Whether or not these changes are made, **fdisk** provides the same prompt, where you can press **m** to list basic **fdisk** commands:

```
Command (m for help): m
Command action
   a   toggle a bootable flag
   b   edit bsd disklabel
   c   toggle the dos compatibility flag
   d   delete a partition
   l   list known partition types
   m   print this menu
   n   add a new partition
   o   create a new empty DOS partition table
   p   print the partition table
   q   quit without saving changes
   s   create a new empty Sun disklabel
   t   change a partition's system id
   u   change display/entry units
   v   verify the partition table
   w   write table to disk and exit
   x   extra functionality (experts only)

Command (m for help):
```

There are a wide variety of commands associated with **fdisk**—and more if you run the **x** command to access **fdisk**'s extra functionality.

Using fdisk: A New Drive with No Partitions

After installing a new drive on Linux, that drive normally isn't configured with partitions. The **fdisk** utility can be used to configure partitions on physical or virtual disks attached to the system. For example, the baseline virtual system for this book includes three drives: /dev/vda, /dev/sda, and /dev/sdb.

on the Job

SATA, PATA, and SCSI drives are now all represented by device files like /dev/sda, /dev/sdb, and so on.

If a newly added drive hasn't been used by the RHEL installation program (or some other disk management program), it'll return the following message the first time it's opened by **fdisk**:

```
Device contains neither a valid DOS partition table, nor Sun, SGI or OSF disklabel
Building a new DOS disklabel with disk identifier 0xa15e5d53.
Changes will remain in memory only, until you decide to write them.
After that, of course, the previous content won't be recoverable.

Warning: invalid flag 0x0000 of partition table 4 will be corrected by w(rite)
```

In other words, even if you don't create a partition after opening it in **fdisk**, it will automatically write a DOS disk label to the drive. Yes, despite the previous warning about DOS-compatible mode, **fdisk** still uses the Disk Operating System commonly associated with Microsoft. But DOS predates Microsoft.

If you need more than four partitions on the new physical disk, configure the first three partitions as primary partitions, and then configure the fourth partition as an extended partition. That extended partition should be pretty big; all logical partitions must fit in that space.

Using fdisk: In a Nutshell

At the **fdisk** command line prompt, start with the print command (**p**) to examine the partition table. This allows you to review the current entries in the partition table. Assuming free space is available, you can then create a new (**n**) partition. Generally, partitions are either primary (**p**) or logical (**l**). If it doesn't already exist, you can also create an extended partition (**e**) to contain logical partitions. Remember that you can have up to four primary partitions, which would correspond to numbers 1 through 4. One of the primary partitions can be redesignated as an extended partition. The remaining partitions are logical partitions, numbered 5 and above. While you might think **fdisk** is old and unmaintained, it actually now supports the creation of more than 16 partitions on a drive.

If free space is available, **fdisk** normally starts the new partition at the first available sector or cylinder. The actual size of the partition depends on disk geometry.

Using fdisk: Create a Partition

The following screen output sample shows the steps used to create (**n**) the first partition, make it bootable (**a**), and then finally write (**w**) the partition information to the disk. (Note that although you may specify a 500MB partition, the geometry of the disk may not allow that precise size.) First, to avoid error messages described earlier, the DOS compatibility flag is unset (**c**) and display units are changed to sectors (**u**).

```
# fdisk /dev/sda

Command (m for help): c
DOS Compatibility flag is not set

Command (m for help): u
Changing display/entry units to sectors

Command (m for help): n
Command action
   e    extended
   p    primary partition (1-4)
p
Partition number (1-4): 1
First sector (2048-2047999, default 2048):
Using default value 2048
Last sector, +sectors or +size{K,M,G} (2048-2047999, default 2047999): +500M

Command (m for help): a
Partition number (1-4): 1

Command (m for help): p
Disk /dev/sda: 1048 MB, 1048576000 bytes
.....
   Device Boot    Start      End    Blocks   Id  System
/dev/sda1    *       2048  1026047   512000   83  Linux

Command (m for help):
```

Note how the number of blocks matches the binary representation of 500MB. Repeat the commands to create any other partitions that you might need.

When partitions are added or changed, you generally don't have to reboot to get Linux to read the new partition table, unless another partition on that drive has been formatted and mounted. If so, an attempt to write the partition table with the **w** command fails temporarily with the following message:

```
WARNING: Re-reading the partition table failed with error 16: Device or resource busy.
 The kernel still uses the old table. The new table will be used at
 the next reboot or after you run partprobe(8) or kpartx(8)
```

If you're able to unmount existing partitions or volumes on the target hard drive, you'd be able to apply the **partprobe** or **kpartx** commands to the device file of that hard drive. For example, until other applicable volumes from that drive are unmounted, the **partprobe /dev/sda** command returns the same error message.

Using fdisk: Many Partition Types

One feature of special interest is based on the **t** command, to change the partition system identifier. If you need space for logical volumes, RAID arrays, or even swap space, that command is important. After pressing **t**, you're prompted to enter the partition number (if there's more than one configured). You can then list available partition types with the **L** command, as shown here. (If there's only one partition on the drive, it is selected automatically.)

```
Command (m for help) : t
Partition number (1-4)
1
Partition ID (L to list options): L
```

The list of available partition identifiers, as shown in Figure 6-1 is impressive. Note how it's not limited to Linux partitions. But as this book covers Linux, Table 6-1 lists associated partition types.

FIGURE 6-1

Linux partition types infdisk

```
 0  Empty            24  NEC DOS           81  Minix / old Lin  bf  Solaris
 1  FAT12            39  Plan 9            82  Linux swap / So  c1  DRDOS/sec (FAT-
 2  XENIX root       3c  PartitionMagic    83  Linux            c4  DRDOS/sec (FAT-
 3  XENIX usr        40  Venix 80286       84  OS/2 hidden C:   c6  DRDOS/sec (FAT-
 4  FAT16 <32M       41  PPC PReP Boot     85  Linux extended   c7  Syrinx
 5  Extended         42  SFS               86  NTFS volume set  da  Non-FS data
 6  FAT16            4d  QNX4.x            87  NTFS volume set  db  CP/M / CTOS / .
 7  HPFS/NTFS        4e  QNX4.x 2nd part   88  Linux plaintext  de  Dell Utility
 8  AIX              4f  QNX4.x 3rd part   8e  Linux LVM        df  BootIt
 9  AIX bootable     50  OnTrack DM        93  Amoeba           e1  DOS access
 a  OS/2 Boot Manag  51  OnTrack DM6 Aux   94  Amoeba BBT       e3  DOS R/O
 b  W95 FAT32        52  CP/M              9f  BSD/OS           e4  SpeedStor
 c  W95 FAT32 (LBA)  53  OnTrack DM6 Aux   a0  IBM Thinkpad hi  eb  BeOS fs
 e  W95 FAT16 (LBA)  54  OnTrackDM6        a5  FreeBSD          ee  GPT
 f  W95 Ext'd (LBA)  55  EZ-Drive          a6  OpenBSD          ef  EFI (FAT-12/16/
10  OPUS             56  Golden Bow        a7  NeXTSTEP         f0  Linux/PA-RISC b
11  Hidden FAT12     5c  Priam Edisk       a8  Darwin UFS       f1  SpeedStor
12  Compaq diagnost  61  SpeedStor         a9  NetBSD           f4  SpeedStor
14  Hidden FAT16 <3  63  GNU HURD or Sys   ab  Darwin boot      f2  DOS secondary
16  Hidden FAT16     64  Novell Netware    af  HFS / HFS+       fb  VMware VMFS
17  Hidden HPFS/NTF  65  Novell Netware    b7  BSDI fs          fc  VMware VMKCORE
18  AST SmartSleep   70  DiskSecure Mult   b8  BSDI swap        fd  Linux raid auto
1b  Hidden W95 FAT3  75  PC/IX             bb  Boot Wizard hid  fe  LANstep
1c  Hidden W95 FAT3  80  Old Minix         be  Solaris boot     ff  BBT
1e  Hidden W95 FAT1
Hex code (type L to list codes):
```

Partition Identifier	Description
5	Extended partition; while not a Linux partition type, such partitions are a prerequisite for logical partitions. Also see 85.
82	Linux swap.
83	Linux; applicable for all standard Linux partition formats.
85	Linux extended partition; not recognized by other operating systems.
88	Linux plaintext partition table; rarely used.
8e	Linux logical volume management for partitions used as physical volumes.
fd	Linux RAID; for partitions used as components of a RAID array.

Unless you're making a change, type in identifier **83**. You'll be returned to the **fdisk** command prompt.

Using fdisk: Delete a Partition

The following example removes the only configured partition. The sample output screen first starts **fdisk**. Then you can print (**p**) the current partition table, delete (**d**) the partition by number (**1** in this case), write (**w**) the changes to the disk, and quit (**q**) from the program. Needless to say, *do not perform this action on any partition where you need the data*. The following output is based on a system where the aforementioned DOS compatibility flag has been disabled and system units have been changed to sectors with the **c** and **u** commands, respectively.

Assuming only one partition on this drive, it is selected automatically after running the **d** command.

```
# fdisk /dev/sda
Command (m for help): p
Disk /dev/sda: 1048 MB, 1048576000 bytes
255 heads, 63 sectors/track, 127 cylinders, total 2048000 sectors
Units = sectors of 1 * 512 = 512 bytes
Sector size (logical/physical): 512 bytes / 512 bytes
I/O size (minimum/optimal): 512 bytes / 512 bytes
Disk identifier: 0x654f1cda

Device     Boot     Start       End     Blocks   Id  System
/dev/sda1            2048    206847     102400   83  Linux
Command (m for help): d
Partition number (1-1): 1
```

This is the last chance to change your mind before deleting the current partition. To avoid writing the change, exit from **fdisk** with the **q** command. If you're pleased with the changes that you've made and want to make them permanent, proceed with the **w** command:

```
Command (m for help): w
```

Unless the aforementioned error 16 message appears, that's it. You should now have an empty hard drive.

Using fdisk: Create a Swap Partition

Now that you know how to create partitions with **fdisk**, just one additional step is required to set up that partition for swap space. Once you have a swap partition of the desired size, run the **t** command to select a partition, and then run the l command to show the partition ID types listed in Figure 6-1.

In this case, at the following prompt, type in **82** for a Linux swap partition:

```
Hex code (type L to list codes): 82
```

For example, I could run the following sequence of commands to set up a new swap partition on the second hard drive. The commands that I type are in boldface. The details of what you see depend on the partitions that you may have created. It'll be a 900MB swap space on the first primary partition (/dev/sdb1).

```
Command (m for help): n
Command action
     e   extended
     p   primary partition (1-4)
p
Partition number (1-4): 1
First sector (2048-2047999, default 2048): 2048
Last sector, +sectors or +size{K,M,G} (2048-2047999, default 2047999): +900M

Command (m for help): p

Disk /dev/sdb: 1048 MB, 1048576000 bytes
...

   Device Boot      Start         End      Blocks   Id  System
/dev/sdb1             2048     1845247      921600   83  Linux

Command (m for help): t
Selected partition 1
```

```
Hex code (type L to list codes): 82
Changed system type of partition 1 to 82 (Linux swap / Solaris)

Command (m for help): w
The partition table has been altered!

Calling ioctl() to re-read partition table.
Syncing disks.
```

The **fdisk** utility doesn't actually write the changes to disk until you run the write (**w**) command. Alternatively, you can cancel these changes with the quit (**q**) command. If you don't have the error 16 message described earlier, the changes are written to disk. As described later in this chapter, additional work is required to implement that swap partition.

The parted Utility

In its different forms, the **parted** utility is becoming increasingly popular. It's an excellent tool developed by the GNU foundation. As with **fdisk**, you can use it to create, check, and destroy partitions, but it can do more. You can also use it to resize and copy partitions, as well as the filesystems contained therein. It's the foundation for multiple GUI-based partition management tools, including GParted and QtParted. For the latest information, see www.gnu.org/software/parted. As discussed later in this chapter, RHEL 6 includes the Disk Utility, available from the gnome-disk-utility package and the **palimpsest** command.

on the **job**

In some ways, the parted utility may be more risky. For example, I accidentally ran the mklabel command from the (parted) prompt on an existing RHEL system. It deleted all existing partitions. Changes were written immediately, while parted was still running. Fortunately, I had a backup of this virtual system and was able to restore it with little trouble.

exam

ⓦatch

Real Linux administrators understand that partition management tools are inexact. While fdisk is improved when sectors are used, parted does not have that option.

During our discussion of **parted**, we'll proceed from section to section assuming that **parted** is still open with the following prompt:

```
(parted)
```

Using parted: Starting, Getting Help, and Quitting

The next screen output lists commands that show how to start the **parted** utility, how to get help, and how to quit the program. In this case, the /dev/sdb drive is associated with the second SATA drive on a regular PC. Your computer may have a different hard drive; you can check the output from the **df** and **mount** commands for clues.

As you can see in Figure 6-2, when **parted** is run, it opens its own command line prompt. Enter **help** for a list of available commands.

There are a wide variety of commands available at the **parted** interface. When compared to **fdisk**, **parted** can do more in some ways; it can even be used to format and resize partitions. Unfortunately, the format functionality is limited and does not allow you to create or resize ext3 or ext4 partitions, at least for RHEL 6. In fact, an attempt to resize a partition with **parted** leads to the following message:

```
WARNING: you are attempting to use parted to operate on (resize) a file system.
parted's file system manipulation code is not as robust as what you'll find in
dedicated, file-system-specific packages like e2fsprogs.
```

FIGURE 6-2

parted command options

```
(parted) help
  align-check TYPE N                          check partition N for TYPE(min|opt)
        alignment
  check NUMBER                                do a simple check on the file system
  cp [FROM-DEVICE] FROM-NUMBER TO-NUMBER      copy file system to another partition
  help [COMMAND]                              print general help, or help on
        COMMAND
  mklabel,mktable LABEL-TYPE                  create a new disklabel (partition
        table)
  mkfs NUMBER FS-TYPE                         make a FS-TYPE file system on
        partition NUMBER
  mkpart PART-TYPE [FS-TYPE] START END        make a partition
  mkpartfs PART-TYPE FS-TYPE START END        make a partition with a file system
  move NUMBER START END                       move partition NUMBER
  name NUMBER NAME                            name partition NUMBER as NAME
  print [devices|free|list,all|NUMBER]        display the partition table,
        available devices, free space, all found partitions, or a particular
        partition
  quit                                        exit program
  rescue START END                            rescue a lost partition near START
        and END
  resize NUMBER START END                     resize partition NUMBER and its file
        system
  rm NUMBER                                   delete partition NUMBER
  select DEVICE                               choose the device to edit
  set NUMBER FLAG STATE                       change the FLAG on partition NUMBER
  toggle [NUMBER [FLAG]]                       toggle the state of FLAG on partition
        NUMBER
  unit UNIT                                   set the default unit to UNIT
  version                                     display the version number and
        copyright information of GNU Parted
(parted)
```

Resizing is a process normally associated with logical volumes. For more information, see the description of the **resize2fs** command later in this chapter.

Using parted: In a Nutshell

At the **parted** command line prompt, start with the **print** the partition table command. This allows you to review the current entries in the partition table, assuming one exists. Assuming sufficient free space is available, you can then make a new (**mkpart**) partition or even make and format the filesystem (**mkpartfs**). For more information about **parted** command options, use the **help** command; for example, the following command (in bold) provides more information about **mkpart**:

```
(parted) help mkpart
  mkpart PART-TYPE [FS-TYPE] START END      make a partition

        PART-TYPE is one of: primary, logical, extended
        FS-TYPE is one of: ext3, ext2, fat32, fat16, hfsx,
        hfs+, hfs, jfs, linux-swap,ntfs, reiserfs, hp-ufs,
        sun-ufs, xfs, apfs2, apfs1, asfs, amufs5, amufs4,
        amufs3, amufs2, amufs1, amufs0, amufs, affs7, affs6,
        affs5, affs4, affs3, affs2, affs1, affs0
        START and END are disk locations, such as 4GB or 10%.
        Negative values count from the end of the disk.
        For example, -1s specifies exactly the last sector.

        mkpart makes a partition without creating a new
        file system on the partition.
        FS-TYPE may be specified to set an appropriate
        partition ID.
```

If that's too much information, just run the command. You'll be prompted for the necessary information. Remember that drives can contain up to four primary partitions, corresponding to numbers 1 through 4. One of the primary partitions can be redesignated as an extended partition. The remaining partitions are logical partitions, numbered 5 and above.

Using parted: A New PC (or Hard Drive) with No Partitions

The first step with any truly new hard drive is to create a partition table. For example, after I add a new hard drive to my virtual RHEL system, just about any command I run in **parted** leads to the following message:

```
Error: /dev/sdb - unrecognised disk label.
```

Before I can do anything else with this drive, I need to create a label. As shown from the list of available commands, I can do so with the **mklabel** command. As strange as it sounds, the default label to be used for Linux is **msdos**; here are the commands I run:

```
(parted) mklabel
New disk label type? msdos
```

Using parted: Create a New Partition

Now you can create a new partition in **parted**, with the **mkpart** command. Naturally, if an extended partition already exists, the only type available will be a logical partition.

```
(parted) mkpart
Partition type? primary/extended? primary
File system type? [ext2]? ext4
Start? 1MB
End? 500MB
```

For **parted**, I use 1MB as some space has to be reserved for the MBR. While only 512 bytes are required for the MBR, a 1MB entry avoids an error message. Now review the results with the **print** command:

```
(parted) print

Disk /dev/sdb: 10.7GBSector size (logical/physical): 512B/512B
Partition Table: msdos

Number  Start   End     Size   Type      File system  Flags
 1      1049kB  500MB   499MB  primary   ext4
```

If this is the first partition you've created, the filesystem type is empty. Unfortunately, **parted** does not work perfectly; even if you've set up an ext4 label, you still need to format it with the **mkfs.ext4** command discussed later in this chapter. But as long as there are no errors, the partition table is already written to disk. But for the purpose of this chapter, don't exit from **parted** just yet.

on the job

The GUI parted tools (GParted, QTParted) do support formatting to a wider variety of filesystem formats, even though they're just "front ends" to parted. They might be available from third-party repositories such as those described in Chapter 7.

Using parted: Delete a Partition

It's easy to delete a partition in **parted**. All you need to do from the **(parted)** prompt is use the **rm** command to delete the target partition, by number.

Of course, before deleting any partition, you should:

- Save any data you need from that partition.
- Unmount the partition.
- Make sure it isn't configured in /etc/fstab, so Linux doesn't try to mount it the next time you boot.
- After starting **parted**, run the **print** command to identify the partition you want to delete, as well as its ID number.

For example, to delete partition /dev/sdb10 from the **(parted)** prompt, run the following command:

```
(parted) rm 10
```

Using parted: Create a Swap Partition

Now let's repeat the process to create a swap partition. If necessary, delete the previously created partition to make room. Make the start of the new partition 1MB after the end of the previous partition. You can still use the same commands, just substitute the **linux-swap** filesystem type as appropriate:

```
(parted) mkpart
Partition type? primary/extended? primary
File system type? [ext2]? linux-swap
Start? 501MB
End? 1000MB
```

Now review the result with the **print** command:

```
(parted) print

Model: ATA QEMU HARDDISK (scsi)
Disk /dev/sdb: 1049MB
Sector size (logical/physical): 512B/512B
Partition Table: msdos

Number  Start   End     Size   Type     File system  Flags
 1      1049kB  500MB   499MB  primary  ext4
 2      501MB   1000MB  500MB  primary
```

Now exit from **parted**. Additional work is required to implement these changes. The commands that follow, **mkswap**, **swapon**, and **mkfs.ext4**, are covered later in this chapter.

```
(parted) quit

# mkswap /dev/sdb2
# swapon /dev/sdb2
```

Now you can format the new regular Linux partition with the following command:

```
# mkfs.ext4 /dev/sdb1
```

Using parted: Set Up a Different Partition Type

When a partition is created in **parted**, you can reset its purpose with the **set** command. If the partitions are still available on that second hard drive (or any other existing hard drive with unused partitions, open it with the **parted** command. For example, the following command opens up that second hard drive:

```
# parted /dev/sdb
```

Run the **print** command. The flags column for existing partitions should be empty. Now you'll set that flag with the **set** command. From the commands shown here, the flags are set to use that first partition of the second drive as an LVM partition:

```
(parted) set
Partition number? 1
Flag to Invert? lvm
New state? [on]/off on
```

Now review the result with the **print** command:

```
(parted) print

Model: ATA QEMU HARDDISK (scsi)
Disk /dev/sdb: 1049MB
Sector size (logical/physical): 512B/512B
Partition Table: msdos

Number  Start   End    Size   Type     File system  Flags
 1      1049kB  500MB  499MB  primary  ext4         lvm
```

Similar steps can be used to configure a partition or a component of a RAID array. It's also a flag; just substitute **raid** for **lvm** in response to the Flag to Invert prompt just shown. If you're following along with a RHEL 6 system, first confirm the result. Exit from **parted**, and run the following commands:

```
# parted /dev/sdb print
# fdisk -l /dev/sdb
```

You'll see the **lvm** flag as shown previously from the **parted** command; you'll see the following confirmation in the output to the **fdisk** command:

```
   Device  Boot  Start    End   Blocks   Id  System
/dev/sda1                  1    263   487424   fd  Linux LVM
```

If you've set up the baseline virtual system described in Chapter 2, this is an excellent opportunity to set up partitions as components of LVM volumes. Now that you have the tools, it does not matter whether you use **fdisk** or **parted** for the purpose. You can choose to use all free space. Just be sure to create a partition on more than one hard disk for this purpose, to help illustrate the power of logical volumes.

Graphical Options

As suggested earlier, excellent graphical front ends are available for disk partitions. The GParted and QtParted options are based on **parted** and are designed for the GNOME and KDE desktop environments, respectively. As they are not available from the Red Hat Network, they are not supported by Red Hat and therefore won't be available for any Red Hat exams.

One graphical option available for RHEL 6 is known simply as Disk Utility, available from the gnome-disk-utility package. Once appropriate packages are installed, you can open Disk Utility from the command line interface with the **palimpsest** command.

The Disk Utility screen shown in Figure 6-3 reveals an application that's far from perfect. The screen depicts the baseline virtual machine created in Chapter 2; it lists the virtual hard drive, device /dev/vda, as if it were a peripheral hard drive. Fortunately, that is a trivial error; the functionality of the tool is not affected. It is still a very capable tool that can organize your drives or destroy all of your data in a number of ways.

The functionality includes the following clickable options:

- **Format Drive** Supports changes to the entire drive.
- **Benchmark** Allows measurements of read and write performance.

- **Unmount Volume**   Front end to the **umount** command.
- **Format Volume**   Front end to the **mkfs** command for a number of filesystem formats.
- **Check Filesystem**   Front end to the **fsck** command.
- **Edit Filesystem Label**   Front end to the **e2label** command; labels were commonly used on RHEL 5.
- **Edit Partition**   Front end to **fdisk**'s Change A Partition's System ID command for different partition types such as Linux swap and Linux LVM.
- **Delete Partition**   Front end to the **fdisk** functionality to delete a partition.
- **Create Partition**   Front end to the **fdisk** functionality to create a new partition.

Not all of these options appear in Figure 6-3; for example, the Create Partition option does not appear unless you've selected a "free" area of the target hard drive. In addition, you may note that the functionality of the Disk Utility goes beyond mere partitioning.

FIGURE 6-3   The Disk Utility

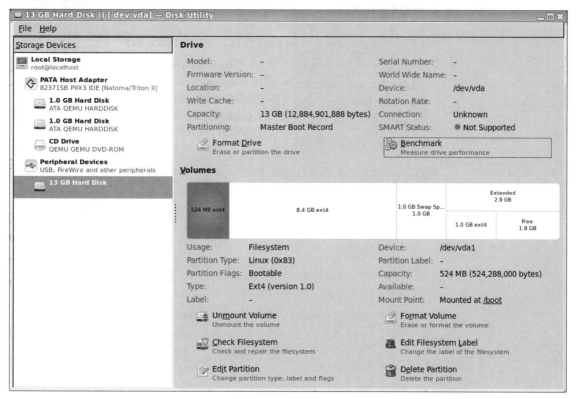

Work with fdisk and parted

In this exercise, you'll work with both the **fdisk** and **parted** utilities. It assumes a new empty drive is available. That does not require additional expense, as a virtual machine–based drive is acceptable for this purpose. For the purpose of this exercise, **fdisk** and **parted** will be used on drives /dev/sda and /dev/sdb, respectively. Feel free to substitute accordingly. Be aware, you'll save the results of this work for exercises that follow later in this chapter.

1. Run the **fdisk -l /dev/sda** command to review the current status of the /dev/sda drive.

2. Open disk /dev/sda with the **fdisk /dev/sda** command.

3. As suggested by the start message, switch off DOS-compatible mode and change display units to sectors with the **c** and **u** commands.

4. Run the **p** command to display any previously configured partitions.

5. Create a new partition with the **n** command. If there are primary partitions available, create one with the **p** command. If options for primary partition numbers are presented, select the first available.

6. When presented with a request similar to the following to specify the first sector of the new partition, specify something else. First try to specify sector 1 to see the response. Then try a sector somewhere after the default. For the purpose of this example, I specify 10,000 here:

   ```
   First sector (2048-2047999, default 2048): 10000
   ```

7. When presented with a request similar to the following to specify the last sector of the new partition, enter a number somewhere in the middle of the listed range. For the purpose of this example, I specify 1,000,000 here:

```
Last sector, +sectors or +size{K,M,G} (10000-2047999, default 2047999):
1000000
```

8. Run the **p** command again to review the result. Run the **w** command to write the result to disk.

9. Review the result on the /dev/sda disk with the **parted /dev/sda print** command.

10. Open the other available free disk /dev/sdb with the **parted /dev/sdb** command.

11. From the (parted) prompt, Run the **print** command to review the current status of partitions. If you see an "unrecognized disk label" error message, run the **mklabel msdos** command and run the **print** command again.

12. Create a new partition with the **mkpart** command. Follow the prompts. It does not matter whether the partition is primary or logical (avoid an extended partition for now). Do not enter a filesystem type; start the partition at **100M** (100MB) and end it at **600M** (600MB). Run the **print** command to confirm the new partition, and identify the partition number.

13. Run the **quit** command to exit from parted.

14. Run the **fdisk -l /dev/sdb** command to review the result. Do you see a problem?

15. Run the **fdisk /dev/sdb** command to open that drive. Run the **p** command. What do you see? Is it familiar?

16. Enter the **c** and **u** commands again. Repeat the **p** command. Do you see the same problem?

17. Exit from **fdisk** with the **q** command.

CERTIFICATION OBJECTIVE 6.02

Filesystem Formats

The number of filesystem types may exceed the number of operating systems. While RHEL can work with many of these formats, the default is ext4. While many users enable other filesystems such as ReiserFS, Red Hat may not support them.

Linux supports a rich variety of filesystems. Linux filesystems can be somewhat inaccurately divided into two categories: "standard" formatting and journaling. While this is an oversimplification, it suffices to describe the filesystems important to Linux. To me, a standard filesystem is an older Linux filesystem that does not log changes.

*There are a large number of filesystem types well described in the Filesystems
HOWTO at www.tldp.org. Strictly speaking, there is no "standard" Linux
filesystem.*

The filesystems described in this book are just a small list of those that can be
configured on an RHEL system. While Red Hat supports a limited list, the Linux
kernel makes it possible to set up more. A list of the filesystems supported by a kernel
is available in its configuration file in the /boot directory, in the **config-`uname -r`**
file, where **uname -r** is a command that, with the backquotes, substitutes the version
number of the currently loaded kernel.

Standard Formatting Filesystems

Linux is a clone of Unix. The Linux filesystems were developed to mimic the
functionality of Unix filesystems available at the time. The first Linux operating
systems used the Extended Filesystem (ext). Until the past few years, Red Hat Linux
operating systems formatted their partitions by default to the Second Extended
Filesystem (ext2). For RHEL 5, the default was the Third Extended Filesystem
(ext3). The new default for RHEL 6 is the Fourth Extended Filesystem (ext4). Both
ext3 and ext4 are journaling filesystems, described in the next section.

Given the growth in filesystem sizes, journaling filesystems are more resilient to
failure. So to some extent, the non-journaling filesystems described in Table 6-2
are legacy filesystems. Of course, filesystems such as ISO 9660 and swap are still in
common use.

Journaling Filesystems

As hard disks and partitions grow in size, Linux distributions use filesystems with
journaling features. Journaling filesystems have two main advantages. First, such as
filesystem is faster for Linux to check during the boot process. Second, if a crash
occurs, a journaling filesystem has a log (also known as a journal) that can be used
to restore the metadata for the files on the relevant partition.

For RHEL 5, the default RHEL filesystem is ext3; for RHEL 6, it's ext4. Those
aren't the only journaling filesystem options available, however. I list a few of the
options commonly used for RHEL in Table 6-3. From this list, Red Hat officially
supports only ext3 and ext4.

TABLE 6-2	**Filesystem Type**	**Description**
Some Standard Filesystems	ext	The first Linux filesystem, used only on early versions of that operating system.
	ext2 (Second Extended)	The foundation for ext3, the default filesystem for RHEL 5. The ext3 filesystem is essentially ext2 with journaling.
	swap	The Linux swap filesystem is associated with dedicated swap partitions. You probably created at least one swap partition when you installed RHEL.
	MS-DOS and VFAT	These filesystems allow you to read MS-DOS-formatted filesystems. MS-DOS lets you read pre–Windows 95 partitions, or regular Windows partitions within the limits of short filenames. VFAT lets you read Windows 9x/NT/2000/XP/Vista/7 partitions formatted to the FAT16 or FAT32 filesystems.
	ISO 9660	The standard filesystem for CD-ROMs. It is also known as the High Sierra File System, or HSFS, on other Unix systems.
	/proc	A Linux *virtual* filesystem. Virtual means that it doesn't occupy real disk space. Instead, files are created as needed. Used to provide information on kernel configuration and device status.
	/dev/pts	The Linux implementation of the Open Group's Unix98 PTY support.

TABLE 6-3	**Filesystem Type**	**Description**
Some Journaling Filesystems	ext3	The default filesystem for RHEL 5.
	ext4	The default filesystem for RHEL 6.
	JFS	IBM's journaled filesystem, commonly used on IBM enterprise servers.
	ReiserFS	The Reiser File System is resizable and supports fast journaling. It's more efficient when most of the files are very small and very large. It's based on the concept of "balanced trees." It is no longer supported by RHEL, or even by its former main proponent, SUSE. For more information, see www.namesys.com.
	xfs	Developed by Silicon Graphics as a journaling filesystem, it supports very large files; as of this writing, xfs files are limited to 9×10^{18} bytes. Do not confuse this filesystem with the X Font Server; both use the same acronym.
	NTFS	The current Microsoft Windows filesystem

The Red Hat move to ext4 is a testament to its use as a server operating system. One improvement with ext4 means that filesystems can be as large as 1 exabyte (EB). The former maximum filesystem size with ext3 was just 16 terabytes (TB). The ext4 filesystem reduces fragmentation, guarantees space for files, supports faster checks, and more. It even supports file timestamps in nanoseconds. As ext4 has been a part of the Linux kernel since 2008, it is proven technology. Given its speed and reliability, Red Hat even uses ext4 as the default filesystem for partitions dedicated to the /boot directory.

Filesystem Format Commands

There are several commands that can help you create a Linux filesystem. They're all based on the **mkfs** command, which works as a front end to filesystem-specific commands such as **mkfs.ext2**, **mkfs.ext3**, and **mkfs.ext4**.

If you want to reformat an existing partition, logical volume, or RAID array, take the following precautions:

- Back up any existing data on the partition.
- Unmount the partition.

There are two ways to apply formatting on a volume. (As noted earlier in this chapter, a volume is a generic name that can describe a partition, a RAID array, or a logical volume.) For example, if you've just created a partition on /dev/sdb5, you can format it to the ext4 filesystem using one of the following commands:

```
# mkfs -t ext4 /dev/sdb5
# mke2fs -t ext4 /dev/sdb5
# mkfs.ext4 /dev/sdb5
```

You can format partitions, logical volumes, and RAID arrays to other filesystems. The options available in RHEL 6 include:

- **mkfs.cramfs** creates a compressed ROM filesystem.
- **mkfs.ext2** formats a volume to the ext2 filesystem.
- **mkfs.ext3** formats a volume to the RHEL 5 default ext3 filesystem.
- **mkfs.ext4** formats a volume to the RHEL 6 default ext4 filesystem.
- **mkfs.msdos** (or **mkfs.vfat** or **mkdosfs**) formats a partition to the Microsoft-compatible VFAT filesystem; it does not create bootable filesystems.

(The inode numbers for all three files are the same; in other words, they are three different names for the same command.)

- **mkfs.xfs** formats a volume to the XFS filesystem developed by the former Silicon Graphics.

- **mkswap** formats a volume to the Linux swap filesystem.

These commands assume that you've configured an appropriate partition in the first place; for example, before the **mkswap** command can be properly applied to a partition, the Linux swap partition ID type must be configured for that partition. If you've created a RAID array or logical volume, as described later in this chapter, similar rules apply.

One advantage of some rebuild distributions is the availability of packages not supported by or available from Red Hat. For example, CentOS 6 includes the ntfsprogs package, which supports the mounting of NTFS partitions.

Swap Volumes

While Linux can use swap files, the swap space that's used essentially as overflow for RAM is generally configured in properly formatted partitions or logical volumes. They're generally not configured from RAID arrays, as redundancy for RAM is generally not useful. To see the swap space currently configured, run the **cat /proc/swaps** command.

As suggested in the previous section, swap volumes are formatted with the **mkswap** command. But that's not enough. First, to test the new swap volume, it must be activated with the **swapon** command. If the new swap volume is recognized, you'll see it in both the /proc/swaps file and the output to the **top** command. Second, you'll need to make sure to configure the new swap volume in the /etc/fstab file, as described later in this chapter.

Filesystem Check Commands

The **fsck** command analyzes the specified filesystem and performs repairs as required. Assume, for example, you're having problems with files in the /var directory, which happens to be mounted on /dev/sda7. If you want to run **fsck**, unmount that filesystem first. In some cases, you may need to go into single-user mode with the

init 1 command before you can unmount a filesystem. To unmount, analyze, and then remount the filesystem noted in this section, run the following commands:

```
# umount /var
# fsck -t ext4 /dev/sda7
# mount /dev/sda7 /var
```

The **fsck** command also serves as a "front end," depending on the filesystem format. For example, if you're formatting an ext2, ext3, or ext4 filesystem, **fsck** by itself automatically calls the **e2fsck** command. In fact, the **fsck.ext2**, **fsck.ext3**, **fsck.ext4**, and **e2fsck** files are all different names for the same command! They have the same inode number. You can confirm this by applying the **ls -i** command to all four files, which are part of the /sbin directory.

Filesystem Conversions

If you're upgrading between versions of Linux, you may also want to upgrade filesystems. It wasn't that long ago that most Linux systems were configured to the ext2 filesystem. In fact, for RHEL 5, ext3 was considered inefficient by many for filesystems such as the /boot directory, so many administrators formatted the associated partition to ext2.

Fortunately, if you have a partition formatted to ext2, it's easy to add the journal associated with ext3. And then it's a straightforward command to add the features associated with ext4 formatting. These commands require a temporary remounting of the filesystem in read-only mode. Alternatively, you could just unmount that directory. For example, if the filesystem in question is mounted on the /dev/vda1 partition, you'd run the following commands to convert from ext2 to ext3, where the **tune2fs -j** command adds a journal.

```
# mount -o remount,ro /dev/vda1
# tune2fs -j /dev/vda1
# mount -o remount,rw /dev/vda1
```

Of course, you'd then have to make appropriate changes to the /etc/fstab configuration file, namely changing the filesystem format column from ext2 to ext3. If necessary, you could convert back with the **tune2fs ^O has_journal** command. But any move from ext2 or ext3 to ext4 is one-way. You can't convert back to ext3 or ext2. If you're ready to make the move to ext4, run the following command:

```
# tune2fs -O extent,uninit_bg,dir_index /dev/vda1
```

In fact, if you try to disable some components of the ext4 filesystem, it may break features such as the **blkid** command described later in this chapter.

If you're converting the volume associated with the top-level root directory (/), it's not possible to even remount that directory in read-only mode. Thus, the process with that directory may require a detour through the rescue mode environment described in Chapter 5.

To confirm the current settings associated with a filesystem, run the following command:

```
# dumpe2fs /dev/vda1 | grep "Filesystem features"
```

You should see the features just described in the output associated with the features of the specified filesystem volume.

EXERCISE 6-2

Format, Check, and Mount Different Filesystems

In this exercise, you'll work with the file format and checking commands **mkfs** and **fsck**, and review the results with the **mount** command. This exercise assumes you've completed Exercise 6-1, or at least have unmounted Linux partitions with no data.

1. Review the current status of partitions on the drives discussed in Exercise 6-1 with the **parted /dev/sda print** and **fdisk -l /dev/sdb** commands.

2. Format the partition created by the first drive with the **mkfs.ext2 /dev/sda1** command. Review the current status of the volume with the **dumpe2fs /dev/sda1 | grep formats** command. What features do you see in the output? Save the output, temporarily. One way to do so is open a new command line console. Check the system with the **fsck.ext2 /dev/sda1** command.

3. Mount the newly formatted partition with **mount /dev/sda1 /mnt** command. Review the output with the **mount** command, by itself. If the mount and format worked, you'll see the following output:

   ```
   /dev/sda1 on /mnt type ext2 (rw)
   ```

4. Unmount the formatted partition with the **umount /mnt** command.

5. Run the **tune2fs -j /dev/sda1** command and rerun the **dumpe2fs** command from the previous step. What's the difference between the output now, and the output when the partition was formatted to the ext2 filesystem?

6. Repeat Steps 3 and 4. What's the difference in the output to the **mount** command?

7. Run the **tune2fs -O extent,uninit_bg,dir_index /dev/sda1** command. Do you see a message in the output?

8. Apply the **fsck.ext4** command on the partition. What do you see?

9. Repeat Step 6.

10. Now on the other partition created in Exercise 6-1, apply the **mkfs.ext4 /dev/sdb1** command.

11. Mount the newly formatted partition on the **/net** directory, and run the **mount** command by itself. Can you confirm the format of the /dev/sdb1 partition?

CERTIFICATION OBJECTIVE 6.03

Basic Linux Filesystems and Directories

Everything in Linux can be reduced to a file. Partitions are associated with *filesystem device nodes* such as /dev/sda1. Hardware components are associated with node files such as /dev/dvd. Detected devices are documented as files in the /proc directory. The Filesystem Hierarchy Standard (FHS) is the official way to organize files in Unix and Linux directories. As with the other sections, this introduction provides only the most basic overview of the FHS. More information is available from the official FHS home page at www.pathname.com/fhs.

Separate Linux Filesystems

There are several major directories associated with all modern Unix/Linux operating systems. Files, drivers, kernels, logs, programs, utilities, and more are organized in these directories. The way these components are organized on storage media is known as a filesystem. It's based on the way the filesystem is formatted, and the directory where that filesystem is mounted. The FHS makes it easier for users of other Unix-based operating systems to understand the basics of Linux.

Every FHS starts with the top-level root directory, also known by its symbol, the single forward slash (/). All of the other directories shown in Table 6-4 are subdirectories of the root directory. Unless mounted separately, you can also find their files on the same partition as the root directory. You may not see some of the directories shown in the table if associated packages have not been installed. Not all directories shown are officially part of the FHS. More importantly, not all listed directories can or should be mounted separately.

Mounted directories are often known as *volumes,* which can span multiple partitions. However, while the root directory (/) is the top-level directory in the FHS, the root user's home directory (/root) is just a subdirectory.

on the ☝ o b

In Linux, the word filesystem has several different meanings. For example, a filesystem can refer to the FHS, an individual volume, or a format such as ext3. A filesystem device node such as /dev/sda1 represents the partition on which a directory can be mounted.

Directories That Can Be Mounted Separately

If space is available, several directories listed in Table 6-4 are excellent candidates to be mounted separately. As discussed in Chapter 1, it's typical to mount directories such as /, /boot, /home, /opt, /srv, /tmp, and /var on separate volumes. Sometimes, it makes sense to mount lower-level subdirectories on separate volumes, such as /var/ftp for an FTP server or /var/www for a web server.

But first, several directories should always be maintained as part of the top-level root directory filesystem. These directories include: /bin, /dev, /etc, /lib, /root, /sbin, and /selinux. Files within these directories are essential to the smooth operation of Linux as an operating system. While the same argument can be made for the /boot directory, it is a special case. The storage of the Linux kernel, Initial RAM Disk, and bootloader files in this directory can help protect the core of the operating system when there are other problems.

This ignores directories with virtual filesystems, including /proc and /sys. Files in these directories are filled only during the boot process and disappear when a system is shut down. As there's nothing to store from these directories, there's no reason to mount them separately. Some directories listed in Table 6-4 are designed for use only as mount points. In other words, they should normally be empty. If you store files on those directories, they won't be accessible if, say, a network share is mounted on them. Typical network mount points include the /media, /mnt, /net, and /smb directories.

TABLE 6-4	Basic Filesystem Hierarchy Standard Directories

Directory	Description
/	The root directory, the top-level directory in the FHS. All other directories are subdirectories of root, which is always mounted on some volume.
/bin	Essential command line utilities. Should not be mounted separately; otherwise, it could be difficult to get to these utilities when using a rescue disk.
/boot	Includes Linux startup files, including the Linux kernel. The default, 500MB, is usually sufficient for a typical modular kernel and additional kernels that you might install during the RHCE or RHCSA exam.
/dev	Hardware and software device drivers for everything from floppy drives to terminals. Do not mount this directory on a separate volume.
/etc	Most basic configuration files. Do not mount this directory on a separate volume.
/home	Home directories for almost every user.
/lib	Program libraries for the kernel and various command line utilities. Do not mount this directory on a separate volume.
/media	The mount point for removable media, including floppy drives, DVDs, and Zip disks.
/misc	The standard mount point for local directories mounted via the automounter.
/mnt	A legacy mount point; formerly used for removable media.
/net	The standard mount point for network directories mounted via the automounter.
/opt	Common location for third-party application files.
/proc	Currently running kernel-related processes, including device assignments such as IRQ ports, I/O addresses, and DMA channels, as well as kernel configuration settings such as IP forwarding. As a virtual filesystem, Linux automatically configures it as a separate filesystem in RAM.
/root	The home directory of the root user. Do not mount this directory on a separate volume.
/sbin	System administration commands. Don't mount this directory separately.
/selinux	Currently configured settings associated with Security Enhanced Linux. Do not mount this directory on a separate volume.
/smb	The standard mount point for remote shared Microsoft network directories mounted via the automounter.
/srv	Commonly used by various network servers on non–Red Hat distributions.
/tftpboot	Included if the TFTP server is installed.
/tmp	Temporary files. By default, Red Hat Enterprise Linux deletes all files in this directory periodically.
/usr	Small programs accessible to all users. Includes many system administration commands and utilities.
/var	Variable data, including log files and printer spools.

CERTIFICATION OBJECTIVE 6.04

Logical Volume Management (LVM)

Logical Volume Management (LVM, also known as the Logical Volume Manager) can allow you to manage the space allocated to appropriate directories. As an example, assume the /var and /home directories are configured on separate logical volumes. If extra space is available on the volume associated with the /var directory, you can reallocate space to the volume associated with the /home directory.

Alternatively, if you are managing a server on a growing network, new users will be common. Periodically, more room may be needed on a volume associated with the /home directory. With LVM, you can add a new physical disk and allocate its storage capacity to an existing /home directory volume.

on the
job

While LVM can be an important tool to manage the space available to different volumes, it does not provide redundancy. However, you can use LVM in concert with a RAID array.

Definitions in LVM

To work with LVM, you need to understand how partitions configured for that purpose are used. First, with the **fdisk** and **parted** utilities, you need to create partitions configured to the LVM partition type. The commands within those utilities were described earlier in this chapter.

Once those partitions are available, they need to be set up as physical volumes (PVs). That process sets up the physical partitions into manageable chunks known as physical extents (PEs). With the right commands, you can then convert those PEs to logical extents (LEs). Those LEs can be organized into logical volumes (LVs). You can then create volume groups (VGs) from part or all of an LV. That VG can then be formatted and mounted on an appropriate directory. For those who are new to LVM, it may be important to break out each definition:

- **Physical volume (PV)**   A PV is a partition, configured to the LVM partition type.
- **Physical extent (PE)**   A PE is a small uniform segment of disk space. PVs are split into PEs.

- **Logical extent (LE)** Every LE is associated with a PE and can be combined into a volume group.
- **Volume group (VG)** A VG is a bunch of LEs grouped together.
- **Logical volume (LV)** An LV is a part of a VG, which can be formatted and then mounted on the directory of your choice.

You'll see this broken down in the following sections. But in essence, to create an LV system, you need to create a new PV, using a command such as **pvcreate**, assign the space from one or more PVs to a VG with a command such as **vgcreate**, and allocate the space from some part of available VGs to an LV with a command such as **lvcreate**.

To add space to an existing LVM system, you need to add free space from an existing VG with a command such as **lvextend**. If you don't have any existing VG space, you'll need to add to it with unassigned PV space with a command such as **vgextend**. If all of your PVs are taken, you may need to create a new PV from an unassigned partition or hard drive with the **pvcreate** command.

Whenever you change an active PV, LV, or VG, unmount the mounted LV first. If it's an essential filesystem such as the top-level root (/) directory, you may need to boot from the RHEL 6 installation CD/DVD into rescue mode.

Create a Physical Volume

The first step is to start with a physical partition. Based on the discussion earlier in this chapter, you should be able to set up partitions set up to match the Linux LVM identifier. Then, to set up a new PV on a properly configured partition, such as /dev /sda1, apply the **pvcreate** command to that partition:

```
# pvcreate /dev/sda1
```

If there is more than one partition to be configured as a PV, the associated device files can all be listed in the same command:

```
# pvcreate /dev/sda1 /dev/sda2 /dev/sdb1 /dev/sdb2
```

Create a Volume Group

From one or more PVs, you can create a volume group (VG). In the following command, substitute the name of your choice for *volumegroup*:

```
# vgcreate volumegroup /dev/sda1 /dev/sda2
```

You can include additional PVs in any VG. Assume there are existing PVs based on /dev/sdb1 and /dev/sdb2 partitions, you can add to the *volumegroup* VG with the following command:

```
# vgextend volumegroup /dev/sdb1 /dev/sdb2
```

Create a Logical Volume

However, a new VG isn't enough since you can't format or mount a filesystem on it. So you need to create a logical volume (LV) for this purpose. The following command creates an LV. You can add as many chunks of disk space, in PEs, as you need.

```
# lvcreate -l number_of_PEs volumegroup -n logvol
```

This creates a device named /dev/*volumegroup*/*logvol*. You can format this device as if it were a regular disk partition, and then mount a directory on that new logical volume.

But this isn't useful if you don't know how much space is associated with each PE. You could use trial and error, using the **df** command to check the size of the volume after mounting a directory on it. Alternatively, you can use the **-L** switch to set a size in MB. For example, the following command creates an LV named flex of 200MB:

```
# lvcreate -L 200M volumegroup -n flex
```

Make Use of a Logical Volume

But that's not the last step. You may not get full credit unless the directory gets mounted on the logical volume when the system is rebooted. This process is described later in this chapter in the discussion of the /etc/fstab configuration file.

More LVM Commands

There are a wide variety of LVM commands related to PVs, LVs, and VGs. Generally, they are **pv***, **lv***, and **vg*** in the /usr/sbin directory. Physical volume commands include those listed in Table 6-5.

As you assign PVs to VGs to LVs, you may need commands to control and configure them. Table 6-6 includes an overview of most related volume group commands.

TABLE 6-5	Physical Volume Command	Description
Physical Volume Management Commands	pvchange	Changes attributes of a PV: the **pvchange -x n /dev/sda10** command disables the use of PEs from the /dev/sda10 partition.
	pvck	Checks the integrity of a physical volume.
	pvcreate	Initializes a disk or partition as a PV; the partition should be flagged with the LVM file type.
	pvdisplay	Displays currently configured PVs.
	pvmove	Moves PVs in a VG from the specified partition to free locations on other partitions; prerequisite to disabling a PE. One example: **pvmove /dev/sda10**.
	pvremove	Removes a given PV from a list of recognized volume: for example, **pvremove /dev/sda10**.
	pvresize	Changes the amount of a partition allocated to a PV. If you've expanded partition /dev/sda10, **pvresize /dev/sda10** takes advantage of the additional space. Alternatively, **pvresize --setphysicalvolumesize 100M /dev/sda10** reduces the amount of PVs taken from that partition to the noted space.
	pvs	Lists configured PVs and the associated VGs, if so assigned.
	pvscan	Similar to **pvs**.

TABLE 6-6	Volume Group Command	Description
Volume Group Commands	vgcfgbackup vgcfgrestore	Backs up and restores the configuration files associated with LVM; by default, they're in the /etc/lvm directory.
	vgchange	Similar to **pvchange**, allows you to activate or deactivate a VG. For example, **vgchange -a** y enables all local VGs.
	vgck	Checks the integrity of a volume group.
	vgconvert	Supports conversions from LVM1 systems to LVM2: **vgconvert -M2 VolGroup00** converts VolGroup00.
	vgcreate	Creates a VG, from two or more configured PVs: for example, **vgcreate vgroup00 /dev/sda10 /dev/sda11** creates vgroup00 from PVs as defined on /dev/sda10 and /dev/sda11.
	vgdisplay	Displays characteristics of currently configured VGs.
	vgexport vgimport	Exports and imports unused VGs from those available for LVs; the **vgexport -a** command exports all inactive VGs.

TABLE 6-6	Volume Group Command	Description
Volume Group Commands (*continued*)	vgextend	If you've created a new PV: **vgextend vgroup00 /dev/sda11** adds the space from /dev/sda11 to vgroup00.
	vgmerge	If you have an unused VG vgroup01, you can merge it into vgroup00 with the following command: **vgmerge vgroup00 vgroup01**.
	vgmknodes	Run this command if you have a problem with VG device files.
	vgreduce	The **vgreduce vgroup00 /dev/sda11** command removes the /dev/sda11 PV from vgroup00, assuming sufficient free space is available.
	vgremove	The **vgremove vgroup00** command removes vgroup00, assuming it is not assigned to any LV.
	vgrename	Allows renaming of LVs.
	vgs	Displays basic information on configured VGs.
	vgscan	Scans and displays basic information on configured VGs.
	vgsplit	Splits a volume group.

As you assign PVs to VGs and then subdivide VGs into LVs, you may need commands to control and configure them. Table 6-7 includes an overview of related LVM commands.

TABLE 6-7	Logical Volume Command	Description
Logical Volume Commands	lvchange	Similar to **pvchange**, changes the attributes of an LV: for example, the **lvchange -a n vgroup00/lvol00** command disables the use of the LV labeled lvol00.
	lvconvert	If there are sufficient available PVs, the **lvconvert -m1 vgroup00/lvol00** command mirrors the LV.
	lvcreate	Creates a new LV in an existing VG. For example, **lvcreate -l 200 volume01 -n lvol01** creates lvol01 from 200 extents in the VG named volume01.
	lvdisplay	Displays currently configured LVs.
	lvextend	Adds space to an LV: the **lvextend -L4G /dev/volume01/lvol01** command extends lvol01 to 4GB, assuming space is available.
	lvreduce	Reduces the size of an LV; if there's data in the reduced area, it is lost.
	lvremove	Removes an active LV: the **lvremove volume01/lvol01** command removes all lvol01 from VG volume01.

TABLE 6-7	Logical Volume Command	Description
Logical Volume Commands (*continued*)	lvrename	Renames an LV.
	lvresize	Resizes an LV; can be done by -L for size. For example, **lvresize -L 4GB volume01/lvol01** changes the size of lvol01 to 4GB.
	lvs	Lists all configured LVs.
	lvscan	Scans for all active LVs.

Here's an example how this works. Try the **vgscan** command. You can verify configured volume groups (VGs) with the **vgdisplay** command. For example, Figure 6-4 illustrates the configuration of VG volgroup.

While there are a number of **lvm*** commands installed, just four of them are active: **lvm**, **lvmconf**, **lvmdiskscan**, and **lvmdump**. The lvm command moves to an **lvm>** prompt. It's rather interesting, as the **help** command at that prompt provides a nearly full list of available LVM commands.

The **lvmconf** command can modify the default settings in the related configuration file, /etc/lvm/lvm.conf. The **lvmdiskscan** command scans all available drives for LVM-configured partitions. Finally, the **lvmdump** command sets up a configuration report in the root administrative user's home directory (/root).

FIGURE 6-4	

Configuration of a volume group (VG)

```
[root@server1 ~]# vgdisplay
  --- Volume group ---
  VG Name               volgroup
  System ID
  Format                lvm2
  Metadata Areas        4
  Metadata Sequence No  2
  VG Access             read/write
  VG Status             resizable
  MAX LV                0
  Cur LV                0
  Open LV               0
  Max PV                0
  Cur PV                4
  Act PV                4
  VG Size               1.92 GiB
  PE Size               4.00 MiB
  Total PE              492
  Alloc PE / Size       0 / 0
  Free  PE / Size       492 / 1.92 GiB
  VG UUID               BBnWnG-iWTl-M8T3-KPwS-Ye31-TsaJ-8TwjZ6

[root@server1 ~]#
```

Before logical volumes are useful, you need to know how to add another LV. For example, if you've added more users, and they need more room than is available on the /home directory, you may need to add more LVs.

Linux can't read files from the /boot directory if it's configured on a logical volume. As those files are essential to the boot process, don't set up a logical volume for that directory.

Remove a Logical Volume

The removal of an existing LV is straightforward, with the **lvremove** command. This assumes that any directories previously mounted on LVs have been unmounted. At that point, the basic steps are simple:

1. Save any data in directories that are mounted on the LV.
2. Unmount any directories associated with the LV. Based on the example in the previous section, you would use the following command:

   ```
   # umount /dev/vg_01/lv_01
   ```

3. Apply the **lvremove** command to the LV with a command such as:

   ```
   # lvremove /dev/vg_01/lv_01
   ```

4. You should now have the LEs from this LV free for use in other LVs.

Resize Logical Volumes

If you need to increase the size of an existing LV, you can add the space from a newly created PV to it. All it takes is appropriate use of the **vgextend** and **lvextend** commands. For example, to add the PEs to the VG associated with a /home directory mounted on a LV, take the following basic steps:

1. Back up any data existing on the /home directory. (This is a standard precaution that isn't necessary if everything goes right. You might even skip this step on the Red Hat exams. But do you really want to risk user data in practice?)
2. Unmount the /home directory from the current LV.
3. Extend the VG to include new partitions configured to the appropriate type. For example, to add /dev/sdd1 to the /home VG, run the following command:

   ```
   # vgextend vg_00 /dev/sdd1
   ```

4. Make sure the new partitions are included in the VG with the following command:

```
# vgdisplay vg_00
```

5. Now you can extend the space given to the current LV. For example, to extend the LV to 2000MB, run the following command:

```
# lvextend -L 2000M /dev/vg_00/lv_00
```

6. The **lvextend** command can increase the space allocated to an LV in KB, MB, GB, or even TB. For example, you could specify a 2000M LV with the following command:

```
# lvextend -L 2G /dev/vg_00/lv_00
```

7. Resize the formatted volume with the **resize2fs** command. If you're using the entire extended LV, the command is simple:

```
# resize2fs /dev/vg_00/lv_00
```

To use just part of the new volume, you can specify the amount of space at the end of the command; for example, the following command suggests a format of 1900MB:

```
# resize2fs /dev/vg_00/lv_00 1900M
```

8. Alternatively, you can reformat the LV, using commands described earlier, so the filesystem can take full advantage of the new space—and then restore data from the backup. (If you've already successfully resized an LV, *don't* reformat it. It isn't necessary and would destroy existing data!)

```
# mkfs.ext4 /dev/vg_00/lv_00
```

9. In either case, you'd finish the process by remounting the newly resized LV.

```
# mount /dev/vg_00/lv_00 /home
```

The GUI Logical Volume Management Tool

If this is all confusing, you might try the GUI Logical Volume Management tool, as shown in Figure 6-5. In general, command line tools are superior. While command line tools can still do more, the Red Hat Logical Volume Management tool is quite capable. In the GNOME desktop, you can start it by running **system-config-lvm** from a GUI command line. In the following sections, I'll show you how to use it to add, remove, and resize logical volumes.

FIGURE 6-5   The Logical Volume Management tool

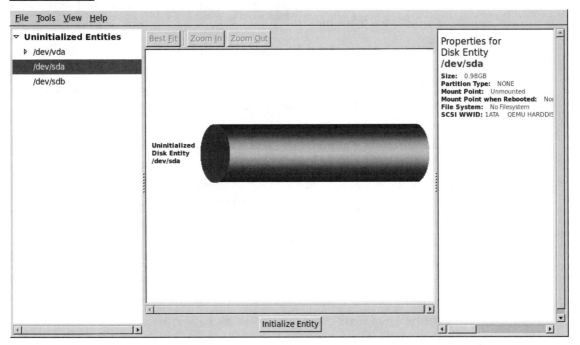

If needed, you can install the system-config-lvm package with the following command:

```
# yum install system-config-lvm
```

If possible, test the options in these three subsections in one sitting. If you test the commands in the first subsection, retain them for the next subsection and so on. These sections effectively repeat the descriptions shown earlier in this chapter based on command line tools.

Add an LV

Assume you've added a new hard drive. For the purpose of this section, I'm using the /dev/sda and /dev/sdb drives associated with the baseline virtual machine used for this book. In addition, I've deleted those partitions. That provides up to 2000MB of space.

Remember that if the GUI commands in this tool don't work, you can always use the associated regular text commands described earlier. Based on the tool shown in Figure 6-5, take the following steps:

1. Create a /test directory. (You should already know how to use the **mkdir** command for this purpose.)

2. Open the GUI Logical Volume Management tool; one method is to run the **system-config-lvm** command inside the GUI.

3. Navigate to the Uninitialized Entities section in the left-hand pane. Based on the standard VM installation, select drive /dev/sda, or a partition configured on that drive.

4. Click the Initialize Entity button that appears at the bottom of the window. This action applies the **pvcreate** command, in this case, to the entire drive.

5. You'll see a warning that all data on the partition will be lost. Assuming that's not a problem for you, click Yes.

6. If you're initializing an entire disk, you'll see a suggestion to create a single partition encompassing the entire drive. Click Yes.

7. Confirm the result from a command line; run the **fdisk -l** command to confirm the new partition of the appropriate LVM type, and the **pvs** command to confirm the creation of the physical volume.

8. If you haven't seen it before, you'll see an Unallocated Volumes category. Select the PV that you've just initialized. You'll see three options:

   ■ The Create New Volume Group option allows you to create a new VG for another filesystem, which corresponds to the **vgcreate** command.

   ■ Add To Existing Volume Group allows you to increase the space associated with the VG of your choice. This corresponds to the **vgextend** command.

   ■ Remove Volume From LVM reverses the process.

   As this section is based on adding a new VG, select Create New Volume Group. You'll see the window shown in Figure 6-6, where you can assign a name and set the size for the new VG; the default uses all available space. For the purpose of this section, I've named the new VG NewVol. Name the volume and click OK.

9. You'll see the new VG in the Volume Groups category. In the left-hand pane, navigate to the name of the new VG, in this case, NewVol, and select the Logical View for this group. Click the Create New Logical Volume button that appears at the bottom of the window, which opens the window shown in Figure 6-7.

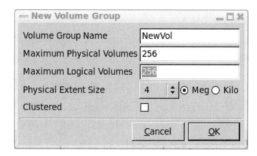

FIGURE 6-6

Create a New
Volume Group.

10. In the Create New Logical Volume window, you can configure the amount
of space assigned to the LV, the format, and the mount point. In Figure 6-7,
I've allocated half the space to NewLV, formatted it to ext4, and set it to be
mounted on the previously created /test directory. If you were to also select
the Mount When Rebooted option, the tool would also configure the LV in
the /etc/fstab file.

This new LV is now ready for a new filesystem; you can copy desired files to the
/test directory, unmount it, and change /etc/fstab to mount it on a different directory.
But for the purpose of this section, complete Step 10, but don't make any further
changes to the /test directory or the /etc/fstab file. If you want to see the changes
reflected in the Logical Volume Management tool, click View | Reload.

FIGURE 6-7

Create a New
Logical Volume

Remove an LV

This section assumes that you've created an LV using the steps described in the preceding section.

1. Unless it's already open, start the GUI Logical Volume Management tool.
2. In the left-hand pane, navigate to NewVol, select Logical View, and click NewLV. This is the LV assigned to and mounted on the /test directory.
3. Click the Remove Logical Volume button, which corresponds to the **lvre-move** command. Confirm when prompted.

on the **job**

Before removing the LV, look at the other options. The Create Snapshot option supports a mirror of the current LV. It works only if there is sufficient unallocated space from available VGs. The Edit Properties option supports changes to the LV settings described in the previous subsection.

You'll see a warning about NewLV containing data from directory /test. Any data copied to that directory will be lost if you click Yes. Go ahead. Technically, that's all you need to remove the LV. But you can do more.

4. Move up a bit in the left-hand pane. Click NewVol and then select Physical View. Navigate down to the partition you created in the previous subsection, and then select Remove Volume From Volume Group, and select Yes when the warning appears.
5. You'll now see the partition in the Unallocated Volumes category, as shown in Figure 6-8. Navigate to and select the subject partition. Do not click Remove Volume From LVM.
6. In preparation for the next subsection, reverse the process. Rerun Steps 9 and 10 from the Add an LV section. Refer to Figure 6-7 if and as needed.

Add to and Increase the Size of an LV

In this subsection, you'll redo the first steps to add an LV from a newly available partition or hard drive, as described in an earlier section. Instead of creating a new LV, you'll add the new space to an existing LV. To do so, take the following steps:

1. Unless it's already open, start the GUI Logical Volume Management tool.
2. Navigate to the Uninitialized Entities associated with the other spare drive, /dev/sdb.

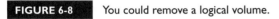

FIGURE 6-8   You could remove a logical volume.

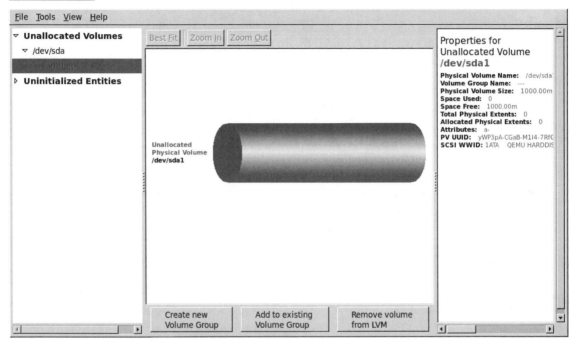

3. Select a partition or a drive; in this case, /dev/sdb1 or /dev/sdb. It should be different from the partition or drive created earlier. Click the Initialize Entity button that appears at the bottom of the window, and confirm when the warning message appears. If you're working with a drive, accept the prompt to create a partition. This action applies the **pvcreate** command to the new partition.

4. In the Unallocated Volumes category, select the PV just initialized. In this case, select Add To Existing Volume Group. You'll see the Add Physical Volume To VG window shown in Figure 6-9.

5. Select the existing volume group of your choice and click Add. If you've followed the instructions so far, the volume group should be named NewVol. Under the Volume Groups heading, navigate to the name of the new LV and click Logical View; for the work done in earlier sections, the name is NewLV, as shown in Figure 6-10.

FIGURE 6-9

Add a PV to a
logical volume.

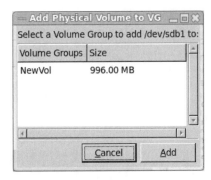

6. Click Edit Properties. You'll see an Edit Logical Volume window similar to
(but not identical to) Figure 6-7. You'll be able to change the amount of
space allocated from the VG to the NewLV Logical Volume. The advantage
here is that it automatically resizes the formatted volume, with the **resize2fs**
command. The process may take several minutes.

Check the result; rerun the **df** command.

FIGURE 6-10   Increase the size of a logical volume.

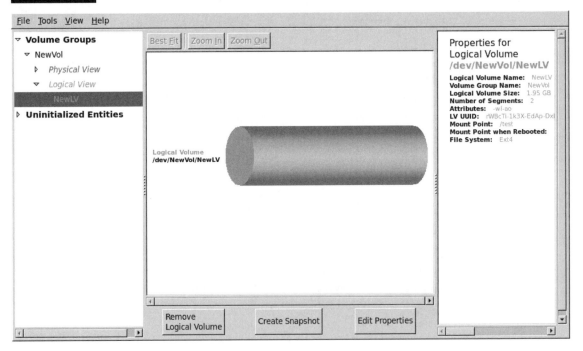

CERTIFICATION OBJECTIVE 6.05

Volume Encryption with the Linux Unified Key Setup

Encryption can help secure data on key devices, such as the volume that may contain critical personal information. One way to encrypt devices on a system is with the Linux Unified Key Setup (LUKS). Encryption with LUKS works on a block level; in other words, it's applied to block device files such as the partitions and LVs associated with storage. If a key computer is lost, the data within is at least a bit more secure, as the LUKS-protected system requires either a passphrase or a keyfile.

Passwords, Passphrases, and More

The discussion of LUKS is the first place in this book where you have to define a passphrase. Thus, it's the first opportunity to explore the difference between a passphrase and a password. So what happens if a laptop with a critical database of credit card numbers, or even social security numbers, is lost? The company that owns the laptop may then have to provide identity protection services, and even more for any users who subsequently suffer financial loss as a result.

Computer users are used to passwords. They're relatively short and they're easy to remember. They have been adequate for networked systems that have been properly secured in other ways. While there are security issues associated with many passwords, users are resistant to change. But given the importance of data stored on many systems, a password is not enough. (Nevertheless, usernames and passwords are still part of the Red Hat exam requirements.)

However, given just a little time, most passwords can be cracked. In fact, the dictionary words used by most people as passwords can be cracked in a matter of seconds. With this fact in mind, computer professionals encourage users to create passwords with some combination of uppercase and lowercase characters, mixed with numbers and punctuation. Perhaps the most difficult passwords to crack are based on the first alphanumeric characters of a favorite phrase. For example, a password like ET,Ie3ppsiR,NC. could stand for "Every Tuesday, I eat 3 pulled pork sandwiches in Raleigh, North Carolina." But given enough time, even passwords of that complexity can be cracked. In general, spaces are not allowed in a password.

Many networks are moving to more secure systems. To that end, it's more common to find partitions and entire drives encrypted with a password, or preferably a passphrase. Passwords are typically 6 to 10 characters. Longer passwords are difficult for users to remember, unless they're based on a favorite phrase.

One advantage of a passphrase is that it can also include spaces, and even complete sentences. Such longer entries, such as "Every Tuesday, I eat 3 pulled pork sandwiches in North Carolina." are more difficult to crack than just a password. But you can go further. Computer security professionals encourage the use of a combination of words and acronyms in a passphrase, perhaps something like "On Tuesday, Ia3pps in North Carolina." Such a combination of words and acronyms in a sentence is even more difficult for a cracker to decrypt. In any case, the use of passphrases is covered in both the RHCSA and RHCE exams. This section covers the use of passphrases to protect LUKS-encrypted storage volumes.

Of course, there are more secure authentication systems available. For example, one RHCE skill discussed in Chapter 11 combines the advantages of passphrases with encryption key cryptography. In addition, RHEL 6 (though not the RHCSA/RHCE exams) includes the drivers associated with fingerprint readers, which can also be set up for user logins.

Encryption During Installation

The easiest way to prepare a LUKS-encrypted volume is during the installation process. Figure 6-11 illustrates the RHEL 6 installation screen where a LUKS-encrypted volume is created on the /test directory.

If you've paid careful attention during the installation process, you may remember that the entire system can be encrypted, as shown back in Chapter 1, in Figure 1-6.

But as suggested at the beginning of this chapter, for the RHCSA, you need to know how to create, configure, mount, and unmount LUKS-encrypted filesystems. While this is normally done with a passphrase entered during the boot process, it also can be set up with a passkey, which can be set up on remote media such as a USB stick.

FIGURE 6-11

Create a LUKS-encrypted volume with Disk Druid.

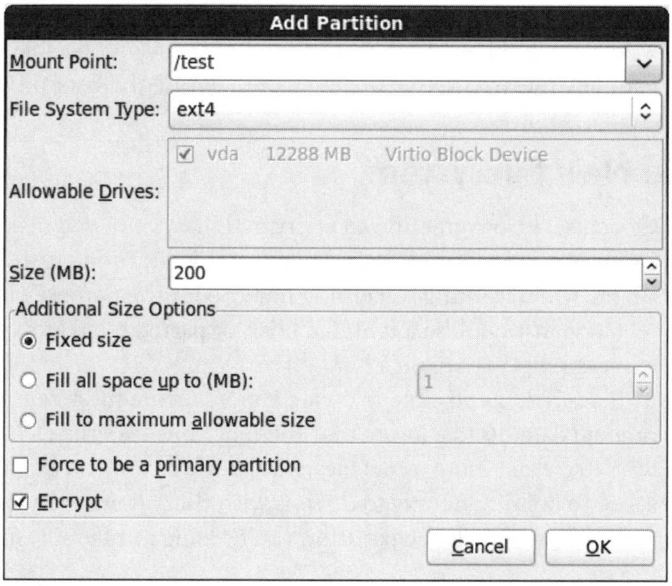

Add Partition	
Mount Point:	/test
File System Type:	ext4
Allowable Drives:	☑ vda 12288 MB Virtio Block Device
Size (MB):	200

Additional Size Options
- ⦿ Fixed size
- ○ Fill all space up to (MB): 1
- ○ Fill to maximum allowable size

☐ Force to be a primary partition

☑ Encrypt

Cancel   OK

Prepare and Initialize Encryption

So in this chapter, you need to learn how to set up an encrypted filesystem mounted on a specific directory. It requires the dm_crypt module, which is installed as part of the baseline RHEL 6 kernel package. It should be shown in the following output to the **lsmod | grep dm_crypt** command:

```
dm_crypt      12860   0
dm_mod        76856   7 dm_crypt,dm_mirror,dm_log
```

If you don't see this output, run the following command:

```
# modprobe dm_crypt
```

You'll also need the cryptsetup-luks RPM package. Install it if needed with the following command:

```
# yum install cryptsetup-luks
```

When a passphrase is configured on a LUKS filesystem, the user that boots a system is prompted for that passphrase during that boot process, with a prompt similar to the following:

```
Password for /dev/vda2 (luks-45b...):**************************
```

Each character of the passphrase, including spaces, is shown with asterisks. A cracker who gets a hold of a LUKS-encrypted system won't be able to boot the system, or at least any filesystems that are encrypted during the boot process.

Prepare the New Filesystem

Of course, before creating an encrypted filesystem, you need a partition. While it can be processed into a logical volume or RAID array first, it's best to keep things simple when learning something new. So for the purpose of this section, start with a regular partition. Use a tool like **fdisk** or **parted** to create a regular partition from existing empty space on a hard drive.

If desired, it's possible to create a more secure filesystem by first filling it with random data. Just be aware that these options take time. While they are excellent ways to create a more secure filesystem, don't do it on an exam unless you're specifically asked to do so! One way to do so is with the following **badblocks** command on device /dev/sda1. If the partition you're using is different, substitute accordingly.

```
# badblocks -c 10240 -s -w -t random -v /dev/sda1
```

This particular command tests 10240 blocks at a time ($2^{10} * 10$) with the number of blocks (**-c**) switch. The **-s** illustrates the progress of the command. The **-w** does the actual writing of data, in a random test pattern (**-t random**), in verbose mode (**-v**). This command took a couple of minutes to add random data to a 1GB partition on my server1.example.com VM system.

An alternative is to use the Linux random number generator device, /dev/urandom. The following command is simpler in a way, as it starts by dumping random data, block by block, on the /dev/sda1 device:

```
# dd if=/dev/urandom of=/dev/sda1
```

This command took about five minutes to add random data to a 1GB partition on my server1.example.com VM system.

Create the New Filesystem

The command that creates a LUKS-based filesystem is **cryptsetup**. The first step is to actually set up the passphrase for the filesystem with the following command. You're prompted for confirmation and a passphrase:

```
# cryptsetup luksFormat /dev/sda1
WARNING!
========
This will overwrite data on /dev/sda1 irrevocably.
Are you sure? (Type uppercase yes): YES
Enter LUKS passphrase:
Verify passphrase:
```

The passphrases that you type in are not shown at the console. The command shown in Figure 6-12 displays header information from the encrypted device. Once again, case matters. If you type in **yes** in lowercase, the command does not prompt for a passphrase, and the volume is not encrypted.

A couple of more steps are needed before the encrypted device is ready for formatting: it must be mapped. In other words, since the /dev/sda1 volume is now encrypted, it can't be read. However, you can create a map to a different device, which is essentially the decrypted version of the device.

First, you need a UUID for the device. The following **cryptsetup** command creates a UUID for the newly encrypted /dev/sda1 device:

```
# cryptsetup luksUUID /dev/sda1
```

FIGURE 6-12

The header of a LUKS-encrypted volume

```
[root@server1 ~]# cryptsetup luksDump /dev/sda1
LUKS header information for /dev/sda1

Version:        1
Cipher name:    aes
Cipher mode:    cbc-essiv:sha256
Hash spec:      sha1
Payload offset: 4096
MK bits:        256
MK digest:      0d 3c 3e 48 48 2e 14 14 ce de d7 b6 0c 65 6c de 4b eb 70 6b
MK salt:        22 3a a2 35 5d 84 b1 f7 0e 5f f9 7d 75 ba ba c3
                48 2d f0 45 fb 81 49 69 d1 8e 22 1c cf 8e e9 cf
MK iterations:  45625
UUID:           70a9f05e-b320-4c80-bc70-597f4e68122d

Key Slot 0: ENABLED
        Iterations:             182774
        Salt:                   75 0e 1c f2 66 dd 8e 28 e6 a5 fb cf 4d a0 42 ed
                                f3 80 b3 16 07 19 d4 d3 76 94 57 87 0c 4e 66 9f
        Key material offset:    8
        AF stripes:             4000
Key Slot 1: DISABLED
Key Slot 2: DISABLED
Key Slot 3: DISABLED
Key Slot 4: DISABLED
Key Slot 5: DISABLED
Key Slot 6: DISABLED
Key Slot 7: DISABLED
[root@server1 ~]#
```

Naturally, that command returns a 128-bit UUID number. Red Hat documentation recommends that you use that number as part of the device file for the encrypted filesystem. You can copy that number to the local buffer by highlighting it in a console. In a GUI console, you should be able to right-click and select Copy in the pop-up menu that appears. In a text console, if the mouse is active, that UUID number should already be in the buffer.

Now type in the following command:

```
# cryptsetup luksOpen /dev/sda1 uuidnumber
```

Paste the UUID number in place of *uuidnumber*. If it's in the GUI console, right-click at the end of the command and click Paste in the pop-up menu that appears. If it's in the command line console, click the middle mouse button (or the left and right mouse buttons together). Alternatively, if mouse buttons are unavailable, you could run the following commands (Of course, the two commands can be combined.):

```
# cryptsetup luksUUID /dev/sda1 > sda1uuid
# cryptsetup luksOpen /dev/sda1 `cat sda1uuid`
```

exam

watch　*Unless required on an exam, there's no reason to use the UUID number of an encrypted device. For example,* *you could run the following alternative cryptographic encryption command:* **cryptsetup luksOpen /dev/sda1 test.**

The mapped device should now appear in the /dev/mapper directory. You should now be able to format that device with a command like **mkfs.ext4**. The following command formats the device I created in my server1.example.com system:

```
# mkfs.ext4 /dev/mapper/test
```

You should now be able to apply the **mount** command on that /dev/mapper device file. Ideally, you should now set that up in the /etc/fstab file to make sure that encrypted filesystem is mounted the next time that system is booted.

If you're already jumping ahead to configuration of the encrypted filesystem in the /etc/fstab file, this UUID corresponds to the original partition and is not associated with the encrypted filesystem. To find the UUID associated with this particular encrypted filesystem, run the following command:

```
# dumpe2fs /dev/mapper/test | grep UUID
```

That UUID number can then be used to represent the encrypted volume in /etc/fstab. The following are two ways such a volume could be configured in that file:

```
/dev/mapper/test        /test      ext4      defaults      1 2
UUID=uuidnumber         /test      ext4      defaults      1 2
```

Alternatively, the aforementioned mkfs.ext4 command would change the associated UUID, as confirmed by the output to the **blkid** command. That UUID in the **blkid** command output can then be used to represent the noted volume in a similar fashion.

If successful, you'll be prompted for the passphrase for any LUKS-encrypted filesystems that may have been created. One common related error is the unloading of the dm_crypt module during the system reboot process.

Finally, you'll also need to add a bit of information to the /etc/crypttab file, in the following format:

```
<directory name w/o slash> <device name> none
```

For example, if the LUKS formatted filesystem /dev/mapper/test is to be mounted on the directory named /shared, you could add one of the following lines in /etc/crypttab:

```
shared /dev/mapper/test none
shared UUID=uuidnumber none
```

CERTIFICATION OBJECTIVE 6.06

Filesystem Management

Before you can access the files in a directory, that directory must be mounted on a partition formatted to some readable filesystem. Linux normally automates this process using the /etc/fstab configuration file. When Linux goes through the boot process, directories specified in /etc/fstab are mounted on configured volumes, with the help of the **mount** command. Of course, you can run that command with any or all appropriate options. So that's an excellent place to start this section.

The remainder of this section focuses on options for /etc/fstab. While it starts with the default using the baseline configuration for the standard virtual machine, it includes options for how you can customize that file for local, remote, and removable filesystems.

The /etc/fstab File

The standard configuration file for filesystems mounted during the boot process is /etc/fstab. To look it over safely, run the **less /etc/fstab** command. From the example shown in Figure 6-13, different filesystems are configured on each line.

The default use of UUIDs is new for RHEL 6, as RHEL 5 used the **LABEL** directive. As you'll see in the next section, UUIDs can represent a partition, a logical volume, or a RAID array. In all cases, that volume should be formatted to the filesystem noted on each line. That volume is mounted on the directory in the second column. The advantage of an UUID, relative to the **LABEL** directive, is that the UUID is automatically created when the volume is formatted with a command like **mkfs.ext4**.

Line wrapping in the /etc/fstab file is now allowed on current versions of Linux, including RHEL 6. It is necessary to accommodate the length of the UUID.

But to some extent, UUIDs are beside the point. As shown in Figure 6-13, there are six fields associated with each filesystem, described from left to right in Table 6-8. You can verify how partitions are actually mounted in the /etc/mtab file, as

```
#
# /etc/fstab
# Created by anaconda on Thu Nov 25 17:53:49 2010
#
# Accessible filesystems, by reference, are maintained under '/dev/disk'
# See man pages fstab(5), findfs(8), mount(8) and/or blkid(8) for more info
#
UUID=ffe37c21-53ab-46ab-b9df-4b856046e18f /                       ext4    defaults        1 1
UUID=1c9fc5ca-aff1-4af0-87d6-2de71938dbef /boot                   ext4    defaults        1 2
UUID=ffad5916-4066-4aed-a284-e966bd936f3b /home                   ext4    defaults        1 2
UUID=9f28f1ab-0a89-4f18-8a4f-c9a05bc8bdc9 swap                    swap    defaults        0 0
tmpfs                   /dev/shm            tmpfs   defaults        0 0
devpts                  /dev/pts            devpts  gid=5,mode=620  0 0
sysfs                   /sys                sysfs   defaults        0 0
proc                    /proc               proc    defaults        0 0
~
~
```

FIGURE 6-14

Sample /etc/mtab

```
[root@server1 ~]# cat /etc/mtab
/dev/vda2 / ext4 rw 0 0
proc /proc proc rw 0 0
sysfs /sys sysfs rw 0 0
devpts /dev/pts devpts rw,gid=5,mode=620 0 0
tmpfs /dev/shm tmpfs rw,rootcontext="system_u:object_r:tmpfs_t:s0" 0 0
/dev/vda1 /boot ext4 rw 0 0
/dev/vda5 /home ext4 rw 0 0
none /proc/sys/fs/binfmt_misc binfmt_misc rw 0 0
sunrpc /var/lib/nfs/rpc_pipefs rpc_pipefs rw 0 0
[root@server1 ~]# █
```

shown in Figure 6-14. Note the differences, especially the use of the device file associated with the partition, LV, or RAID array.

When adding a new partition, you could just add the device file associated with the partition, LV, or LUKS volume to the first column. The last four lines include virtual filesystems and are discussed later in this chapter.

TABLE 6-8

Description of /etc/fstab by Column, Left to Right

Field Name	Description
Device	Lists the device to be mounted; you may substitute the UUID or LABEL.
Mount Point	Notes the directory where the filesystem will be mounted.
Filesystem Format	Describes the filesystem type. Valid filesystem types include ext, ext2, ext3, ext4, msdos, vfat, devpts, proc, tmpfs, udf, iso9660, nfs, smb, and swap.
Mount Options	Covered in the following section.
Dump Value	Either 0 or 1. A value of 1 means that data is automatically saved to disk by the **dump** command when you exit Linux.
Filesystem Check Order	Determines the order that filesystems are checked by the **fsck** command during the boot process. The root directory (/) filesystem should be set to 1, and other local filesystems should be set to 2. Removable filesystems such as those associated with CD/DVD drives should be set to 0, which means that they are not checked during the Linux boot process.

Universally Unique Identifiers in /etc/fstab

In /etc/fstab, note the focus on UUIDs, short for Universally Unique Identifiers. Every formatted volume has an UUID, a unique 128-bit number. Each UUID represents either a partition, a logical volume, or a RAID array.

To identify the UUID for available volumes, run the **blkid** command. The output should sort of match volumes from partitions, LVs, RAID arrays, and LUKS-encrypted filesystems to their UUIDs, as defined in /etc/fstab. To that end, both LVs and LUKS filesystems use /dev/mapper devices. For one of the LVs and the VGs created in this chapter, that device file would be /dev/mapper/vg_00-lv_00. To verify, run the **ls -l** command on both device files (/dev/mapper/vg_00-lv_00 and /dev/vg_00/lv_00). You should see both device files linked to the same /dev/dm-0 (the dm-* number can vary) device file. In the same way, you can verify that the /dev/mapper file for the LUKS encrypted volume is linked to another /dev/dm-* device file.

Alternatively, you could use the **dumpe2fs** command on available volumes; for example, the following command identifies the UUID associated with the noted LV:

```
# dumpe2fs /dev/vg_00/lv_00 | grep UUID
```

As UUIDs are not limited to LVs, you should be able to get equivalent information for a partition from a command like the following:

```
# dumpe2fs /dev/vda1 | grep UUID
```

Of course, the same is true with a properly configured and formatted LUKS volume (in this case, the UUID starts with a 7), with a command like the following:

```
# dumpe2fs /dev/mapper/7* | grep UUID
```

But the **dumpe2fs** command does not work with swap volumes, whether they be partitions or logical volumes. To identify the UUID associated with swap space, you just have to rely on the output of the **blkid** command.

The mount Command

The **mount** command can be used to attach local and network partitions to specified directories. Mount points are not fixed; you can mount a CD drive or even a shared network directory to any empty directory if appropriate ownership and permissions are set. Closely related is the **umount** (not unmount) command, which unmounts selected volumes from associated directories.

First, try the **mount** command by itself. It'll display all currently mounted filesystems, along with important mount options. For example, the following output suggests that the top-level root directory is mounted in read-write mode, on the /dev/vda2 partition, formatted to the ext4 filesystem:

```
/dev/vda2 on / type ext4 (rw)
```

As suggested earlier, the **mount** command is closely related to the /etc/fstab file. If you've unmounted a directory, and have made changes to the /etc/fstab file, the easiest way to implement the currently configured /etc/fstab file is with the following command:

```
# mount -a
```

However, if a filesystem is already mounted, this command doesn't change its status, no matter what has been done to the /etc/fstab file. But if the system is subsequently rebooted, the options configured in /etc/fstab are used automatically.

If you're not sure about a possible change to the /etc/fstab file, it's possible to test it out with the **mount** command. For example, the following command remounts the volume associated with the /home directory, in read-only mode:

```
# mount -o remount,ro /home
```

You can confirm the result by rerunning the **mount** command. The following output should reflect the result on the /home directory:

```
/dev/vda5 on /home type ext4 (ro)
```

If you've read this book from the beginning, you've already seen the **mount** command at work with access control lists (ACLs), and even the ISO files associated with downloaded CD/DVDs. To review, the following command remounts the noted /home directory with ACLs:

```
# mount -o remount,acl /dev/vda5 /home
```

And for ISO files, the following command mounts the noted RHEL 6 ISO file on the /mnt directory:

```
# mount -o loop rhel-server-6.0-x86_64-dvd.iso /mnt
```

More Filesystem Mount Options

Many **mount** command options are appropriate for the /etc/fstab file. One option most commonly seen in that file is **defaults**. While that is the appropriate mount option for most /etc/fstab filesystems, there are other options, such as those listed in Table 6-9. If you want to use multiple options, separate them by commas. Don't use spaces between options. The list in Table 6-9 is not comprehensive, and these options can also be used with the **mount** command. You can find out more from the mount man page, available with the **man mount** command.

TABLE 6-9	Mount Option	Description
Options for the mount command and /etc/fstab	async	Data is read and written asynchronously.
	atime	The inode associated with each file is updated each time the file is accessed.
	auto	Searches through /etc/filesystems for the appropriate format for the partition; normally associated with a floppy or removable drive.
	defaults	Uses default mount options **rw**, **suid**, **dev**, **exec**, **auto**, **nouser**, and **async**.
	dev	Permits access to character devices such as terminals or consoles and block devices such as drives.
	exec	Allows binaries (compiled programs) to be run on this filesystem.
	noatime	The inode associated with each file is not updated when accessed.
	noauto	Requires explicit mounting. Common option for CD and floppy drives.
	nodev	Devices on this filesystem are not read or interpreted.
	noexec	Binaries (compiled programs) cannot be run on this filesystem.
	nosuid	Disallows **setuid** or **setgid** permissions on this filesystem.
	nouser	Only root users are allowed to mount the specified filesystem.
	remount	Remounts a currently mounted filesystem. Also an option for the **mount** command.
	ro	Mounts the filesystem as read-only.
	rw	Mounts the filesystem as read/write.
	suid	Allows **setuid** or **setgid** permissions on programs on this filesystem.
	sync	Reads and writes are done at the same speed (synchronously) on this filesystem.
	user	Allows nonroot users to mount this filesystem. By default, this also sets the **noexec**, **nosuid**, and **nodev** options.

There are more options available, including **noatime**, **noauto**, **nodev**, **noexec**, **nosuid**, and **nouser**, which are the opposites of **atime**, **auto**, **dev**, **exec**, **suid**, and **user**, respectively.

Virtual Filesystems

This section describes the virtual filesystems configured in the /etc/fstab configuration file. The four standard virtual filesystem configuration lines are:

```
tmpfs    /dev/shm    tmpfs    defaults        0 0
devpts   /dev/pts    devpts   gid=5,mode=620  0 0
sysfs    /sys        sysfs    defaults        0 0
proc     /proc       proc     defaults        0 0
```

■ The **tmpfs** filesystem is a virtual memory filesystem that uses both RAM and swap space.

■ The **devpts** filesystem relates to pseudo-terminal devices.

■ The **sysfs** filesystem provides dynamic information about system devices. Explore the associated /sys directory. You'll find a wide variety of information related to the devices and drivers attached to the local system.

■ The **proc** filesystem is especially useful, as it provides dynamically configurable options for changing the behavior of the kernel. As an RHCE skill, you may learn more about options in the proc filesystem in Chapter 12.

Add Your Own Filesystems to /etc/fstab

If you need to set up a special directory, it sometimes makes sense to set it up on a separate volume. Different volumes for different directories means that files in that volume can't overload critical directories such as /boot. While it's nice to follow the standard format of the /etc/fstab file, it is an extra effort. If required on a Red Hat exam, it'll be in the instructions that you see.

So in most cases, it's sufficient to set up a new volume in /etc/fstab with the associated device file, such as a /dev/vda6 partition, a /dev/mapper/* LUKS encrypted volume, or a /dev/NewVol/NewLV LV. Make sure the device file reflects the new volume that you've created, the intended mount directory (such as /special), and the filesystem format that you've applied (such as ext4).

Removable Media and /etc/fstab

In general, removable media should not be mounted automatically during the boot process. That's possible in the /etc/fstab configuration file with an option like **noauto**. But in general, it's not standard in RHEL to set up removable media in /etc/fstab.

To read removable media such as smart cards and CD/DVDs, RHEL somewhat automates the mounting of such media in the GNOME or KDE Desktop Environments. While the details of this process are not part of the Red Hat Exam Prep guide, the process is based on configuration files in the /etc/udev/rules.d directory. If RHEL detects your hardware, click Places; in the menu that appears, select the entry for the removable media. If multiple removable media options are loaded, you can select the media to mount in the Removable Media submenu.

If that doesn't work for some reason, you can use the **mount** command directly. For example, the following command mounts a CD/DVD in a drive.

```
# mount -t iso9660 /dev/sr0 /mnt
```

The **-t** switch specifies the type of filesystem (iso9660). The device file /dev/sr0 represents the first CD/DVD drive; /mnt is the directory through which you can access the files from the CD/DVD after mounting. But /dev/sr0? How is anyone supposed to remember that?

Linux addresses that in a couple of ways. First, it sets up links from more sensibly named files such as /dev/cdrom, which you can confirm with the **ls -l /dev/cdrom** command. Second, try the **blkid** command. If removable media (other than a CD/DVD) are connected, you'll see it in the output to the command, including the associated device file.

Just remember that it is important to unmount removable media such as USB keys before removing them. Otherwise, the data that you thought was written to the disk might still be in the unwritten RAM cache. In that case, you would lose that data.

Given these examples of how removable media can be mounted, you should have a better idea on how such media can be configured in the /etc/fstab configuration file. The standard **defaults** option is inappropriate in most cases, as it mounts a system in read-write mode (even for read-only DVDs), attempts to mount automatically during the boot process, and limits access to the root administrative user. But that can be changed with the right options. For example, to configure a CD drive that can be mounted by regular users, you could add the following line to /etc/fstab:

```
/dev/sr0 /cdrom auto ro,noauto,users 0 0
```

This line sets up a mount in read-only mode, does not try to mount it automatically during the boot process, and supports access by regular users.

As desired, similar options are possible for removable media such as USB keys. But that can be more problematic with multiple USB keys; one may be detected as /dev/sdc once, and then later detected as /dev/sdd, if there's a second USB key installed. However, if properly configured, each USB key should have unique UUIDs. As described earlier, UUIDs are the RHEL 6 way to identify different volumes to be mounted in /etc/fstab.

Networked Filesystems

The /etc/fstab file can be used to automate mounts from shared directories. The two major sharing services of interest are NFS and Samba. This section provides only a brief overview to how such shared directories can be configured in the /etc/fstab file; for more information, see Chapters 15 and 16.

In general, shares from networked directories should be assumed to be unreliable. People step on power lines, on Ethernet cables, and so on. If your system uses a wireless network, that adds an additional level of unreliability. In other words, the settings in the /etc/fstab file should account for that. So if there's a problem either in the network connection, or perhaps a problem like a power failure on the remote NFS server, that problem should not lead to a "hang" of a client, where the terminal (or more) is frozen due to the lost connection. Similar issues do not apply to Samba.

A connection to a shared NFS directory is based on its hostname or IP address, along with the full path to the directory on the server. So to connect to a remote NFS server on system *server1* that shares the /var/ftp/pub directory, you could mount that share with the following command (assuming the /share directory exists):

```
# mount -t nfs server1.example.com:/pub /share
```

But that mount has some risks. The Red Hat Storage Administration Guide suggests the following entry in /etc/fstab:

```
server1:/pub  /share  nfs rsize=8192,wsize=8192,timeo=14,intr,udp 0 0
```

The **rsize** and **wsize** variables specify the size of the blocks of data to be read and written in bytes, respectively. The **timeo=14** directive specifies that the client will wait 1.4 seconds for the connection request to be completed. The **intr** allows the client to interrupt a connection; that's useful when the NFS server is not responding. The **udp** specifies a connection using the User Datagram Protocol (UDP). If the connection is to a NFS version 4 server, substitute **nfs4** for **nfs** in the third column.

In contrast, such variables are not required for shared Samba directories. The following line is generally all that's needed for a share of the same directory and server:

```
//server/pub  /share  cifs rw,username=user,password=pass, 0 0
```

Older Samba servers may require a substitution of **smbfs** for **cifs**, which are acronyms for the Samba File System and its successor, the Common Internet File System. If you're disturbed by the open display of a username and password in the /etc/fstab file, which is world-readable, try the following option:

```
//server/pub  /share  cifs rw,credentials=/etc/secret 0 0
```

You can then set up the /etc/secret file as accessible only to the root administrative user, with the username and password in the following format:

```
username=user
password=password
```

CERTIFICATION OBJECTIVE 6.07

The Automounter

With network mounts and portable media, problems may come up if connections are lost or media are removed. During the server configuration process, you could be mounting directories from a number of remote systems. You may also want temporary access to removable media such as USB keys or Zip drives. The automount daemon, also known as the automounter or autofs, can help. It can automatically mount specific directories as needed. It can unmount a directory automatically after a fixed period of time.

Mounting via the Automounter

Once a partition is mounted, it stays mounted until you unmount it or shut down the system. The permanence of the mount can cause problems. For example, if you've mounted a USB key and then physically remove the key, Linux may not have had a chance to write the file to the disk. Data would be lost. The same issue applies to secure digital cards or other hotswappable removable drives.

Another issue: mounted NFS directories may cause problems if the remote computer fails or the connection is lost. Systems may slow down or even hang as the local system looks for the mounted directory.

This is where the automounter can help. It relies on the **autofs** daemon to mount configured directories as needed, on a temporary basis. In RHEL, the relevant configuration files are auto.master, auto.misc, auto.net, and auto.smb, all in the /etc directory. If you use the automounter, keep the /misc and /net directories free. Red Hat configures automounts on these directories by default, and they won't work if local files or directories are stored there. Subsections will cover each of these files, and a hypothetical auto.home file for automatically mounting directories from a remote server on the local /home directory.

on the **Job**

You won't even see the /misc and/or /net directories unless you properly configure /etc/auto.master and the autofs daemon is running.

Default automounter settings are configured in /etc/sysconfig/autofs. The default settings include a timeout of 300 seconds; in other words, if nothing happens on an automount within that time, the share is automatically unmounted:

```
TIMEOUT=300
```

The **BROWSE_MODE** can allow you to search from available mounts. The following directive disables it by default:

```
BROWSE_MODE="no"
```

There are a wide variety of additional settings available, as commented in the /etc/sysconfig/autofs file, which also assumes that the **autofs** daemon is active.

/etc/auto.master

The standard /etc/auto.master file includes a series of comments, with three default commands. The first refers to the /etc/auto.misc file as the configuration file for this directory. The **/net -hosts** command allows you to specify the host to automount a network directory, as specified in /etc/auto.net.

```
/misc /etc/auto.misc
/net  -hosts
+auto.master
```

In any case, these commands point to configuration files for each service. Shared directories from each service are automatically mounted, on demand, on the given directory (/misc and /net).

You can set up the automounter on other directories. One popular option is to set up the automounter on the /home directory. In this way, you can configure user home directories on remote servers, mounted on demand. Users are given access to their home directories upon login, and based on the **TIMEOUT** directive in the /etc/sysconfig/autofs file, all mounted directories are automatically unmounted 300 seconds after that user logs off the system.

```
# /home /etc/auto.home
```

This works only if a /home directory doesn't already exist on the local system. As the Red Hat exam requires the configuration of a number of regular users, your systems should include a /home directory for regular users. In that case, you could substitute a different directory, leading to a line like the following:

```
/shared /etc/auto.home
```

One method that can be used to create the auto.home directory is discussed shortly. Just remember, for any system accessed over a network, you'll need to be sure that the firewall allows traffic associated with the given service.

/etc/auto.misc

Red Hat conveniently provides standard automount commands in comments in the /etc/auto.misc file. It's helpful to analyze this file in detail. I use the default RHEL version of this file. The first four lines are comments, which I skip. The first directive is:

```
cd      -fstype=iso9660,ro,nosuid,nodev    :/dev/cdrom
```

In RHEL, this directive is active by default, assuming you've activated the **autofs** service. In other words, if you have a CD in the /dev/cdrom drive, you can access its files through the automounter with the **ls /misc/cd** command, even as a regular user. The automounter accesses it using the ISO9660 filesystem. It's mounted read-only (**ro**); set user ID permissions are not allowed (**nosuid**); and devices on this filesystem are not used (**nodev**).

With the **TIMEOUT** interval defined in /etc/sysconfig/autofs, the CD is unmounted 300 seconds after the last time it's accessed. There are a number of other sample commands, commented out, ready for use. Of course, you would have to delete the comment character (#) before using any of these commands. And you'd have to adjust names and device files accordingly; for example, /dev/hda1 is no longer used as a device file on the latest Linux systems, even for PATA hard drives.

As suggested by one of the comments, "The following entries are samples to pique your imagination." The first of these commented commands allows you to set up a /misc/linux mount point from a shared NFS directory, /pub/linux, from the ftp. example.org computer:

```
#linux   -ro,soft,intr     ftp.example.org:/pub/linux
```

The next command assumes that the /boot directory is stored on the /dev/hda1 partition. With this command, you don't need to mount /boot when you start Linux. Instead, this command allows you to automount it with the **mount /misc/boot** command.

```
#boot    -fstype=ext2      :/dev/hda1
```

The following three commands apply to a floppy disk drive. Don't laugh; floppies are fairly easy to create and configure on most virtual machine systems. The first command, set to an "auto" filesystem type, searches through /etc/filesystems to try to match what's on your floppy. The next two commands assume that the floppy is formatted to the ext2 filesystem.

```
#floppy      -fstype=auto      :/dev/fd0
#floppy      -fstype=ext2      :/dev/fd0
#e2floppy    -fstype=ext2      :/dev/fd0
```

The next command points to the first partition on the third drive. The **jaz** at the beginning suggests this is suitable for an Iomega-type Jaz drive.

```
#jaz         -fstype=ext2      :/dev/sdc1
```

Finally, the last command is based on an older system where the automounter is applied to a legacy PATA drive. Of course, the /dev/hdd device file is no longer used, so substitute accordingly. But the **removable** at the beginning suggests this is also suitable for removable hard drives. Of course, you'd likely have to change the filesystem format to something like ext4. As suggested earlier in this chapter, the **blkid** command can help identify available device files from removable systems like USB keys and portable drives.

```
#removable   -fstype=ext2        :/dev/hdd
```

In general, you'll need to modify these lines for available hardware.

/etc/auto.net

With the /etc/auto.net configuration script, you can review and read shared NFS directories. It now works with the hostnames or IP addresses of NFS servers. By default, executable permissions are enabled on this file.

Assuming the automounter is active, and can connect to an NFS server with an IP address of 192.168.122.1, you can review shared NFS directories on that system with the following command:

```
# /etc/auto.net 192.168.122.1 -fstype=nfs,hard,intr,nodev,nosuid \
    /srv/ftp 192.168.122.1:/srv/ftp
```

This output tells me that the /srv/ftp directory on the 192.168.122.1 system is shared via NFS. Based on the directives in /etc/auto.master, you could access this share (assuming appropriate firewall and SELinux settings) with the following command:

```
# ls /net/192.168.122.1/srv/ftp
```

/etc/auto.smb

One of the problems associated with the configuration of a shared Samba or CIFS directory is that it works, at least in its standard configuration, only with public directories. In other words, if you activate the /etc/auto.smb file, it'll only work with directories shared without a username or a password.

If you accept these unsecure conditions, it's possible to set up the /etc/auto.smb file in the same way as the /etc/auto.net file. First, you'd have to add it to the /etc/auto.master file in a similar fashion, with the following directive:

```
/smb  /etc/auto.smb
```

You'd then need to specifically stop and restart the automounter service with the following commands:

```
# /etc/init.d/autofs stop
# /etc/init.d/autofs start
```

You'll then be able to review shared directories with the following command; substitute a hostname or IP address if desired. Of course, this won't work unless the Samba server is activated on the noted server1.example.com system, and the firewall is configured to allow access through associated TCP/IP ports.

```
# /etc/auto.smb server1.example.com
```

/etc/auto.home

Yes, it's possible to set up shared home directories from a central server using the automounter. However, that requires a central authentication database, such as the Network Information Service (NIS) or the Lightweight Directory Access Protocol (LDAP). Of course, it also requires a shared /home directory from that remote system. However, NIS is no longer part of the Red Hat exams, and LDAP client configuration is only part of the RHCSA exam requirements.

Therefore, if you're asked to configure a shared /home directory filesystem with the automounter, it would be only with the help of an existing LDAP server. LDAP and other authentication options are covered in Chapter 8.

To that end, automounter configuration requires the activation of five directives in the /etc/sysconfig/autofs file:

```
DEFAULT_MAP_OBJECT_CLASS="automountMap"
DEFAULT_ENTRY_OBJECT_CLASS="automount"
DEFAULT_MAP_ATTRIBUTE="automountMapName"
DEFAULT_ENTRY_ATTRIBUTE="automountKey"
DEFAULT_VALUE_ATTRIBUTE="automountInformation"
```

You'd then configure the shared home directory, per exam requirements, in the /etc/auto.home file. It may be something simple, similar to the following directive:

```
* -rw,soft,intr server1.example.com:/home/&
```

In this case, the shared directory is mounted with read-write permissions, soft interrupts that assume the network connection is completely reliable, and permission for signals to interrupt file operations.

Activate the Automounter

Once appropriate files have been configured, you can start, restart, or reload the automounter. As it is governed by the **autofs** daemon, you can stop, start, restart, or reload that service with one of the following commands:

```
# service autofs stop
# service autofs start
# service autofs restart
# service autofs reload
```

With the default command in the /etc/auto.misc file, you should now be able to mount a CD on the /misc/cd directory, automatically, just by accessing the configured directory. Once you have a CD in the drive, the following command should work:

```
# ls /misc/cd
```

If you navigate to the /misc/cd directory, the automounter would ignore any timeouts. Otherwise, /misc/cd is automatically unmounted according to the timeout, which according to the **TIMEOUT** directive in /etc/sysconfig/autofs is 300 seconds.

EXERCISE 6-3

Configure the Automounter

In this exercise, you'll test the automounter. You'll need at least a CD. Ideally, you should also have a USB key, or a secure digital (SD) card. First, however, you need to make sure that the **autofs** daemon is in operation, modify the appropriate configuration files, and then restart **autofs**. You can then test the automounter in this lab.

1. From the command line interface, run the following command to make sure the **autofs** daemon is running:

   ```
   # service autofs start
   ```

2. Review the /etc/auto.master configuration file in a text editor. The defaults are sufficient to activate the configuration options in /etc/auto.misc and /etc/auto.net.

3. Check the /etc/auto.misc configuration file in a text editor. Make sure it includes the following line (which should already be there by default). Save and exit from /etc/auto.misc.

   ```
   cd     -fstype=iso9660,ro,nosuid,nodev    :/dev/cdrom
   ```

4. Now reload the **autofs** daemon. Since it's already running, all you need to do is make sure it rereads associated configuration files.

   ```
   # service autofs reload
   ```

5. The automounter service is now active. Insert a CD or DVD into an appropriate drive and run the following command. If successful, it should display the contents of the CD or DVD:

   ```
   # ls /misc/cd
   ```

6. Run the **ls /misc** command immediately. You should see the CD directory in the output.

7. Wait at least five minutes, and repeat the previous command. What do you see?

SCENARIO & SOLUTION

You need to configure several new partitions for a standard Linux partition, for swap space, and for a logical volume.	Use the **fdisk** or **parted** utility to create partitions, and then modify their partition types with the **t** or **set** commands.
You want to set up a mount during the boot process based on the UUID.	Identify the UUID of the volume with the **dumpe2fs** or **blkid** commands, and use that UUID in the /etc/fstab file.
You need to configure a volume to the ext2, ext3, or ext4 filesystem type.	Format the target volume with a command like **mkfs.ext2**, **mkfs.ext3**, or **mkfs.ext4**.
You want to set up a logical volume.	Use the **pvcreate** command to create PVs; use the **vgcreate** command to combine PVs in VGs; use the **lvcreate** command to create an LV; format that LV for use.
You want to add new filesystems without destroying others.	Use the free space available on existing or newly installed hard drives.
You need to encrypt a volume with sensitive data.	Configure and format a special volume with the **cryptsetup** command; be prepared with an appropriate passphrase.
You want to expand the space available to an LV.	Use the **lvextend** command to increase the space available to an LV, and then use the **resize2fs** command to expand the formatted filesystem accordingly.
You need to configure automated mounts to a shared network filesystem.	Configure the filesystem either in /etc/fstab or through the automounter.

CERTIFICATION SUMMARY

As a Linux administrator, you should know how to create and manage new filesystem volumes. To create a new filesystem, you need to know how to create, manage, and format partitions, as well as how to set up those partitions for logical volumes. With the increasing focus on security, you also need to know how to encrypt those volumes with LUKS.

RHEL 6 also supports the configuration of logical volumes. The process is a bit intricate, as it requires the configuration of a partition as a PV. Multiple PVs can then be configured as a VG. Logical volumes can then be configured from desired portions of a VG. Associated commands are **pv***, **vg***, and **lv***; those and others can be accessed from the **lvm>** prompt. The GUI Logical Volume Management tool is also useful for this purpose.

Linux supports the format of partitions, RAID arrays, and logical volumes to a wide variety of filesystems. While the default is ext4, Linux supports formats and checks associated with regular and journaling filesystems associated with Linux, Microsoft, and other operating systems.

Once configured, partitions and logical volumes, whether they be encrypted or not, can be configured in the /etc/fstab file. That configuration is read during the boot process and can also be used by the **mount** command. If desired, removable filesystems and shared network directories can also be configured in /etc/fstab.

The /etc/fstab file is not the only option to set up mounts. You can automate this process for regular users with the automounter. Properly configured, it allows users to access shared network directories, removable media, and more through paths defined in /etc/auto.master.

✓ # TWO-MINUTE DRILL

Here are some of the key points from the certification objectives in Chapter 6.

Storage Management and Partitions

❑ The **fdisk** and **parted** utilities can help you create and delete partitions.

❑ Both **fdisk** and **parted** can be used to configure partitions for logical volumes and RAID arrays.

❑ The RHEL 6 Disk Utility, which can be started with the **palimpsest** command, can serve as a front end not only for partition management, but also for mounting, formatting, and filesystem checks.

Filesystem Formats

❑ Linux tools can be used to configure and format volumes to a number of different filesystems.

❑ Examples of standard filesystems include MS-DOS and ext2.

❑ Journaling filesystems, which include logs that can restore metadata, are more resilient; the default RHEL 6 filesystem is ext4.

❑ RHEL 6 supports a variety of **mkfs.*** filesystem format and **fsck.*** filesystem check commands.

Basic Linux Filesystems and Directories

❑ Linux files and filesystems are organized into directories based on the FHS.

❑ Some Linux directories are well suited to configuration on separate filesystems.

Logical Volume Management (LVM)

❑ LVM is based on physical volumes, logical volumes, and volume groups.

❑ You can create and add LVM systems with a wide variety of commands starting with **pv***, **lv***, and **vg***.

❑ The space from new partitions configured as PVs can be allocated to existing volume groups with the **vgextend** command; they can be added to LVs with the **lvextend** command.

❑ The extra space can be used to extend an existing filesystem with the **resize2fs** command.

❑ The GUI LVM tool is an alternative for those who don't remember all of the commands required to manage logical volumes.

Volume Encryption with the Linux Unified Key Setup

❑ The passphrases that can be used with LUKS can be considerably more secure than regular passwords.

❑ Volumes can be LUKS-encrypted during the installation process.

❑ LUKS encryption after installation depends on the dm_crypt module and commands in the cryptsetup-luks package.

❑ The safety of encrypted volumes can be enhanced with random data, added with either the **badblocks** command from the /dev/urandom random number generator.

❑ The **cryptsetup luksFormat /dev/sda1** command sets up a passphrase on the given partition. Once configured, you can format the /dev/mapper device that's created.

Filesystem Management

❑ Standard filesystems are mounted as defined in /etc/fstab.

❑ Filesystem volumes are now identified by their UUIDs; for a list, run the **blkid** command.

❑ The **mount** command can either use the settings in /etc/fstab or mount filesystem volumes directly.

❑ It's also possible to configure mounts of shared network directories from NFS and Samba servers in /etc/fstab.

❑ With the right commands, you can convert an ext2 formatted filesystem to ext3, and then convert an ext3 formatted filesystem to ext4.

The Automounter

❑ With the automounter, you can configure automatic mounts of removable media and shared network drives.

❑ Key automounter configuration files are auto.master, auto.misc, and auto.net, in the /etc directory.

❑ It's possible to configure an /etc/auto.home file to make home directories available from a remote shared network server.

SELF TEST

The following questions will help measure your understanding of the material presented in this chapter. As no multiple-choice questions appear on the Red Hat exams, no multiple-choice questions appear in this book. These questions exclusively test your understanding of the chapter. Getting results, not memorizing trivia, is what counts on the Red Hat exams. There may be more than one answer to many of these questions.

Storage Management and Partitions

1. What **fdisk** command lists configured partitions from all attached hard drives?

   _____

2. After creating a swap partition, what command activates it?

   _____

Filesystem Formats

3. What is the primary advantage of a journaling filesystem such as ext4?

   _____

4. What command formats /dev/sdb3 to the default Red Hat filesystem format?

   _____

Basic Linux Filesystems and Directories

5. What directory is mounted on a partition separate from the top-level root directory in the default RHEL 6 installation?

   _____

6. Name three directories just below /, not suitable for mounting separately from the volume with the top-level root directory.

   _____

Logical Volume Management (LVM)

7. Once you've created a new partition and set it to the Logical Volume Management filetype, what command adds it as a PV?

_____

8. Once you've added more space to an LV, what command would expand the formatted filesystem to fill the new space?

_____

Volume Encryption with the Linux Unified Key Setup

9. What command configures the /dev/sdc1 partition with a LUKS passphrase?

_____

Filesystem Management

10. To change the mount options for a local filesystem, what file would you edit?

_____

11. What would you add to the /etc/fstab file to set up access control lists on the /home directory, mounted on partition /dev/vda6, with other default options? Assume you can't find the UUID of /dev/vda6. Assume a dump value of 1 and a filesystem check order of 2.

_____

The Automounter

12. If you've started the **autofs** daemon and want to read the list of shared NFS directories from the server1.example.com computer, what automounter-related command would you use?

_____

13. Name three configuration files associated with the default installation of the automounter on RHEL 6.

_____

LAB QUESTIONS

Several of these labs involve format exercises. You should do these exercises on test machines only. The instructions in these labs delete all of the data on a system. The second Lab sets up KVM for this purpose. However, some readers may not have hardware that supports KVM. Options to KVM include virtual machine solutions such as VMware, available from www.vmware.com or Virtualbox, open-source edition, available from www.virtualbox.org.

Red Hat presents its exams electronically. For that reason, most of the labs in this and future chapters are available from the CD that accompanies the book, in the Chapter5/ subdirectory. It's available in .doc, .html, and .txt formats, in the filename starting with 56505-labs. In case you haven't yet set up RHEL 6 on a system, refer to the first lab of Chapter 2 for installation instructions. However, the answers for each lab follow the self test answers for the fill-in-the-blank questions.

SELF TEST ANSWERS

Storage Management and Partitions

1. The **fdisk** command that lists configured partitions from all attached hard drives is **fdisk -l**.

2. After creating a swap partition, the **swapon** *devicename* command activates it; just substitute the device file associated with the volume (such as /dev/sda1 or /dev/VolGroup00/LogVol03) for *devicename*.

Filesystem Formats

3. The primary advantage of a journaling filesystem such as ext4 is faster data recovery if power is suddenly cut.

4. The command that formats /dev/sdb3 to the default Red Hat filesystem format is **mkfs.ext4 /dev/sdb3**. The **mkfs -t ext4 /dev/sdb3** and **mke2fs -t ext4 /dev/sdb3** commands are also acceptable answers.

Basic Linux Filesystems and Directories

5. The /boot directory is mounted separately from /.

6. There are many correct answers to this question; some directories not suitable for mounting separately from / include /bin, /dev, /etc, /lib, /root, and /sbin. (In contrast, several directories are essentially shown as placeholders for mounting, including /media and /mnt. Other directories such as /proc and /sys are virtual filesystems; in other words, as they don't include files kept on storage media, they should not be mounted separately from / for other reasons.)

Logical Volume Management (LVM)

7. Once you've created a new partition and set it to the Logical Volume Management filetype, the command that adds it as a PV is **pvcreate**. For example, if the new partition is /dev/sdb2, the command is **pvcreate /dev/sdb2**.

8. Once you've added more space to an LV, the command that would expand the formatted filesystem to fill the new space is **resize2fs**.

Volume Encryption with the Linux Unified Key Setup

9. The command that encrypts the /dev/sdc1 partition with a passphrase is **cryptsetup luksFormat /dev/sdc1**.

Filesystem Management

10. To change the mount options for a local filesystem, edit /etc/fstab.

11. Since the UUID is unknown, you'll need to use the device file for the volume, in this case, /dev/vda6. Thus, the line to be added to /etc/fstab is:

```
/dev/vda6 /home    ext4     defaults,acl,usrquota        1 2
```

The Automounter

12. If you've started the **autofs** daemon and want to read the list of shared NFS directories from the first.example.com computer, the automounter-related command you'd use to list those directories is **/etc/auto.net server1.example.com**.

13. The configuration files associated with the default installation of the automounter include auto. master, auto.misc, auto.net, and auto.smb, all in the /etc directory, as well as /etc/sysconfig/autofs. The /etc/auto.home directory is not a part of the default installation.

LAB ANSWERS

One of the assumptions with these labs is that where a directory such as /test1 is specified, that you create it before mounting a volume device file on it, or including it in a key configuration file such as /etc/fstab. Otherwise, you'll possibly encounter unexpected errors.

Lab 1

1. It shouldn't matter whether partitions are created in the **fdisk** or the **parted** utility. As long as the partition types were correctly configured, you should see one Linux partition and one Linux swap partition in the configured hard drives, in the output to the **fdisk -l** command.

2. If you're confused about what UUID to use in /etc/fstab, run the **blkid** command. If the given partitions have been properly formatted (with the **mkfs.ext4** and **mkswap** commands), you'll see the UUID for the new partitions in the output to **blkid**.

3. You should be able to test the configuration of a new partition and directory in /etc/fstab with the **mount -a** command. Then a **mount** command by itself should be able to confirm appropriate configuration in /etc/fstab.

4. You should be able to confirm the configuration of a new swap partition in the output to the **cat /proc/swaps** command. If you add the space allocated to each swap partition, you should also be able to verify the result in the **Swap** line associated with the **top** command.

5. Remember, all changes should survive a reboot. For the purpose of this lab, you may want to reboot this system to confirm this. However, reboots take time; if you have multiple tasks during an exam, you may want to wait until completing as much as possible before rebooting a system.

Lab 2

This discussion is focused on how you can verify the results of this lab. Even if you've configured the exact spare partitions described in this lab and followed exact instructions, it's quite possible that your LV won't be exactly 900M. Some of that variance comes from the differences between cylinders and sectors; others come from the difference between base 2 and base 10 numbers. Don't panic; that variance is normal. The same proviso applies to Lab 3 as well.

Keep in mind that logical volumes are based on appropriately configured partitions, set up as PVs, collected into a VG, and then subdivided into an LV. That LV is then formatted and then mounted on an appropriate directory; for the purpose of this lab, that directory is /test2. The UUID of that formatted volume can then be used to set up that LV as a mount in the /etc/fstab file.

1. To verify appropriate partitions prepared for logical volumes, run the **fdisk -l** command. Appropriate partitions should appear with the "Linux LVM" label.

2. To verify the configuration of appropriate PVs, run the **pvs** command. The output should report the devices and space allocated to PVs.

3. To verify the configuration of an appropriate VG, run the **vgs** command. The output should list the VG created during the lab from available PVs, including the space available.

4. To verify the configuration of an appropriate LV, run the **lvs** command. The output should list the LV, the VG from where it was created, and the amount of space allocated to that LV.

5. To verify the UUID of the newly formatted volume, run the following command:

```
# blkid
```

6. If the /etc/fstab file is properly configured, you should be able to run the **mount -a** command. Then you should see the /dev/mapper/volgroup1-logvol1 (or whatever the name of the LV device file is) mounted on the /test2 directory.

7. As with Lab 1, all changes should survive a reboot. At some point, you'll want to reboot the local system to check for success or failure of this and other labs.

Lab 3

Based on the information from Lab 2, you should already know what the size of the current LV is. The associated **df** command should confirm the result; the **df -m** command, with its output in MB, could help.

The key command in this lab is **resize2fs**. While there are a number of excellent switches available, all you really need with that command is the device file for the LV along with the desired size. As with Lab 2, the result can be confirmed after an appropriate **mount** and **df** command. However, full success can't be confirmed until the /etc/fstab file has been revised, and the **mount -a** command run to confirm that everything in /etc/fstab, including the new line, actually works. Of course, based on the instructions in the lab, you could focus with the **mount /test3** command. Since the remaining information is in /etc/fstab, the device file for the mount should not be required.

Lab 4

There are several steps associated with confirming the successful creation of a LUKS-encrypted filesystem. The **blkid** command should specify crypto_LUKS in the output associated with those volumes that have been encrypted. There should also be a /dev/mapper device associated with that volume. That /dev/mapper device file should be mountable; if so, it confirms an appropriate format for the encrypted filesystem.

If you've encountered problems with many of these commands, you may need to load associated modules with a command like **modprobe dm_crypt**.

Lab 5

The configuration of a LUKS-encrypted filesystem in the /etc/fstab file can be a bit tricky. A number of LUKS-related commands won't work unless the dm_crypt module is loaded. If you made certain kinds of mistakes in Lab 4, the dm_crypt module won't be reloaded on the next reboot.

If you're uncertain about the process, first try to use the associated /dev/mapper device in the /etc/fstab file. Afterwards, find the appropriate UUID, as shown in the output to the **blkid** command. And if you forget to configure the /etc/crypttab file, the system won't ask for the passphrase during the boot process, which would make the encryption of the protected filesystem somewhat worthless. Just be sure to include the **none** directive after the name and UUID of the unencrypted device.

However, if everything works, the system should prompt for the passphrase during the boot process, and then mount the encrypted volume automatically.

Lab 6

The configuration of the automounter on a shared NFS directory is easier than it looks. Before you begin, make sure the shared NFS directory is available from the remote computer with the **showmount -e remoteNFSipaddr** command, where remoteNFSipaddr is the IP address of the remote NFS server. If that doesn't work, you may have skipped a step described in the lab. For more information on NFS servers, refer to Chapter 16.

Of course, there's the CD/DVD. If the automounter is running and a CD/DVD drive is in the appropriate location, you should be able to read the contents of that drive with the **ls /misc/cd** command. That matches the default configuration of the /etc/auto.master and /etc/auto.misc files.

As for the shared NFS directory, there are two approaches. You could modify the following commented sample NFS configuration directive. Of course, you'd have to at least change ftp.example.org to the name or IP address of the NFS server, and /pub/linux to /tmp (or whatever is the name of the directory being shared).

```
linux   -ro,soft,intr   ftp.example.org:/pub/linux
```

Or you could just directly take advantage of the **/etc/auto.net** script. For example, if the remote NFS server is on IP address 192.168.122.50, run the following command:

```
# /etc/auto.net 192.168.122.50
```

You should see the /tmp directory shared in the output. If so, you'll be able to access it more directly with the following command:

```
# ls /net/192.168.122.50/tmp
```

If you really want to learn the automounter, try modifying the aforementioned directive in the /etc/auto.misc configuration file. Assuming the automounter is already running, you can make sure the automounter rereads the applicable configuration files with the **/etc/init.d/autofs reload** command.

If you use the same first directive in the aforementioned line, you'll be able to use the automounter to access the same directory with the **ls /misc/linux** command.

7
Package
Management

After installation is complete, after systems are secured, filesystems are administered, and more, you still have work to do. To customize the system as needed, you may need to add or remove packages, among other tasks. To make sure the right updates are installed, you need to know how to get a system working with the Red Hat Network (RHN) or the repository associated with a rebuild distribution.

To accomplish these tasks, you need to understand how to use the **rpm** and **yum** commands in detail. While they're "just" two commands, they are rich in detail. Entire books have been dedicated to the **rpm** command, such as the *Red Hat RPM Guide*, by Eric Foster-Johnson. For many, that degree of in-depth knowledge of the **rpm** command is no longer necessary, given the capabilities of the **yum** command, and the additional package management tools provided on RHEL 6.

INSIDE THE EXAM

Administrative Skills

As the management of RPM packages is a fundamental skill for Red Hat administrators, it's reasonable to expect to use the **rpm**, **yum**, and related commands on the RHCSA exam. In fact, the RHCE exam effectively assumes knowledge of such commands and more as effective prerequisite skills. The RHCSA objectives include two requirements addressed in this chapter:

■ Install and update software packages from the RHN, a remote repository, or the local filesystem.

■ Update the kernel package appropriately to ensure a bootable system.

A couple of other, closely related objectives are covered in other chapters. A predecessor to the RPM package are the compressed archives described in Chapter 9. An RHCE skill covered in Chapter 12 supports the configuration of an RPM package for "a single file."

Now let's break down these skills a bit. If you don't have access to the RHN, don't be intimidated. When you use a **yum** command to install and update packages from the RHN, it's no different from the commands that you would use to install and update packages from a remote repository.

CERTIFICATION OBJECTIVE 7.01

The Red Hat Package Manager

One of the major duties of a system administrator is software management. New applications are installed. Services are updated. Kernels are patched. Without the right tools, it can be difficult to figure out what software is on a system, what is the latest update, and what applications depend on other software. Worse, you may install a new software package only to find it has overwritten a crucial file from a currently installed package.

The Red Hat Package Manager (RPM) was designed to alleviate these problems. With RPM, software is managed in discrete *packages*. An RPM package includes the software with instructions for adding, removing, and upgrading those files. When properly used, the RPM system can back up key configuration files before proceeding with upgrades and removals. It can also help you identify the currently installed version of any RPM-based application.

RPMs and the **rpm** command are far from ideal, which is why it has been supplemented with the **yum** command. With a connection to a repository such as that available from the RHN or third-party "rebuilds" such as Scientific Linux, you'll be able to use **yum** to satisfy dependencies.

What Is a Package?

In the generic sense, an RPM package is a container of files. It includes the group of files associated with a specific program or application, which normally includes binary installation scripts as well as configuration and documentation files. It also includes instructions on how and where these files should be installed and uninstalled.

An RPM package name usually includes the version, the release, and the architecture for which it was built. For example, the fictional penguin-3.4.5-26.x86_64.rpm package is version 3.4.5, build 26, and the x86_64 indicates that it is suitable for computers built to the AMD/Intel 64-bit architecture.

*Many RPM packages are CPU-specific. You can identify the CPU type for the system with the **uname -i** or **uname -p** commands. More information is available from the contents of the /proc/cpuinfo file.*

What Is a Red Hat Package?

At the heart of this system is the RPM database. Among other things, this database tracks the version and location of each file in each RPM. The RPM database also maintains an MD5 checksum of each file. With the checksum, you can use the **rpm -V** *package* command to determine whether any file from that RPM package has changed. The RPM database makes it easy to add, remove, and upgrade individual packages, as it's configured to know which files to handle and where to put them.

RPM also manages conflicts between packages. For example, assume you have two different packages that use configuration files with the same name. Call the original configuration file /etc/*someconfig.conf*. You've already installed package X. If you then try to install an update package Y, RPM packages are designed to back up the original /etc/*someconfig.conf* file (with a filename like /etc/*someconfig.conf. rpmsave*) before installing package Y.

While RPM upgrades are supposed to preserve or save existing configuration files, there are no guarantees, especially if the RPM is designed by someone other than Red Hat. It's best to back up all applicable configuration files before upgrading any associated RPM package.

What Is a Repository?

RPM packages are frequently organized into repositories. Generally, such repositories include groups of packages with different functions. When downloading a package, you may need to navigate to a different directory, depending on the function of the repository. For example, the RHN includes the following RHEL 6 Server repositories (additional repositories are available):

- **Red Hat Enterprise Linux Server** The main repository, which includes both the packages associated with the original installation of RHEL 6, along with updates.
- **RHN Tools** A repository associated with the management of RHN connections, along with virtualization tools and utilities for automating Kickstart installation on virtual machines.
- **RHN Server Supplementary** A collection of packages released under licenses other than open source, such as Java and Acrobat reader.
- **RHEL V2VWIN** A single package that includes support for reading Microsoft-formatted partitions on RHEL virtual machines.

■ **RHEL Server Optional** A large group of packages not normally associated with server systems. It includes desktop packages and more.

In contrast, the repository categories for third-party rebuild distributions vary. Generally, they include categories such as main and extras, along with supplementary packages and more. In most cases, while the main repository includes just the packages available from the released DVD, updated packages are configured in their own repositories.

Each repository includes a database of packages in a repodata/ subdirectory. That database includes information on each package, including dependencies. That database allows installation requests to that directory to include all dependencies. If you have a subscription to the RHN, access to these repositories is enabled in the rhnplugin.conf file, in the /etc/yum/pluginconf.d directory. That file is discussed later in this chapter.

Later in this chapter, you'll examine how to configure connections to repositories with the configuration files associated with the **yum** command.

on the job

A dependency is a package that needs to be installed to make sure all the features of a target package is available.

Install an RPM Package

There are three basic commands *that may* install an RPM. They won't work if there are dependencies (packages that need to be installed first). For example, if you haven't installed the SELinux policy analysis command line tools package (setools-console) and try to install the SELinux configuration tool package (policycoreutilis-gui), you'll get the following message (version numbers may vary):

```
# rpm -i policycoreutils-gui-2.0.83-19.1.el6.x86_64.rpm
error: Failed dependencies:
        policycoreutils-python = 2.0.83-19.1.el6 is needed by policycoreutils-gui-
2.0.83-19.1.el6.x86_64
        setools-console is needed by policycoreutils-gui-2.0.83-19.1.el6.x86_64
```

One way to test this is to mount the RHEL 6 DVD with the **mount /dev/cdrom /media** command. Next, find the noted policycoreutils-gui package in the Packages/ subdirectory. Alternatively, you could download that package directly from the Red Hat Network or a configured repository with the **yumdownloader policycoreutils-gui** command. This and other **yum** commands are discussed later in this chapter. Just be aware, some Linux GUI desktop environments automatically mount CD/DVD media that is inserted into associated drives. If so, you'll see the mount directory in the output to the **mount** command.

When dependency messages are shown, **rpm** does not install the given package. Note the dependency messages. First, it requires a policycoreutils-python package of the same version number, and a less-defined setools-console package.

Sure, you can use the --force option to make rpm ignore dependencies, but that can lead to other problems, unless you install those dependencies as soon as possible. The best option is to use an appropriate yum command, described later in this chapter. In this case, a yum install policycoreutils-gui command would automatically install the other dependent RPM as well.

If you're not stopped by dependencies, there are three basic commands that can install RPM packages:

```
# rpm -i packagename
# rpm -U packagename
# rpm -F packagename
```

The **rpm -i** option installs the package, if it isn't already installed. The **rpm -U** option upgrades any existing package or installs it if an earlier version isn't already installed. The **rpm -F** option upgrades only existing packages. It does not install a package if it wasn't previously installed.

I like to add the **-vh** options with the **rpm** command. These options add verbose mode and use hash marks that can help monitor the progress of the installation. So when I use **rpm** to install a package, I run the following command:

```
# rpm -ivh packagename
```

There's one more thing associated with a properly designed RPM package. When unpacked with the **rpm** command, it checks to see whether it would overwrite any configuration files. The **rpm** command tries to make intelligent decisions about what to do in this situation. As suggested earlier, if the **rpm** command chooses to replace an existing configuration file, it provides a warning (in most cases) similar to:

```
# rpm -i penguin-3.26.i386.rpm
warning: /etc/someconfig.conf saved as /etc/someconfig.conf.rpmsave
```

The **rpm** command normally works in the same fashion when a package is erased with the **-e** switch. If a configuration file has been changed, it's also saved with a .rpmsave extension in the same directory.

It's up to you to look at both files and determine what modifications, if any, need to be made. Of course, as not every RPM package is perfect, there's always a risk that such an update would overwrite that critical customized configuration file. In that case, backups are important.

In general, the **rpm** commands to upgrade a package work only if the package being installed is of a newer version. Sometimes, an older version of a package is desirable. As long as there are no security issues with the older package, more administrators may be familiar with slightly older releases. Bugs that may be a problem on a newer package may not exist in an older version of that package. So if you want to "downgrade" a package with the **rpm -i**, **-U**, or **-F** commands, the **--force** switch can help.

If you've already customized a package and upgraded it with rpm, go to the saved configuration file. Use it as a guide to change the settings in the new configuration file. But remember, with upgrades, there may be additional required changes. Therefore, you should test the result for every conceivable production environment.

Uninstall an RPM Package

The **rpm -e** command uninstalls a package. But first, RPM checks a few things. It performs a dependency check to make sure no other packages need what you're trying to uninstall. If dependent packages are found, **rpm -e** fails with an error message identifying these packages.

With properly configured RPMs, if you have modified related configuration files, RPM makes a copy of the file, adds an .rpmsave extension to the end of the filename, and then erases the original. It can then proceed with the uninstallation. When the process is complete, it removes the package name from the database.

Be very careful about which packages you remove from a system. Like many other Linux utilities, RPM may silently let you shoot yourself in the foot. For example, if you were to remove the packages that include /etc/passwd or the kernel, it could render that system unusable.

Install RPMs from Remote Systems

With the RPM system, you can even specify package locations similar to an Internet address, in URL format. For example, if you want to apply the **rpm** command to the foo.rpm package on the /pub directory of the ftp.rpmdownloads.com FTP server, you can install this package with a command such as:

```
# rpm -ivh ftp://ftp.rpmdownloads.com/pub/foo.rpm
```

Assuming you have a network connection to that remote server, this particular **rpm** command logs on to the FTP server anonymously and downloads the file. Unfortunately, an attempt to use wildcards in the package name with this command leads to an error message associated with "file not found." The complete package name is required, which can be an annoyance.

If you installed RHEL 6 from an FTP server as instructed in Chapters 1 and 2, you could substitute the associated URL, along with the exact name of the package. For example, based on the FTP server configured in Chapter 1 and the aforementioned policycoreutils-gui package, the appropriate command would be:

```
# rpm -ivh ftp://192.168.122.1/pub/inst/policycoreutils-gui-2.0.83-19.1.el6.
x86_64.rpm
```

If the FTP server requires a username and password, you can include them in the following format: ftp://*username:password@hostname:port/path/to/remote/package/file*.rpm, where *username* and *password* are the username and password you need to log on to this system, and *port,* if required, specifies a nonstandard port used on the remote FTP server. One of the drawbacks of FTP is that all information is transmitted in clear text. When that information includes usernames and passwords, that can be a security risk. For such reasons, anonymous FTP servers may be preferred.

Based on the preceding example, if the username is *mjang* and the password is *Ila451MS*, you could install an RPM directly from a server with the following command:

```
# rpm -ivh ftp://mjang:Ila451MS@192.168.122.1/pub/inst/policycoreutils-gui-
2.0.83-19.1.el6.x86_64.rpm
```

The key to this system is the **rpm** command. Unfortunately, globbing no longer works with this command, at least when tested on RHEL 6. So the exact name of the package to be installed is required.

RPM Installation Security

Security can be a concern, especially with RPM packages downloaded over the Internet. If a cracker were to somehow penetrate the RHN, or perhaps a third-party repository, how would you know that packages from those sources were genuine? The key is the GNU Privacy Guard (GPG) key, which is the open-source implementation of Pretty Good Privacy (PGP).

If you haven't imported or installed a GPG key, you might have noticed something similar to the following message when packages are installed:

```
warning: vsftpd-2.2.2-6.el6.i686.rpm: Header V3 RSA/SHA256
Signature, key ID f21541eb: NOKEY
```

If you're concerned about security, this warning should raise alarm bells. During the RHEL 6 installation process, GPG keys are stored in the /etc/pki/rpm-gpg directory. Take a look at the contents of this directory. You'll find files like RPM-GPG-KEY-redhat-release. To actually use the key to verify packages, it has to be imported. And the command to import the GPG key is fairly simple:

```
# rpm --import /etc/pki/rpm-gpg/RPM-GPG-KEY-redhat-release
```

If there's no output, the **rpm** command probably successfully imported the GPG key. Even if this command succeeds, if you repeat it, an "import failed" message will appear. In addition, the GPG key is now included in the RPM database, which can be verified with the **rpm -qa gpg-pubkey** command.

In the /etc/pki/rpm-gpg directory, there are normally five GPG keys available, as described in Table 7-1.

Later in this chapter, you'll see how GPG keys are imported automatically from remote repositories when new packages are installed.

TABLE 7-1	GPG Key	Description
rpm --query **Options**	RPM-GPG-KEY-redhat-beta	Packages built for the RHEL 6 beta
	RPM-GPG-KEY-redhat-legacy-former	Packages for pre–November 2006 releases (and updates)
	RPM-GPG-KEY-redhat-legacy-release	Packages for post–November 2006 releases
	RPM-GPG-KEY-redhat-legacy-rhx	Packages associated with Red Hat Exchange
	RPM-GPG-KEY-redhat-release	Released packages for RHEL 6

Special RPM Procedures with the Kernel

Kernel updates incorporate new features, address security issues, and generally help Linux systems work better. However, kernel updates can also be a pain in the rear end, especially if specialized packages that depend on an existing version of a kernel have been installed.

In any case, don't upgrade a kernel if you're not ready to repeat every step taken to customize software with the existing kernel, whether it's specialized drivers, recompiling to incorporate additional filesystems, or more. For example, the drivers for a few wireless network cards and printers may be tied to a specific version of a kernel. Some virtual machine software components (not including KVM) may be installed against a specific version of a kernel. In those cases, upgrading a kernel may mean that you'd also have to rebuild associated drivers to keep those network cards, printers, and virtual machine systems operational.

If you see an available update for a kernel RPM, the temptation is to run the **rpm -U** *newkernel* command. Don't do it! It overwrites your existing kernel, and if the updated kernel doesn't work with the system, you're out of luck. (Well, not completely out of luck, but if you reboot and have problems, you'll have to use **linux rescue** mode discussed in Chapter 5 to boot a system and reinstall the existing kernel. In the days where there was a separate Troubleshooting and System Maintenance section on the Red Hat exams, that might have made for an interesting test scenario.)

The best option for upgrading to a new kernel is to install it, specifically with a command such as:

```
# rpm -ivh newkernel
```

If you're connected to an appropriate repository, the following command works just as well:

```
# yum install kernel
```

This installs the new kernel, along with related files, side by side with the current working kernel. One example of the result is shown in Figure 7-1, in the output to the **ls /boot** command.

FIGURE 7-1

New and existing kernel files in the /boot directory

```
[root@server1 ~]# ls /boot/
config-2.6.32-71.7.1.el6.x86_64          lost+found
config-2.6.32-71.el6.x86_64              symvers-2.6.32-71.7.1.el6.x86_64.gz
efi                                      symvers-2.6.32-71.el6.x86_64.gz
grub                                     System.map-2.6.32-71.7.1.el6.x86_64
initramfs-2.6.32-71.7.1.el6.x86_64.img   System.map-2.6.32-71.el6.x86_64
initramfs-2.6.32-71.el6.x86_64.img       vmlinuz-2.6.32-71.7.1.el6.x86_64
initrd-2.6.32-71.7.1.el6.x86_64kdump.img vmlinuz-2.6.32-71.el6.x86_64
[root@server1 ~]#
```

You'll note different files for various parts of the boot process in the boot directory, briefly described in Table 7-2. In many cases, you won't see a new initrd file with a new kernel, unless the system has sufficient RAM (several GB) to support kernel crash dumps. On my system, RHEL 6 did not support crash dumps until I upgraded from 4GB to 8GB of RAM. So unless you have more than 4GB of RAM, don't be concerned if you don't see a new initrd-* file when a new kernel is installed.

The installation of a new kernel adds options to boot the new kernel in the boot loader menu, as defined in the GRUB configuration file (/boot/grub/grub.conf), without erasing existing options. One example of the revised GRUB configuration file is shown in Figure 7-2.

TABLE 7-2

Files in the /boot Directory

File	Description
config-*	Kernel configuration settings; a text file
efi/	Extensible firmware interface (EFI) directory; includes an interface between GRUB and the newer UEFI
grub/	Directory with GRUB configuration files
initramfs-*	The initial RAM disk filesystem, a root filesystem called during the boot process to help load other components
initrd-*	A root filesystem used for kernel crash dumps
symvers-*	List of modules
System.map-*	Map of system names for variables and functions, with their locations in memory
vmlinuz	The actual Linux kernel

FIGURE 7-2

FIGURE 7-2

GRUB with a
second kernel

```
#          root (hd0,0)
#          kernel /vmlinuz-version ro root=/dev/vda2
#          initrd /initrd-[generic-]version.img
#boot=/dev/vda
default=0
timeout=5
splashimage=(hd0,0)/grub/splash.xpm.gz
hiddenmenu
title Red Hat Enterprise Linux Server (2.6.32-71.7.1.el6.x86_64)
       root (hd0,0)
       kernel /vmlinuz-2.6.32-71.7.1.el6.x86_64 ro root=UUID=d92cce5c-d3da-40f
8-9924-6ebe137560a2 rd_NO_LUKS rd_NO_LVM rd_NO_MD rd_NO_DM LANG=en_US.UTF-8 SYS
FONT=latarcyrheb-sun16 KEYBOARDTYPE=pc KEYTABLE=us crashkernel=auto rhgb quiet
       initrd /initramfs-2.6.32-71.7.1.el6.x86_64.img
title Red Hat Enterprise Linux (2.6.32-71.el6.x86_64)
       root (hd0,0)
       kernel /vmlinuz-2.6.32-71.el6.x86_64 ro root=UUID=d92cce5c-d3da-40f8-99
24-6ebe137560a2 rd_NO_LUKS rd_NO_LVM rd_NO_MD rd_NO_DM LANG=en_US.UTF-8 SYSFONT
=latarcyrheb-sun16 KEYBOARDTYPE=pc KEYTABLE=us crashkernel=auto rhgb quiet
       initrd /initramfs-2.6.32-71.el6.x86_64.img
~
~
```

A careful reading of the two stanzas reveals that the only difference is in the version numbers listed in the title, for the Linux kernel, and for the Initial RAM disk filesystem. In addition, the default kernel is the newly installed kernel. So if that kernel does not work, you can restart the system, access the GRUB menu, and then boot from the older kernel, which presumably still works.

If for some reason an updated kernel does not update the GRUB bootloader, all you need to do is make a copy of one stanza, and revise the version number for the title, the kernel, and the Initial RAM disk filesystem filenames.

CERTIFICATION OBJECTIVE 7.02

More RPM Commands

The **rpm** command is rich with details. All this book can do is cover some of the basic ways **rpm** can help you manage RHEL. You've already read about how **rpm** can install and upgrade packages in various ways. Queries can help you identify what's installed, in detail. Validation tools can help you check the integrity of packages and individual files. You can use related tools to help identify the purpose of different RPMs, as well as a full list of those RPMs already installed.

The RHCE objectives include a requirement to create a simple RPM package. The building of source code, along with related commands, is discussed in Chapter 12.

Package Queries

The simplest RPM query verifies whether a specific package is installed. The following command verifies the installation of the Upstart package (the version number you see may vary):

```
# rpm -q upstart
upstart-0.6.5-6.1.el6_0.1.x86_64
```

You can do more with RPM queries, as described in Table 7-3. Note how queries are associated with **-q** or **--query**; full-word switches such as **--query** are usually associated with a double-dash.

Package Signatures

RPM uses several methods for checking the integrity of a package. You've seen how to import the GPG signature. Some of these methods are shown in the output to the **rpm --checksig** *pkgname* command. (The **-K** switch is equivalent to **--checksig**.) For example, if you've downloaded a package from a third party such as the hypothetical pkg-1.2.3-4.noarch.rpm package, and want to check it against the imported GPG signature, run the following command:

```
# rpm --checksig pkg-1.2.3-4.noarch.rpm
```

If successful, you'll see output similar to the following:

```
pkg-1.2.3-4.noarch.rpm: rsa sha1 (md5) pgp md5 OK
```

TABLE 7-3	rpm Query Command	Meaning
rpm --query **Options**	rpm -qa	Lists all installed packages.
	rpm -qf /path/to/file	Identifies the package associated with /path/to/file.
	rpm -qc *packagename*	Lists only configuration files from *packagename*.
	rpm -qi *packagename*	Displays basic information for *packagename*.
	rpm -ql *packagename*	Lists all files from *packagename*.
	rpm -qR *packagename*	Notes all dependencies; you can't install *packagename* without them.

You may already recognize the algorithms used to verify package integrity:

- **rsa** Named for its creators, Rivest, Shamir, and Adlemen, it's a public key encryption algorithm.
- **sha1** A 160-bit message digest Secure Hash Algorithm; a cryptographic hash function.
- **md5** Message Digest 5, a cryptographic hash function.
- **pgp** PGP, as implemented in Linux by GPG.

File Verification

The verification of an installed package compares information about that package with information from the RPM database on a system. The **--verify** (or **-v**) switch checks the size, MD5 checksum, permissions, type, owner, and group of each file in the package. Verification can be done in a number of ways. Here are a few examples:

- Verify all files. Naturally, this may take a long time on your system. (Of course, the **rpm -Va** command performs the same function.)

  ```
  # rpm --verify -a
  ```

- Verify all files within a package against a downloaded RPM.

  ```
  # rpm --verify -p vsftpd-2.2.2-6.el6.i686.rpm
  ```

- Verify a file associated with a particular package.

  ```
  # rpm --verify --file /bin/ls
  ```

If the integrity of the files or packages is verified, you will see no output. Any output means that a file or package is different from the original. There's no need to panic if certain changes appear; after all, administrators do edit configuration files. There are eight tests. If there's been a change, the output is a string of up to eight failure code characters, each of which tells you what happened during each test.

If you see a dot (.), that test passed. The following example shows /bin/vi with an incorrect group ID assignment:

```
# rpm --verify --file /bin/vi
......G.   /bin/vi
```

Table 7-4 lists the failure codes and their meanings.

TABLE 7-4	Failure Code	Meaning
rpm --verify **Codes**	5	MD5 checksum
	S	File size
	L	Symbolic link
	T	File modification time
	D	Device
	U	User
	G	Group
	M	Mode

Now here's an interesting experiment: When you have one version of a package installed, use the **rpm --verify -p** command with a second version of the same package. Finding such a package should not be too difficult, as Red Hat updates packages for feature updates, security patches, and yes, bug fixes, frequently. For example, when I wrote this book for RHEL 6, I had access to both vsftpd-2.2.2-1.el6.i686.rpm and vsftpd-2.2.2-6.el6.i686.rpm When the latter version was installed, I ran the following command:

```
# rpm --verify -p vsftpd-2.2.2-1.el6.i686.rpm
```

and got a whole list of changed files, as shown in Figure 7-3. That command provides information on what was changed between different versions of the vsFTP server package.

FIGURE 7-3	
Verifying changes between packages	

```
[root@server1 SPECS]# rpmbuild -bp --target=`uname -m` kernel.spec
Building target platforms: x86_64
Building for target x86_64
error: Failed build dependencies:
        gcc >= 3.4.2 is needed by kernel-2.6.32-71.7.1.el6.x86_64
        redhat-rpm-config is needed by kernel-2.6.32-71.7.1.el6.x86_64
        patchutils is needed by kernel-2.6.32-71.7.1.el6.x86_64
        elfutils-libelf-devel is needed by kernel-2.6.32-71.7.1.el6.x86_64
        zlib-devel is needed by kernel-2.6.32-71.7.1.el6.x86_64
        binutils-devel is needed by kernel-2.6.32-71.7.1.el6.x86_64
        hmaccalc is needed by kernel-2.6.32-71.7.1.el6.x86_64
[root@server1 SPECS]# 
```

Different Databases of Installed Packages

There are two basic databases of installed RPMs. Through RHEL 5, the basic list was stored in /var/log/rpmpkgs. However, as that database was updated only once a day, it's often best to just get the current list of installed packages with the following command:

```
# rpm -qa
```

The /root/install.log file includes all packages included when RHEL was installed on this system. It's not updated after installation. So once a new or updated package is installed, that file is out of date. If desired, you can set up that same /var/log/rpmpkgs database in RHEL 6, by installing the rpm-cron package.

CERTIFICATION OBJECTIVE 7.03

Dependencies and the yum Command

The **yum** command makes it easy to add and remove software packages to a system. It maintains a database regarding the proper way to add, upgrade, and remove packages. This makes it relatively simple to add and remove software with a single command. That single command overcame what was known as "dependency hell."

The **yum** command was originally developed for Yellow Dog Linux. The name is based on the Yellow Dog updater, modified. Given the trouble associated with dependency hell, Linux users were motivated to find a solution. It was adapted for Red Hat distributions with the help of developers from Duke University.

The configuration of **yum** depends on package libraries known as repositories. Red Hat repositories are configured through the RHN. As the repositories of third-party rebuild distributions can't use RHN (without a subscription), they use publicly available servers. In either case, it's important to know the workings of the **yum** command, how it installs and updates individual packages as well as package groups.

An Example of Dependency Hell

To understand more about the need for the **yum** command, examine Figure 7-4. The packages listed in that figure are what's required to build an RPM. While the building of an RPM package is a RHCE requirement, the associated packages provide an excellent illustration of the need for **yum**.

FIGURE 7-4

Packages required
to build RPMs

```
[root@server1 SPECS]# rpmbuild -bp --target=`uname -m` kernel.spec
Building target platforms: x86_64
Building for target x86_64
error: Failed build dependencies:
        gcc >= 3.4.2 is needed by kernel-2.6.32-71.7.1.el6.x86_64
        redhat-rpm-config is needed by kernel-2.6.32-71.7.1.el6.x86_64
        patchutils is needed by kernel-2.6.32-71.7.1.el6.x86_64
        elfutils-libelf-devel is needed by kernel-2.6.32-71.7.1.el6.x86_64
        zlib-devel is needed by kernel-2.6.32-71.7.1.el6.x86_64
        binutils-devel is needed by kernel-2.6.32-71.7.1.el6.x86_64
        hmaccalc is needed by kernel-2.6.32-71.7.1.el6.x86_64
[root@server1 SPECS]# █
```

You could try to use the **rpm** command to install each of these packages. To do so, take the following steps:

1. Include the RHEL 6 DVD. Insert it into its drive, or make sure it's included in the configuration for the target virtual machine.

2. Unless it's already mounted, mount that DVD with the following command. Of course, a different empty directory can be substituted for /media.

   ```
   # mount /dev/sr0 /media
   ```

3. Navigate to the directory where the DVD is mounted, /media or some subdirectory of /media.

4. The RPM packages on the RHEL 6 DVD can be found in the Packages/ subdirectory of the DVD. Navigate to that subdirectory.

5. Enter the **rpm -ivh** command, and then type in the names of the packages listed in Figure 7-4. It may be easiest to use command completion for this purpose; for example, if you were to type in:

   ```
   # rpm -ivh gcc-
   ```

You could then press the TAB key twice, and review available packages that start with *gcc-*. You could then enter additional keys and press the TAB key again to complete the name of the package. After a bit of work, you'd end up with something similar to the command and results shown in Figure 7-5. What actually appears depends on the current revision level of each package, as well as what's already installed on the local system.

FIGURE 7-5

These
packages have
dependencies.

```
[root@tester1 Packages]# rpm -ivh gcc-4.4.4-13.el6.x86_64.rpm redhat-rpm-config-9.0.3-25.el6.
noarch.rpm patchutils-0.3.1-3.1.el6.x86_64.rpm elfutils-libelf-devel-0.148-1.el6.x86_64.rpm z
lib-devel-1.2.3-25.el6.x86_64.rpm binutils-devel-2.20.51.0.2-5.11.el6.x86_64.rpm hmaccalc-0.9
.12-1.el6.x86_64.rpm
warning: gcc-4.4.4-13.el6.x86_64.rpm: Header V3 RSA/SHA256 Signature, key ID fd431d51: NOKEY
error: Failed dependencies:
        cloog-ppl >= 0.15 is needed by gcc-4.4.4-13.el6.x86_64
        cpp = 4.4.4-13.el6 is needed by gcc-4.4.4-13.el6.x86_64
        glibc-devel >= 2.2.90-12 is needed by gcc-4.4.4-13.el6.x86_64
[root@tester1 Packages]# █
```

6. The next step is to try to include these dependencies in the list of packages to be installed. When I try this step, it leads to more dependencies, as shown in Figure 7-6.

At this point, the addition of more packages to the installation becomes somewhat more difficult. How would you know, except from experience, that the ppl-* and mpfr-* packages would satisfy the first three "Failed Dependencies" error messages? Even if you do already understand, the inclusion of such packages is not enough. There's even one more level of dependent packages. This pain is known as dependency hell.

Relief from Dependency Hell

Before **yum**, some attempts to use the **rpm** command were stopped by the dependencies described earlier. Sure, you could install those dependent packages with the same command, but what if those dependencies themselves have dependencies? That perhaps is the biggest advantage of the **yum** command.

Before **yum**, RHEL incorporated dependency resolution into the update process. Through RHEL 4, this was done with **up2date**. Red Hat incorporated **yum** starting

FIGURE 7-6

There are
even more
dependencies.

```
[root@tester1 Packages]# rpm -ivh gcc-4.4.4-13.el6.x86_64.rpm redhat-rpm-config-9.0.3-25.el6.
noarch.rpm patchutils-0.3.1-3.1.el6.x86_64.rpm elfutils-libelf-devel-0.148-1.el6.x86_64.rpm z
lib-devel-1.2.3-25.el6.x86_64.rpm binutils-devel-2.20.51.0.2-5.11.el6.x86_64.rpm hmaccalc-0.9
.12-1.el6.x86_64.rpm cloog-ppl-0.15.7-1.2.el6.x86_64.rpm cpp-4.4.4-13.el6.x86_64.rpm glibc-de
vel-2.12-1.7.el6.x86_64.rpm
warning: gcc-4.4.4-13.el6.x86_64.rpm: Header V3 RSA/SHA256 Signature, key ID fd431d51: NOKEY
error: Failed dependencies:
        libppl.so.7()(64bit) is needed by cloog-ppl-0.15.7-1.2.el6.x86_64
        libppl_c.so.2()(64bit) is needed by cloog-ppl-0.15.7-1.2.el6.x86_64
        libmpfr.so.1()(64bit) is needed by cpp-4.4.4-13.el6.x86_64
        glibc-headers is needed by glibc-devel-2.12-1.7.el6.x86_64
        glibc-headers = 2.12-1.7.el6 is needed by glibc-devel-2.12-1.7.el6.x86_64
[root@tester1 Packages]# █
```

with RHEL 5. The **yum** command uses subscribed RHN channels and any other repositories configured in the /etc/yum.repos.d directory.

All you need to do to install the packages listed in Figure 7-4 is run the following command:

```
# yum install gcc redhat-rpm-config patchutils elfutils-libelf-devel zlib-devel
binutils-devel hmaccalc
```

If so prompted, accept the request to install additional dependent packages, and then all of the noted dependencies are installed automatically. (Yes, the **-y** switch would perform the same function.) If updates are available from connected repositories, the latest available version of each package is installed. The **yum** command is described in more detail later in this chapter.

But if you're running RHEL 6 without a connection to the RHN, nothing happens. Shortly, you'll see how to create a connection between **yum** and the installation server created in Chapter 1.

There are a number of third-party repositories available for RHEL. They include several popular applications that are not supported by Red Hat. For example, I use one to install packages associated with my laptop wireless network card.

While the owners of these repositories work closely with some Red Hat developers, there are some reports where dependencies required from one repository are unavailable from other repositories, leading to a different form of "dependency hell." However, at least the more popular third-party repositories are excellent; I've never encountered "dependency hell" from using these repositories.

on the job

There are two main reasons why Red Hat does not include most proven and popular packages available from third-party repositories. Some are not released under open-source licenses, and others are packages that Red Hat simply chooses not to support.

Basic yum Configuration

Relief from dependency hell depends on the proper configuration of **yum**. Not only do you need to know how to configure **yum** to connect to repositories over the Internet, but also you need to know how to configure **yum** to connect to repositories on a local network. With this knowledge, you can connect **yum** to repositories on the RHN, to repositories configured by third parties, and to custom repositories configured for specialized networks. And remember, during the Red Hat exams, you won't have access to the Internet.

To that end, you to understand how yum is configured in some detail. It starts with the /etc/yum.conf configuration file and continues with files in the /etc/yum and /etc/yum.repos.d directories. To get the full list of yum configuration directives and their current values, run the following command:

```
# yum-config-manager
```

This command requires the installation of the yum-utils package.

The Basic yum Configuration File: yum.conf

This section analyzes the default version of the /etc/yum.conf file, line by line. While you won't make changes to this file in most cases, you need to understand at least the standard directives in this file, if something goes wrong. The following lines are straight excerpts from the default version of this file. The first directive is a header; the **[main]** header suggests that all directives that follow apply globally to **yum**.

```
[main]
```

The **cachedir** directive specifies where caches of packages, package lists, and related databases are to be downloaded. Based on the standard 64-bit architecture for RHEL 6, this translates to the /var/cache/yum/x86_64/6Server directory.

```
cachedir=/var/cache/yum/$basearch/$releasever
```

The **keepcache** boolean directive specifies whether **yum** actually stores downloaded headers and packages in the directory specified by **cachedir**. The standard shown here suggests that caches are not kept, which helps make sure that a system is kept up to date with the latest available packages.

```
keepcache=0
```

The **debuglevel** directive is closely related to the **errorlevel** and **logfile** directives, as they specify the detail associated with debug and error messages. Even though the **errorlevel** directive is not shown, both it and **debuglevel** are set to 2 by default. The available range is 0–10, where 0 provides almost no information, and 10 provides perhaps too much information even for developers.

```
debuglevel=2
logfile=/var/log/yum.log
```

The **exactarch** boolean directive makes sure the architecture matches the actual processor type, as defined by the **arch** command.

```
exactarch=1
```

The **obsoletes** boolean directive can support the uninstallation of obsolete packages in conjunction with a **yum update** command.

```
obsoletes=1
```

The **gpgcheck** boolean directive makes sure the **yum** command actually checks the GPG signature of downloaded packages.

```
gpgcheck=1
```

The **plugins** boolean directive provides a necessary link to Python-based RHN plugins in the /usr/share/yum-plugins directory. It also refers indirectly to plugin configuration files in the /etc/yum/pluginconf.d directory.

```
plugins=1
```

The **installonly_limit** directive provides a safeguard of sorts, making sure that Linux kernel packages are always installed and not upgraded, for reasons described earlier in this chapter:

```
installonly_limit=3
```

To make sure the header data downloaded from the RHN (and any other repositories) are up to date, the **metadata_expire** directive specifies a lifetime for headers. The default is shown in comments. In other words, if you haven't used the **yum** command in 90 minutes, the next use of the **yum** command downloads the latest header information.

```
#metadata_expire=90m
```

The final directive of interest, in comments, happens to be the default; it's a reference to the noted directory for actual configuration information for repositories:

```
# PUT YOUR REPOS HERE OR IN separate files named file.repo
# in /etc/yum.repos.d
```

Configuration Files in the /etc/yum/pluginconf.d Directory

The default files in the /etc/yum/pluginconf.d directory configure a connection between **yum** and the Red Hat network. If you're studying from a RHEL rebuild distribution such as Scientific Linux, you'll see a different set of files in this directory. In Scientific Linux, the files in this directory are focused on connecting the local system to better repositories over the Internet. But as this is a Red Hat book, the focus will be on the two basic files in the RHEL 6 installation.

If you've installed the Kickstart Configurator discussed in Chapter 2, there will be two additional files in this directory: blacklist.conf and whiteout.conf. They are not relevant to the Red Hat exams.

Red Hat Network Plugins with rhnplugin.conf

If you have a subscription to the RHN, the rhnplugin.conf file in this directory is especially important. While the directives, as follows, may seem simple, they enable access and check GPG signatures:

```
[main]
enabled = 1
gpgcheck = 1
```

In comments, this file suggests that different settings can be configured for different repositories. The repositories entitled in brackets should match those associated with the actual RHN repositories (or the repositories of third-party rebuilds).

Red Hat Network Plugins with refresh-packagekit.conf

The refresh-packagekit-conf file is designed to connect the **yum** system to the PackageKit. As discussed later in this chapter, PackageKit is a system designed to work with all types of update commands, including **yum**, **apt**, and others. It's a simple file, with two directives, which enables a connection between **yum** and the GUI package management tools discussed later in this chapter.

```
[main]
enabled=1
```

Configuration Files in the /etc/yum.repos.d Directory

The configuration files in the /etc/yum.repos.d directory are designed to connect systems to actual repositories. If you're running a rebuild distribution such as Scientific Linux, you'll see files that connect to public repositories on the Internet. If you're running RHEL 6, this directory may be empty, unless that system was installed locally from the RHEL 6 DVD. In that case, you'll see a packagekit-media. repo file in that directory, which is designed to get further updates from the DVD.

A couple of elements in common for configuration files in the /etc/yum.repos.d directory is the file extension (.repo) and the documentation, available with the **man yum.conf** command.

A properly configured .repo file in the /etc/yum.repos.d directory can be a terrific convenience, to enable the installation of groups of packages with the **yum** command. As the /etc/yum.repos.d directory may be empty on a RHEL 6 system, you should know how to create that file from scratch, using data for the installation server and information available in the yum.conf man page.

Deal with the packagekit-media.repo File

However, as the latest updates are available, it is often best to disable that file. In fact, you may not even have the RHEL 6 installation DVD available during an exam. While you could just delete that file, other software components regenerate that file when RHEL 6 is rebooted. So the best approach to the packagekit-media. repo file is to disable it by adding the following directive to the end of the file:

```
enabled=0
```

If you're experienced with various versions of Fedora Linux, this solution hasn't always worked. However, it works in current tests of RHEL 6 systems installed from DVD (as opposed to the RHCSA objective of installing RHEL 6 over a network).

Understand /etc/yum.repos.d Configuration Files for Rebuild Distributions

If you're running a rebuild distribution, the files in the /etc/yum.repos.d directory may connect the local system to one or more remote repositories. One example comes from Scientific Linux 6, as shown in Figure 7-7. While it includes a number of different repositories, you can learn from the pattern of directives configured for each repository.

There are four stanzas of data shown in Figure 7-7. Each stanza represents a connection to a Scientific Linux repository. For example, the first stanza includes the basic elements of a repository and more. The first line, in brackets, provides a name for the repository. In this case, the [sl] just happens to match the initials of Scientific Linux. It doesn't represent the directory where the associated packages are installed. That's a difference with the /etc/yum/pluginconf.d/rhnplugin.conf file described earlier.

```
[sl]
```

FIGURE 7-7

Several repositories configured in one file

```
[sl]
name=Scientific Linux $releasever - $basearch
baseurl=http://ftp.scientificlinux.org/linux/scientific/$releasever/$basearch/os/
              http://ftp1.scientificlinux.org/linux/scientific/$releasever/$basearch/os/
              http://ftp2.scientificlinux.org/linux/scientific/$releasever/$basearch/os/
              ftp://ftp.scientificlinux.org/linux/scientific/$releasever/$basearch/os/
#mirrorlist=http://ftp.scientificlinux.org/linux/scientific/mirrorlist/sl-base-6.txt
enabled=1
gpgcheck=1
gpgkey=file:///etc/pki/rpm-gpg/RPM-GPG-KEY-sl file:///etc/pki/rpm-gpg/RPM-GPG-KEY-dawson

[sl-testing]
name=Scientific Linux $releasever Testing - $basearch
baseurl=http://ftp.scientificlinux.org/linux/scientific/6rolling/testing/$basearch/
              http://ftp1.scientificlinux.org/linux/scientific/6rolling/testing/$basearch/
              http://ftp2.scientificlinux.org/linux/scientific/6rolling/testing/$basearch/
              ftp://ftp.scientificlinux.org/linux/scientific/6rolling/testing/$basearch/
enabled=0
gpgcheck=0
gpgkey=file:///etc/pki/rpm-gpg/RPM-GPG-KEY-sl file:///etc/pki/rpm-gpg/RPM-GPG-KEY-dawson

[sl-source]
name=Scientific Linux $releasever Alpha - Source
baseurl=http://ftp.scientificlinux.org/linux/scientific/$releasever/SRPMS/
              http://ftp1.scientificlinux.org/linux/scientific/$releasever/SRPMS/
              http://ftp2.scientificlinux.org/linux/scientific/$releasever/SRPMS/
              ftp://ftp.scientificlinux.org/linux/scientific/$releasever/SRPMS/
enabled=0
gpgcheck=1
gpgkey=file:///etc/pki/rpm-gpg/RPM-GPG-KEY-sl file:///etc/pki/rpm-gpg/RPM-GPG-KEY-dawson

[sl-testing-source]
name=Scientific Linux $releasever Testing - Source
baseurl=http://ftp.scientificlinux.org/linux/scientific/6rolling/testing/SRPMS/
              http://ftp1.scientificlinux.org/linux/scientific/6rolling/testing/SRPMS/
              http://ftp2.scientificlinux.org/linux/scientific/6rolling/testing/SRPMS/
              ftp://ftp.scientificlinux.org/linux/scientific/6rolling/testing/SRPMS/
enabled=0
gpgcheck=0
gpgkey=file:///etc/pki/rpm-gpg/RPM-GPG-KEY-sl file:///etc/pki/rpm-gpg/RPM-GPG-KEY-dawson
```

However, when you run the **yum update** command to update the local database of those remote packages, it includes **sl** as the name of the repository, in output similar to the following, which suggests that it took ten seconds to download the 1.6MB database of existing repository data.

```
sl              | 1.6MB   00:10
```

While the name of the repository follows, it's just for documentation purposes and does not affect how packages or package databases are read or downloaded. However, the inclusion of the **name** directive does avoid a nonfatal error message.

```
name=Scientific Linux $releasever - $basearch
```

Note the several **baseurl** directives that follow. While only one is required, multiple **baseurl** directives specify the URL to different remote servers with a copy of the actual repository of packages. It can work with either the HTTP or the FTP protocol. (It can even work with local directories or mounted Network File System shares, as described in Exercise 7-1.)

```
baseurl=http://ftp.scientificlinux.org/linux/scientific/$releasever/$basearch/os/
```

Alternatively, these repositories can be set up in a file downloaded with the **mirrorlist** directive:

```
#mirrorlist=http://ftp.scientificlinux.org/linux/scientific/mirrorlist/sl-base-6.txt
```

While repositories configured in .repo files in the /etc/yum.repos.d directory are **enabled** by default, the following directive provides an easy way to deactivate a connection to such (**enabled=0** would deactivate the connection):

```
enabled=1
```

If you want **yum** to check the GPG signatures of each package to be downloaded, the following command puts that wish into effect:

```
gpgcheck=1
```

Of course, any GPG check requires a GPG key; the following directive specifies two keys from the local /etc/pki/rpm-gpg directory for that purpose:

```
gpgkey=file:///etc/pki/rpm-gpg/RPM-GPG-KEY-sl file:///etc/pki/rpm-gpg/RPM-GPG-KEY-dawson
```

Create Your Own /etc/yum.repos.d Configuration File

You'll want to know how to create a local configuration file in the /etc/yum.repos.d directory. It enables the use of the **yum** command, which is the easiest way to install groups of packages like the Apache web server from Chapter 1 or any of the groups of packages discussed in the RHCE part of this book.

To do so, you'll need to set up a text file with a .repo extension in the /etc/yum .repos.d directory. All that file needs is three lines. In fact, if you're willing to accept some nonfatal errors, two lines are sufficient.

On RHEL 6, especially during an exam, the /etc/yum.repos.d directory may be empty. So you may not have access to examples such as those available for Scientific Linux, as shown in Figure 7-7. The first guidance comes from the following comments at the bottom of the /etc/yum.conf file, which confirm that the file must have a .repo extension in the /etc/yum.repos.d directory:

```
# PUT YOUR REPOS HERE OR IN separate files named file.repo
# in /etc/yum.repos.d
```

In addition, you could configure the three lines in the /etc/yum.conf file. If you forget what three lines to add, there is an example in the man page for the yum.conf file, as shown in Figure 7-8.

FIGURE 7-8
 	
Excerpt from man yum.conf for a new /etc/yum .repos.d file
	`[repository] OPTIONS`
	`        The repository section(s) take the following form:`
	
	`        Example: [repositoryid]`
	`        name=Some name for this repository`
	`        baseurl=url://path/to/repository/`
	
	`        repositoryid Must be a unique name for each repository, one`
	`        word.`
	
	`        name A human readable string describing the repository.`
	
	`        baseurl Must be a URL to the directory where the yum reposi-`
	`        tory's 'repodata' directory lives. Can be an http://, ftp:// or`
	`        file:// URL. You can specify multiple URLs in one baseurl state-`
	`        ment. The best way to do this is like this:`
	`        [repositoryid]`
	`        name=Some name for this repository`
	`        baseurl=url://server1/path/to/repository/`
	`                url://server2/path/to/repository/`
	`                url://server3/path/to/repository/`
	
	`        If you list more than one baseurl= statement in a repository you`
	`        will find yum will ignore the earlier ones and probably act`
	`        bizarrely. Don't do this, you've been warned.`
	
	`:▮`

If you forget what to do, run the **man yum.conf** command, and scroll down to this part of the man page. The identifier for the repository is shown in brackets. Unless specified by the RHCSA exam, it doesn't matter what single word you put between the brackets as the identifier.

For the purpose of this chapter, I open a new file named whatever.repo in the /etc/yum.repos.d directory. (To some extent, the filename of the .repo file does not matter, as long as it has a .repo extension in the /etc/yum.repos.d directory.) In that file, I add the following identifier:

```
[test]
```

Next comes the **name** directive for the repository. As suggested by the listing in the man page, that name should be "human readable." In Linux parlance, that also means the name does not affect the functionality of the repository. To demonstrate, I add the following directive:

```
name=somebody likes Linux
```

Finally, there's the **baseurl** directive, which can be configured to point to an installation server. Per the RHCSA requirements, you need to know how to install Linux from a remote server. It also suggests that you need to know how to install and update packages from a remote repository. To meet either objective, you need to know the URL of that remote server or repository. It's reasonable to expect that URL to be provided during the exam. In Chapter 1, you created FTP and HTTP installation servers on the host system for virtual machines, which are "remote" from those systems.

The FTP and HTTP installation servers that you created in Chapter 1 can also be used as remote repositories. To set up access to those repositories, all you need to include is one of the following **baseurl** directives:

```
baseurl=ftp://192.168.122.1/pub/inst
baseurl=http://192.168.122.1/inst
```

As suggested in the yum.conf man page, you should not include both URLs in separate **baseurl** directives. Make a choice and save the resulting file. That's all you need. Unless directed during the exam to do so, there's no reason (except for better security) to include the **enabled**, **gpgcheck**, or **gpgkey** directives described earlier. Of course security is important in real life, but if your focus is on the exam, the best advice is often to keep things as simple as possible.

Once the file is saved, run the following commands, to first clear out databases from previously accessed repositories, and then to update the local database from the repository newly configured in the /etc/yum.repos.d/whatever.repo file.

```
# yum clean all
# yum update
```

For a system not registered with the RHN, it'll lead to the following output:

```
Loaded plugins: refresh-packagekit, rhnplugin
This system is not registered with RHN.
RHN support will be disabled.
test                                        |  3.7 kB      00:00
test/primary_db                             |  2.9 MB      00:00
Setting up Update Process
No Packages marked for Update
```

The system is now ready for the installation of new packages. Try running the following command:

```
# yum install system-config-printer
```

Given the virtual machines configured earlier in this book, you might see the result shown in Figure 7-9. If confirmed, the **yum** command would download and then install not only the system-config-printer RPM, but also the four dependent packages shown in the figure to make sure the system-config-printer package is fully supported.

FIGURE 7-9

Installation of one package can include dependencies.

```
Dependencies Resolved

================================================================================
 Package                      Arch       Version          Repository    Size
================================================================================
Installing:
 system-config-printer        x86_64     1.1.16-17.el6    test          444 k
Installing for dependencies:
 gnome-python2-gnomekeyring   x86_64     2.28.0-4.el6     test           24 k
 libsmbclient                 x86_64     3.5.4-68.el6     test          1.7 M
 notify-python                x86_64     0.1.1-10.el6     test           26 k
 system-config-printer-libs   x86_64     1.1.16-17.el6    test          651 k

Transaction Summary
================================================================================
Install       5 Package(s)
Upgrade       0 Package(s)

Total download size: 2.8 M
Installed size: 12 M
Is this ok [y/N]: 
```

EXERCISE 7-1

Create a yum Repository from the RHEL 6 DVD

This exercise requires access to the RHEL 6 DVD. If you don't have a lot of space for this exercise, it's acceptable to set up the repository directly on the mounted DVD. Alternatively, you can copy the contents to a specified directory. It also assumes an available installation repository, such as one of those created in Chapter 1.

This exercise assumes you'll be starting with no files in the /etc/yum.repos.d directory described in this chapter.

1. If there are existing files in the /etc/yum.repos.d directory, copy them to a backup location such as the root user's home directory, /root.

2. If you're working with a rebuild distribution such as CentOS 6, copy the rhel-debuginfo.repo file from the book CD's Chapter5/ subdirectory to your system's /etc/yum.repos.d directory.

3. Mount the RHEL 6 DVD on the /mnt directory with the following command:

   ```
   # mount /dev/sr0 /mnt
   ```

   Alternatively, if you have only the RHEL 6 DVD as an ISO file, mount it with the following command:

   ```
   # mount -o loop rhel-server-6.0-i386-dvd.iso /mnt
   ```

   Of course, if desired, you can copy the files from a different mount point such as /media to the /mnt directory with a command like **cp -ar /media/. /mnt**. The dot (.) in front of the /media directory ensures the copying of hidden files from the mounted DVD.

4. Open a new file in a text editor. Use a name like rhel6.repo.

5. Edit the rhel6.repo file. Create a new stanza of directives. Use an appropriate stanza title such as **[rhel]**.

6. Specify an appropriate **name** directive for the repository.

7. Include a **baseurl** directive set to **file:///mnt/**. Include an **enabled=1** directive.

8. Save and close the file.

9. Assuming you're running RHEL 6 (and not a rebuild distribution), open the rhnplugin.conf file in the /etc/yum/pluginconf.d directory, and set **enabled=0**.

10. Run the **yum clean all** and **yum update** commands.

11. If successful, you should see the following output:

```
Loaded plugins: refresh-packagekit

rhel      | 3.7 kB      00:00 ...
rhel/primary_db      | 2.3 MB      00:00 ...
Setting up Update Process
No Packages marked for Update
:
```

You've now set up a repository on the local /mnt directory.

12. Restore the original files. Open the rhnplugin.conf file in the /etc/yum/pluginconf.d directory, and set **enabled=1**. Restore the files backed up to the /root directory to the /etc/yum.repos.d directory. If you want to restore the original configuration, delete or move the rhel6.repo file from that directory. Run the **yum clean all command** again.

Third-Party Repositories

Other groups of third-party developers create packages for RHEL 6. They include packages for some popular software not supported by Red Hat. The web sites for two of these third parties can be found at https://rpmrepo.org/RPMforge and http://atrpms.net.

To add third-party repositories to a system, you'd create a custom .repo file in the /etc/yum.repos.d directory. For example, I often use Axel Thimm's third-party repository for my RHEL and Fedora Core systems. It's available from http://ATrpms.net. To make it work with my RHEL system, I use the instructions available from that web site and add the following information to atrpms.repo in the /etc/yum.repos.d directory:

```
[atrpms]
name=atrpms for RHEL $releasever - $basearch
baseurl=http://dl.atrpms.net/el6-i386/atrpms/stable
gpgkey=http://atrpms.net/RPM-GPG-KEY.atrpms
gpgcheck=1
```

If you want to disable any repository in the /etc/yum.repos.d directory, add the following directive to the applicable repository file:

```
enabled=0
```

Basic yum Commands

If you want to learn more about the intricacies of the **yum** command, run the command by itself. You'll see the following output scroll by, probably far too fast. Of course, you can pipe the output to the **less** command pager with the **yum | less** command.

```
# yum
Loaded plugins: refresh-packagekit, rhnplugin
You need to give some command
usage: yum [options] COMMAND

List of Commands
```

You'll examine how a few of these commands and options work in the following sections. While you won't have Internet access during a Red Hat exam, you might have a network connection to a locally configured repository. Such configurations are even supported by a variation of the RHN known as the RHN Satellite Server. So you should be ready to configure an appropriate file in the /etc/yum.repos.d directory, as described earlier, and use the **yum** command during either Red Hat exam. Besides, it's an excellent tool for administering Red Hat systems.

Start with a simple command: **yum list**. It'll return a list of all packages, whether they're installed or available, along with their version numbers and repositories. If you want more information about a specific package, the **yum info** command can help. For example, the following command is functionally equivalent to **rpm -qi samba**:

```
# yum info samba
```

The **rpm -qi** command works if the queried package is already installed. The **yum info** command is not subject to that limitation.

Installation Mode

There are two basic installation commands. If you haven't installed a package before, or you want to update it to the latest stable version, run the **yum install** *packagename* command. For example, if you're checking for the latest version of the Samba RPM, the following command will update it or add it if it isn't already installed on the target system.

```
# yum install samba
```

If you just want to keep the packages on a system up to date, run the **yum update** *packagename* command. For example, if you already have the Samba RPM installed, the following command makes sure it's updated to the latest version:

```
# yum update samba
```

If you haven't installed Samba, this command doesn't add it to your installed packages. In that way, the **yum update** command is analogous to the **rpm -F** command.

Of course, the **yum** command is not complete without options that can uninstall a package. The first one is straightforward, as it uninstalls the Samba package along with any dependencies.

```
# yum erase samba
```

The **yum update** command by itself is powerful; if you want to make sure that all installed packages are updated to the latest stable versions, run the following command:

```
# yum update
```

The **yum update** command may take some time as it communicates with the RHN or other repositories. It downloads the current database of packages with all dependencies. It then finds all packages with available updates, and adds them to the list of packages to be updates. It then finds all dependent packages if they're not already included in the list of updates.

What if you just want a list of available updates? The **yum list updates** command can help there. It's functionally equivalent to the **yum check-update** command.

But what if you aren't quite sure what to install? For example, if you want to install the Evince document reader, and think the operational command includes the term "evince," the **yum whatprovides */*evince** command can help.

Alternatively, to search for all instances of files with the .repo extension, run the following command:

```
# yum whatprovides */*.repo
```

It lists all instances of the packages with files that end with the .repo extension, with the associated RPM package. The first wildcard is required, since the **whatprovides** option requires the full path to the file. It accepts partial filenames; for example, the **yum whatprovides /etc/init/*** command returns the RPM associated with files in the /etc/init directory. Once the needed package is known, you can proceed with the **yum install** *packagename* command.

on the Job

*In many cases, problems with yum can be solved with the **yum clean all** command. If there are recent updates to RHN packages (or third-party repositories), this command flushes the current cache of headers, allowing you to resynchronize headers with configured repositories, without having to wait the default 90 minutes before the cache is automatically flushed (as defined by the metadata_expire directive in /etc/yum.conf).*

Security and yum

Security can be a concern, especially with RPM packages downloaded over the Internet. If a cracker were to somehow penetrate the RHN, or perhaps a third-party repository, how would you know that packages from those sources were genuine? The answer is the GNU Privacy Guard (GPG) key, which is the open-source implementation of Pretty Good Privacy (PGP). It's the same system described earlier in this chapter for RPM packages. As an example, look at the output the first time a new package is installed over a network on RHEL 6:

```
# yum install samba
```

After packages are downloaded, you'll see something similar to the following messages:

```
warning: rpmts_HdrFromFdno: Header V3 RSA/SHA256 Signature, key ID f21541eb: NOKEY

 rhel/gpgkey      | 6.3 kB      00:00 ...
Importing GPG key 0xF21541EB "Red Hat, Inc. (release key 2) <security@redhat.com>"
from
/etc/pki/rpm-gpg/RPM-GPG-KEY-redhat-release
Is this ok [y/N]: y
Importing GPG key 0x2FA658E0 "Red Hat, Inc. (auxiliary key) <security@redhat.com>"
from
/etc/pki/rpm-gpg/RPM-GPG-KEY-redhat-release
Is this ok [y/N]: y
```

If you're simultaneously downloading packages from other repositories, additional GPG keys may be presented for approval. As suggested by the last line, **N** is the default response; you actually have to type in **y** to proceed with the download and installation; not only of the GPG key, but also of the package in question.

You may note that the GPG key used is from the same directory of keys associated with the **rpm** command earlier in this chapter. And that makes sense, as the **yum** command is essentially just a capable front end to the **rpm** command.

Updates and Security Fixes

Red Hat maintains a public list of errata at http://rhn.redhat.com/errata/. Such errata are classified by RHEL releases. If you have an RHEL subscription, affected packages are normally made available through the RHN. All you need to do is run the **yum update** command periodically. This list is useful for those third parties who use RHEL source code, such as CentOS, Scientific Linux, or even Oracle Linux.

Package Groups and yum

The **yum** command can do more. It can install and remove packages in groups. These are the groups defined in the .xml files described in Chapter 2. One location for that file is on the RHEL 6 DVD, in the /repodata subdirectory. At the start of most of those stanzas, you'll see the **<id>** and **<name>** XML directives, which list two identifiers for each of those groups.

But that's a lot of work to find a package group. The **yum** command makes it simpler. With the following command, you can identify available package groups from configured repositories:

```
# yum grouplist
```

Note how the groups are divided into installed and available groups. Some of the groups listed may be of particular interest, such as "Remote Desktop Clients", some of which you'll use in Chapter 9. To find out more about this group, run the following command, with output shown in Figure 7-10.

```
# yum groupinfo "Remote Desktop Clients"
```

FIGURE 7-10

Packages in the Remote Desktop Clients group

```
[root@server1 yum.repos.d]# yum groupinfo "Remote Desktop Clients"
Loaded plugins: refresh-packagekit, rhnplugin
This system is not registered with RHN.
RHN support will be disabled.
Setting up Group Process

Group: Remote Desktop Clients
 Optional Packages:
   rdesktop
   spice-client
   spice-xpi
   tigervnc
   tsclient
   vinagre
[root@server1 yum.repos.d]# ▌
```

Note how the packages are all listed as "Optional Packages". In other words, they're not normally installed with the package group. Thus, suppose you were to run the following command:

```
# yum groupinstall "Remote Desktop Clients"
```

Nothing would be installed. Desired packages from this package group have to be specifically named to be installed with commands like the following:

```
# yum install rdesktop
```

But optional packages are not the only category. The following command lists all packages in the Print Server package group, with output shown in Figure 7-11.

```
# yum groupinfo "Print Server"
```

Packages in this group are classified in two other categories. Mandatory packages are always installed with the package group. Default packages are normally installed with the package group; however, specific packages from this group can be excluded with the **-x** switch, unless changes are made during the RHEL installation process. For example, the following command installs the two mandatory and five default packages:

```
# yum groupinstall "Print Server"
```

FIGURE 7-11

Packages in the Print Server group

```
[root@server1 yum.repos.d]# yum groupinfo "Print Server"
Loaded plugins: refresh-packagekit, rhnplugin
This system is not registered with RHN.
RHN support will be disabled.
Setting up Group Process

Group: Print Server
 Description: Allows the system to act as a print server.
 Mandatory Packages:
   cups
   printer-filters
 Default Packages:
   foomatic-db-ppds
   gutenprint
   gutenprint-cups
   hpijs
   paps
[root@server1 yum.repos.d]# 
```

In contrast, the following command excludes the paps and the gutenprint-cups packages from the list of those to be installed:

```
# yum groupinstall "Print Server" -x paps -x gutenprint-cups
```

The options to the **yum** command are not complete unless there's a command that can reverse the process. As suggested by the name, the **groupremove** option uninstalls all packages from the noted package group:

```
# yum groupremove "Print Server"
```

Exclusions are not possible with the **groupremove** switch. If you don't want to remove all packages listed in the output to the command, it may be best to remove target packages individually.

More yum Commands

A number of additional **yum**-related commands are available. Two of them may be of particular interest to those studying for the Red Hat exams: **yum-config-manager** and **yumdownloader**, which can display all current settings for each repository as well as download individual RPM packages. One more related command is **createrepo**, which can help you set up a local repository.

View All Directives with yum-config-manager

To some extent, the directives listed in the yum.conf and related configuration files provide only a small snapshot of available directives. To review the full list of directives, run the **yum-config-manager** command. Pipe it to the **less** command as a pager. It includes 100 lines. The excerpt from the [main] repository shown in Figure 7-12 is based on the connection to the RHN.

Many of the directives associated with **yum** are not filled in, such as **assumeyes**; some don't really matter, such as the color directives. Some of the other significant directives are shown in Table 7-5. It is not a comprehensive list. If you're interested in a directive not shown, it's defined in the man page for the yum.conf file.

Package Downloads with yumdownloader

As suggested by the name, the **yumdownloader** command can be used to download packages from yum-based repositories. It's a fairly simple command. For example, the

FIGURE 7-12

A partial list of
yum directives

```
diskspacecheck = True
distroverpkg = redhat-release
enable_group_conditionals = True
enabled = True
enablegroups = True
errorlevel = 2
exactarch = True
exactarchlist =
exclude =
failovermethod = priority
gaftonmode =
gpgcheck = True
group_package_types = mandatory,
    default
groupremove_leaf_only =
history_record = True
history_record_packages = yum,
    rpm
http_caching = all
installonly_limit = 3
installonlypkgs = kernel,
    kernel-bigmem,
    kernel-enterprise,
    kernel-smp,
    kernel-debug,
    kernel-unsupported,
    kernel-source,
    kernel-devel,
    kernel-PAE,
```

following command reviews the contents of configured repositories for a package
named cups.

```
# yumdownloader cups
```

Either the RPM package is downloaded to the local directory, or the command
returns the following error messages:

```
No Match for argument cups
Nothing to download
```

Sometimes, more specifics are required. If there are multiple versions of a package
stored on a repository, the default is to download the latest version of that package.
That may not always be what you want. For example, if you want to use the
originally released RHEL 6 kernel, the following command downloads the original
RHEL 6 version of the kernel package:

```
# yumdownloader kernel-2.6.32-71.el6
```

TABLE 7-5	Configuration Parameters from yum-config-manager

Configuration Directive in yum	Description
alwaysprompt	Prompts for confirmation on package installation or removal.
assumeyes	Set to no by default; if set to 1, **yum** proceeds automatically with package installation and removal.
cachedir	Set to the directory for database and downloaded package files.
distroverpkg	Refers to the /etc/redhat-release file with the name of the release.
enablegroups	Supports **yum group*** commands.
installonlypkgs	Lists packages that should never be updated; normally includes Linux kernel packages.
logfile	Specifies name of file with log information, normally /var/log/yum.log.
pluginconfpath	Notes the directory with plugins, normally /etc/yum/pluginconf.d.
reposdir	Specifies the directory with repository configuration files.
ssl*	Supports the use of the Secure Sockets Layer (SSL) for secure updates.
tolerant	Determines whether **yum** stops if an error is made in update package names.

Create Your Own Repository with createrepo

An earlier version of the RHCE objectives for RHEL 6 suggested that you should know how to "create a private yum repository." While that objective has since been removed, it's a logical future direction for the Red Hat exams.

Custom repositories can provide additional control. Enterprises who want to control the packages installed on their Linux systems can create their own customized repositories. While it can be based on the standard repositories developed for a distribution, it can include additional packages such as custom software unique to an organization. Just as easily, it can omit packages that may violate organizational policies such as games. Limits on the choices for certain functions such as browsers can minimize related support requirements.

To create a customized repository, you need to collect desired packages in a specific directory. The **createrepo** command can process all packages in that directory. The database is created in XML files in a repodata/ subdirectory. An example of this package database already exists in the repodata/ subdirectory of the RHEL 6 DVD.

The RHN enables support of customized repositories with related products, including the Red Hat Proxy Server and the Red Hat Satellite Server. For more information on repository management, see *Linux Patch Management*, written by this author, published by Prentice Hall.

More Package Management Tools

Whether a system is connected to the RHN or remote repositories provided by a distribution like CentOS or Scientific Linux, it uses the same basic package management tools. Each of these alternatives uses the **rpm** command to process RPM packages. They use the **yum** command to satisfy dependencies and install groups of packages. And that makes sense, as the rebuild distributions are built on the same source code as RHEL 6.

Those similarities extend to GUI-based package management tools. While the identity of these tools have changed between RHEL 5 and RHEL 6, they're still front ends to the **rpm** and **yum** commands. They take advantage of the package groups configured in the .xml file described in Chapter 2. Since Red Hat uses GNOME as the default GUI desktop environment, the associated tools for RHEL 6 are based on that interface.

However, one thing that the rebuild distributions don't have is access to the RHN. That situation may only be temporary, Red Hat has recently started to release RHN software under open-source licenses. And developer groups are at work with projects like Spacewalk. That's important for the enterprise, as the RHN provides tools to administer groups of systems remotely from a single Web-based interface.

on the job

Subscriptions to the RHN includes access to the actual RHEL 6 operating system releases. Trial subscriptions support RHN access for that trial period. However, if you or your organization can't afford RHN subscriptions for every system, consider the tools provided by the Spacewalk project. It provides all of the functionality of the RHN, except for timely access to updates.

For RHEL 6, GUI-based package management tools are based on the PackageKit. However, it's quite possible that the PackageKit won't be available on a server, or perhaps even a system configured for a Red Hat exam. If you absolutely need the PackageKit, install the required RPMs with the **yum install gnome-packagekit** command. Of course, if you're already comfortable with the **yum** command, you may not need the PackageKit.

e x a m

ⓦatch   *While the RHN is listed as part of the RHCSA objectives, it's listed in context as a choice. Whether you're installing or updating software packages from the RHN, "a remote repository, or*   *a local filesystem," the rpm and yum commands are the same. Of course, it would be simplest if you did have an official subscription the RHN.*

The GNOME Software Update Tool

If you're running a GUI in RHEL 6, the standard graphical software tool is based on the PackageKit application, configured for GNOME. It starts with the Software Update tool, which you can start from a GUI command line with the **gpk-update-viewer** command. Alternatively, from the GNOME Desktop Environment, click System | Administration | Software Update. The tool as shown in Figure 7-13 lists packages that are available for update.

It's a pretty straightforward interface. It's effectively a front end to the **yum update** command. Note the additional information, with a description of changes. Updates may be classified in up to six different categories, as shown in Figure 7-14, an excerpt from www.packagekit.org/pk-faq.html. The update categories shown in Figure 7-13 are enhancements, bug fixes, and security.

Automated Updates

It may be important to make sure the latest security updates are installed as quickly as possible. To that end, open the Software Update Preferences tool shown in Figure 7-15. You can open it by clicking System | Preferences | Software Updates, or from a GUI command line with the **gpk-prefs** command. You can configure the system to check for updates on an hourly, daily, or a weekly basis, or not at all. When updates are found, you can configure automatic installation of all available updates, of only security updates, or of nothing at all.

FIGURE 7-13

The GNOME
Software Update
tool

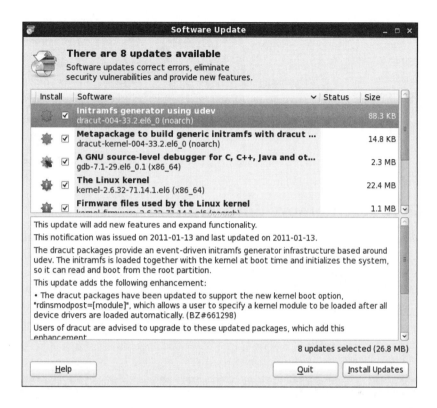

Changes made through the Software Preferences tool are stored in the authorized user's home directory, in a %gconf.xml file in the .gconf/apps/gnome-packagekit/ update-icon subdirectory. Just be aware, changes may not be written to this file until the user logs out of the GUI.

FIGURE 7-14

PackageKit
update types

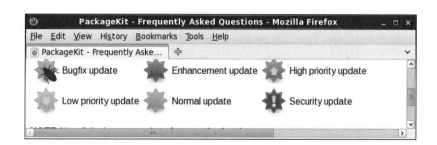

FIGURE 7-15

FIGURE 7-15

The GNOME
Software Update
Preferences tool

GNOME Add/Remove Software Tool

You can add, update, and remove packages with a graphical tool. To start the
Add/Remove Software tool from a GUI command line, run the **gpk-application**
command, or click System | Administration | Add/Remove Software. It opens the
tool shown in Figure 7-16. Here you can install more than one package or package
group at a time. Once packages are selected (or deselected), the tool automatically
calculates dependencies and installs (or removes) them, along with the selected
packages.

FIGURE 7-16

The GNOME
Add/Remove
Software tool

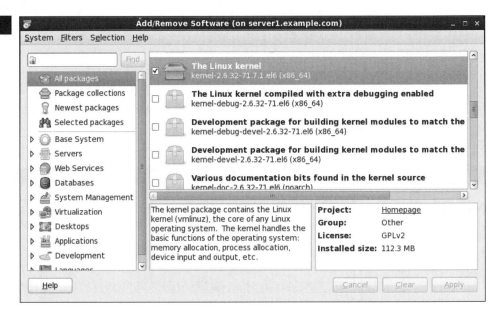

You can use the Add/Remove Software tool to add the packages or package groups of your choice. In the upper-left part of the screen, there are four basic options:

- **All Packages**   All packages from available repositories are listed in alphabetic order of RPM package name.
- **Package Collections**   Options in this list are packages collected in groups; these are the same groups shown in the output to the **yum grouplist** command described earlier.
- **Newest Packages**   Packages in this list do not include earlier versions.
- **Selected Packages**   Packages in this list are in the queue for installation or removal, awaiting an in-process step such as downloads.

The package collections associated with the **yum grouplist** command are further subdivided in the lower-left part of the screen. When you select an individual group, every package member of the group is open for selection. That includes the mandatory, default, and optional packages described earlier in the XML package file described in Chapter 2; none of those packages are selected by default.

The options are straightforward. When a package or package group is selected or deselected for installation or removal, the Apply button becomes clickable. Once clicked, the tool uses the **yum** command to calculate dependencies. If there are no dependencies, the installation proceeds immediately. If there are dependencies, the entire list of packages to be installed or removed is presented for your approval.

EXERCISE 7-2

Installing More with yum and the Add/Remove Software Tool

This exercise requires a network connection to a remote repository, or at least a RHEL 6 DVD copied or mounted as a repository as configured earlier in this chapter. If you're using a rebuild of RHEL 6, you'll need to make sure the connection to the core repository is active, perhaps with a **ping** command to the URL of that repository as defined in the appropriate file in the /etc/yum.repos.d directory. Given the possible variations, exact steps are not possible there.

1. Run the **yum list** command. Assuming an active network connection and a responsive repository, you'll see a full list of available packages, including those already installed. Note the label in the right column; it will either show

the repository where a package is available or note that the package is already installed.

2. Enter the **gpk-application** command in a GUI command line. This should open the Add/Remove Software tool.

3. In a second command line console, type in the **yum grouplist** command. In the Add/Remove Software tool, select Package Collections. Compare the list of package groups in each output.

4. Review available package groups in the Add/Remove Software tool. For example, click the arrow next to Servers. Under the options that appear, click CIFS Server. (CIFS stands for the Common Internet File System.) There's only one official package in the RHEL 6 configuration of this group. If you see more than one package, they are different versions of the same package. Select the latest available version of the package, which will be installed when you click Apply.

5. Click the All Packages option. Review the list of available packages. Packages that are already selected (or don't even have a check box) are currently installed. If you select or deselect a package, it will be installed or removed (with dependencies) when you click Apply.

6. Locate the text box in the upper-left corner of the Add/Remove Software tool. Type in a common search term such as *gnome* and watch as a long list of packages are shown. Compare the result to the output of the **yum search gnome** command.

7. Use a less common search term such as *iptables*. Highlight the iptables package and review it in the lower-right part of the screen. Compare the result to the output of the **yum info iptables** command.

8. Once you've selected some packages, click Apply. If there are dependencies, you'll see a window with a list of packages that you've selected for installation and removal. Depending on whether the packages are to be installed or removed, you'll see an Install or Remove button and a Cancel button.

9. Wait as downloads packages are installed. When finished, click System | Quit to exit from the Add/Remove Software tool.

The Red Hat Network

Before you use the RHN to administer RHEL 6 systems, those systems must be registered. To that end, you'll need either a registration code or available entitlements on the subject RHN account. Alternatively, you can configure RHEL and rebuild (and even Fedora) systems on a Spacewalk server. For more information, see http://spacewalk.redhat.com/. Remember, the related objective suggests that all you need to know is how to install and update packages from the RHN. And that skill was already covered with the **rpm** and **yum** commands, along with the related GUI tools discussed in most of this chapter.

If you have a limited budget and can afford some RHEL subscriptions, it's technically feasible to set up mirrors of downloaded packages on a Spacewalk server. (I do not know whether such a mirror of binary Red Hat RPM packages would violate any agreements associated with a RHN subscription.) Of course, while Red Hat does sponsor Spacewalk, it does not include official support for that software. Alternatively, you could purchase supported access to RHN Proxy Server and Satellite Server products.

Perhaps the key benefit of the RHN or a substitute like Spacewalk is the ability to manage all RHEL and rebuild distribution systems remotely, over a Web-based interface. Once an appropriate connection is configured from the client systems, RHN can even run remote commands on any schedule. If you're administering a whole bunch of systems, RHN supports configuration of systems in groups. For example, if there are ten systems configured as RHEL 6-based web servers, you can configure those systems as a single group. You can then schedule a single command that's applied to all of those systems remotely.

The following list of capabilities highlight the features of RHN:

- Pre-scheduled commands
- Remotely installed packages
- The ability to edit and add custom configuration files
- Options to create Kickstart installations
- The ability to create snapshots

It also allows you to configure different subscription channels for each system, and more. For more information on the RHN, see the latest version of the reference guide, available from https://rhn.redhat.com/rhn/help/reference/.

If a system isn't already registered, the following steps support registration of an RHEL 6 system from the command line:

1. Run **rhn_register** from the command line. If the system is already registered, you're prompted with the opportunity to leave the registration process.

2. You'll see a screen related to the configuration of software updates. The exact wording varies, depending on whether the registration is proceeding at the console or the GUI. If you need more information about the RHN, select Why Should I Connect To RHN; otherwise, select Next or Forward to continue. (Next is the option in the console; Forward is the option in the GUI.)

3. In the GUI version, you'll see options associated with the RHN Proxy and Satellite servers. The console version of the registration tool skips this step.

4. You'll see a screen where you can enter RHN login information. Do so and select Next or Forward to continue.

5. Now choose whether to register a system profile and whether to send basic hardware information about your system; make appropriate decisions and select Next or Forward to continue.

6. Next, choose to include a list of installed packages, which helps the RHN check whether you need software and security updates. Make any desired changes and select Next or Forward to continue.

7. Finally, choose whether to send your system profile to the RHN. If you click Cancel, the tool stops, and your system is not registered. If you want to register, select Next or Forward to continue.

8. Your system attempts to contact the RHN server (or possibly your RHN Satellite Server). If a free subscription entitlement is available, a message eventually appears that the system is successfully registered with the RHN.

CERTIFICATION SUMMARY

This chapter focuses on the management of RPM packages. With different switches, you also looked at how the **rpm** command installs, removes, and upgrade packages, as well as how it works locally and remotely. When presented with a new version of a kernel, it's important to never "upgrade." A properly configured installation of a later kernel version does not overwrite, but brings kernels together, side by side. You'll then be able to boot into either kernel.

With the **rpm** command, you also learned how to query packages, to examine to which package a file belongs, to validate a package signature, to find the current list of installed RPMs. You also looked at the difficulties associated with dependencies, which drove developers to the **yum** command.

The **yum** command is, in part, a front end to the **rpm** command. When there are dependencies, it installs those packages simultaneously. You learned how to configure Red Hat and other repositories to work with the **yum** command. You should now be able to configure even the RHEL 6 DVD as its own repository. As you saw, the **yum** command also can install or remove package groups, as defined by the XML database file of packages on the RHEL 6 DVD. The **yum** command is fully compatible with the RHN.

While additional package management tools are available from the GUI, they are front ends to the **yum** and **rpm** commands. With the **gpk-update-viewer** command, you started the Software Update tool to identify and install available updates. With the **gpk-prefs** command, you started the Software Update Preferences tool that can check for and install security or all available updates on a regular schedule. With the **gpk-application** command, you opened the Add/Remove Software tool, which also can be used to add or remove packages and package groups. If you have an RHEL subscription, systems can also be kept up to date through the RHN's Web-based interface.

✓ TWO-MINUTE DRILL

Here are some of the key points from the certification objectives in Chapter 7.

The Red Hat Package Manager

❑ The RPM database tracks where each file in a package is located, its version number, and much more.

❑ The **rpm -i** command installs RPM packages.

❑ The **rpm -e** command uninstalls RPM packages.

❑ The **rpm** command can even install RPMs directly from remote servers.

❑ RPM package verification is supported by the GPG keys in the /etc/pki/rpm-gpg directory.

❑ Kernel RPMs should always be installed, never upgraded.

❑ The Upgrade mode of RPM replaces the old version of the package with the new one.

More RPM Commands

❑ The **rpm -q** determines whether packages are installed on a system; with additional switches, it can list more about a package and identify the package for a specific file.

❑ Package signatures can be checked with the **rpm --checksig** (or **-K**) command.

❑ The **rpm -V** command can identify files that have changed from the original installation of the package.

❑ The **rpm -qa** command lists all currently installed packages.

Dependencies and the yum Command

❑ By including additional required packages, the **yum** command can help avoid "dependency hell."

❑ The behavior of the **yum** command is configured in the /etc/yum.conf file, plugins in the /etc/yum/pluginconf.d directory, and repositories configured in the /etc/yum.repos.d directory.

❑ Red Hat organizes packages in several different repositories for RHEL 6.

❑ Repositories for rebuild distributions and from third parties are accessible online.

❑ The **yum** command can install, erase, and update packages. It also can be used to search in different ways.

❑ The **yum** command uses the GPG keys developed for RPM packages.

❑ The **yum** command can install, remove, and list package groups.

More Package Management Tools

❑ RHEL 6 package management tools are based on the PackageKit, built for GNOME.

❑ With PackageKit tools, you can install and remove packages and package groups.

❑ The PackageKit also includes tools focused on current updates. It can also set up updates of security or all packages on a schedule.

❑ The RHN or Spacewalk can help you manage subscribed systems remotely using a Web-based interface.

SELF TEST

The following questions will help measure your understanding of the material presented in this chapter. As no multiple-choice questions appear on the Red Hat exams, no multiple-choice questions appear in this book. These questions exclusively test your understanding of the chapter. It is okay if you have another way of performing a task. Getting results, not memorizing trivia, is what counts on the Red Hat exams. There may be more than one answer to many of these questions.

The Red Hat Package Manager

1. What command would you use to install the penguin-3.26.i386.rpm package, with extra messages in case of errors? The package is on the local directory.

    _____

2. What command would you use to upgrade the penguin RPM with the penguin-3.27.i386.rpm package? The package is on the ftp.remotemj02.abc server.

    _____

3. If you've downloaded a later version of the Linux kernel to the local directory, and the package filename is kernel-2.6.32-100.el6.x86_64.rpm, what's the best command to make it a part of your system?

    _____

4. What directory contains GPG keys on an installed system?

    _____

More RPM Commands

5. What command lists all currently installed RPMs?

    _____

6. What file lists the RPMs installed during the system installation process?

    _____

7. If you've downloaded an RPM from a third party called third.i386.rpm, how can you validate the associated package signature?

    _____

Dependencies and the yum Command

8. What is the full path to the directory where the location of **yum** repositories are normally configured?

_____

9. What command searches **yum** repositories for the package associated with the /etc/passwd file?

_____

More Package Management Tools

10. What command-line command lists the package groups shown in the Add/Remove Software tool?

_____

11. Name two allowable time periods for automatic updates, as defined by the Software Update Preferences tool.

_____

_____

12. What command from the console starts the process of registration on the RHN?

_____

LAB QUESTIONS

Red Hat presents its exams electronically. For that reason, most of the labs in this chapter are available from the CD that accompanies the book, in the Chapter7/ subdirectory. They're available in .doc, .html, and .txt format, to reflect standard options associated with electronic delivery on a live RHEL 6 system. In case you haven't yet set up RHEL 6 on a system, refer to the first lab of Chapter 2 for installation instructions. The answers for each lab follows the Self Test answers for the fill-in-the-blank questions.

SELF TEST ANSWERS

The Red Hat Package Manager

1. The command that installs the penguin-3.26.i386.rpm package, with extra messages in case of errors, from the local directory, is

```
# rpm -iv penguin-3.26.i386.rpm
```

Additional switches that don't change the functionality of the command, such as **-h** for hash marks, are acceptable. This applies to subsequent questions as well.

2. The command that upgrades the aforementioned penguin RPM with the penguin-3.27.i386.rpm package from the ftp.remotemj02.abc server is

```
# rpm -Uv ftp://ftp.remotemj02.abc/penguin-3.26.i386.rpm
```

If you use the default vsFTP server, the package may be in the pub/Packages/ subdirectory. In other words, the command would be

```
# rpm -Uv ftp://ftp.remotemj02.abc/pub/Packages/penguin-3.26.i386.rpm
```

Yes, the question is not precise. But that's what you see in real life.

3. If you've downloaded a later version of the Linux kernel to the local directory, and the package filename is kernel-2.6.32-100.el6.x86_64.rpm, the best way to make it a part of your system is to install it—and not upgrade the current kernel. Kernel upgrades overwrite existing kernels. Kernel installations allow kernels to exist side by side; if the new kernel doesn't work, you can still boot into the working kernel. Since the desired package is already downloaded, you'd use a command similar to the following:

```
# rpm -iv kernel-2.6.32-100.el6.x86_64.rpm
```

Variations of the **rpm** command, such as **rpm -i** and **rpm -ivh**, are acceptable. However, variations that upgrade, with the **-U** or **-F** switches, are incorrect.

4. The directory with GPG keys on an installed system is /etc/pki/rpm-gpg. The GPG keys on the RHEL 6 CD/DVD are not "installed" on a system.

More RPM Commands

5. The command that lists all installed RPMs is

```
# rpm -qa
```

6. The file that lists the RPMs installed when you first installed the local system is /root/install.log. The /var/log/rpmpkgs file is complete but is updated only once per day.

7. If you've downloaded an RPM from a third party, call it third.i386.rpm, you'll first need to download and install the RPM-GPG-KEY file associated with that repository. You can then validate the associated package signature with a command like (note the uppercase **-K**); **--checksig** is equivalent to **-K**.

```
# rpm -K third.i386.rpm
```

Dependencies and the yum Command

8. The **yum** command repositories are normally configured in files in the /etc/yum.repos.d directory. Technically, **yum** command repositories can also be configured directly in the /etc/yum.conf file.

9. The **yum whatprovides /etc/passwd** command identifies packages associated with that file.

More Package Management Tools

10. This is a slightly tricky question, as the **yum grouplist** command lists the package groups also shown in the Add/Remove Software tool.

11. Allowable time periods for updates, as defined by the Software Update Preferences tool, are hourly, daily, and weekly.

12. The **rhn_register** command starts the process of registering a system on the RHN.

LAB ANSWERS

Lab 1

When complete, run the following commands to verify the connection:

```
# yum clean all
# yum update
```

The output should include output similar to the following:

```
Loaded plugins: refresh-packagekit
inst                  | 3.7 kB      00:00 ...
inst/primary_db       | 2.3 MB      00:00 ...
Setting up Update Process
```

This output verifies a successful connection to the FTP server. If you see something significantly different, check the following in the /etc/yum.repos.d/file.repo file:

- Make sure the stanza in this file starts with [**inst**].
- Check the URL associated with the **baseurl** directive. It should match the URL of the FTP server defined in Chapter 1, Lab 2. You should be able to run the **lftp** or **ftp** commands with that URL from a command line interface. If that doesn't work, either the FTP server is not running, or messages to that server are blocked by a firewall.
- If there were problems, fix them. Then try the previous commands again.

Lab 2

One way to check all of the files in the /usr/sbin directory is to use the **rpm -Va | grep /usr/sbin** command.

If successful, you'll identify the /usr/sbin/vsftpd and /etc/vsftpd/vsftpd.conf files as different from their original versions as installed from the RPM. Changes to a configuration file are not a big deal, especially if it's been customized in any way. However, changes to the binary file are a reason for suspicion.

Assuming standard Red Hat RPM packages, removal and reinstallation should preserve changes to the vsftpd.conf file in a vsftpd.conf.rpmsave file.

If you really do have a security concern, additional measures are appropriate. For example, some security professionals might compare all files on a suspect system to the files on a verified baseline system.

In that case, it may be simplest to take a copy or clone of the baseline system, reinstall the vsftpd RPM, and reconfigure it as needed. Assuming the baseline system is secure, you'd then be reasonably sure the new server would also be secure.

The changes made by the script to this lab set a new modification time for the /usr/sbin/vsftpd binary and appended a comment to the end of the vsftpd.conf configuration file. If you want to restart with fresh copies of these packages, back up your current vsftpd.conf file and run the **rpm -e vsftpd** command to uninstall the package. If the RPM package has been properly configured, you should see at least the following warning message:

```
warning: /etc/vsftpd/vsftpd.conf saved as /etc/vsftpd/vsftpd.conf.rpmsave
```

You can then reinstall the original package from either the installation DVD or a remote repository. Alternatively, you could delete (or move) the changed files and then run the following command to force the **rpm** command to provide the original copies of these files from the associated package. The version number is based on the RHEL 6.0 DVD.

```
# rpm -ivh --force vsftpd-2.2.2-6.el6.x86_64.rpm
```

Lab 3

This lab is intended to help you examine what the **yum update** command can do. It's the essential front end to GUI update tools. As you can see from the update.txt file created in this lab, the messages display how **yum** appears for all newer packages from configured repositories or the RHN, downloads their headers, and uses them to check for dependencies that also need to be downloaded and installed.

Lab 4

This lab should be straightforward, as it involves the use of the Software Update Preferences tool, which you can start from a GUI command line with the **gpk-prefs** command. If successful, you'll see these changes in the %gconf.xml file, in the .gconf/apps/gnome-packagekit/update-icon subdirectory of your home directory. For example, the following excerpt suggests that updates are made every 86400 seconds, which corresponds to 24 hours.

```
<entry name="frequency_get_updates" mtime="1299287329" type="int" value="86400">
```

Bonus bit: if you are familiar with Linux, you may recognize the **mtime** as the number of seconds since the Unix epoch of January 1, 1970. To find the actual date associated with that modification time, run the following command:

```
# date -ud @1299287328
```

Lab 5

This lab is somewhat self-explanatory and is intended to help you explore what happens when you properly install a new kernel RPM. As with other Linux distributions, when you install (and do not use upgrade mode) for a new kernel, two areas are affected.

The new kernel is added as a new option in the GRUB configuration menu. The existing kernel should be retained as an option in that menu. When you reboot the system, try the new kernel. Don't hesitate to reboot the system again, and try the other option, probably the older kernel.

When you review the /boot directory, all of the previously installed boot files should be there. The new kernel RPM should add matching versions of all of the same files—with different revision numbers.

To keep this all straight, it helps if you made copies of the original versions of the GRUB configuration file and the file list in the /boot directory. If you choose to retain the newly installed kernel, great. Otherwise, uninstall the newly installed kernel. This is one case where revision numbers are required with the **rpm -e** command; the following is based on the removal of the kernel and kernel-firmware packages, based on version number 2.6.32-71.14.1el6:

```
# rpm -e kernel- 2.6.32-71.14.1el6.x86_64
# rpm -e kernel-firmware-2.6.32-71.14.1el6
```

If the revision number of the kernel or kernel-firmware package that you installed during this lab is different, adjust the commands accordingly.

Lab 6

This lab is designed to give you practice with both the **yum** command and the Add/Remove Software tool. It should help you prepare for Chapter 9, and provide the skills required to install services for other chapters. You should realize by now that since all packages in the Remote Desktop Clients package group are optional, the **yum groupinstall "Remote Desktop Clients"** command doesn't install anything. You'll need to install each of the optional packages by name.

To identify the names of the packages to be installed, run the **yum groupinfo "Remote Desktop Clients"** command. Be sure to install every package from that group on both systems. The best method is with the **yum install** *package1 package2* ... command, where package1, package2, and so on, are names of packages in the "Remote Desktop Clients" package group.

8

User
Administration

F undamental to the tasks associated with Linux administration is the management of users and groups. In this chapter, you'll examine different ways to manage the variety of users and groups available to Linux. Important skills in this area range from the simple login to user account management, group membership, group collaboration, and network authentication. The configuration of administrative privileges for Linux users can help the master administrator distribute responsibilities to others.

You'll see how to manage these tasks from the command line, with the help of the files of the shadow password suite. You'll also use tools like the User Manager and the Authentication Configuration tool to set up some of these tasks. As you should expect, Red Hat GUI tools can't do it all, which emphasizes the importance of understanding user management from the command line.

INSIDE THE EXAM

This chapter addresses several RHCSA objectives. Briefly explained, these objectives include the following:

- Log in and switch users in multi-user runlevels

Briefly, that means you need to know how to log in with regular accounts when RHEL 6 is running in standard runlevels 3 and 5. To switch users, you need to know how to log out and log back in with a second account. Simple enough.

- Create, delete, and modify local user accounts
- Change and adjust password aging for local user accounts
- Create, delete, and modify local groups , adjust group memberships

You could use commands like **useradd**, **usermod**, **groupadd**, **groupmod**, and **chage**, as

well as the User Manager to accomplish these tasks. While this chapter explains how you can use both types of tools, there is no guarantee that the User Manager will be available during an exam.

- Create and configure set-gid directories for collaboration

When the RHCT exam was active, the related objective was to "Configure filesystem permissions for collaboration." In other words, the objective is now more specific— you're told how to set one or more directories for collaboration between a group of users.

- Configure a system to use an existing LDAP directory service for user and group information

In other words, you need to know how to take advantage of a Lightweight Directory Access Protocol (LDAP) server with changes to appropriate configuration files.

CERTIFICATION OBJECTIVE 8.01

User Account Management

You need to know how to create and configure users. This means knowing how to configure and modify accounts, work with passwords, and organize users in groups. You also need to know how to configure the environment associated with each user account: in configuration files and in user settings.

If you've installed RHEL 6 via Kickstart or in text mode, or somehow otherwise avoided the First Boot process described in Chapter 1, the default Red Hat installation includes just a single login account: root. While no other accounts are required, it's important to set up some regular user accounts. Even if you're going to be the only user on the system, it's a good idea to create at least one nonadministrative account for day-to-day work. Then you can use the root account only when it's necessary to administer the system. Accounts can be added to Red Hat Enterprise Linux systems using various utilities, including direct editing of password configuration files (the manual method), the **useradd** command (the command line method), and the User Manager utility (the graphical method).

Different Kinds of Users

There are three basic types of Linux user accounts: administrative (root), regular, and service. The administrative root account is automatically created when Linux is installed, and it has administrative privileges for all services on a Linux system. A cracker who has a chance to take control of this account can take full control of that system.

For the times when you do log in as an administrator, RHEL builds in safeguards for root users. Log in as the root user, and then run the **alias** command. You'll see entries such as the following:

```
alias rm='rm -i'
```

Due to this particular alias, when the root user runs the **rm** command, the shell actually executes the **rm -i** command, which prompts for confirmation before the **rm** command deletes a file. Unfortunately, a command such as **rm -rf** *directoryname* supersedes this safety setting.

As suggested by the technical editor, some administrators set a different alias for the rm command: alias rm='mv -t ~/.Trash'. Files in that directory are like a standard trashbin; some administrators may set up a cron job, such as those described in Chapter 9, to delete files from that directory on a periodic basis. A trash directory is already available in the GNOME desktop, in each user's .local/share/Trash/files/ subdirectory.

Regular users have the necessary privileges to perform standard tasks on a Linux computer. They can access programs such as word processors, databases, and web browsers. They can store files in their own home directories. Since regular users do not normally have administrative privileges, they cannot accidentally delete critical operating system configuration files. You can assign a regular account to most users, safe in the knowledge that they can't disrupt a system with the privileges they have on that account.

Services such as Apache, Squid, mail, games, and printing have their own individual service accounts. These accounts exist to allow each of these services to interact with Linux systems. Normally, you won't need to change any service account, but if you see that someone has logged in through one of these accounts, be wary. Someone may have broken into your system.

One resource for checking whether your system has been cracked is the Distributed Intrusion Detection System at www.dshield.org. Check your public IP address against its database. If your system has been cracked, it's likely that someone is using it to attack other systems. While there are "false positives," IP addresses that have been cracked are logged in the www.dshield.org database.

To review recent logins, run the utmpdump /var/log/wtmp | less command. If the login is from a remote location, it will be associated with a specific IP address outside your network.

The Shadow Password Suite

When Unix was first developed back in the 1960s and 1970s, security was not such a serious concern. Everything required for user and group management was contained in the /etc/passwd and /etc/group files. As suggested by the name, passwords were originally in the /etc/passwd file. The problem is that file is "world-readable." Anyone with a copy of that file, before the shadow password suite, would have a copy of the password for every user. Even passwords that are encrypted in that file can eventually be decrypted. That is the motivation behind the development of the shadow password suite, where more sensitive information was moved to other files, readable only by the root administrative user.

The four files of the shadow password suite are /etc/passwd, /etc/group, /etc/shadow, and /etc/gshadow. Defaults in these files are driven by the /etc/login.defs file.

The /etc/passwd File

The /etc/passwd file contains basic information about every user. Open that file in a text editor. Browse around a bit. Atop the file is basic information for the root administrative user. Other users in this file may relate to services such as mail, ftp, and sshd. They may be specific users designed for logins.

There are seven columns of information in the /etc/passwd file, delineated by colons. Each column in /etc/passwd includes specific information described in Table 8-1.

TABLE 8-1	The Anatomy of /etc/passwd	
Field	**Example**	**Purpose**
Username	mj	The user logs in with this name. Usernames can include hyphens (-) or underscores (_). However, they should not start with a number or include uppercase letters.
Password	x	The password. You should see either an *x*, an asterisk (*), or a seemingly random group of letters and numbers. An *x* points to /etc/shadow for the actual password. An asterisk means the account is disabled. A random group of letters and numbers represents the encrypted password.
User ID	500	The unique numeric user ID (UID) for that user. By default, Red Hat starts user IDs at 500.
Group ID	500	The numeric group ID (GID) associated with that user. By default, RHEL creates a new group for every new user, and the number matches the UID. Some other Linux and Unix systems assign all users to the default Users group (GID=100).
User info	Michael Jang	You can enter any information of your choice in this field. Standard options include the user's full name, telephone number, e-mail address, or physical location. You can leave this blank.
Home Directory	/home/mj	By default, RHEL places new home directories in /home/*username*.
Login Shell	/bin/bash	By default, RHEL assigns users to the bash shell. You can change this to any legal shell that you have installed.

The RHEL 6 version of /etc/passwd includes more secure features for user accounts when compared to some other Linux distributions. The only accounts with a real login shell are user accounts. If a cracker somehow breaks into a service account such as mail or nobody, with the false /sbin/nologin shell, that user doesn't automatically get access to the command line.

The /etc/group File

Every Linux user is assigned to a group. By default in RHEL 6, every user gets his own private group. The user is the only member of that group, as defined in the /etc/group configuration file. Open that file in a text editor. Browse around a bit. The first line in this file specifies information for the root administrative user's group. Some service users include other users as members of that group. For example, user qemu is a member of the kvm group, which gives services associated with the QEMU emulator privileges with the Kernel-based Virtual Machine (KVM).

There are four columns of information in the /etc/group file, delineated by colons. Each column in /etc/group specifies information described in Table 8-2.

The /etc/shadow File

The /etc/shadow file is a supplement to /etc/passwd. While it contains eight columns of information, the first column contains the same list of usernames as documented in /etc/passwd. As long as there's an *x* in the second column of each /etc/passwd entry, Linux knows to look at /etc/shadow for more information. Open that file in a text editor. Browse around a bit. You'll see the same pattern of information, starting with information for the root administrative user.

As shown in Table 8-3, while it includes the encrypted password in the second column, the remaining information relates to the way passwords are managed. In fact, the first two characters of the second column are based on the encryption hash for the password. If you see a $1, the password is hashed to the Message Digest 5 (MD5) algorithm, the standard through RHEL 5. If you see a $6, the password is protected with the 512-bit Secure Hash Algorithm (SHA-512), the standard for RHEL 6.

The /etc/gshadow File

The /etc/gshadow file is the group configuration file in the shadow password suite. It includes the administrator for the group. If desired, you can even configure a hashed password for that group administrator. Table 8-4 describes the columns in /etc/gshadow, from left to right.

TABLE 8-2	Field	Example	Purpose
The Anatomy of /etc/group	Groupname	mj	Each user gets his own group, with the same name as his username. You can also create unique group names.
	Password	x	The password. You should see either an *x* or a seemingly random group of letters and numbers. An *x* points to /etc/gshadow for the actual password. A random group of letters and numbers represents the encrypted password.
	Group ID	500	The numeric group ID (GID) associated with that user. By default, RHEL creates a new group for every new user. If you want to create a special group such as managers, you should assign a GID number outside the standard range; otherwise, Red Hat GIDs and UIDs would probably get out of sequence.
	Group members	mj,vp	Lists the usernames that are members of the group. If it's blank, and there is a username that is identical to the group name, that user is the only member of that group.

TABLE 8-3	Column	Field	Description
The Anatomy of /etc/shadow	1	Username	Username
	2	Password	Encrypted password; requires an *x* in the second column of /etc/passwd
	3	Password history	Date of the last password change, in number of days after January 1, 1970
	4	mindays	Minimum number of days that a user must keep a password
	5	maxdays	Maximum number of days after which a password must be changed
	6	warndays	Number of days before password expiration when a warning is given
	7	inactive	Number of days after password expiration when an account is made inactive
	8	disabled	Number of days after password expiration when an account is disabled

TABLE 8-4	Field	Example	Purpose
The Anatomy of /etc/gshadow	Groupname	mj	Each user gets his own group, with the same name as his username. Specific users may be assigned as administrators for unique groups.
	Password	!	Most groups have a *!*, which indicates no password; some groups may have a hashed password similar to that shown in the /etc/shadow file.
	Group ID	500	The numeric group ID (GID) associated with that user. By default, RHEL creates a new group for every new user. If you want to create a special group such as managers, you should assign a GID number outside the standard range; otherwise, Red Hat GIDs and UIDs would probably get out of sequence.
	Group members	mj,vp	A comma-delineated list of usernames that are members of the group. If it's blank, and there is a username that is identical to the group name, that user is the only member of that group.

The /etc/login.defs File

The /etc/login.defs file provides the baseline for a number of parameters in the shadow password suite. This section provides a brief analysis of each active directive in the default version of this file. As you'll see, the directives go somewhat beyond authentication. The first directive specifies the directory with locally delivered e-mail, listed by username:

```
MAIL_DIR /var/spool/mail
```

The next four directives relate to default password aging information. The directives are explained in the file comment, and in Table 8-5.

TABLE 8-5	Directive	Purpose
/etc/login.defs Password Aging Directives	PASS_MAX_DAYS	After this number of days, the password must be changed.
	PASS_MIN_DAYS	Passwords must be kept for at least this number of days.
	PASS_MIN_LEN	A warning is given when a user tries to use a password shorter than this length.
	PASS_WARN_AGE	Users are warned this number of days before PASS_MAX_DAYS.

As suggested earlier, User ID (UID) and Group ID (GID) numbers for regular users and groups start at 500. Since Linux supports UID and GID numbers above 4 billion (actually, up to 2^{32}), the maximum UID and GID numbers of 60000 as defined in the /etc/login.defs file may seem strange. However, it leaves higher numbers available for other authentication databases, such as those associated with LDAP and Microsoft Windows (via Samba). As suggested by the directives, **UID_MIN** specifies the minimum UID, **UID_MAX** specifies the maximum UID, and so on:

```
UID_MIN   500
UID_MAX   60000
GID_MIN   500
GID_MAX   60000
```

Normally, when the **useradd** command is run to create a new user, it automatically creates home directories as well, which is confirmed by the following directive:

```
CREATE_HOME yes
```

As described later in this chapter, other files drive a value of umask. But if those other files did not exist, this directive would govern the default umask for regular users:

```
UMASK    077
```

The following directive is critical in the implementation of the User Private Group scheme, where new users are also made members of their own private group, normally with the same UID and GID numbers. It means when new users are created (or deleted), the associated group is also added (or deleted):

```
USERGROUPS_ENAB yes
```

Finally, the following directive determines the algorithm used to encrypt passwords, normally SHA 512 for RHEL 6:

```
ENCRYPT_METHOD SHA512
```

Different encryption methods may be set up with the Authentication Configuration tool described later in this chapter.

Command Line Tools

There are two basic ways to add users through the command line interface. You can add users directly by editing the /etc/passwd file in a text editor such as vi. To this end, the **vipw** and **vigr** were described in Chapter 3. Alternatively, you can use text commands customized for the purpose.

Adding Users Directly

Open the /etc/passwd file in the text editor of your choice. As described in Chapter 3, you can do so with the **vipw** command. However, if you add users by directly editing the files of the shadow password suite, you'll have to do two more things:

■ Add a user home directory. For example, for user donna, you'd have to add the /home/donna home directory, making sure that user donna and group donna both have ownership of that directory.

■ Populate the user home directory. The default option is to copy the files from the /etc/skel directory, discussed later in this chapter. You'd also have to make sure that user donna and group donna have ownership of those files copied to the /home/donna directory.

Add Users to a Group Directly

Every Linux user is normally assigned to a group, at least his own private group. As implied in Chapter 3, the GID number listed in the /etc/group file has to match that shown for that user in the /etc/passwd file. The user is the only member of that group.

Of course, users can be members of other groups as well. For example, if to create a group named project, you could add the entries to the /etc/group and /etc/gshadow files. One way to do so in a text editor is with the **vigr** command. For example, the following entry might be appropriate for a group named project:

```
project:x:60001:
```

The number 60001 is used, as that is beyond the limit of the **GID_MAX** directive from the /etc/login.defs file described earlier. But that's just arbitrary. There's no prohibition against a lower number, as long as it is above 500 and does not interfere with existing GIDs. However, it is convenient when the UID and GID numbers of regular users match. In fact, it's important, as you'll see in the discussion of the /etc/bashrc file later in this chapter.

Of course, for a group to be useful, you'd have to add users already configured in the /etc/passwd file at the end of the line. The following example assumes these users already exist.

```
project:x:60001:michael,elizabeth,stephanie,tim
```

You'd also have to add this group to the /etc/gshadow file. You could do so directly with the **vigr -s** command. Alternatively, to set up a group administrator with a password, you could run the **gpasswd** command. For example, the **gpasswd project** command would set up a password for administering the group, associated with the **newgrp** and **sg** commands described later in this chapter. It would automatically add the encrypted password with the given group name to the /etc/gshadow file.

Add Users at the Command Line

Alternatively, you can automate this process with the **useradd** command. The **useradd pm** command would add user pm to the /etc/passwd file. In addition, the **useradd** command creates the /home/pm home directory; adds the standard files from the /etc/skel directory; and assigns the default shell, /bin/bash. But **useradd** is versatile. It includes a number of command options shown in Table 8-6.

TABLE 8-6	Option	Purpose
useradd Command Options	-u *UID*	Overrides the default assigned *UID*. By default, in RHEL this starts at 500 and can continue sequentially the maximum number of users supported by kernel 2.6, which is 2^{32}, something over four billion users.
	-g *GID*	Overrides the default assigned *GID*. By default, RHEL uses the same *GID* and *UID* numbers to each user. If you assign a *GID*, it must be either 100 (users) or already otherwise exist.
	-c *info*	Enters the comment of your choice about the user, such as her name.
	-d *dir*	Overrides the default home directory for the user, /home/*username*.
	-e *YYYY-MM-DD*	Sets an expiration date for the user account.
	-f *num*	Specifies a number of days after password expiration when the account is disabled.
	-G *group1,group2*	Makes the user a member of *group1* and *group2*, based on their current names as defined in the /etc/group file. A space between *group1* and *group2* would lead to an error.
	-s *shell*	Overrides the default shell for the user, /bin/bash.

Assign a Password

Once a new user is created, you can use the **passwd** *username* command to assign a password to that user. For example, the **passwd pm** command prompts you to assign a new password to user pm. RHEL is configured to discourage passwords that are based on dictionary words, shorter than five characters, too simple, based on palindromes, and other, similar criteria for security reasons. Nevertheless, such passwords are legal, and such a password is accepted by the **passwd** command when entered a second time.

Add or Delete a Group at the Command Line

When it's appropriate to add a special group to the shadow password suite, you may want to use the **groupadd** command. Generally, you'll want to use it with the **-g** switch. For example, the following command would set up a special project group with a GID of 60001:

```
# groupadd -g 60001 project
```

If you don't use the **-g** switch, the **groupadd** command takes the next available GID number. For example, if two regular users are configured on a system, they each have UID and GID numbers of 500 and 501, respectively. If you've run the **groupadd project** command without specifying a GID number, the project group is assigned a GID of 502. The next regular user that's created would get a UID of 502 and a GID of 503, which could lead to confusion.

Fortunately, the command to delete a group is simpler. If the project group has completed its work, you can delete that group from the shadow password suite database with the following command:

```
# groupdel project
```

EXERCISE 8-1

Add a User with the Red Hat User Manager

If the GUI is available, one alternative to user management commands such as **useradd** and **usermod** is the Red Hat User Manager. If possible, try to open it remotely over an **ssh -X** connection described in Chapter 2. For example, if you've configured the server1.example.com system as described in earlier chapters, connect to that system from a remote GUI with the **ssh -X root@192.168.122.50** command. Once logged in, enter the **system-config-users** command.

1. In the Red Hat User Manager, click the Add User button, or choose File | Add User. This will open the Create New User window, as shown here:

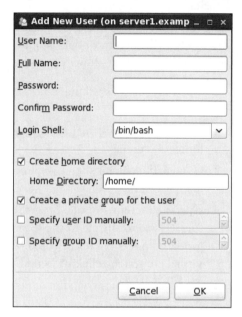

2. Complete the form. All entries are required, except Full Name. The entries are fairly self-explanatory (see the earlier discussions of each field). The password should be at least six characters and should ideally contain a mix of upper- and lowercase letters, numbers, and punctuation to keep it more secure from the standard password-cracking programs.

3. Enter the identical password in the Confirm Password field.

4. Note the number associated with the Specify User ID Manually and Specify Group ID Manually options; those are the UID and GID numbers that will be assigned to the new user. Click OK when you are done.

5. Repeat the process as desired for any additional new users that may be required. Make sure to create at least one new user prior to running Exercise 8-2.

EXERCISE 8-2

Real and Fake Shells

Do not run this exercise unless a regular user has already been created on the local system. Otherwise, an error might require a cold restart of the system. If desired, run Exercise 8-1 first, as that allows you to create a new regular user on the target system.

1. Open the /etc/passwd file. Find a current regular user, with a UID of 500 or above.

2. Identify the default shell. It's specified in the last column, normally /bin/bash for regular users.

3. Change the default shell to /sbin/nologin, and save the changes to the /etc/passwd file.

4. Open a different console. Press the CTRL-ALT-F2 keys to open a different console. (If you're already in the second virtual console, substitute F3, F4, F5, or F6 for F2. If you're in a KVM-based VM in the GUI, you can move to the second virtual console by clicking Send Key | CTRL-ALT-F2.)

5. Try logging in as the modified user. What happens?

6. Return to the original console. If it's the GUI, it should be accessible with either the ALT-F1 or ALT-F7 key combinations. If that is not possible (such as when the GUI is not installed), you should still be able to log in as the root administrative user.

7. Reopen the /etc/passwd file. Restore the /bin/bash shell to the target regular user.

Delete a User

The removal of a user account is a straightforward process. The easiest way to delete a user account is with the **userdel** command. By default, this command does not delete that user's home directory, so administrators can transfer files from that user perhaps to an employee who has taken over the tasks of the deleted user. Alternatively, the **userdel -r** *username* command deletes that user's home directory along with all of the files stored in that home directory.

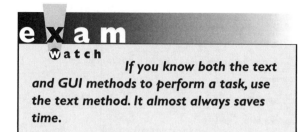

This is a lot faster than the GUI method, for which you start the X Window System, open the Red Hat User Manager, select the user, and then click Delete. While it's probably easier for a less experienced user to remember the GUI method, text commands are faster.

Modify an Account

As a Linux administrator, you may want to add some limitations to user accounts. The easiest way to illustrate some of the changes is with the User Manager tool. Start the User Manager, select a currently configured user, and then click Properties to open the User Properties dialog box.

Click the Account Info tab for the account expiration information shown in Figure 8-1. As shown in the figure, you can limit the life of an account so that it expires on a specific date, or you can disable an account by locking it.

Click the Password Info tab. As shown in Figure 8-2, you can set several characteristics related to an individual user's password. Even when good passwords are set, frequent password changes can help provide additional security. The categories shown in the figure are self-explanatory; a 0 in any of these text boxes means that the limit does not apply.

FIGURE 8-1

Manage user account life.

> **User Properties (on server1.example.com)** _ □ ×
>
> Under Data | Account Info | Password Info | Groups
>
> ☑ Enable account expiration
>
> Account expires (YYYY-MM-DD): [ ] - [ ] - [ ]
>
> ☑ Local password is locked
>
> Cancel   OK

FIGURE 8-2

Configure
password
information.

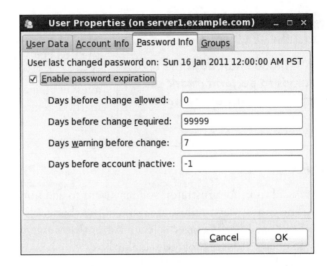

Click the Groups tab. Users can belong to more than one group in Linux. Under the Groups properties tab shown in Figure 8-3, you can assign the target user to other groups. For example, to collect the files supporting the managers into one directory, you can assign appropriate users to the group named managers. Alternatively, you can then assign members of that project team to the project group through the Groups tab.

More User and Group Management Commands

While the Red Hat User Manager GUI utility is convenient, it's often faster to perform the associated administrative functions at the command line interface. I've described some of these commands such as **useradd**, **userdel**, **groupadd**, and **groupdel**. Three other key user administration commands are **usermod**, **groupmod**, and **chage**.

usermod

The **usermod** command modifies various settings in /etc/passwd. In addition, it also allows you to set an expiration date for an account or an additional group. For example, the following command sets the account associated with user test1 to expire on June 8, 2011:

```
# usermod -e 2011-06-08 test1
```

FIGURE 8-3

Assign a group.

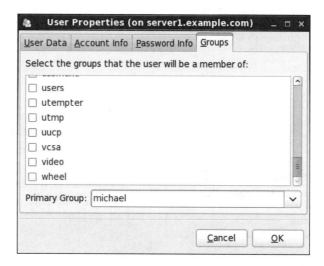

The following command makes user test1 a member of the special group:

```
# usermod -G special test1
```

The **usermod** command is closely related to the **useradd** command; in fact, the **usermod** command can use all of the **useradd** command switches listed in Table 8-6. The **usermod** command includes several additional switches listed in Table 8-7.

groupmod

The **groupmod** command is relatively simple. It has two practical uses. The following command changes the GID number of the group named project, in this case, to 60002:

```
# groupmod -g 60002 project
```

TABLE 8-7

usermod
Command
Options

Option	Purpose
-aG *group1*	Appends to existing group memberships; multiple groups may be specified, split with a comma, with no spaces.
-l *newlogin*	Changes the username to *newlogin*, without changing the home directory.
-L	Locks a user's password.
-U	Unlocks a user's password.

In contrast, the following command changes the name of the group named project to secret:

```
# groupmod secret project
```

ⓦatch *The chage command is an excellent way to address the RHCE objective to "adjust password aging for local user accounts."*

chage

The **chage** command is primarily used to manage aging information for a password, as stored in the /etc/shadow file. While some of the parameters can also be set with the **useradd** and **usermod** commands, most of the switches are different, as described in Table 8-8.

TABLE 8-8	Option	Purpose
chage Command Options	-d YYYY-MM-DD	Sets the last change date for a password; output shown in /etc/shadow as the number of days after January 1, 1970.
	-E YYYY-MM-DD	Assigns the expiration date for an account; output shown in /etc/shadow as the number of days after January 1, 1970.
	-I *num*	Locks an account *num* days after a password has expired; can be set to -1 to make the account permanent.
	-l	Lists all aging information.
	-m *num*	Sets a minimum number of days that a user must keep a password.
	-M *num*	Sets a maximum number of days that a user is allowed to keep a password; can be set to -1 to remove that limit.
	-W *num*	Specifies the number of days before a password must be changed; a user is warned at that time.

CERTIFICATION OBJECTIVE 8.02

Administrative Control

As the root administrative user is all-powerful, it's important for administrators to execute most actions as the regular user. Limits on regular users can help protect Linux systems from accidents. Regular users who have the root administrative password can temporarily take root privileges with the **su** command. The **su** command can do more with other accounts. In contrast, the **sg** command is associated with privileges on special groups.

While the **su** command is adequate for small networks, no administrator should work alone. With the help of the **sudo** command configured in the /etc/sudoers file, it's possible to set up dedicated administrators with partial or complete root administrative privileges.

The Ability to Log In as root

It's possible to keep users from logging in directly as the root administrative user. Local access is regulated in the /etc/securetty file. By default, it contains access directives for 12 virtual consoles. While only six virtual consoles are enabled in the /etc/init/start-ttys.conf file discussed in Chapter 5, it is possible to configure 12 (based on the number of function keys on a keyboard).

The virtual consoles listed in /etc/securetty determine the consoles where the root administrative user is allowed to log in. If the directives in this file were commented out, administrators would not be able to log in directly to the root account. They'd have to log in to a regular account and use either the **su** or **sudo** command for administration.

While it's still possible to log in remotely as the root administrative user with the **ssh** command, that ability can also be regulated. The configuration of the SSH server in this manner is an RHCE skill described in Chapter 12.

EXERCISE 8-3

Limit root Logins

In this exercise, you'll examine the effect of eliminating the consoles in the /etc/securetty file. But first, you'll confirm that the root administrative user can log in to the standard consoles on virtual terminals 1 through 6. This exercise assumes that a regular account is available on the local system.

1. Move to the second virtual console. Press CTRL-ALT-F2; alternatively, in a KVM VM, click Send Key | CTRL-ALT-F2. At the *login:* prompt that appears, log in as the root user.

2. Repeat the process with the first, third, fourth, fifth, and sixth virtual consoles. Unless /etc/securetty has already been changed, you should be able to log in as the root user in all of these consoles.

3. Back up the current /etc/securetty file.

4. Open the /etc/securetty file in a text editor. Comment out all of the directives. Save the file.

5. Log out of the console. Try logging back in as the root administrative user. What happens? Repeat the process in other virtual consoles. What happens?

6. Log in to a console as a regular user. Does it work? Run the **su -** command to assume root privileges. Restore the original /etc/securetty file.

7. If a regular user account doesn't exist on the system, you'll have to reboot the system in single-user mode, as discussed in Chapter 5. You'll then be able to restore the /etc/securetty file from the prompt that appears.

The Ability to Log In

Beyond the /etc/securetty file is /etc/security/access.conf, which regulates access by all users. While the default version of this file is completely commented out, the comments provide useful examples. The first example would disallow (with the -) access to the first virtual console (tty1) to ALL users but root:

```
-:ALL EXCEPT root:tty1
```

Jump ahead in the file. The following line is a slightly more complex example that would disallow access to all users, except users who are members of the wheel group, along with the shutdown and sync users, on the LOCAL system.

```
-:ALL EXCEPT (wheel) shutdown sync:LOCAL
```

Scroll down further in the file. The following lines allow (with the +) the root user to access the system from three specific remote IP addresses, along with the localhost address:

```
+ : root : 192.168.200.1 192.168.200.4 192.168.200.9
+ : root : 127.0.0.1
```

If you're protecting a system from outside networks, this type of limitation on direct root administrative access makes sense. As long as the **su** or **sudo** command allows, users who log in remotely as regular users can still elevate their privileges accordingly.

Be aware, the directives in this file are considered in order. So if directives that allow access (with the +) come first, then the following directive denies access to all other users from all other local or remote systems:

```
- : ALL : ALL
```

The Proper Use of the su Command

In some cases, such as Red Hat exams, it's appropriate to log in as the root administrative user. But in practice, it's best to log in as a regular user. As a regular user, you can temporarily log in with root administrative privileges with the **su** command. Normally, that command prompts for the password of the root administrative user. After you've completed administrative tasks, it's best to log out of the root administrative account; the **exit** command would return to the regular account of that user.

The **su -** command is slightly different, as it accesses the full privileges of the root administrative account. If the password is accepted, it navigates to the root user's home directory, /root.

If you have the password of a second user, you can use the **su -** *username* command to log in directly to that account. For example, if I wanted to log in to user dickens' account, I'd run the **su - dickens** command. When I enter her password successfully, the command takes me to the /home/dickens directory.

Finally, the **su -c** command can be used to assume administrative privileges for one command. For example, the following command can be used to modify the first virtual drive on a system (assuming the root administrative password is successfully entered in response to the prompt:

```
$ su -c '/sbin/fdisk /dev/vda'
```

Limit Access to su

As discussed earlier, the ability to log in directly as the root administrative user can be regulated. Further limitations on administrative access are possible. For example, you can limit the users who are allowed to run the **su** command. This requires two basic steps.

First, you'll need to list the users who should have access to the **su** command. Make them a part of the wheel group. By default, this line in /etc/group looks like:

```
wheel:x:10:root
```

You can add selected users to the end of this line directly, with the **usermod -G wheel** *username* command, or with the User Manager.

Second, this requires a change to the configuration of Pluggable Authentication Modules (PAM). While PAM, as described in Chapter 10, is an RHCE objective, there's a commented directive available in the /etc/pam.d/su file ready for this purpose.

```
# auth    required pam_wheel.so use_uid
```

If this line is activated, only users who are members of the wheel group are allowed to use the **su** command.

The Proper Use of the sg Command

With the **sg** command, you can execute another command with the rights associated with a special group. This assumes you've set up a group password for the project group with the **gpasswd project** command. Then the **sg project -c** command allows you access to files and directories owned by the group named project. For example, if the /home/secret directory is owned by the project group, and you know the password set with the **gpasswd** command, the following command copies the important.doc file to the noted directory:

```
$ sg project -c 'cp important.doc /home/project'
```

Custom Administrators with the sudo Command

Alternatively, you can limit access to the **sudo** command. Regular users who are authorized in /etc/sudoers can access administrative commands with their own password. You don't need to give out the administrative password to everyone who thinks they know as much as a Red Hat certified professional.

To access /etc/sudoers in the vi editor, run the **visudo** command. The following directive is active by default, which allows the root user full access to administrative commands:

```
root     ALL=(ALL) ALL
```

Other users can be given administrative access. For example, if you want to allow user boris full administrative access, add the following directive to /etc/sudoers:

```
boris    ALL=(ALL) ALL
```

In this case, all boris needs to do to run an administrative command is to preface it with the **sudo** command. For example, if boris runs the following command, he's prompted for his own regular user password before the noted service is started.

```
$ sudo service vsftpd start
Password:
```

Alternatively, you can allow special users administrative access without a password. As suggested by the comments, the following directive in /etc/sudoers would allow all users who are members of the wheel group to run administrative commands without a password:

```
%wheel   ALL=(ALL)  NOPASSWD: ALL
```

But you don't have to allow full administrative access. For example, if you want to allow users who are members of the %users group to shut down the local system, activate the following directive:

```
%users  localhost=/sbin/shutdown -h now
```

In many Linux configuration files, the % sign in front of a directive specifies a group. Even though the users group has a GID of 100, it's acceptable to make regular users members of that group. For example, another directive shown in comments specifies a group of commands that can be run by users who are members of the %sys group:

```
%sys ALL = NETWORKING, SOFTWARE, SERVICES, STORAGE, DELEGATING, PROCESSES,
LOCATE, DRIVERS
```

Each of the directives can be associated with a set of commands. For example, users in the sys group, who are allowed to run NETWORKING directives, can run the commands associated with the following directive:

```
Cmnd_Alias NETWORKING = /sbin/route, /sbin/ifconfig, /bin/ping, /sbin/dhclient,
/usr/bin/net, /sbin/iptables, /usr/bin/rfcomm, /usr/bin/wvdial, /sbin/iwconfig,
/sbin/mii-tool
```

In a similar fashion, you could set up a netadmin group of users who are allowed to run these commands with the following directive:

```
%netadmin ALL = NETWORKING
```

This assumes that groups such as netadmin exist in the /etc/group and /etc/gshadow files.

Other Administrative Users

Various services may be configured with their own groups of administrative users. For example, examine the following directive from the /etc/cups/cupsd.conf file:

```
SystemGroup sys root
```

Members of groups listed with the **SystemGroup** get administrative privileges on the RHEL 6 print server.

CUPS is no longer an acronym, to avoid concerns with the word "UNIX" as a trademark. CUPS is still the name of the default Linux print server.

CERTIFICATION OBJECTIVE 8.03

User and Shell Configuration

Each user on any Red Hat Enterprise Linux system has an *environment* when logged on to the system. The environment defines directories where Linux looks for programs to run, the look of the login prompt, the terminal type, and more. This section explains how you can configure the default environment for local users. All system-wide shell configuration files are kept in the /etc directory. These files are bashrc, profile, and the scripts in the /etc/profile.d directory. These files and scripts are supplemented by hidden files in each user's home directory, as just described. Let's take a look at these files.

Home Directories and /etc/skel

When a new user is created, with standard commands such as **useradd** or utilities such as the User Manager, a default set of configuration files is copied to the user's home directory from the /etc/skel directory.

Home Directory

The home directory is where a user starts when logging in to a RHEL system. The home directory for most users is /home/*username*, where *username* is the user's login name. Every user should normally have write permission in his own home directory, so each user is free to read and write his own files.

/etc/skel

The /etc/skel directory contains default environment files for new accounts. The **useradd** command and the Red Hat User Manager copies these files to the home directory for new users. The contents of /etc/skel may vary. While the standard files in this directory are hidden, administrators are free to add more files for new users. Standard files from one copy of /etc/skel are described in Table 8-9.

TABLE 8-9	File	Purpose
Standard files in the /etc/skel Directory	.bashrc	This basic bash configuration file may include a reference to the general /etc/bashrc configuration file. Can include commands to run when the bash shell is started. One example is an alias such as **rm='rm -i'**.
	.bash_logout	This file is executed when you exit a bash shell and can include commands appropriate for this purpose, such as commands for clearing a screen.
	.bash_profile	Configures the bash startup environment. Appropriate place to add environment variables or modify the directories in your user account PATH.
	.gnome2/	Includes settings for the GNOME Desktop Environment.
	.kde/	Specifies settings for the K Desktop Environment. Not added to /etc/skel and not copied to user home directories if KDE is not installed.
	.mozilla/	Includes options associated with the Firefox web browser, developed by the Mozilla project.

e x a m

ⓦ a t c h
Linux includes many hidden files that start with a dot (.). To list these files, run the ls -a command. For example, if you want to list all of the files in the /etc/skel directory, run the ls -a /etc/skel command.

If you've installed more than a standard set of software packages on RHEL, additional configuration files and subdirectories may appear in the /etc/skel directory. For example, the installation of certain packages may include configuration files associated with emacs and the z shell (zsh) in this directory.

As the system administrator, you can edit these files or place custom files in /etc/skel. When new users are created, these files are propagated to the new users' home directories.

/etc/bashrc

The /etc/bashrc file is used for aliases and functions on a system-wide basis. Open this file in the text editor of your choice. Read each line in this file. Even if you don't understand the programming commands, you can see that this file sets the following bash shell parameters for each user. For example:

- It assigns a value of **umask**, which creates the default permissions for newly created files. It supports one set of permissions for root and system users (with user IDs below 200), and another for regular users. (Officially, RHEL reserves all user IDs above 500 for regular users; however, that is not reflected in /etc/bashrc.)
- It assigns and defines a prompt, which is what you see just before the cursor at the command prompt.
- It includes settings from *.sh files in the /etc/profile.d/ directory.

The settings here are supplemented by the .bashrc file in each user's home directory. The settings are supplemented by the .bash_profile and .bash_logout files in each user's home directory.

/etc/profile and /etc/profile.d

The /etc/profile file is used for system-wide environments and startup files.

The first part of the file sets the PATH for searching for commands. Additional directories are added to the PATH with the **pathmunge** command. (Unless you use the Korn shell, ignore the **ksh workaround** stanza.) Then it exports the **PATH**,

USER, LOGNAME, MAIL, HOSTNAME, HISTSIZE, and **HISTCONTROL**
variables and finally runs the scripts in the /etc/profile.d directory. You can check the
current value of any of these variables with the **echo $***variable* command.

/etc/profile.d

The /etc/profile.d directory is designed to contain scripts to be executed by the
/etc/profile file. The following is a partial listing of the files; those with .sh extensions
apply to the default bash shell:

```
colorls.csh    gnome-ssh-askpass.csh   udisks-bash-completion.sh
colorls.sh     gnome-ssh-askpass.sh    vim.csh
cvs.csh        lang.csh                vim.sh
cvs.sh         lang.sh                 which2.csh
glib2.csh      less.csh                which2.sh
glib2.sh       less.sh
```

In most cases, there are two versions of a script, customized for different shell
environments. Look at the files in the /etc/profile script directory. You can see
that any script in this directory that ends with an .sh is included as part of the
configuration with /etc/profile. Scripts with other extensions, such as .csh, relate
to a different command shell.

EXERCISE 8-4

Another Way to Secure a System

One more way to help secure a system is to change the default permissions for new
files and directories. In this exercise, you'll reconfigure a system to remove access
permissions for default files from other users or groups.

1. Back up the current version of the /etc/bashrc file.
2. Open the /etc/bashrc file in a text editor. Two lines in the file set the **umask**.
   One of the two lines is selected, depending on the **if** statement above them.
   See if you can determine which value of **umask** is assigned to an average
   (nonroot) user.
3. The **if** statement tests to see whether the user ID (**UID**) and group ID (**GID**)
   are the same, and that the **UID** is greater than 199. (On RHEL, you can—
   but don't have to—change this to 499.)

In other words, the **umask** value of 002 is given to users with UIDs of 200 and above. A umask value of 022 is given to users with UID of 199 and below.

4. Change the first **umask** statement to exclude all permissions for groups and others. In other words, replace the **umask** of 002 with a **umask** of 077.

5. Save and exit the file.

6. Log in as a regular nonprivileged user. Use the **touch** command to make a new empty file. Use **ls -l** to verify the permissions on that file.

7. Log in as root. Again, use the **touch** command to make a new empty file and use **ls -l** to verify the permissions on that new file.

You have just changed the default umask for all regular users. While this is an excellent option for security, it would affect the steps used in other chapters. Therefore, one final step is important:

8. Restore the original version of /etc/bashrc from the backup created in Step 1.

Shell Configuration Files in User Home Directories

As described earlier, each user gets a copy of all files from the /etc/skel directory. Most of them are hidden, revealed only with commands like **ls -a**. As users start working with their accounts, more configuration files may be added to their home directories. Some users may work primarily with the default bash shell, while others include additional configuration in configuration files related to their GUI desktop environments such as GNOME.

The default Linux shell is bash, and until recently, it was specifically included as the only shell described in associated Red Hat exam objectives. While bash is no longer specifically included in the objectives, it is the default for RHEL 6.

Login, Logout, and User Switching

While this may seem like a "no-brainer" topic for Linux users with even a couple of days of experience, one of the RHCSA topics is to "Log in and switch users in multi-user runlevels." It includes concepts from different chapters. As discussed in Chapter 5, the multi-user runlevels are 2, 3, 4, and 5. Command-line logins are available at all of these runlevels. For the first RHEL 6 release, command-line logins appear as follows:

```
Red Hat Enterprise Linux Server release 6.0 (Santiago)
Kernel 2.6.32-71.el6.x86_64 on an x86_64

server1 login:
```

The hostname, as well as the versions of RHEL 6 and the kernel, will vary. But that's irrelevant to actual logins; all you need to do is type in a username, press ENTER, and type in a password when prompted.

Logouts from the command line are even simpler; the **exit**, **logout**, and CTRL-D commands all perform logouts from the command line. Of course, once you've logged out from a system, the login prompt just shown will appear.

As discussed earlier in this chapter, there's a different way to switch user accounts. For example, to switch from the current account to user donna's account, run the following command:

```
$ su - donna
```

The same **exit**, **logout**, and CTRL-D commands can be used to exit from user donna's account.

Of course, users can log in to and log out of the GUI. While the steps vary a bit by desktop environment, they are as simple as the steps required to log in to and log out of any other operating system.

CERTIFICATION OBJECTIVE 8.04

Users and Network Authentication

By default, access to a Linux computer requires a valid username and password. One problem with a large network of Linux systems is that without some central database, each user would require an account on every Linux computer.

Several services are available that can be used as a central authentication database. One now-obsolete option for the Red Hat exams is the Network Information Service (NIS). In contrast, the Lightweight Directory Access Protocol (LDAP) is specifically listed in the RHCSA objectives. Other services are available, namely Samba, which can be configured to support access by Linux systems and users to networks governed by a Microsoft database. In any of these cases, one database of passwords and usernames exists for a network.

e x a m

ⓦ a t c h   *In the RHCSA objectives, the only requirement is to be able to connect a client to a LDAP server. You're not required to actually create an LDAP server. In addition, NIS is no longer part of the objectives.*

The focus of this section is LDAP as a client. You'll configure an RHEL 6 system as an LDAP client, set up authentication in the name service switch file, and repeat the process with Red Hat network authentication tools. First, I'll show you how you can configure LDAP clients using the command line interface and then use the Red Hat Authentication Configuration tool to repeat the process. So you'll know two methods for configuring LDAP clients.

In contrast to NIS, LDAP services can be configured on a variety of platforms. Of course, LDAP servers can be configured on RHEL 6, but they are not part of the current RHCSA or RHCE exam objectives. LDAP authentication databases can even be configured on Microsoft-based Active Directory (AD) services.

on the
job

LDAP directory services and authentication is one focus of Red Hat's RH423 course. While Red Hat allows students with "equivalent experience" to take RH423, the RHCE is an acceptable prerequisite. So you're not expected to know LDAP servers for the RHCSA exam. If you want to set up a simplified LDAP server, explore the FreeIPA (Identity, Policy, and Audit) project at www.freeipa.org.

LDAP Client Configuration

To configure a RHEL computer as an LDAP client, you'll need the openldap-clients, openldap, and nss-pam-ldapd RPM packages. The openldap-clients and nss-pam-ldapd RPMs are both optional parts of the Directory Client package group. The openldap package, as a mandatory part of the Server package group, should be installed by default on the RHEL 6 systems for this book.

To configure an LDAP client, you'll need to configure various LDAP configuration files, namely /etc/pam_ldap.conf and /etc/openldap/ldap.conf. While the files can get quite complex, you don't have to reconfigure a lot just to set up an LDAP client.

/etc/pam_ldap.conf

The default version of the /etc/pam_ldap.conf file includes a number of different commands and comments. Standard changes required to set up a basic LDAP client are based on several directives shown in Table 8-10. Encryption-related directives in this file may be associated with both the Secure Sockets Layer (SSL) and its successor, Transport Layer Security (TLS). If TLS is shown, the SSL directives work with them.

	Directive	Description
TABLE 8-10 Client Configuration Parameters in /etc/pam_ldap .conf	host 127.0.0.1	Specifies the IP address for the LDAP server. This command assumes the LDAP server is on the local computer. Should be changed to the actual IP address of the LDAP server.
	base dc=example,dc=com	Sets the default **base** distinguished name, in this case, example.com. Should be changed to the domain of the network that is being served.
	ssl start_tls	Required if TLS support is used to encrypt passwords that are sent to the LDAP server.
	pam_password	Supports encryption schemes for passwords; options include **crypt**, **nds** (Novell Directory Services), and **ad** (Active Directory).
	nss_init, groups_ignoreusers root, ldap	Assumes no supplemental groups in the LDAP directory server.

As suggested by the name of the file, the pam_ldap.conf file applies Pluggable Authentication Modules to LDAP authentication. It is almost identical to the /etc/ldap.conf file from RHEL 5; the differences do not affect the successful configuration of an LDAP client.

Related directives are included at the end of the file; they may include the following. First, the Uniform Resource Identifier, as specified by the **uri**, should redirect the client to the actual IP address of the LDAP server.

```
uri ldap://127.0.0.1/
```

If secure communication is used, you may change **ldap** to **ldaps**; if you're also configuring the LDAP server, that corresponds to TCP/IP ports 389 and 636, respectively. An LDAP server won't work if a firewall blocks these ports. Of course, if secure communication is being used to LDAP, you'd want to change this to **ssl yes**:

```
ssl no
```

Of course, to enable secure connections, LDAP needs access to appropriate certificates. While TLS is the successor to SSL, it's commonly used in concert with SSL directives. The following directive specifies the directory with those certificates:

```
tls_cacertdir /etc/openldap/cacerts
```

While OpenLDAP does support the SHA512 passwords now included by default in the shadow password suite, the default is based on MD5 hashes.

```
pam_password md5
```

If you prefer the SHA512 hash, replace that directive with:

```
pam_password exop
```

/etc/openldap/ldap.conf

You'll need to specify the **URI**, **BASE**, and **TLS_CACERTDIR** variables in this file, just as was done in the /etc/pam_ldap.conf configuration file. Given the parameters in the preceding section, you may even see a fourth directive in that file:

```
URI ldap://127.0.0.1
HOST tester1.example.com
BASE dc=example,dc=com
TLS_CACERTDIR /etc/openldap/cacerts
```

If the LDAP server is not on the local system, and the network domain is not example.com, substitute accordingly. Individual users can supersede this file in a hidden .ldaprc file in their home directories.

The Name Service Switch File

The Name Service Switch file, /etc/nsswitch.conf, governs how a computer searches for key files such as password databases. It can be configured to look through LDAP and other server databases. For example, when an LDAP client looks for a computer hostname, it might start with the following entry from /etc/nsswitch.conf:

```
hosts: files ldap dns
```

This line tells your computer to search through name databases in the following order:

1. Start with the database of hostnames and IP addresses in /etc/hosts.
2. Search for the hostname in a map file based on LDAP.
3. If none of these databases includes the desired hostname, refer to the DNS server.

You can configure the /etc/nsswitch.conf configuration file to look at an LDAP server for the desired databases. For example, to set up a centralized username and password database for your network, you'll need to configure at least the following commands in /etc/nsswitch.conf:

```
passwd:    files ldap
shadow:    files ldap
group:     files ldap
```

Other authentication databases can be configured; NIS is associated with the **nis** directive; Microsoft authentication before LDAP-based AD services is associated with **winbind**.

Red Hat Network Authentication Tools

If you're not familiar with LDAP, it may be simpler to configure a system with the Red Hat Authentication Configuration tool. In RHEL 6, you can start it in the GUI with the **system-config-authentication** command or in the console with the **authconfig-tui** command. This opens an Authentication Configuration tool; the GUI version is shown in Figure 8-4.

The Authentication Configuration tool has changed. By default, it's set to look at only the local authentication database. But if you click the drop-down text box, it presents three other options. LDAP is all that matters under the current

FIGURE 8-4

Authentication
Configuration
Options

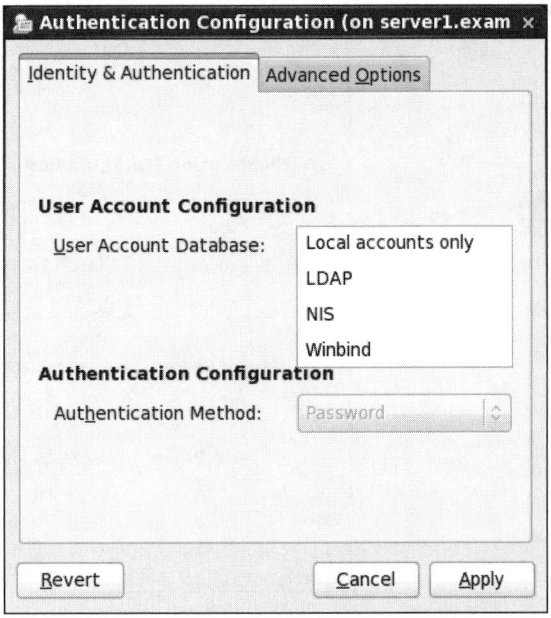

RHCSA objectives. When selected, the window changes, as shown in Figure 8-5. It defaults to the Kerberos Password Authentication Method, associated with client authentication under that system discussed in Chapter 11.

So if you see Kerberos in the window, click the associated text box, and select LDAP Password. The window changes again and provides the following warning:

```
You must provide ldaps:// server address or use TLS for LDAP authentication.
```

To eliminate that warning, select the Use TLS To Encrypt Connections option. If successful, what you see should resemble Figure 8-6.

This section assumes you're using LDAP as the User Account Database. The Authentication Configuration tool requires you to select the Use TLS To Encrypt Connections option. Those options won't be changed.

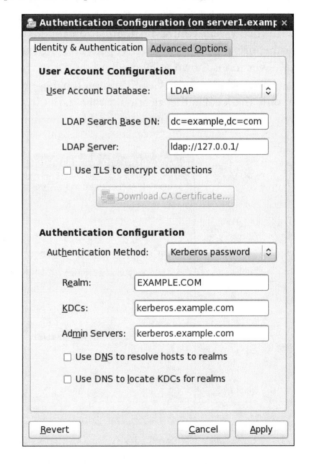

FIGURE 8-5

LDAP Authentication Configuration Options

LDAP
Authentication
Configuration
Options

The remaining options may vary:

1. The LDAP Search Base DN text box includes the domain name for the LDAP server. For example, if the local system domain is my-domain.com, the text box should contain the following:

   dc=my-domain,dc=com

2. The LDAP server text box should include the URI of that server. If it's the local computer, you can use the 127.0.0.1 IP address. But that's unlikely, especially on an exam.

3. If LDAP is associated with a Certificate Authority (CA) certificate, click Download CA Certificate. It opens a window that allows you to specify the URL with the CA Certificate with the .pem extension.

Now select the other tab, Advanced Options. The options are shown in Figure 8-7. It's just for reference, and not related to the configuration of an LDAP client.

FIGURE 8-7

Advanced
Authentication
Options

Once you've made desired changes, click OK; it may take a few seconds for the Authentication Configuration tool to write the changes to the noted configuration files.

CERTIFICATION OBJECTIVE 8.05

Special Groups

In the past, Linux groups of regular users allowed its members to share files. Red Hat has helped change this with the way it assigns unique UID and GID numbers to each user. When regular users are all made members of the same group, that also means everyone in that group has access to the home directories of all other group members. And that's often not desirable. Users may not want to share the files in their home directories with others.

On the other hand, RHEL gives each user a unique user ID and group ID in /etc/passwd. This is known as the *user private group* scheme. Users get exclusive access to their own groups and don't have to worry about other users reading the files in their home directories.

Standard and Red Hat Groups

In RHEL, each user gets her own special private group by default. As noted earlier, UIDs and GIDs normally start at 500, are assigned matching numbers, and proceed in ascending order. In addition, you can set up special groups of dedicated users, ideally with higher GIDs. For example, an administrator might configure accgrp for the accounting department, perhaps with a GID of 70000.

Shared Directories

Most people work in groups. They may want to share files. There may be good reasons for people in those groups to keep their information hidden from others. To support such groups, you can set up a shared directory, with access limited to the members of that group.

Assume you want to set up a shared directory, /home/accshared, for a group of accountants. To that end, you can set up a shared directory with the following basic steps:

1. Create the shared directory:

   ```
   # mkdir /home/accshared
   ```

2. Create a group for the accountants. Call it accgrp. Give it a group ID that doesn't interfere with existing group or user IDs. One way to do this is to add a line such as the following to the /etc/group file, or with the User Manager. Substitute desired usernames.

   ```
   accgrp:x:70000:robertc,alanm,victorb,roberta,alano,charliew
   ```

3. Set up appropriate ownership for the new shared directory. The following commands prevent any specific user from taking control of the directory and assign group ownership to accgrp:

   ```
   # chown nobody.accgrp /home/accshared
   # chmod 2770 /home/accshared
   ```

Any user who is a member of the accgrp group can now create files in and copy files to the /home/accshared directory. Any files generated within or copied to that directory will be owned by the accgrp group.

This is made possible by the 2770 permissions that assigned to the /home/accshared directory. Break that down into its component parts. The first digit (2) is the *set group ID bit,* also known as the *SGID bit.* When a SGID bit is set on a directory, any files created in that directory automatically have their group ownership set to be the same as the group owner of the directory. In addition, group ownership of files copied from other directories is reassigned, in this case, to the group named accgrp. There is a second way to set the SGID bit for the /home/accshared directory:

```
chmod g+s /home/accshared
```

The remaining digits are basic knowledge for any experienced Linux or Unix user. The **770** sets read, write, and execute permissions for the user and group that own the directory. Other users get no permissions to that directory. But since the user owner of the directory is the nonprivileged user named nobody, the group owner of the directory is most important. In this case, members of the accgrp group have read, write, and execute permissions to files created in this directory.

EXERCISE 8-5

Control Group Ownership with the SGID Bit

In this exercise, you will create new files in a directory designed to be shared by a group of users. You'll also see the difference in what happens before and after the SGID bit is set.

1. Add users called test1, test2, and test3. Specify passwords when prompted. Check the /etc/passwd and /etc/group files to verify that each user's private group was created:

```
# useradd test1; passwd test1
# useradd test2; passwd test2
# useradd test3; passwd test3
```

2. Edit the /etc/group file and add a group called tg1. Make the test1 and test2 accounts members of this group. You could add the following line to /etc/group directly or use the Red Hat User Manager:

```
tg1:x:99999:test1,test2
```

Before you proceed, make sure the group ID assigned to group tg1 (in this case, 99999) is not already in use. Make sure to add the following line to /etc/shadow. A group password is not required:

```
tg1:!::
```

3. Create a directory intended for use by the tg1 group:

```
# mkdir  /home/testshared
```

4. Change the user and group ownership of the shared directory:

```
# chown  nobody.tg1  /home/testshared
```

5. Log in as user test1. Make sure the login navigates to the /home/test1 directory. Run the **umask** command to confirm that files created from this account will have appropriate permissions. (The output of the **umask** command for regular users such as test1 should be 0002.) If there's a problem with the home directory or the **umask** output, you may have made an error earlier in this chapter with user settings. If so, repeat Steps 1–5 on a different VM.

6. Run the **cd /home/testshared** command. Now try to create a file with the following commands. What happens?

```
$ date  >>test.txt
$ touch abcd
```

7. Now as the root user, set group write permissions on the testshared directory.

```
# chmod 770 /home/testshared
```

8. Log in again as user test1, navigate back to the /home/testshared directory, and then try to create a file in the new directory. So far, so good.

```
$ cd /home/testshared
$ date  >> test.txt
$ ls -l test.txt
```

9. Remove all permissions for other users on new files in the /home/testshared directory:

```
# chmod o-rwx /home/testshared/*
```

10. Now with the following command, check the ownership on the new file. Do you think other users in the tg1 group can access this file? If in doubt, log in as user test2 and see for yourself.

    ```
    $ ls -l
    ```

11. From the root account, set the SGID bit on the directory:

    ```
    # chmod g+s  /home/testshared
    ```

    (Yes, if you are efficiency-minded, you may know that the **chmod 2770 /home/testshared** command combines the effect of this and the previous **chmod** commands.)

12. Switch back to the test1 account, navigate back to the /home/testshared directory, and create another file. Remove permissions for other users on the newly created file. Check the ownership on the newly created file. Do you think that user test2 can now access this file? (To see for yourself, try it from the test2 account.)

    ```
    $ date >> testb.txt
    $ chmod o-rwx /home/testshared/testb.txt
    $ ls  -l
    ```

13. Now log in as the test2 account. Go into the /home/testshared directory. Try accessing the testb.txt file. Create a different file, and use **ls -l** to check permissions and ownership again. (To see that it worked, try accessing this file from the test1 account.)

14. Switch to the test3 account and check whether that user can or cannot create files in this directory, and whether that user can or cannot view the files in this directory.

CERTIFICATION SUMMARY

You can manage users and groups with the files of the shadow password suite. These files can be modified directly, with the help of commands such as **useradd** and **groupadd**, or the User Manager tool. The way users are configured is based on the /etc/login.defs file. Any variables or system-wide functions you may need to run can be kept in the /etc/bashrc or /etc/profile script. They can be modified by files in user home directories.

There are several ways to limit the use of administrative privileges. The ability to log in can be regulated in files such as /etc/securetty and /etc/security/access. conf. Access to the **su** command can be limited with the help of PAM. Partial and complete administrative privileges can be configured for the **sudo** command in the /etc/sudoers file.

You can use centralized network account management with the LDAP service. RHEL 6 systems can be configured as an LDAP client with the help of the /etc/pam_ldap.conf and /etc/openldap/ldap.conf files.

By default, Red Hat Enterprise Linux assigns unique user and group ID numbers to each new user. This is known as the user private group scheme. This scheme supports the configuration of special groups for a specific set of users. The users in the group can be configured with read and write privileges in a dedicated directory, courtesy of the SGID bit.

✓ # TWO-MINUTE DRILL

Here are some of the key points from the certification objectives in Chapter 8.

User Account Management

❑ After installation, a system may have only a single login account: root. For everyday operation, it's best to create one or more regular accounts.

❑ The shadow password suite is configured in the /etc/passwd, /etc/shadow, /etc/group, and /etc/gshadow files.

❑ Administrators can add user and group accounts by directly editing the files of the shadow password suite, or with commands like **useradd** and **groupadd**. The way accounts are added are defined by the /etc/login.defs file.

❑ Accounts can be added with the Red Hat User Manager tool. You can also use this tool or related commands such as **chage** and **usermod** to modify other account parameters.

Administrative Control

❑ Logins as the root user can be regulated by the /etc/securetty file.

❑ Logins in general can be regulated by the /etc/security/access.conf file.

❑ Access to the **su** command can be regulated through the /etc/pam.d/su file.

❑ Custom administrative privileges can be configured in the /etc/sudoers file.

User and Shell Configuration

❑ The home directory for new login accounts is populated from the /etc/skel directory.

❑ Each user has an environment when logged on to the system, based on /etc/profile, and if the shell is bash, /etc/bashrc.

❑ All users have hidden shell configuration files in their home directories.

Users and Network Authentication

❏ LDAP allows you to configure one centrally managed username and password database with other Linux and Unix systems on a LAN.

❏ LDAP clients are configured in /etc/pam_ldap.conf and /etc/openldap/ldap.conf.

❏ Changes are required to /etc/nsswitch.conf to make a system look for a remote authentication database such as LDAP.

❏ Red Hat includes GUI and console tools that can help configure a system as an LDAP client.

Special Groups

❏ Red Hat's user private group scheme configures users with their own unique user and group ID numbers.

❏ With appropriate SGID permissions, you can configure a shared directory for a specific group of users.

❏ Setting the SGID bit is easy; use **chown** to set nobody as the user owner and the name of the group as the group owner. Then run the **chmod 2770** command on the shared directory.

SELF TEST

The following questions will help measure your understanding of the material presented in this chapter. As no multiple choice questions appear on the Red Hat exams, no multiple choice questions appear in this book. These questions exclusively test your understanding of the chapter. It is okay if you have another way of performing a task. Getting results, not memorizing trivia, is what counts on the Red Hat exams. There may be more than one answer to many of these questions.

User Account Management

1. What's the standard minimum user ID number for regular users on Red Hat distributions?

_____

2. What command at a GUI-based text console starts the Red Hat User Manager?

_____

Administrative Control

3. What file regulates the local consoles where the root user can log in?

_____

4. What file supports the configuration of custom administrators?

_____

5. When a regular user uses the **sudo** command to run an administrative command, what password is required?

_____

User and Shell Configuration

6. If you want to add files to every new user account, what directory should you use?

_____

7. The system-wide configuration file associated with the bash shell is

_____

Users and Network Authentication

8. If the LDAP domain is example.org, what is the LDAP Search Base DN?

   dc=_____

   dc=_____

9. What's the full path to the file that refers to an LDAP database for authentication?

   _____

Special Groups

10. What command would set the SGID bit on the /home/developer directory?

    _____

11. What command would set up ownership of the developer group on the /home/developer directory?

    _____

12. What command would add user alpha to the developer group? This question assumes the alpha user and the developer group already exists and alpha belongs to no group other than his own.

    _____

LAB QUESTIONS

Red Hat presents its exams electronically. For that reason, the labs in this chapter are available from the CD that accompanies the book, in the Chapter8/ subdirectory. They're available in .doc, .html, and .txt formats, to reflect standard options associated with electronic delivery on a live RHEL 6 system. In case you haven't yet set up RHEL 6 on a system, refer to the first lab of Chapter 2 for installation instructions. The answers for each lab follows the Self Test answers for the fill-in-the-blank questions.

SELF TEST ANSWERS

User Account Management

1. The minimum user ID number for regular users on Red Hat distributions is 500.

2. The command in a GUI-based text console that starts the Red Hat User Manager is **system-config-users**.

Administrative Control

3. The file that regulates the local consoles where the root user can log in is /etc/securetty.

4. The file that supports the configuration of custom administrators is /etc/sudoers.

5. When a regular user uses the **sudo** command to run an administrative command, the regular password of that user is required.

User and Shell Configuration

6. To automatically add files to every new user account, you should use the /etc/skel directory.

7. The system-wide configuration file associated with the bash shell is /etc/bashrc.

Users and Network Authentication

8. If the LDAP domain is example.org, the LDAP Search Base DN is dc=example,dc=org.

9. The full path to the file that points to an LDAP database for authentication is /etc/nsswitch.conf.

Special Groups

10. The command that would set the SGID bit on the /home/developer directory is **chmod g+s /home/developer**. Numeric options such as **chmod 2770 /home/developer** are not correct, as they go beyond just setting the SGID bit.

11. The command would set up ownership of the developer group on the /home/developer directory is **chgrp developer /home/developer**.

12. The command that adds user alpha to the developer group is **usermod -G developer alpha**.

LAB ANSWERS

Lab 1

While there are a number of methods available to create new users and groups, they should all come to the same result.

1. The output to the **ls -l /home** command should include the following output, substituting today's date:

```
drwx------.   4 newguy   newguy   4096 Jan 19 12:13 newguy
drwx------.   4 intern   intern   4096 Jan 19 12:13 intern
```

2. Run the **ls -la /etc/skel** command. The output should include a number of hidden files, owned by the user root and the group root.

3. Run the **ls -la /home/newguy** and **ls -la /home/intern** commands. The output should include the same hidden files as in /etc/skel, but owned by the users associated with each home directory.

4. The end of the /etc/passwd and /etc/shadow file should include entries for both users. If you've set up a password for these users, it should be in encrypted format in the second column of /etc/shadow.

5. The following entry should exist somewhere in the middle of the /etc/group file. It is acceptable if other users are included at the end of the line.

```
users:x:100:newguy
```

6. The following line should be near to or at the end of the /etc/group file; the order of the users in the fourth column does not matter.

```
peons:x:123456:newguy,intern
```

Lab 2

The simplest way to limit root logins to the sixth virtual console is in the /etc/securetty file. The only active directives in that file should be:

```
vc/6
tty6
```

Of course, there are other ways to do just about anything in Linux. To try it out, press CTRL-ALT-F1 and try logging in as the root user. Press CTRL-ALT-F2, and repeat the process through virtual terminal 6.

Lab 3

Use the answers to the first part of Lab 1 as guidance to verify the ownership and permissions set /home/senioradm directory, along with the files therein. With respect to **sudo** privileges, you should see the following line in the /etc/sudoers file:

```
senioradm     ALL=(ALL)         ALL
```

To test the result, log in as the senioradm user, and run an administrative command, prefaced by a sudo. For example, try the following command:

```
# sudo system-config-firewall
```

Unless you've run the **sudo** command in the last few minutes, this action will prompt for a password. Enter the password created for user senioradm. It should open the Firewall Configuration tool.

Lab 4

Use the answers to Lab 1 as guidance to verify the ownership and permissions of the /home/junioradm directory, along with the files therein. With respect to **sudo** privileges, you should see the following line in the /etc/sudoers file:

```
junioradm     ALL=/sbin/fdisk
```

Next, try running the **fdisk** command such as:

```
$ sudo /sbin/fdisk -l
```

You'll be prompted for a password. Enter the password created for user junioradm. Unless the passwords are identical, the root password would not work. If successful, you should see a list of partitions for connected drives in the output.

Lab 5

Use the answers to Lab 1 as guidance to verify the ownership and permissions on /home/infouser directory, along with the files therein. If successful, that directory will include an info-*/ subdirectory. In addition, the /etc/skel directory should also include an info-*/ subdirectory. That subdirectory should have the same files as those shown in the /usr/share/doc/info-* directory. Of course, that works only if you copy the contents of the info-*/ subdirectory from the /usr/share/info directory to /etc/skel.

Lab 6

This is a straightforward process, using the following basic steps:

1. Create accounts for mike, rick, terri, and maryam if required. You can use the **useradd** command, edit the /etc/passwd file directly, or work through the User Manager.

2. Set up a group for these users. Configure a group ID outside the range of regular users in /etc/group with a line such as:

   ```
   galley:x:88888:mike,rick,terri,maryam
   ```

3. Create the /home/galley directory. Give it proper ownership and permissions with the following commands:

   ```
   # mkdir /home/galley
   # chown nobody.galley
   # chmod 2770 /home/galley
   ```

9

RHCSA-Level System Administration Tasks

A s the final chapter related to the RHCSA exam, this covers those functional system administration tasks not already covered in other chapters. One part of remote access not already covered is based on the GUI-based sharing enabled through Virtual Network Computing (VNC).

The system administration tasks discussed in this chapter include process management and the use of archives. Furthermore, this chapter also helps you work with repetitive system administration tasks. Some of it happens when you want to have a "life," more when you'd rather be asleep. In this chapter, you'll learn how to schedule both one-time and periodic execution of jobs. That's made possible with the cron and at daemons. In this case, "at" is not a preposition, but a service that monitors a system for one-time scheduled jobs. In a similar fashion, cron is a service that monitors a system for regularly scheduled jobs.

When troubleshooting, system logging often provides the clues that you need to solve a lot of problems. The focus in this chapter is local logging; the network logging capabilities of the rsyslog service is an RHCE skill covered in Chapter 17.

INSIDE THE EXAM

Remote Access

Linux administrators are frequently responsible for a variety of systems in remote locations. You reviewed client options associated with SSH in Chapter 2. In this chapter, you'll learn about the VNC part of this objective:

■ Access remote systems using SSH and VNC

System Administration

Linux administrators work on Linux systems in a number of ways. In this chapter, you'll learn various methods for meeting the fol-

lowing RHCSA objectives. The first of these objectives involves fundamental command skills:

■ Archive, compress, unpack, and uncompress files using **tar**, **star**, **gzip**, and **bzip2**

These other objectives are more closely related to system administration:

■ Identify CPU/memory intensive processes; adjust process priority with **renice**, **kill** processes

■ Schedule tasks using cron

■ Locate and interpret system log files

CERTIFICATION OBJECTIVE 9.01

Configure Access with VNC

If you're skilled enough with Linux to go for the RHCSA, you've probably already used VNC. It's the standard viewer for KVM-based virtual machines. Given the seamless way it's integrated with the virtual machine manager, the use of VNC to view the VMs created so far in this book is essentially painless.

But VNC can do so much more. It's an excellent option for viewing remote systems in another room or another continent. While VNC is not secure, it can be redirected over secure communication systems such as SSH. VNC communication normally proceeds on port 5900, so that port (and those immediately above it) must be open to enable communication. For example, the first connection to a VNC server would also use port 5901; the second connection would use port 5902, and potentially up to port 5909, as port 5910 is normally reserved for a different service. This communication proceeds through the TCP protocol.

As the intent is to provide remote access to a GUI, this section assumes some GUI desktop environment is installed on the local system. In addition, there are three types of VNC Server packages available for RHEL 6.

- The display associated with a KVM-based virtual machine.
- The GNOME-based VNC server known as vino. It's suitable for users who want others such as tech support to see what they're doing.
- The TigerVNC server, based on the TightVNC server. It's suited for administrators who want remote access to a GUI on a different system.

The VNC display associated with a KVM-based virtual machine is integrated into that system. As no additional configuration is required, beyond the steps discussed in Chapter 2, this chapter does not discuss the display associated with KVM. However, that display does not work simultaneously with vino on RHEL 6.

Just be aware, such connections to VNC displays are inherently less secure than a standard login, as all that's required is knowledge of the right port and perhaps a password. Someone who connects remotely via VNC does not even have to have a username. In addition, the TightVNC and vino servers should not be run on the same system simultaneously.

Install and Configure a TigerVNC Server

While alternatives are available, the simplest way to configure remote VNC communication is with TigerVNC. It includes client and server packages: tigervnc and tigervnc-server. But you don't need tigervnc to connect to tigervnc-server. Some users may prefer an alternative GUI client such as the Remote Desktop Viewer.

As always, the simplest method to install these packages is with the **yum install vinagre tigervnc tigervnc-server** command. Once they are installed, you can start the configuration process in the /etc/sysconfig/vncservers file. The last two lines in the default version of the file are sample configuration directives:

```
# VNCSERVERS="2:myusername"
# VNCSERVERARGS[2]="-geometry 800x600 -nolisten tcp -localhost"
```

The first directive would work for a single username; for example, the following line would work for two usernames. The username associated with the number does not matter; however, the numbers should be consecutive. In addition, the numbers shown here correspond to VNC port numbers. For example, the line shown here matches user michael and elizabeth to port numbers 5901 and 5902, respectively.

```
VNCSERVER="1:michael 2:elizabeth"
```

For now, just specify the geometry with the following directive, which supports connections over TCP and does not require tunneling through an SSH connection.

```
# VNCSERVERARGS[2]="-geometry 800x600"
```

Now save the changes and get the VNC service going. The following sequence of actions will seem counterintuitive. To start the VNC service, you first have to make sure it's stopped, with the following command:

```
# /etc/init.d/vncserver stop
```

Now set up one of the users associated with the VNCSERVER directive just configured. You'll have to do so from that user's account with the **vncserver** command. The first available port is assumed, unless one is specified. The following command specifies a connection through port 5902 (not 2):

```
$ vncserver :2
```

Now check the result with the following command. It should confirm that VNC servers are actually running.

```
# /etc/init.d/vncserver status
```

More detailed configuration is possible. The following command adds more information, which in this case overrides the GUI window dimensions set in the /etc/sysconfig/vncservers configuration file:

```
$ vncserver :2 -geometry 640x400
```

The command adds configuration options to the subject user's home directory, in the .vnc/ subdirectory, which will be discussed shortly. The number included after the colon (:) with the **vncserver** command determines the communications port for that connection. In this case, remote users will be able to connect to this system over port 5902. For the command with the :1, a connection to that system can be made over port 5901. In either case, the **vncserver** command normally prompts for a password, which is used for the connection from the remote system.

The GNOME-Based vino Server

The GNOME-based vino server allows administrators to view the current state of remote GUI desktop environments. The necessary tools are included in the package of the same name. Once it is installed, run the **vino-preferences** command from the desired account, to open the Remote Desktop Preferences window shown in Figure 9-1.

FIGURE 9-1

Remote Desktop
Preferences
with vino

Remote Desktop Preferences (on server1.example.com) ×

Sharing

☐ Allow other users to view your desktop

☑ Allow other users to control your desktop

Nobody can access your desktop.

Security

☑ You must confirm each access to this machine

☐ Require the user to enter this password:

☐ Configure network automatically to accept connections

Notification Area

○ Always display an icon

◉ Only display an icon when there is someone connected

○ Never display an icon

Help   Close

The options associated with the Remote Desktop Preferences window are straightforward. In addition, in most cases, if you hover a cursor over an option, the tool provides additional explanation. As the objective is to share the local desktop environment over a network, all other options are grayed out unless you activate the first option: Allow Other Users To View Your Desktop.

When you activate that first option, the Remote Desktop Preferences window changes; it evaluates the current configuration to identify whether and how the desktop may be accessible over the local network. That changes, depending on the other now-active options in the window. Each option is described as follows:

- **Allow Other Users To Control Your Desktop**   If this option is active, remote users will be able to enter keystrokes and mouse clicks remotely onto your desktop environment.

- **You Must Confirm Each Access To This Machine**   If this option is active, you'll get a chance to confirm remote requests to access the local GUI desktop environment. It's an excellent way to allow local users to retain control over their local systems, perhaps until prompted by a technical support person who is trying to help them.

- **Require The User To Enter This Password**   If this option is active, it provides one additional security measure for the local user.

- **Configure Network To Automatically Accept Connections**   If a local network router works with universal plug and play (UPnP), this option enables access from remote networks.

Only one of the final three options can be active. As they relate to a notification icon, they have no bearing on the configuration of vino as a server. They just determine if and when an icon associated with the vino server is shown in the upper-right corner area of the GNOME desktop environment.

The vino server does not work with the standard configuration of a physical host and virtual machines created in the first two chapters of this book. If KVM-based virtual machines are currently running, they should be deactivated. You'll then be able to connect to the vino-based VNC server from a physically remote system, using either the **vncviewer** command or an option like the Remote Desktop Preferences tool.

Incidentally, the Remote Desktop Preferences tool saves its settings in an XML file in the subject user's home directory, in the .gconf/desktop/gnome/remote_access subdirectory.

Although the vino server requires the same open ports as the aforementioned TigerVNC server, the two VNC servers should not be run simultaneously. If you're running into a problem with vino, I did warn you about this issue earlier in the chapter.

Install and Configure a VNC Client

You should then be able to test the result locally, with the **vncviewer** command. But strangely enough, that action fails with a "couldn't find suitable pixmap" error message. If you're already on a remote system, that command will work with the IP address of the VNC Server, coupled with the associated port. For example, if the previous **vncserver :2** command has been run on a local 192.168.122.1 system, you should be able to connect remotely through port 5902 with the following command:

```
# vncviewer 192.168.122.1:2
```

To test a VNC server on a local system, you can use the Remote Desktop Viewer, which can be started from a GUI desktop with the **vinagre** command or from the GNOME desktop by clicking Applications | Internet | Remote Desktop Viewer. It opens the Remote Desktop Viewer window. Click Connect to open the Remote Desktop Viewer window shown in Figure 9-2.

FIGURE 9-2

Remote Desktop Preferences

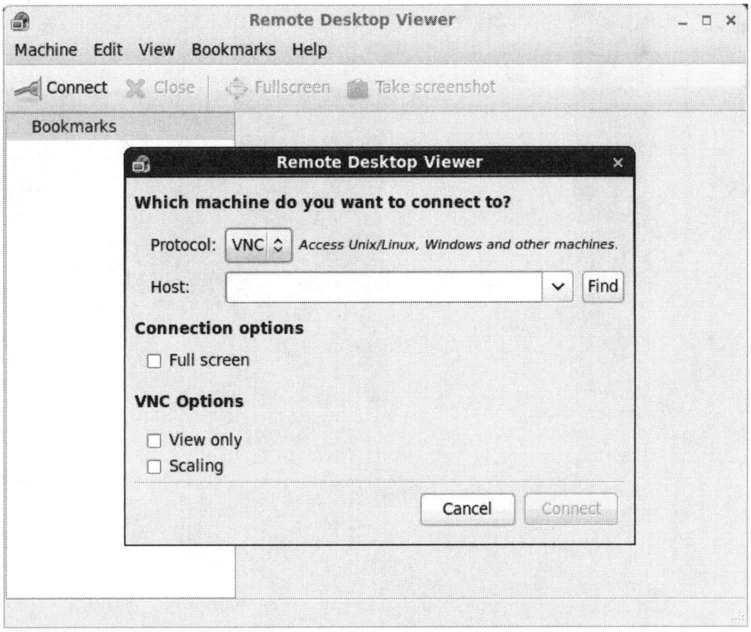

The options are as follows:

- **Protocol** VNC is assumed in this chapter; however, the Remote Desktop Viewer can be used with a variety of protocols.
- **Host** Specify the hostname or the IP address of the system to which you want to connect.
- **Full Screen** If selected, the remote connection occupies the full screen of the local system.
- **View Only** If selected, no actions are allowed over the connection.
- **Scaling** When selected, changes the screen to allow viewing in different-sized GUI environments.

If successful, it'll open up another Remote Desktop Viewer window, with a request for the password, and a Remember This Credential option, which would store that password. If a connection is made, you'll see the "remote" desktop on the local system, as shown in Figure 9-3.

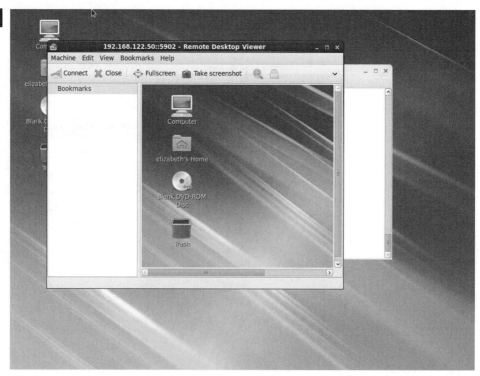

FIGURE 9-3

A local connection to a "Remote" Desktop via VNC

But that's just a local connection. Before proceeding to Firewall Options, use this command to make sure this VNC server is running the next time this system is booted:

```
# chkconfig vncserver on
```

There's a limit. Only one connection can be made per port. For example, if the previous vncviewer command used port 5902, you can't use the Remote Desktop Viewer to connect to the same port.

Firewall Options

The ports to be open in a firewall depend on the number of connections that may be made to the local VNC server. At minimum, you'll need to open ports 5900 and 5901. The additional ports that you open depend on the number of connections needed from remote systems. While firewalls are covered in Chapters 4 and 10, the following is a brief description of one way you can open ports 5900 through 5905 through a firewall.

1. Run the **system-config-firewall-tui** command.
2. In the console window that appears, select Customize and press ENTER.
3. In the Trusted Services window that appears, select Forward and press ENTER.
4. In the Other Ports window, select Add to open the Port And Protocol window shown in Figure 9-4. The entries shown specify ports 5900 through 5905, over the TCP protocol. Type in those entries, select OK, and then press ENTER.
5. Select Close and press ENTER.
6. Back in the Firewall Configuration window, select OK and press ENTER.
7. When the warning appears about overriding the existing firewall configuration, select Yes and press ENTER.
8. To confirm the new firewall, run the **iptables -L** command. The following line from the output confirms that the ports associated with vnc-server in the /etc/services file, 5900 (the vnc-server port), through 5905, are open in the firewall.

```
ACCEPT tcp -- anywhere anywhere state NEW tcp dpts:vnc-server:5905
```

The local system is now ready to transmit VNC server connections to remote systems, using connection tools such as the Remote Desktop Viewer and the **vncviewer** command.

FIGURE 9-4

Firewall Ports and
Protocol

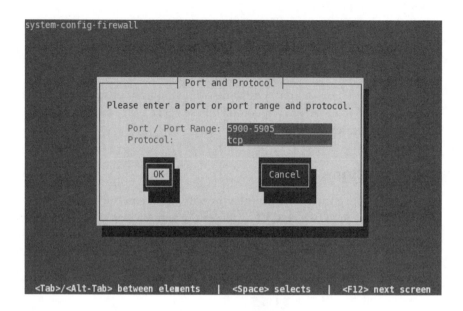

Confirm Access to a VNC Server

This is one case where the **telnet** and **nmap** tools discussed in Chapter 2 may be helpful. The messages associated with the start of various VNC servers may be cryptic. To confirm that a system is listening on appropriate ports from a local system, try the following command:

```
# nmap localhost
```

For my physical host system, that results in the following output:

```
Starting Nmap 5.21 ( http://nmap.org ) at 2011-01-26 12:18 PST
Nmap scan report for localhost (127.0.0.1)
Host is up (0.000011s latency).
rDNS record for 127.0.0.1: localhost.localdomain
Not shown: 993 closed ports
PORT      STATE SERVICE
22/tcp    open  ssh
25/tcp    open  smtp
5900/tcp  open  vnc
5901/tcp  open  vnc-1
5902/tcp  open  vnc-2
```

The last three lines confirm the availability of three ports for connections to VNC servers. To reiterate, ports 5901 and 5902 are used for different VNC terminals. The ports can be confirmed with **telnet** commands such as the following:

```
# telnet localhost 5900
```

The following output indirectly confirms a connection to a VNC server, as the **RFB** shown in the output refers to a remote framebuffer, a protocol for network access to a GUI:

```
RFB 003.008
```

Of course, remote access to VNC servers won't work unless there's access through the firewall just configured earlier. You can use both the **nmap** and **telnet** commands for that purpose from remote systems. Just substitute the IP address or the hostname of the VNC server for localhost in the commands just shown.

Route Through a Secure Shell

For this example, assume you've configured a VNC server on the server1.example.com system. Furthermore, assume you've set up /etc/sysconfig/vncservers to point to the appropriate port, and have run the following command to set up user elizabeth's account for remote access over port 5903:

```
$ vncserver :3
```

Now navigate to a remote system such as tester1.example.com. From that system, run the following command to set up an SSH tunnel:

```
$ ssh -L 5903:server1.example.com:5903 elizabeth@server1.example.com
```

That **ssh** command with the **-L** specifies that communications from local port 5903 are to be bound to communications over port 5903 from the server1.example.com system. Since the secure shell requires a user login, the **ssh** command requires access via an account on that remote system. Since this communication proceeds over port 5903, it does not interfere with normal ssh communication. However, it also means that you would need to open port 5903 for this particular VNC server.

Once that communications tunnel is established, open up a second command line console, or the Remote Desktop Viewer on the local system. Connect to the **localhost:3** system. That connection is transmitted over port 5903 through the now established SSH tunnel.

More VNC Configuration

When a user establishes a connection by entering a command like **vncserver :3**, that action sets up configuration files in that user's home directory, in the .vnc/ subdirectory. That command sets up four files in the .vnc/ subdirectory: the password, a log file, a process identifier (PID) file, and a configuration file.

When the **vncserver :3** command prompts for a password, an encrypted version of that entry is stored in the passwd file.

The activity associated with a VNC server is a process, with a PID number. On the server1.example.com system, that file is server1.example.com.pid. That file includes the actual PID number. The **kill** command can be used to stop this process, as discussed later in this chapter.

The last two files are more important. The server1.example.com.log file provides information on what happened, and what is happening with the connection. The configuration file is xstartup, which is preconfigured to start the local default desktop environment.

A User VNC Configuration File

The following is a line-by-line analysis of the VNC configuration file that's created when a user activates a VNC server for her system. To review, the file is xstartup in the .vnc/ subdirectory of the target user. The first line is common to many scripts, as it establishes the bash shell via a soft link as the shell for the script:

```
!#/bin/sh
```

The following line sets up the VNC window as an icon:

```
vncconfig -iconic
```

The **unset** command applied to the SESSION_MANAGER variable allows the new GUI to create its own communications socket:

```
unset SESSION_MANAGER
```

The unset command applied to the DBUS_SESSION_BUS_ADDRESS variable supports the creation of a new message bus for the GUI to be created:

```
unset DBUS_SESSION_BUS_ADDRESS
```

While it's useful to confirm the operating system is Linux with the OS=`uname -s` directive, the **if** loop that follows applies only to the PATH variable associated with the SUSE Linux distribution. Since this book covers RHEL, that loop is not shown here.

The two **if** loops that follow execute the commands within the /etc/X11/xinit/xinitrc script. The only difference is the **-x** and the **-f** switches, which execute the script depending on whether the noted file has executable permissions. You may already recognize the xinitrc script as the standard script associated with the **startx** command, which starts the GUI from the command line interface.

```
if [ -x /etc/X11/xinit/xinitrc ]; then
  exec /etc/X11/xinit/xinitrc
fi
if [ -f /etc/X11/xinit/xinitrc ]; then
  exec sh /etc/X11/xinit/xinitrc
fi
```

CERTIFICATION OBJECTIVE 9.02

Elementary System Administration Commands

There are several system administration commands in the RHCSA objectives not covered in previous chapters. They're associated with system resource management and archives. System resource management allows you to see what processes are running, to check the resources they're using, and to kill or restart those processes. Archive commands support the consolidation of a group of files in a single archive, which can then be compressed.

System Resource Management Commands

Linux includes a variety of commands that can help you identify those processes that are monopolizing a system. The most basic of those commands is **ps**, which provides a snapshot of currently running processes. Those processes can be ranked with the **top** command, which can display running Linux tasks in order of their resource usage. With **top**, you can identify those processes that are using the most CPU and RAM memory. Commands that can adjust process priority include **nice** and **renice**. Sometimes it's not enough to adjust process priority, at which point it

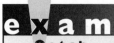

e x a m
ⓦatch

The objective related to system resource management is to "Identify CPU/memory intensive processes, adjust process priority with renice, and kill processes."

may be appropriate to stop a process with commands like **kill** and **killall**. If you need to monitor system usage, the **sar** and **iostat** commands can also be helpful.

Process Management with the ps Command

It's important to know what's running on a Linux computer. To help with that task, the **ps** command has a number of critical switches. When trying to diagnose a problem, it's common to get the fullest possible list of running processes, and then look for a specific program. For example, if the Firefox Web browser were to suddenly crash, you'd want to kill any associated processes. The **ps aux | grep firefox** command could then help you identify the process(es) that you need to kill.

The **ps** command by itself is usually not enough. All it does is identify those processes running in the current command line shell. Unless you've started a running process with the ampersand (&) to return the command to a shell prompt, that command typically returns just the process associated with the current shell, and the **ps** command process itself.

To identify those processes associated with a username, the **ps -u** *username* command can help. Sometimes there are specific users who may be problematic for various reasons. So if you're suspicious of a user like mjang, the following command can help you review every process currently associated with that user:

```
$ ps -u mjang
```

As an administrator, you may choose to focus on a specific account for various reasons, such as activity revealed by the **top** command, described in the next section. If a bigger picture view is required, you may want to audit all currently running processes with a command like the following:

```
$ ps aux
```

The output is a more complete database of currently running processes, in order of their PIDs. The **a** lists all running processes, the **u** classifies those processes by user, and the **x** lifts the standard limitation that listed processes must be associated with a terminal or console. One example is shown in Figure 9-5. While the output can include hundreds of processes and more, the output can be redirected to a file for further analysis with commands like **grep**. The output columns shown Figure 9-5 are described in Table 9-1.

FIGURE 9-5

Output from the
ps aux command

```
USER       PID %CPU %MEM    VSZ   RSS TTY      STAT START   TIME COMMAND
root         1  0.0  0.0  19244  1340 ?        Ss   Jan19   0:05 /sbin/init
root         2  0.0  0.0      0     0 ?        S    Jan19   0:00 [kthreadd]
root         3  0.0  0.0      0     0 ?        S    Jan19   0:00 [migration/0]
root         4  0.0  0.0      0     0 ?        S    Jan19   0:00 [ksoftirqd/0]
root         5  0.0  0.0      0     0 ?        S    Jan19   0:00 [watchdog/0]
root         6  0.0  0.0      0     0 ?        S    Jan19   0:00 [migration/1]
root         7  0.0  0.0      0     0 ?        S    Jan19   0:01 [ksoftirqd/1]
root         8  0.0  0.0      0     0 ?        S    Jan19   0:00 [watchdog/1]
root         9  0.0  0.0      0     0 ?        S    Jan19   0:00 [migration/2]
root        10  0.0  0.0      0     0 ?        S    Jan19   0:05 [ksoftirqd/2]
root        11  0.0  0.0      0     0 ?        S    Jan19   0:00 [watchdog/2]
root        12  0.0  0.0      0     0 ?        S    Jan19   0:00 [migration/3]
root        13  0.0  0.0      0     0 ?        S    Jan19   0:01 [ksoftirqd/3]
root        14  0.0  0.0      0     0 ?        S    Jan19   0:00 [watchdog/3]
root        15  0.0  0.0      0     0 ?        S    Jan19   0:01 [events/0]
root        16  0.0  0.0      0     0 ?        S    Jan19   0:24 [events/1]
root        17  0.0  0.0      0     0 ?        S    Jan19   0:12 [events/2]
root        18  0.0  0.0      0     0 ?        S    Jan19   0:04 [events/3]
root        19  0.0  0.0      0     0 ?        S    Jan19   0:00 [cpuset]
root        20  0.0  0.0      0     0 ?        S    Jan19   0:00 [khelper]
root        21  0.0  0.0      0     0 ?        S    Jan19   0:00 [netns]
root        22  0.0  0.0      0     0 ?        S    Jan19   0:00 [async/mgr]
:
```

TABLE 9-1

Columns of
Output from
ps aux

Column Title	Description
USER	The username associated with the process
PID	Process Identifier
%CPU	Current CPU usage
%MEM	Current RAM usage
VSZ	Virtual memory size of the process in KB
RSS	Physical memory in use by the process, not including swap space, in KB
TTY	Associated terminal console
STAT	Process status
START	Start time of the process; if you just see a date, the process started more than 24 hours ago
TIME	Cumulative CPU time used
COMMAND	Command associated with the process

Incidentally, you may note that the **ps aux** command does not include the familiar dash in front of the **aux** switches. In this case, the command works with and without the dash (slightly differently); the following alternative includes current environmental variables.

```
$ ps eux
```

Processes can be organized in a tree format. Specifically, the first process, with a PID of 1, is init. That process is the base of the tree, which may be shown with the **pstree** command. In a few cases, it's not possible to use standard **kill** commands described shortly to kill a process. In such cases, it may be possible to kill a process by killing its "parent" in the tree. To that end, the following command identifies the parent of a process, known as the PPID:

```
$ ps axl
```

The **l** switch is not compatible with the **u** switch; in other words, you can't set up the output of the **ps** command to include both the user who started the process and the PPID. You can view the PID and PPIDs of all running processes in Figure 9-6.

With the **-Z** switch (that's an uppercase Z), the **ps** command can also identify the SELinux contexts associated with a process. For example, the following command includes the SELinux contexts of each process at the start of the output. If you've read Chapter 4, the contexts should already seem familiar. For example, contrast the context of the vsFTP server process, with the following excerpt:

```
system_u:system_r:ftpd_t:s0-s0:c0.c1023 2059 ? Ss     0:00 /usr/sbin/vsftpd
/etc/vsftpd/vsftpd.conf
```

	F	UID	PID	PPID	PRI	NI	VSZ	RSS	WCHAN	STAT	TTY	TIME	COMMAND
FIGURE 9-6	4	0	1	0	20	0	19244	1340	poll_s	Ss	?	0:05	/sbin/init
	1	0	2	0	20	0	0	0	kthrea	S	?	0:00	[kthreadd]
Output from the	1	0	3	2	-100	-	0	0	migrat	S	?	0:00	[migration/0]
ps axl command	1	0	4	2	20	0	0	0	ksofti	S	?	0:00	[ksoftirqd/0]
	5	0	5	2	-100	-	0	0	watchd	S	?	0:00	[watchdog/0]
	1	0	6	2	-100	-	0	0	migrat	S	?	0:00	[migration/1]
	1	0	7	2	20	0	0	0	ksofti	S	?	0:01	[ksoftirqd/1]
	5	0	8	2	-100	-	0	0	watchd	S	?	0:00	[watchdog/1]
	1	0	9	2	-100	-	0	0	migrat	S	?	0:00	[migration/2]
	1	0	10	2	20	0	0	0	ksofti	S	?	0:05	[ksoftirqd/2]
	5	0	11	2	-100	-	0	0	watchd	S	?	0:00	[watchdog/2]
	1	0	12	2	-100	-	0	0	migrat	S	?	0:00	[migration/3]
	1	0	13	2	20	0	0	0	ksofti	S	?	0:01	[ksoftirqd/3]
	5	0	14	2	-100	-	0	0	watchd	S	?	0:00	[watchdog/3]
	1	0	15	2	20	0	0	0	worker	S	?	0:01	[events/0]
	5	0	16	2	20	0	0	0	worker	S	?	0:25	[events/1]
	1	0	17	2	20	0	0	0	worker	S	?	0:12	[events/2]
	1	0	18	2	20	0	0	0	worker	S	?	0:04	[events/3]
	1	0	19	2	20	0	0	0	worker	S	?	0:00	[cpuset]
	1	0	20	2	20	0	0	0	worker	S	?	0:00	[khelper]

Contrast that with the context of the actual daemon. The object role works with the actual daemon; you can review it with other daemons in the /usr/sbin directory. The vsftpd daemon works with the associated configuration file with the ftpd_t type. In contrast, the vsftpd daemon alone is executable with the ftpd_exec_t type.

```
-rwxr-xr-x. root root system_u:object_r:ftpd_exec_t:s0 /usr/sbin/vsftpd
```

The role of different daemons and their corresponding processes should match and contrast in a similar fashion. If they don't, the daemon should not work, and the problem should be documented in the SELinux audit log described in Chapter 4 in the /var/log/audit directory.

View Loads with the top Task Browser

The **top** command sorts active processes first by their CPU load and RAM memory usage. Take a look at Figure 9-7. It provides an overview of the current system status, starting with the current up time, number of connected users, active and sleeping tasks, CPU load, and more. The output is in effect a task browser.

The default sort field is CPU load. In other words, the process that's taking the most in CPU resources is listed first. You can change the sort field with the help of the left and right directional (<, >) keys. Most of the columns are the same as shown in Figure 9-6, as detailed in Table 9-1. The additional columns are described in Table 9-2.

FIGURE 9-7

Output from the top command

```
top - 20:10:14 up 4 days, 20:25,  7 users,  load average: 0.05, 0.04, 0.05
Tasks: 256 total,   1 running, 255 sleeping,   0 stopped,   0 zombie
Cpu(s):  3.2%us,  2.8%sy,  0.0%ni, 94.1%id,  0.0%wa,  0.0%hi,  0.0%si,  0.0%st
Mem:   7985904k total,  6257164k used,  1728740k free,   205204k buffers
Swap:  9775512k total,    25400k used,  9750112k free,  2429716k cached

  PID USER      PR  NI  VIRT  RES  SHR S %CPU %MEM    TIME+  COMMAND
 1231 qemu      20   0 1137m 633m 3048 S  6.6  8.1 117:24.28 qemu-kvm
 2619 root      20   0  230m  64m  28m S  4.0  0.8 156:45.17 Xorg
 2971 michael   20   0 1405m 544m  29m S  3.3  7.0 417:44.30 firefox
18809 michael   20   0 1256m  81m  16m S  2.3  1.0 126:40.65 python
 2874 michael   20   0  334m  15m  10m S  2.0  0.2   5:36.19 wnck-applet
 1063 root      20   0  592m  16m 4516 S  1.3  0.2  18:33.44 libvirtd
 3077 michael   20   0 1834m 106m  24m S  1.0  1.4 439:11.63 plugin-containe
 2932 michael   20   0 4784m 775m  51m S  0.7  9.9  31:14.37 swriter.bin
 6137 michael   20   0 15072 1308  900 R  0.7  0.0   0:13.75 top
 2827 michael   20   0  575m  18m 9508 S  0.3  0.2   1:00.75 gnome-settings-
 2844 michael   20   0  433m  19m  10m S  0.3  0.3   2:24.75 metacity
 2893 michael   20   0  289m  15m 9628 S  0.3  0.2   0:37.65 gnome-terminal
 2957 michael   20   0  256m  11m 5580 S  0.3  0.1   0:33.13 gnome-screensav
10870 michael   20   0  244m 9544 7516 S  0.3  0.1   0:00.06 screenshot
    1 root      20   0 19244 1276 1056 S  0.0  0.0   0:05.30 init
    2 root      20   0     0    0    0 S  0.0  0.0   0:00.04 kthreadd
    3 root      RT   0     0    0    0 S  0.0  0.0   0:00.24 migration/0
```

TABLE 9-2	Column Title	Description
Additional Columns of Output from top	PR	The priority of the task; for more information, see the **nice** and **renice** commands
	NI	The nice value of the task, an adjustment to the priority
	VIRT	The virtual memory used by the task
	RES	Physical memory in use by the process, not including swap space, in KB (similar to RSS in the output to the **ps aux** command)
	SHR	Shared memory used by a task, which can be reallocated
	S	Process status (same to STAT in the output to the **ps aux** command)

One problem with the **top** and **ps** commands is that they display the status of processes on a system as a snapshot in time. That may not be enough. Processes may load a system for just a blip of time, or even periodic blips in time. One way to find more information about the overall load on a system is with two commands from the sysstat package: **sar** and **iostat**. That system activity information is logged courtesy of the **sa1** and **sa2** commands associated with the /etc/cron.d/sysstat script, which will be described shortly.

System Activity Reports with the sar Command

The **sar** command, in essence, can be used to provide a system activity report. For example, Figure 9-8 shows the output of the **sar -A** command. As you can see, the output shows various CPU measures at different points in time. The default settings measure CPU load at ten-minute intervals. There are four CPU cores on this system, which are measured individually and as a whole. The large idle numbers shown in the figure are a good sign that the CPU is not being overloaded; however, the figure shows the load for less than an hour.

The ten-minute intervals associated with the **sar** command output are driven by a regular job in the /etc/cron.d directory. The output from those reports are collected in log files in the /var/log/sa directory. The filenames are associated with the numeric day of the month; for example, system activity report status for the fifteenth of the month can be found in the sa15 file in the noted directory. However, such reports are normally stored at least for the last seven days, based on the following default in the /etc/sysconfig/sysstat file:

```
HISTORY=7
```

FIGURE 9-8 Output from the sar -A command

```
Linux 2.6.32-71.el6.x86_64 (Maui)      01/24/2011     _x86_64_      (4 CPU)

12:00:01 AM    CPU    %usr   %nice    %sys  %iowait  %steal    %irq   %soft  %guest   %idle
12:10:01 AM    all    5.09    0.00    2.57    0.18    0.00    0.01    0.01    0.02   92.13
12:10:01 AM      0    4.69    0.00    4.15    0.07    0.00    0.02    0.01    0.04   91.01
12:10:01 AM      1    6.86    0.00    1.40    0.03    0.00    0.02    0.01    0.01   91.67
12:10:01 AM      2    4.00    0.00    3.44    0.55    0.00    0.00    0.01    0.02   91.97
12:10:01 AM      3    4.79    0.00    1.28    0.06    0.00    0.00    0.01    0.00   93.85
12:20:01 AM    all    5.41    0.00    2.74    0.24    0.00    0.02    0.01    0.02   91.56
12:20:01 AM      0    4.39    0.00    4.29    0.10    0.00    0.01    0.01    0.02   91.17
12:20:01 AM      1    7.98    0.00    1.54    0.03    0.00    0.04    0.01    0.00   90.40
12:20:01 AM      2    3.60    0.00    3.81    0.70    0.00    0.01    0.02    0.04   91.83
12:20:01 AM      3    5.69    0.00    1.33    0.11    0.00    0.00    0.01    0.00   92.85
12:30:01 AM    all    6.20    0.00    2.61    0.19    0.00    0.02    0.02    0.02   90.94
12:30:01 AM      0    5.31    0.00    4.53    0.05    0.00    0.03    0.02    0.03   90.03
12:30:01 AM      1    7.84    0.00    1.52    0.02    0.00    0.05    0.02    0.01   90.54
12:30:01 AM      2    4.36    0.00    3.21    0.63    0.00    0.00    0.03    0.03   91.75
12:30:01 AM      3    7.29    0.00    1.21    0.06    0.00    0.00    0.01    0.00   91.43
12:40:01 AM    all    4.80    0.00    2.38    0.22    0.00    0.02    0.01    0.02   92.56
12:40:01 AM      0    4.45    0.00    3.92    0.07    0.00    0.02    0.01    0.03   91.49
12:40:01 AM      1    6.31    0.00    1.27    0.01    0.00    0.07    0.01    0.01   92.32
12:40:01 AM      2    3.39    0.00    3.28    0.67    0.00    0.00    0.02    0.02   92.61
12:40:01 AM      3    5.03    0.00    1.06    0.11    0.00    0.00    0.00    0.00   93.79
--More--
```

CPU and Storage Device Statistics with iostat

In contrast to **sar**, the **iostat** command reports more general input/output statistics for the system, not only for the CPU, but also for connected storage devices, such as local drives and mounted shared NFS directories. An example shown in Figure 9-9 displays information for the CPU and the storage devices on the server1.example. com system.

Variations on sar with sa1 and sa2

The **sa1** and **sa2** commands are often used to collect system activity report data. In the /etc/cron.d/sysstat script, the **sa1** command is used to gather disk activity data every ten minutes. In that same script, the **sa2** command collects all **sar** data in a daily report. As noted in the script, that report is processed every day, at seven minutes before midnight.

nice and renice

The **nice** and **renice** commands can be used to manage the priority of different processes. While the **nice** command is used to start a process with a different priority, the **renice** command is used to change the priority of a currently running process.

FIGURE 9-9

CPU and storage
device statistics

```
[root@server1 ~]# iostat
Linux 2.6.32-71.el6.x86_64 (server1.example.com)          01/26/2011      _x86_64_
(2 CPU)

avg-cpu:  %user   %nice %system %iowait  %steal   %idle
           0.05    0.00    0.03    0.03    0.00   99.88

Device:            tps    Blk_read/s    Blk_wrtn/s    Blk_read    Blk_wrtn
sda               0.00          0.01          0.00        2368           0
sdb               0.00          0.01          0.00        2144           0
scd0              0.00          0.03          0.00        7392           0
vda               0.21          2.70          1.97      765626      556858
dm-0              0.00          0.00          0.00         256           0

[root@server1 ~]#
```

Process priorities in Linux specify numbers that seem counterintuitive. The range of available nice numbers can vary from -20 to 19. A process given a priority of -20 takes precedence over all other processes. In contrast, a process given a priority of 19 will wait until the system is almost completely free before taking any resources. The default nice number of a process is 0.

The **nice** command prefaces other commands. For example, if you have an intensive script to be run at night, you might choose to start it with a command like the following:

```
$ nice -n 19 ./intensivescript
```

This command starts the noted script with the lowest possible priority. If started at night (or at some other time when a system is not loaded by other programs), the script is run until just about any other jobs, such as a script in one of the /etc/cron.* directories, is scheduled for execution. As such scripts are run on a schedule, they normally should take priority over some user-configured programs.

Sometimes a program is just taking up too many resources. If you need to make sure that program continues to run, one step before killing the associated process is to lower its priority with the **renice** command. Normally, the easiest way to identify a process that's taking up too many resources is by its PID in the output to the **top** command. That PID number is in the left-hand column of the output. For example, if you identify a process that's monopolizing current CPU and memory resources, copy the PID number of that process. If that number were 1234, the following command would change the nice number of that process to -10, which gives that process a higher priority than the default of 0.

```
# renice -10 1234
```

Even though the output refers to the "priority," it really is just listing the old and new "nice" numbers for the process:

```
1234: old priority 0, new priority, -10
```

The new nice number is shown in the output to the **top** command, under the NI column.

Process Killing Commands

Sometimes, it's not enough to reprioritize a process. Some processes can just overwhelm a system. With some other operating systems, such situations require a reboot. Linux is different. In most cases, you can stop such difficult processes with the **kill** and **killall** commands. In many cases, you can kill a process directly from the **top** task browser.

If there's a situation where a process is taking up a lot of memory or CPU, it's probably slowing down everything else running on that system. As shown in Figure 9-10, Firefox has loaded the CPU of the noted system pretty heavily. If it were slowing down my system, I'd press **k** from the top task browser.

FIGURE 9-10

The top task browser with heavy Firefox load

```
top - 09:45:25 up 5 days, 10:00,  7 users,  load average: 0.05, 0.14, 0.10
Tasks: 262 total,   2 running, 260 sleeping,   0 stopped,   0 zombie
Cpu(s): 13.1%us,   3.4%sy,  0.0%ni, 83.5%id,  0.0%wa,  0.0%hi,  0.0%si,  0.0%st
Mem:   7985904k total,  6257932k used,  1727972k free,   134668k buffers
Swap:  9775512k total,    26272k used,  9749240k free,  2319512k cached
PID to kill: 2971
  PID USER      PR  NI  VIRT  RES  SHR S %CPU %MEM    TIME+  COMMAND
 2971 michael   20   0 1426m 584m  29m S 40.2  7.5 484:48.60 firefox
 2619 root      20   0  242m  65m  29m S  8.3  0.8 174:59.88 Xorg
 2932 michael   20   0 4787m 773m  45m S  6.0  9.9  36:40.56 swriter.bin
 1231 qemu      20   0 1127m 635m 3024 S  5.0  8.2 172:23.96 qemu-kvm
 3077 michael   20   0 1847m 119m  24m S  1.7  1.5 458:21.41 plugin-containe
18809 michael   20   0 1263m  78m  15m S  1.7  1.0 145:13.97 python
 2844 michael   20   0  435m  21m  10m S  1.0  0.3   2:44.51 metacity
 1063 root      20   0  592m  16m 4504 S  0.7  0.2  27:23.08 libvirtd
17881 michael   20   0  266m 157m  21m S  0.7  2.0  33:26.73 acroread
19436 michael   20   0 15072 1316  900 S  0.7  0.0   2:56.68 top
 2874 michael   20   0  334m  15m 9996 S  0.3  0.2   5:57.49 wnck-applet
 4039 michael   20   0  649m 117m  17m S  0.3  1.5   0:16.04 opera
    1 root      20   0 19244 1272 1052 S  0.0  0.0   0:05.94 init
    2 root      20   0     0    0    0 S  0.0  0.0   0:00.04 kthreadd
    3 root      RT   0     0    0    0 S  0.0  0.0   0:00.25 migration/0
    4 root      20   0     0    0    0 S  0.0  0.0   0:01.04 ksoftirqd/0
    5 root      RT   0     0    0    0 S  0.0  0.0   0:00.00 watchdog/0
```

As shown in the figure, the **k** command reveals the PID To Kill: prompt, where I enter the PID of the Firefox process, 2971. It applies the **kill** command to the process with that PID number.

Of course, you could apply the **kill** command directly to a PID number. For example, the following command is equivalent to the steps just described in the **top** task browser:

```
# kill 2971
```

The **kill** command can be run by the owner of a process from his account. Thus, user michael could run the **kill 2971** command from his regular account, as he has administrative privileges over processes associated with his username.

The **kill** command can send a wide variety of signals to different processes. For a full list, run the **kill -l** command. Before the advent of scripts in the /etc/init.d directory, the **kill -1** command was used to send a restart signal to service daemons. For example, if the PID number of the process associated with the vsFTP server is 2059, the following command is functionally equivalent to the **/etc/init.d/vsftpd restart** command:

```
# kill -1 2059
```

Without the **-1** switch (and that's a dash number 1), the **kill** command, under normal circumstances, would stop the given process. In this case, it would stop the vsFTP server. But sometimes, processes get stuck in loops. In some such cases, the **kill** command does not work by itself. The process continues running. In that case, you can try two things.

First, you could try the **kill -9** command, which attempts to stop a process "uncleanly." If it is successful, other related processes may still remain in operation.

Sometimes there are a number of processes running under the same name. For example, as you'll see in Chapter 14, the Apache web server starts several processes that run simultaneously. It's at best inefficient to kill just one process; the following command would kill all currently running server processes, assuming no other issues:

```
# killall httpd
```

Archives and Compression

Linux includes a variety of commands to archive groups of files. Some archives can be reprocessed into packages such as RPMs. Other archives are just used as backups. In either case, archives can be a terrific convenience, especially when compressed. To that end, this section explores those archive and compression commands specifically cited in the RHCSA objectives. These "essential tools" include the **gzip**, **bzip2**, **tar**, and **star** commands.

gzip and bzip2

The **gzip** and **bzip2** commands are functionally similar, as they compress and decompress files, using different algorithms. The **gzip** command uses the Lempel-Ziv algorithm, found in some Microsoft compression algorithms. The **bzip2** command uses the Burrows-Wheeler block sorting algorithm. While they both work well, the **bzip2** command makes a big file a bit smaller. For example, either of the two following commands could be used to compress a big picture file named big.jpg:

```
# gzip big.jpg
# bzip2 big.jpg
```

It adds a .gz or a .bz2 suffix to the file, compressed to the associated algorithms. With the **-d** switch, you can use the same commands to reverse the process:

```
# gzip -d big.jpg.gz
# bzip2 -d big.jpg.bz2
```

tar

The **tar** command was originally developed for archiving data to tape drives. However, it's commonly used today for collecting a series of files, especially from a directory. For example, the following command backs up the information from the /home directory in the home.tar.gz file:

```
# tar czvf home.tar.gz /home
```

Like the **ps** command, this is one of the few commands that does not require a dash in front of the switch. This particular command creates (**c**) an archive, compresses (**z**) it, in verbose (**v**) mode, with the filename (**f**) that follows. Alternatively, you can extract (**x**) from that file with the following command:

```
# tar xzvf home.tar.gz /home
```

The compression specified (**z**) is associated with the **gzip** command; if you wanted to use **bzip2** compression, substitute the **j** switch. But there are drawbacks to the **tar** command, as such archives do not store access control list settings or SELinux attributes. But if a tar archive is all that's available, you can use commands like **restorecon**, as described in Chapter 4, to restore the contexts of an archive that have been restored to their original directories.

star

The **star** command is more appropriate for archiving files in a SELinux system. As the **star** command is not normally installed, you'll need to install it; one method is with the following command:

```
# yum install star
```

Unfortunately, the **star** command doesn't quite work in the same fashion as **tar**. If you ever have to use the **star** command, some practice is appropriate. For example, the following command would create an archive, with all SELinux contexts, from the current /home directory:

```
# star -xattr -H=exustar -c -f=home.star /home/
```

The **-xattr** switch saves the extended attributes associated with SELinux. The **-H=exustar** records the headers associated with ACLs. The **-c** creates a new archive file. The **-f** specifies the name of the archive file.

Once the archive is created, it can be unpacked with the following command, which extracts the archive:

```
# star -x -f=home.star
```

If desired, the archive can be compressed with the aforementioned **gzip** or **bzip2** commands. However, with an archive created with the **star** command, such compressed files can't be uncompressed with the **gzip -d** or **bzip2 -d** command. Nevertheless, the **star -x** command can detect and restore files from archives configured with various compression schemes. For example, based on a gzip-compressed archive, the **star** command unpacks that archive, as noted by the following log information message:

```
star: WARNING: Archive is 'gzip' compressed, trying to use the -z option.
```

Control Services Through Daemons

A *daemon* is a process that runs in the background. It is resident in system RAM and watches for signals before it goes into action. For example, a network daemon such as httpd, the Linux web server known as Apache, waits for a request from a browser before it actually serves a web page.

Many Linux daemons are designed to work on a network. Unfortunately, networks don't always work. Sometimes you need to restart a network daemon to implement a configuration change. As discussed in Chapter 5, RHEL makes it easy to control network service daemons through the scripts in the /etc/rc.d/init.d directory. This directory includes scripts that can control installed Linux network services (and more) for everything from the Network File System (NFS) to sendmail. The actual daemon itself is usually located in the /sbin or /usr/sbin directory.

CERTIFICATION OBJECTIVE 9.03

Automate System Administration: cron and at

The cron system is essentially a smart alarm clock. When the alarm sounds, Linux runs the commands of your choice automatically. You can set the alarm clock to run at all sorts of regular time intervals. Many cron jobs are scheduled to run during the middle of the night, when user activity is lower. Of course, that timing can be adjusted. Alternatively, the at system allows users to run the commands of their choice, once, at a specified time in the future.

RHEL installs the cron daemon by default. There have been significant changes in cron since RHEL 5, as the cron daemon now incorporates the anacron system. The cron daemon starts jobs on a regular schedule. The anacron system helps the cron daemon work on systems that are powered off at night. This helps enterprises that want to save energy.

Because cron always checks for changes, you do not have to restart cron every time a change has been made.

It's configured to check the /var/spool/cron directory for jobs by user. In addition, it incorporates jobs defined in the /etc/anacrontab file, based on the 0anacron script in the /etc/cron.hourly directory. It also checks for scheduled jobs for the computer described in the /etc/crontab file and in the /etc/cron.d directory.

The System crontab and Components

The /etc/crontab file is set up in a specific format. Each line can be blank, a comment (which begins with #), a variable, or a command. Naturally, blank lines and comments are ignored. Through RHEL 5, that file included a schedule of jobs. At this point, the crontab file just includes the format for other related configuration files.

Users run regular commands. Anyone who runs a regular command, whether it be you or a daemon, is limited by various environmental variables. To see the environmental variables for the current user, run the **env** command. If that user is your account, some of the standard variables in RHEL include **HOME**, which should match your home directory, **SHELL**, which should match the default shell, and **LOGNAME** as the username.

Other variables can be set in the /etc/crontab and related files such as /etc/anacrontab and /etc/cron.d/0hourly in the following format:

```
Variable=Value
```

Some variables are already set for you. For example, **MAIL** for me is /var/spool/mail/michael, **LANG** is en_US.UTF-8, and **PATH** is where the shell looks for commands. You can set these variables to different values in various cron configuration files. For example, the default /etc/crontab file includes the following variables:

```
SHELL=/bin/bash
PATH=/sbin:/bin:/usr/sbin:/usr/bin
MAILTO=root
HOME=/
```

Note that the values of **PATH**, **MAILTO**, and **HOME** are different from standard environment variables. The **PATH** variable in a cron configuration file may be different from the **PATH** variable associated with a shell. In fact, the two variables are independent. Therefore, you'll want to know the exact path of every command in each cron configuration file. Specify the absolute path with the command if it isn't in the crontab **PATH**.

on the job

*The **MAILTO** variable can help you administer several Linux systems. The cron daemon sends output by e-mail. Just add a line such as MAILTO=me@example.net to route all cron messages associated with that file to that e-mail address.*

The format of a line in /etc/crontab is now detailed in comments, as shown in Figure 9-11. Each of these columns is explained in more detail in Table 9-3.

If you see an asterisk in any column, the **cron** daemon runs that command for all possible values of that column. For example, an * in the minute field means that the command is run every minute during the specified hour(s). Consider another example, as shown here:

```
1  5  3  4  *  ls
```

FIGURE 9-11

The format of a
crontab

```
SHELL=/bin/bash
PATH=/sbin:/bin:/usr/sbin:/usr/bin
MAILTO=root
HOME=/
█
# For details see man 4 crontabs

# Example of job definition:
# .---------------- minute (0 - 59)
# |  .------------- hour (0 - 23)
# |  |  .---------- day of month (1 - 31)
# |  |  |  .------- month (1 - 12) OR jan,feb,mar,apr ...
# |  |  |  |  .---- day of week (0 - 6) (Sunday=0 or 7) OR sun,mon,tue,wed,thu,f
ri,sat
# |  |  |  |  |
# *  *  *  *  *  command to be executed

"/etc/crontab" 16L, 448C
```

This line runs the **ls** command every April 3 at 5:01 A.M. The asterisk in the day
of week column simply means that it does not matter what day of the week it is;
crontab still runs the **ls** command at the specified time.

The entries associated with the cron daemon are flexible. For example,
a 7–10 entry in the hour field would run the specified command at 7:00 A.M.,
8:00 A.M., 9:00 A.M., and 10:00 A.M. A list of entries in the minute field such as
0,5,10,15,20,25,30,35,40,45,50,55 would run the specified command every five
minutes. But that's a lot of numbers. The */5 in the minute field would lead to
the same result. The **cron** daemon also recognizes abbreviations for months and
the day of the week.

TABLE 9-3

Columns in a cron
Configuration File

Field	Value
minute	0–59
hour	Based on a 24-hour clock; for example, 23 = 11 P.M.
day of month	1–31
month	1–12, or jan, feb, mar, etc.
day of week	0–7; where 0 and 7 are both Sunday; or sun, mon, tue, etc.
command	The command to be executed, sometimes listed with the username to run the command

The actual command is the sixth field. You can set up new lines with a percent (%) symbol. This is useful for formatting standard input. The example of a cron file follows formats input for an e-mail message:

```
# crontab -l
# Sample crontab file
#
# Force /bin/sh to be my shell for all of my scripts.
SHELL=/bin/bash
# Run 15 minutes past Midnight every Saturday
15 0 * * sat   $HOME/scripts/scary.script
# Do routine cleanup on the first of every Month at 4:30 AM
30 4 1 * *     /usr/scripts/removecores >> /tmp/core.tmp 2>>&1
# Mail a message at 10:45 AM every Friday
45 10 * * fri  mail -s "Project Update employees%Can I have a status
update on your project?%%Your Boss.%
# Every other hour check for alert messages
0 */2 * * * /usr/scripts/check.alerts
```

Hourly cron Jobs

Now it's time for some sample cron files. The files and scripts discussed are limited to those seen on the server1.example.com system. A number of different packages add their own cron jobs. Certain jobs associated with the cron daemon are run every hour, based on the 0hourly script in the /etc/cron.d directory. It includes the same variables as the /etc/crontab file just described. For hourly jobs, it includes one line:

```
01 * * * * root run-parts /etc/cron.hourly
```

Given the information provided in the preceding section, you should be able to read this line. The **run-parts** command executes each script in the directory that follows; the scripts in that directory are executed as the root user. Of course, the first five columns specify the time; the scripts are run at one minute past the hour, every hour, every day, every month, on each day of the week.

The script of interest in the /etc/cron.hourly directory is 0anacron. That script reviews the contents of the /var/spool/anacron/cron.daily file, to see if the **anacron** command has been run in the past day. If not, and if the system is running on AC power, the **/usr/sbin/anacron -s** command is executed, which runs scripts defined in the /etc/anacrontab configuration file.

The system status script described earlier is stored in the /etc/cron.d/sysstat file. There are two active commands in that file. The first command, **sa1**, is run every ten minutes, as depicted by the */10. That command is run every hour, every day, etc.

```
*/10 * * * * root /usr/lib64/sa/sa1 -S DISK 1 1
```

The second command, sa2, is run at 53 minutes after the hour, on the 23rd hour of each day. In other words, the system activity report is not collected until 11:53 P.M. at night.

```
53 23 * * * root /usr/lib64/sa/sa2 -A
```

Regular Anacron Jobs

The 0anacron script in the /etc/cron.hourly directory described earlier executes the **anacron** command after a system has been powered up. That command executes three scripts defined in the /etc/anacrontab file. It includes three environment variables that should seem familiar:

```
SHELL=/bin/sh
PATH=/sbin:/bin:/usr/sbin:/usr/bin
MAILTO=root
```

The SHELL directive may appear a bit different, but the **ls -l /bin/sh** command should confirm a soft link to the /bin/bash command, which starts the default bash shell. The following directive means that scripts are run at a random time of up to 45 minutes after the scheduled time:

```
RANDOM_DELAY=45
```

With the following directive, anacron jobs are run only between the hours of 3 A.M. and 10:59 P.M.

```
START_HOURS_RANGE=3-22
```

While the format of /etc/anacrontab is similar to those listed in a script for a regular cron job, there are differences. The order of data in each line is specified by the following comment:

```
#period in days   delay in minutes   job-identifier   command
```

The period in days is 1, 7, or @monthly, since the number of days in a month varies. The delay in minutes is associated with the **RANDOM_DELAY** directive. Since the /etc/anacrontab file is executed through the /etc/cron.d/0hourly script, the clock starts one minute after the hour, after the system has been started. The delay in minutes comes before the **RANDOM_DELAY** directive.

In other words, based on the following line, the scripts in the /etc/cron.daily directory may be run anywhere from 5 to 50 minutes after the **anacron** command is run, or 6 to 51 minutes after the hour.

```
1  5  cron.daily     nice run-parts /etc/cron.daily
```

For more examples, review some of the scripts in the /etc/cron.daily directory. Three key scripts include *logrotate*, for rotating log files; *mlocate.cron*, which updates the *locate* file database; and *tmpwatch*, which wipes files from /tmp and /var/tmp after a specific amount of time.

The only SELinux settings associated with cron support automated relabeling and enable access for the fcron scheduler, associated with the cron_can_ relabel and fcron_crond booleans.

Setting Up cron for Users

Each user can use the **crontab** command to create and manage **cron** jobs for their own accounts. There are four switches associated with the **crontab** command:

- ■ **-u** *user*   Allows the root user to edit the crontab of another specific user.
- ■ **-l**   Lists the current entries in the crontab file.
- ■ **-r**   Removes **cron** entries.
- ■ **-e**   Edits an existing **crontab** entry. By default, **crontab** uses vi.

To set up **cron** entries on your own account, start with the **crontab -e** command. Normally, it opens a file in the vi editor, where you can add appropriate variables and commands, similar to what you've seen in other cron job files.

Once the cron job is saved, you can confirm the job with either the **crontab -l** command, or by reading the contents of a file in the /var/spool/cron directory associated with a username. All current cron jobs for a user can be removed with the **crontab -r** command.

EXERCISE 9-1

Create a cron Job

In this exercise, you will modify the basic Red Hat **cron** job settings to read a text file at 1:05 P.M. every Monday in the month of January. To do so, you'll need to create a directory for yearly **cron** jobs. To do this, use the following steps:

1. Log in as a regular user.
2. Create a /etc/cron.yearly directory. Add a file called taxrem, which reads a text file from your home directory. A command such as the following in the taxrem file should suffice:

```
cat ~/reminder
```

Make sure to add appropriate lines to the reminder file in your home directory, such as "Don't forget to do your taxes!" Make sure the taxrem file is executable with the **chmod +x /etc/cron.yearly/taxrem** command.

3. Open up the crontab for your account with the **crontab -e** command.
4. Add an appropriate command to the crontab. Based on the conditions described, it would read as follows:

```
5 13 * 1 1 root run-parts /etc/cron.yearly
```

5. Don't forget directives such as **SHELL=/bin/bash** at the start of the script.
6. Save and exit. Confirm the existence of the user cron file in the /var/spool/cron directory. That file should have the same name as the user.

Running a Job with the at System

Like **cron**, the **at** daemon supports job processing. However, you can set an **at** job to be run once. Jobs in the **cron** system must be set to run on a regular basis. The **at** daemon works in a way similar to the print process; jobs are spooled in the /var/spool/at directory and run at the specified time.

You can use the **at** daemon to run the command or script of your choice. For the purpose of this section, assume that user michael has created a script named 797 in his home directory to process some airplane sales database to another file in the same directory called sales.

From the command line, you can run the **at *time*** command to start a job to be run at a specified *time*. That *time* can be now; in a specified number of minutes, hours, or days; or at the time of your choice. Several examples are illustrated in Table 9-4.

You can use one of the example commands shown in Table 9-4 to open an **at** job. It opens a different command line interface, where you can specify the command of your choice. For this example, assume you're about to leave work and want to start the job in an hour. From the conditions specified, run the following commands:

```
$ at now + 1 hour
at> /home/michael/797 > /home/michael/sales
at> Ctrl-D
```

The CTRL-D command exits the **at** shell and returns to the original command line interface. The **atq** command, as shown here, checks the status of current **at** jobs. All jobs that are pending are listed in the output to the **atq** command:

```
$ atq
1        2012-12-21 03:00 a michael
```

If there's a problem with the job, you can remove it with the **atrm** command. For example, you can remove the noted job, labeled as job 1, with the following command:

```
$ atrm 1
```

Secure cron and at

You may not want everyone to be able to run a job in the middle of the night. If the system has a security flaw, someone may download important data or worse, and it could be days before the security breach is found.

TABLE 9-4	Time Period	Example	Start Time for jobs
Examples of the at Command	Minutes	at now + 10 minutes	In 10 minutes
	Hours	at now + 2 hours	In 2 hours
	Days	at now + 1 day	In 24 hours
	Weeks	at now + 1 week	In 7 days
	n/a	at teatime	At 4:00 P.M.
	n/a	at 3:00 12/21/12	On December 21, 2012, at 3:00 A.M.

TABLE 9-5		/etc/cron.deny exists	/etc/cron.deny does not exist
Security Effects of cron.allow and cron.deny	/etc/cron.allow exists	Only users listed in /etc/cron.allow can run **crontab -e**; contents of /etc/cron.deny are ignored.	Only users listed in /etc/cron.allow can run **crontab -e**.
	/etc/cron.allow does not exist	All users listed in /etc/cron.deny cannot use **crontab -e**.	Only the root user can run **crontab -e**.

Users can be configured in /etc/cron.allow and /etc/cron.deny files. If neither of these files exist, **cron** usage is restricted to the root administrative user. If the +/etc/cron.allow file exists, only users named in that file are allowed to use **cron**. If there is no /etc/cron.allow file, only users named in /etc/cron.deny can't use **cron**.

These files are formatted as one line per user; if you include the following entries in /etc/cron.deny, and the /etc/cron.allow file does not exist, users elizabeth and nancy aren't allowed to set up their own **cron** scripts:

```
elizabeth
nancy
```

However, if the /etc/cron.allow file does exist, with the same list of users, it takes precedence. In that case, both users elizabeth and nancy are allowed to set up their own cron scripts. The range of possibilities is summarized in Table 9-5.

User security for the at system is almost identical. The corresponding security configuration files are /etc/at.allow and /etc/at.deny. The range of possibilities is summarized in Table 9-6.

If you're paranoid about security, it may be appropriate to include only desired users in the /etc/cron.allow and /etc/at.allow files. Otherwise, a security breach in a service account may allow a cracker to run a cron or at script from the associated account.

TABLE 9-6		/etc/at.deny exists	/etc/at.deny does not exist
Security Effects of at.allow and at.deny	/etc/at.allow exists	Only users listed in /etc/at.allow can run the **at** command; contents of /etc/at.deny are ignored.	Only users listed in /etc/at.allow can run the **at** command.
	/etc/at.allow does not exist	All users listed in /etc/at.deny cannot run the **at** command.	Only the root user can run the **at** command.

Local Log File Analysis

An important part of maintaining a secure system is monitoring those activities that take place on the system. If you know what usually happens, such as understanding when users log in to a system, you can use log files to spot unusual activity. Red Hat Enterprise Linux comes with new system monitoring utilities that can help identify the culprit if there is a problem.

RHEL 6 comes with an enhanced logging daemon known as rsyslog. It includes the functionality of the kernel and system logging services used through RHEL 5. The rsyslogd service logs all process activity. You can use the log files so generated to track activities on a system. The configuration of rsyslog as a log server for multiple systems is an RHCE skill covered in Chapter 17.

The rsyslog daemon is active by default and can be activated by the /etc/init.d/rsyslog script. The way it logs files is based on the configuration defined in the /etc/rsyslog.conf file. If you're familiar with the RHEL 5 syslogd and klogd daemons, the concepts in the rsyslog.conf file should be familiar.

In many cases, services such as SELinux, Apache, and Samba have their own log files, defined within their own configuration files. Details are addressed with the chapters associated with those services.

System Log Configuration File

You can configure what is logged through the /etc/rsyslog.conf configuration file. As shown in Figure 9-12, it includes a set of rules for different facilities (if the corresponding packages are installed): authpriv, cron, kern, mail, news, user, and uucp.

Each facility is associated with several different levels of logging, known as the priority. In ascending order, log priorities are **debug**, **info**, **notice**, **warn**, **err**, **crit**, **alert**, **emerg**. There's also a generic **none** priority that logs no messages of the specific facility; for example, a authpriv.none directive would omit all authentication messages.

For each facility and priority, log information is sent to a specific log file. For example, consider the following line from /etc/syslog.conf:

```
*.info;mail.none;news.none;authpriv.none;cron.none          /var/log/messages
```

FIGURE 9-12

The rsyslog.conf log configuration file

```
#### RULES ####

# Log all kernel messages to the console.
# Logging much else clutters up the screen.
#kern.*                                                  /dev/console

# Log anything (except mail) of level info or higher.
# Don't log private authentication messages!
*.info;mail.none;authpriv.none;cron.none                /var/log/messages

# The authpriv file has restricted access.
authpriv.*                                              /var/log/secure

# Log all the mail messages in one place.
mail.*                                                  -/var/log/maillog


# Log cron stuff
cron.*                                                  /var/log/cron

# Everybody gets emergency messages
*.emerg                                                 *

# Save news errors of level crit and higher in a special file.
uucp,news.crit                                          /var/log/spooler

# Save boot messages also to boot.log
local7.*                                                /var/log/boot.log
```

This line sends log information from all of the given facilities to the /var/log/messages file. This includes:

- All facility messages of info level and higher
- Except for log messages related to the **mail, news, authpriv** (authentication), and **cron** services

You can use the asterisk as a wildcard in /etc/syslog.conf. For example, a line that starts with ***.*** tells the **rsyslogd** daemon to log everything. A line that starts with **auth.*** means you want to log all messages from the **authpriv** service.

By default, **rsyslogd** logs all messages of a given priority or higher. In other words, a **cron.err** line will include all log messages from the **cron** daemon at the **err, crit, alert,** and **emerg** levels.

Most messages from the **rsyslogd** daemon are written to files in the /var/log directory. You should scan these logs on a regular basis and look for patterns that could indicate a security breach. It's also possible to set up cron jobs to look for such patterns.

Log File Management

Logs can easily become very large and difficult to read. By default, the logrotate utility creates a new log file on a weekly basis, using the directives in the /etc/logrotate.conf file, which also pulls in directives from files in the /etc/logrotate.d directory. As shown in Figure 9-13, the directives in the file are straightforward and well explained by the comments.

Specifically, the default settings rotate log files on a weekly basis, storing the past four weeks of logs. New log files are created during the rotation, and older files have the date of rotation as a suffix. Different provisions are given to wtmp and btmp logs, related to authentication.

FIGURE 9-13

Log rotation configured in /etc/logrotate.conf

```
# see "man logrotate" for details
# rotate log files weekly
weekly

# keep 4 weeks worth of backlogs
rotate 4

# create new (empty) log files after rotating old ones
create

# use date as a suffix of the rotated file
dateext

# uncomment this if you want your log files compressed
#compress

# RPM packages drop log rotation information into this directory
include /etc/logrotate.d

# no packages own wtmp and btmp -- we'll rotate them here
/var/log/wtmp {
    monthly
    create 0664 root utmp
        minsize 1M
    rotate 1
}

/var/log/btmp {
    missingok
    monthly
    create 0600 root utmp
    rotate 1
}

# system-specific logs may be also be configured here.
```

A Variety of Log Files

Various log files and their functionality are described in Table 9-7. These files are created based on the previously described configuration of the /etc/rsyslog.conf file. All files shown are in the /var/log directory. If you haven't installed, activated, or used the noted service, the associated log file may not appear. In contrast, you may see log files not shown here based on additional installed services.

TABLE 9-7   Standard Red Hat Log Files

Log Files	Description
anaconda.*	Specifies six log files: anaconda.log for installation messages; anaconda.program.log for storage detection messages; anaconda.storage.log for format messages; anaconda.syslog for the first **dmesg**, anaconda.xlog for the first start of the GUI server; and anaconda.yum.log for package installation
audit/	Includes the audit.log file, which collects messages from the kernel 2.6 audit subsystem
boot.log	Associated with services that start and shut down process
btmp	Lists failed login attempts; readable with the **utmpdump btmp** command
ConsoleKit/	Tracks user logins with consoles and input device hardware
cron	Collects information from scripts run by the **cron** daemon
cups/	Directory of printer access, page, and error logs
dmesg	Includes basic boot messages
gdm/	Directory of messages associated with starting via the GNOME Display Manager; includes login failures
httpd/	Directory of log files associated with the Apache Web server
lastlog	Lists login records; readable with the **lastlog** command
maillog	Collects log messages related to e-mail servers
mcelog	Specifies machine check exception data on 64-bit systems
messages	Includes messages from other services as defined in /etc/syslog.conf
ntpstats/	Directory with NTP server data
pm-*	Specifies two log files related to power management
ppp/	Directory with Point to Point Protocol statistics; usually associated with telephone modems
prelink/	Directory with logs of prelinked libraries and binaries designed to speed the boot process
rpmpkgs	Current list of installed RPM packages
sa/	Directory with system activity reports
samba/	Directory of access and service logs for the Samba server

| TABLE 9-7 | Standard Red Hat Log Files (*continued*) | |

Log Files	Description
scrollkeeper.log	Notes log information related to GNOME documentation
secure	Lists login and access messages
setroubleshoot/	Directory of messages associated with the SELinux troubleshooting tool
spooler	Shows a log file that might include critical messages
squid/	Directory of files related to Squid Proxy Server access, cache, and storage
sssd/	Directory of messages associated with the System Security Services Daemon
tallylog	Supports pam_tally, which locks out a user after excessive login attempts
up2date	Includes access messages to a Red Hat Network update server
wtmp	List of logins, in binary format; can be read with the **utmpdump** command
xferlog	Adds messages associated with file transfers from a local FTP server
Xorg.0.log	Notes setup messages for the X Window System; may include configuration problems
yum.log	Specifies logs packages installed, updated, and erased with **yum**

Service Specific Logs

As suggested earlier, a number of services control their own log files. The log files for the vsFTP server, for example, are configured in the vsftpd.conf file in the /etc/vsftpd directory. As noted from that file, the following directive enables the logging of both uploads and downloads in the /var/log/xferlog file:

```
xferlog_enable=YES
```

The logging of other services may be more complex. For example, separate log files are configured for access and errors in the Apache Web server in the /var/log/httpd directory.

EXERCISE 9-2

Learn the Log Files

In this exercise, you'll inspect the log files on a local system to try to identify different problems.

1. Restart the Linux computer. Log in as the root user. Use the wrong password once.

2. Log in properly with the correct password as the root user.

3. In a console, navigate to the /var/log directory and open the file named secure. Navigate to the "FAILED LOGON" message closest to the end of the file. Close the file.

4. Review other logs in the /var/log directory. Use Table 9-7 for guidance. Look for messages associated with hardware. What log files are they in? Does that make sense?

5. Most, but not all, log files are text files. Try reading the lastlog file in the /var/log directory as a text file. What happens? Try the **lastlog** command. Are you now reading the contents of the /var/log/lastlog file? Can you confirm this from the associated man page?

SCENARIO & SOLUTION

Can't connect to a local VNC server.	Make sure the VNC server is running with the **/etc/init.d/vncserver restart** or **vino-preferences** command.
Can't connect to a remote VNC server.	Make sure you're connecting to the right port; for example, a connection to 192.168.100.1:1 requires open ports 5900 and 5901. Review open ports with appropriate **nmap** and **telnet** commands.
Regular users can't access the crontab command or the at prompt.	Review the cron.allow and cron.deny files in the /etc directory. If all regular users are allowed access, make sure the cron.deny file exists but is empty and to delete cron.allow. (Similar guidelines apply for the at prompt.)
Log files don't include sufficient information.	Revise /etc/rsyslog.conf. Focus on the desired facility such as authpriv, mail, or cron, and revise the priority to include more detailed information.

CERTIFICATION SUMMARY

RHEL 6 includes two VNC servers that can help you configure remote connections to a local GUI desktop environment. They require open ports starting with 5900 and up, depending on the number of remote GUI connections that you want to allow. Such communication can be encrypted over an SSH connection. Be aware, the viewer for the KVM graphical console also uses VNC.

A variety of system administration commands can help you as an administrator to monitor and manage the resources used on a system. These commands include **ps**, **top**, **kill**, **nice**, and **renice**. In addition, with the right commands, you can create archives. However, special commands are required to back up files with specialized attributes such as those based on ACLs and SELinux.

The cron and at daemons can help you manage what jobs are run on a system on a schedule. With related configuration files, access to these daemons can be limited to certain users. While cron configuration files follow a specific format documented in /etc/crontab, those configuration directives have been integrated with the anacron system that supports job management on systems that are powered off on a regular basis.

RHEL 6 includes the rsyslog daemon, configured primarily for local systems in the /etc/rsyslog.conf file. Log files are normally collected in the /var/log directory. The rsyslog daemon also supports the creation of a logging server that can collect log file information from a variety of systems.

✓ TWO-MINUTE DRILL

Here are some of the key points from the certification objectives in Chapter 9.

Configure Access with VNC

❑ VNC communication is normally configured over ports 5900 up to 5909; to enable remote access, configured firewalls need to let such traffic through.

❑ On RHEL 6, VNC servers can be configured with the TightVNC server and the vino server.

❑ RHEL 6 also uses VNC to provide a graphical view of KVM-based virtual machines.

❑ Capable VNC client software includes the **vncviewer** command and the Remote Desktop Viewer that you can start with the **vinagre** command.

❑ VNC communication can be encrypted by routing it through a SSH connection.

Elementary System Administration Commands

❑ The **ps** command can identify currently running processes.

❑ The **top** command starts a task browser that can identify processes taking excessive load on a system.

❑ The **sar** and related commands provide system activity reports.

❑ The **iostat** command can provide CPU and storage device statistics.

❑ The **nice** and **renice** commands can be used to reprioritize processes.

❑ The **kill** and **killall** commands can be used to stop currently running processes and even daemons with a variety of signals.

❑ Archives can be created, extracted, and compressed with the **gzip**, **bzip2**, **tar**, and **star** commands.

❑ The **chkconfig** command can help control services at the daemon level.

Automate System Administration: cron and at

❑ The cron system allows users to schedule jobs so they run at given intervals.

❑ The at system allows users to configure jobs to run once at a scheduled time.

❑ The **crontab** command is used to work with cron files. Use **crontab -e** to edit, **crontab -l** to list, or **crontab -r** to delete cron files.

❑ The /etc/cron.allow and /etc/cron.deny files are used to control access to the cron job scheduler; the /etc/at.allow and /etc/at.deny files are used to control access to the at job scheduler in a similar fashion.

Local Log File Analysis

❑ Red Hat Enterprise Linux includes the rsyslog daemon, which monitors a system for kernel messages as well as other process activity, as configured in /etc/rsyslog.conf.

❑ You can use log files generated in the /var/log directory to track activities on a system.

❑ Other log files may be created and configured through service configuration files.

❑ Log files may be rotated on a regular basis, as configured in the /etc/logrotate.conf file.

SELF TEST

The following questions will help measure your understanding of the material presented in this chapter. As no multiple-choice questions appear on the Red Hat exams, no multiple-choice questions appear in this book. These questions exclusively test your understanding of the chapter. It is okay if you have another way of performing a task. Getting results, not memorizing trivia, is what counts on the Red Hat exams.

Configure Access with VNC

1. What two port numbers are associated with the first connection to a VNC server?

   _____

   _____

2. What **vncserver** command would you use to connect to the third VNC server window, where the VNC Server is on IP address 192.168.200.1?

   _____

3. Name a software package associated with the VNC server. Version numbers are not required, just the name of the package that can be used with the **yum** command for installation.

   _____

Elementary System Administration Commands

4. What command identifies all running processes in the current terminal console?

   _____

5. What is the highest priority number that you can set for a process with the **nice** command?

   _____

6. What command can be used to archive the files of an existing directory while saving its SELinux contexts?

   _____

Automate System Administration: cron and at

7. You want to schedule a maintenance job, maintenance.pl, to run from your home directory on the first of every month at 4:00 A.M. You've run the **crontab -e** command to open your personal

job file. Assume you've added appropriate **PATH** and **SHELL** directives. What directive would you add to run the specified job at the specified time?

_____

8. If you see the following entry in the output to the **crontab -l** command,

```
42 4 1 * * root run-parts /etc/cron.monthly
```

when is the next time Linux will run the jobs in the /etc/cron.monthly directory?

_____

9. If the users tim and stephanie are listed in both the /etc/cron.allow and the /etc/cron.deny files, and users donna and elizabeth are listed only in the /etc/cron.allow file, which of those users is allowed to run the **crontab -e** command?

_____

10. What file documents how log files are managed over time?

_____

Local Log File Analysis

11. What entry in the /etc/rsyslog.conf file would notify logged-in users whenever there is a serious problem with the kernel?

_____

12. There are several files in the /var/log directory related to what happened during the installation process. What is the first word shared by the name of these log files?

_____

LAB QUESTIONS

Several of these labs involve exercises that can seriously affect a system. You should do these exercises on test machines only. The second Lab of Chapter 1 sets up KVM for this purpose. However, some readers may not have hardware that supports KVM. Alternatives to KVM include virtual machine solutions such as VMware, available from www.vmware.com, or Virtualbox, open source edition, available from www.virtualbox.org.

Red Hat presents its exams electronically. For that reason, the labs for this chapter are available on the CD that accompanies the book, in the Chapter9/ subdirectory. It's available in .doc, .html, and .txt formats, in the filename starting with 56509-labs. In case you haven't yet set up RHEL 6 on a system, refer to the first lab of Chapter 2 for installation instructions. However, the answers for each lab follows the Self Test answers for the fill-in-the-blank questions.

SELF TEST ANSWERS

Configure Access With VNC

1. The two port numbers associated with the first connection to a VNC server are 5900 and 5901.

2. The appropriate command to connect to the third VNC server window on the given IP address is **vncserver 192.168.200.1:3**.

3. Two software packages that install VNC servers are tigervnc and vino.

Elementary System Administration Commands

4. This is a bit of a trick question, as the **ps** command by itself identifies any currently running processes in the current console.

5. The highest priority number that can be used with the **nice** command is -20. Remember, priority numbers for processes are counter-intuitive.

6. The command that preserves SELinux contexts in an archive is **star**.

Automating System Administration: cron and at

7. The directive that runs the maintenance.pl script from a home directory at the noted time is

```
00 4 1 * * ~/maintenance.pl
```

8. Based on the noted entry in /etc/crontab, the next time Linux will run the jobs in the /etc/cron. monthly directory is on the first of the upcoming month, at 4:42 A.M.

9. When usernames exist in both the /etc/cron.allow and /etc/cron.deny files, users listed in /etc/cron.deny are ignored. Thus, all four users listed are allowed to run various **crontab** commands.

10. The file associated with the management of log files over time is /etc/logrotate.conf.

Local Log File Analysis

11. There's a commented entry in the /etc/rsyslog.conf file that meets the requirements of the question. Just activate it to notify you (and everyone) whenever a serious problem with the kernel occurs:

```
kern.*        /dev/console
```

Of course, that means there are other acceptable ways to meet the requirements of the question.

12. The log files in /var/log that are most relevant to the installation process start with **anaconda**.

LAB ANSWERS

Lab 1

One way to modify the login messages as noted is with the following steps (I can think of at least one other method, related to the /etc/cron.d directory):

1. Log in as the root user.

2. Run the **crontab -e** command.

3. Add appropriate environment variables, at least the following:

```
SHELL=/bin/bash
```

4. Add the following commands to the file to overwrite /etc/motd at the appropriate times:

```
0 7  * * * /bin/echo 'Coffee time!' > /etc/motd
0 13 * * * /bin/echo 'Want some ice cream?' > /etc/motd
0 18 * * * /bin/echo 'Shouldn't you be doing something else?' > /etc/motd
```

5. Save the file. As long as the **cron** daemon is active (which it is by default), the next user who logs into the console after one of the specified times should see the message upon a successful login. If you want to test the result immediately, the **date** command can help. For example, the following command

```
# date 06120659
```

sets a date of June 12, at 6:59 A.M., just before the **cron** daemon should execute the first command in the list. (Of course, you'll want to substitute today's date, and wait one minute before logging in to this system from another console.)

Lab 2

To set up an at job to start 24 hours from now, start with the **at** command. It'll take you to an at> prompt.

Currently installed RPMs are shown in the output to the **rpm -qa** command. Since there is no PATH given at the at> prompt, you should include the full path. So one way to create a list of currently installed RPMs in the /root/rpms.txt file, in a one-time job starting five minutes from now, is with the following commands:

```
# at now + 5 min
at> /bin/rpm -qa > /root/rpms.txt
at> Ctrl+d
#
```

Within five minutes, you should see an rpms.txt file in the home directory of the root user, /root. If five minutes is too long to wait (as it might be during the RHCSA exam), proceed to Lab 3 and come back to this problem afterward. Don't forget to set up the other at job to be run in 24 hours.

Lab 3

Given the hardware discussed so far in this book, successful configuration of a remote VNC server can only be confirmed indirectly. However, if you have a second physical system with RHEL installed, it's not hard to confirm the availability of a VNC server remotely. For example, if the VNC server can be found on the 192.168.122.200 system, on the second terminal, you can connect to that VNC server with the **vncviewer 192.168.122.200:2** command.

Lab 4

There are no secret solutions in this lab; the intent is to get you to review the contents of key log files to see what should be there.

When you review the anaconda.* files in /var/log and compare them to other files, you may gain some insight on how to diagnose installation problems. In future chapters, you'll examine some of the log files associated with specific services; many are located in subdirectories such as /var/log/samba and /var/log/httpd.

The failed login should be readily apparent in the /var/log/secure file. You may be able to get hints in the output to the **utmpdump btmp** command.

When you review the /var/log/cron file, you'll see when standard **cron** jobs were run. Most of the file should be filled (by default) by the standard hourly job, **run-parts /etc/cron.hourly**, from the /etc/crontab configuration file. If you've rebooted, you may see the anacron service, and you should be able to search for the job of the same name.

While /var/log/dmesg includes the currently booted kernel, it may be the same kernel as the one associated with /var/log/anaconda.syslog, if you haven't upgraded kernels. At the end of /var/log/dmesg, you can find the filesystems mounted to the EXT4 format, as well as currently mounted swap partitions. For example, the following lists partitions from a KVM-based virtual drive:

```
EXT4-FS (vda1): mounted filesystem with ordered data mode.
SELinux: initialized (dev vda1, type ext4), uses xattr
```

```
EXT4-FS (vda5): mounted filesystem with ordered data mode.
SELinux: initialized (dev vda5, type ext4), uses xattr
Adding 1023992k swap on /dev/vda3. Priority:-1 extents:1 across:979956k
```

As you've hopefully discovered, the /var/log/maillog file does not include any information on mail clients, but only servers.

Red Hat included a GUI configuration tool in RHEL 5. The automatic configuration for hardware graphics is now sufficiently reliable; there's no longer even a standard xorg.conf configuration file.

10

A Security Primer

A s you start the first chapter of the RHCE section of this book, you'll start with security. Many administrators and enterprises move toward Linux because they believe it's more secure. Since most Linux software is released under open-source licenses, the source code is available to all. Some believe that provides advantages for crackers who want to break into a system.

However, Linux developers are believers in collaboration. "Linus' Law," according to the open-source luminary Eric Raymond is that "given enough eyeballs, all bugs are shallow." Some of those eyes are from the U.S. National Security Agency (NSA), which has contributed a lot of code to Linux, including the foundations of SELinux.

The NSA has also contributed a number of other concepts adapted by Red Hat, which have been integrated into a layered security strategy. It includes system firewalls, wrappers on packets, and security by service. It includes both user- and host-based security. It includes access controls such as ownership, permissions, and SELinux. (A number of these layers were covered in earlier chapters.) The fundamentals of these layers of security, as they apply to RHCE objectives, are also covered here.

RHEL comes with a large and varied assortment of tools for handling security. These include tools for managing the security on individual Linux computers and tools for managing security for an entire network of systems, both Linux and otherwise. In this chapter, you'll examine some of the tools provided by RHEL for managing security. You'll start with some fundamentals, and continue with detailed analysis of firewalls, Pluggable Authentication Modules (PAM), TCP Wrappers, and more.

This is not the only chapter to focus on security. Strictly speaking, it covers only two of the RHCE objectives. However, this chapter covers the themes associated with security on Linux systems. And those themes can help you understand the security options associated with every service in this book.

CERTIFICATION OBJECTIVE 10.01

The Layers of Linux Security

The best computer security comes in layers. If there's a breach in one layer, such as penetration through a firewall, a compromised user account, or a buffer overflow that messes up a service, there's almost always some other security measure that prevents or at least minimizes further damage.

INSIDE THE EXAM

This chapter is the first one in this book focused on RHCE requirements. As described in the RHCE objectives, security starts with firewalls developed with the **iptables** command. The related objective is

■ Use iptables to implement packet filtering and configure Network Address Translation (NAT)

But as suggested in the introduction, security is an issue for all services covered in the RHCE objectives. This chapter provides a foundation for a discussion of security, including several methods to

■ Configure host-based and user-based security for the service

While host-based security can start with **iptables**-based firewalls, host and user-based security measures can involve the Extended Internet Super-Server, TCP Wrappers, and Pluggable Authentication Modules.

These options start with bastion hosts, which minimizes the functionality associated with an individual Linux system. The best defenses come in concert with other Linux developers, when you keep up to speed with the latest security updates. Beyond the firewall and SELinux come security options associated with individual services. Isolation options such as chroot jails are generally configured as part of a service. A number of these options are based on recommendations from the NSA.

While the sections on bastion systems are intended to be a lead-in to the security measures used for RHCE-level services, they also incorporate those security options often associated with the RHCSA exam, which are described in earlier chapters.

Bastion Systems

Properly configured, a bastion system minimizes the risk of a security breach. It's based on a minimal installation, with less software than was installed on the systems configured in Chapters 1 and 2. A bastion system is configured with two services. One service defines the functionality of the system. It could be a web server, a file server, an authentication server, or something similar. The other service supports remote access, such as SSH, or perhaps VNC over SSH.

Before virtualization, the use of bastion system was frequently limited. Only the wealthiest enterprises could afford to dedicate different physical systems to each service. If redundancy was required, the costs only increased further.

With virtualization, bastion systems are within reach of even smaller businesses. All that's needed is a standard minimal installation. With a few Kickstart files, you as an administrator of such a network could easily create a whole group of bastion systems. Each system could then be customized with and dedicated to a single server.

Well-constructed bastion systems follow two principles:

- If you don't need the software, uninstall it.
- If you need the software but aren't using it, make sure it's not active.

In general, crackers can't take advantage of a security flaw if the associated service isn't installed. If you do have to install the service for test purposes, keep that service inactive. That can help keep risks to a minimum. Of course, firewalls configured for each bastion system should allow traffic through only for the dedicated service and the remote access method.

Best Defenses with Security Updates

The best defenses come from security updates. You can review available updates with the Software Update tool. You can start that tool in a GUI with the **gpk-update-viewer** command. As discussed in Chapter 7, you can set up automatic security updates with the Software Updates Preferences tool that you can start in a GUI with the **gpk-prefs** command.

In practice, security is often a race. When a vulnerability is discovered, responsible developers in the open-source community post a public notice of the problem. They get to work on updates. Until that update is available and installed, any affected services might be vulnerable.

As a Linux professional, it's your job to know these vulnerabilities. If you maintain servers like Apache, vsFTP, and Samba, monitor the information feeds from these developers. Security news may come in various forms, from message board updates to RSS feeds. Normally, Red Hat also keeps up to speed on such issues. However, if you've subscribed to the forums maintained by the developers of a service, it's best to hear about problems and planned solutions directly from the source. To some extent, that is a province of service-specific security.

Service-Specific Security

Most major services have some level of security that can be configured within. In many cases, you can configure a service to limit access by host, by network, by user, and by group. As listed in the RHCE objectives, you need to know how to configure host- and user-based security for each listed service, as listed by protocol. SELinux options are also available that can help secure each of these services. While details are discussed in appropriate upcoming chapters, the following is a brief overview of service-specific security options.

HTTP/HTTPS Service-Specific Security

While there are alternatives, the primary service for the HTTP and HTTPS protocol on Linux is the Apache web server. In fact, Apache is the dominant web server on the Internet. No question, Apache configuration files are complex. But they need to be, as the security challenges on the Internet are substantial. Some options for responding to these challenges are covered in Chapter 14.

Apache includes a good number of optional software components. Don't install more than is absolutely necessary. If there's a security breach in a Common Gateway Interface (CGI) script and you haven't installed Apache support for CGI scripts, that security issue doesn't affect you. But as the RHCE specifies an objective to deploy a "basic CGI application," you don't have that luxury.

Fortunately, with Apache, you can limit access in a number of ways. Limits can be created on the server, or on individual virtual hosts. Different limits can be created on regular and secure web sites. In addition, Apache supports the use of secure certificates.

DNS Service-Specific Security

Domain Name Service (DNS) servers are a big target for crackers. With that in mind, RHEL 6 includes the bind-chroot package, which configures the necessary files, devices, and libraries in an isolated subdirectory. That subdirectory provides a limit for any user who breaks through DNS security known as a chroot jail. It's designed to limit the directories where a cracker can navigate if he does break into the service. In other words, crackers who do break into a RHEL 6 DNS server should not be able to "escape" the subdirectory configured as a chroot jail.

Since RHCE exam candidates are not expected to create a master or a slave DNS server, the challenges and risks are somewhat limited. Nevertheless, in Chapter 17, you'll see how to limit access to the configured DNS server by host.

FTP Service-Specific Security

While there are alternatives, the primary FTP server for RHEL 6 is vsFTP. While you created a basic FTP server in Chapter 1 with that service, no additional configuration was required. In Chapter 16, you'll configure the main vsFTP configuration files to limit access by user and by chroot jail. While you can use options like TCP Wrappers and **iptables** to limit access by IP address, such limits are not directly available in the vsFTP configuration files.

NFS Service-Specific Security

With the move to the Network File System, version 4, it is now possible to set up Kerberos authentication to support user-based security. However, the configuration of servers for Kerberos and LDAP is beyond the scope of the RHCE objectives. Thus, the discussion in Chapter 16 is focused on host-based security options.

SMB Service-Specific Security

The SMB listed in the RHCE objectives stands for the Server Message Block protocol. It's the networking protocol originally developed by IBM, later modified by Microsoft as the network protocol for its operating systems. While Microsoft now refers to it as the Common Internet File System (CIFS), the Linux implementation of this networking protocol is still known as Samba.

As implemented for RHEL 6, you can take advantage of Microsoft authentication databases. Samba supports the mapping of such users and groups into a Linux authentication database. Samba also supports both user- and host-based security on a global and a shared directory level, as discussed in Chapter 15.

The standard Samba for RHEL 6 is version 3.5.4. While there's a Samba version 4 package available from the RHEL 6 repositories, it is not yet ready for production use. When it is ready, you'll be able to set up RHEL 6 as an Active Directory Domain Controller.

SMTP Service-Specific Security

RHEL supports two different services for e-mail communication through the Simple Mail Transport Protocol (SMTP): Postfix and sendmail. Both are released under open-source licenses. The sendmail service is listed in lowercase, to distinguish it from the commercial release of Sendmail.

The default SMTP e-mail service for RHEL 6 is Postfix, which is a change—the default for RHEL 5 is sendmail. You can configure either service to meet the associated RHCE objective. In either case, the service normally only listens on the localhost address, which is one level of security. Other levels of security are possible based on hosts, usernames, and more. For more information, see Chapter 13.

SSH Service-Specific Security

The SSH service is installed by default even in the minimal installation of RHEL 6. That encourages its use as a remote administration tool. However, there are risks associated with the SSH server that can be minimized. For example, it's not necessary to send even encrypted passwords over a network. Remote logins to the root account do not have to be allowed. Security can be further regulated by user.

Host-Based Security

Host-based security refers to access limits, not only by the system hostnames, but also by their fully qualified domain names and IP addresses. The syntax associated with host-based security can vary. For example, while every system recognizes a specific IP address such as 192.168.122.50, the use of wildcards or Classless Inter-Domain Routing (CIDR) notation for a range of IP addresses varies by service. Depending on the service, you may use one or more of the following options for the noted range of network addresses:

```
192.168.122.0/255.255.255.0
192.168.122.0/24
192.168.122.*
192.168.122.
192.168.122
```

Just be careful, some of these options may lead to syntax errors on some but not all network services. In a similar fashion, any of the following options may or may not work to represent all of the systems on an example.com network:

```
*.example.com
.example.com
example.com
```

User-Based Security

User-based security includes users and groups. Generally, users and groups who are allowed or denied access to a service are collected in a list. That list could include a user on each line, as in files like /etc/cron.allow, or it could be in a list that follows a directive, such as

```
valid users = michael donna @book
```

Sometimes the syntax of a user list is unforgiving; in some cases, an extra space after a comma or at the end of a line may result in an authentication failure.

Groups are frequently included in a list of users, with a special symbol in front, such as an **@** or an **+**.

Sometimes, users who are allowed access to a system are configured in a separate authentication database, such as that associated with the Samba server, configured with the **smbpasswd** command.

Console Security

As discussed in Chapter 8, console security is regulated in the /etc/securetty and /etc/security/access.conf files. It can help you regulate local console access to root and regular users.

But console access is not just local. For a full view of console security, you need to be able to configure limits on remote console access. Two primary options are SSH, as discussed earlier, and Telnet. While the **telnet** command has its uses, as described in Chapter 2, communications to Telnet servers are inherently insecure. Usernames, passwords, and other communication to and from a Telnet server are transmitted in clear text. That means a network protocol analyzer such as Ethereal could be used to read those usernames, passwords, and any other critical information.

Even though Kerberos-based options are available for Telnet servers, most security professionals avoid Telnet for remote consoles at almost all costs. And that's consistent with the recommendations from the NSA.

Recommendations from the U.S. National Security Agency

The NSA has taken a special interest in Linux, and specifically Red Hat Enterprise Linux. Not only has the NSA taken the time to develop SELinux, but also it has created guides to help administrators like yourself create a more secure RHEL configuration. (Yes, the "super-secret" NSA has released SELinux code under open-source licenses for all to see.) They recognize the importance of Linux in the infrastructure of computer networks. Observers of RHEL may notice how changes between RHEL 5 and RHEL 6 follow NSA recommendations.

The NSA includes five general principles for securing operating systems in general and RHEL in particular.

- ■ **Encrypt Transmitted Data Whenever Possible**   NSA recommendations for encryption include communications over what should be private and secure networks. SSH, with the security options described in Chapter 11, are an excellent step in this process.

- ■ **Minimize Software to Minimize Vulnerability**   As suggested by the NSA, "The simplest way to avoid vulnerabilities in software is to avoid installing that software." The NSA pays special attention to any software that can communicate over a network, including the Linux GUI. The minimal installation of RHEL 6 includes far fewer packages than the comparable installation of RHEL 5.

- ■ **Run Different Network Services on Separate Systems**   This is consistent with the concept of bastion servers described earlier in this chapter. Implementation is made easier by the flexibility afforded by virtual machine technologies such as KVM.

- ■ **Configure Security Tools to Improve System Robustness**   The RHCSA and RHCE objectives have this well covered, with the use of **iptables**-based firewalls, SELinux, and appropriate log collection services.

- ■ **Least Privilege**   In principle, you should give users the minimum privileges required to accomplish their tasks. Not only does that mean minimize access to the root administrative account, but also careful use of the **sudo** command privileges. SELinux options such as the user_u role for confinement described in Chapter 4 may also be helpful to that end.

The PolicyKit

The PolicyKit is one more security mechanism designed to help protect different administrative tools. When starting an administrative tool in the GUI from a regular account, most tools prompt for the root administrative password with a window similar to Figure 10-1.

Alternatively, you might see a slightly different window similar to that shown in Figure 10-2. Functionally, the effect is the same. As described in the window, authentication by the superuser is required. In this case, you'd still have to enter the root administrative password. However, there's a difference, as shown under details. The action specifies the policy required by the "vendor," in this case, the system-config-firewall command.

FIGURE 10-1

Access to
Administrative
Tools in the GUI
requires the root
password.

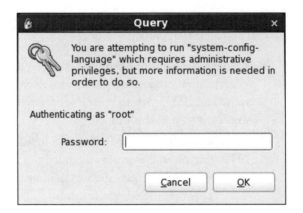

The action noted is "org.fedoraproject.config.firewall.auth," which is associated with a policy file in the /usr/share/polkit-1/actions directory. Policy configuration files are stored in this directory; the corresponding file for the **system-config-firewall** tool is org.fedoraproject.config.firewall.policy.

These policy files are configured in XML format and may be modified further to support fine-grained control by individual users. However, since the PolicyKit only works within the GUI, its fine-grained controls do not affect the use of administrative tools from the console. It certainly does not prevent administrators from configuring or otherwise controlling important services. If fine-grained control is required, the better tool is the /etc/sudoers file described in Chapter 8.

FIGURE 10-2

Access to
Administrative
Tools may be
limited by the
PolicyKit.

Authenticate

**Authentication is required to
read and modify firewall settings**

An application is attempting to perform an action
that requires privileges. Authentication as the super
user is required to perform this action.

Password for root: |

▽ **Details**

Action: org.fedoraproject.config.firewall.auth
Vendor: System Config Firewall

Cancel | Authenticate

CERTIFICATION OBJECTIVE 10.02

Firewalls and Network Address Translation

Typically, firewalls reside between internal LANs and outside insecure networks such as the Internet. A firewall can be configured to examine every network packet that passes into or out of your LAN. When configured with appropriate rules, it can filter out those packets that may pose a security risk to the systems on the LAN.

However, to follow the spirit of the recommendations from the NSA, you'll configure a firewall on every system. While Network Address Translation uses the same **iptables** command, its use is generally still most appropriate for those systems on the gateway or router between a LAN and an outside network.

Definitions

Firewalls based on the **iptables** command work by reading the headers of each packet of network data. Based on the information contained in the headers, **iptables**-based rules can be used to filter each packet. To understand how *packet filtering* works, you have to understand a little bit about how information is sent across networks.

Before a message is sent over a network, that message is broken down into smaller units called *packets*. Administrative information, including the type of data, the source address, and the destination address, is added to the header of each packet. The packets are reassembled when they reach the destination computer. A firewall examines the fields in each header. Based on existing rules, the firewall may then take one of four actions with that packet:

- Allow the packet into the system.
- Forward the packet to other systems if the current system is a gateway or router between networks.
- Reject the packet with a message sent to the originating IP address.
- Drop the packet without sending any sort of message.

Whatever the result, the decision can be logged. If there are a substantial number of packets that are rejected or dropped, a log file may be useful.

RHEL 6 comes with everything you need to configure a system to be a firewall, including the **iptables** and **ip6tables** commands for IPv4 and IPv6 networks.

In contrast, NAT hides the IP address of the computers of a LAN that connect to outside networks. NAT replaces the internal source address with the IP address of the gateway or router system with the firewall. That internal source address is cached on the gateway, so it knows which computer made the request.

When the firewall receives data such as a web page, the process is reversed. As the packets pass through the firewall, the originating computer is identified in the cache. The header of each packet is modified accordingly before the packets are sent on their way.

This approach is useful for several reasons. Hiding that internal IP addresses makes it harder for a cracker to know what IP address to use to break into an internal network. NAT supports connections between systems with private IP addresses and external networks such as the Internet. It's the reason why IPv4 addressing has survived for so long. In the Linux world, this process is known as *IP masquerading*.

The Structure of the iptables Command

The way **iptables** commands are assembled into a firewall is based on "chains." A chain of firewall rules may be applied to each network packet, in order. Each rule in a chain does two things: it specifies the conditions a packet must meet to match the rule, and it specifies the action if the packet matches.

The **iptables** command uses the following basic format:

```
iptables -t tabletype <action direction> <packet pattern> -j
<what to do>
```

Now analyze this command, item by item. The first item is the **-t** *tabletype* switch. There are three basic *tabletype* options of interest for **iptables**:

■ **filter**   Sets a rule for filtering packets.

■ **nat**   Configures Network Address Translation, also known as masquerading, discussed later in this chapter.

■ **mangle**   Changes packet headers.

The default is **filter**; if you don't specify a **-t** *tabletype,* the **iptables** command assumes that you're trying to create a filtering rule.

The next item is the **<*action direction*>**. There are four basic actions associated with **iptables** rules:

■ **-A (--append)**   Appends a rule to the end of a chain.

- **-D (--delete)**   Deletes a rule from a chain. Specify the rule by the number or the packet pattern.
- **-L (--list)**   Lists the currently configured rules in the chain.
- **-F (--flush)**   Flushes all of the rules in the current **iptables** chain.

If you're appending to (**-A**) or deleting from (**-D**) a chain, you'll want to apply it to network data traveling in one of three directions. In most cases for a regular firewall that protects a system from external data, the appropriate direction to apply is **INPUT**:

- **INPUT**   All incoming packets are checked against the rules in this chain.
- **OUTPUT**   All outgoing packets are checked against the rules in this chain.
- **FORWARD**   All packets being sent to another computer are checked against the rules in this chain.

Next, you need to configure a *<packet pattern>*. All **iptables** firewalls check every packet against this pattern. The simplest pattern is by IP address:

- **-s *ip_address***   All packets are checked for a specific source IP address.
- **-d *ip_address***   All packets are checked for a specific destination IP address.

Packet patterns can be more complex. In TCP/IP, most packets are transported using the Transport Control Protocol (TCP), the User Datagram Protocol (UDP), or the Internet Control Message Protocol (ICMP) protocols. You can specify the protocol with the **-p** switch, followed by the destination port (**--dport**). For example, the **-p tcp --dport 80** extension affects users outside your network who are trying to use an HTTP connection.

Once the **iptables** command finds a packet pattern match, it needs to know what to do with that packet, which leads to the last part of the command, **-j *<what to do>***. There are three basic options:

- **DROP**   The packet is dropped. No message is sent to the requesting computer.
- **REJECT**   The packet is dropped. An error message is sent to the requesting computer.
- **ACCEPT**   The packet is allowed to proceed as specified with the **-A** action: **INPUT, OUTPUT,** or **FORWARD**.

Take a look at some examples of how you can use **iptables** commands to configure a firewall. A good first step is to see what is currently configured, with the following command:

```
# iptables -L
```

If **iptables** is properly configured, it should return chain rules in three different categories: **INPUT**, **FORWARD**, and **OUTPUT**.

The following rule rejects all traffic from the 192.168.75.0 subnet, and it sends a "destination unreachable" error message back to any client from that network address who tried to connect:

```
# iptables -A INPUT -s 192.168.75.0/24 -j REJECT
```

This rule stops users from the computer with an IP address of 192.168.25.200 from "pinging" your system, as the **ping** command uses the ICMP protocol:

```
# iptables -A INPUT -s 192.168.25.200 -p icmp -j DROP
```

The following command guards against TCP SYN attacks from outside the local system, associated with packet floods and denial of service attacks. Assume that the IP address of the LAN to be protected is 192.168.1.0. The exclamation point (!) inverts the meaning; in this case, the command applies to all IP addresses except those with a 192.168.1.0 network address (and a 255.255.255.0 subnet mask).

on the job

*SYN is not an acronym, but a type of packet that is sent from a client using TCP. The response is an SYN-ACK packet, which is an acknowledgment. The client then sends an ACK message to the server. The associated **iptables** rule stops potential attacks at the SYN level.*

```
# iptables -A INPUT -s !192.168.1.0/24 -p tcp -j DROP
```

Then, if you want to delete the rule related to the **ping** command in this list, use the following command:

```
# iptables -D INPUT -s 192.168.25.200 -p icmp -j DROP
```

The default rule for **INPUT**, **OUTPUT**, and **FORWARD** is to **ACCEPT** all packets. One way to stop packet forwarding is to add the following rule:

```
# iptables -A FORWARD -j DROP
```

The Default Firewall

Now that you've seen the effect of various firewall rules, it's an appropriate time to look at the default firewall for RHEL 6, based on the VM systems installed in Chapters 1 and 2. While you can use the **iptables -L** command for that purpose, the firewall rules implemented during the boot process are stored in the /etc/sysconfig/iptables file. (For IPv6 networks, the corresponding firewall configuration file is /etc/sysconfig/ip6tables.) The meaning of each of these lines is described in Chapter 4.

Recommendations from the NSA

Simple firewalls are frequently the most secure. On an exam, it's best to keep everything, firewalls included, as simple as possible. But the NSA would go further. It has recommendations with respect to the default rules, limitations on the **ping** command, and blocks from suspicious groups of IP addresses. To those recommendations, I add a couple to reduce risks to a SSH system that may be applicable to other services. While these recommendations go beyond what's suggested by the RHCE objectives, read this section. If you're less than comfortable with the **iptables** command, this section can help.

To implement these changes on multiple systems, it may be most efficient to edit the /etc/sysconfig/iptables file directly. While you could implement these changes with the Custom Rules option in the Firewall Configuration tool, that is less efficient than a script that directly edits the noted file. Unfortunately, the Firewall Configuration tool overwrites any such changes. So if you administer the firewall on multiple systems with scripts, make sure to back up that /etc/sysconfig/iptables file. Nevertheless, the Custom Rules option in the Firewall Configuration tool is an excellent choice if you're just changing the firewall for one or two systems.

Then you can test any of these suggestions on a system like the server1.example.com VM created in Chapter 2. To do so, edit the /etc/sysconfig/iptables file. And then to put such changes into effect, run the following command:

```
# /etc/init.d/iptables restart
```

e x a m

ⓦatch   *The suggested changes to iptables-based firewalls are just recommendations. However, since the requirement to "implement packet filtering" is generic, it's useful to examine a variety of examples.*

Recommended Changes to Default Rules

It recommends changes to default rules that are appropriate on bastion servers such as the VMs configured early in this book. The default is

```
:INPUT ACCEPT [0:0]
:FORWARD ACCEPT [0:0]
```

The NSA recommendation would change this to

```
:INPUT DROP [0:0]
:FORWARD DROP [0:0]
```

While the rules that allow network traffic into the system still apply, these changes provide another limit on traffic into a system, and traffic that may be forwarded to another system.

Just be careful. When I tried these changes on a gateway system, specifically the physical host system for my VMs, it stopped communication by dropping packets between VMs and external networks. I should have limited such changes to the VMs. So test any changes before implementing them on production systems.

Regulate the ping Command

One earlier attack on various Internet systems involved the **ping** command. From Linux, it's possible to flood another system with the **-f** switch. It may transmit thousands of packets per second. It's important to be able to defend a system from such attacks, as they can prevent others from accessing your web sites and more.

on the job

The -f switch to the ping command was described solely to point out one of the major risks on a network. In many cases, it is illegal to run such a command on or against someone else's system. For example, one Wikipedia article suggests that such an attack could be a violation of the Police and Justice Act in the United Kingdom with a penalty of up to ten years in prison. Similar laws exist in other countries.

One potentially troublesome rule in the default firewall is

```
-A INPUT -p icmp -j ACCEPT
```

However, ICMP messages go both ways. If you run the **ping** command on a remote system, the remote system responds with an ICMP packet. So if you want to limit ICMP messages, the following rules allow "acceptable" responses to a **ping**:

```
-A INPUT -p icmp --icmp-type echo-reply -j ACCEPT
-A INPUT -p icmp --icmp-type destination-unreachable -j ACCEPT
-A INPUT -p icmp --icmp-type time-exceeded -j ACCEPT
```

The following rule limits the rate at which a **ping** command can be applied to a system:

```
-A INPUT -p icmp --icmp-type echo-request -m limit --limit 1/s -j ACCEPT
```

While the Firewall Configuration tool discussed later in this chapter can limit the effect of ICMP messages in most of the same ways, it does not have the ability to regulate the rate of **ping** network packets accepted onto a system.

Block Suspicious IP Addresses

Crackers who want to break into a system may hide their source IP address. As nobody is supposed to use a private, multicast, or experimental IPv4 address on the public Internet, such addresses are one way to hide. The following additions to the /etc/sysconfig/iptables file would drop packets sourced from the specified IPv4 network address blocks:

```
-A INPUT -i eth0 -s 10.0.0.0/8 -j DROP
-A INPUT -i eth0 -s 172.16.0.0/12 -j DROP
-A INPUT -i eth0 -s 192.168.0.0/16 -j DROP
-A INPUT -i eth0 -s 224.0.0.0/4 -j DROP
-A INPUT -i eth0 -s 240.0.0.0/5 -j DROP
```

Regulate Access to SSH

Since SSH is such an important means for the administration of remote systems, additional measures to protect such services are important. It's certainly possible to set up a nonstandard port for SSH communication. Such a measure can be a part of a layered security strategy. However, tools like **nmap** can detect the use of SSH on such nonstandard ports. So it's generally better to set up the configuration of the SSH server as discussed in Chapter 11 along with firewall rules such as the following. The first rule shown here creates a new chain, SSH_CHAIN, for all TCP traffic to port 22:

```
-A INPUT -i eth0 -p tcp -m tcp --dport 22 -m state --state NEW -j SSH_CHAIN
```

The next rule starts the SSH_CHAIN, by limiting access requests to three per minute.

```
-A SSH_CHAIN -i eth0 -p tcp -m tcp --dport 22 -m state --state NEW -m recent
--update --seconds 60 --hitcount 3 --rttl --name SSH -j DROP
```

Make Sure the Firewall Is Running

Once desired changes are saved to the /etc/sysconfig/iptables configuration file, it's important to make sure the Firewall is in operation, with the new rules. Since the reload option is not available in the iptables service script, you'll need to do so with the following command:

It's critical to understand how to secure a Red Hat Enterprise Linux system against unauthorized access.

```
# service iptables restart
```

As discussed in Chapter 11, this is functionally equivalent to the **/etc/init.d/iptables restart** command.

IP Masquerading

Red Hat Enterprise Linux supports a variation of NAT called *IP masquerading*. IP masquerading supports Internet access from multiple computers with a single public IP address. IP masquerading maps multiple internal IP addresses to that single valid external IP address. That helps as all public IPv4 address blocks have now been allocated. IPv4 addresses are often still available from these third parties, at a price. That cost is one more reason for IP Masquerading. On the other hand, systems on IPv6 networks may not need masquerading, as it's relatively easy for many requesting users to get their own subnet of public IPv6 addresses. Nevertheless, even on IPv6 networks, masquerading can help keep that system secure.

The RHCE objectives specify the use of iptables to configure network address translation.

IP Masquerading is a fairly straightforward process. It's implemented on a gateway or router, where the system has two or more network cards. One network card is connected to an outside network such as the Internet, and the second (and additional) network card is connected to a LAN. The card connected to the outside network may connect through an external device such as a cable "modem" or Digital Subscriber Line (DSL) adapter. The following assumptions are made for the configuration:

■ The public IP address is assigned to the network card that is directly connected to the outside network.

- Network cards on the LAN get IP addresses associated with a single private network.
- One network card on the gateway or router system gets an IP address on that same private network.
- The same **iptables** command and configuration files used to set up a firewall are also used to set up IP masquerading.
- IP forwarding is enabled on the router or gateway system, as discussed later in this chapter.
- Each system on the LAN is configured with the private IP address of the router or gateway system as the default gateway address.

When a computer on a LAN wants a web page on the Internet, it sends packets to the firewall. The firewall replaces the source IP address on each packet with the firewall's public IP address. It then assigns a new port number to the packet. The firewall caches the original source IP address and port number.

When a packet comes in from the Internet to the firewall, it should include a port number. If the firewall can match an associated rule with the port number assigned to a specific outgoing packet, the process is reversed. The firewall replaces the destination IP address and port number with the internal computer's private IP address and then forwards the packet back to the original client on the LAN.

In practice, the following command uses **iptables** to enable masquerading. The noted command assumes that eth1 represents the network card that is directly connected to the Internet, with a private IP network of 192.168.0.0/24:

```
# iptables -t nat -A POSTROUTING -s 192.168.0.0/24 -o eth1 -j MASQUERADE
```

In most cases, the private IP network address is not required, as most LANs protected by a masquerade are configured on a single private IP network.

If you're using separate private networks, such as for the KVM-based virtual machines configured in Chapters 1 and 2, masquerading of those networks enables communication between those systems. In that configuration, masquerading rules would be applied to the firewall of the physical host system. On my system, I have the following masquerading rules:

```
# iptables -t nat -A POSTROUTING -o wlan0 -j MASQUERADE
# iptables -t nat -A POSTROUTING -o virbr0 -j MASQUERADE
# iptables -t nat -A POSTROUTING -o virbr1 -j MASQUERADE
```

These rules work hand in hand with the IP forwarding rules discussed next. Just be aware, masquerading substitutes the IP address of the router for that of the originating system. So if you set up masquerading on the physical host system for two VMs, communication from one VM appears to be coming from the IP address of the physical host system. If that's not desirable, you may prefer to configure IP forwarding.

IP Forwarding

IP forwarding is more commonly referred to as *routing*. Routing is critical to the operation of the Internet or any IP network. Routers connect and facilitate communication between multiple networks. When you set up a computer to find a site on an outside network, it needs a gateway address. This corresponds to the IP address of a router on the LAN.

A router looks at the destination IP address of each packet. If the IP address is on one of its LANs, it routes the packet directly to the proper computer. Otherwise, it sends the packet to another gateway closer to its final destination. To use a Red Hat Enterprise Linux system as a router, you should enable IP forwarding in the /etc/sysctl.conf configuration file by changing

```
net.ipv4.ip_forward = 0
```

to

```
net.ipv4.ip_forward = 1
```

These settings take effect on the next reboot. Until then, IPv4 forwarding can be enabled with the following command:

```
echo 1 > /proc/sys/net/ipv4/ip_forward
```

But that is not enough. You'll also need to enable routing through the firewall for communications to other networks. For example, with the KVM-based VM systems on two virtual networks, they include two virtual network devices in the output to the **ifconfig** command on the physical host: virbr0 and virbr1. On the system that I'm using to write this book, it also includes the local wireless network device, wlan0. For a physical host with a regular wired Ethernet card, you may need to substitute eth0 for wlan0.

```
# iptables -A FORWARD -o wlan0 -j ACCEPT
# iptables -A FORWARD -o virbr0 -j ACCEPT
# iptables -A FORWARD -o virbr1 -j ACCEPT
```

If you actually need to configure a connection to external networks such as the Internet, a change is also required to the /etc/resolv.conf file on the VMs. Normally, it sets the default DNS server to the IP address of the virbr0 and virbr1 networks on the physical host system. You may need to change that DNS server IP address to that used for other systems on the local network. However, that should not be necessary, as Internet access is not available during the Red Hat exams.

The Red Hat Firewall Configuration Tool

The basic functionality of the Red Hat Firewall Configuration tool was discussed in Chapter 4, with respect to RHCSA objectives. The Firewall Configuration tool can do more. Start it with the **system-config-firewall** command or by clicking System | Administration | Firewall. This is a tool with a number of capabilities, as shown in Figure 10-3. In general, you can immediately implement any changes made with the Apply button. But for that reason, you may want to back up the current version of the /etc/sysconfig/iptables file before doing anything with the Firewall Configuration tool.

FIGURE 10-3

The Firewall Configuration tool

Similar functionality is available from the console version of the tool. You can open it with the **system-config-firewall-tui** command. Select Customize for access to the same options shown in Figure 10-3. The following sections address those options not previously discussed in Chapter 4.

Trusted Interfaces

In the Firewall Configuration tool, click Trusted Interfaces to reveal the window shown in Figure 10-4. Routers and gateways have two or more network cards. Administrators who trust the systems on the internal network may choose to disable the firewall on that interface. However, it can be a risky practice. Threats can come from within as well as from outside a network.

The options shown in Figure 10-4 would apply to all interfaces of each type, as listed in Table 10-1. They all end with a +, which is effectively like a wildcard. For example, eth+ is associated with device eth0, eth1, and so on.

In most cases, the gateway or router system will have two Ethernet devices. Assume those devices are eth0 and eth1, where eth0 is connected to an external network. If the local network is to be trusted, then you might set up device eth1 as the trusted device.

Sometimes wireless devices appear as other names. In some configurations, wireless hardware appear as Ethernet devices such as eth0 or eth1. In other cases, I've seen wireless devices appear as wlan0 or even ath0. So it's important to know the device files associated with each network device on a system.

Click Add to open the Interface window shown in Figure 10-5. Then enter the device name of the interface, in this case, eth1.

TABLE 10-1	Device	Description
Network Interface Types	eth+	Ethernet devices
	ippp+	Integrated Services Digital Network (ISDN) devices for Point to Point Protocol (PPP) communication
	isdn+	Regular ISDN devices
	ppp+	PPP devices, normally associated with telephone modems
	tun+	Tunneling devices, often associated with virtual private networks
	wlan+	Wireless LAN devices

FIGURE 10-4

Trusted Interfaces

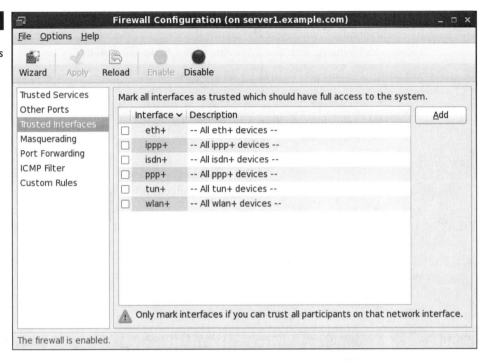

FIGURE 10-5

A user-defined
trusted interface

Once applied, trusted interfaces add rules to the /etc/sysconfig/iptables file. For example, if you select the wlan+ devices, all devices with that name are trusted, as documented with the following directive in the noted file:

```
-A INPUT -i wlan+ -j ACCEPT
```

which accepts all network packets that come into all "wireless" devices. In contrast, the following directive is more specific, based on the user-defined trusted interface from Figure 10-5.

```
-A INPUT -i eth1 -j ACCEPT
```

You should also note these rules appear just after a similar rule for the loopback device, lo. These rules appear before any other rule that allows packets in through certain ports, such as 22 for SSH communication.

Masquerading

In the Firewall Configuration tool, click Masquerading to reveal the window shown in Figure 10-6. Routers and gateways have two or more network devices. In most

FIGURE 10-6	
Masquerading with the Firewall Configuration tool	

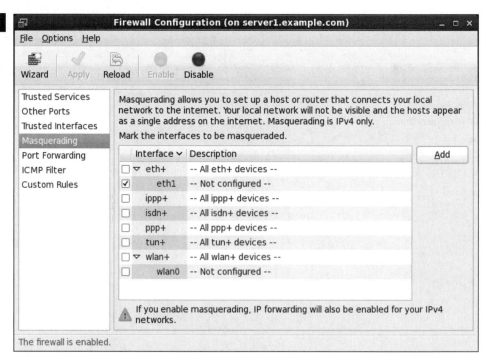

cases, you should set up masquerading for the systems on an internal network. That has three advantages:

- It hides the IP address identity of the internal systems from external networks.
- It requires only one public IP address.
- It sets up forwarding across the configured network devices.

As with trusted interfaces, you should know the device filename associated with each network card. If you've selected a specific device as a trusted interface, such as eth1, that device should also appear in this section. Otherwise, it's selectable in a similar fashion.

Administrators can choose to set up masquerading on the network interface of their choice. The selected network interface should be the one connected to an external network such as the Internet. The action adds several commands to the /etc/sysconfig/iptables file. The following example is based on the eth1 device as the network interface connected to the external network.

The first line specifies the table type, associated with the **iptables -t** switch. The **nat** option stands for network address translation, the functionality associated with masquerading.

```
nat
```

The four lines that follow accept data for forwarding, before routing (PREROUTING), as output to another network (OUTPUT), and after routing has been determined (POSTROUTING) back out through the eth1 interface with outside networks. The COMMIT directive actually commits the commands to the firewall.

```
:PREROUTING ACCEPT [0:0]
:OUTPUT ACCEPT [0:0]
:POSTROUTING ACCEPT [0:0]
-A POSTROUTING -o eth1 -j MASQUERADE
COMMIT
```

Several directives are also added toward the end of the firewall, applied to packets that are to be forwarded. The first FORWARD directive shown here continues communication that is already in process:

```
-A FORWARD -m state --state ESTABLISHED,RELATED -j ACCEPT
```

The next directive accepts **ping** and other ICMP packets, which you may want to change.

```
-A FORWARD -p icmp -j ACCEPT
```

The next two options accept packets forwarded through the loopback adapter (lo), and back out (-o) through the interface to the external network (eth1).

```
-A FORWARD -i lo -j ACCEPT
-A FORWARD -o eth1 -j ACCEPT
```

Port Forwarding

In the Firewall Configuration tool, select Port Forwarding. As suggested in the description, forwarding in this fashion works only in combination with masquerading. With such rules, port forwarding can be used to set up communication to one port on a specific network interface to a port on a remote system, as defined by its IP address. One example is shown in Figure 10-7.

The options shown in the figure would include two additional rules, which redirect traffic destined for port 22 on the eth1 network device to a remote destination, with

FIGURE 10-7

Port forwarding with the Firewall Configuration tool

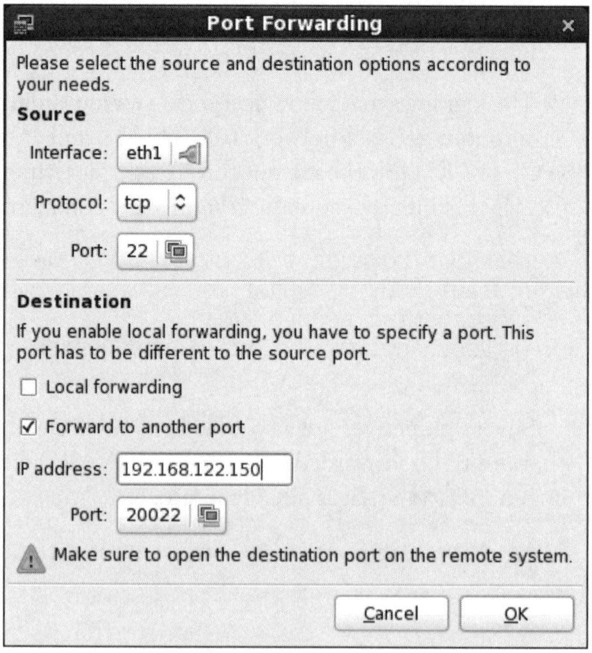

an IP address of 192.168.122.150. The port on that remote system is 20022. The second rule makes sure that information forwarded to that port on the noted IP address is accepted and forwarded through the firewall.

```
-A PREROUTING -i eth1 -p tcp --dport 22 -j DNAT --to-destination
192.168.122.150:20022
-A FORWARD -i eth1 -m state --state NEW -m tcp -p tcp -d 192.168.122.150 --dport
20022 -j ACCEPT
```

ICMP Filter

In the Firewall Configuration tool, click ICMP filter to open the screen shown in Figure 10-8. As suggested in the description, the options listed related to different messages associated with the ICMP protocol. This is not limited to the **ping** command and responses. The options shown are further described in Table 10-2. If a filter in that table is activated, the packets of the noted filter are blocked.

As shown in Figure 10-8, if you hover the cursor over an option, the Firewall Configuration tool provides more information.

FIGURE 10-8	

ICMP filters with the Firewall Configuration tool

Filter	**Description**
Destination Unreachable	A host not found message in response to a **ping** command
Echo Reply	Regular response messages to the **ping** command
Echo Request	A packet associated with the actual **ping** command
Parameter Problem	Error message not otherwise defined
Redirect	For a routing message
Router Advertisement	Periodic message to other routers of a multicast IP address
Router Solicitation	A request for a router advertisement
Source Quench	Response to a host to slow down packet transfers
Time Exceeded	Error message if a "Time To Live" message in a packet is exceeded

TABLE 10-3

ICMP Filter
Options

Custom Rules

The developers behind Red Hat and Fedora have done excellent work to improve the flexibility of the Firewall Configuration tool. A Linux guru who wants to create a custom firewall might uninstall both firewall tools by uninstalling the system-config-firewall and system-config-firewall-tui packages. As suggested earlier, that would help ensure that custom rules created by scripts aren't overwritten by the Firewall Configuration tool. However, someone who is administering just a few systems can use the Red Hat Firewall Configuration tool to set up a file with custom rules. For the purpose of this section, I created a file, /root/iptables-custom, with the following lines:

```
-A INPUT -m state --state NEW -m tcp -p tcp --dport 2222 -j ACCEPT
-A INPUT -m state --state NEW -m tcp -p tcp --dport 8080 -j ACCEPT
```

In the Firewall Configuration tool, I then selected Custom Rules and clicked Add to open the Custom Rules File window shown in Figure 10-9.

If you understand the **iptables** command, it's easier to set up a custom file. Such files are easier to transfer form system to system. Figure 10-9, in fact, shows the result after I clicked the File button and selected the /root/iptables-custom file that I created for this purpose. The name of the custom file that you may choose to create does not matter. When the change is applied, the rules are added to the /etc/sysconfig/iptables file in an appropriate location.

FIGURE 10-9

Take advantage of custom rules.

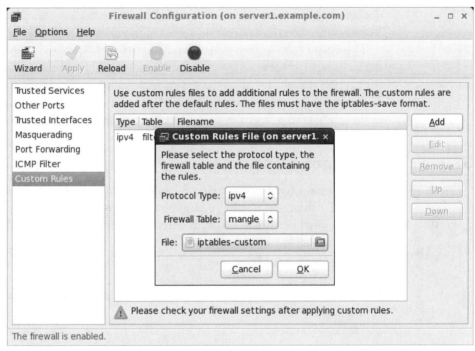

CERTIFICATION OBJECTIVE 10.03

The Extended Internet Super-Server

Linux typically supports network communication between clients and servers. For example, even though it's insecure, it is still possible to use Telnet on Linux to connect to a remote system. The Telnet client on a local computer makes a connection with a Telnet server daemon on the remote system. This section assumes that you've installed the default RHEL xinetd and telnet-server packages. The use of Telnet in this section is for illustration purposes only. This book does not endorse the use of Telnet or any clear-text protocol for private data.

While the focus in this section is on Telnet, other xinetd packages of note include rsync, which is popular for backups and cvs, which is popular for software development version control. As no xinetd service is explicitly cited in the RHCE objectives, I keep the coverage of xinetd services to a minimum. Nevertheless, xinetd services are "Network Services," an important subset of the exam objectives.

The **xinetd** (also known as the Extended Internet Services Daemon) service can start a number of server daemons simultaneously. The **xinetd** service listens for connection requests for all *active* servers with scripts in the /etc/xinetd.d directory. There's a generic configuration file for xinetd services, /etc/xinetd.conf. The scripts in the /etc/xinetd.d directory function as service-specific configuration files.

Generic xinetd Configuration

The generic configuration for xinetd services is stored in the /etc/xinetd.conf file. As RHCE candidates need to configure services only for "basic operation," this chapter analyzes only the active directives in this file. First, a number of default settings are enabled with the following command:

```
defaults
```

This allows services such as rsync to retain their default TCP/IP ports (873) within the xinetd service.

This is followed by

```
log_type = SYSLOG daemon info
```

which specifies logging through the rsyslog daemon as described in Chapters 9 and 17, as configured in /etc/rsyslog.conf.

This is followed by

```
log_on_failure = HOST
```

which specifies the logging information when a login through an xinetd-controlled service fails. Naturally, this specifies the hostname (or IP address) of the client host. It might help to add USERID to the list, which lists the UID number associated with the failed login. This can help you identify compromised accounts.

This line,

```
log_on_success = PID HOST DURATION EXIT
```

specifies the logging information associated with a successful connection. For example, once I logged off a Telnet connection from a remote system, and this led to the following entries in /var/log/messages:

```
Jan 31 08:46:55 server1 xinetd[16543]: START: telnet pid=16582
from=::ffff:tester1.example.com
```

```
Jan 31 08:47:01 server1 xinetd[16543]: EXIT: telnet status=0 pid=16582
duration=6(sec)
```

The effect from /etc/xinetd.conf is straightforward. The next active line is

```
cps = 50 10
```

The **cps** command prevents attempts to "flood" any xinetd service; this line limits connections to 50 per second. If this limit is exceeded, xinetd waits 10 seconds before allowing a remote user to try again.

The next line,

```
instances = 50
```

limits the number of active services for a particular service; in this case, no more than 50 users can be logged into the local Telnet server simultaneously. That number goes down if other xinetd services are running.

This is followed by a related directive:

```
per_source = 10
```

which limits the number of connections from each IP address.

The next active directive is almost self-explanatory:

```
v6only = no
```

If this were set to **yes**, access would be limited to systems with IPv6 addresses.

A couple of environment directives follow, which allow execution with the xinetd group, or one defined with the **group** directive (singular), since there is no default xinetd group.

```
groups = yes
umask = 002
```

Finally, the last active line supports the use of the other configuration files specified in the /etc/xinetd.d directory:

```
includedir /etc/xinetd.d
```

Service-Specific xinetd Configuration

Each file in the /etc/xinetd.d directory specifies a particular service for xinetd to manage. By default, scripts in this directory are disabled. The following code shows a sample of the /etc/xinetd.d/telnet configuration file, with this service disabled.

```
# default: on
# description: The telnet server serves telnet sessions; it uses
#              unencrypted username/password pairs for authentication.
service telnet
{
    flags              = REUSE
    socket_type        = stream
    wait               = no
    user               = root
    server             = /usr/sbin/in.telnetd
    log_on_failure     += USERID
    disable            = yes
}
```

This is a typical /etc/xinetd.d configuration file. The variables (and a few additional variables that you can use) are described in Table 10-3. This is a versatile configuration file; other fields are described in the man pages for xinetd.conf. Do read the xinetd. conf man page; the **only_from** and **no_access** directives may be of particular interest, as they can help you "configure host-based and user-based security for the service."

You can enable any xinetd service by changing **disable = yes** to **disable = no**.

TABLE 10-3	Field	Description of Field Entry
Standard Parameters for xinetd Configuration Files	flags	Supports different parameters for the service; **REUSE** is a default that supports continuous use of the service. Options include IPv6 to set this as a service for those types of networks.
	socket_type	Specifies the communication stream.
	wait	Set to **yes** for single-threaded applications or **no** for multithreaded applications.
	user	Account under which the server should run.
	group	Group under which the server should run.
	server	The server program.
	only_from	Hostname or IP address allowed to use the server. CIDR notation (such as 192.168.0.0/24) is okay.
	no_access	Hostname or IP address not allowed to use the server. CIDR notation is okay.
	log_on_failure	If there's a failed login attempt, this specifies the information sent to a log file.
	disable	By default, set to **yes**, which disables the service.

Always remember to make sure that a service will be active after a reboot. The chkconfig servicename on command is one way to do this for xinetd services. Otherwise, anything you configure may not work after a system is rebooted.

There are two ways to activate an xinetd service. You can edit the configuration file directly by changing the **disable** field from **no** to **yes**. Then make the xinetd daemon reread the configuration files with the **service xinetd reload** command.

Alternatively, you can use the **chkconfig** *servicename* **on** command, which automatically makes this change and makes xinetd reread the configuration file.

EXERCISE 10-1

Configure xinetd

In this exercise, you will enable the Telnet service using xinetd. This exercise assumes that the telnet-server package is already installed. Before starting this exercise, try to establish a Telnet session using the command **telnet localhost**. If you're successful, Telnet was previously enabled; in that case, disable it first with the **chkconfig telnet off** command.

1. Edit /etc/xinetd.d/telnet and change the value of **disable** from **yes** to **no**.

2. Tell xinetd to reread its configuration file using this command:

   ```
   # service xinetd reload
   ```

3. Try the **telnet localhost** command again. It should work.

4. Try to log in with an incorrect username or password.

5. Log in to another terminal. What do you see when you run **utmpdump /var/log/wtmp**?

6. Now log in with a correct username and password.

7. What do you see in /var/log/messages?

8. Log out of the Telnet session. What do you see now in /var/log/messages?

9. Use the **chkconfig** command to disable Telnet. (Remember that the name of the service is telnet.) Try connecting to the Telnet server again. Do you have to restart or reload xinetd?

10. What happens when you use **chkconfig** to disable Telnet? Does it change the /etc/xinted.d/telnet configuration file?

11. For the security of this system, uninstall the associated package with the **rpm -e telnet-server** command. As suggested by the NSA, crackers can't exploit weaknesses in uninstalled software.

CERTIFICATION OBJECTIVE 10.04

TCP Wrappers

As suggested by its name, TCP Wrappers protects those services that communicate using the TCP protocol. It was originally designed to help protect services configured through the Extended Internet Super-Server just described. But TCP wrappers protection is no longer limited to such services; the protection can apply to all services statically and dynamically linked to the associated library wrapper file, libwrap.so.0.

The way TCP wrappers protects a service is defined in the /etc/hosts.allow and /etc/hosts.deny configuration files.

Is a Service Protected by TCP Wrappers?

The **strings** command can be used to identify those daemons protected by TCP Wrappers. It does so by listing the strings associated with various components of binary files. The string associated with TCP Wrappers is hosts_access. Daemons can be found in the /sbin and /usr/sbin directories. Thus, the quickest way to scan the daemons in these directories for the host_access string is with the following commands:

```
# strings /sbin/* | grep hosts_access
# strings /usr/sbin/* | grep hosts_access
```

The output depends on installed packages. One example is the SSH daemon, /usr/sbin/sshd. You can then use the full path to that daemon to confirm a link to the TCP Wrappers library, libwrap.0.so.

The library dependencies command, **ldd**, can list the libraries used by the **sshd** daemon. To identify those dependencies, run the following command:

```
# ldd /usr/sbin/sshd
```

But that's not convenient, as it returns the files for more than a couple of dozen library files. As an expert at the Linux command line, you should know how to pipe that output to the **grep** command to see if it's associated with the TCP Wrappers library file: libwrap.so.0:

```
# ldd /usr/sbin/sshd | grep libwrap.0.so
```

And from the output, it's confirmed:

```
libwrap.so.0 => /lib64/libwrap.so.0 (0x00007f231674e000)
```

Now it's confirmed. You can use the TCP Wrappers configuration files to help protect the SSH service. That protection comes over and above any settings included in standard **iptables** command firewalls, the SSH server configuration file, SELinux, and so on. But such redundant protection is important in a layered security strategy.

TCP Wrappers Configuration Files

When a system receives a network request for a service linked to the libwrap.so.0 library, it passes the request on to TCP Wrappers. This system logs the request and then checks its access rules. If there are no limits on the particular host or IP address, TCP Wrappers passes control back to the service.

The key files are hosts.allow and hosts.deny. The philosophy is fairly straightforward: users and clients listed in hosts.allow are allowed access; users and clients listed in hosts.deny are denied access. As users and/or clients may be listed in both files, the TCP Wrappers system takes the following steps:

1. It searches /etc/hosts.allow. If TCP Wrappers finds a match, it grants access. No additional searches are required.

2. It searches /etc/hosts.deny. If TCP Wrappers finds a match, it denies access.

3. If the host isn't found in either file, access is automatically granted to the client.

You use the same access control language in both /etc/hosts.allow and /etc/hosts.deny files. The basic format for commands in each file is as follows:

```
daemon_list : client_list
```

The simplest version of this format is

```
ALL : ALL
```

This specifies all services and makes the rule applicable to all hosts on all IP addresses. If you set this line in /etc/hosts.deny, access is prohibited to all services. Of course, since that is read after /etc/hosts.allow, services in that file are allowed.

Of course, you can create finer-grained filters than just prohibiting access to ALL daemons from ALL systems. For example, the following line in /etc/hosts.allow allows the client with an IP address of 192.168.122.50 to connect to the local system through the Secure Shell:

```
sshd : 192.168.122.50
```

The same line in /etc/hosts.deny would prevent the computer with that IP address from using SSH to connect. If the same line exists in both files, /etc/hosts.allow takes precedence, and users from the noted IP address will be able to connect through SSH, assuming other security settings such as **iptables**-based firewalls allow it. You can specify clients a number of different ways, as shown in Table 10-4.

As you can see in Table 10-4, there are two different types of wildcards. **ALL** can be used to represent any client or service, and the dot (**.**) specifies all hosts with the specified domain name or IP network address.

You can set up multiple services and addresses with commas. Exceptions are easy to make with the **EXCEPT** operator. Review the following example excerpt from a /etc/hosts.allow file:

```
#hosts.allow
ALL : .example.com
sshd : 192.168.122.0/255.255.255.0 EXCEPT 192.168.122.150
rpc.mountd, in.tftpd : 192.168.100.100
```

TABLE 10-4   Sample Commands in /etc/hosts.allow and /etc/hosts.deny

Client	Description
.example.com	Domain name. Since this domain name begins with a dot, it specifies all clients on the example.com domain.
172.16.	IP address. Since this address ends with a dot, it specifies all clients with an IP address of 172.16.x.y.
172.16.72.0/255.255.254.0	IP network address with subnet mask. CIDR notation not recognized.
ALL	Any client, any daemon.
user@linux1.example.com	Applies to the specific user on the given computer.

The first line in this file is simply a comment. The next line opens **ALL** services to all computers in the example.com domain. The following line opens the SSH service to any computer on the 192.168.122.0 network, except the one with an IP address of 192.168.122.150. Then the mount and TFTP services are opened to the computer with an IP address of 192.168.100.100. You may want to add the localhost IP address network to the noted daemons in the /etc/hosts.allow file, as follows:

```
sshd : 127. 192.168.122.0/255.255.255.0 EXCEPT 192.168.122.150
rpc.mountd, in.tftpd : 127. 192.168.100.100
```

Otherwise, attempts to connect from the local system may be denied based on directives in the /etc/hosts.deny file that follows.

The code that follows contains a hosts.deny file to see how lists can be built to control access:

```
#hosts.deny
ALL EXCEPT in.tftpd : .example.org
sshd : ALL EXCEPT 192.168.122.150
ALL:ALL
```

The first line in the hosts.deny file is a comment. The second line denies all services except TFTP to computers in the example.org domain. The third line states that the only computer allowed to access the local SSH server has an IP address of 192.168.122.100. Finally, the last line is a blanket denial; all other computers are denied access to all services controlled by TCP Wrappers.

EXERCISE 10-2

Configure TCP Wrappers

In this exercise, you will use TCP Wrappers to control access to network resources. Since such controls are enabled by default, you shouldn't have to make any modifications to installed services.

1. Try to connect to the local telnet server using the address localhost. You may need to do several things first:

   A. Install the Telnet server service, from the telnet-server RPM.

   B. Activate the service with the **chkconfig telnet on** command.

   C. Allow Telnet through any active firewall, on the default port of 23.

    D. Add the following line to /etc/hosts (substitute your computer's hostname for server1 and server1.example.com).

```
127.0.0.1   server1 server1.example.com   localhost.localdomain  localhost
```

    E. Recognize that the Telnet service included with RHEL 6 does not normally allow root logins.

2. Edit /etc/hosts.deny and add the following line (don't forget to write the file):

```
ALL : ALL
```

3. What happens when you try to telnet to the address localhost?

4. Edit /etc/hosts.allow and add the following line:

```
in.telnetd : 127.0.0.1
```

5. Now what happens when you try to telnet to the address localhost? Do you need to add anything else to the /etc/hosts.allow file? Try to add the hostname localhost.

6. If other network services associated with TCP Wrappers are available on the local system, try restricting access to those daemons in the /etc/hosts.allow and /etc/hosts.deny files.

7. Undo any changes made when finished. If you agree that a clear-text communications protocol such as Telnet is inherently insecure, that should include the removal of the telnet-server package.

CERTIFICATION OBJECTIVE 10.05

Pluggable Authentication Modules

RHEL uses the Pluggable Authentication Modules (PAM) system as another layer of security primarily for administrative tools and related commands. PAM includes a group of dynamically loadable library modules that govern how individual applications verify their users. You can modify PAM configuration files to customize security requirement for different administrative utilities. Most PAM configuration files are stored in the /etc/pam.d directory.

PAM modules also standardize the user authentication process. For example, the login program uses PAM to require usernames and passwords at login. Open the /etc/pam.d/login file. Take a look at the first line:

```
auth [user_unknown=ignore success=ok ignore=ignore default=bad] \
    pam_securetty.so
```

To interpret, this line means that root users can log in only from secure terminals as defined in the /etc/securetty file, and unknown users are ignored.

on the Job

A backslash in a command line "escapes" the meaning of the next character; in the preceding command, pam_securetty.so is added to the end of the command line. Due to limits in the format of this series, I've had to change the spacing of some lines and add backslashes to others.

The configuration files shown in the /etc/pam.d directory often have the same name as the command that starts the administrative utility. These utilities are "PAM aware." In other words, you can change the way users are verified for applications such as the console login program. Just modify the appropriate configuration file in the /etc/pam.d directory.

Configuration Files

Take a look at the configuration files in a typical /etc/pam.d directory, as shown in Figure 10-10. Depending on what's installed, you may see a somewhat different list of files.

As suggested earlier, most of the filenames in the /etc/pam.d directory are descriptive. Take a look at some of these files. In most cases, they refer to PAM modules. These modules can be found in the /lib64/security directory (on 32-bit systems, in the /lib/security directory). Excellent descriptions of each module can be found in the /usr/share/doc/pam-*versionnumber* directory, in the txt/ and html/ subdirectories. For example, the functionality of the pam_securetty.so module is described in the README.pam_securetty file.

In fact, there's an HTML version of the Linux-PAM System Administrators' Guide available in the /usr/share/doc/pam-*versionnumber*/html directory, starting with the Linux-PAM_SAG.html file.

FIGURE 10-10

PAM configuration
files in the
/etc/pam.d
directory

```
[root@server1 ~]# ls /etc/pam.d/
atd                  halt                 smartcard-auth-ac
authconfig           ksu                  smtp
authconfig-gtk       login                smtp.postfix
authconfig-tui       newrole              sshd
chfn                 other                su
chsh                 passwd               sudo
config-util          password-auth        sudo-i
crond                password-auth-ac     su-l
cups                 polkit-1             system-auth
cvs                  poweroff             system-auth-ac
eject                reboot               system-config-authentication
fingerprint-auth     remote               system-config-date
fingerprint-auth-ac  rhn_register         system-config-kdump
gdm                  run_init             system-config-keyboard
gdm-autologin        runuser              system-config-network
gdm-fingerprint      runuser-l            system-config-network-cmd
gdm-password         setup                system-config-users
gdm-smartcard        smartcard-auth       xserver
[root@server1 ~]#
```

Control Flags

The PAM system divides the process of verifying users into four separate tasks. These are the four different types of PAM flags:

- **Authentication management (auth)**   Establishes the identity of a user. For example, a PAM **auth** command decides whether to prompt for a username and/or a password. Related options may even grant group membership.

- **Account management (account)**   Allows or denies access according to the account policies. For example, a PAM **account** command may deny access according to time, password expiration, or a specific list of restricted users.

- **Password management (password)**   Manages other password policies. For example, a PAM **password** command may limit the number of times a user can try to log in before a console is reset.

- **Session management (session)**   Applies settings for an application. For example, the PAM **session** command may set default settings for a login console.

The code shown in Figure 10-11 is from an example PAM configuration file, /etc/pam.d/login. Every line in all PAM configuration files is written in the following format:

```
module_type   control_flag   module_path   [arguments]
```

<table>
<tr><td>

FIGURE 10-11

The PAM
/etc/pam.d/login
configuration file

</td><td>

```
#%PAM-1.0
auth█[user_unknown=ignore success=ok ignore=ignore default=bad] pam_securetty.so
auth        include      system-auth
account     required     pam_nologin.so
account     include      system-auth
password    include      system-auth
# pam_selinux.so close should be the first session rule
session     required     pam_selinux.so close
session     required     pam_loginuid.so
session     optional     pam_console.so
# pam_selinux.so open should only be followed by sessions to be executed in the
user context
session     required     pam_selinux.so open
session     required     pam_namespace.so
session     optional     pam_keyinit.so force revoke
session     include      system-auth
-session    optional     pam_ck_connector.so
~
~
~
~
"/etc/pam.d/login" 16L, 728C
```

</td></tr>
</table>

The **module_type**, as described previously, can be **auth**, **account**, **password**, or **session**. The **control_flag** determines what PAM does if the module succeeds or fails. The **module_path** specifies the location of the actual PAM module file. Finally, as with regular shell commands, you can specify arguments for each module.

The **control_flag** field requires additional explanation. It determines how the configuration file reacts when a module flags success or failure. The five different control flags are described in Table 10-5.

TABLE 10-5

PAM Control
Flags

control_flag	Description
required	If the module works, the command proceeds. If it fails, PAM proceeds to the next command in the configuration file—but the command controlled by PAM will still fail.
requisite	Stops the process if the module fails.
sufficient	If the module works, the login or other authentication proceeds. No other commands need be processed.
optional	PAM ignores success or failure of this module, unless no other modules are used.
include	Includes all **module_type** directives from the noted configuration file; for example, if the directive is **password include system-auth**, this includes all password directives from the PAM system-auth file.

To see how control flags work, take a look at the commands from the /etc/pam.d/reboot configuration file:

```
auth     sufficient      pam_rootok.so
```

The first **auth** command checks the pam_rootok.so module. In other words, if the root user runs the **reboot** command, the **control_flag** is **sufficient**, and the other **auth** commands in this file are ignored. Linux runs the **reboot** command. This is explained in the README.pam_rootok file in the /usr/share/doc/pam-*versionnumber*/txts directory.

```
auth     required      pam_console.so
```

Given the purpose of the first line, this second **auth** command is run only for nonroot users, to govern permissions within the console. In this case, it just confirms console ownership to any user who is logged in to that console.

```
#auth     include      system-auth
```

The third line is commented out by default. If you make this line active, it includes the commands from the system-auth configuration file, which requires root user privileges. Remote users who connect with root privileges are still allowed to reboot the system.

```
account     required      pam_permit.so
```

The module associated with the **account** command (pam_permit.so) accepts all users, even those who've logged in remotely. In other words, this configuration file would allow any root user, local or remote, to reboot the Linux system, unless rejected by a previous directive.

The Format of a PAM File

This section is a little complex. It starts with the /etc/pam.d/login configuration file shown in Figure 10-12. In addition, as the file includes references to the /etc/pam.d/system-auth configuration file, you'll need to go back and forth between files to follow along with this section.

When a user opens a text console and logs in, Linux goes through this configuration file line by line. As previously noted, the first line in /etc/pam.d/login limits root user access to secure terminals as defined in the /etc/securetty file:

```
auth [user_unknown=ignore success=ok ignore=ignore default=bad] \
 pam_securetty.so
```

FIGURE 10-12   The PAM /etc/pam.d/system-auth configuration file

```
#%PAM-1.0
# This file is auto-generated.
# User changes will be destroyed the next time authconfig is run.
auth        required        pam_env.so
auth        sufficient      pam_fprintd.so
auth        sufficient      pam_unix.so nullok try_first_pass
auth        requisite       pam_succeed_if.so uid >= 500 quiet
auth        required        pam_deny.so

account     required        pam_unix.so
account     sufficient      pam_localuser.so
account     sufficient      pam_succeed_if.so uid < 500 quiet
account     required        pam_permit.so

password    requisite       pam_cracklib.so try_first_pass retry=3 type=
password    sufficient      pam_unix.so sha512 shadow nullok try_first_pass use_au
thtok
password    required        pam_deny.so

session     optional        pam_keyinit.so revoke
session     required        pam_limits.so
session     [success=1 default=ignore] pam_succeed_if.so service in crond quiet
use_uid
session     required        pam_unix.so
~
"/etc/pam.d/system-auth" 22L, 937C
```

The next line includes the **auth** commands from the system-auth PAM configuration file:

```
auth    include     system-auth
```

The system-auth configuration file shown in Figure 10-12 includes five **auth** directives:

```
auth        required     pam_env.so
auth        sufficient   pam_fprintd.so
auth        sufficient   pam_unix.so nullok try_first_pass
auth        requisite    pam_succeed_if.so uid >= 500 quiet
auth        required     pam_deny.so
```

In order, they set up environment variables, check authentication via a fingerprint reader (pam_fprintd.so) if available, and check passwords (pam_unix.so). The **sufficient** flag associated with those modules means that authentication works if a valid fingerprint or password has been entered. The User ID of the account must be

500 and above. If these conditions are not met, the user is locked out (pam_deny.so).

Now return to the /etc/pam.d/login file. The next line, which looks for an **account** module type, checks for accounts not allowed to log in as listed in the /etc/nologin file:

```
account    required    pam_nologin.so
```

The following account module includes the **account** modules from the /etc/pam.d/system-auth configuration file:

```
account    include    system-auth
```

These are the **account** module type lines from /etc/pam.d/system-auth:

```
account    required      pam_unix.so
account    sufficient    pam_localuser.so
account    sufficient    pam_succeed_if.so uid < 500 quiet
account    required      pam_permit.so
```

The first line refers to the pam_unix.so module in the /lib/security directory, which brings up the normal username and password prompts. Based on the pam_localuser. so module, users found in /etc/passwd are automatically accepted. Based on the pam_succeed_if.so module, service users (with user IDs less than 500) are automatically logged in, without messages (quiet). The pam_permit.so module always returns success.

Now return to the /etc/pam.d/login file. The next line is a **password** module, which includes other password module type lines from the /etc/pam.d/system-auth file:

```
password    include    system-auth
```

These are the **password** module type lines from /etc/pam.d/system-auth:

```
password requisite    pam_cracklib.so try_first_pass retry=3
password sufficient   pam_unix.so sha512 shadow nullok try_first_pass \
use_authok
password required     pam_deny.so
```

The first command from this list allows the use of a previously successful password (**try_first_pass**) and then sets a maximum of three retries. The next command encrypts passwords using the SHA512 hash, supports the Shadow Password Suite described in Chapter 8, allows the use of null (zero-length) passwords, allows the use of a previously successful password (**try_first_pass**), and prompts the user for a password (**use_authok**). The **password required pam_deny.so** directive is trivial; as noted in README.pam_deny in the /usr/share/doc/pam-*versionlevel*/txt directory, that module always fails, so PAM moves on to the next directive.

Finally, there are eight **session** commands in the /etc/pam.d/login file. Take them four at a time:

```
session    required    pam_selinux.so close
session    required    pam_loginuid.so
session    optional    pam_console.so
session    required    pam_selinux.so open
```

The first and fourth lines deactivate (**pam_selinux.so close**) and reactivate SELinux (**pam_selinux.so open**), just for this part of the login process. The second line (**pam_loginuid.so**) records the user ID for audits. The third line gives ownership of the process to the user logged in to the console (**pam_console.so**).

```
session    required    pam_namespace.so
session    optional    pam_keyinit.so force revoke
session    include     system-auth
session    optional    pam_ck_connector.so
```

The fifth **session** command makes sure the user's home directory has standard /etc/skel files. The following command, even though it's listed as optional, revokes any existing unique session keyring. Jumping ahead, the last of this group of commands allows logins to work with the Console Kit described in Chapter 9. The command that precedes it includes the following **session** module–type commands from the system-auth file:

```
session    optional       pam_keyinit.so revoke
session    required       pam_limits.so
session    [success=1 default=ignore] pam_succeed_if.so service in crond quiet
use_uid
session    required       pam_unix.so
```

The first of these commands repeats the revoke of the keyring already accomplished in the main /etc/pam.d/login file. The next command sets limits (pam_limits.so) on individual users through /etc/security/limits.conf. The following command relates to cron jobs. The final command logs the result when the user logs out.

EXERCISE 10-3

Configure PAM

In this exercise, you can experiment with some of the PAM security features of Red Hat Enterprise Linux 6.

1. Make a backup copy of /etc/securetty with the following command:

   ```
   # cp /etc/securetty /etc/securetty.sav
   ```

2. Edit /etc/securetty and remove the lines for tty3 through tty11. Save the changes and exit.

3. Use ALT-F3 (CTRL-ALT-F3 if you're running X Window) to switch to virtual console number 3. Try to log in as root. What happens?

4. Repeat Step 3 as a regular user. What happens? Do you know why?

5. Use ALT-F2 to switch to virtual console number 2 and try to log in as root.

6. Review the messages in /var/log/secure. Do you see where you tried to log in as root in virtual console number 3?

7. Restore the original /etc/securetty file with the following command:

   ```
   # mv /etc/securetty.sav /etc/securetty
   ```

One thing to remember is that the /etc/securetty file governs the consoles from which you can log in to Linux as the root user. Therefore, the changes that were made do not affect regular (nonroot) users.

PAM and User-Based Security

In this section, you'll learn how to configure PAM to limit access to specific users. The key to this security feature is the pam_listfile.so module. The location varies with architecture; it may be in the /lib64/security or /lib/security directories. If you've installed the vsFTP server, the /etc/pam.d/vsftpd file includes an example of this module.

As described earlier, four settings are available for each PAM configuration command. First, the following line clears out any existing keyrings, making sure the authentication options that follow are actually used.

```
session optional pam_keyinit.so   force revoke
```

To make sure that the command respects what's done with this module, this directive should come next:

```
auth required pam_listfile.so
```

The way PAM limits user access is in the last part of the command—in the details. For example, if you added the following line to a PAM configuration file, access to the associated tool would be limited to any users listed in /etc/special:

```
auth required pam_listfile.so item=user sense=deny \
file=/etc/vsftpd/ftpusers onerr=succeed
```

To understand how this works, break this command into its component parts. You already know the first three parts of the command from the previous section. The switches that are shown are associated with the pam_listfile.so module, as described in Table 10-6.

TABLE 10-6	pam_listfile Switch	Description
Options for the pam_listfile.so Module	item	This switch can be used to limit access to a terminal (**tty**), users in a specific file (**user**), groups (**group**), or more.
	sense	If the item is found in the specified **file**, take the noted action. For example, if the user is in /etc/special, and **sense=allow**, then this command allows use of the specified tool.
	file	Configures a file with a list, such as **file = /etc/special**.
	onerr	If there is a problem, tell the module what to do. The options are **onerr=succeed** or **onerr=fail**.

Thus, for the specified command (**onerr=succeed**), an error, strangely enough, returns success (**item=user**), based on a specific list of users. If the user is in the specified list (**file=/etc/special**), allow that user (**sense=allow**) to access the specified tool. To see how this works, run through the steps in Exercise 10-4.

e x a m

ⓦ a t c h   *Make sure you understand*   *everything in PAM before making any*
how Red Hat Enterprise Linux handles user   *changes, because any errors that you make*
authorization through the /etc/pam.d   *to a PAM configuration file can disable your*
configuration files. When you test these   *system completely (PAM is that secure).*
files, make sure you create a backup of

EXERCISE 10-4

Use PAM to Limit User Access

You can also use the PAM system to limit access to regular users. In this exercise, you'll limit access by adding one or more users to the /etc/nologin file. It should work hand-in-hand with the default /etc/pam.d/login security configuration file, specifically the following line:

```
account   required  pam_nologin.so
```

1. Look for an /etc/nologin file. If it doesn't already exist, create one with a message such as:

   ```
   I'm sorry, access is limited to the root user
   ```

2. Access another terminal with a command such as CTRL-ALT-F2. Try logging in as a regular user. What do you see?

3. If the message flashes by too quickly for you, log in as the root user. You'll see the same message; but as the root user, you're allowed access.

4. Inspect the /var/log/secure file. Did your system reject the attempted login from the regular user? What were the associated messages for the root user?

SCENARIO & SOLUTION

You have only one official IP address, but you need to provide Internet access to all of the systems on your LAN. Each computer on the LAN has its own private IP address.	Use **iptables** to implement IP masquerading. Make sure IP forwarding is active.
You have installed an SSH server on a corporate network and want to restrict access to certain departments. Each department has its own subnet.	Use the /etc/hosts.deny file in the tcp_wrappers package to block SSH access, using the sshd daemon, to the unwanted subnets. A better alternative would be to use /etc/hosts.allow to support access to desired departments, and then use /etc/hosts.deny to deny access to everyone else. Similar options are possible based on **iptables** firewall rules.
You want to modify the commands associated with halting and rebooting your computer so that they're accessible only to the root user.	Set up the appropriate Pluggable Authentication Module configuration files in /etc/pam.d to use the **system-auth** module.
You want to modify the local firewall to defend against ICMP attacks such as **ping** command floods.	Modify the firewall to reject or deny certain types of ICMP packets. Many such settings are available with the Firewall Configuration tool.

CERTIFICATION OBJECTIVE 10.06

Secure Files and More with GPG2

With the importance of security on current networks, you should know how to encrypt files for secure transmission. The computer standard for file encryption is known as Pretty Good Privacy (PGP). The open source implementation of PGP is known as the GNU Privacy Guard (GPG). The version released for RHEL 6 is more advanced and capable, documented as GPG version 2 (GPG2) You've likely already used GPG2 to verify the authenticity of RPM packages as discussed in Chapter 7. This section takes such checks one step further; you'll generate private and public keys, and use those keys to encrypt and decrypt selected files.

While GPG is not listed in the RHCE objectives, it's a security topic consistent with other security objectives discussed in this book. It is also part of Red Hat's prep course for the RHCE, RH254. I believe it's an excellent topic that might be included in future versions of the RHCE exam.

GPG2 Commands

There's a new version of the GPG package, implemented for RHEL 6. It includes a more modular approach to encryption and authentication. There's even a related package used for smart card authentication. But that's not the point of the new **gpg2** commands. Available GPG commands are briefly described in Table 10-7.

Table 10-7 is just intended to describe the range of capabilities associated with the RHEL 6 GPG2 packages. The focus of this section is on the encryption and decryption of files.

Current GPG2 Configuration

While the man page for the **gpgconf** command suggests that it's just used to modify the directory with associated configuration files, that command does more. By itself, it defaults to the **--list-components** switch, which specifies the full path to related executable files. With the **--check-programs** switch, it makes sure all related programs can be executed. It can also be used to check the syntax of a GPG2

TABLE 10-7	Command	Description
GPG2 Commands	gpg	Executable file soft-linked to the **gpg2** command
	gpg2	The GPG2 encryption and signing tool
	gpg-agent	GPG2 key management command
	gpgconf	Status command for GPG2 components
	gpg-connect-agent	Communicate with an active GPG2 agent
	gpg-error	Command to interpret a GPG2 error number
	gpg-error-config	Command to build applications based on a GPG2 error
	gpgkey2ssh	Conversion command for GPG2 keys for SSH
	gpgparsemail	Under development
	gpgsplit	Command to split a GPG2 message into packets
	gpgv	Executable file soft-linked to the **gpg2v** command
	gpgv2	Command to verify GPG signatures; requires a signature file
	gpg-zip	Command to encrypt and sign files into an archive

configuration file. One typical option is in the current user's home directory, in the .gnupg/ subdirectory. Another typical option is in the /etc/gnupg directory.

GPG2 Encryption Options

The development of a GPG2 key includes a choice of three different cryptographic algorithms. Each of these algorithms include a public and a private key. The public key can be distributed to others, for use in encrypting files and messages. The private key is used by the owner, and is the only way to decrypt the file or message.

- **RSA** Named for its developers, Rivest, Shamir, and Adelman. While typical RSA keys are 1024 or 2048 bits in length, they can be up to 4096 bits. Shorter keys of 512 bits have been cracked. It is in the public domain.

- **DSA** The Digital Signature Algorithm. Owned by the U.S. National Institute of Science and Technology, it has been made available for worldwide use, royalty-free. This is a U.S. Government standard that uses Secure Hash Algorithm (SHA) versions SHA-1 and SHA-2 as message digest hash functions. SHA-1 is being phased out; SHA-2 includes four hash functions with message digests of up to 512 bits, also known as SHA-512, the same hash as is now used for the RHEL 6 shadow password suite.

- **ElGamel** Developed by Taher Elgamel, this probabilistic encryption scheme predates the others. The choices for the number of bits for encryption keys range from 1024 to 3072 bits. While it was never patented, it may be covered under the patent for the Diffie-Hellman key exchange protocol.

Generate a GPG2 Key

The **gpg2 --gen-key** command can be used to set up key pairs with one of four types of encryption schemes. Before running the command, be prepared with answers to the following questions:

- The number of bits for the encryption keys. Normally, the maximum number of bits is 4096, but an encryption key that complex may take a number of minutes to develop.

- The desired lifetime of the keys. Especially if you set up keys with a smaller number of bits, you should assume that a determined cracker would be able to decrypt the key within some number of months or weeks.

■ A name, an e-mail address, and a comment. While the name and e-mail address do not have to be real, they will be seen by others as part of the public key.

■ A passphrase. Good passphrases should include spaces, lower- and uppercase letters, numbers, and punctuation.

As given, the **gpg2 --gen-key** command prompts for one of four different encryption schemes. As suggested by the (sign only) label associated with choices 3 and 4, those options work just as digital signatures, not for encryption.

```
Please select what kind of key you want:
    (1) RSA and RSA (default)
    (2) DSA and Elgamal
    (3) DSA (sign only)
    (4) RSA (sign only)
Your selection?
```

All four options follow a similar sequence of steps. For example, if you select option 2, the following output appears:

```
DSA keys may be between 1024 and 3072 bits long.
What keysize do you want? (2048)
```

The default is 2048 bits, which is selected if you just press ENTER. The command then prompts for a key lifetime:

```
Requested keysize is 2048 bits
Please specify how long the key should be valid.
        0 = key does not expire
    < >  = key expires in n days
    < >w = key expires in n weeks
    < >m = key expires in n months
    < >y = key expires in n years
Key is valid for? (0) 2m
```

In this case, I've selected two months. The command responds with a date and time two months into the future and prompts for confirmation.

```
Key expires at Sun 03 Apr 2011 11:14:17 AM PDT
Is this correct? (y/N) y
```

At this point, the **gpg2** command prompts for identifying information for the key. The "User ID" requested here is not related to the UID in the standard Linux authentication database. In this example, I've responded to the prompts in bold:

```
Real name: Michael Jang
Email address: michael@example.com
Comment: DSA and Elgamel key
You selected this USER-ID:
    "Michael Jang (DSA and Elgamel key) <michael@example.com>"

Change (N)ame, (C)omment, (E)mail or (O)kay/(Q)uit? o
```

The system should now prompt for a passphrase. If you're working in the GNOME Desktop Environment, the window shown in Figure 10-13 would appear.

As you type in a passphrase, the system evaluates its quality, based on the length, use of upper- and lowercase characters, numbers, and punctuation. Of course, a similar window appears a second time to allow you to type in the passphrase a second time.

At this point, the **gpg2** command goes to work. Especially with larger keys, it may seem to pause for a few minutes with a message about creating random bytes. You might need to run some other programs to stimulate the process. When complete, it displays a message similar to the following:

```
gpg: key D385AFDD marked as ultimately trusted
public and secret key created and signed.
```

To make sure the public and private keys were actually written, run the following command:

```
$ gpg2 --list-key
```

The output should include the latest key, along with any others created from the user's home directory, in the .gnupg/ subdirectory. For the given options, if this is the only key pair on the local account, you'll see something similar to the following output:

```
/home/michael/.gnupg/pubring.gpg
--------------------------------
pub   2048D/1665FE84 2011-02-02 [expires: 2011-04-03]
uid   Michael Jang (DSA and ElGamel) <michael@example.com>
sub   2048g/EEC05210 2011-02-02 [expires: 2011-04-03]
```

FIGURE 10-13	

Prompting for a passphrase

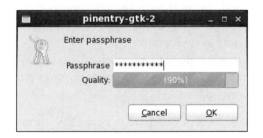

Use a GPG2 Key to Secure a File

Now you can send the public key to a remote system. To start the process, you'll need to export the public key. For the key pair just created, you could do so with the following command. Substitute your name for "Michael Jang."

```
$ gpg2 --export Michael Jang > gpg.pub
```

Now copy that key to a remote system. The delivery vehicle, such as e-mail, a USB stick, or the **scp** command shown here, is not important. This particular command from user michael's account would copy the gpg.pub key to user michael's home directory on the tester1.example.com system. If you prefer, substitute the IP address.

```
$ scp gpg.pub tester1.example.com:
```

Now go to the remote system, in this case, tester1.example.com. Log in to user michael's account (or the account home directory to which you copied the gpg.pub key). If desired, you can even log in to that system remotely with a command like **ssh**. Once connected to that system, first check for existing GPG keys with the following command:

```
$ gpg2 --list-key
```

If this is a system without previous GPG keys, the list should be empty, and nothing will appear in the output to this command. Now import the gpg.pub file into the list of local GPG keys with the following command:

```
$ gpg2 --import gpg.pub
```

Confirm the import by running the **gpg2 --list-key** command again.

Now on the remote system, you can encrypt a file with the **gpg2** command. The following example encrypts the local keepthis.secret file:

```
$ gpg2 --out underthe.radar --recipient 'Michael Jang' --encrypt
keepthis.secret
```

The username in this case is 'Michael Jang'. If you've just imported a private key, the username as shown in the output to the **gpg2 --list-key** command may be different. Substitute as appropriate.

Now when the underthe.radar file is copied to the original system, server1.example.com, you can start the decryption process with the private key with the following command:

```
$ gpg --out keepthis.secret --decrypt underthe.radar
```

FIGURE 10-14

Prompting for a
passphrase for
decryption

```
Please enter the passphrase to unlock the secret key for the OpenPGP
certificate:
"Michael Jang (DSA and ElGamel) <michael@example.com>"
2048-bit ELG key, ID EEC05210,
created 2011-02-02 (main key ID 1665FE84).


Passphrase *************█_____

          <OK>                                            <Cancel>
```

In a console, you'd be prompted for the passphrase created earlier, with a screen similar to that shown in Figure 10-14.

CERTIFICATION SUMMARY

To help defend the data, the services, and the systems on a network, Linux provides layers of security. If a service is not installed, a cracker can't use it to break into a system. Those systems that are installed should be kept up to date. Such services can be protected by firewalls, along with host- and user-based security options. Many services include their own layers of security. RHEL 6 incorporates several recommendations from the NSA, including SELinux.

Firewalls based on the **iptables** command can regulate and protect gateways as well as individual systems. That same command can be used to set up packet forwarding, as well as masquerading of private networks. Such options can be configured directly in the /etc/sysconfig/iptables file, or set up with the help of the Firewall Configuration tool.

Some services are still configured through the Extended Internet Super-Server, xinetd. Those systems can be regulated and protected through the /etc/xinetd.conf file and service-specific configuration files in the /etc/xinetd.d directory.

Those systems connected to the TCP Wrappers library can be protected by appropriate settings in the /etc/hosts.allow and /etc/hosts.deny files. If there is a conflict, /etc/hosts.allow is read first. Regulation through TCP Wrappers is possible by user or host.

PAM supports user-based security for a number of administrative tools. They're configured individually through files in the /etc/pam.d directory. These files refer to modules in the /lib64/security directory.

Linux supports encryption with the help of GPG. RHEL 6 includes GPG2 for this purpose. It includes commands like **gpg2** to set up private/public key pairs using the RSA, DSA, or ElGamel schemes.

✓ TWO-MINUTE DRILL

The following are some of the key points from the certification objectives in Chapter 10.

The Layers of Linux Security

❏ Bastion systems are more secure, as they're configured with a single service. With virtualization, bastion systems are now a practical option even for smaller organizations.

❏ You may choose to automate at least security updates with the Software Updates Preference tool.

❏ Many services include their own security options in their configuration files.

❏ Host-based security can be configured by domain name or IP address.

❏ User-based security includes specified users and groups.

❏ The PolicyKit can regulate security of administrative tools run from the GNOME desktop environment.

Firewalls and Network Address Translation

❏ The main firewall configuration command is **iptables**, configured in the /etc/sysconfig/iptables file.

❏ With **iptables**, you can regulate packet traffic into, out of, and forwarded through a system.

❏ With **iptables**, you can also masquerade the IP addresses from one network on an outside network such as the Internet.

❏ Listed **iptables** options can also be configured with the help of the Firewall Configuration tool, which you can start with the **system-config-firewall** command.

The Extended Internet Super-Server

❏ Some services are still regulated by the xinetd service.

❏ Services configured can be activated and protected through individual configuration files in the /etc/xinetd.d directory.

TCP Wrappers

❑ The **strings /sbin/*** and **strings /usr/sbin/*** commands can identify daemons with the hosts_access setting, to identify services that can be regulated by TCP Wrappers.

❑ You can confirm regulation by TCP Wrappers with the **ldd** command, applied to the full path to the daemon. The TCP Wrappers library file for 64-bit systems is /lib64/libwrap.so.0.

❑ Clients and users listed in /etc/hosts.allow are allowed access; clients and users listed in /etc/hosts.deny are denied access.

❑ Services can also be configured in /etc/hosts.allow and /etc/hosts.deny. Remember to use the actual executable name of the daemon, normally in /usr/sbin, such as **in.tftpd**.

Pluggable Authentication Modules

❑ RHEL 6 uses the Pluggable Authentication Modules (PAM) system to check for authorized users.

❑ PAM modules are called by configuration files in the /etc/pam.d directory. These configuration files are usually named after the service or command that they control.

❑ There are four types of PAM modules: authentication, account, password, and session management.

❑ PAM configuration files include lines that list the module_type, the control_flag, and the path to the actual module, followed by arguments.

❑ PAM modules are well documented in the /usr/share/doc/pam-*versionnumber*/txts directory.

Secure Files and More with GPG2

❑ GPG is the Linux implementation of PGP.

❑ RHEL 6 includes more advanced encryption known as GPG2.

❑ The **gpgconf** command can reveal the current GPG2 configuration.

❑ GPG2 encryption can use the DSA, RSA, and ElGamel schemes.

❑ GPG2 keys can be created with the **gpg2 --gen-key** command, and listed with the **gpg2 --list-key** command.

SELF TEST

The following questions will help measure your understanding of the material presented in this chapter. As no multiple-choice questions appear on the Red Hat exams, no multiple-choice questions appear in this book. These questions exclusively test your understanding of the chapter. It is okay if you have another way of performing a task. Getting results, not memorizing trivia, is what counts on the Red Hat exams. There may be more than one answer to many of these questions.

The Layers of Linux Security

1. What security option is best for a service that isn't currently required on a system?

_____

Firewalls and Network Address Translation

2. Consider the following command:

```
# iptables -A INPUT -s 192.168.77.77 -j REJECT
```

Once saved to a firewall, what effect will this have when the client with an IP of 192.168.77.77 tries to connect to this system?

_____

3. What file includes rules associated with the **iptables** command?

_____

4. You are setting up a small office and would like to provide Internet access to a small number of users but don't have the money for dedicated IPv4 address for each system on the network. What can you do?

_____

5. What **iptables** command switch sets up masquerading?

_____

The Extended Internet Super-Server

6. In what directory are files associated with individual xinetd services located?

_____

7. What command rereads the configuration files associated with the xinetd service?

_____

TCP Wrappers

8. You are using the xinetd program to start services. With TCP Wrappers configuration files, how could you limit Telnet access to clients on the 192.168.170.0 network? Hint: The telnet daemon, when installed, is in /usr/sbin/telnetd.

_____

9. What happens to a service if you allow the service in /etc/hosts.allow and prohibit it in /etc/hosts.deny?

_____

Pluggable Authentication Modules

10. What are the four basic PAM module types?

_____

_____

_____

_____

11. You are editing the PAM configuration file by adding a module. Which control flag immediately terminates the authentication process if the module succeeds?

_____

Secure Files and More with GPG

12. What command lists the GPG public keys loaded on the current local account?

_____

LAB QUESTIONS

Several of these labs involve exercises that can seriously affect a system. You should do these exercises on test machines only. The second Lab of Chapter 1 sets up KVM for this purpose. However, some readers may not have hardware that supports KVM. Options to KVM include virtual machine solutions such as VMware, available from www.vmware.com, or Virtualbox, open-source edition, available from www.virtualbox.org.

Red Hat presents its exams electronically. For that reason, the labs for this chapter are available from the CD that accompanies the book, in the Chapter10/ subdirectory. It's available in .doc, .html, and .txt formats, with filenames starting with 56510-labs. In case you haven't yet set up RHEL 6 on a system, refer to the first lab of Chapter 2 for installation instructions. However, the answers for each lab follows the Self Test answers for the fill-in-the-blank questions.

SELF TEST ANSWERS

The Layers of Linux Security

1. The security option that is best for a service that isn't currently required on a system is to not install that service.

Firewalls and Network Address Translation

2. Based on the given command, any connection attempt (including packets sent with the **ping** command) from the 192.168.77.77 system is rejected.

3. Rules associated with **iptables**-based firewalls are stored in /etc/sysconfig/iptables.

4. To set up a small office while providing Internet access to a small number of users, all you need is one dedicated IP address. The other addresses can be on a private network. Masquerading makes this possible.

5. The **iptables** command switch that sets up masquerading is **-t nat**.

The Extended Internet Super-Server

6. The configuration files for individual xinetd services are stored in the /etc/xinetd.d directory.

7. Several acceptable options are available to reread the configuration files associated with the xinetd service. The standard option is **/etc/init.d/xinetd reload**; the **service xinetd reload** command is functionally equivalent. While you could substitute **restart** for **reload**, that's an inferior answer. A "restart" kicks off any connected users.

TCP Wrappers

8. You are using the xinetd program to start services. To limit Telnet access to clients on the 192.168.170.0 network, you'd allow access to the network in /etc/hosts.allow and deny it to all others in /etc/hosts.deny. As /usr/sbin is in the root user path, you can cite the **telnetd** daemon directly and add the following directive to /etc/hosts.allow:

```
telnetd : 192.168.0.170/255.255.255.0
```

Then add the following to /etc/hosts.deny:

```
telnetd : ALL
```

9. If you allow a service in /etc/hosts.allow and prohibit it in /etc/hosts.deny, the service is allowed.

Pluggable Authentication Modules

10. The four basic PAM types are: **auth**, **account**, **password**, and **session**. The **include** type refers to one or more of the other PAM types in a different file.

11. The **sufficient** control flag immediately terminates the authentication process if the module succeeds.

Secure Files and More with GPG

12. The command that lists currently loaded public keys is **gpg2 --list-key**. The **gpg --list-key** command is acceptable.

LAB ANSWERS

Lab 1

Verifying this lab should be straightforward. If it works, you should be able to confirm with the following command on the tester1.example.com system:

```
$ gpg2 --list-keys
```

It should include the GPG2 public key just imported to that system. Of course, if the encryption, file transfer, and decryption worked, you should also be able to read the decrypted 56510-labs.txt file in a local text editor.

Lab 2

This lab is somewhat self-explanatory, in that it can help you think about how to make a system more secure. As discussed in the chapter, it starts with a minimal installation. The minimal installation of RHEL 6 happens to include the SSH server, for remote administrative access.

While RHEL 6 has greatly reduced the number of standard services installed, most users will find some services that are not required. For example, how many administrators actually need Bluetooth services for a RHEL 6 system installed on a virtual machine?

Lab 3

If you want to set up an RHEL computer as a secure web server, it's a straightforward process described in Chapter 14. But firewall configuration is part of the process covered in this chapter. To that end, you'll want to set up a firewall to block all but the most essential ports. This should include TCP/IP ports 80 and 443, which allow outside computers to access local regular and secure web services. Open ports should also include port 22, for SSH communication.

The easiest way to set this up is with the Red Hat Firewall Configuration tool, which you can start with the **system-config-firewall** command. Once in the Firewall Configuration tool, take the following steps, which vary slightly between the GUI- and console-based versions of the tool.

1. Customize the firewall.

2. Select the Trusted Services window. (If you're in the text-based tool, click Customize to open the Firewall Configuration – Customize window.) Activate the WWW (HTTP) option. This allows access from outside the local computer to the local regular web site. Activate the Secure WWW (HTTPS) option as well. Make sure the SSH option remains active.

3. Make sure to apply any changes, and exit from the Firewall Configuration tool.

4. Enter the following command to check the resulting firewall:

   ```
   # iptables -L
   ```

5. Once you've configured a web service as described in Chapter 14, users will be able to access both the regular and secure web servers from remote systems.

Lab 4

Several steps are required to set up any xinetd service such as Telnet. You'll need to modify the xinetd Telnet configuration file. The following steps demonstrate three different methods to limit access to the noted system on IP address 192.168.122.150. Any of the three methods would be acceptable. These methods secure Telnet in three ways: in the /etc/xinetd.d/telnet configuration file, through TCP Wrappers, or with the appropriate firewall commands. In a "real-world" scenario, you might use all three methods in a layered security strategy. These steps assume you're performing this lab on the server1.example.com system.

1. Make sure that the telnet-server RPM is installed. Back up the current version of the /etc/xinetd.d/telnet configuration file.

2. Activate Telnet. Use the **chkconfig telnet on** command to revise the /etc/xinetd.d/telnet configuration script.

3. Edit the /etc/xinetd.d/telnet configuration file. Add the **only_from = 192.168.122.150** line, which represents the tester1.example.com system.

4. Save the configuration file and reload the xinetd service script with the **service xinetd reload** command. Try accessing Telnet from the local computer. What happens?

5. Try accessing Telnet from the computer with the IP address of 192.168.122.150. What happens? Try again from a different system on the LAN.

6. Restore the previous /etc/xinetd.d/telnet configuration file. Don't forget to reload the xinetd service script with the **service xinetd reload** command.

7. Back up the current version of the /etc/hosts.deny file. Open that file in a text editor. Add the **telnetd : ALL EXCEPT 192.168.122.150** line.

8. Try accessing Telnet from the computer with the IP address of 192.168.122.50. What happens? Try again from a different computer on your LAN.

9. Restore the previous /etc/hosts.deny file.

10. Save any existing **iptables** chains. Back up the current /etc/sysconfig/iptables file.

11. Flush current firewall rules with the **iptables -F** command.

12. Block the Telnet port, 23, for all IP addresses except 192.168.122.150 with the **iptables -A INPUT -s ! 192.168.122.150 -p tcp --dport 23 -j DROP** command.

13. Activate the firewall with the **/etc/init.d/iptables restart** command.

14. Try accessing the Telnet server from the computer with the IP address of 192.168.122.150. What happens? Try again from a different computer on the LAN.

15. Restore any previous firewall rules; restore the original version of /etc/sysconfig/iptables from backup. Reload the firewall with the **/etc/init.d/iptables restart** command.

16. Bonus: Repeat these commands for the SSH service on port 22.

Lab 5

To confirm that TCP Wrappers can be used to help protect the SSH service, run the following command:

```
# ldd /usr/sbin/sshd | grep libwrap
```

Output, which includes a reference to the libwrap.so.0 library, confirms a library link to the TCP Wrappers library. In general, it's safest to deny access to all services by including the following entry in the /etc/hosts.deny file:

```
ALL : ALL
```

You can then set up access to the SSH service with a line like the following in the /etc/hosts.allow file:

```
sshd : 192.168.122.50
```

While in most cases, the use of the fully qualified domain name for the noted IP address (server1.example.com) should work too, the use of the IP address is often appropriate. Limits by IP address don't depend on connections to DNS servers.

Of course, this is not the only way to limit access to the SSH to one system. It's possible within the /etc/hosts.deny file with a directive such as the following:

```
sshd : ALL EXCEPT 192.168.122.50
```

It's possible to set this up with other security options such as **iptables** command–based firewalls.

Lab 6

Before this lab can work, however, you'll need to activate one SELinux boolean, ftp_home_dir. It's listed in the SELinux Management tool as "Allow ftp to read and write files in the user home directories." While this boolean setting is covered in Chapter 11, the basic management of SELinux, including the activation of boolean settings, is an RHCSA skill covered in Chapter 4. Therefore, with the key boolean identified, you should be able to set up vsFTP as described.

The description in this lab should point you to the /etc/pam.d/vsftpd configuration file. The model command line in this file is

```
auth required  pam_listfile.so item=user sense=deny file=/etc/vsftpd/ftpusers
onerr=succeed
```

which points to the /etc/vsftpd/ftpusers file, a list of users to "deny" access. As the conditions in the lab suggest that you need a list of (one) user to which access is to be allowed, a second line of a similar type in this file is appropriate. To verify this lab, I included the following line:

```
auth required  pam_listfile.so item=user sense=allow file=/etc/vsftpd/testusers
onerr=succeed
```

which allows all users listed in the /etc/vsftpd/testusers file. The **onerr=succeed** directive means that the vsFTP server still works if there's an error elsewhere in the line. For example, if there is no testusers file in the /etc/vsftpd directory, the directives in this line are forgiving, allowing the conditions for the **auth** module type to succeed.

As an experiment, try this lab with the boolean ftp_home_dir variable set and unset. That should demonstrate the power of SELinux and serve as an appropriate preview of Chapter 11.

11

System Services
and SELinux

T his is a "big picture" chapter with respect to the RHCE objectives. Those objectives are focused on common tasks that you'll perform on the job. These tasks relate to the detailed configuration of RHCE-level services.

RHEL 6 incorporates basic system configuration files in the /etc/sysconfig directory. These files are called by different services in the /etc/init.d directory. The services then use custom configuration files in dedicated locations. Integral to this process is the configuration of SELinux, as it includes a substantial number of custom options for various services.

These tools will be tested on the one service that you might install on all bastion systems, SSH. As it is the common service for all such systems, crackers everywhere want to find a weakness in SSH. So this chapter also describes how you can make SSH services more secure. This is the first chapter where the three virtual machines created in Chapters 1 and 2 will be used.

In this chapter, you'll also the boolean options used by SELinux to secure those server services associated with the RHCE objectives. While SELinux is a common source of frustration, it is easier to handle when you know the options that support desired features.

In addition, this chapter covers the basic procedure that should be followed to make sure the service is operational, accessible from remote systems, and up the next time the system is rebooted.

INSIDE THE EXAM

This section includes tasks that will be repeated in the remainder of this book.

- Install the packages needed to provide the service

Whether you're installing the Samba file server or a DNS caching-only nameserver, the same tools are used. Yes, these are the same **rpm** and **yum** commands, along with

the Package Management tools described in Chapter 7. To save time, you might use these commands to install the services described in Chapters 12 through 17.

- Configure the service to start when the system is booted
- Configure SELinux to support the service

While the detailed configuration of individual services is the province of each chapter, the steps required to configure a service to start during the boot process are based on common commands like **chkconfig**. In addition, the configuration of SELinux to support a service requires access to and the configuration of similar options. As suggested in the introduction, there's a special focus on the SSH service.

■   Configure key-based authentication

With key-based authentication, you'll be able to connect to remote systems by using private/public key pairs. Password transmission over the network would no longer be required. The 1024 or more bits associated with such authentication are a lot harder to crack than a password transmitted over a network. Given the importance of SSH security, you'll also

■   Configure additional options described in documentation

CERTIFICATION OBJECTIVE 11.01

Red Hat System Configuration

In this section, you'll review basic information on how services are configured on Red Hat systems. The actual process associated with a service is a daemon. Such daemons are executable files, normally stored in the /usr/sbin and /sbin directories. Red Hat configures custom parameters and more in the /etc/sysconfig directory.

Service Management

As discussed throughout the book, services are controlled with scripts in the /etc/init.d directory. But those scripts just put things together. As described in Chapter 4, they can be used to **start**, **stop**, or **restart** a service. In many cases, those scripts can be used to **reload** the service with modified configuration files, without kicking off currently connected users.

While the real daemons are in the /sbin and /usr/sbin directories, the /etc/init.d scripts do more. They call the daemons with parameters configured in the /etc/sysconfig directory. The daemons then call service-specific configuration files.

In any case, the scripts in the /etc/init.d directory are hard-linked to the scripts in the /etc/rc.d/init.d directory. And the **service** command in the /sbin directory is a front end to those scripts. In other words, the following commands are functionally identical:

```
# /etc/init.d/sshd restart
# /etc/rc.d/init.d/sshd restart
# service sshd restart
```

System Services

The files in the /etc/sysconfig directory are normally used with /etc/init.d scripts. They're as varied as the services included in the /etc/init.d directory. As they include basic configuration options for each daemon, they drive the basic operation of each service. These files are briefly described in Table 11-1. While the list goes beyond the services covered in the RHCSA and RHCE objectives, the list does not include files in /etc/sysconfig subdirectories. While the descriptions frequently refer to discussions in other chapters, most files in this directory are rarely edited by administrators. In many cases, these files aren't even described in the noted chapters. They're listed to help give you a feel for the depth and breadth of Red Hat services. Remember, the RHCSA and RHCE are separate exams, covered in Chapters 1 through 10 and 11 through 17, respectively.

TABLE 11-1	Files in the /etc/sysconfig Directory
File	**Description**
atd	Supports limits on the number of jobs and time interval between jobs, as described in Chapter 9.
auditd	Includes switches for the audit daemon.
authconfig	Specifies the options for the Authentication Configuration tool, described in several chapters.
autofs	Works with the automounter, discussed in Chapter 6.
cgconfig, cgred.conf	Controls the control group rules daemon.
clock	Notes the current time zone, discussed in Chapter 5.
cpuspeed	Supports changes in CPU speeds based on workloads.
crond	Includes options for the cron daemon, as described in Chapter 9.

TABLE 11-1	Files in the /etc/sysconfig Directory (continued)
File	**Description**
ebtables-config	Configures data-link-level firewalls.
firstboot	Specifies whether the First Boot process will be run; if you change this to yes, the First Boot process is run upon the next reboot.
grub	Sets the boot drive and can set other boot parameters, discussed in Chapter 5.
httpd	Configures options for the Apache web server daemon, as described in Chapter 14.
i18n	Specifies the currently configured language.
init	Sets options during the boot process before the scripts in the /etc/init directory, discussed in Chapter 5.
ip6tables	Sets firewall configuration rules for IPv6 networking.
ip6tables-config	Defines firewall service options for IPv6.
iptables	Sets firewall configuration rules for IPv4 networking, discussed in Chapters 4 and 10.
iptables-config	Defines firewall service options for IPv4.
irqbalance	Configures how interrupts are loaded.
kadmin	Sets up Kerberos administration.
kexec	Sets up the boot into a different kernel.
kernel	Configures how new kernels are updated, briefly described in Chapter 5.
keyboard	Notes parameters of the current keyboard.
krb5kdc	Specifies arguments for starting the Kerberos key distribution center.
ksm	Sets up kernel page swaps for virtual machines.
ldap	Includes daemon options for the LDAP server.
libvirtd	Sets up basic parameters for virtualization support.
libvirt-guests	Configures the startup or shutdown of virtual machine guests.
mcelog	Specifies options for the kernel machine check log.
named	Sets up options for the standard Red Hat DNS server, described in Chapter 17.
netconsole	Supports remote logging.
network	Configures basic network parameters, described in Chapter 4.
nfs	Sets up specific NFS parameters and port numbers, discussed in Chapter 16.
nspluginwrapper	Supports plugins for web browsers.
ntpd	Includes basic options for the NTP server, described in Chapter 17.

TABLE 11-1	Files in the /etc/sysconfig Directory (*continued*)
File	**Description**
ntpdate	Includes basic options for the NTP client, as discussed in Chapter 5.
openct	Specifies control options for smart card readers.
prelink	Configures library management.
raid-check	Options for the weekly job to check RAID arrays.
readahead	Specifies caching information for the boot process.
readonly-root	Sets read/write settings during the boot process.
rsyslog	Includes options for the rsyslog daemon, as discussed in Chapters 9 and 17.
samba	Supports options for three Samba daemons, smbd, nmbd, and winbindd, as discussed in Chapter 15.
sandbox	Works with limits on users, such as xguest discussed in Chapter 8.
saslauthd	Helps configure authentication support.
sa-update	Supports nightly system activity reports.
smartmontools	Configures support for hard disk monitoring.
spamd	Specifies options for the spamd daemon.
sysstat	Includes log and compression options for system status tools.
sysstat.ioconf	Lists available drive devices for sysstat.
system-config-firewall	Summarizes non-default firewall rules.
system-config-users	Configures basic options for the user manager.
tgtd	Sets up basic SCSI and iSCSI parameters.
udev	Supports caching of device files.
vncservers	Configures basic VNC server options, as discussed in Chapter 7.
wpa_supplicant	Supports options for Wi-Fi Protected Access (WPA).
xinetd	Sets up the Extended Internet Super-Server, described in Chapter 10.

In most cases, each of these files supports the use of switches as described in associated man pages. For example, the /etc/sysconfig/httpd file can be used to set up custom options for starting the Apache web server. In that file, the **OPTIONS** directive would pass switches to the /usr/sbin/httpd daemon, as defined in the httpd man page.

Bigger Picture Configuration Process

In general, when you configure a network server service on Linux, take the following steps. The following guidelines are general; for example, sometimes it's appropriate to modify SELinux options first. Sometimes, you'll want to test a service locally and remotely before making sure the service starts automatically upon the next reboot.

1. Install the service, normally with a command like **rpm** or **yum**. In some cases, the RHCE exam or real-life needs require the installation of additional packages.

2. Edit the service configuration files. In some cases, there are one or more configuration files; for example, you may need to modify and customize several configuration files to set up the Postfix e-mail server in the /etc/postfix directory.

3. Modify SELinux booleans. As discussed later in this chapter, different services have a variety of options controlled by SELinux. For example, SELinux changes are required to allow the Samba file server to share files in read/write or in read-only mode.

4. Start the service, as typically controlled by a script in the /etc/init.d directory. You'll also need to make sure the service starts the next time the system is booted, as discussed later in this chapter.

5. Test the service locally. Make sure it works from appropriate client(s) on the local system.

6. Open applicable firewall ports, based on **iptables**, TCP wrappers, and more. Configure access to desired users and systems.

7. Test the service remotely. If the right ports are open, the service should work as well as when you connect locally. The service should not work for undesired users.

Available Configuration Tools

In general, it's most efficient to configure various services from the command line interface. An administrator who knows a service well will be able to set it up at least for basic operation in just a few minutes. However, all but the most capable administrators can't specialize in everything. To that end, Red Hat has developed a number of configuration tools. When used properly, these tools will modify the right configuration files. Some are installed with each service, others have to be installed separately. Most of these tools are accessible from a GUI command line interface with a **system-config-*** command.

The tools used in this book (and a couple more) are summarized in Table 11-2.

There are actually fewer GUI configuration tools for RHEL 6 when compared to RHEL 5. For example, RHEL 5 included GUI configuration tools to configure a DNS server and the GUI display. Personally, I find it easier to edit DNS server configuration files directly. To me, the RHEL 5 GUI tool was cumbersome.

TABLE 11-2	Tool	Command	Function
Red Hat Configuration Tools	Add/Remove Software	**gpk-application**	Front end to **yum** command; manages current software configuration
	Authentication Configuration	**authconfig*,** **system-config-authentication**	Connection between clients and authentication databases
	Date/Time Properties	**system-config-date**	Management of the current time zone, NTP client
	Firewall Configuration	**system-config-firewall**	Configuration of **iptables** firewalls, masquerading, and forwarding
	Language Selection	**system-config-language**	Language selection within the GUI
	Network Management	**system-config-network**	Network device / DNS configuration at the console
	Network Connections	**nm-connection-editor**	Detailed network device configuration tool
	Printer Configuration	**system-config-printer**	Management of the CUPS print server
	SELinux Management	**system-config-selinux**	Configuration of SELinux booleans, labels, users, etc.
	Software Update	**gpk-update-viewer**	Review and install available updates to installed packages
	User Manager	**system-config-users**	Management and configuration of users and groups

CERTIFICATION OBJECTIVE 11.02

Security-Enhanced Linux

Security-Enhanced Linux (SELinux) provides one more layer of security. Developed by the U.S. National Security Agency, SELinux makes it more difficult for crackers to use or access any file or service if they break in. SELinux assigns different contexts to each file, known as *subjects*, *objects*, and *actions*.

Basic SELinux options were covered in Chapter 4, as it is also a requirement for the RHCSA certification. For the RHCE, the focus of SELinux relates to various services. Specifically, you need to know how to configure SELinux to support the Apache web server, Domain Name System (DNS) services, an FTP server, Network File System (NFS) servers, Samba file servers, Simple Mail Transport Protocol (SMTP) servers, Secure Shell (SSH) servers, and Network Time Protocol (NTP) servers.

The requirements for each of these services are covered in this and later chapters of this book. As the SELinux configuration for each service requires the use of the same commands and tools, they're covered here.

Perhaps the key commands and tools discussed in this section are **getsebool**, **setsebool**, **chcon**, **ls -Z**, and the SELinux Management Tool. While these are the same tools used in Chapter 4, the focus is different. To review, the **getsebool** and **setsebool** commands set boolean options in the files of the /selinux/booleans directory. A boolean is a binary option, 1 or 0, which corresponds to yes and no.

Options in the SELinux Booleans Directory

When configuring SELinux for a service, you'll generally make changes to boolean settings in the **/selinux/booleans** directory. Take a look at the files in this directory. The file names are somewhat descriptive.

For example, the ftp_home_dir boolean either allows or denies access to user home directories via an FTP server. It is disabled by default. In other words, if you configure the vsFTP server in Chapter 16 to support logins to user home directories without changes to SELinux, users won't be able to log in to their home directories via FTP.

Problems like this are a common source of frustration for administrators of RHEL systems. They do all the work to configure a service, they test out the configuration, they check their documentation, they think they've done everything right, and yet the service doesn't work as they want. The solution is to make SELinux a part of what you do to configure a service.

In other words, run the following command:

```
$ cat /selinux/booleans/ftp_home_dir
```

By default, the output should be

```
0 0
```

That's two 0s. Supposedly one boolean is for the current setting, the other is for the permanent setting. In practice, the numbers don't reflect the differences, at least for RHEL 6. But the differences are still there. Because of this issue, the best way to see the current state of a boolean is the **getsebool** command. For example, the command

```
$ getsebool ftp_home_dir
```

leads to the following output:

```
ftp_home_dir --> off
```

Bottom line, if the current setting is 0, either of the following commands would activate the ftp_home_dir boolean only until the system is rebooted:

```
# setsebool ftp_home_dir 1
# togglesebool ftp_home_dir
```

As suggested by the name, the **togglesebool** command changes the current boolean from 0 to 1 and back. To repeat from Chapter 4, the way to make the change permanent from the command line is with the **setsebool -P** command, in this case:

```
# setsebool -P ftp_home_dir 1
```

---

e x a m

ⓦatch   *Many service-related*   *command. If you don't have access to the*
SELinux booleans are described in local   *GUI SELinux Management tool during the*
documentation; for a list of associated   *exam, that could be a lifesaver.*
man pages, run the man -k _selinux

Service Categories of SELinux Booleans

There are about 170 files in the /selinux/booleans directory. As the filenames in the /selinux/booleans directory are descriptive, you can use database filter commands like grep to help classify those booleans. Based on some of the services discussed in this book, the following would be some appropriate filtering commands:

```
$ ls /selinux/booleans | grep http
$ ls /selinux/booleans | grep ftp
$ ls /selinux/booleans | grep nfs
```

You'll explore each of these categories of booleans in more detail shortly. For a brief description of available booleans with their current status, run the **semanage boolean -l** command. The **semanage** command is part of and can be installed through the policycoreutils-python package.

Boolean Configuration with the SELinux Management Tool

One of the benefits of GUI tools is a view of the "big picture." With the SELinux Management tool, you can review the active booleans and quickly get a sense of whether SELinux is set to allow few or many options associated with a service. As discussed in Chapter 4, you can start the SELinux Management tool in a GUI desktop environment with the **system-config-selinux** command. In the left-hand pane, click Boolean. It opens access to a group of booleans in the right side of the window. Note the **ftp** filter added in Figure 11-1. It filters the system for all booleans related to FTP.

Compare the list to the output of the **ls /selinux/booleans | grep ftp** command described earlier. Note the differences. Some booleans shown through the SELinux Management tool don't show up directly with a **grep** of the file list in the /selinux/booleans directory. In general, booleans like user_tcp_server are only tangentially related to FTP services.

There are a number of categories shown in the left pane of the SELinux Management Tool window; they are described in the following sections. Most of the focus here will be in the Boolean category, where most of SELinux policies are customized.

In some cases, the boolean is associated with a requirement for a SELinux file context. For example, the allow_httpd_anon_write boolean works only if associated files and directories are labeled with the public_content_rw_type. To set that type on, say, the /var/www/html/files directory (and subdirectories), you would run the following command:

```
# chcon -R -t public_content_rw_type /var/www/html/files
```

FIGURE 11-1   Filter booleans with the SELinux Management tool.

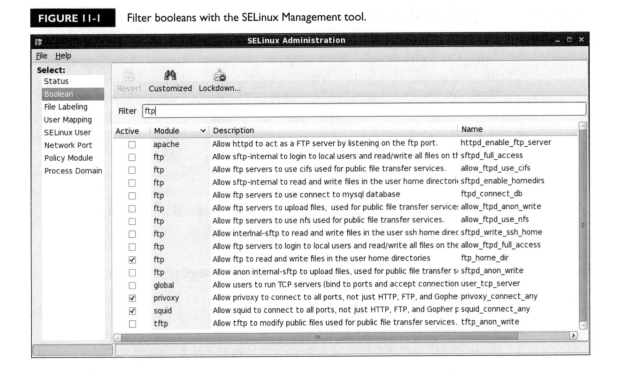

Boolean Settings

The boolean settings discussed in the following sections fall into a number of categories. They're based on the services defined in the RHCE objectives. The SELinux settings do not stand alone. For example, if you enable the httpd_enable_homedirs boolean, you'll still have to configure the /etc/httpd/conf/httpd.conf file to support access to user home directories. Only after both SELinux and Apache are configured with such support can users connect to their home directories through that Apache server.

As there are no current SELinux booleans related to the Network Time Protocol (NTP) service, there is no separate section for NTP booleans in the following list.

Regular and Secure HTTP Services

There are a number of SELinux directives available to help secure the Apache web server, as summarized in the following bullets. Most are straightforward and self-explanatory. They are ordered by the filename of the boolean as shown in the /selinux/booleans directory. While these booleans should apply to any web service, Red Hat assumes the use of the Apache web server. The descriptions specify the configuration if the boolean is active.

- **allow_httpd_anon_write**   Allows the web service to write to files labeled with the public_content_rw_t type.
- **allow_httpd_mod_auth_ntlm_winbind**   Permits access to the Microsoft NT LAN Manager (NTLM) and winbind authentication databases; requires an installed and active mod_auth_ntlm_winbind module for Apache.
- **allow_httpd_mod_auth_pam**   Supports PAM access for user authentication; requires an installed and active mod_auth_pam module for Apache.
- **allow_httpd_sys_script_anon_write**   Allows HTTP scripts to write to files labeled with the public_content_rw_t type.
- **httpd_builtin_scripting**   Permits access to scripts, normally associated with PHP. Enabled by default.
- **httpd_can_check_spam**   Supports the use of SpamAssassin for web-based e-mail applications.
- **httpd_can_network_connect**   Supports access by scripts to external systems; normally disabled to minimize risks to other systems.
- **httpd_can_network_connect_cobbler**   Supports access by scripts to an external Cobbler installation server; if this boolean is enabled, you should disabled the httpd_can_network_connect boolean.
- **httpd_can_network_connect_db**   Allows connections to database server ports; more specific than httpd_can_network_connect.
- **httpd_can_network_memcache**   Enables access to memory object caching; associated with the Pootle language translation project.
- **httpd_can_network_relay**   Supports access to standard relay ports, such as those associated with HTTP and FTP; more specific than httpd_can_network_connect.
- **httpd_can_sendmail**   Allows outgoing SMTP access from web-based e-mail applications.

- **httpd_dbus_avahi** Supports access to automated IP addressing, using the avahi service, via the D-bus message system. Allowed by default.

- **httpd_enable_cgi** Supports access to Common Gateway Interface (CGI) scripts. Allowed by default; requires scripts to be labeled with the httpd_sys_script_exec_t file type.

- **httpd_enable_ftp_server** Allows Apache to listen on the FTP port (normally 21) and work as an FTP server.

- **httpd_enable_homedirs** Enables configuration of Apache to read user home directories.

- **httpd_execmem** Supports programs such as those written in Java or Mono that require memory addresses that are executable and writable.

- **httpd_read_user_content** Allows the Apache web server to read all files in user home directories, not just those labeled with various httpd_*_t file types.

- **httpd_setrlimit** Allows changes to Apache file descriptor limits.

- **httpd_ssi_exec** Supports executable Server Side Includes (SSIs).

- **httpd_tmp_exec** Lets Apache run executable files from the /tmp directory.

- **httpd_tty_comm** Supports access by the apache user (lower case) for access to the files with secure certificates. Allowed by default.

- **httpd_unified** Enables access to all httpd_*_t labeled files, whether they be read-only, writable, or executable. Allowed by default.

- **httpd_use_cifs** Supports access from Apache to shared Samba files and directories labeled with the cifs_t file type.

- **httpd_use_gpg** Allows Apache to use GPG for encryption.

- **httpd_use_nfs** Supports access from Apache to shared NFS files and directories labeled with the nfs_t file type.

- **privoxy_connect_any** Enables access by the Privoxy web proxy server through standard Apache ports.

- **squid_connect_any** Enables access by the Squid web proxy server through standard Apache ports.

- **varnishd_connect_any** Enables access by the Varnish web proxy server through standard Apache ports.

Name Service

The name service daemon (**named**) is based on the Berkeley Internet Name Domain (BIND) software, which is the RHEL 6 DNS service. If you maintain an authoritative DNS zone, it's appropriate to activate the named_write_master_zones boolean. Then local DNS software can overwrite master zone files.

In general, this does not apply to the RHCE, as the objectives state that all you need to do is configure DNS as a caching or a forwarding name server. Such servers by definition cannot be authoritative for a specific domain. As such DNS servers do not have master zone files, the noted DNS boolean does not apply.

FTP

While there aren't quite as many configuration options for FTP servers when compared to those available for the Apache web server, they are varied and important. While these booleans should apply to any FTP server, Red Hat assumes the use of the vsFTP server. While there are a number of options associated with the FTP server associated with SSH, the boolean settings associated with the **sftp** commands are not active, and in any case they are not part of the configuration associated with the vsFTP server. In any case, changes to the sftp-booleans had no effect on my ability to perform the associated actions. Therefore, **sftp**-related SELinux settings are not covered in this book. None of these booleans are enabled by default.

- **allow_ftpd_anon_write**   Supports uploads from anonymous users, to directories labeled with the public_content_rw_t type.
- **allow_ftpd_full_access**   Supports full access to all directories shared via the FTP server, beyond those allowed by the allow_ftp_anon_write and the ftp_home_dir booleans.
- **allow_ftpd_use_cifs**   Enables access to files labeled with the cifs_t file type, which is assigned to files from mounted Samba directories.
- **allow_ftpd_use_nfs**   Enables access to files labeled with the nfs_t file type, which is assigned to files from mounted NFS directories.
- **ftpd_connect_db**   Supports connections from an FTP server to a database.
- **ftp_home_dir**   Allows access to user home directories.

NFS

More of the basic SELinux booleans associated with the Network File Service (NFS) servers are enabled by default. So in some basic configurations, you'll be able to share certain directories with the NFS server without changes to SELinux booleans. But alas, that's not always true. In fact, if you don't want to allow others to set up an NFS server, it may be safest to disable such booleans.

- **cdrecord_read_content**   Supports access by the **cdrecord** command to shared files from network and locally mounted directories.
- **nfs_export_all_ro**   Allows shared NFS directories to be exported with read-only permissions. Enabled by default.
- **nfs_export_all_rw**   Allows shared NFS directories to be exported with read/write permissions. Enabled by default.
- **qemu_use_nfs**   Enables access from KVM-based virtual machines of files from NFS mounted filesystems. Enabled by default.
- **use_nfs_home_dirs**   Supports access of home directories from remote systems. Enabled by default.
- **virt_use_nfs**   Enables access with the libvirt daemon of files from NFS mounted filesystems.

Samba

Samba booleans are generally not enabled by default. So in most configurations, you'll need to make changes to SELinux to match changes to the Samba configuration files. These booleans include the following:

- **allow_smbd_anon_write**   Supports writing to public directories, where access by specific users is not otherwise regulated. Requires directories labeled with the public_content_rw_t file type.
- **samba_create_home_dir**   Allows Samba to create new home directories, such as for users who connect from other systems, using network authentication databases.
- **samba_domain_controller**   Enables the configuration of the local Samba server as a local domain controller on a Microsoft Windows style network.
- **samba_enable_home_dirs**   Supports the sharing of user home directories.
- **samba_export_all_ro**   Allows files and directories to be shared in read-only mode.
- **samba_export_all_rw**   Allows files and directories to be shared in read/write mode.

- **samba_run_unconfined** Allows Samba to run scripts stored in the /var/lib/samba/scripts directory; it has the samba_unconfined_script_exec_t tag.
- **samba_share_fusefs** Supports sharing of filesystems mounted under FUSE filesystems (fusefs).
- **samba_share_nfs** Supports sharing of filesystems mounted under NFS.
- **use_samba_home_dirs** Enables the use of applications shared from remote Samba servers on local home directories.
- **virt_use_samba** Allows virtual machines to use files shared from Samba.

SMTP

The two SELinux booleans associated with SMTP services both work with the default Postfix server. The httpd_can_sendmail boolean was previously described. The other Postfix boolean is enabled by default:

- **allow_postfix_local_write_mail_spool** Supports sharing of filesystems mounted under NFS.

Be aware, if you use the Exim SMTP service, a different set of SELinux booleans are available. Nevertheless, Exim is not included on the RHEL 6 DVD.

SSH

The two SELinux booleans associated with SSH connections, in my opinion, should never be enabled. Fortunately, neither option is enabled by default:

- **allow_ssh_keysign** Allows host-based authentication; would not require usernames or public/private passphrase based authentication.
- **ssh_sysadm_login** Supports access by users configured with the sysadm_r role. This does not include the root administrative user; in general, it's more secure to log in as a regular user, connecting with passphrases, before authenticating with administrative privileges.

SELinux File Contexts

Changes made with the **chcon** command are not permanent. While they do survive a reboot, they do not survive a *relabel*. SELinux relabels of a system can happen when SELinux is disabled and then re-enabled. The **restorecon** command relabels a target directory. The configured SELinux contexts are stored in the /etc/selinux/targeted/contexts/files directory.

The default version of this directory includes three files:

- **file_contexts** Baseline file contexts for the entire system
- **file_contexts.homedirs** File contexts for the /home directory, and all subdirectories
- **media** File contexts for removable devices that may be mounted after installation

If you need a change to file system contexts to survive a reboot, the **semanage** command can help. For example, if you need to set up the /www directory for virtual web sites, the following command makes sure the file contexts are appropriate for that directory (and subdirectories) even after a relabel:

```
# semanage fcontext -a -s system_u -t httpd_sys_content_t /www/*
```

The noted command creates a file_contexts.local file in the /etc/selinux/targeted/contexts/files directory.

While the **semanage** command manages a variety of SELinux policies, the focus here is on file contexts, as represented by the **fcontext** option. The switches shown are described in Table 11-3.

TABLE 11-3	Switch	Description
	-a	Add
Command	-d	Delete
Switches for	-D	Delete all
semanage	-f	File type
fcontext	-l	List
	-m	Modify
	-n	No heading
	-r	Range
	-s	SELinux user name; used for user roles
	-t	SELinux file type

EXERCISE 11-1

Configure a New Directory with Appropriate SELinux Contexts

In this exercise, you'll set up a new directory, /ftp, with SELinux contexts that match the standard directory for FTP servers. This exercise demonstrates how this is done with the **chcon** command, along with the effect of the **restorecon** and **semanage** commands.

1. Create the /ftp directory. Use the **ls -Zd /ftp** command to identify the SELinux contexts on that directory. Contrast that with the contexts on the /var/ftp directory.

2. Change the contexts on the /ftp directory to match those on the /var/ftp directory. The most efficient method is with the following command:

   ```
   # chcon -R --reference /var/ftp /ftp
   ```

   While the **-R** switch is not required, I include it to help you get used to the idea of changing contexts recursively.

3. Run the **ls -Zd /ftp** command to review the changed contexts on that directory. It should now match the contexts on the /var/ftp directory.

4. Run the following command to see what happens when SELinux is relabeled.

   ```
   # restorecon -R /ftp
   ```

   What did this command do to the contexts of the /ftp directory? (If desired, include the **-v** switch; if successful, it specifies the changes that have been made.)

5. To make changes to the /ftp directory permanent, you need help from the **semanage** command, with the **fcontext** option. As there is no analogue to the **chcon --reference** command switch, the following command specifies the user role and file type, based on the default settings for the /var/ftp directory:

   ```
   # semanage fcontext -a -s system_u -t public_content_t /ftp/*
   ```

6. Review the results. First, the **semanage** command does not change the current SELinux contexts of the /ftp directory. Next, review the contents of file_contexts.local in the /etc/selinux/targeted/contexts/files directory. It should reflect the **semanage** command just executed.

7. Rerun the **restorecon** command from Step 4. Does it change the SELinux contexts of the /ftp directory now?

CERTIFICATION OBJECTIVE 11.03

The Secure Shell Server

Red Hat Enterprise Linux installs the Secure Shell (SSH) server packages by default, using the openssh-server, openssh-clients, and openssh RPMs. Chapter 2 addressed SSH client programs including **ssh**, **scp**, and **sftp**. The focus of this section is on the SSH server. The secure daemon, **sshd**, listens for all inbound traffic on TCP port 22. The SSH server configuration files are located in the /etc/ssh directory.

As SSH is an important tool for administering systems remotely, it's important to understand the basics of how it encrypts communication between a client and the SSH server. Then you'll see how to create a public/private keypair, so connections won't even put passwords at risk. Finally, you'll examine how to configure the SSH server configuration file in detail. But first, it may be helpful to review some basic information about SSH configuration commands and files.

SSH Configuration Commands

There are a few SSH-oriented utilities you need to know about:

- **sshd** The daemon service; this must be running to receive inbound Secure Shell client requests.

- **ssh-agent** A program to hold private keys used for Digital Signature Algorithm (DSA) and Rivest, Shamir, Adelman (RSA) authentication. The idea is that the **ssh-agent** command is started in the beginning of an X session or a login session, and all other windows or programs are started as clients to the **ssh-agent** program.

- **ssh-add** Adds RSA identities to the authentication agent, **ssh-agent**.

- **ssh** The Secure Shell command, **ssh**, is a secure way to log in to a remote machine, similar to Telnet or **rlogin**. The basic use of this command was discussed in Chapter 2. To make this work securely, you need a private key on the server and a public key on the client. Take the public key file, identity.pub or id_dsa.pub, created later in this section. Copy it to the client. Place it in the home directory of an authorized user, in the ~/.ssh/authorized_keys file.

- **ssh-keygen** A utility that creates private/public keypairs for SSH authentication. The **ssh-keygen -t** *keytype* command will create either *keytype*, DSA or RSA.
- **ssh-copy-id** A command that transmits a public key to a target remote system.

All you need to do is transfer the public key, with the .pub extension, to an authorized user. You can do this directly, using a method such as a USB key. Alternatively, you can transmit that key over the network with the **ssh-copy-id** command. It's important to add a passphrase to protect that digital signature. It's important to protect that passphrase. In the worst case, a cracker could use the passphrase to steal your account identity.

SSH Configuration Files

Systems configured with SSH include configuration files in two different directories. For the local system, basic SSH configuration files are stored in the /etc/ssh directory. The functionality of these files are summarized here:

- **moduli** Supports the Diffie-Hellman Group Exchange key method with prime numbers and random key generators.
- **ssh_config** Includes configuration for the local SSH client, discussed in Chapter 2.
- **sshd_config** Specifies the configuration of the SSH server; discussed in detail later in this chapter.
- **ssh_host_dsa_key** Includes the host private key for the local system, based on the DSA algorithm.
- **ssh_host_dsa_key.pub** Includes the host public key for the local system, based on the DSA algorithm.
- **ssh_host_key** Obsolete; private host key for SSH protocol version 1, which has been cracked.
- **ssh_host_key.pub** Obsolete; public host key for SSH protocol version 1, which has been cracked.
- **ssh_host_rsa_key** Includes the host private key for the local system, based on the RSA algorithm.
- **ssh_host_rsa_key.pub** Includes the host public key for the local system, based on the RSA algorithm.

But just as important are the configuration files in each user's home directory, in the .ssh/ subdirectory. Those files configure how the given user is allowed to connect to remote systems. When both DSA and RSA keys are included, the typical user .ssh/ subdirectory includes the following files, which should for the most part be familiar from the previous discussion of files in the /etc/ssh directory.

- ■ **authorized_keys**   Includes a list of public keys from remote systems. Users with public encryption keys in this file can connect to remote systems. The system users and names are listed at the end of each public key copied to this file.
- ■ **id_dsa_key**   Includes the local private key based on the DSA algorithm.
- ■ **id_dsa_key.pub**   Includes the local public key for the system based on the DSA algorithm.
- ■ **id_rsa_key**   Includes the local private key based on the RSA algorithm.
- ■ **id_rsa_key.pub**   Includes the local public key for the system based on the RSA algorithm.
- ■ **known_hosts**   Contains the public RSA keys from remote systems. The first time a user logs in to a system, he's prompted to accept the key. The contents of the remote /etc/ssh/ssh_host_rsa_key.pub file are added to the local known_hosts file at that time.

Older RHEL systems included id_dsa.keystore and id_rsa.keystore files with copies of both public and private keys. That is no longer necessary.

Basic Encrypted Communication

Basic encryption in computer networking normally requires a private key and a public key. The principle is the same as GPG communications discussed in Chapter 10. The private key is stored on the server, and the public key is sent to administrative workstations. When the pair is properly configured, administrators on those workstations can connect to the noted servers remotely. Data that is sent through an SSH connection is encrypted with the public key. The SSH server can unscramble the message with the private key.

Encryption keys are based on random numbers. The numbers are so large (typically 768 bits or more) that the chance that someone will break into the server system, at least with a PC, is quite small. Private and public encryption keys are based on a matched set of these random numbers.

Private Keys

The private key must be secure. It is accessible only to the user owner of that key, in the .ssh subdirectory of that user's home directory. Anything that is sent over the SSH connection is then digitally signed and encrypted with the public key. Only the recipient, in this case, the SSH server, will be able to decrypt the message.

Public Keys

The public key is just that, publicly available. Public keys created in this chapter are exclusive to the SSH server in use. They're designed to be copied to appropriate user's .ssh/ subdirectories, in files with .pub extensions. The public keys for SSH servers belong on administrative workstations, so systems managers like yourself can connect to those systems remotely.

The example shown in Figure 11-2 lists the directories and files associated with SSH usage as well as a public key that has been added to the local "keyring."

This key is like a password used to encrypt communications data. But it's not a standard password by any means. Imagine trying to remember the 1024-bit number expressed in hexadecimal format as shown here:

```
3081 8902 8181 00D4 596E 01DE A012 3CAD 51B7
7835 05A4 DEFC C70B 4382 A733 5D62 A51B B9D6
29EA 860B EC2B 7AB8 2E96 3A4C 71A2 D087 11D0
E149 4DD5 1E20 8382 FA58 C7DA D9B0 3865 FF6E
88C7 B672 51F5 5094 3B35 D8AA BC68 BBEB BFE3
9063 AE75 8B57 09F9 DCF8 FFA4 E32C A17F 82E9
7A4C 0E10 E62D 8A97 0845 007B 169A 0676 E7CF
5713 1423 96E0 8E6C 9502 0301 0001
```

That is why the applications save this value for you, on a "public keyring." You can add as many public keys from other users, sites, and services as needed.

FIGURE 11-2

Keys in a User's .ssh/ subdirectory

```
michael@Maui:~$ ls -l .ssh/
total 44
-rw-------. 1 michael michael  1822 Feb  8 16:55 authorized_keys
-rw-------. 1 michael michael   736 Jun  5  2008 id_dsa
-rw-r--r--. 1 michael michael  3576 Jun 17  2008 id_dsa.keystore
-rw-r--r--. 1 michael michael   606 Jun  5  2008 id_dsa.pub
-rw-------. 1 michael michael  1743 Feb  5  2010 id_rsa
-rw-r--r--. 1 michael michael  2506 Feb  5  2010 id_rsa.keystore
-rw-r--r--. 1 michael michael   398 Feb  5  2010 id_rsa.pub
-rw-r--r--. 1 michael michael 15162 Jan 21 09:05 known_hosts
michael@Maui:~$ 
```

The private key is similar, *but you must keep it private*, or this whole system fails. Keeping it private means no one should have access to the server systems. If your PC is public, secure your system with a passphrase (password). The procedure to set up a passphrase is described next. Don't forget the passphrase, or you'll have to remove and reinstall the Secure Shell.

Set Up a Private/Public Pair for Key-Based Authentication

The **ssh-keygen** command is used to set up a public/private key pair. While it creates an RSA key by default, it also can be used to create DSA keys. For example, some users may need DSA keys to comply to certain U.S. government standards. An example of the command sequence is shown in Figure 11-3.

As shown in the figure, the command prompts for a passphrase, twice. When the identical passphrase is confirmed, the private key is saved in the id_rsa file, and the corresponding public key is stored in the id_rsa.pub file. Both files for user michael are stored in the /home/michael/.ssh directory.

FIGURE 11-3

Commands
to generate
encryption keys

```
[michael@server1 ~]$ ssh-keygen
Generating public/private rsa key pair.
Enter file in which to save the key (/home/michael/.ssh/id_rsa):
Enter passphrase (empty for no passphrase):
Enter same passphrase again:
Your identification has been saved in /home/michael/.ssh/id_rsa.
Your public key has been saved in /home/michael/.ssh/id_rsa.pub.
The key fingerprint is:
c4:60:26:5a:38:53:e9:22:c8:97:a7:51:d6:16:f9:ff michael@server1.example.com
The key's randomart image is:
+--[ RSA 2048]----+
|    o+.=.o       |
|    +o.* *        |
|o .++ . +        |
|o..+.. . .       |
| ...+  S .       |
|   .     .       |
|          .      |
|        E        |
|                 |
+-----------------+
[michael@server1 ~]$ ▮
```

If desired, you can set up RSA keys with a larger number of bits. In my testing, I was able to set up key pairs with up to 8192 bits fairly quickly, even on a 768MB virtual machine system. The command which starts the process is

```
$ ssh-keygen -b 8192
```

Alternatively, if a DSA key is needed, the following command can help. Unfortunately, only 1024-bit DSA keys are allowed. The process after this command is the same as shown in Figure 11-3.

```
$ ssh-keygen -t dsa
```

The next step is to transmit the public key to a remote system. It might be one of the servers that you administer. If you're willing to transmit that public key over the network (once per connection), the following command can work:

```
$ ssh-copy-id -i .ssh/id_rsa.pub michael@tester1.example.com
```

Strictly speaking, the **-i** option defaults to transmitting the .ssh/id_rsa.pub key. It's included in the command for clarity. The command automatically appends the noted local RSA public key to the end of the *remote* .ssh/authorized_keys file. In this case, that file can be found in the /home/michael directory. Of course, you may choose to substitute the IP address for the hostname.

e x a m

ⓦatch

Sometimes, the public key is not immediately accessible on the remote system. If you get an "agent admitted failure to sign using the key" error followed by a password prompt, log out of the console or the GUI and log back in. In most cases, the ssh command will prompt for the passphrase.

You should then be able to immediately connect to that remote system. In the preceding case, the appropriate command is either one of the following:

```
$ ssh -l michael tester1.example.com
$ ssh michael@tester1.example.com
```

When run on a console, the **ssh** command uses the following prompt for the passphrase:

```
Enter passphrase for key '/home/michael/.ssh/id_rsa'
```

When run in a GUI-based command line, it prompts with a window similar to that shown in Figure 11-4.

If the public key is available to all, there should be no hesitation about sending it over the network. However, it does mean transmitting the public key over the network, once. As that's a "public" key, that shouldn't cause heartburn. However, you may want to limit access to that pubic key. To do so, you can use a USB key or other portable media to physically carry the public key to the target remote system. You'd then copy the contents of the public key to the end of the target user's .ssh/authorized_keys file.

Configure an SSH Server

You don't have to do much to configure an SSH server for basic operation. Install the packages described earlier, activate the service, make sure it's active the next time the system is rebooted. As discussed in Chapter 1, the standard SSH port 22 is open in the default RHEL 6 firewall.

However, the RHCE objectives specify that you should be prepared to "configure additional options described in documentation." Because of the general nature of that objective, this section will address every active and commented option in the default version of the SSH server configuration file.

The SSH server configuration file is /etc/ssh/sshd_config. The commands in comments are generally defaults. So if you want to set a nonstandard port for the SSH service, you could change the following commented directive

```
#Port 22
```

to something like

```
Port 2222
```

<table>
<tr><td>**FIGURE 11-4**</td></tr>
<tr><td>Prompt for a
passphrase</td></tr>
</table>

Assuming the firewall allows access through this port, you'd then be able to connect from a remote system with the **ssh -p 2222 server1.example.com** command. If the SSH server is different, substitute for server1.example.com.

While the default shown here listens for both IPv4 and IPv6 addresses,

```
#AddressFamily any
```

it's possible to limit access to one of these types of addresses, where **inet** corresponds to IPv4 and **inet6** corresponds to IPv6.

```
AddressFamily inet
AddressFamily inet6
```

The default shown with the following ListenAddress directives is to listen for SSH communications on all local IPv4 and IPv6 addresses:

```
#ListenAddress 0.0.0.0
#ListenAddress ::
```

You can limit SSH to listening on the IPv4 or IPv6 addresses of certain network cards. That can help limit access to the SSH server to certain networks.

The first active directive configures SSH version 2. As noted earlier, SSH version 1 has been cracked and is therefore insecure.

```
Protocol 2
```

Since SSH version 1 is not used, you should not have to activate the following directive:

```
#HostKey /etc/ssh/ssh_host_key
```

The standard RSA and DSA keys are documented here; generally, there's no reason to change their locations:

```
#HostKey /etc/ssh/ssh_host_rsa_key
#HostKey /etc/ssh/ssh_host_dsa_key
```

The commented directives that follow relate to an SSH version 1 key. Such keys would be regenerated every hour, with 1024 bits. But that would still be insecure.

```
#KeyRegenerationInterval 1h
#ServerKeyBits 1024
```

The first directive sends all logging attempts, successful and otherwise, to the appropriate log file; in this case, /var/log/secure. It's as defined in the /etc/rsyslog.conf file. The level of information is INFO and above.

```
SyslogFacility AUTHPRIV
#LogLevel INFO
```

To limit unauthorized password attempts, the default LoginGraceTime shown here is two minutes. In other words, if a connection has not been completed in that time, the SSH server automatically disconnects from the remote client.

```
#LoginGraceTime 2m
```

The directive that follows documents that the root administrative user can log in from a remote location.

```
#PermitRootLogin yes
```

Direct root logins over SSH can be inherently insecure. If you've set up private/public key-based passphrase authentication from an administrative account on a laptop system, that's a risk. A cracker who gets a hold of that laptop system might then be able to connect to the remote server with administrative privileges. For that reason, I always change that directive on my personal systems to

```
PermitRootLogin no
```

But if that's not a requirement when you take the RHCE exam, don't make that change. In fact, it could be counted as an error on the exam.

Administrators who log in as regular users can use the **su** or **sudo** command as appropriate to take administrative privileges with fewer risks. Next, it's more secure to retain the following directive, especially with respect to private and public keys:

```
#StrictModes yes
```

As noted with the following directive, the default number of authentication attempts per connection is six. You could reduce that number, for users who know their passphrases:

```
#MaxAuthTries 6
```

The following directive suggests that you could open up to ten SSH connections on different consoles:

```
#MaxSesssions 10
```

The following directive is used only with SSH version 1. Hopefully, you didn't activate that version of SSH.

```
#RSAAuthentication yes
```

On the other hand, the following directive is critical if you want to set up passphrase-based private/public key authentication on the standard SSH version 2:

```
#PubkeyAuthentication yes
```

The following directive confirms the use of the authorized_keys file on the remote system to confirm public keys for authentication:

```
#AuthorizedKeysFile .ssh/authorized_keys
```

The two directives that follow are typically ignored:

```
#AuthorizedKeysCommand none
#AuthorizedKeysCommandRunAs nobody
```

The following Rhosts directive is generally not used, as it applies to SSH version 1, and the less-secure Remote Shell (RSH):

```
#RhostsRSAAuthentication no
```

While the following directive could support the use of the /etc/hosts.equiv file to limit hosts that connect, that's not normally encouraged. Nevertheless, it is one method for SSH host-based security, beyond what's possible with an alternative such as TCP wrappers discussed in Chapter 10.

```
#HostbasedAuthentication no
```

As described earlier, the .ssh/known_hosts file stores RSA keys from remote systems, and is read because of the following default:

```
#IgnoreUserKnownHosts no
```

The following directive may help administrators who are converting from RSH to SSH, as they use .rhosts and .shosts files. But as it's not used by default, the following option is sensible:

```
#IgnoreRhosts yes
```

For systems and users where private/public passphrases aren't used, password-based authentication is needed, as enabled by this default:

```
#PasswordAuthentication yes
```

In general, you should never permit empty passwords, due to the security risks:

```
#PermitEmptyPasswords no
```

Challenge-response authentication is normally associated with one-time passwords common with remote terminals. While it can also work with PAM, it is normally disabled on SSH:

```
ChallengeResponseAuthentication = no
```

If you do set up a Kerberos system for the local network, as discussed in Chapter 12, you could set up some of the following options. The first two are almost self-explanatory, as they can enable Kerberos verification of a user and set up alternative Kerberos or local password authentication.

```
#KerberosAuthentication no
#KerberosOrLocalPasswd yes
```

The next two options relate to Kerberos authentication tickets and associated Andrew File System (AFS) tokens:

```
#KerberosTicketCleanup yes
#KerberosGetAFSToken no
```

This is followed by a directive that supports authentication using the Generic Security Services Application Programming Interface (GSSAPI) for client/server authentication:

```
GSSAPIAuthentication = yes
```

The following directive destroys GSSAPI credentials upon logout.

```
GSSAPICleanupCredentials = yes
```

Normally, hostname checks are strict:

```
GSSAPIStrictAcceptorCheck = yes
```

But normally authentication doesn't rely on SSH keys, as described here:

```
GSSAPIKeyExchange = yes
```

Access to PAM modules is supported:

```
UsePAM yes
```

The following directives allow the client to set several environmental variables. The details are normally trivial between two Red Hat Enterprise Linux systems:

```
AcceptEnv LANG LC_CTYPE LC_NUMERIC LC_TIME LC_COLLATE LC_MONETARY LC_MESSAGES
AcceptEnv LC_PAPER LC_NAME LC_ADDRESS LC_TELEPHONE LC_MEASUREMENT
AcceptEnv LC_IDENTIFICATION LC_ALL
AcceptEnv XMODIFIERS
```

With the following setting, the **ssh-agent** command can be used to forward private keys to other remote systems:

```
#AllowAgentForwarding yes
```

In a similar fashion, TCP communications can be forwarded over an SSH connection:

```
#AllowTCPForwarding yes
```

The GatewayPorts directive is normally disabled to keep remote hosts from connecting to forwarded ports:

```
#GatewayPorts no
```

The following directive is important for anyone who needs remote access to a GUI tool:

```
X11Forwarding yes
```

For example, when I'm working from a remote location, I can connect to and open GUI tools from Red Hat systems in my office when I use SSH to connect with the following command:

```
# ssh -X michael@Maui.example.com
```

The next directive helps avoid conflicts between local and remote GUI displays. The default should be adequate, unless there are more than ten GUI desktop environments open on the SSH server system.

```
#X11DisplayOffset 10
```

Normally, no changes are required to the following default, related to how the GUI display is bound on the SSH server:

```
#X11UseLocalhost yes
```

When SSH users log in remotely, the following setting means they see the contents of the /etc/motd file. Different messages are possible, based on the cron script configured in Chapter 9.

```
#PrintMotd yes
```

This is one useful setting for administrators, as it documents the date and time of the last login to the noted system:

```
#PrintLastLog yes
```

The **TCPKeepAlive** directive can keep a system from crashing if a network connection, the SSH server, or any connected SSH client goes down:

```
#TCPKeepAlive yes
```

Generally, you should not enable this option, as it is incompatible with **X11Forwarding**:

```
#UseLogin no
```

The privilege separation associated with the following directive sets up separate processes for the user and for network communication:

```
#UsePrivilegeSeparation yes
```

The following directive does not supersede the default **AuthorizedKeysFile** setting earlier in the file:

```
#PermitUserEnvironment no
```

Compression often helps speed communications over an SSH connection. The default is to delay compression until the password is accepted or the private/public key pair is matched to authenticate the user:

```
#Compression delayed
```

Sometimes, it's important to have the SSH server make sure the user still wants to transmit data. It's how clients are disconnected from sensitive systems such as bank accounts. But for an administrative connection, the following option disables such checks:

```
#ClientAliveInterval 0
```

If the **ClientAliveInterval** is set to some number, the following directive specifies the number of messages that may be sent before that client is automatically disconnected:

```
#ClientAliveCountMax 3
```

The following option for a patch level applies only to SSH version 1:

```
#ShowPatchLevel no
```

To minimize the risks of spoofing, the following option checks remote hostnames against a DNS server or an /etc/hosts file:

```
#UseDNS yes
```

The PID file listed here contains the process ID number of the running SSH server process:

```
#PidFile /var/run/sshd.pid
```

When a cracker tries to break into a SSH server, he may try to set up a bunch of terminals, all attempting to log in simultaneously. The following directive limits the number of terminals that the SSH server will work with. For a SSH server on an administrative system, it's something that you might consider reducing.

```
#MaxStartups 10
```

The following directive, if activated, would support device forwarding:

```
#PermitTunnel no
```

The following directive may seem like good idea but could be difficult to put into practice. Any directory specified should contain all of the commands, devices, and configuration files within that directory tree:

```
#ChrootDirectory none
```

The final directive supports the use of SSH encryption for secure FTP file transfers:

```
Subsystem  sftp   /usr/libexec/openssh/sftp-server
```

User-Based Security for SSH

User-based security can be configured in the /etc/ssh/sshd_config file. To that end, I like to add directives that limit the users allowed to access a system via SSH. The key is the **AllowUsers** directive. You can limit by user with a directive such as

```
AllowUsers michael donna
```

Alternatively, you can limit access by each user to certain hosts with a directive such as the following, which combines aspects of both user- and host-based security.

```
AllowUsers michael@192.168.122.50 donna@192.168.122.150
```

Just be aware, if access is coming from a remote network, an **iptables**-based masquerading configuration may assign the IP address of the router to the remote system. In that case, the IP address of the router serves as a proxy to limit access to all systems you won't be able to specify a single system (except the router) on a remote network.

Related directives that can be included in the /etc/ssh/sshd_config file are **AllowGroups**, **DenyUsers**, and **DenyGroups**. Such directives can be used in similar ways to limit the users who connect. But if you want to limit access to SSH to a very few users, the **AllowUsers** directive is all that's needed. For the first **AllowUsers** directive just shown, only users michael and donna can connect to this SSH server. A corresponding **DenyUsers** or **DenyGroups** directive is not required. Even the root user can't connect via SSH under those circumstances.

While the SSH server would prompt other users for a password, access is denied even when the remote user enters the correct password. The /var/log/secure log file would reflect that with something similar to the following message:

```
User dickens from 192.168.122.150 not allowed because not listed in AllowUsers.
```

Host-Based Security for SSH

While there are methods for configuring host-based security through the SSH configuration files, the process is needlessly complex. It involves changes to both servers and clients, and involves risks that I believe are not necessary. It's also possible to set up host-based security through **iptables**-based firewalls.

The simplest method for host-based SSH security is based on TCP Wrappers, as discussed in Chapter 10. For the purpose of this chapter, I've included the following directive in /etc/hosts.allow, which accepts SSH connections from the noted network addresses.

```
sshd : 127. 192.168.122.
```

To make sure access is limited to systems on the noted networks, it's also important to include the following line in /etc/hosts.deny:

```
sshd : ALL
```

Of course, it would be more secure to include **ALL : ALL** in /etc/hosts.deny. But that may block communications with services that you've worked hard to configure in other ways. In addition, other ports should already be protected by an appropriate **iptables**-based firewall. So it may be an option to avoid during a Red Hat exam.

CERTIFICATION OBJECTIVE 11.04

A Security and Configuration Checklist

A number of steps required to install, configure, and secure a service are repetitive. I therefore summarize them in this section. If desired, you can use this section to help prepare for Chapters 12 through 17. It will help you install required services, make sure those services are active, and make sure those services are accessible through a firewall configured with appropriate open ports.

Installation of Server Services

The RHCE objectives directly address eight different services. This section addresses some of the different ways that you can install these services. If you've read Chapter 7, this should be mostly review. But it will also give you an opportunity to prepare a system such as the server1.example.com virtual machine for testing in Chapters 12 through 17.

In this section, you'll review commands like **rpm** and **yum**, in the context of the server services needed for upcoming chapters. If you prefer to use the GUI Add/Remove Software application, refer to Chapter 7. Generally, you can use any of these options to install desired services.

Install the vsFTP Server with the rpm Command

In general, the installation of most services require the installation of more than one RPM package. One exception is the RPM package associated with the vsFTP server. To that end, if you've mounted the RHEL 6 DVD on the /media directory, you can install the vsFTP server with the following command (the version number may vary):

```
# rpm -ivh /media/Packages/vsftpd-2.2.2-6.el6.x86_64.rpm
```

Install Server Services with the yum Command

As discussed in Chapter 7, the **yum** command can be used to install packages with dependencies. Sometimes, dependencies are simple. For example, for the e-mail services configured in Chapter 13, you may be more familiar with open-source sendmail, as opposed to the default Postfix SMTP service.

Of course, you'd also have to make sure the focus is on sendmail, but that's a detailed configuration topic discussed in Chapter 13. One way to install the sendmail package with dependencies is with the following command:

```
# yum install sendmail
```

As needed, you can use the **yum install** command to install a package in a way that automatically identifies and also installs all dependent packages.

Install Server Package Groups with the yum Command

Also noted in Chapter 7 is the way RHEL 6 packages are organized in groups. Each of those groups have names, which can be identified with the **yum grouplist** command. The relevant groups for the RHCE exam are listed in Table 11-4. The capitalization of each package group is as shown in the output to the **yum grouplist** command.

You can identify different packages in each group with the **grouplist** switch; for example, the following command lists the different packages that are part of the Web Server package group:

```
# yum groupinfo "Web Server"
```

The output for RHEL 6 is shown in Figure 11-5.

Packages are classified in three categories: mandatory, default, and optional. If you run the following command:

```
# yum groupinstall "Web Server"
```

TABLE 11-4	Package Group	Description
RHCE-Related Server Package Groups	CIFS file server	Package group for the Samba file server.
	E-mail server	Support packages for SMTP and Internet Message Access Protocol (IMAP) services; the default services are Postfix and Dovecot. The sendmail server is an optional package in this group.
	FTP server	Package group for the vsFTP server.
	iSCSI Storage Client	Client packages for connections to remote iSCSI systems.
	NFS file server	Setup packages for the NFS server.
	Network Infrastructure Server	Blanket package group for the DNS and rsyslog servers; all packages in this group are optional.
	Network Storage Server	Associated with iSCSI connections, discussed in Chapter 12.
	Network file system client	Includes clients for the automounter, Samba, and NFS.
	Web Server	Includes basic Apache web server packages; however, packages for CGI applications required in the objectives are listed as optional.

FIGURE 11-5	
Packages in the Web Server package group	

```
Group: Web Server
 Description: Allows the system to act as a web server, and run Perl and Pytho
web applications.
  Mandatory Packages:
   httpd
  Default Packages:
   crypto-utils
   httpd-manual
   mod_perl
   mod_ssl
   mod_wsgi
   webalizer
  Optional Packages:
   certmonger
   libmemcached
   memcached
   mod_auth_kerb
   mod_auth_mysql
   mod_auth_pgsql
   mod_authz_ldap
   mod_nss
   perl-CGI
   perl-CGI-Session
   perl-Cache-Memcached
   python-memcached
   squid
[root@Maui ~]#
```

Only packages in the mandatory and default categories are installed. In most cases, that's not a problem. But the RHCE objectives related to web servers suggest the need to "deploy a basic CGI application." And the CGI-related packages are listed as optional. While there are ways to set up the installation of optional packages with the **groupinstall** switch, it's easier for our purposes to just install needed packages separately by name. But for our purposes, the httpd package includes a CGI module, sufficient for a basic CGI application discussed in Chapter 14.

In a similar fashion, you can install the Samba File Server covered in Chapter 15 with the following command:

```
# yum groupinstall "CIFS file server"
```

There's actually just one package in this group, samba. For that reason, the following command would work equally well:

```
# yum install samba
```

For Chapter 17, the Network Infrastructure Server package group includes packages associated with logging and DNS. However, as all packages in this group are optional, the **yum groupinstall** command would not install any packages from that group. Fortunately, the rsyslog package is already installed by default, even in a minimal RHEL 6 installation. But you will want to install DNS to address one of the RHCE objectives. One way to set up the DNS service for Chapter 17 is with the following command:

```
# yum install bind
```

For a number of server services, you should make sure that appropriate client packages are installed. The Network file system client package group can help in that respect; the following command would install clients for the automounter, Samba, and NFS:

```
# yum groupinstall "Network file system client"
```

A different kind of network server relates to iSCSI storage. There are two package groups of interest: the Network Storage Server and the iSCSI Storage Client. They each are associated with a single package, which will be discussed in Chapter 12.

Finally, there are a couple of packages of interest that are not included in standard package groups. They set up the NTP server and authentication to remote databases. If not already installed, you'll need to install them. One method is with the following command:

```
# yum install ntp sssd
```

I focus on command line installation methods, as they are generally fastest. Of course, you could install packages with the GUI Add/Remove Software tool discussed in Chapter 7.

Basic Configuration

While the current RHCE objectives are more specific than ever, it's best to keep what you change as simple as possible. As noted in the objectives, you'll be asked to "configure the service for basic operation." Basic operation is simpler. It is frequently more secure. If you do less to configure a service, it takes less time. You'll have a better chance to finish the exam. You'll be able to do more on the job.

Of course, the details associated with basic configuration are covered in upcoming chapters.

Make Sure the Service Survives a Reboot

In Chapter 5, you looked at when a service starts or does not start during the boot process. The simplest method is associated with the **chkconfig** command. To review, the **chkconfig --list** command lists whether a service controlled by scripts in the /etc/init.d directory. For the services discussed in the following chapters, once the appropriate packages have been installed, you'll want to make sure they start during the boot process with the following commands:

```
# chkconfig httpd on
# chkconfig iscsi on
# chkconfig iscsid on
# chkconfig named on
# chkconfig nfs on
# chkconfig nmb on
# chkconfig ntpd on
# chkconfig ntpdate on
# chkconfig rpcbind on
# chkconfig rsyslog on
# chkconfig smb on
# chkconfig sshd on
# chkconfig vsftpd on
```

This list is not complete. On the other hand, on an actual exam, while all of these services are "fair game," you may not be required to install them all. For example, if there's no requirement to install an NTP server (or client), you need not install the ntp package. Without that package, the **chkconfig ntpd on** command would lead to an error message.

Sometimes, there are mutually exclusive alternatives. For example, for SMTP services, RHEL 6 makes it possible to configure either Postfix or sendmail. In Chapter 13, you'll examine a different way to make sure only one service is set to run.

Of course, it is always possible that during an exam, you'll be told to make sure a service does *not* start during the boot process. And in a production environment, the installation of so many services on a single system is rare, because of the security risks.

Review Access Through Layers of Security

The first place to check a service is from the local system. For example, if you can connect to an FTP server from that system, that confirms a good configuration of that service. Some issues relate to SELinux; others relate to various user and host-based firewalls. For issues beyond SELinux, the network command tools installed in Chapter 2 can be quite helpful.

Troubleshoot SELinux Issues

If the configuration is good but still does not work, that suggests an SELinux issue. Not all SELinux issues are readily visible. However, you can check two basic issues with respect to SELinux:

- The list of boolean settings related to the configuration option in question. For example, users who try to connect to remote home directories through the FTP server can be configured through the main vsFTP configuration file. However, problems don't always appear in the SELinux logs.
- The SELinux file contexts. The contexts of the target directories should match those of default directories. In other words, when you run the **ls -Z** command on a shared FTP directory, the file contexts should match that of the default shared FTP directory.

The next step is to test the connection from a remote system. It's appropriate to test the connection in a number of ways:

1. Can the remote client system communicate with the remote server? That's most easily confirmed with the **ping** command.

2. Can the remote client communicate over the assigned port? That can be confirmed with the **telnet** command. For example, the following command attempts to establish a connection on TCP/IP port 21:

    ```
    $ telnet 192.168.122.50 21
    ```

    If the connection is successful, the vsFTP server is identified by name. Type in the **quit** command and press ENTER to exit from the connection.

3. If the **telnet** connection to the appropriate port does not work, then there may be a firewall problem. There are actually subtle differences:

    a. Firewalls exist on several levels. The **iptables** command firewall discussed in Chapters 4 and 10, as configured in /etc/sysconfig/iptables, must support access through the noted port number and can't limit it from desired hosts.

    b. The TCP Wrappers system works with daemons associated with the libwrap.so.0 library, allowing and limiting access in /etc/hosts.allow and /etc/hosts.deny.

If all firewalls are clear, and the service still does not work as intended, then there may be a configuration problem with the server. Some servers include their own limits, based on hosts, IP addresses, and usernames.

Troubleshoot iptables-Based Firewall Issues

In general, **iptables**-based firewalls are straightforward. If a system allows access for server communications, you'll see it in the port numbers documented in the /etc/sysconfig/iptables file and the output to the **iptables -L** command.

Specifically, you should expect to see a line like the following in /etc/sysconfig/iptables to allow communications through the standard port for the SSH server:

```
-A INPUT -m state --state NEW -m tcp -p tcp --dport 22 -j ACCEPT
```

When the iptables service is started with the **/etc/init.d/iptables start** command, the file is read into memory; you should be able to see the following excerpt from the **iptables -L** command for the noted port:

```
ACCEPT     tcp  --  anywhere      anywhere       state NEW tcp dpt:ssh
```

Let's translate that line into something closer to English. This rule accepts packets. It checks the packet for the use of the TCP protocol. It then checks the IP addresses of the header but allows packets that come from any address, with a destination of any address. The packet is new, with a TCP destination port (**dpt**) associated with **ssh**. The /etc/services file translates **ssh** to the standard SSH port of 22.

Of course, you could just use the Firewall Configuration tool described in Chapters 4 and 10, but what if those tools are flawed? The bottom line for iptables-based firewalls is based on the noted file and the rules shown with the **iptables -L** command.

Unless this port is open in the firewall, an attempt to connect to that server is rejected with a message like the following:

```
ssh: connect to host server1.example.com port 22: No route to host
```

In contrast, the **telnet server1.example.com 22** command leads to a similar message:

```
telnet: connect to address 192.168.122.50: No route to host
```

Troubleshoot TCP Wrappers Firewall Issues

In contrast, if the service is protected by TCP wrappers, the error message behavior is different. For this section, I configured the /etc/hosts.allow and /etc/hosts.deny files on the server1.example.com system to allow access only from .example.com systems on the 192.168.122.0/24 network. That means access is not allowed from systems such as outsider1.example.org on IP address 192.168.100.100.

In that case, when I tried accessing the server1.example.com system with the **ssh** command, I received the following error message:

```
ssh_exchange_identification: Connection closed by remote host
```

In contrast, the **telnet server1.example.com 22** command from the same system returns the following messages, which stops for a moment:

```
Trying 192.168.122.50
Connected to server1.example.com.
Escape character is /^]'
```

For a few moments, it appears the system is about to connect. But then the block from TCP Wrappers results in the following message:

```
Connection closed by foreign host.
```

EXERCISE 11-2

Review the Different Effects of iptables and TCP Wrappers

This exercise assumes an operational vsFTP server, similar to the one configured in Chapter 1 for installations. It is assumed that you'll configure that vsFTP server on the server1.example.com system. You'll then make sure the firewall blocks traffic on the standard vsFTP port, 21, before checking the effect from a remote blocked system, outsider1.example.org. To review, these systems as configured in Chapters 1 and 2 are on IP addresses 192.168.122.50 and 192.168.100.100, respectively.

Then you'll open up the firewall on port 21 and then limit access using TCP Wrappers. There are a lot of steps in this exercise; in fact, each numbered step requires several commands or actions. In some cases, the required command is implied. Exact steps are not possible since there are two versions of the Firewall Configuration tool.

1. If it is not already installed, install the vsFTP server, as discussed in the chapter. Make sure that server is active with the **/etc/init.d/vsftpd start** command.

2. Start the Firewall Management tool with the **system-config-firewall** command. Make sure FTP is not activated in the list of Trusted Services. Make sure the changes are applied and then exit from the Firewall Management tool.

3. Try connecting to the vsFTP server from the local system with a command like **lftp localhost**. It should work, which you can confirm from the lftp localhost:/> prompt with the **ls** command. Exit from the vsFTP server with the **quit** command.

4. Move to the outsider1.example.org system. It's acceptable to connect to it via SSH; in fact, that may be the only method available to connect to that system on an exam (and in real life).

5. Try pinging the system with the vsFTP server with the **ping 192.168.122.50** command. Remember to press CTRL-C to stop the process. Try connecting to the vsFTP server with the **lftp 192.168.122.50** command. What happens? Try to connect to the system with the **telnet 192.168.122.50 21** command. What happens?

6. Return to the server1.example.com system. Open the Firewall Configuration tool again, and this time, make FTP a trusted service. Don't forget to apply the change, before exiting from the Firewall Configuration tool.

7. Open the /etc/hosts.allow file, and include the following entry:

   ```
   vsftpd : localhost 127. 192.168.122.150
   ```

8. Open the /etc/hosts.deny file, and include the following entry:

   ```
   vsftpd : ALL
   ```

9. Return to the outsider1.example.com system as discussed in Step 4. Repeat Step 5. What happens after each attempt to connect?

10. Go back to the server1.example.com system. Open the /etc/hosts.allow and /etc/hosts.deny files, and delete the lines created in Steps 7 and 8.

11. Once again, move to the outsider1.example.org system. Repeat Step 5. Both commands should result in a successful connection. The **quit** command should exit in both cases.

12. BONUS: Review connections via the contents of the /var/log/secure file. Review the originating IP addresses in that file. Use that information to configure **iptables** to deny access to all but one IP address.

SCENARIO & SOLUTION

You want to limit SSH access to two users.	Specify the desired usernames in the SSH server configuration file, /etc/ssh/sshd_config, with the AllowUsers directive.
You're told to limit SSH access to systems on the 192.168.122.0/24 network.	Use TCP Wrappers. Configure /etc/hosts.allow to allow access to the **sshd** daemon from systems on the noted network. Configure /etc/hosts.deny to restrict access to **sshd** from **ALL** systems.
U.S. Government contracts require SSH passphrase compliance.	Set up passphrases with the **ssh-keygen -t dsa** command to set up a private/public key pair that uses DSA encryption.
You need to make sure SELinux user and file types survive a relabel.	Use the **semanage fcontext -a** command to specify the desired user and file types for desired directories.
A server is accessible only locally.	Check security options for **iptables** command firewall rules, TCP Wrappers; make sure the service allows remote access.
A server is properly configured but still is not accessible.	Check for SELinux booleans and file label types.

CERTIFICATION SUMMARY

This chapter focused on the general steps required to configure, secure, and access various services. Daemons are controlled by scripts in the /etc/init.d directory, which are started based on parameters in various /etc/sysconfig files. Access to various aspects of server services may be controlled by different SELinux booleans.

The information was tested on the SSH server service. With the **ssh-keygen** command, you can create private/public key passphrase-protected pairs that can keep users from having to transmit passwords over a network. The sshd_config configuration file includes a substantial number of options for configuring that service.

To configure a service, you'll need to install the right packages and make sure the services are active after the next reboot. You'll also need to navigate through the variety of available security options, including SELinux, **iptables**-based firewalls, and TCP Wrappers–based security in the /etc/hosts.allow and /etc/hosts.deny files.

TWO-MINUTE DRILL

The following are some of the key points from the certification objectives in Chapter 11.

Red Hat System Configuration

❑ System services can be started with scripts in the /etc/init.d directory or with the **service** command.

❑ System services use basic configuration files in the /etc/sysconfig directory. Such files often include basic parameters for service daemons.

❑ When configuring a network server, you'll need to be concerned about SELinux booleans, **iptables**-based firewalls, TCP Wrappers, and more.

❑ Services should be tested locally and remotely.

Security-Enhanced Linux

❑ Individual services are frequently protected by multiple SELinux booleans.

❑ SELinux booleans are stored in the /selinux/booleans directory, with descriptive filenames.

❑ SELinux booleans can be changed with the **setsebool -P** command or the SELinux Management tool. From the command line, make sure to use the **-P** switch, or the change won't survive a reboot.

❑ SELinux file contexts can be changed with the **chcon** command. However, the change does not survive a relabel unless documented with the **semanage fcontext -a** command. Changes are documented in the file_contexts.local file, in the /etc/selinux/targeted/contexts/files directory.

The Secure Shell Package

❑ SSH server configuration commands include **sshd**, **ssh-agent**, **ssh-add**, **ssh-keygen**, **ssh-copy-id**, and **ssh**.

❑ SSH server configuration files in the /etc/ssh directory include client and server configuration files, along with public and private host keys, encrypted with RSA and DSA formats.

❑ User home directories include their own .ssh subdirectory of configuration files, with private and public identification keys, suitable for passphrases.

❑ Private/public keypairs can be configured with passphrases with the **ssh-keygen** command.

❑ Public keys can be transmitted to users' home directory on remote systems with the **ssh-copy-id** command.

❑ The SSH server configuration file, sshd_config, can be set up with user-based security.

❑ The easiest way to set up host-based SSH security is through TCP Wrappers.

A Security and Configuration Checklist

❑ You'll need to install a number of services to prepare for the RHCE exam, with commands like **rpm** and **yum**.

❑ One way to make sure services survive a reboot is with the **chkconfig** command; a full list of such commands related to RHCE services are listed in the chapter.

❑ You'll need to configure access to a service through layers of security, including SELinux, **iptables**-based firewalls, and TCP Wrappers.

SELF TEST

The following questions will help measure your understanding of the material presented in this chapter. As no multiple-choice questions appear on the Red Hat exams, no multiple-choice questions appear in this book. These questions exclusively test your understanding of the chapter. It is okay if you have another way of performing a task. Getting results, not memorizing trivia, is what counts on the Red Hat exams. There may be more than one answer to many of these questions.

Red Hat System Configuration Files

1. What is the name of the configuration file for iptables-based firewalls in the /etc/sysconfig directory?

   _____

2. What command is equivalent to the **/etc/init.d/smb reload** command?

   _____

Security-Enhanced Linux

3. What directory contains boolean options associated with SELinux? Specify the full path.

   _____

4. What man page contains SELinux options associated with NFS daemons?

   _____

5. What command restores the default settings on a given directory?

   _____

6. If the file_contexts file contains SELinux labels for different directories, what file is created with the help of **semanage fcontext -a** command? It's in the /etc/selinux/targeted/contexts/files directory.

   _____

The Secure Shell Server

7. What command configures a private/public key pair using DSA?

   _____

8. What subdirectory of a user home directory contains the authorized_keys file?

_____

9. What directive specifies the port number of the local SSH server in the associated configuration file?

_____

10. What directive specifies a list of allowed users in the SSH server configuration file?

_____

A Security and Configuration Checklist

11. What command displays a list of all available package groups?

_____

12. What command can help the abcd service survive a reboot?

_____

LAB QUESTIONS

Several of these labs involve configuration exercises. You should do these exercises on test machines only. It's assumed that you're running these exercises on virtual machines such as KVM.

Red Hat presents its exams electronically. For that reason, the labs in this and future chapters are available from the CD that accompanies the book, in the Chapter11/ subdirectory. In case you haven't yet set up RHEL 6 on a system, refer to Chapter 1 for installation instructions.

The answers for the labs follow the Self Test answers for the fill-in-the-blank questions.

SELF TEST ANSWERS

Red Hat System Configuration Files

1. Slight trick question: the file in the /etc/sysconfig directory where **iptables**-command firewalls are configured is iptables.

2. Two commands equivalent to **/etc/init.d/smb reload** are

```
/etc/rc.d/init.d/smb reload
service smb reload
```

Security-Enhanced Linux

3. The directory with SELinux booleans is /selinux/booleans.

4. The nfs_selinux man page contains some SELinux booleans for that service.

5. The command that restores file contexts to a given directory is **restorecon**.

6. The name of the file that is created by the noted command is file_contexts.local.

The Secure Shell Server

7. The command is **ssh-keygen -t dsa**.

8. Every user with public keys stored in the authorized_keys file can find that file in the .ssh/ subdirectory of her home directories.

9. The directive is **Port**.

10. The directive is **AllowUsers**.

A Security and Configuration Checklist

11. The command that lists all available package groups is **yum grouplist**.

12. Assuming the abcd service is also a script in the /etc/init.d directory, the command that would help it survive a reboot is **chkconfig abcd on**. Variations on this command such as **chkconfig --level 35 on** are acceptable.

LAB ANSWERS

Lab 1

This lab should give you an idea of what can be done with /etc/sysconfig files, and how it changes the way a daemon is started. It should also demonstrate the risks; the wrong change, such as that demonstrated in the lab, means that the service won't work.

Lab 2

There are three measures of success in this lab.

1. There will be an id_rsa file and an id_rsa.pub file in the client /home/hawaii/.ssh directory.
2. You'll be able to connect to the remote system without a password. Just enter the "I love Linux!" passphrase (without quotes) when prompted.
3. You'll find the contents of the client's id_rsa.pub file in the remote authorized_keys file in the /home/hawaii/.ssh directory.

Lab 3

Much as in Lab 2, there are three measures of success in this lab.

1. There will be an id_dsa and an id_dsa.pub file in the client /home/tonga/.ssh directory.
2. You'll be able to connect to the remote system without a password. Just enter the "I love Linux!" passphrase when prompted.
3. You'll find the contents of the client's id_dsa.pub file in the remote authorized_keys file in the /home/hawaii/.ssh directory.

Lab 4

The simplest way to implement this lab is to add the following directive to the /etc/ssh/sshd_config file:

```
AllowUsers hawaii
```

Just don't forget to reload or restart the SSH service after making the change; otherwise, other users will still have access.

In case you're curious, user tonga on the client is still able to access the hawaii account on the SSH server with the passphrase, as it is connections to the user hawaii account that are being allowed. The identity of the remote account does not matter to the AllowUsers directive.

If you've made too many changes to the /etc/ssh/sshd_config file and want to start fresh, move that file and run the **yum reinstall openssh-server** command. It'll set up a fresh copy of that configuration file. If you want to connect from other accounts in the future, make sure the **AllowUsers hawaii** directive is disabled.

Oh yes, did you need to activate the **PermitRootLogin no** directive to prevent SSH logins to the root account?

Lab 5

Success in this lab is confirmed by a good SSH connection from client to server. If you just want to make sure, use the **ssh -p 8022** command from the client. If you haven't disabled the AllowUsers directive on the server, that connection would have to be to the hawaii account.

In addition, this lab should give you a sense of the effort required to set up obscure ports. However, while the **nmap** command would detect an opening on port 8022, it would be obscure; the relevant output would be

```
PORT        STATE       SERVICE
8022/tcp    open        unknown
```

Go to the client system. Change the client configuration file (/etc/ssh/ssh_config) to point to port 8022. Try connecting to the SSH server. Remember, you'll also need to open port 8022 in the firewall of the SSH server.

When this lab is complete, restore the original port numbers on the SSH client and server.

Lab 6

Confirmation of success in this lab is straightforward. Run the **ls -Zd** commands on the noted directories. The SELinux contexts for the /virtual/web and /var/www directories should match with the following contexts:

```
system_u:object_r:httpd_sys_content_t:s0
```

The contexts for the /virtual/web/cgi-bin and /var/www/cgi-bin directories should also match:

```
system_u:object_r:httpd_sys_script_exec_t:s0
```

It should go without saying that any changes that you make should survive a SELinux relabel. Otherwise, how do you expect to get credit for your work? If you've run the **semanage fcontext -a** command on the correct directories, you'll see these contexts listed in the file_contexts.local file, in the /etc/selinux/targeted/contexts/files directory:

```
/virtual/web        system_u:object_r:httpd_sys_content_t:s0
/virtual/web/cgi-bin    system_u:object_r:httpd_sys_script_exec_t:s0
```

12

RHCE Administrative Tasks

T he automation of system maintenance is an objective for both the RHCSA and RHCE exams. For the RHCE, you need to know how to create a shell script for that purpose. You'll study some example scripts used on RHEL 6. Standard scripts may be used on an hourly, daily, or even weekly basis. The Linux kernel is flexible and highly customizable. With different run-time parameters configured in the /proc directory, kernels can be modified to meet the needs of your users.

One of the special challenges of the RHCE exam is the configuration of a custom RPM package. It's easier than you think. RHEL 6 already includes excellent tools to help you create that custom RPM.

The RHCE objectives also include a number of special network options. You need to know how to set up a system as a Kerberos client. In a complex network, you may need to configure a special route between networks. Finally, with the variety of systems that can be configured, you should know how to connect to remote storage over a network; the RHCE specifies the Internet Small Computer Systems Interface (iSCSI) for that purpose.

INSIDE THE EXAM

This chapter directly addresses six RHCE objectives. The first is a basic skill for systems administration, specifically, to

■ Use scripting to automate system maintenance tasks

Administrative scripts combine a series of commands in a single executable file. Automated scripts are normally run on a regular schedule, which makes the cron daemon perfect for that purpose.

Some Linux administrative tasks can be met through kernel run-time parameters, how the kernel manages the operating system. That's made possible by the files in the /proc/sys directory and the **sysctl** command and is summarized by the following objective:

■ Use /proc/sys and sysctl to modify and set kernel run-time parameters

As RHEL and other Linux distributions are configured with RPM packages, it can be helpful to know how to create your own RPM. The following RHCE objective is step one in that process, to

■ Build a simple rpm that packages a single file

This chapter also addresses several network tasks from the RHCE objectives. The configuration of an iSCSI initiator, as described in the following objective, is the configuration of a client:

■ Configure system as an iSCSI Initiator persistently mounting existing Target

The following objective relates to the configuration of a system as a Kerberos client:

■ Configure system to authenticate using Kerberos

Finally, the following objective is related to the nitty-gritty of enterprise networking:

■ Route IP traffic and create static routes

CERTIFICATION OBJECTIVE 12.01

Automate System Maintenance

As discussed in Chapter 9, RHEL 6 includes a number of standard scripts for system maintenance, driven by the /etc/crontab and the /etc/anacrontab configuration files. In that chapter, you can review basic information on when scripts in various /etc/cron.* directories are run. In this chapter, you'll get into the details of some of the standard scripts in the /etc/cron.* directories and then analyze various script commands in detail. With that information in hand, you'll be able to create administrative scripts too.

Standard Administrative Scripts

Start with the scripts in the /etc/cron.hourly directory. While the intent of the 0anacron script was summarized in Chapter 9, you'll analyze it in detail here. But first, start with a simpler script, mcelog.cron, which logs machine check exception data on an hourly basis. That script has two lines. The first line is standard on most scripts, as it specifies that the commands that follow are governed by the syntax of the bash shell:

```
#!/bin/bash
```

Normally, lines that start with the pound symbol (#) are comments. This line is an exception. The second line is a straightforward execution of the **mcelog** command, which would exit silently if a device is not found (**--ignorenodev**) and filters out (**--filter**) known problems, before appending the messages (**>>**) to the end of the /var/log/mcelog file.

```
/usr/sbin/mcelog --ignorenodev --filter >> /var/log/mcelog
```

Next, examine the contents of the /etc/cron.daily directory. A slightly more complex script is logrotate. It starts with what seems to be a different shell operator:

There's actually a bug related to the 0anacron script; for more information, search for bug 675077 at https://bugzilla.redhat.com.

```
#!/bin/sh
```

But that command is soft-linked to the /bin/bash command, the bash shell. The next line in the file is executed automatically. The **logrotate** command rotates logs as defined in the /etc/logrotate.conf file, as described in Chapter 9. Standard logging messages are sent to /dev/null, which is essentially the Linux trash bin. Error messages, as signified by the **2>**, are sent to the standard exit value, as indicated by the **&1**.

Some Linux distributions (not Red Hat) link the /bin/sh command to a shell other than bash. Unless #!/bin/bash is specified in the script, it may not be transferable to other distributions.

```
/usr/sbin/logrotate /etc/logrotate.conf >/dev/null 2>&1
```

The following line assigns the standard exit value to a variable named **EXITVALUE**:

```
EXITVALUE=$?
```

Success has an exit value of 0. If there's a problem, the exit value is some other number. The **if** command starts a conditional statement. The bang character (!), which looks like an exclamation point, in effect means "not" or "anything but." So the following if conditional is true when the value of **EXITVALUE** is something other than 0:

```
if [ $EXITVALUE != 0 ];
```

So if **EXITVALUE** is not 0, the command inside the **if** conditional is executed, which can help an administrator identify a problem with the logrotate script or related log files.

```
/usr/bin/logger -t logrotate "ALERT exited abnormally with [$EXITVALUE]"
```

The **fi** command that follows ends the conditional statement that started with the **if**. The last directive returns 0, an indication of success:

```
exit 0
```

Since that may have been confusing for users who are newer to scripts, it's a good time to look at some of the basic commands available for scripts.

Script Commands

Scripts are filled with various command constructs. Some groups of commands are organized in a loop, which continues to run as long as the conditions are met. These command constructs are also known as *operators*. Common operators include **for**, **if**, and **test**. The end of a loop may be labeled with an operator such as **done** or **fi**. Some operators only exist in the context of others, which will be described in the subsections that follow.

Test Operators with if

The **if** operator is primarily used to check if a file is of a certain type. For example, the following command checks to see if the /var/cache/man/whatis file, a local database of man pages, is anything but a regular file:

```
if [ ! -f /var/cache/man/whatis ]
```

As suggested earlier, the bang (!) is "anything but." The **-f** checks to see if the filename that follows is a currently existing regular file. The key is the test operators common in bash shell scripts. Some of these operators are listed in Table 12-1.

The **if** operator normally is associated with a **then**, and possibly an **else** operator. For example, take the following hypothetical loop:

```
if [ -e /etc/inittab ];
then
    /bin/ls /home > /root/homedirs
else
    /bin/echo "Don't reboot, /etc/inittab is missing!"
fi
```

For this loop, if the /etc/inittab file exists (courtesy of the **-e**), the command associated with the **then** operator is run. If that file is missing, then the noted message is run.

Operator	Description
-b	Checks for a block file.
-d	Looks to see if the file is a directory.
-e	Asks if the file exists.
-eq	Checks for equality of the noted variables or values.
-f	Works if the file is a regular file.
-ge	Looks to see if the first value is greater than or equal to the second.
-le	Looks to see if the first value is less than or equal to the second.
-lt	Looks to see if the first value is less than the second.
-ne	Looks to see if the first value is not equal to the second.
-r	Checks the file for read permissions.
-s	Checks to see if the size of the file is greater than zero.
-w	Inspects the file for write permissions.
-x	Looks to the file for execute permissions.
||	Asks if the previous expression is false.
&&	Asks if the previous expression is true.

Test Operators with test

The **test** operator is sometimes used as a conditional within the **if**. For example, the original version of the 0anacron script in the /etc/cron.hourly directory includes the following line:

```
if test -x /var/spool/anacron/cron.daily;
```

which is functionally equivalent to

```
if [ -x /var/spool/anacron/cron.daily ];
```

The do Loop

The **do** loop normally exists within other loops. It's fairly simple; the following example continues until some condition related to variable **n** is met:

```
do
     echo "I love Linux #$n"
done
```

A more complex example exists within the tmpwatch script, in the /etc/cron.daily directory, as it is combined with an **if** operator:

```
do
    if [ -d "$d" ]; then
        /usr/sbin/tmpwatch "$flags" -f 30d "$d"
    fi
done
```

This loop executes the noted **tmpwatch** command for all noted files from variable **d** that are confirmed as directories [-d "$d"].

The for directive with a do Loop

An example of a **for** directive exists in the tmpwatch script, in the /etc/cron.daily directory. It includes the **do** loop just described. The **for** directive specifies the value of variable **d** based on existing directories such as /var/cache/man/cat1.

```
for d in /var/{cache/man,catman}/{cat?,X11R6/cat?,local/cat?}; do
    if [ -d "$d" ]; then
        /usr/sbin/tmpwatch "$flags" -f 30d "$d"
    fi
done
```

That combination may seem complex. I've written a simpler script for Exercise 12-1.

Create Your Own Administrative Scripts

If this is the first time you're creating a script, keep it simple. There may be a command that you run often on a Linux system. For example, sometimes I configure my server to collect pictures from an outside camera every second. After a few days, that results in a lot of files. The **rm** command by itself can't handle too many files. I can never remember the exact command, so I've set up a script for this purpose:

```
#!/bin/sh
/usr/bin/find /home/camera/ -type f -name "outside*" -exec rm -f {} \
```

This particular script finds all regular files (**-type f**) with the given name and passes it off to the **rm** command. Commands of any such complexity are perfect candidates for scripts. I could set up that script to be run on a regular basis with a cron job associated with the user named camera, assuming the files in that directory are owned by that user. Similar cron jobs were discussed in Chapter 9.

EXERCISE 12-3

Create a Script

In this lab, you'll create a simple script that lists the .doc files in the local home directory. Of course, there are easier ways to identify local .doc files. If there are no .doc files in an appropriate directory, you can use the **touch** command to create them, or substitute a different kind of file, such as those with a .pdf or a .conf extension. The purpose of this exercise is to help users who are newer to scripts understand how they work.

1. Use the /etc/cron.daily/cups script as a template. Copy it to your home directory with a command like **cp /etc/cron.daily/cups ~/testscript**.

2. Take ownership of the script from your regular user account with the **chown** command. For more information on **chown**, see Chapter 4. Confirm appropriate permissions in the newly copied file with the **ls -l ~/testscript** command. Scripts should be executable.

3. Open the script. Consider the first line. It's acceptable to leave it as is or change it to **#!/bin/bash**.

4. Consider the second line. It reads the file names in the /var/spool/cups/tmp directory. How would you change it to read .doc files in your local home directory? For user michael, one option is the following:

```
for d in /home/michael/*.doc
```

In some cases, a different directory such as /home/michael/Documents might be more appropriate.

5. Consider the **if** loop that follows. The **-d** operator checks to see if the file is a directory. An option like **-f** is more appropriate, as it checks to see if the contents of the variable is a regular file. While other options may work, change the noted line to read

```
if [ -f "$d" ]; then
```

6. As the objective is simply to identify .doc files in the local directory, it's best to send the output to another file. One method is with the following line, where the >> appends the output to the end of a file.

```
/bin/ls -l "$d" >> docfiles
```

7. You may retain the remaining lines; where the **fi** ends the **if** loop, the **done** ends the **do** loop, and the **exit 0** returns a success message:

```
    fi
done
exit 0
```

8. Save the changes. Execute the script from the local directory. Since the script name is testscript, the following command executes its contents from the local directory:

```
$ ./testscript
```

9. Check the contents of the docfiles file. If the script worked, you'll find existing .doc files in that directory.

CERTIFICATION OBJECTIVE 12.02

Kernel Run-Time Parameters

Kernel run-time parameters, as defined in the RHCE objectives, relate to files in the /proc/sys directory and the **sysctl** command. Closely related is the /etc/sysctl.conf configuration file, as that's used by the **sysctl** command during the boot process to add parameters to various files in the /proc/sys directory. So it's appropriate to start this section with a look at that sysctl.conf file.

How sysctl Works with /etc/sysctl.conf

The /etc/sysctl.conf file was briefly discussed in Chapter 1, as it controls IPv4 forwarding. To review, you can enable IPv4 forwarding in two steps. First, change the following boolean directive to activate IPv4 forwarding in the configuration:

```
net.ipv4.ip_forward = 1
```

Then make the system re-read the configuration file with the following command:

```
# sysctl -p
```

Let's examine this process in a bit more detail. First, kernel run-time parameters are documented in various files in the /proc/sys directory. Add the net.ipv4.ip_forward variable to that directory. That's interpreted as the ip_forward file, in the net/ipv4/ subdirectory. In other words, IPv4 forwarding is documented in the ip_forward file, in the /proc/sys/net/ipv4 directory.

As that file contains either a 0 or a 1, it is a boolean variable. So the value 1 for the net.ipv4.ip_forward variable activates IPv4 forwarding.

What if you want to add IPv6 forwarding? While that's not configured in the /etc/sysctl.conf file, it's a feature that you can add. IPv6 forwarding can be set in a file named forwarding, in the /proc/sys/net/ipv6/conf/all directory. In other words, to set IPv6 forwarding on reboot, you'd include the following directive in /etc/sysctl.conf:

```
net.ipv6.conf.all.forwarding=1
```

Similar directives would work for other settings associated with files in the /proc/sys directory. Look at the icmp_* directives in the /proc/sys/net/ipv4 directory. Some of you may recognize that the Internet Control Message Protocol (ICMP) is most frequently associated with the **ping** command. In fact, a **ping** command is a request for an echo. So the icmp_echo_ignore_all and icmp_echo_ignore_broadcasts relate to a direct **ping** command, as well as a **ping** command associated with the broadcast address.

In other words, if you add the following directives to the /etc/sysctl.conf file:

```
net.ipv4.icmp_echo_ignore_all = 1
net.ipv4.icmp_echo_ignore_broadcasts = 1
```

the local system won't respond to a direct **ping** command, nor will it respond to a request made by a **ping** to the broadcast address for the network.

Settings in the /etc/sysctl.conf File

The settings in the /etc/sysctl.conf file are a small fraction of what can be configured. It's fair to assume that RHEL 6 includes the options in that file for a reason, and those settings are most likely to be addressed in a RHCE exam. You've already examined the first directive for IPv4 forwarding. The next directive, if active, makes sure that packets that come in from an external network are in fact external:

```
net.ipv4.conf.default.rp_filter = 1
```

The following directive is normally disabled, to keep crackers on outside networks from routing data via third parties. Such routing is a common tactic in attacks, as it can help mask the identity of the attacker.

```
net.ipv4.conf.default.accept_source_route = 0
```

Also known as the kernel magic sysrq key, developers may enable this directive for development purposes. Generally, you should retain the following setting:

```
kernel.sysrq = 0
```

If there's a crash of the Linux kernel, this option includes the PID number with the kernel core dump file to help identify the culprit:

```
kernel.core_uses_pid = 1
```

Another standard method used by crackers to overload a system is a flood of SYN packets. It's similar to the so-called "ping of death." The following setting regulates their use:

```
net.ipv4.tcp_syncookies = 1
```

A bridge is an older term for a switch that can regulate traffic within a single network. The following directives disable the use of the noted **iptables**, **ip6tables**, and **arptables** commands on such bridges.

```
net.bridge.bridge-nf-call-ip6tables = 0
net.bridge.bridge-nf-call-iptables = 0
net.bridge.bridge-nf-call-arptables = 0
```

Such bridges relate to virtualization on physical host systems; they don't apply within KVM-based virtual machines.

EXERCISE 12-2

Disable Responses to the ping Command

In this exercise, you'll use kernel parameters to disable responses to the **ping** command. While this exercise can be run on any two connected systems, this exercise assumes that you'll be configuring the server1.example.com system and testing the result from the tester1.example.com system.

1. On the server1.example.com system, review the current setting related to responses to **ping** messages with the following command:

   ```
   # cat /proc/sys/net/ipv4/icmp_echo_ignore_all
   ```

2. Assuming the output is a 0, try the **ping localhost** command. What happens? Don't forget to press CTRL-C to exit from the output stream. If the output is 1, skip to Step 5.

3. Confirm the result from a remote system such as tester1.example.com. In some situations, you may not have physical access to that system, so connect with the appropriate **ssh** command. From the remote system, try the **ping server1.example.com** or **ping 192.168.122.50** commands.

4. Return to the server1.example.com system. Change the kernel setting described in Step 1 with the following command:

   ```
   # echo "1" > /proc/sys/net/ipv4/icmp_echo_ignore_all
   ```

   Confirm by repeating the command from Step 1. Try the **ping localhost** command again. What happens?

5. Restore the original 0 setting to the icmp_echo_ignore_all option.

CERTIFICATION OBJECTIVE 12.03

Create an RPM Package

If you've never created an RPM before, the RHCE objective to "build a simple RPM that packages a single file" may seem like a big challenge. With the help of some relatively new tools, it's easier than it looks.

While you won't have access to the Internet during the exam, you can download source RPMs to help study for the exam. Source RPMs, when installed, set up a structure of subdirectories. The location depends on the user. If the source RPM is installed by user michael (and yes, regular users can now load source code), source RPM subdirectories can be found in the /home/michael/rpmbuild directory.

In production, it's risky to install and compile a source RPM as the root administrative user. Mistakes in the source RPM could easily compromise a production system.

The source code unpacked from a source RPM (SRPM) can serve as a model for the one that you will create. RHEL 6 tools are now available to help set up a spec file. That spec file can then be used to build an actual binary RPM that others can use to install the single file on their own systems.

Source RPMs

On Red Hat systems, when the GNU General Public License (GPL) refers to source code, it refers to source RPMs. In fact, Red Hat complies with such open-source licenses in part by releasing source RPMs on their public servers at ftp.redhat.com. The source code includes the programs and files, as created by the developers. Source code can then be built into the binary packages used for installing RHEL 6 and additional software after installation is complete.

In this section, you'll download and install the source-code RPM associated with the vsFTP server. One way to do so is with the **lftp** command described in Chapter 2. To use that command to connect to the Red Hat FTP server, run the following command:

```
$ lftp ftp.redhat.com
```

That command connects to the Red Hat public FTP server anonymously and initiates the lftp ftp.redhat.com> prompt. To connect to the directory with source-code packages for the RHEL 6 server, run the following command from the noted prompt:

```
lftp ftp.redhat.com> cd /redhat/linux/enterprise/6Server/en/os/SRPMS
```

Command completion features work at the **lftp** prompt; in other words, if you're not sure what directories are available after typing in the **cd** command, just press TAB once or twice.

At the noted directory, you can then download the source code for the vsFTP server with the following command (the version number will vary with updates):

```
get vsftpd-2.2.2-6.el6.src.rpm
```

You can then run the **quit** command to exit from the **lftp** prompt and return to the regular command line interface. The source-code SRPM should now be available in the local directory. Even as a regular user, you'll be able to unpack that SRPM with the **rpm** command. For example, the following command run from my regular account unpacks that source code into /home/michael/rpmbuild subdirectories:

```
$ rpm -ivh vsftpd-*.src.rpm
```

The command doesn't install the vsFTP server, as it would with a regular RPM package. It unpacks the SRPM into specific subdirectories.

The Directory Structure of an RPM Source

SRPMs, when installed, are unpacked. The source code from such packages are loaded onto the rpmbuild/SPECS and rpmbuild/SOURCES subdirectories. As suggested by the names, the source code is in the SOURCES subdirectory. Figure 12-1 illustrates the list of files unpacked from the vsFTP source code.

Most of the files in the noted directory are patches, updates to the source code. Some of the files are configuration files to be loaded into the /etc/vsftpd directory by the binary package. The actual source code is compressed in a gzip-compressed tar archive, in .tar.gz format. Note how the version number is included in the source-code archive. Such archives can be created and unpacked with the help of the **tar** command.

Source code can also be compressed using the bzip2 algorithm.

FIGURE 12-1

Source code in an rpmbuild/ SOURCES subdirectory

```
[michael@server1 SOURCES]$ ls
vsftpd-2.0.5-greedy.patch              vsftpd-2.2.2-clone.patch
vsftpd-2.1.0-build_ssl.patch           vsftpd-2.2.2-isolate.patch
vsftpd-2.1.0-configuration.patch       vsftpd-2.2.2.tar.gz
vsftpd-2.1.0-filter.patch              vsftpd-2.2.2-v6only.patch
vsftpd-2.1.0-libs.patch                vsftpd-close-std-fds.patch
vsftpd-2.1.0-pam_hostname.patch        vsftpd_conf_migrate.sh
vsftpd-2.1.0-tcp_wrappers.patch        vsftpd.ftpusers
vsftpd-2.1.0-trim.patch                vsftpd.init
vsftpd-2.1.0-userlist_log.patch        vsftpd.pam
vsftpd-2.1.1-daemonize_plus.patch      vsftpd.user_list
vsftpd-2.2.0-openssl.patch             vsftpd.xinetd
vsftpd-2.2.0-wildchar.patch
[michael@server1 SOURCES]$
```

To create an RPM, you're going to have to set up a similar archive in the same rpmbuild/SOURCES subdirectory. Once configured, you'll also have to create a spec file, to be stored in the rpmbuild/SPECS subdirectory. You'll then be able to compile that package with the **rpmbuild** command.

Install and Analyze the rpmbuild Command

The **rpmbuild** command is used to build a binary RPM from source code, as configured with a spec file. As the command is not available by default, you'll have to install it from the rpm-build package. You should also install the rpmdevtools package, which will be useful shortly. To speed up the process, it's more efficient to use administrative privileges to use the **yum** command to install all of these packages, using the procedures described in Chapter 7.

```
# yum install rpm-build rpmdevtools
```

In general, if you want more information on how it works, run the **rpmbuild** command with the **-v** or **-vv** switch. Most documentation assumes the **rpmbuild** command uses a spec file in the rpmbuild/SPECS directory. In that case, you'd use the **-b** switch. Options with the **-t** switch are associated with a spec file included in the actual source-code archive in .tar or compressed .tar.gz format. Given current documentation, it's assumed that you'll configure a separate .spec file and would therefore use one of the **-b** switches described in Table 12-2.

TABLE 12-2	Switch	Description
Switches for the rpmbuild Command	-ba	Builds both binary and source RPM packages.
	-bb	Builds the binary RPM package.
	-bc	Executes the %prep and %build commands from the .spec file.
	-bi	Executes the %prep, %build, and %install commands from the .spec file.
	-bl	Checks for the existence of cited files.
	-bp	Executes just the %prep stage of the .spec file.
	-bs	Builds just the source RPM package.

In general, you'd apply either the **rpmbulid -ba** or **rpmbuild -bb** command to the spec file from the rpmbuild/SPECS subdirectory.

Use the rpmbuild Command

If you unpacked the vsFTP source RPM described earlier, there will be a .spec file in the rpmbuild/SPECS subdirectory. The following rpmbuild command can be used to build both the source and binary RPMs for the vsFTP server, from a regular user's home directory:

```
$ rpmbulid -ba rpmbuild/SPECS/vsftpd.spec
```

In many cases, the process of building an RPM from source code requires the installation of development packages. For example, when I ran the noted **rpmbuild** command on the standard server1.example.com system, it cited a need for four other packages:

```
pam-devel is needed by vsftpd-2.2.2-6.el6.x86_64
libcap-devel is needed by vsftpd-2.2.2-6.el6.x86_64
openssl-devel is needed by vsftpd-2.2.2-6.el6.x86_64
tcp_wrappers-devel is needed by vsftpd-2.2.2-6.el6.x86_64
```

The GNU C Compiler package, gcc, is also required. With dependencies, several other packages will probably be required on your system. So before the noted **rpmbuild** command works, you should install the noted packages with a command like

```
# yum install gcc pam-devel libcap-devel openssl-devel tcp_wrappers-devel
```

Once these developmental and related compiler packages are installed, a regular user will be able to run the aforementioned **rpmbuild** command to compile the source code for the vsFTP server to create a binary and a source RPM.

Once the build process is complete, the compiled binary RPM can be found in the rpmbuild/RPMS/x86_64 subdirectory; of course, the last bit would vary with the architecture. The collected source RPM can be found in the rpmbuild/SRPMS subdirectory.

Create Custom Source Code

With what you now know about the build process for the vsFTP source RPM, you should be able to create a source-code package. For the purpose of this chapter, I've created a corporate_policies.pdf file. Since source code that's built into an RPM is configured as a gzip compressed tar archive that will be expanded into a directory, it should be copied to a directory created for that purpose. In addition, the **rpmbuild** command, with standard .spec files, requires access to an executable file named configure. It can be an empty file.

For my own user account, I took the following steps:

1. I copied the given corporate_policies.pdf file to a newly created /home/michael/CorPor-1.0 directory. The -1.0 represents the version number of the package.

2. I created an empty file named *configure* and assigned it executable permissions with the following commands:

```
$ cd /home/michael/CorPor-1.0
$ touch configure
$ chmod u+x configure
$ cd /home/michael
```

3. I used the following command to create an appropriate gzip-compressed tar archive:

```
$ tar czvf CorPor-1.0.tar.gz CorPor-1.0
```

4. I then copied the archive to the rpmbuild/SOURCES subdirectory.

If you're following along in a regular account, download a PDF file, such as RHEL 6 documentation available from http://docs.redhat.com/docs/en-US/Red_Hat_ Enterprise_Linux/index.html. Copy the downloaded PDF, and change that filename with a command such as **mv** to corporate_policies.pdf.

That rpmbuild/SOURCES subdirectory can also contain the source code for the previously discussed vsFTP server. Don't be concerned about all of the patch and other files, as the RHCE objective is to create an RPM with one file. With a properly configured spec file, the source code for multiple packages can co-exist in this directory.

One More Prep Package

The next step is to create a spec file. If you've looked at the vsftpd.spec file in the rpmbuild/SPECS subdirectory, don't be too concerned. First, your spec file doesn't have to be nearly so complex. Second, there's no need to memorize the format of a .spec file, as long as the rpmdevtools package is installed. It depends on the fakeroot package, which supports root-type privileges for regular users.

Once installed, two commands from the rpmdevtools package are of special interest. The **rpmdev-setuptree** command creates the rpmbuild/ subdirectory, with appropriate subdirectories. The **rpmdev-newspec** command creates a newpackage. spec file in the local directory, with a template that can be used to create an RPM.

Thus, if the RHCE exam expects you to build an RPM, you'd run the **rpmdev-setuptree** command to build the directory structure, and then copy the gzip compressed archive to the rpmbuild/SOURCES subdirectory. Now you can create a spec file to process that archive.

Create Your Own spec File

You can create a newpackage.spec file with the **rpmdev-newspec** command. From that template, you can configure a spec file that can process the CorPor.tar.gz archive into an RPM package. The file as shown in Figure 12-2 essentially prompts for all needed information.

Compare this file to the contents of the vsftpd.spec file described earlier for hints. For this section, make a copy of that file as corpor.spec in the rpmbuild/SPECS subdirectory. Only the .spec file extension matters; it could be named mytest.spec. Examine the spec file line by line.

The first line is the name of the spec file. While the given Name doesn't matter, it becomes the name for the RPM package:

```
Name: CorPor
```

The version number is also added to the RPM; 1.0 is standard:

```
Version: 1.0
```

The release number is added afterward; this default adds a **1.el6** for RHEL 6:

```
Release: 1%(?dist)
```

While the summary should describe the contents of the package, it doesn't affect how the RPM is created.

```
Summary: A package with one file
```

The Group is related to the package groups listed in the XML file described in Chapter 7. To set up a package as part of a package group, you'd need to assign a real package group; for example, the vsFTP server is part of the System Environment /Daemons package group. But for our purposes, the assigned package group does not matter.

```
Group:  Miscellaneous
```

| **FIGURE 12-2** | ```
Name:
Version:
Release:        1%{?dist}
Summary:

Group:
License:
URL:
Source0:
BuildRoot:      %{_tmppath}/%{name}-%{version}-%{release}-root-%(%{__id_u} -
n)

BuildRequires:
Requires:

%description


%prep
%setup -q


%build
%configure
make %{?_smp_mflags}


%install
rm -rf $RPM_BUILD_ROOT
make install DESTDIR=$RPM_BUILD_ROOT


%clean
rm -rf $RPM_BUILD_ROOT


%files
%defattr(-,root,root,-)
%doc
"newpackage.spec" 42L, 488C
``` |
| A newpackage spec file | |

Open-source software may be released under a variety of different licenses. Most RHEL 6 software is released under the GPL.

```
License: McGraw-Hill
```

You can either comment out the URL, or add an appropriate address, as shown here:

```
URL: http://www.mheducation.com/
```

The Source0 is perhaps most important. It specifies the name of the gzip compressed tar archive file, either from a remote URL or from the local rpmbuild/SOURCES/
```

subdirectory. While the vsftpd.spec file includes Source1, Source2, and later directives, it's not required. All that's needed is the full name of the compressed archive file.

```
Source0: CorPor-1.0.tar.gz
```

Most packages don't include a BuildArch directive, as most packages are built to the architecture of the local system. However, for those packages that are supposed to be architecture-independent, it's appropriate to include the following BuildArch line:

```
BuildArch: noarch
```

If you forget, don't worry. The BuildArch line is not required unless you're told to set up a single RPM package that can be installed on systems with all architectures.

The lines that follow are dependencies. The BuildRequires line specifies packages that must be installed before the RPM and SRPM packages can be built with this spec file. Review the vsftpd.spec file for this line. There are actually four BuildRequires lines in that file, which specify the developmental packages listed as dependencies when you applied the **rpmbuild -ba** command to that vsftpd.spec file. In contrast, the Requires line would specify actual dependencies. For an RPM package from a single file, especially one related to documentation, there's generally no reason to have BuildRequires or Requires dependencies. In that case, you'd comment out these lines:

```
#BuildRequires
#Requires
```

The %description directive that follows allows you to include a brief paragraph description of the package. One word would be sufficient.

```
%description
This is a package with one file, associated with corporate policies.
```

The %prep section is associated with any commands required to prepare the source code. The line that follows is a bit strange. Even though it starts with a %, it is a command. The **%setup -q** is a command macro that unpacks the compressed tar archive in the rpmbuild/SOURCES directory.

```
%prep
%setup -q
```

The %build section that follows includes commands that configure and compile the source code. It normally points to scripts within the source code, commonly set up with script filenames like **configure** and **make**. With a one-file RPM, there's nothing to configure or compile, so it is appropriate to comment out or erase these options.

```
%build
#%configure
#make %{?_smp_mflags}
```

The %install section includes commands that actually adds the files from the package to noted directories. It normally starts with the following command to delete the directory tree associated with any previous builds of this package:

```
%install
rm -rf $RPM_BUILD_ROOT
```

As noted before, the **make** command is normally used to compile actual source code. Unless you've included some script, command, or executable in the source code, it's also not necessary. For RPM packages with one file, you should in fact erase or comment out that line:

```
#make install DESTDIR=$RPM_BUILD_ROOT
```

However, that means you need to configure a directory where the specified package is actually getting installed. I actually found an excellent model for this purpose in a package for fonts for a language from Ethiopia, in the abyssinica-fonts. spec file. The key excerpt is shown in Figure 12-3.

The directives from Figure 12-3 also provide a slightly different perspective. For example, %{buildroot} is equivalent to $RPM_BUILD_ROOT. As there's nothing to compile in a group of fonts, there's no "make" command in that file.

I've modified those options a bit. The **install -d** directive creates a directory, with (**-m**) mode (**chmod**-style octal permissions) of 0755. The system is built on some hypothetical root to be defined, in the /opt/CorPor-1.0 subdirectory.

FIGURE 12-3	
An RPM model for file placement	

```
%install
rm -rf %{buildroot}

#fonts
install -d -m 0755 %{buildroot}%{_fontdir}
install -m 0644 *.ttf %{buildroot}%{_fontdir}
```

The corporate_policies.pdf file is then installed, with 0644 permissions, in the directory just created.

```
install -d -m 0755 $RPM_BUILD_ROOT/opt/CorPor-1.0
install -m 0644 corporate_policies.pdf $RPM_BUILD_ROOT/opt/CorPor-1.0/corporate_
policies.pdf
```

After the source code is compiled, it is cleaned with the following directive:

```
%clean
rm -rf $RPM_BUILD_ROOT
```

The locations of the files and directories can be confirmed:

```
%files
%dir /opt/CorPor-1.0
%defattr(-,root,root,-)
/opt/CorPor-1.0/corporate_policies.pdf
```

If desired, you can set up different ownership. For example, if user and group michael were substituted for root in the %defattr(-,root,root,-) directive, the corporate_policies.pdf file that follows would be owned by the user and group michael.

Once the changes are made, you can proceed with the building of an RPM.

Build Your Own RPM

With the packages installed so far in this chapter, the **rpmbuild -ba** command can be run by a regular user to create binary and source RPM packages. For the corpor.spec file just described, user michael, from his home directory, could build the RPM from the directives specified in that file with the following command:

```
$ rpmbuld -ba rpmbuild/SPECS/corpor.spec
```

If successful, the last message should indicate success, as follows:

```
+ exit 0
```

If there's a problem, the last message might provide a clue. For example, the following message is straightforward, associated with a typographical error in a file. It also shows the location of the $RPM_BUILD_ROOT variable in the .spec file.

```
RPM build errors:
    File not found: /home/michael/rpmbuild/BUILDROOT/CorPor-1.0-1.el6.x86_64/
opt/CorPor-1.0/corporate_policies.pdf
```

Some error messages are even more straightforward. When I avoided an entry in the License field, the **rpmbuild** command returned the following message:

```
error: License field must be present in package: (main package)
```

Other error messages may seem more cryptic, but they point to a file which actually generates the RPM:

```
make: *** No targets specified and no makefile found.  Stop.
|error: Bad exit status from /var/tmp/rpm-tmp.tF080m (%build)
```

The extension of the rpm-tmp file varies. For more information, examine the contents of the latest rpm-tmp.* file the /var/tmp directory. Sometimes, the error message includes a line number. In some cases, the **rpmbuild -ba -vv** command provides very verbose (thus the **-vv** switch) information.

The Built RPMs

Once built, you'll be able to find the RPMs in the same rpmbuild/ subdirectory tree. With the **rpmbuild -ba** command described previously, both source and binary RPMs are built in that tree. Source RPMs can be found in the rpmbuild/SRPMS subdirectory; binary RPMs can be found in a subdirectory like rpmbuild/RPMS/noarch or rpmbuild/RPMS/x86_64. The actual directory classifies RPMs built in an architecture-independent manner, or for systems with 64-bit CPUs.

To view the differences, I built the CorPor RPM with and without the **BuildArch: noarch** directive in the .spec file. The resulting packages are

```
rpmbuild/RPMS/noarch/CorPor-1.0-1.el6.noarch.rpm
rpmbuild/RPMS/x86_64/CorPor-1.0-1.el6.x86_64.rpm
```

While the fakeroot package made it possible to run the **rpmbuild** command as a regular user, installation of the new package still requires administrative privileges. When installed, it loaded the noted corporate_policies.pdf file in the /opt/CorPor-1.0 directory. And an **rpm -qi** command applied to that package led to the output shown in Figure 12-4.

Compare that output to the information added to the corpor.spec file described earlier. That should help you better understand the purpose of each entry in the spec file.

FIGURE 12-4

Information on
the single-file
RPM package

```
[michael@server1 ~]$ rpm -qi CorPor
Name        : CorPor              Relocations: (not relocatable)
Version     : 1.0                     Vendor: (none)
Release     : 1.el6               Build Date: Wed 16 Feb 2011 09:2
2:44 AM PST
Install Date: Wed 16 Feb 2011 09:23:04 AM PST    Build Host: server1
Group       : Miscellaneous       Source RPM: CorPor-1.0-1.el6.src
.rpm
Size        : 7702360                License: McGraw-Hill
Signature   : (none)
URL         : http://www.mheducation.com
Summary     : A package with one file
Description :
This is a package with one file, associated with corporate policies.
[michael@server1 ~]$ ▮
```

CERTIFICATION OBJECTIVE 12.04

Special Network Options

This section relates to three different network options, each associated with an objective for the RHCE exam. The first is related to routing, which requires an understanding of routing tables, the **route** command, and associated configuration tools and files. The second relates to the configuration of a system as a Kerberos client. It's not the first time client side–only configuration has been required on Red Hat exams, as the previous version of the RHCE exam required only the configuration of a system as a Network Information Service (NIS) or a Lightweight Directory Access Protocol (LDAP) client. Just be aware, a Kerberos client does not work unless Network Time Protocol (NTP) clients on both systems are configured to synchronize with the same NTP server.

For the third option, you need to know how to set up an iSCSI client, which can connect to storage over a standard network connection. Just to be clear, as an iSCSI client does not require SCSI hardware, there's no need to look for that now-older type of server storage media.

Configure Special IP Routes

As described in the RHCE objectives, you need to know how to "Route IP traffic and create static routes." That's really two tasks. First, it's a standard part of network configuration to set up a default route to an outside network. But there's also the related task, when a system has two or more network devices, of setting up a special route, using a nondefault device, to a specific network.

Configure a Default Route

The default route is the path taken by a network message, when the destination address is on an outside network. When a Dynamic Host Configuration Protocol (DHCP) server is working, and is configured to assign gateway addresses, a default route is assigned with the dynamic IP address. That's normally evident in the output to the **route -n** and **netstat -nr** commands discussed in Chapter 5. One sample of such output for a system that uses a DHCP server is shown here:

```
Destination     Gateway         Genmask         Flags Metric Ref Use Iface
192.168.122.0   0.0.0.0         255.255.255.0   U     0      0     0 eth0
0.0.0.0         192.168.122.1   0.0.0.0         UG    0      0     0 eth0
```

To review, the default IPv4 address is 0.0.0.0, so the default route goes through the gateway address of 192.168.122.1. In a similar fashion, the default route for a statically configured network system is configured with the GATEWAY directive in its configuration file. Such configuration files are stored in the /etc/sysconfig/network-scripts directory, with names like ifcfg-eth0.

But there are situations, such as a temporary disconnect on a network cable, where the default route is not given by a DHCP server. Perhaps the DHCP server has to be replaced, and you'll have to set up static IP address information. In such cases, the output to the **route -n** command might look more like the following:

```
Destination     Gateway         Genmask         Flags Metric Ref Use Iface
192.168.122.0   0.0.0.0         255.255.255.0   U     0      0     0 eth0
```

In other words, since the default IP address of 0.0.0.0 is missing, there is no default route. That route can be added temporarily with the **route add** command. For example, the following command would restore the default route shown earlier:

```
# route add default gw 192.168.122.1
```

If multiple network devices exist on the local system, you can specify it; just for variety, the following command specifies the second Ethernet adapter, eth1:

```
# route add default gw 192.168.122.1 dev eth1
```

To make sure that default route survives a reboot, you'll need to make sure either the system configures that default gateway IP address as part of a static configuration, or the DHCP server used for the network can assign that gateway IP address. To review, Figure 12-5 reflects the way the default gateway IPv4 address is configured

FIGURE 12-5

A static network configuration with a default gateway

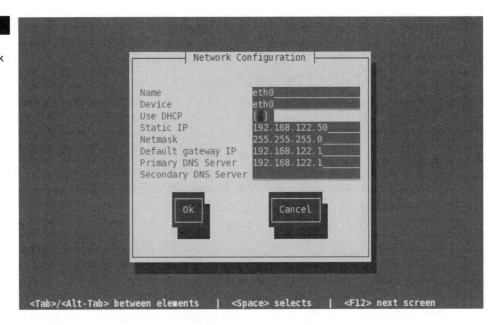

```
┌──────────┤ Network Configuration ├──────────┐
│                                               │
│    Name                eth0                    │
│    Device              eth0                    │
│    Use DHCP            [ ]                      │
│    Static IP          192.168.122.50           │
│    Netmask            255.255.255.0            │
│    Default gateway IP 192.168.122.1            │
│    Primary DNS Server 192.168.122.1            │
│    Secondary DNS Server                        │
│                                               │
│         ┌────────┐         ┌────────┐         │
│         │   Ok   │         │ Cancel │         │
│         └────────┘         └────────┘         │
│                                               │
└───────────────────────────────────────────────┘

  <Tab>/<Alt-Tab> between elements  |  <Space> selects  |  <F12> next screen
```

with the Network Configuration tool. In addition, you'll need to make sure the added default route survives a reboot, either by a direct change to the ifcfg-eth*x* configuration file or indirectly with the Network Configuration tool.

Some systems may have multiple network devices connected to the same network. In that case, you may need to configure a special route. As you might see, special routes are not possible with the console-based Network Configuration tool.

Configure a Special Route

One way to configure a special route is with the Network Connections tool. As discussed in Chapter 5, you can start it from a GUI console with the **nm-connection-editor** command. Select an existing wired or wireless network device, and click Edit. Under either the IPv4 or IPv6 tab, there's a Routes button for special routes. Click it to see the window shown in Figure 12-6.

on the job

The Network Connections tool does not work unless the NetworkManager service in the /etc/init.d directory is active.

FIGURE 12-6

A special route
for a specific
network device

When applied, it writes a route-eth0 file in the /etc/sysconfig/network-scripts directory. The following is the complete contents of that file:

```
ADDRESS0=192.168.0.0
NETMASK0=255.255.255.0
GATEWAY0=192.168.122.1
```

When the network service is restarted, it's applied to the routing table. Based on the previously configured routing table, the following is the result:

```
Destination    Gateway         Genmask         Flags Metric Ref Use Iface
192.168.0.0    192.168.122.1   255.255.255.0   UG    0      0     0 eth0
192.168.122.0  0.0.0.0         255.255.255.0   U     1      0     0 eth0
0.0.0.0        192.168.122.1   0.0.0.0         UG    0      0     0 eth0
```

Set Up a Kerberos Client

For the purpose of an exam, as well as on the job, it's almost always best to keep the solutions as simple as possible. That's where the Authentication Configuration tool can help. To see what this tool does to help configure a Kerberos client, you could back up the files in the /etc/sssd directory, along with the /etc/nsswitch.conf configuration file. It's related to the System Security Services Daemon, controlled by the /etc/init.d/sssd script. If you've previously configured a system to authenticate via an LDAP server in Chapter 8, the sssd service may already be running.

As there is no RHCE objective related to the configuration of a Kerberos server, that process will not be covered in this book. What you should know is that Kerberos servers as configured on RHEL 6 don't have their own authentication databases. So for a valid client connection to a Kerberos server, you'll also need a connection to a network authentication database such as LDAP.

If you configure a Kerberos server, make sure port 88 is open in the relevant firewalls.

What Is Kerberos

Kerberos is a network authentication protocol originally developed at the Massachusetts Institute of Technology (MIT) that supports secure identification of networked systems. On RHEL 6, a separate protocol such as LDAP is normally configured for user-based authentication.

Two systems configured with and confirmed by Kerberos can communicate in encrypted format, with a symmetric key. That key is granted by a Key Distribution Center (KDC), which consists of an Authentication Server (AS) and a Ticket Granting Server (TGS). When authentication is confirmed, the Kerberos client gets a ticket good for a limited time, typically eight hours.

Given the importance of time to Kerberos, it may not work unless configured clients and servers also use NTP services, as discussed in Chapters 5 and 17.

The Graphical Authentication Configuration Tool

One way to open the GUI version of the Authentication Configuration tool is with the **authconfig-gtk** command. That should open the Authentication Configuration tool with the two tabs shown in Figure 12-7. While other authentication databases are supported, the focus is on LDAP, especially since LDAP is the selected network client authentication option for the RHCSA exam. The options in the LDAP half of the Identity And Authentication tab were discussed in Chapter 8.

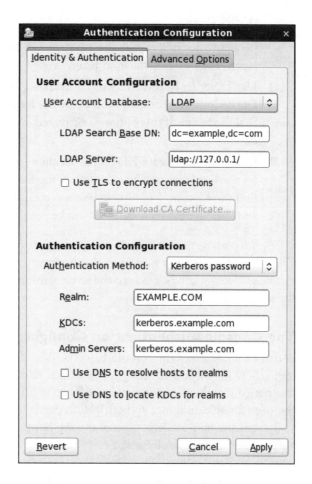

FIGURE 12-7

Configure a
Kerberos-based
client with
the graphical
Authentication
Configuration
Tool.

The focus of this section is on the second half of the tab. For a Kerberos-based client, you'd retain Kerberos Password as the Authentication Method. The other options are

- **Realm** By convention, the Kerberos realm is the same as the domain name for the network, in uppercase letters. It's necessary if you configure DNS support for Kerberos.
- **KDCs** The KDC is the Kerberos Key Distribution Center. The entry here should correspond either to the Fully Qualified Domain Name (FQDN) or the IP address of the actual Kerberos server.

- **Admin Servers** The administrative server associated with the KDC is frequently located on the same system. On the Kerberos administrative server, the kadmind daemon is running.
- **Use DNS To Resolve Hosts To Realms** Where a trusted DNS server exists for the local network, you can allow the local system to use a DNS server to find the realm. If this option is activated, the Realm text box will be blanked out.
- **Use DNS To Locate KDCs For Realms** Where a trusted DNS server exists for the local network, you can allow the local system to use a DNS server to find the KDC and administrative server. If this option is activated, the KDCs and Admin Servers text boxes will be blanked out.

For the purpose of this section, accept the default options as shown in Figure 12-7. Click Apply. After a few moments, the Authentication Configuration window will close and changes will be made to the aforementioned configuration files. In addition, the sssd service will be started.

The Console Authentication Configuration Tool

Perhaps a weakness of the console-based version of the Authentication Configuration tool is how it's possible to set up a system as a Kerberos client without a connection to a network authentication database. If you're using the console tool, keep in mind the need for an actual user authentication database to go with Kerberos.

To start the text-mode version of the Authentication Configuration tool, run the **authconfig-tui** command. As shown in Figure 12-8, you'll need to activate LDAP at least for authentication.

After selecting Next, the tool prompts for LDAP settings information, as discussed in Chapter 8. After that screen, you'll see the Kerberos Settings screen shown in Figure 12-9. The default options shown here are the same as those shown in the graphical version of the tool from Figure 12-7.

You may also need to set up changes to configuration files, described next.

Changes to Configuration Files

Several changes are made to local configuration files, specifically /etc/nsswitch.conf and /etc/sssd/sssd.conf, based on the configuration of a Kerberos client.

FIGURE 12-8

Configure a
Kerberos-based
client with
the console
Authentication
Configuration
tool.

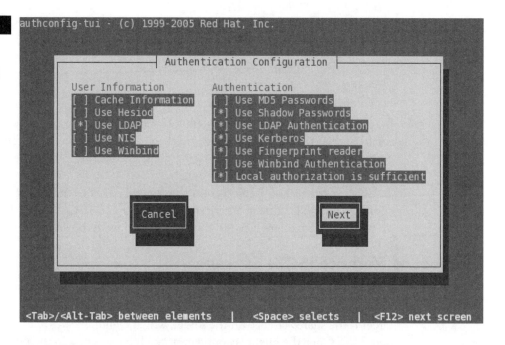

```
authconfig-tui - (c) 1999-2005 Red Hat, Inc.

                    ┤ Authentication Configuration ├
  User Information            Authentication
  [ ] Cache Information       [ ] Use MD5 Passwords
  [ ] Use Hesiod             [*] Use Shadow Passwords
  [*] Use LDAP               [*] Use LDAP Authentication
  [ ] Use NIS                [*] Use Kerberos
  [ ] Use Winbind            [*] Use Fingerprint reader
                             [ ] Use Winbind Authentication
                             [*] Local authorization is sufficient

              Cancel                        Next

<Tab>/<Alt-Tab> between elements  |  <Space> selects  |  <F12> next screen
```

FIGURE 12-9

Specify Kerberos
client settings.

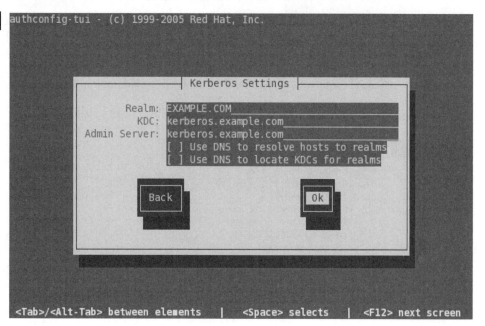

```
authconfig-tui - (c) 1999-2005 Red Hat, Inc.

                    ┤ Kerberos Settings ├
          Realm: EXAMPLE.COM
            KDC: kerberos.example.com
   Admin Server: kerberos.example.com
                 [ ] Use DNS to resolve hosts to realms
                 [ ] Use DNS to locate KDCs for realms

              Back                          Ok

<Tab>/<Alt-Tab> between elements  |  <Space> selects  |  <F12> next screen
```

First, look at the changes to the /etc/nsswitch.conf file, where the **sss** setting is added to the authentication files shown here:

```
passwd:    files sss
shadow:    files sss
group:     files sss
```

In other words, when the local system looks for usernames and passwords, the files of the local shadow password suite are checked. If the username is not found there, control is turned over to the sssd daemon described earlier. Those files are configured in the /etc/sssd directory.

Changes to the sssd daemon configuration are added to the end of /etc/sssd/sssd. conf file. The added directives are shown in Figure 12-10 and are explained in Table 12-3. The directives are listed in the order that they're shown in the figure.

Connect to Remote iSCSI Storage

The relevant RHCE objective is to "configure a system as an iSCSI initiator that persistently mounts an iSCSI target." The iSCSI initiator is a client. The iSCSI target is the shared storage on the server, which communicates with the client over port 3260. Once the client is configured, you'll have access to the iSCSI target; that target will look like just another hard drive. Of course, the response will probably be slower, but that depends on the speed of and the traffic on that network.

To set up an iSCSI client, you'll need the iscsi-initiator-utils packages, along with any dependencies. Then you'd use the **iscsiadm** command to discover available iSCSI targets. One method is with the following command:

```
# iscsiadm -m discoverydb -t st -p 192.168.122.1 -D
```

FIGURE 12-10

Kerberos
Configuration in
/etc/sssd/sssd.conf

```
[domain/default]
auth_provider = krb5
cache_credentials = True
ldap_id_use_start_tls = False
debug_level = 0
krb5_kpasswd = kerberos.example.com
ldap_search_base = dc=example,dc=com
krb5_realm = EXAMPLE.COM
chpass_provider = krb5
id_provider = ldap
ldap_uri = ldap://127.0.0.1/
krb5_kdcip = kerberos.example.com
ldap_tls_cacertdir = /etc/openldap/cacerts
```

TABLE 12-3	Directive	Description
Kerberos-Based Directives in /etc/sssd/sssd.conf	auth_provider	Set to krb5 for Kerberos authentication.
	cache_credentials	Stores authentication information locally if set to true.
	ldap_id_use_start_tls	Requires Transport Layer Security (TLS) to encrypt connections to the LDAP server, if set to true.
	debug_level	Configures when messages are logged; may be set between 0 to limit logging to critical messages and 10 for more information.
	krb5_kpasswd	Can specify the FQDN of the applicable server.
	ldap_search_base	Specifies the domain components of the LDAP server.
	krb5_realm	Notes the name of the Kerberos realm; should be in all uppercase letters.
	chpass_provider	Specifies the provider for the Kerberos password.
	id_provider	Configures the identity provider for the domain, usually ldap.
	ldap_uri	Includes the Uniform Resource Identifier (URI) for the LDAP server.
	krb5_kdcip	Notes the IP addresses or FQDN of Kerberos servers; multiple servers can be included.
	ldap_tls_cacertdir	Specifies the directory with a secure certificate for the LDAP server.

To interpret, this **iscsiadm** command queries iSCSI targets. It works in discovery database (**discoverydb**) mode (**-m**), where the discovery type (**-t**) requests that iSCSI servers actually send available targets (**sendtargets** or **st**), with a portal (**-p**) of the noted IP address, to discover (**-D**) shared storage.

If successful, you'll see output similar to the following:

```
192.168.122.1:3260,1 iqn.2011-02.com.example:for.all
```

You should then be able to start the iSCSI service with a command like

```
# /etc/init.d/iscsi start
```

If successful, you'll be able to review the available iSCSI shared storage, with the **/etc/init.d/iscsi status** command. The output should be similar to that shown in Figure 12-11.

FIGURE 12-11

Discovered iSCSI
storage

```
[root@server1 ~]# /etc/init.d/iscsi status
iSCSI Transport Class version 2.0-870
version 2.0-872
Target: iqn.2011-02.com.example:for.all
        Current Portal: 192.168.122.1:3260,1
        Persistent Portal: 192.168.122.1:3260,1
                **********
                Interface:
                **********
                Iface Name: default
                Iface Transport: tcp
                Iface Initiatorname: iqn.1994-05.com.redhat:dd2d45d064b4
                Iface IPaddress: 192.168.122.50
                Iface HWaddress: <empty>
                Iface Netdev: <empty>
                SID: 6
                iSCSI Connection State: LOGGED IN
                iSCSI Session State: LOGGED_IN
                Internal iscsid Session State: NO CHANGE
                *************************
                Negotiated iSCSI params:
                *************************
                HeaderDigest: None
                DataDigest: None
                MaxRecvDataSegmentLength: 262144
                MaxXmitDataSegmentLength: 8192
                FirstBurstLength: 65536
                MaxBurstLength: 262144
                ImmediateData: Yes
                InitialR2T: Yes
                MaxOutstandingR2T: 1
                *************************
                Attached SCSI devices:
                *************************
                Host Number: 7  State: running
                scsi7 Channel 00 Id 0 Lun: 0
[root@server1 ~]#
```

e**x**a m
ⓦatch   *To set up an iSCSI client,*   *open on that server, making it accessible*
you'll need access to an iSCSI target, acting   *with the iscsiadm command described in*
as a server. Normally, port 3260 will be   *this chapter.*

You should then be able to manage the shared storage as if it were a new hard
drive on the local system. The hard drive device file will show up in the /var/log/
messages file with information like the following, which points to device file /dev/sg3.

```
server1 kernel: scsi 7:0:0:0: Attached scsi generic sg3 type 12
```

You should then be able to create partitions and more on the new /dev/sg3 drive just as if it were a local drive, based on the techniques discussed in Chapter 6. Of course, a "persistent mount" as described in the relevant RHCE objective requires that you make sure the iSCSI service starts the next time the system is rebooted with a command like

```
# chkconfig iscsi on
```

To make sure there's an actual mount, you may also need to set up a partition that's actually mounted in the /etc/fstab file. In practice, the actual device file for the iSCSI drive may vary on each reboot. Therefore, such mounts should be configured with the Universally Unique Identifier (UUID) numbers described in Chapter 6.

You do not need to create an iSCSI target storage server for the RHCE exam. But as the configuration of an iSCSI server is relatively simple, you might consider creating one for that purpose. Red Hat developer Daniel Berrangé has created an excellent introduction to the creation of an iSCSI storage server at http://berrange.com/tags/tgtadm/.

SCENARIO & SOLUTION

You need to set up a daily task to back up files in the /home directory.	Set up a script in the /etc/cron.daily directory with appropriate backup commands to copy files from /home.
You've been told to set up IPv6 forwarding on a system.	Include the **net.ipv6.conf.all.forwarding=1** setting in /etc/sysctl.conf, and activate it with the **sysctl -p** command.
You need to set up source code for a single-file RPM.	Set up the single file, along with an executable **configure** script in a dedicated directory; then set it up in a compressed tar archive.
You need to set up a special static route over device eth1.	Use the Network Connections tool to set up that special route, given the network address, subnet mask, and desired gateway IP address.
You need to set up a system as a Kerberos client.	Use the GUI Authentication Configuration tool; the realm should be the uppercase listing for the domain. You'll also need the FQDN for the KDC and Kerberos administration servers (which may be the same).
You need to set up an iSCSI initiator.	Install the iscsi-initiator-utils package, use the **iscsiadm** command to discover available iSCSI targets, and make sure the iscsi service is active on reboot.

CERTIFICATION SUMMARY

Linux administrators need to configure scripts on a regular basis. Sample scripts are already available in different /etc/cron.* directories. Normally, scripts start with the **#!/bin/bash** line, which sets up the language for the rest of the script. Administrative scripts can use bash commands, along with operators such as **for, if, do,** and **test.** Kernel run-time parameters can be found in the /proc/sys directory. But changes to such files are temporary. For more permanent changes, you'd set up options in the /etc/sysctl.conf file. Changes to that file can be implemented with the **sysctl -p** command. Many standard options relate to networking.

One new RHCE requirement is to create an RPM from a single file. To do so, you need to know how to set up a source-code archive. The rpmdevtools and rpm-build packages can help. The **rpmdev-setup** tree command can help set up the needed directories. The **rpmdev-newspec** command can help create a template for a .spec file. The **rpmbuild** command can then be used to process the instructions in the spec file along with the packaged source code into an SRPM and an RPM package that can be installed on different systems.

The RHCE objectives include requirements for several special network options. With the help of the Network Connections tool, special IP routes can be configured in a file in the /etc/sysconfig/network-scripts directory. Kerberos clients can be configured in the /etc/sssd/sssd.conf file, referenced through the /etc/nsswitch.conf file. Perhaps the easiest way to configure a Kerberos client is with the GUI Authentication Configuration tool.

✓ TWO-MINUTE DRILL

Here are some of the key points from the certification objectives in Chapter 12.

Automate System Maintenance

- ❑ Standard administrative scripts can provide a model for custom scripts to automate system maintenance tasks.
- ❑ Various command operators within scripts include **do**, **for**, **if**, and **test**.
- ❑ Many Linux administrative scripts start with **#!/bin/bash**, a reference to the bash shell.

Kernel Run-Time Parameters

- ❑ Kernel run-time parameters are located in the /proc/sys directory.
- ❑ Many kernel run-time parameters relate to network options such as forwarding and security.
- ❑ Kernel run-time parameters can be configured on a permanent basis with the help of the /etc/sysctl.conf file.

Create an RPM Package

- ❑ Available source RPMs can be used as a model to help create your own RPMs.
- ❑ RPM source-code components can be found in user home directories, in the rpmbuild/ subdirectory, as configured with the **rpmdev-setuptree** command.
- ❑ The actual source code can be found in the rpmbuild/SOURCES subdirectory.
- ❑ RPMs are built with the **rpmbuild** command, based on a .spec file in the rpmbuild/SPECS subdirectory. You can create a standard .spec template with the **rpmdev-newspec** command.
- ❑ Built RPMs can be found in the rpmbuild/SRPMS and rpmbuild/RPMS subdirectories.

Special Network Options

❑ The default network route to an outside network goes through a gateway IP address.

❑ Special routes to different networks can be configured through certain IP specific network devices.

❑ To configure a Kerberos client, you need to modify the /etc/sssd/sssd.conf file.

❑ A connection to the Kerberos client also requires a connection to a network authentication service such as LDAP.

❑ To configure an iSCSI client, you need the iscsi-initiator-utils package, which can be used to connect to iSCSI storage with the **iscsiadm** command.

❑ To make sure the iSCSI connection survives a reboot, you'll need to activate the iscsi service.

SELF TEST

The following questions will help measure your understanding of the material presented in this chapter. As no multiple-choice questions appear on the Red Hat exams, no multiple-choice questions appear in this book. These questions exclusively test your understanding of the chapter. It is okay if you have another way of performing a task. Getting results, not memorizing trivia, is what counts on the Red Hat exams.

Automate System Maintenance

1. What exit number is associated with success in a script?

   _____

2. What operator means "anything but"?

   _____

Kernel Run-Time Parameters

3. What's the full path to the file associated with the **net.ipv4.ip_forward** parameter?

   _____

Create an RPM Package

4. When source code is installed from an SRPM by user stephanie in her home directory, what is the full path to the actual source code?

   _____

5. What's the name of the package with a command that can be used to create a spec file template?

   _____

6. What common file is needed in a source-code directory to process standard source-code packages? Bonus: what should be different about permissions on that file, when compared to a regular file?

   _____

7. What command can be used to create just a regular RPM from source code, based on the test. spec file in the rpmbuild/SPECS subdirectory? Assume all required source code is in the correct location.

---

8. When user tim builds a regular RPM associated with 64-bit systems, what's the full path to the directory with that RPM?

Special Network Options

9. What are the three types of IP addresses associated with a special route?

---

10. In what file is a Kerberos client configured?

---

11. What is the standard Kerberos realm for the server1.example.com system?

---

12. What service script that should be running on reboot on a properly configured iSCSI target?

LAB QUESTIONS

Several of these labs involve configuration exercises. You should do these exercises on test machines only. It's assumed that you're running these exercises on virtual machines such as KVM.

Red Hat presents its exams electronically. For that reason, the labs in this and future chapters are available from the CD that accompanies the book, in the Chapter12/ subdirectory. In case you haven't yet set up RHEL 6 on a system, refer to Chapter 1 for installation instructions.

The answers for the labs follow the Self Test answers for the fill-in-the-blank questions.

SELF TEST ANSWERS

Automate System Maintenance

1. The exit number associated with success in a script is 0.

2. In a script, the operator that means "anything but" is the exclamation point (!). (It's also known as a "bang" in the world of Linux.)

System Run-Time Parameters

3. The full path to the file associated with the **net.ipv4.ip_forward** parameter is /proc/sys/net/ipv4/ip_forward.

Create an RPM Package

4. The full path to the actual source code, installed from an SRPM by user stephanie, is /home/stephanie/rpmbuild/SOURCES.

5. The name of the package with a command that can be used to create a spec file template is **rpmdev-newspec**.

6. The common file needed in standard source-code packages is named configure. Bonus: That file should also have executable permissions.

7. The command that can be used to create just a regular RPM from source code under the given conditions is **rpmbuild -ba rpmbuild/SPECS/test.spec**.

8. When user tim builds a regular RPM associated with 64-bit systems, the full path to the directory with that RPM is /home/tim/rpmbuild/RPMS/x86_64.

Special Network Options

9. The three types of IP addresses associated with a special route are the network address, the network or subnet mask, and the gateway address.

10. On RHEL 6, Kerberos clients are normally configured in the /etc/sssd/sssd.conf file.

11. The standard Kerberos realm for the server1.example.com system is EXAMPLE.COM.

12. The service script that should be active on reboot on a properly configured iSCSI target is iscsi.

LAB ANSWERS

Lab 1

Success in this lab should be straightforward. If you've run the **date** command as suggested in the body of the lab, the files from the /etc directory should be copied to the /backup directory a minute later.

The simplest way to set up that script to be run on an hourly basis is to configure it in the /etc/cron.hourly directory. The script needs only two lines. The following is one example of the lines you might include in that script:

```
#!/bin/bash
   /bin/cp -ar /etc /backup
```

Of course, for that script to work, it requires executable permissions. For the purpose of this lab, I created a script named whatever.cron in that directory with the two lines just shown. The name of the script does not matter, as long as it's saved to the /etc/cron.hourly directory.

As defined in the 0hourly script in the /etc/cron.d directory, hourly scripts are executed one minute past every hour. Since I'm by nature impatient (and tested this file on April 14), I ran the following command to advance the clock to the next hour (11 A.M.):

```
# date 04141100
```

One minute later, I found the contents of the /etc directory in the /backup directory.

Given the importance of the system clock for Kerberos-based authentication, you should restore the original time.

Lab 2

If you've followed the instructions in this lab, the /etc/sysctl.conf file should now have the following entry:

```
net.ipv4.icmp_echo_ignore_all = 1
```

That just makes sure the new setting survives a reboot. You may have also set the associated file, /proc/sys/net/ipv4/icmp_echo_ignore_all, to 1, or run the **sysctl -p** command to implement the change before the system is rebooted.

Of course, success can be confirmed with a **ping** command both from local and remote systems. If you want to restore the original configuration, return to the server1.example.com system, and then remove the net.ipv4.icmp_echo_ignore_all option from the /etc/sysctl.conf file.

Lab 3

If successful, you'll have a dedicated spec file in the rpmbuild/SPECS directory, and at least a binary RPM in a directory like rpmbuild/RPMS/noarch. Yes, you'll have to take administrative privileges to run the **rpm** command; when installed, the vsftpd.conf file should be installed in the /opt/sampleftp directory.

   If that doesn't work, you may need to refer back to the body of the chapter for more information. To summarize, remember to perform the following steps:

1. Set up a compressed archive for the directory with the vsftpd.conf file.

2. Install the rpm-build, rpmdevtools, and gcc packages, along with the dependencies shown when running the **rpmbuild -ba** command on the newly created spec file.

3. Use the **rpmdev-setuptree** command to configure a directory tree to build the new RPM.

4. Use the **rpmdev-newspec** command to set up a newpackage.spec file to process the RPM source code.

5. In the spec file, make sure to fill in the name, version, release number, summary, group, license, and a description. You should comment out the BuildRequires and Requires options, as there are no dependencies for this one file RPM.

6. Make sure to set up %install directives at the end of the file; for example, the following directives would make sure the binary RPM, when installed, sets up the file in the specified directory.

```
install -d -m 0755 $RPM_BUILD_ROOT/opt/sampleftp
install -m 0644 vsftpd.conf $RPM_BUILD_ROOT/opt/sampleftp/vsftpd.conf
```

7. Make sure the following directives confirm the noted directories, ownership, and filename from the source code. Of course, you can change the ownership of the loaded file with the help of the **defattr** directive.

```
%files
%dir /opt/sampleftp
%defattr(-,root,root,-)
/opt/sampleftp/vsftpd.conf
```

8. Save the file and apply the **rpmbuild -ba** command to the spec file.

9. Address any build errors that may appear in the **rpmbuild -ba** command output, or the latest /var/tmp/rpm-tmp.* file.

10. Use the **rpm** command to install the newly configured RPM from an rpmbuild/RPMS/noarch (or rpmbuild/RPMS/x86_64) subdirectory.

Lab 4

As with Lab 3, you'll have a different dedicated .spec file in the rpmbuild/SPECS directory, and at least a binary RPM in a directory like rpmbuild/RPMS/x86_64. Yes, you'll have to take administrative privileges to run the **rpm** command; when installed, the OVERVIEW file should be installed in the /opt/postfixinfo directory.

If you're ready, this can be a bit of a preview of the next chapter. The OVERVIEW file provides background information on the philosophy behind the Postfix service.

Lab 5

If you use the Network Connections tool to set up a special route, it should set up a special file in the /etc/sysconfig/network-scripts directory. If the specified network adapter is eth0, that special file would be route-eth0. Given the parameters used for the outsider1.example.org network as discussed in Chapter 1, that file would contain the following three lines:

```
ADDRESS0=192.168.100.0
NETMASK0=255.255.255.0
GATEWAY0=192.168.122.1
```

Of course, if the outsider1.example.org system is on a different network, the contents of the route-eth0 file would change accordingly.

Lab 6

Success in this lab means the following:

1. The sssd service is running and is set to run the next time the system is booted, with commands like **/etc/init.d/sssd start** and **chkconfig sssd on**.

2. The /etc/nsswitch.conf file includes the following entries for the shadow password suite:

```
passwd:    files sss
shadow:    files sss
group:     files sss
```

3. The /etc/sssd/sssd.conf file should include the following entries:

```
[domain/default]
ldap_id_use_start_tls = False
cache_credentials = True
auth_provider = krb5
debug_level = 0
krb5_kpasswd = maui.example.org
ldap_schema = rfc2307
ldap_search_base = dc=example,dc=org
krb5_realm = EXAMPLE.ORG
chpass_provider = krb5
id_provider = ldap
ldap_uri = ldap://192.168.100.1
krb5_kdcip = maui.example.org
ldap_tls_cacertdir = /etc/openldap/cacerts
```

13

Electronic Mail Servers

L inux offers a number of alternative methods for handling incoming and outgoing e-mail. RHEL 6 includes sendmail and Postfix for this purpose. Yes, it includes Dovecot, Fetchmail, and Procmail as well, but since the RHCE objectives focus on services associated with the Simple Mail Transfer Protocol (SMTP), this chapter focuses on sendmail and Postfix, as they are the two supported services associated with SMTP.

The default RHEL 6 SMTP service is now Postfix. That service was first developed in the late 1990s as an alternative to sendmail. It was designed to be easier to configure. It's feasible for most administrators to directly edit the associated configuration files. Now that Red Hat has changed default SMTP services from sendmail to Postfix, they've reached another milestone.

Despite Red Hat's move toward Postfix, sendmail is perhaps still the most common server for SMTP services. It was the default service through RHEL 5. Red Hat still supports it for RHEL 6. Once it is installed and configured, sendmail can be configured as an e-mail server for anything from an enterprise to a smart host for a personal system, subject to the limitations of an ISP. RHEL includes the open-source version of sendmail; the commercial version is the Sentrion Message Processing Engine from the company known as Sendmail (with the capital S).

For the purpose of this chapter, both Postfix and sendmail were installed on the physical host system. Smart host versions of each server were installed on the server1.example.com system. Access tests were performed from the VMs configured in Chapters 1 and 2, representing different external networks.

on the Job

A number of alternatives to Postfix and sendmail are not covered in this book; they include procmail, mail.local, exim, Cyrus IMAP, and uucp.

INSIDE THE EXAM

The objectives related to e-mail services on the RHCE exam are relatively simple. First, as the focus is on SMTP services, the focus is on services directly associated with SMTP. The major SMTP services available for RHEL 6 are Postfix and sendmail. While Postfix is installed by default, you're certainly

free to install and configure sendmail as an alternative to meet the noted requirements, specifically to

■ Configure a mail transfer agent (MTA) to accept inbound e-mail from other systems

- ■ Configure an MTA to forward (relay) e-mail through a smart host

  A related clue comes from the Red Hat prep course for the RHCE, which includes an objective to "configure an SMTP server for basic operation (null client, receiving mail, smarthost relay)."

  A null client is a system that can only send mail. A system that can receive mail is normally limited to the local network; however, such systems can be configured to receive e-mail from other networks as well. Mail can also be sent to remote systems. If a firewall or perhaps an ISP requires e-mail to be sent through their servers, you can configure SMTP services as smart hosts, which forwards information to such services.

  In addition, you also need to meet the basic RHCE objectives that apply to all network services, as discussed in Chapter 11.

CERTIFICATION OBJECTIVE 13.01

A Variety of E-Mail Agents

With either Postfix or sendmail comes serious configuration files that may seem cryptic to administrators who are newer to e-mail administration. Do not let the size of the configuration files intimidate you. Just a few changes are required to meet the requirements associated with the RHCE objectives. In this section, you'll explore where SMTP services fit in the hierarchy of e-mail services.

Definitions and Protocols

A mail server has four major components, as described in Table 13-1. On any Linux computer, you can configure a mail transfer agent (MTA) such as Postfix or sendmail for various outbound services, such as forwarding, relaying, smart host communication with other MTAs, aliases, and spooling directories. Other MTAs, such as Dovecot, are designed to handle only incoming e-mail services, based on the protocols it serves, POP3 (Post Office Protocol, version 3) and IMAP4 (Internet Message Access Protocol, version 4).

Abbreviation	Meaning	Examples
MTA	Mail transfer agent	Postfix, sendmail, Dovecot
MUA	Mail user agent	mutt, Evolution, mail, Thunderbird
MDA	Mail delivery agent	procmail
MSA	Mail submission agent	Postfix, sendmail

E-mail systems are heavily dependent on name resolution. While you could handle name resolution through /etc/hosts on a small network, any mail system that requires Internet access needs access to a fully functional DNS server. For spam protection and more, it's important to make sure that the system that intends to send an e-mail is actually transmitting with the assigned IP address.

But that is only one component of how e-mail works, from transmission to delivery. E-mail messages start with a mail user agent (MUA), a client system for sending and receiving e-mail such as mutt, Evolution, or Thunderbird. With the help of a Mail Submission Agent (MSA), such mail is normally sent to an MTA such as Postfix or sendmail. A Mail Delivery Agent (MDA) such as Procmail works locally to transfer e-mail from a server to an inbox folder. Procmail can also be used to filter e-mail. Red Hat also supports additional MTA services such as Dovecot to enable POP3 and/or IMAP (or the secure cousins, POP3s and IMAPs) to receive e-mail.

SMTP, the Simple Mail Transfer Protocol, has become one of the most important service protocols of the modern era. Much of the Internet-connected world lives and dies by e-mail and relies on SMTP to deliver it. Like POP3 and IMAP, SMTP is a *protocol*, a set of rules for transferring data used by various mail transfer agents.

Relevant Mail Server Packages

The packages associated with sendmail and Postfix are both part of the "E-mail server" package group. Key packages are listed in Table 13-2. You can install them with the **rpm** or **yum** command. Just remember that you do not need to install everything in this table.

When installed, the default E-mail server package group includes packages for the Postfix and Dovecot servers, along with the Spamassassin filter. Since you may not need all of these packages, it may be faster to install just Postfix or sendmail with the **rpm** or **yum** command, especially if you're configuring your Linux computer from the text console. It takes time to start the GUI.

TABLE 13-2	RPM Package	Description
Mail Server Packages	cyrus-imapd*	Installs the Cyrus IMAP enterprise e-mail system (several packages); may require perl-Cyrus.
	cyrus-sasl	Adds the Cyrus implementation of the Simple Authentication and Security Layer (SASL).
	dovecot	Supports both the IMAP and the POP incoming e-mail protocols.
	dovecot-mysql, dovecot-pgsql, dovecot-pigeonhole	Includes database back ends and related plugins for Dovecot.
	mailman	Supports e-mail discussion lists.
	postfix	Includes an alternative to sendmail.
	sendmail	Installs the most popular open-source mail server of the same name.
	sendmail-cf	Adds a number of templates that you can use to generate your sendmail configuration file; required to process many sendmail configuration files.
	spamassassin	Includes the spam fighting package of the same name.

watch

If you choose to work with sendmail, you should also install the sendmail-cf package to support the use of sendmail macro files.

Use alternatives to Select an E-Mail System

The **alternatives** command, with the **--config** switch, supports choices between different services such as Postfix and sendmail. Before using **alternatives**, you should stop the currently running SMTP service with the appropriate one of the following commands:

```
# /etc/init.d/postfix stop
# /etc/init.d/sendmail stop
```

Now run the following **alternatives** command, with the **--config** switch, to select the preferred MTA:

```
# alternatives --config mta
```

The command leads to the following output, which allows you to choose from installed SMTP e-mail servers. Other SMTP services, if installed, would be included in the list that follows:

```
There are 2 programs which provide 'mta'.

  Selection     Command
-------------------------------------------------
*+ 1            /usr/sbin/sendmail.sendmail
   2            /usr/sbin/sendmail.postfix

Enter to keep the current selection[+], or type selection number:
```

When making a selection, **alternatives** changes the appropriate runlevel scripts for each service, which can be confirmed with the following commands:

```
# chkconfig --list sendmail
# chkconfig --list postfix
```

In fact, the **chkconfig** command, when used to list the runlevels associated with an inactive service, may return an error message (with a proposed solution) similar to the following:

```
service sendmail supports chkconfig, but is not referenced in any runlevel (run
'chkconfig --add sendmail')
```

The **alternatives** command does not by itself stop or start a service. If you did not stop the original service earlier, the daemon will still be running. In that case, you'd have to use the **kill** command described in Chapter 9 to kill the undesired SMTP service. And it's important to have only one SMTP service running on a system. Interactions between sendmail and Postfix would lead to errors.

In addition, you'd have to use the appropriate script in the /etc/init.d directory (**sendmail** or **postfix**) to start the desired SMTP service.

General User Security

By default, all users are allowed to use locally configured SMTP services, without passwords. You'll see how this can be changed for both Postfix and sendmail in appropriate sections later in this chapter. This section assumes appropriate limitations have been configured.

In some cases, you may want to set up local users just so they have access to such services. If you don't want such users to log in to the server with regular accounts, one option is to make sure that such users don't have a login shell. For example, the following command can set up a user named tempworker on a local system without a login shell:

```
# useradd tempworker -s /sbin/nologin
```

That tempworker user can then set up his own e-mail manager such as Evolution, Thunderbird, or even Outlook Express to connect to networked Postfix or sendmail SMTP services. Any attempts by that user to log in directly to the server are rejected.

Of course, access is limited to configured users, whether or not their accounts are configured with a login shell. That's configured courtesy of the Simple Authentication and Security Layer (SASL). As implemented for RHEL 6, it's based on the cyrus-sasl package, as configured in the /etc/sasl2 directory. While that directory may include different configuration files for Postfix (smtpd.conf) and sendmail (Sendmail.conf, yes, that's an uppercase S), both configuration files refer back to the same authentication scheme with the following directive:

```
pwcheck_method:saslauthd
```

The /etc/sysconfig/saslauthd configuration file confirms the standard mechanism for password checks with the following directive:

```
MECH=pam
```

That's a reference to the Pluggable Authentication Modules (PAM) described in Chapter 10. In other words, users who are configured on the local system are controlled by associated files in the /etc/pam.d directory, namely smtp.postfix and smtp.sendmail. However, you'll need to make a few changes to Postfix to actually make it read the authentication database.

Mail Logging

Most log messages associated with SMTP services can be found in the /var/log/maillog file. Messages that you might expect to see in this file relate to

- Restarts of both sendmail and Postfix
- Successful and failed user connections
- Sent and rejected e-mail messages

Common Security Issues

By default, the SMTP service uses port 25. If you open port 25 on the firewall, outside users may have access to that server. If you need to know how to open that port, see Chapter 10. One option for **iptables**-based firewalls is based on source IP addresses. As both Postfix and sendmail are SMTP services, both use port 25.

To create a source address option with the Firewall Configuration tool, you'll need to use the Custom Rules option. As shown in Figure 13-1, you can see custom files added to the firewall configuration, from the /usr/share/netcf directory.

To create a custom rule that supports access only from systems on the 192.168.122.0 network, I've included the following entry in that file:

```
-A INPUT -m state --state NEW -m tcp -p tcp -s 192.168.122.0/24 --dport 25 -j
ACCEPT
```

The entry is in the same format as the commands in the /etc/sysconfig/iptables file. The **iptables** service, when started, reads the contents of the /etc/sysconfig/iptables file along with files cited in the Custom Rules section. Just remember, when you add a file as a custom rule, to make sure the Firewall Table option shown in Figure 13-2 refers to a filter, consistent with standard **iptables**-based firewall rules.

FIGURE 13-1

Custom Rules

FIGURE 13-2

Custom Rules file

Alternatively, you could edit the /etc/sysconfig/iptables file directly. But any future use of the Firewall Configuration tool would overwrite such custom rules.

In general, SELinux is not an issue for SMTP services. Only one SELinux boolean applies to the Postfix service, allow_postfix_local_write_mail_spool. It's active by default. As suggested by the name, it allows the Postfix service to write e-mail files to user spools in the /var/spool/postfix directory.

Testing an E-Mail Server

Besides the **telnet** command described later in this chapter, the appropriate way to test an e-mail server is with an e-mail client. Of course, it would be convenient to have a GUI e-mail client available. But as discussed in Chapter 2, only text clients like **mutt** may be available.

EXERCISE 13-1

Create Users Just for E-Mail

In this exercise, you will create three users on the local system, just so they can access the local SMTP server. It is understood that additional configuration is required to set up access or limits for these users on the Postfix or sendmail SMTP services. The users are mailer1, mailer2, and mailer3.

    1. Review the **useradd** command. Identify the switch associated with the default login shell.

2. Review the contents of the /etc/passwd file. Find a shell not associated with logins. It should be

   ```
   /sbin/nologin
   ```

3. Run commands like **useradd mailer1 -s /sbin/nologin** to add a new user. Make sure to assign that user a password.

4. Review the result in /etc/passwd.

5. Repeat Step 3 for the other noted users.

6. Try logging in to one of the new accounts as a regular user. It should fail. Review associated messages in the /var/log/secure file.

7. Keep the new users.

CERTIFICATION OBJECTIVE 13.02

The Configuration of Postfix

The Postfix mail server is one way to manage the flow of e-mail on a system and for a network. Standard configuration files are stored in the /etc/postfix directory. The **postconf** command can be used to test the configuration. As installed, Postfix accepts e-mail from only the local system. The configuration changes required to set up Postfix to accept incoming e-mail, and to forward e-mail through a smart host are relatively simple.

The details of Postfix configuration files include options for user- and host-based security. If you already know how to configure Postfix for basic operation and just want to know what's required to meet the SMTP objectives for Postfix, jump ahead to the sections associated with /etc/postfix/access, accepting incoming e-mail and smart hosts.

Configuration Files

The configuration files are stored in the /etc/postfix directory. The main configuration file, main.cf, is somewhat simpler than the sendmail alternative, sendmail.cf. It's still complex, as it includes nearly 700 lines.

Except for the .cf files, any changes must first be processed into a database with the **postmap** command. For example, if you've added limits to the access file, it can be processed into a binary access.db file with the following command:

```
# postmap access
```

In many cases, the contents of files in the /etc/postfix directory is a commented version of the associated man page. The following sections do not cover the main.cf or the master.cf files, as those are covered later. It also does not cover the header_checks file, as that's more of a message filter.

After any changes are made to Postfix configuration files, it's normally best to reload them into the daemon with the following command:

```
# /etc/init.d/postfix reload
```

It's best to reload most services, as that avoids kicking off currently connected users. And that can avoid users who complain about lost e-mails. But watch the output. It should include the following:

```
Reloading postfix:    [ OK ]
```

Without that output, there may be a different kind of problem with Postfix. Sometimes that problem can be addressed by restarting the service with the following command:

```
# /etc/init.d/postfix restart
```

The Postfix access File

The access file may be configured with limits on users, hosts, and more. It includes a commented copy of the associated man page, which can also be called with the **man 5 access** command. When limits are included in that file, they're configured in the following pattern:

```
pattern action
```

Patterns can be set up in a number of ways. As suggested by the man page, you can limit users with patterns such as

```
username@example.com
```

Patterns can be configured with individual IP addresses, IP address networks, and domains, such as with the following examples. Pay attention to the syntax, specifically the lack of a dot at the end of the 192.168.100 and the beginning of the example.org expressions. These expressions still are inclusive of all systems on the 192.168.100.0/24 network and the *.example.org domain.

```
192.168.122.50
server1.example.com
192.168.100
example.org
```

Of course, such patterns have no meaning without an action. Typical actions include **REJECT** and **OK**. The following examples of active lines in the /etc/postfix/ access file follow the pattern action format:

```
192.168.122.50 OK
server1.example.com OK
192.168.100 REJECT
example.org REJECT
```

e x a m

watch

One way to configure host- and user-based security for Postfix is through the access file in the /etc/postfix directory. Another way to configure host-based security is with iptables command– based firewalls described in Chapter 10. While there are more complex methods to configure user-based security, the RHCE objectives suggest that you "configure the service for basic operation."

The Postfix canonical and generic Files

The files named canonical and generic in the /etc/postfix directory works like an alias file. In other words, when users move from place to place, or if a company moves from one domain to another, the canonical file can ease that transition. The difference is while the canonical file applies to incoming e-mail from other systems, the generic file applies to e-mail being sent to other systems.

Similar to the access file, options in these files follow a pattern:

```
pattern result
```

The simplest iteration is the following, which forwards e-mail sent to a local user to a regular e-mail address:

```
michael michael@example.com
```

For companies that use different domains, the following line would forward e-mail directed to michael@example.org to michael@example.com. It would forward other example.org e-mail addresses in a similar fashion.

```
@example.org @example.com
```

Don't forget to process the resulting files into databases with the **postmap canonical** and **postmap generic** commands. If you modify the relocated, transport, or the virtual files in the /etc/postfix directory, apply the **postmap** command to those files as well.

The Postfix relocated File

The /etc/postfix/relocated file is designed to contain information for users who are now on external networks, such as users who have left a current organization. The format is similar to the aforementioned canonical and generic files in the same directory. For example, the following entry might reflect forwarding from a local corporate network to a personal e-mail address:

```
john.doe@example.com  john.doe@example.net
```

The Postfix transport File

The /etc/postfix/transport file may be useful in some situations where mail is forwarded, such as from a smart host. For example, the following entry forwards e-mail directed to the example.com network to an SMTP server such as Postfix on the server1.example.com system:

```
example.com  smtp:server1.example.com
```

The Postfix virtual File

The /etc/postfix/virtual file can forward e-mail addressed in a normal fashion, such as to elizabeth@example.com, to the user account on a local system. For example, if user elizabeth is actually the administrator on a system, the following entry forwards mail sent to the noted e-mail address to the root administrative user:

```
elizabeth@example.com root
```

The main.cf Configuration File

Back up this file and open it in a text editor. There are several things that you should configure in this file to get it working. Properly configured, the changes should limit access to the local system and network. This section also describes the function of other active directives, based on the default version of the file.

First, Postfix queues, which include e-mail that has yet to be sent, or e-mail that has been received, can be found in the queue_directory:

```
queue_directory = /var/spool/postfix
```

The following directory is a standard. It describes the location of most Postfix commands.

```
command_directory = /usr/sbin
```

Postfix includes a substantial number of executable files, for configuration in the master.cf file. The daemon_directory directive specifies their location:

```
daemon_directory = /usr/libexec/postfix
```

Postfix includes writable data files in the following directory; it normally includes a master.lock file with the PID of the Postfix daemon:

```
data_directory = /var/lib/postfix
```

As defined in the comments of the main.cf file, some files and directories should be owned by the root administrative user; others should be owned by the specified mail_owner. In the /etc/groups file, you can confirm that there's a dedicated group named postfix, which is also part of the group named mail.

```
mail_owner = postfix
```

While Postfix works for the local system "out of the box," more has to be done to get it working for a network. To that end, you'll need to activate and modify the following **myhostname** directive to point to the name of the local system. For example, you might change the entry

```
#myhostname = host.domain.tld
```

to an alternative like

```
myhostname = server1.example.com
```

on the
Job

> ***An authoritative DNS server may be configured to point to an SMTP e-mail server in its database.***

While an SMTP server is located on a specific system, normally such SMTP servers are configured for an entire network. That's configured with the **mydomain** directive. To that end, you should change the following comment:

```
#mydomain = domain.tld
```

to reflect the domain name or IP network address of the local network:

```
mydomain = example.com
```

Normally, you'd just uncomment the following **myorigin** directive, to label e-mail addresses coming from this Postfix server with an origination domain. In this case, the origination domain is example.com:

```
myorigin = $mydomain
```

By default, the following active directive limits the scope of the Postfix service to the local system.

```
#inet_interfaces = all
inet_interfaces = localhost
```

In most cases, you'd change the active directive so that Postfix listens on all active network cards:

```
inet_interfaces = all
#inet_interfaces = localhost
```

Normally, Postfix listens on both IPv4 and IPv6 networks, based on the following inet_protocols directive:

```
inet_protocols = all
```

The mydestination directive specifies the systems served by this Postfix server. Based on the previous settings, the following default directive means that accepted mail may be sent to the local system's FQDN (server1.example.com), the localhost address on the example.com network, and the localhost system:

```
mydestination = $myhostname, localhost.$mydomain, localhost
```

For a Postfix server configured for the local network, you should add the name of the local domain, already assigned to the mydomain directive:

```
mydestination = $mydomain, $myhostname, localhost.$mydomain, localhost
```

In addition, you'll want to set up the **mynetworks** directive to point to the IP network address to be covered by this Postfix server. The default commented directive does not point to the example.com network defined for this book:

```
#mynetworks = 168.100.189.0/28, 127.0.0.0/8
```

So for systems like server1.example.com, this directive should be changed to

```
mynetworks = 192.168.122.0/24, 127.0.0.0/8
```

Once changes are made to the main.cf file (and any other files in the /etc/postfix directory) are complete and saved, you may want to review current Postfix parameters. To do so, run the following command:

```
# postconf
```

Of course, most of these parameters are defaults. To review the parameters changed by the main.cf file, run the following command:

```
# postconf -n
```

The output is shown in Figure 13-3.

One setting from the **postconf -n** output is important to authentication. Specifically, when the following directive is added to the main.cf file, Postfix will require authorized usernames and passwords for access:

```
smtpd_sender_restrictions = permit_sasl_authenticated, reject
```

In addition, Postfix includes a syntax checker in the basic daemon. Run the following command to see if there are any fatal errors in the main.cf file:

```
# postfix check
```

FIGURE 13-3

Custom Postfix
settings, based
on /etc/postfix/
main.cf

```
[root@Maui postfix]# postconf -n
alias_database = hash:/etc/aliases
alias_maps = hash:/etc/aliases
command_directory = /usr/sbin
config_directory = /etc/postfix
daemon_directory = /usr/libexec/postfix
data_directory = /var/lib/postfix
debug_peer_level = 2
html_directory = no
inet_interfaces = all
inet_protocols = all
mail_owner = postfix
mailq_path = /usr/bin/mailq.postfix
manpage_directory = /usr/share/man
mydestination = $myhostname, localhost.$mydomain, localhost
mydomain = example.com
myhostname = maui.example.com
mynetworks = 192.168.122.0/24, 127.0.0.0/8
newaliases_path = /usr/bin/newaliases.postfix
queue_directory = /var/spool/postfix
readme_directory = /usr/share/doc/postfix-2.6.6/README_FILES
sample_directory = /usr/share/doc/postfix-2.6.6/samples
sendmail_path = /usr/sbin/sendmail.postfix
setgid_group = postdrop
unknown_local_recipient_reject_code = 550
[root@Maui postfix]#
```

The /etc/aliases Configuration File

Another directive from the /etc/postfix/main.cf file includes the database hash from the /etc/aliases file, which is processed into the /etc/aliases.db file when the Postfix system is restarted.

```
alias_maps = hash:/etc/aliases
```

The /etc/aliases file is normally configured to redirect e-mail sent to system accounts to the root administrative user. As you might see at the end of that file, e-mail messages sent to root can be redirected to a regular user account:

```
# root    marc
```

While there are a number of additional directives available in this file, they're beyond the basic configuration associated with the RHCE objectives. When changes are complete, you can and should process this into an appropriate database with the **newaliases** command. As the /etc/aliases file works for both Postfix and sendmail, the **newaliases** command can process the /etc/aliases file for both MTAs.

The master.cf Configuration File

Generally, you should not have to make changes to the master.cf file. It's configured to set up Postfix for regular SMTP services. As shown in the first page of the file, it does include options for the submission protocol on port 587, which is required for a smart host relay to some ISP's e-mail servers. It also supports the configuration of secure SMTP.

Test the Current Postfix Configuration

As noted in previous chapters, the **telnet** command is an excellent way to review the current status of a service on a local system. Based on the default configuration of Postfix, an active version of this service should be listening on port 25. In that case, a **telnet localhost 25** command should return messages similar to the following:

```
Trying 127.0.0.1...
Connected to localhost.
Escape character is '^]'.
220 Maui.example.com ESMTP Postfix
```

If IPv6 networking is enabled on the local system, the IPv4 loopback address (127.0.0.1) would be replaced by the regular IPv6 loopback address (::1). The **quit** command can be used to exit from this connection. But don't quit yet. The **EHLO localhost** command is important; the EHLO is the enhanced HELO command, which introduces the basic parameters of an SMTP server.

```
EHLO localhost
250-maui.example.com
250-PIPELINING
250-SIZE 10240000
250-VRFY
250-ETRN
250-ENHANCEDSTATUSCODES
250-8BITMIME
250 DSN
```

For our purposes, the most important information is what's missing. No authentication is required on this server. When authentication is properly configured on Postfix, you'll also see the following line in the output:

```
250-AUTH GSSAPI
```

Configure Postfix Authentication

When authentication is configured in Postfix, user limits can apply. But as there are no hints in the standard main.cf configuration file, you'll have to refer to Postfix documentation for clues. As suggested in Chapter 3, most packages include some level of documentation in the /usr/share/doc directory. Fortunately, Postfix documentation in that directory is rather extensive. For RHEL 6, you'll be able to find that documentation in the postfix-2.6.6/ subdirectory.

The directives that you need to add to the main.cf file to set up authentication are shown in the README-Postfix-SASL-RedHat.txt file in that directory. The key excerpt is shown in Figure 13-4.

For the first step listed, it's sufficient to copy the four directives listed to the end of the main.cf file, first to enable SASL authentication for Postfix connections:

```
smtpd_sasl_auth_enable = yes
```

Next, this disables anonymous authentication:

```
smtpd_sasl_security_options = noanonymous
```

FIGURE 13-4	Quick Start to Authenticate with SASL and PAM:

Directions to set up Postfix authentication

```
If you don't need the details and are an experienced system
administrator you can just do this, otherwise read on.

1) Edit /etc/postfix/main.cf and set this:

smtpd_sasl_auth_enable = yes
smtpd_sasl_security_options = noanonymous
broken_sasl_auth_clients = yes

smtpd_recipient_restrictions =
  permit_sasl_authenticated,
  permit_mynetworks,
  reject_unauth_destination

2) Turn on saslauthd:

  /sbin/chkconfig --level 345 saslauthd on
  /sbin/service saslauthd start

3) Edit /etc/sysconfig/saslauthd and set this:

  MECH=pam

4) Restart Postfix:

  /sbin/service postfix restart
:
```

The directive that follows allows authentication from nonstandard clients such as Microsoft Outlook Express:

```
broken_sasl_auth_clients = yes
```

This allows authenticated users, allows access from networks configured with the **mynetworks** directive, and rejects destinations other than the Postfix server:

```
smtpd_recipient_restrictions = permit_sasl_authenticated,
    permit_mynetworks, reject_unauth_destination
```

Configure Incoming E-Mail

The directives required to set up Postfix to accept incoming e-mail from other system have been previously described in the description of the main.cf file. But that was a more comprehensive description of that file. This section just covers the minimum requirements to configure Postfix, in the words of the RHCE objectives, "to accept inbound e-mail from other systems." Given a Postfix server configured on the server1.example.com system, on the 192.168.122.0/24 network, you'd make the following changes to the main.cf file in the /etc/postfix directory:

```
myhostname = server1.example.com
mydomain = example.com
myorigin = mydomain
inet_interfaces = all
mynetworks = 192.168.122.0/24, 127.0.0.0/8
```

Each of these options replaces either a comment or an active directive in the default /etc/postfix/main.cf file. For example, you should at least comment out the following directive:

```
#inet_interfaces = localhost
```

Configure a Relay Through a Smart Host

A smart host has all of the functionality of a regular SMTP server, except for the forwarding of all e-mail through a second SMTP server. The location of the smart host can be specified with the **relayhost** directive. For example, if the remote smart host is outsider1.example.org, you'd add the following directive to the /etc/postfix/main.cf file:

```
relayhost = outsider1.example.org
```

For smart hosts to work, you'll need to make sure that e-mail messages intended for users on the local system are properly forwarded. And that's possible through the aforementioned /etc/aliases file. At the least, you should configure e-mail intended for the root administrative user as forwarded to a regular local user, with a line such as

```
root    michael
```

EXERCISE 13-2

Switch Services

This exercise presumes you've installed and want to test the sendmail SMTP service. If you're set on Postfix, there is no need to run this exercise. It assumes that both the sendmail and sendmail-cf packages are installed.

1. Deactivate the Postfix service with the **/etc/init.d/postfix stop** command.
2. Run the **alternatives --config mta** command. From the menu that appears, select the sendmail SMTP service.
3. Start the sendmail service with the **/etc/init.d/sendmail start** command.
4. Review currently running SMTP processes with the **ps aux | grep postfix** and the **ps aux | grep sendmail** commands.
5. Stop the sendmail service with the **/etc/init.d/sendmail stop** command.
6. Run the **alternatives --config mta** command. From the menu that appears, select the Postfix SMTP service.
7. Restart the Postfix service with the **/etc/init.d/postfix start** command.

CERTIFICATION OBJECTIVE 13.03

The Other SMTP Service: sendmail

The sendmail e-mail server may still be the most popular SMTP service on the Internet. It is the older Red Hat way to manage the flow of e-mail on a system and for a network. It was the default SMTP service through RHEL 5. Standard configuration files are stored in the /etc/mail directory. As sendmail is quite complex, configuration is normally done with the help of macros.

As with Postfix, the sendmail software as installed accepts e-mail only from the local system. Based on an understanding of associated macro files, the configuration changes required to modify sendmail to accept incoming e-mail from a network and to forward e-mail through a smart host are relatively simple.

If you already know sendmail, and just want to know what's required to meet the RHCE objectives for that SMTP service, jump ahead to the sections associated with the /etc/mail/access, file, accepting incoming e-mail, and smart hosts.

The Basics of sendmail

When sendmail starts, it reads the /etc/mail/sendmail.cf and /etc/mail/submit.cf files. The sendmail.cf file is a long (around 1800 lines) file that may seem difficult to decipher but includes a wealth of helpful comments. The submit.cf file is nearly as long. This file provides detailed rules (organized into rulesets) on how sendmail should process e-mail addresses, filter spam, talk to other mail servers, and more.

This file is extremely complex and uses cryptic syntax. Fortunately, most of the directives included in this file are standards that you don't need to change. Many are required by various Internet agreements relating to e-mail address, mail transfer agents, and so on.

Red Hat simplifies this process with a smaller file, /etc/mail/sendmail.mc, which contains only the most relevant configuration directives. It is composed entirely of macros that define key sendmail.cf settings. Once appropriate changes are made, you can run the **make** command to compile a new, custom sendmail.cf file. However, the default RHEL version of this file is still around 200 lines long. In most cases, you might have to change two or three of those lines.

Of course, once files are created or revised and compiled in the /etc/mail directory, you'll want to make the sendmail service reread these configuration files with the following command:

```
# /etc/init.d/sendmail reload
```

If successful, you'll see the following output (the second "reloading" is in lowercase):

```
Reloading sendmail:   [ OK ]
reloading sm-client:  [ OK ]
```

Without this output, you should assume that sendmail did not re-read the configuration files, and other measures are required, such as a restart.

Configuration Files

The following is a brief description of the standard configuration files in the /etc/mail directory. Additional files with a .db extension are database files processed from some of these listed here:

- **access**   Supports access control. The default version of this file supports access from the local computer. You can add hostnames or networks to this list, with a message to **REJECT** with an error message, **DISCARD** without an error message, or **RELAY** to accept and send the e-mail. It is one way to configure host- and even user-based security.
- **aliasesdb-stamp**   Supports date checks of existing database files.
- **domaintable**   Allows mapping different domains. For example, if a company is moving its users from mheducation.com to mcgraw-hill.com, people might still send e-mails to addresses such as michael@mheducation.com. The following line would forward that e-mail to michael@mcgraw-hill.com.

```
mheducation.com  mcgraw-hill.com
```

- **helpfile**   Supports help commands from the sendmail prompt, accessible with the **telnet localhost 25** command.
- **local-host-names**   Allows added hostnames or aliases for a sendmail server. Enter one alias per line.
- **mailertable**   Information added to this file may be used as a substitute for DNS searches.
- **makefile**   Supports compiling the sendmail.mc file.
- **sendmail.cf**   Specifies the main sendmail configuration file.
- **sendmail.mc**   Name of a macro file that can be used to generate a new sendmail.cf file.
- **spamassassin/**   A directory that includes configuration files to help minimize spam. The following line in /etc/procmailrc helps it work with Procmail for locally received e-mail:

```
INCLUDERC=/etc/mail/spamassassin/spamassassin-default.rc
```

on the job

If you forget how spamassassin is used with sendmail, run the rpm -qi spamassassin command. You'll see it in the description.

- **statistic**   Collects statistics on sendmail usage in binary format. You can read it with the **mailstats** command. Does not exist until the sendmail service starts processing mail.
- **submit.cf**   The main outgoing sendmail configuration file.
- **submit.mc**   A macro that you can edit and then generate a new submit.cf file.
- **trusted-users**   Lists special users that can send e-mail without warnings.
- **virtusertable**   Supports e-mail forwarding; if some users from outside local networks use the local sendmail server, this file supports e-mail forwarding from those domains.

Some of these files require the other sendmail package, sendmail-cf. Use the **rpm -qa | grep sendmail** command to confirm whether these packages are installed.

Many of these files are cited in the sendmail.mc file. For example, the following directive incorporates /etc/mail/virtusertable in the default sendmail.mc configuration file:

```
FEATURE(`virtusertable',`hash -o /etc/mail/virtusertable.db')dnl
```

You may notice several versions of these files with .db extensions. These are the database files used by sendmail. When you edit files in the /etc/mail directory, the **/etc/mail/make** command, described shortly, processes these files into the .db databases.

There's one more important file, /etc/aliases, already described earlier in this chapter. It has the same functionality for both Postfix and sendmail. In other words, it includes a list of forwarders on a local system, from system addresses to the root account, or from one regular user account to another. The **newalises** command processes this file for sendmail as well.

The sendmail.mc Macro File

Even the main sendmail macro file, sendmail.mc, can seem intimidating. But very few changes are required to actually get sendmail working. Nevertheless, in case you encounter a slightly different question on an exam, or a somewhat nonstandard question on the job, it's important to understand the contents of the sendmail.mc file.

Macro files for sendmail start with the following **divert** directive:

```
divert(-1)dnl
```

Each line in the file either starts or ends with the **dnl**, which is the functional equivalent of the comment character. All information after the **dnl** is ignored by the sendmail macro processor. If coupled with a **divert(0)dnl**, all information between the two **divert** directives is ignored.

The comments that follow provide important directions; the **make** command in the /etc/mail directory in fact processes all files in the /etc/mail directory:

```
dnl # This is the sendmail macro config file for m4. If you make changes to
dnl # /etc/mail/sendmail.mc, you will need to regenerate the
dnl # /etc/mail/sendmail.cf file by confirming that the sendmail-cf
dnl # package is installed and then performing a
dnl #
dnl #     /etc/mail/make
```

The command that follows includes the noted c4.m4 macro processor, from the sendmail-cf package:

```
include(`/usr/share/sendmail-cf/m4/cf.m4')dnl
```

The **include** directive instructs the **make** command to read the contents of the named file and insert it at the current location in the output. The quotes in the sendmail.mc file do not conform to standard English usage. This is how additional standard configuration information is left out of the main sendmail.mc macro file.

Incidentally, quoted parameters start with a back quote mark (`) and end with a single quote mark (').

The **VERSIONID** that follows provides a label for the current configuration:

```
VERSIONID(`setup for linux')dnl
```

The **OSTYPE** directive that follows specifies the configured operating system:

```
OSTYPE(`linux')dnl
```

The **define** directive sets files or enables possibly desirable features. Some examples in sendmail.mc support a list of e-mail aliases in the **ALIAS_FILE** (/etc/aliases), identify where procmail lives (**PROCMAIL_MAILER_PATH**), and set basic authentication options (**confAUTH_OPTIONS**).

One useful option is to avoid advertising the version of sendmail in use, which would otherwise be shown in e-mail message headers. If you activate the following **define** feature, others don't have to know that you've configured sendmail version 8.14.4.

```
dnl define(`confSMTP_LOGIN_MSG', `$j Sendmail; $b')dnl
```

The commented **define** directive for a SMART_HOST that follows would be the simplest way to set up forwarding to a smart host, as discussed later in this chapter.

```
dnl define(`SMART_HOST', `smtp.your.provider')dnl
```

Most of the active **define** options that follow relate to the performance of the sendmail service. The exceptions, shown next, support the use of Procmail for filtering, enable /etc/aliases for substitute e-mail addresses, and require authentication to receive e-mail:

```
define(`PROCMAIL_MAILER_PATH', `/usr/bin/procmail')dnl
define(`ALIAS_FILE', `/etc/aliases')dnl
define(`confAUTH_OPTIONS', 'A')dnl
```

The problem with the last of these **define** directives is that it allows plain text authentication. Like the Telnet service, it allows people to send their usernames and passwords over the network in clear text, where anyone who is listening can read that authentication information. Clear text may be appropriate for initial tests and generally conforms to the "basic operation" concept associated with the RHCE objectives. However, for a sendmail service that requires some form of encryption, you could substitute the following directive, which is commented out by default:

```
dnl define(`confAUTH_OPTIONS', `A p')dnl
```

That authentication mechanism, if active, should be coupled with authentication options. The commented directives that follow provide some suggested solutions.

While there's no evidence from the RHCE objectives of an authentication requirement for SMTP services, it is listed in the public Red Hat RH254 course outline, which suggests that you do need to understand the use of Secure Sockets Layer (SSL) certificates, and its successor, Transport Layer Security (TLS). While it's likely unnecessary for SMTP services, it may be helpful to become familiar with some of these authentication mechanisms, as a preview of Chapter 14. To that end, the following commented directives support a variety of authentication mechanisms:

```
dnl TRUST_AUTH_MECH(`EXTERNAL DIGEST-MD5 CRAM-MD5 LOGIN PLAIN')dnl
dnl define(`confAUTH_MECHANISMS', `EXTERNAL GSSAPI DIGEST-MD5 CRAM-MD5 LOGIN
PLAIN')dnl
```

To support encryption, the following commented section describes the commands required to create a SSL/TLS certificate for sendmail, and its location in the directory tree:

```
dnl # Rudimentary information on creating certificates for sendmail TLS:
dnl #    cd /etc/pki/tls/certs; make sendmail.pem
```

```
dnl # Complete usage:
dnl #     make -C /etc/pki/tls/certs usage
dnl #
dnl define(`confCACERT_PATH', `/etc/pki/tls/certs')dnl
dnl define(`confCACERT', `/etc/pki/tls/certs/ca-bundle.crt')dnl
dnl define(`confSERVER_CERT', `/etc/pki/tls/certs/sendmail.pem')dnl
dnl define(`confSERVER_KEY', `/etc/pki/tls/certs/sendmail.pem')dnl
```

The **define** directive that follows, if activated, would support the use of LDAP authentication:

```
dnl define(`confDONT_BLAME_SENDMAIL', `groupreadablekeyfile')dnl
```

The **define** directives that follow relate to sendmail behavior for message delays and do not affect basic configuration. The only active directive shown disables timeouts when the server waits for an identification (IDENT) query.

```
dnl define(`confTO_QUEUEWARN', `4h')dnl
dnl define(`confTO_QUEUERETURN', `5d')dnl
dnl define(`confQUEUE_LA', `12')dnl
dnl define(`confREFUSE_LA', `18')dnl
define(`confTO_IDENT', `0')dnl
dnl FEATURE(delay_checks)dnl
```

The **FEATURE** directives enable specific features. Some administrators configure sendmail to use the submission protocol, in place of SMTP. In that case, you'd want to disable the following directive, which keeps sendmail from listening on port 587:

```
FEATURE(`no_default_msa', 'dnl')dnl
```

Other **FEATURES** relate to specific executable and configuration files. The following specifies the locations of the sendmail shell (smrsh), along with the aforementioned mailertable and virtualusertable databases.

```
FEATURE(`smrsh', `/usr/sbin/smrsh')dnl
FEATURE(`mailertable`hash -o /etc/mail/mailertable.db')dnl
FEATURE(`virtusertable', `hash -o /etc/mail/virtusertable.db')dnl
```

The **FEATURE** directives that follow support redirection to other e-mail addresses, add the local domain name to an e-mail address if one is not listed, and use files like trusted-users and local-host-names:

```
FEATURE(redirect)dnl
FEATURE(always_add_domain)dnl
FEATURE(use_cw_file)dnl
FEATURE(use_ct_file)dnl
```

While this feature supports repeated attempts for e-mail delivery:

```
FEATURE(local_procmail, `', 'procmail -t -Y -a $h -d $u')dnl
```

The following options are prerequisites for host-based security, as they look to the /etc/mail/access file for (allowed and) blacklisted users, systems, and even networks:

```
FEATURE(`access_db', `hash -T<TMPF> -o /etc/mail/access.db')dnl
FEATURE(`blacklist_recipients')dnl
```

If the root user tries to send e-mail through this SMTP server, the following option requires that user's full e-mail address:

```
EXPOSED_USER(`root')dnl
```

By default, the following **DAEMON_OPTIONS** directive limits the sendmail service to the local system. For basic operation, it's simplest to comment out this directive:

```
DAEMON_OPTIONS(`Port=smtp,Addr=127.0.0.1, Name=MTA')dnl
```

No additional directives are required in the sendmail.mc file to support access from other systems on a network. However, security also depends on the /etc/mail/access file, which also by default limits access to the localhost system.

To configure sendmail on the aforementioned submission port 587, you'd activate the following directive:

```
dnl DAEMON_OPTIONS(`Port=submission, Name=MSA, M=Ea')dnl
```

If you've compiled the previously described TLS certificates, you can activate the following directive to listen for secure SMTP connections on port 465:

```
dnl DAEMON_OPTIONS(`Port=smtps, Name=TLSMTA, M=s')dnl
```

For IPv6 networking, the following directive would listen to only the localhost system:

```
dnl DAEMON_OPTIONS(`port=smtp,Addr=::1, Name=MTA-v6, Family=inet6')dnl
```

Alternatively, the following directive listens for both IPv4 and IPv6 traffic:

```
dnl DAEMON_OPTIONS(`Name=MTA-v4, Family=inet, Name=MTA-v6, Family=inet6')
```

The following **FEATURE** directive allows sendmail to **accept_unresolvable_domains**. This allows sendmail to accept mail even if it can't figure out the domain of the user who sent the e-mail. Specifically, a domain is regarded as unresolvable when a reverse IP address search does not find the associated domain name. However, if reliable DNS service is available, deactivating this option can reduce spam.

```
FEATURE(`accept_unresolvable_domains')dnl
```

If active, the following directive accepts the use of MX records from DNS servers for the locations of remote e-mail servers:

```
dnl FEATURE(`relay_based_on_MX')dnl
```

The following directive is needed to make sure the sendmail service accepts e-mail from local users:

```
LOCAL_DOMAIN(`localhost.localdomain')dnl
```

If you want to substitute a different domain for e-mail addresses, the following directives, if active, specify a substitute:

```
dnl MASQUERADE_AS(`mydomain.com')dnl
dnl FEATURE(masquerade_envelope)dnl
dnl FEATURE(masquerade_entire_domain)dnl
```

The masquerading can be extended. The following directives, if active, would get sendmail to substitute the **MASQUERADE_AS** domain for the localhost, localhost.localdomain, mydomainalias.com, and mydomain.lan domain names.

```
dnl MASQUERADE_DOMAIN(localhost)dnl
dnl MASQUERADE_DOMAIN(localhost.localdomain)dnl
dnl MASQUERADE_DOMAIN(mydomainalias.com)dnl
dnl MASQUERADE_DOMAIN(mydomain.lan)dnl
```

Finally, the following **MAILER** directives specifies the servers in use:

```
MAILER(smtp)dnl
MAILER(procmail)dnl
dnl MAILER(cyrusv2)dnl
```

The submit.mc Macro File

In most cases, no changes are needed to the submit.mc file. If changed, it can also be processed by the same **make** command in the /etc/mail directory. In general, if the network is configured to use the Network Information Service (NIS) for an authentication database, you would comment out the following directive:

```
define(`confDONT_INIT_GROUPS', `True')dnl
```

But NIS is not secure. It just so happens that for RHEL 6, Red Hat has removed NIS from its exam objectives.

If the local network is set up to use only IPv6 addressing, you would change the last line in this file from

```
FEATURE(`msp', `[127.0.0.1]')dnl
```

to

```
FEATURE(`msp', `[IPv6:::1]')dnl
```

Configure sendmail to Accept E-Mail from Other Systems

This section satisfies the RHCE objective to set up sendmail for basic operation. Navigate to the /etc/mail directory. Back up the sendmail.mc macro file. Open that file in a text editor. Review the following directive, which limits sendmail access to the local computer:

```
DAEMON_OPTIONS(`Port=smtp,Addr=127.0.0.1, Name=MTA')dnl
```

You can allow other computers to use your sendmail server by commenting out this line. As described earlier, this requires a **dnl** directive in front, as shown:

```
dnl DAEMON_OPTIONS(`Port=smtp,Addr=127.0.0.1, Name=MTA')dnl
```

Next, if reliable DNS access is available, comment out the **FEATURE** directive that allows the sendmail service to **accept_unresolvable_domains**. This action, which requires verification of sender e-mail addresses, can help block spammers. A spammer may fake his domain. Users from "unresolvable domains" aren't allowed access to this service—unless the **accept_unresolvable_domains** option is active—who use just an IP address, or spammers who fake their domain name to hide themselves:

```
dnl FEATURE(`accept_unresolvable_domains')dnl
```

But that's not enough. To allow remote system access to the local sendmail server, you'll need to add their names or IP addresses to the /etc/mail/access file. For example, to allow access to the 192.168.122.0 domain, you'd add the following line to that file:

```
Connect:192.168.122          RELAY
```

Watch the notation; unlike with other services, there is no dot (.) at the end of the address. It covers all computers on the 192.168.122.0 network. Alternatively, you could designate the example.com domain or a specific computer name or IP address.

Back up the current sendmail.cf file. Then you can generate a new sendmail.cf file, process the other files in /etc/mail, and restart sendmail services with the following commands:

```
# /etc/mail/make
# /etc/init.d/sendmail restart
```

Now you can reconfigure e-mail clients such as Mozilla Thunderbird, Novell Evolution, or even Microsoft Outlook Express to send outgoing e-mail through the newly configured sendmail server. You'll need to set the sendmail computer domain name or IP address as the SMTP outgoing mail server.

Configure sendmail to Relay E-Mail to a Smart Host

In addition to the options described for the sendmail.mc file, it's easy to configure sendmail to relay e-mail to a smart host. The default sendmail.mc file provides a hint with the following commented directive:

```
dnl define(`SMART_HOST', `smtp.your.provider')dnl
```

If the remote smart host is smtp.example.org, you'd activate the directive as follows:

```
define(`SMART_HOST', `smtp.example.org')dnl
```

Configure User- and Host-Based sendmail Security

As suggested in the discussion of the /etc/mail/access file, host-based security can be configured there. For example, as long as the limitation to the 127.0.0.1 system is removed from or commented out of the sendmail.mc macro, host-based security is controlled through the /etc/mail/access file. For example, the following entry rejects all users named michael:

```
michael@ REJECT
```

In addition, unlike Postfix, sendmail can be protected with TCP Wrappers, as discussed in Chapter 10. In other words, you could use the hosts.allow and hosts. deny files in the /etc directory to limit access to certain users and hosts.

Test the Current sendmail Configuration

As with Postfix, the **telnet** command can be used to review the current status of the sendmail service. Based on the default configuration of Postfix, an active version of this service should be listening on port 25. In that case, a **telnet localhost 25** command should return something similar to the following messages:

```
Trying ::1...
telnet: connect to address ::1: Connection refused
Trying 127.0.0.1...
Connected to localhost.
Escape character is '^]'.
220 server1.example.com ESMTP Sendmail 8.14.4/8.14.4; Wed, 23 Feb 2011 16:58:20
-0800
```

The first connection refused message confirms that the sendmail configuration file does not normally listen to IPv6 networking. To set up sendmail.mc for both IPv4 and IPv6 beyond the localhost system, deactivate the following directive (by adding the **dnl** in front):

dnl DAEMON_OPTIONS(`Port=smtp,Addr=127.0.0.1, Name=MTA')dnl

And activate the following directive:

```
DAEMON_OPTIONS(`Name=MTA-v4, Family=inet, Name=MTA-v6, Family=inet6')
```

But that's required only if IPv6 networking is required, which is not always the case. If only IPv4 networking is required, comment out this directive as well.

SCENARIO & SOLUTION

You're told to configure an SMTP server for the 192.168.0.0/24 network.	Use the default Postfix server; modify the **myhostname, mydomain, myorigin, inet_interfaces**, and **mynetworks** directives in /etc/postfix/main.cf. Remember to process the non-cf files into databases with the **postmap** command.
You're told to allow access just to the SMTP server for user1, user2, and user3.	Create the noted users with a /sbin/nologin default shell.
You're told to set up sendmail on RHEL 6.	Stop the Postfix service, and use **alternatives** to change the default MTA to sendmail.
You're told to configure sendmail to allow access to all systems.	Comment out the **DAEMON_OPTIONS** directive associated with the loopback address.

CERTIFICATION SUMMARY

Red Hat includes two servers associated with the SMTP protocol: Postfix and sendmail. Red Hat has switched default SMTP services between RHEL 5 and RHEL 6; it is now Postfix. Whichever SMTP service you select, it's just one part of the hierarchy of services for e-mail. Both Postfix and sendmail are part of the "E-mail server" package group. If you want to switch between SMTP services, the **alternatives --config mta** command can help. Mail log information can be found in the /var/log/maillog file. You can test the current status of both SMTP services from the local system with the **telnet localhost 25** command.

Postfix is somewhat easier to configure than sendmail. Different Postfix configuration files can be found in the /etc/postfix directory. User and host limits can be configured in the access file. Several other files relate to redirected or renamed e-mail accounts or domains. You'll need to modify several Postfix configuration directives in the /etc/postfix/main.cf file, including **myhostname**, **mydomain**, **myorigin**, **inet_interfaces**, and **mynetworks**. The **relayhost** directive can help configure forwarding to a smart host. If you need to configure Postfix authentication, refer to additional directives in the /usr/share/doc/postfix-2.6.6 directory, in the README-Postfix-SASL-RedHat.txt file.

The sendmail service may still be the most popular SMTP server on the Internet. It has configuration files in the /etc/mail directory. The two main configuration files are: sendmail.cf and submit.cf. You can configure these files through macros configured in the sendmail.mc and submit.mc files. You can configure user- and host-based security with the help of the /etc/mail/access file. The sendmail.mc file includes a commented example directive to help you configure a connection to a remote smart host.

✓ # TWO-MINUTE DRILL

Here are some of the key points from the certification objectives in Chapter 13.

A Variety of E-Mail Agents

❑ RHEL 6 allows you to select between Postfix and sendmail. Both are MTAs. Don't activate both.

❑ You can use the **alternatives --config mta** command to switch between Postfix and sendmail.

❑ Mail server information is logged in the /var/log/maillog file.

The Configuration of Postfix

❑ The Postfix server is easier to configure through configuration files in the /etc/postfix directory. In fact, you can configure the main.cf file directly.

❑ You can configure Postfix user and host security Postfix in /etc/aliases.

❑ You can set up various kinds of e-mail forwarding in files like canonical, generic, and relocated, all in the /etc/postfix directory.

❑ The /usr/share/doc/postfix-2.6.6 directory includes information on user authentication options in the README-Postfix-SASL-RedHat.txt file.

❑ The **relayhost** command can be used to set up a connection to a smart host.

❑ You can test a standard Postfix configuration from the local system with the **telnet localhost 25** command. (The same command works for a standard sendmail configuration as well.)

The Other SMTP Service: sendmail

❑ The main sendmail configuration file is /etc/mail/sendmail.cf. It's easier to configure sendmail through its macro file, /etc/mail/sendmail.mc.

❑ You can open up access to all systems in the sendmail.mc file by commenting out the **DAEMON_OPTIONS** directive.

❑ The sendmail.mc file includes a commented suggestion to configure a connection to a smart host.

❑ You can customize the computers allowed to access a sendmail server through the access and virtusertable files in the /etc/mail directory.

❑ The **/etc/mail/make** command processes all files in the **/etc/mail** directory.

SELF TEST

The following questions will help measure your understanding of the material presented in this chapter. As no multiple-choice questions appear on the Red Hat exams, no multiple-choice questions appear in this book. These questions exclusively test your understanding of the chapter. It is okay if you have another way of performing a task. Getting results, not memorizing trivia, is what counts on the Red Hat exams. There may be more than one answer to many of the questions.

A Variety of E-Mail Agents

1. List two examples of an MTA supported on RHEL 6.

   _____

2. What command can be used to switch between installed Postfix and sendmail services?

   _____

The Configuration of Postfix

3. How would you change the following directive in /etc/postfix/main.cf to open Postfix to all systems?

   ```
   inet_interfaces = localhost
   ```

   _____

4. If you use /etc/aliases for forwarding e-mail, what command processes these files into an appropriate database file for Postfix?

   _____

5. What file supports limits on hosts that can connect to Postfix?

   _____

6. What directive in the main.cf file is used to specify the domain served by the Postfix server?

   _____

7. What directive in the main.cf file is used to specify the IP address network served by the Postfix server?

   _____

8. In what directory can you find documentation associated with the Postfix server?

_____

The Other SMTP Service: sendmail

9. In what file would you store forwarding e-mail addresses?

_____

10. Why would you want to comment out the following directive in sendmail.mc?

```
DAEMON_OPTIONS(`Port=smtp,Addr=127.0.0.1, Name=MTA')dnl
```

_____

11. What do you need if you want to comment out the following directive in sendmail.mc?

```
FEATURE(`accept_unresolvable_domains')dnl
```

_____

12. What command processes all files in /etc/mail?

_____

LAB QUESTIONS

Several of these labs involve configuration exercises. You should do these exercises on test machines only. It's assumed that you're running these exercises on virtual machines such as KVM. For this chapter, it's also assumed that you may be changing the configuration of a physical host system for such virtual machines.

Red Hat presents its exams electronically. For that reason, the labs in this and future chapters are available from the CD that accompanies the book, in the Chapter13/ subdirectory. In case you haven't yet set up RHEL 6 on a system, refer to Chapter 1 for installation instructions.

The answers for each lab follow the Self Test answers for the fill-in-the-blank questions.

SELF TEST ANSWERS

A Variety of E-Mail Agents

1. Three examples of MTAs supported on RHEL 6 are Postfix, sendmail, and Dovecot.

2. The command that can be used to help switch between the Postfix and sendmail MTAs is **alternatives --config mta**.

The Configuration of Postfix

3. The simplest solution is to change the directive to

```
inet_interfaces = all
```

4. Forwarding e-mail addresses for both sendmail and Postfix are normally stored in /etc/aliases. Make sure to process these files into appropriate databases; for /etc/aliases, the database is updated with the **newaliases** command.

5. The file that supports limits on hosts that can connect to Postfix is /etc/postfix/access.

6. The directive in the main.cf file that is used to specify the domain served by the Postfix server is **mydomain**.

7. The directive in the main.cf file is used to specify the IP address network served by the Postfix server is **mynetworks**.

8. You find documentation associated with the Postfix server in the /usr/share/doc/postfix-2.6.6 directory.

The Other SMTP Service: sendmail

9. Forwarding e-mail addresses for both sendmail and Postfix are normally stored in /etc/aliases. If you're forwarding e-mail for entire domains, the appropriate file is /etc/mail/domaintable. Make sure to process these files into appropriate databases; for /etc/aliases, the database is updated with the **newaliases** command. For /etc/mail/domaintable, the database is updated with the **/etc/mail/make** command.

10. If you comment out the noted directive, access is supported by all systems allowed to connect.

11. If you comment out the noted directive in sendmail.mc, a reliable DNS server is not required.

12. The command that processes all files in the /etc/mail directory is **/etc/mail/make**.

LAB ANSWERS

For most of these labs, you may be using an e-mail client like **mutt**. To send an e-mail to user michael@localhost, take the following steps:

1. Run the **mutt michael@localhost** command. The **To: michael@localhost** message should appear.

2. Press ENTER. At the **Subject:** prompt, enter an appropriate test subject name and press ENTER.

3. You're taken to a blank screen in the vi editor. Use commands appropriate to that editor to a screen similar to that shown in Figure 13-5.

4. From the screen shown in Figure 13-5, press **y** to send the noted message.

In addition, you may be verifying e-mail receipt in a username file in the /var/spool/mail directory. Normally, such e-mail can be reviewed from within a user account with the **mail** command. In addition, you may be verifying access to a running SMTP server with the **telnet *ip_address* 25** command, where *ip_address* is the IP address of the SMTP server.

After making a configuration change, don't forget to process the file appropriately. For Postfix, the **postmap *filename*** command processes the file. For sendmail, the /etc/mail/make script processes files in the /etc/mail directory. For the common /etc/aliases file, the **newaliases** command processes the file. And don't forget to make sure the service actually re-reads the new configuration files.

Lab I

In Postfix, to disable local-only access in the /etc/postfix/main.cf file, change the **inet_interfaces** directive to accept **all** connections:

```
inet_interfaces = all
```

FIGURE 13-5	
The mutt e-mail client	

```
y:Send  q:Abort  t:To  c:CC  s:Subj  a:Attach file  d:Descrip  ?:Help
        From:  root <root@>
          To:  michael@localhost
          Cc:
         Bcc:
     Subject:  this is a test
    Reply-To:
         Fcc:  ~/sent
    Security:  Clear


-- Attachments
- I     1 /tmp/mutt-Maui-0-607-0                 [text/plain, 7bit, us-ascii, 0.1K]


-- Mutt: Compose [Approx. msg size: 0.1K   Atts: 1]--------------------------------
```

But to meet the requirements of the lab, you'll want to retain the default value of that directive:

```
inet_interfaces = localhost
```

Make sure Postfix is active (and any alternative mail servers such as sendmail are not).

In general, to verify authentication on an SMTP server, connect from the local system with the **telnet localhost 25** command. When you see a message similar to

```
220 maui.example.com ESMTP Postfix
```

type in the following command:

```
EHLO localhost
```

Depending on the configuration, you should see messages similar to the following:

```
250-AUTH LOGIN PLAIN
```

```
250-AUTH=LOGIN PLAIN
```

To verify receipt of e-mail in a user account, log in to that account, or at least verify the time stamp associated with the username in the /var/mail directory. To make sure e-mail directed to the root user is redirected to a regular user account, you'd add a line like the following to the /etc/aliases file:

```
root:  michael
```

Given the wording for the question, any standard user account would be acceptable. Of course, to implement this change, you'll have to run the **newaliases** command, which processes this file into the /etc/aliases.db file.

To make sure this works, you'll want to use a command line client such as **mutt** or even **mail** as defined in Chapter 2. For example, if you send a test e-mail to the local root user, the message should be received by user michael (or whomever is configured in the /etc/aliases file to receive e-mail forwarded from the root user).

Lab 2

To enable access from more than just the localhost, you'll need to modify the inet_interfaces directive in /etc/postfix/main.cf to

```
inet_interfaces = all
```

The next job is to limit access to a specific network, in this case, example.com. While there are options in /etc/postfix files, perhaps the most efficient way to limit access to a specific network is with an appropriate **iptables**-based firewall rule. For example, the following custom rule would limit access to TCP port 25 to systems on the given IP address network. The network shown is based on the originally defined configuration for example.com, the 192.168.122.0/24 network:

```
-A INPUT -m state --state NEW -m tcp -p tcp -s 192.168.122.0/24 --dport 25 -j
ACCEPT
```

In addition, you'll need to set up this network in the /etc/postfix/access file with a rule like the following:

```
192.168.122 OK
```

Once Postfix is running, you should be able to confirm the result with an appropriate **telnet** command from a remote system. For example, if Postfix is configured on a system with a 192.168.122.50 IP address, the command would be

```
# telnet 192.168.122.50 25
```

The configuration of a smart host in Postfix is based on the **relayhost** directive. For the parameters given in the Lab, if the physical host is located on system maui.example.com, the directive in the main.cf file would be

```
relayhost = maui.example.com
```

If Postfix on the server1.example.com system is properly configured as a smart host, e-mails to the forwarded host should be reliably delivered, and even logged into the appropriate /var/log/maillog file.

Lab 3

With the **iptables** rule shown in Lab 2, access should already be prohibited from other networks. However, if you did not include the 192.168.122.0/24 network address in the **iptables** rule shown in the answer to Lab 2, a different approach is available. You can use options available in the /etc/postfix/access file, such as the following to reject messages from the example.org network. If your example.org network uses a different IP address, revise accordingly.

```
192.168.100 REJECT
```

It should be easy to verify connections to the SMTP server from a remote system. From prohibited networks, when you run a command like: **telnet 192.168.122.50 25** from a host on the 192.168.100.0/24 network, you should see the following output:

```
Trying 192.168.122.50...

telnet: connect to address 192.168.122.50: No route to host
```

Lab 4

This lab should be straightforward. As long as sendmail and sendmail-cf are installed on the local system, the basic steps to make the move from Postfix to sendmail are as follows:

1. Stop the Postfix service with a command like **/etc/init.d/postfix stop**.

2. Run the **alternatives --config mta** script, and select sendmail.

Lab 5

IPv6 networking is not enabled on some systems. But when it is, open the sendmail.mc file in the /etc/mail directory. To configure sendmail to accept connections from both IPv4 and IPv6 addresses, first disable the following directive. The added **dnl** in front turns it into a comment.

```
dnl DAEMON_OPTIONS(`Port=smtp,Addr=127.0.0.1, Name=MTA')dnl
```

Next, to let sendmail listen for both IPv4 and IPv6 traffic, activate the following directive:

```
DAEMON_OPTIONS(`Name=MTA-v4, Family=inet, Name=MTA-v6, Family=inet6')
```

If successful, you should be able to connect to the system with either of the following commands:

```
# telnet ::1 25
# telnet 127.0.0.1 25
```

Forwarding from the root account can be enabled through the /etc/aliases file, as explained in the answer to Lab 1.

Lab 6

In sendmail, to disable local-only access in the /etc/mail/sendmail.mc file, comment out the following line. Unlike in most Linux configuration files, the comment code is a **dnl** at the start of this line:

```
DNL DAEMON_OPTIONS(`Port=smtp,Addr=127.0.0.1, Name=MTA')dnl
```

The **dnl** at the end of the line does not affect the command to its left.

Next, you'll want to enable support through /etc/mail/access. To allow access to the example.com network as discussed in this book, add the following line to that file:

```
192.168.122               RELAY
```

For this lab, assume the sendmail system is on server1.example.com, with IP address 192.168.122.50, and the physical system is on maui.example.com on IP address 192.168.122.1. Return to the sendmail.mc file, and then look at this directive:

```
dnl define(`SMART_HOST', `smtp.your.provider')dnl
```

Based on the conditions given, you'd change that directive to

```
define(`SMART_HOST', `maui.example.com')dnl
```

Lab 7

This lab is quite similar to Lab 2. While there are options in the sendmail configuration files, the most efficient way to limit access to a specific network is still with an appropriate **iptables**-based firewall rule. The rule discussed in the answer to Lab 2 would also work in this case. Alternatively, you can configure access limits in the /etc/mail/access file, such as

```
Connect: 192.168.122 OK
Connect: 192.168.100 REJECT
```

14

The Apache
Web Server

U nix was developed by AT&T in the late 1960s and early 1970s, and it was freely distributed among a number of major universities during those years. When AT&T started charging for Unix, a number of university developers tried to create clones of this operating system. One of these clones, Linux, was developed and released in the early 1990s.

Many of these same universities were also developing the network that evolved into the Internet. With current refinements, this makes Linux perhaps the most Internet-friendly network operating system available. The extensive network services available with Linux are not only the tops in their field, but they create one of the most powerful and useful Internet-ready platforms available today at any price.

Currently, Apache is the most popular web server on the Internet. According to the Netcraft (www.netcraft.com) survey, which tracks the web servers associated with virtually every site on the Internet, Apache is currently used by more Internet web sites than all other web servers combined. Apache is included with RHEL 6.

This chapter deals with the basic concepts surrounding the use the Apache web server at a basic level of configuration.

INSIDE THE EXAM

This chapter directly addresses four RHCE objectives. While the objectives specify the HTTP (Hypertext Transfer Protocol) and HTTPS (HTTP, secure) protocols, that is an implicit reference to the Apache web server. It's the only web server currently supported on RHEL 6. In general, regular and secure web sites are configured in different files. The objectives are to

■ Configure a virtual host

Virtual hosts are the bread and butter of Apache, which supports the configuration of multiple web sites on the same server.

■ Configure private directories

The private directory on an Apache web server is sort of halfway in between a regular and a secure web site. It's a directory that's accessible by one user.

■ Configure group-managed content

Sometimes groups of users have to maintain the content of a web site jointly. As private directories can be configured for individual users in their home directories, directories can be configured for groups of users in a shared directory.

■ Deploy a basic CGI application

Don't worry if you don't know the Common Gateway Interface (CGI). But dynamic content on web pages depend on scripts such as those associated with CGI. While you won't have to write a CGI script, you will have to set up Apache to support its deployment.

In addition, there are the standard requirements for all network services, discussed in Chapters 10 and 11. To review, you need to install the service, make it work with SELinux, make sure it starts on boot, configure the service for basic operation, and set up user- and host-based security.

CERTIFICATION OBJECTIVE 14.01

The Apache Web Server

Apache is by far the most popular web server in use today. Based on the HTTP daemon (**httpd**), Apache provides simple and secure access to all types of content using the regular HTTP protocol as well as its secure cousin, HTTPS.

Apache was developed from the server code created by the National Center for Supercomputing Applications (NCSA). It included so many patches that it became known as "a patchy" server. The Apache web server continues to advance the art of the web and provides one of the most stable, secure, robust, and reliable web servers available. This server is under constant development by the Apache Software Foundation (www.apache.org).

For a full copy of Apache documentation, make sure to include the httpd-manual RPM during the installation process. It'll provide a full HTML copy of the Apache manual in the /var/www/manual directory.

Apache 2.2

As befits its reliability and stability, RHEL 6 includes an updated version of Apache 2.2. RHEL 5 also included a slightly older version of Apache 2.2. But no matter, the Apache 2.2 included with RHEL 6 has all of the updates needed to support the latest web pages, with the best possible security from the risks associated with the Internet.

The LAMP Stack

One of the powers of Apache as a web server is the way it can be integrated with other software components. The most common version of such is known as the LAMP stack, which refers to its components: Linux, Apache, MySQL, and one of three scripting languages (Perl, Python, or PHP).

There's no expectation from the RHCE objectives that you'll have to install a Structured Query Language database system such as MySQL (My Structured Query Language). However, they do explain many of the modules available as part of the Apache configuration files. And, of course, Apache works with other SQL databases along with other scripting languages.

Installation

The RPM packages required by Apache are included in the Web Server package group. The simplest way to install Apache after installation is with the following command:

```
# yum install httpd
```

But additional packages are required. It may be simpler to install the mandatory and default packages associated with the Web Server package group with the following command:

```
# yum groupinstall "Web Server"
```

If you don't remember the names of available groups, run the **yum grouplist** command. The standard method to start Linux services is with a script in the /etc/init.d directory. It contains an **httpd** script. However, you can stop and start Apache, as well as reload the configuration file gracefully with the following commands:

```
# apachectl stop
# apachectl start
# apachectl graceful
```

No configuration is required for the most basic operation. Once Apache is running, start a web browser and enter a URL of **http://localhost**. For example, Figure 14-1 displays the default home page for Apache, based on the default configuration, in the **elinks** web browser.

The web page is based on the contents of the /etc/httpd/conf.d/welcome.conf file, which refers to the /var/www/error/noindex.html file for more information.

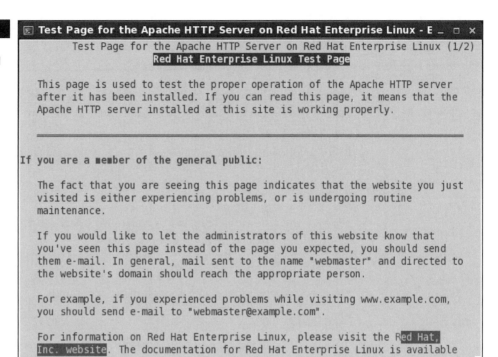

FIGURE 14-1

Default installed Apache home page

Test Page for the Apache HTTP Server on Red Hat Enterprise Linux - E _ □ ×

Test Page for the Apache HTTP Server on Red Hat Enterprise Linux (1/2)
Red Hat Enterprise Linux Test Page

This page is used to test the proper operation of the Apache HTTP server after it has been installed. If you can read this page, it means that the Apache HTTP server installed at this site is working properly.

If you are a member of the general public:

The fact that you are seeing this page indicates that the website you just visited is either experiencing problems, or is undergoing routine maintenance.

If you would like to let the administrators of this website know that you've seen this page instead of the page you expected, you should send them e-mail. In general, mail sent to the name "webmaster" and directed to the website's domain should reach the appropriate person.

For example, if you experienced problems while visiting www.example.com, you should send e-mail to "webmaster@example.com".

For information on Red Hat Enterprise Linux, please visit the Red Hat, Inc. website. The documentation for Red Hat Enterprise Linux is available
http://www.redhat.com/   [------]

EXERCISE 14-1

Install the Apache Server

In this exercise, you'll install all of the packages generally associated with the Apache server. Then you'll configure the system so Apache is active the next time Linux is booted. The twist here is that you'll do it all from the command line interface. This assumes you've already taken the steps discussed in Chapter 7 to either register with the Red Hat Network or connect the system to the RHEL 6 (or rebuild DVD) media as a repository.

1. If you're in the GUI, open a command line console. Press ALT-F2 and log in as the root user.

2. Run the following command to review available groups. You should see "Web Server" near the end of the list.

```
# yum groupinfo
```

3. You can install all default packages in the "Web Server" package group with the following command:

```
# yum groupinstall "Web Server"
```

If you just install the httpd RPM package, other important packages may not get installed, including mod_ssl, for the secure web sites cited in the RHCE objectives.

4. Run the following command to see if Apache is already configured to start in any runlevels:

```
# chkconfig --list httpd
```

5. Now use the following command to make sure Apache starts in runlevels 2, 3, 4, and 5 the next time Linux boots normally:

```
# chkconfig httpd on
```

6. Start the Apache service with the following command:

```
# apachectl start
```

7. If you haven't already done so in Chapter 2, install a text-based web browser. The RHEL 6 standard is **elinks**, which you can install with the following command:

```
# yum install elinks
```

8. Now start the ELinks browser, pointing to the local system, with the following command:

```
# elinks 127.0.0.1
```

9. Review the result. Do you see the Apache test page?

10. Exit from the ELinks browser. Press Q, and when the Exit ELinks text menu appears, press Y to exit Elinks.

11. Back up the default httpd.conf configuration file; a logical location is your home directory.

12. Run the **rpm -q httpd-manual** command, to confirm the installation of Apache documentation. Since that package is a default part of the Web Server package group, you shouldn't get a package "not installed" message.

But if you do get that message, install that package with the
yum httpd-manual command.

The Apache Configuration Files

The two key configuration files for the Apache web server are httpd.conf in the
/etc/httpd/conf directory and ssl.conf in the /etc/httpd/conf.d directory. The default
versions of these files create a generic web server service. There are other configuration
files in two directories: /etc/httpd/conf and /etc/httpd/conf.d. They're illustrated in
Figure 14-2.

Apache can work with a lot of other software, such as Python, PHP, the Squid
Proxy server, and more. If installed, associated configuration files can generally be
found in the /etc/httpd/conf directory.

To configure a regular and a secure web server, you'll need to understand the
httpd.conf and ssl.conf configuration files in some detail.

Analyze the Default Apache Configuration

Apache comes with a well-commented set of default configuration files. In this
section, you'll examine some key directives in the httpd.conf configuration file.
Browse through this file in your favorite text editor or using a command pager such
as **less**. Before beginning this analysis, remember that the main Apache configuration
file incorporates the files in the /etc/httpd/conf.d directory with the following
directive:

```
Include conf.d/*.conf
```

There are a couple of basic constructs in httpd.conf. First, directories, files, and
modules are configured in "containers." The beginning of the container starts with

| FIGURE 14-2 | ```
[root@server1 ~]# ls /etc/httpd/conf
httpd.conf  magic
[root@server1 ~]# ls /etc/httpd/conf.d/
manual.conf     perl.conf  ssl.conf        welcome.conf
mod_dnssd.conf  README     webalizer.conf  wsgi.conf
[root@server1 ~]# █
``` |
|---|---|
| Apache configuration files | |
```

the name of the directory, file, or module to be configured, contained in directional brackets (< >). Examples of this include

```
<Directory "/var/www/icons">
<Files ~ "^\.ht">
<IfModule mod_mime_magic.c>
```

The end of the container is also an expression inside brackets (<>), which starts with a forward slash (/). For the same examples, the ends of the containers would look like

```
</Directory>
</Files>
</IfModule>
```

Next, Apache includes a substantial number of directives—commands that Apache can understand that have some resemblance to English. For example, the **ExecCGI** directive supports executable CGI scripts.

While this provides an overview, the devil is often in the details, which are analyzed (briefly) in the next section. If you've installed the httpd-manual RPM, get the Apache server going, and navigate to http://localhost/manual.

The Main Apache Configuration File

This section examines the default Apache configuration file, httpd.conf. I recommend that you follow along on a test system such as server1.example.com. Only the default active directives in that file are discussed here. Read the comments; they include more information and options.

Once Apache and the httpd-manual RPMs is installed per Exercise 14-1, refer to http://localhost/manual/mod/quickreference.html. It'll provide detailed information on each directive. The default directives are summarized in the following three tables. Table 14-1 specifies directives associated with Section 1: Global Environment.

In all three tables, directives are listed in the order shown in the default version of httpd.conf. If you want to experiment with different values for each directive, save the change and then use **apachectl restart** to restart the Apache daemon or **apachectl graceful** to just reread the Apache configuration files.

Table 14-2 specifies directives associated with Section 2: Main Server Configuration.

TABLE 14-1	Directive	Description
Global Environment Directives	ServerTokens	Specifies the response code at the bottom of error pages; options include OS, Prod, Major, Minor, Min, and Full.
	ServerRoot	Sets the default directory; other directives are subdirectories.
	PidFile	Names the file with the Process ID (and locks the service).
	Timeout	Limits access time for both sent and received messages.
	KeepAlive	Supports persistent connections.
	MaxKeepAliveRequests	Limits requests during persistent connections (unless set to 0, which is no limit).
	KeepAliveTimeout	Sets a time limit, in seconds, before a connection is closed.
	StartServers	Adds child Apache processes; normally set to 8, which means 9 Apache processes run upon startup.
	MinSpareServers	Specifies a minimum number of idle child servers.
	MaxSpareServers	Specifies a maximum number of idle child servers; always at least +1 greater than **MinSpareServers**.
	ServerLimit	Sets a limit on configurable processes; cannot exceed 20000.
	MaxClients	Limits the number of simultaneous requests; other requests to the server just have to wait.
	MaxRequestsPerChild	Limits the requests per child server process.
	MinSpareThreads	Specifies the minimum number of spare threads to handle additional requests.
	MaxSpareThreads	Specifies the maximum number of available idle threads to handle additional requests.
	ThreadsPerChild	Sets the number of threads per child server process.
	Listen	Specifies a port and possibly an IP address (for multihomed systems) to listen for requests.
	LoadModule	Loads various modular components, such as authentication, user tracking, executable files, and more.
	Include	Adds the content of other configuration files.
	User	Specifies the username run by Apache on the local system.
	Group	Specifies the group name run by Apache on the local system.

| TABLE 14-2 | Main Server Configuration Directives |

Directive	Description
ServerAdmin	Sets the administrative e-mail address; may be shown (or linked to) on default error pages.
UseCanonicalName	Supports the use of **ServerName** as the referenced URL.
DocumentRoot	Assigns the root directory for web site files.
Options	Specifies features associated with web directories, such as ExecCGI, FollowSymLinks, Includes, Indexes, MultiViews, and SymLinksIfOwnerMatch.
AllowOverride	Supports overriding of previous directives from .htaccess files.
Order	Sets the sequence for evaluating **Allow** and **Deny** directives.
Allow	Configures host computers that are allowed access.
Deny	Configures host computers that are denied access.
UserDir	Specifies location of user directories; can be set to enable or disable for all or specified users.
DirectoryIndex	Specifies files to look for when navigating to a directory; set to index.html by default.
AccessFileName	Sets a filename within a directory for more directives; normally looks for .htaccess.
Satisfy	Specifies result when both user and host restrictions are used; may be set to Any or All.
TypesConfig	Locates mime.types, which specifies file types associated with extensions.
DefaultType	Sets a default file type if not found in mime.types.
MIMEMagicFile	Normally looks to /etc/httpd/conf/magic to look inside a file for its MIME type.
HostNameLookups	Requires URL lookups for IP addresses; results are logged.
ErrorLog	Locates the error log file, relative to **ServerRoot**.
LogLevel	Specifies the level of log messages.
LogFormat	Sets the information included in log files.
CustomLog	Creates a customized log file, in a different format, with a location relative to **ServerRoot**.
ServerSignature	Adds a list with server version and possibly ServerAdmin e-mail address to error pages and file lists; can be set to **On**, **OFF**, or **EMail**.
Alias	Configures a directory location; similar to a soft link.
DAVLockDB	Specifies the path to the lock file for the WebDAV (Web-based Distributed Authoring and Versioning) database.
ScriptAlias	Similar to **Alias**; for scripts.
IndexOptions	Specifies how files are listed from a **DirectoryIndex**.

TABLE 14-2	Main Server Configuration Directives (*continued*)

Directive	Description
AddIconByEncoding	Assigns an icon for a file by MIME encoding.
AddIconByType	Assigns an icon for a file by MIME type.
AddIcon	Assigns an icon for a file by extension.
DefaultIcon	Sets a default icon for files not otherwise configured.
ReadmeName	Configures a location for a **README** file to go with a directory list.
HeaderName	Configures a location for a **HEADER** file to go with a directory list.
IndexIgnore	Adds files that are not included in a directory list.
AddLanguage	Assigns a language for filename extensions.
LanguagePriority	Sets a priority of languages if not configured in client browsers.
ForceLanguagePriority	Specifies action if a web page in the preferred language is not found.
AddDefaultCharset	Sets a default character set; you may need to change it for different languages.
AddType	Maps filename extensions to a specified content type.
AddHandler	Maps filename extensions to a specified handler; commonly used for scripts or multiple languages.
AddOutputFilter	Maps filename extensions to a specified filter.
BrowserMatch	Customizes responses to different browser clients.

Table 14-3 specifies directives associated with Section 3: Virtual Hosts. While virtual host directives are disabled by default, I include those directives in the commented example near the end of the default httpd.conf file. While these directives were already used in other sections, you can—and generally should—customize them for individual virtual hosts to support different web sites on the same Apache server. In many cases, each virtual host stanza will include directives from the main part of the httpd.conf configuration file, customized for that virtual host.

Basic Apache Configuration for a Simple Web Server

As described earlier, Apache looks for web pages in the directory specified by the **DocumentRoot** directive. In the default httpd.conf file, this directive points to the /var/www/html directory. In other words, all you need to get your web server up and running is to transfer web pages to the /var/www/html directory.

TABLE 14-3	Directive	Description
Virtual Host Configuration Directives	NameVirtualHost	Specifies an IP address and port number for multiple virtual hosts.
	ServerAdmin	Assigns an e-mail address for the specified virtual host.
	DocumentRoot	Sets a root directory for the virtual host.
	ServerName	Names the URL for the virtual host.
	ErrorLog	Creates an error log; the location is based on the **DocumentRoot**.
	CustomLog	Creates an custom log; the location is based on the **DocumentRoot**.

The default **DirectoryIndex** directive looks for an index.html web page file in this directory. A standard RHEL 6 index.html page is available in the /usr/share/doc/HTML/en-US directory. Copy that file to the /var/www/html directory, and navigate to http://localhost with a browser such as ELinks.

The base location of configuration and log files is determined by the **ServerRoot** directive. The default value from httpd.conf is

```
ServerRoot "/etc/httpd"
```

Figure 14-1 confirms that the main Apache configuration files are stored in the conf/ and conf.d/ subdirectories of the **ServerRoot**. Run the **ls -l /etc/httpd** command. Note the soft-linked directories. You should see a link from the /etc/httpd/logs directory to the directory with the actual log files, /var/log/httpd.

Apache Log Files

As suggested earlier, while Apache log files are configured in the /etc/httpd/logs directory, they're actually stored in the /var/log/httpd directory. Standard logging information from Apache is stored in two baseline log files. Custom log files may also be configured. Such log files may have different names, depending on how virtual hosts are configured, how secure web sites are configured, and how logs are rotated.

Based on the standard Apache configuration files, access attempts are logged in the access_log file and errors are recorded in the error_log file. Standard secure log files include ssl_access_log, ssl_error_log, and ssl_request_log.

In general, it's helpful to set up different sets of log files for different web sites. To that end, you should also set up different log files for the secure versions of a web site. The traffic on a web site is important when choosing a log rotation frequency.

There are standard Apache log file formats. For more information, take a look at the **LogFormat** directive in Figure 14-3. Four different formats are shown: combined, common, the referrer (the web page with the link used to get to your site), and the agent (the user's web browser). The first two **LogFormat** lines include a number of percent signs followed by lowercase letters. These directives determine what goes into the log.

You can then use the **CustomLog** directive to select a location for the log file, such as logs/special_access_log, and the desired log file format, such as common. For more information on log files and formats, refer to http://localhost/manual/logs.html.

on the ! Job

Some web log analyzers have specific requirements for log file formats. For example, the popular open-source tool awstats (advanced Web Stats) requires the combined log format. It will fail to run if you leave the default common format. Awstats is a great tool for graphically displaying site activity. You can download it from a site such as awstats.sourceforge.net.

FIGURE 14-3

Specific log formats

```
# LogLevel: Control the number of messages logged to the error_log.
# Possible values include: debug, info, notice, warn, error, crit,
# alert, emerg.
#
LogLevel warn


#
# The following directives define some format nicknames for use with
# a CustomLog directive (see below).
#
LogFormat "%h %l %u %t \"%r\" %>s %b \"%{Referer}i\" \"%{User-Agent}i\"" combined
LogFormat "%h %l %u %t \"%r\" %>s %b" common
LogFormat "%{Referer}i -> %U" referer
LogFormat "%{User-agent}i" agent

# "combinedio" includes actual counts of actual bytes received (%I) and sent (%O);
 this
# requires the mod_logio module to be loaded.
#LogFormat "%h %l %u %t \"%r\" %>s %b \"%{Referer}i\" \"%{User-Agent}i\" %I %O" co
mbinedio

#
```

Standard Apache Security Configuration

You can configure several layers of security for the Apache web server. Firewalls based on the **iptables** command can limit access to specific hosts. Security options based on rules in Apache configuration files can also be used to limit access to specific users, groups, and hosts. Of course, secure Apache web sites can encrypt communication. If there is a problem, SELinux can limit the risks.

Ports and Firewalls

With the **Listen** and **NameVirtualHost** directives, the Apache web server specifies the standard communication ports associated with both the HTTP and HTTPS protocols, 80 and 443. To allow external communication through the noted ports, you can set up both ports as trusted services in the Firewall Configuration tool.

Of course, for systems where HTTP and HTTPS are configured on nonstandard ports, you'll have to adjust the associated **iptables** rules accordingly.

If you just open these ports indiscriminately, it allows traffic from all systems. It may be appropriate to set up a custom rule to limit access to one or more systems or networks. For example, the following custom rules allows access to every system on the 192.168.122.0 network except the one with IP address 192.168.122.150, over port 80. To review, these rules are applied to the **iptables** command, in order.

```
-A INPUT -m state --state NEW -m tcp -p tcp -s 192.168.122.150
--dport 80 -j REJECT
-A INPUT -m state --state NEW -m tcp -p tcp -s 192.168.122.0/24
--dport 80 -j ACCEPT
```

Similar rules may be required for port 443. Of course, that depends on the requirements of the job, and possibly the RHCE exam.

Apache and SELinux

Take a look at the SELinux settings associated with Apache. To review, SELinux settings, as they relate to a service, mostly fall into two categories: boolean settings and file labels. Start with the file labels.

Apache and SELinux File Labels

The default file labels for Apache configuration files are consistent, as shown in the output to the **ls -Z /etc/httpd** and **ls -Z /var/www** commands. Individual files use the same contexts as their directory. The differences in the file contexts are shown in Table 14-4.

The first five are just the default SELinux contexts for standard directories. For web sites where scripts read and or append data to web forms, you'd consider the last two contexts, which support read/write (rw) and read/append (ra) access.

Create a Special Web Directory

In many cases, you'll create dedicated directories for each virtual web site. It's better to segregate the files for each web site in its own directory tree. But with SELinux, you can't just create a special web directory. You'll want to make sure that new directory at least matches the SELinux contexts of the default /var/www directory.

Run the **ls -Z /var/www** command. Note the SELinux contexts. For most directories, the user context is system_u and the type is http_sys_content_t. For a newly created /www directory, you could just change the SELinux contexts with the following commands. The **-R** applies the changes recursively, so the new contexts are applied to files and subdirectories.

```
# chcon -R -u system_u /www/
# chcon -R -t httpd_sys_content_t /www/
```

Of course, if scripts are required for the associated web site, you'll want to run the following command to make sure the SELinux changes survive a relabel:

```
# semanage fcontext -a -s system_u -t httpd_sys_content_t /www/
```

TABLE 14-4	Directory	SELinux Context Type
SELinux File Contexts	/etc/httpd, /etc/httpd/conf, /etc/httpd/conf.d, /var/run/httpd	httpd_config_t
	/usr/lib64/httpd/modules	httpd_modules_t
	/var/log/httpd	httpd_log_t
	/var/www, /var/www/error, /var/www/html, /var/www/icons, /var/www/manual, /var/www/usage	httpd_sys_content_t
	/var/www/cgi-bin	httpd_sys_script_exec_t
	n/a	httpd_sys_content_rw_t
	n/a	httpd_sys_content_ra_t

This command creates a file_contexts.local file in the /etc/selinux/targeted/ contexts/files directory. If there's also a cgi-bin/ subdirectory, you'll want to set up appropriate contexts for that subdirectory as well with the following command:

```
# semanage fcontext -a -s system_u -t httpd_sys_script_exec_t \
/www/cgi-bin/
```

Apache and SELinux Boolean Settings

Boolean settings are more extensive. For display purposes, I've isolated them in the SELinux Administration tool, as shown in Figure 14-4. Only a few SELinux boolean settings are enabled by default, and they're described in Table 14-5.

| **FIGURE 14-4** | Apache-related SELinux boolean settings |

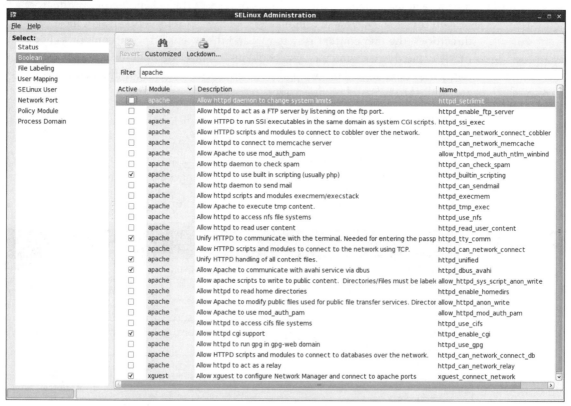

TABLE 14-5	Active Boolean	Description
	httpd_builtin_scripting	Provides permissions to scripts in httpd_t labeled directories; sometimes used for PHP content.
Default Active Apache-Related SELinux Boolean Settings	httpd_dbus_avahi	Supports access from HTTP services to automated IP address configuration.
	httpd_enable_cgi	Allows HTTP services to execute GCI scripts, labeled with the httpd_sys_script_exec_t type.
	httpd_tty_comm	Enables communication with controlling terminals; useful for SSL certificates.
	httpd_unified	Supports full read/write/execute access by all httpd_t files.
	xguest_connect_network	Allows access from secured guests.

Out of the many other SELinux options, the one of particular interest for this chapter is **httpd_enable_homedirs**, which supports access to files from user home directories. Other scripts of potential interest relate to interactions with other services, specifically, httpd_enable_ftp_server, httpd_use_cifs, and httpd_use_nfs. These options allow Apache to act as an FTP server, as well as to read shared Samba / NFS directories.

The uses of these and the other unenabled SELinux Apache-related options from Figure 14-4 are summarized in Table 14-6. All descriptions are based on the perspective "What would happen if the boolean were enabled?" For variety, the terms HTTP and Apache are used interchangeably; strictly speaking, Apache is one option for HTTP and HTTPS services.

Module Management

The Apache web server includes many modular features. For example, it's not possible to set up SSL-secured web sites without the mod_ssl package, which includes the mod_ssl.so module along with the ssl.conf configuration file.

A number of other similar systems are organized in modules. Loaded modules are included in standard Apache configuration files with the **LoadModule** directive. A full list of available modules is located in the /usr/lib64/httpd/modules directory (for 32-bit systems, the directory is /usr/lib/httpd/modules). But available modules aren't used unless they're loaded with the LoadModule directive in appropriate Apache configuration files.

TABLE 14-6   Default Inactive Apache-Related SELinux Boolean Settings

Inactive Boolean	Description
allow_httpd_anon_write	Allows the web server to write to files labeled with the public_content_rw_t file type.
allow_httpd_mod_auth_ntlm_winbind	Supports access to Microsoft authentication databases, if the mod_auth_ntlm_winbind module is loaded.
allow_httpd_mod_auth_pam	Enables access to PAM authentication modules, if the mod_auth_pam module is loaded.
allow_httpd_sys_script_anon_write	Configures write access by scripts to files labeled with the public_content_rw_t file type.
httpd_can_check_spam	Works with web-based e-mail applications to check for spam.
httpd_can_network_connect	Supports Apache access to connections on remote ports; normally disabled to minimize risk of attacks on other systems.
httpd_can_network_connect_cobbler	Allows Apache to connect to the Cobbler installation server; should not be activated simultaneously with httpd_can-network_connect.
httpd_can_network_connect_db	Allows Apache to connect to a database server.
httpd_can_network_memcache	Enables HTTP memory caching access; originally set up for a translation server.
httpd_can_network_relay	Supports the use of the HTTP service as a proxy.
httpd_can_sendmail	Allows the use of HTTP-based e-mail services; does not require the use of the sendmail SMTP server described in Chapter 13.
httpd_enable_homedirs	Configures access via HTTP to files in user home directories.
httpd_execmem	Supports operation of executable programs that require executable and writable memory addresses; normally disabled to minimize risk of buffer overflows.
httpd_read_user_content	Enables access to scripts from user home directories.
httpd_setrlimit	Allows Apache to modify maximum number of file descriptors.
httpd_ssi_exec	Allows Apache to access Server Side Include (SSI) scripts; similar to httpd_enable_cgi.
httpd_tmp_exec	Supports those Apache-based scripts that require access to the /tmp directory.
httpd_use_cifs	Enables Apache access to shared Samba directories, when labeled with the cifs_t file type.
httpd_use_gpg	Allows access to systems that require GPG encryption.
httpd_use_nfs	Enables Apache access to shared Samba directories, when labeled with the nfs_t file type.

Security Within Apache

You've read about (and hopefully tested) Apache security options related to **iptables**-based firewalls as well as SELinux. Now you'll examine the security options available in the main Apache configuration file, httpd.conf. That file can be modified to secure the entire server or to configure security on a directory-by-directory basis. Directory controls secure access by the server, as well as users who connect to the web sites on the server. To explore the basics of Apache security, start with the first default active line in httpd.conf:

```
ServerTokens OS
```

This line looks deceptively simple; it limits the information displayed about a web server you navigate to a nonexistent page to the following message:

```
Apache/2.2.15 (Red Hat) Server at localhost Port 80
```

Contrast that output with what happens with a **ServerTokens Full** line:

```
Apache/2.2.15 (Red Hat) DAV/2 mod_ssl/2.2.15 OpenSSL/1.0.0-fips mod_wsgi/3.2
Python/2.6.5 mod_perl/2.0.4 Perl/v5.10.1 Server at localhost Port 80
```

In other words, with one option, outsiders can see whether modules such as Perl, Python, and PHP have been loaded, along with their version numbers. As not everyone updates their software in a perfectly timely manner, what happens when a cracker sees a version that has been compromised, your servers will face additional risks.

Next, you can restrict access to the directory defined by the **ServerRoot** directive as shown here:

```
<Directory />
    Options FollowSymLinks
    AllowOverride None
</Directory>
```

This configures a very restrictive set of permissions. The **Options FollowSymLinks** line supports the use of symbolic links for web pages. The **AllowOverride None** line disables any .htaccess files. The ServerRoot directive points to /etc/httpd, which contains Apache configuration files. Without the **AllowOverride None** line, a cracker who inserts a malicious .htaccess file can configure permissions that allows any user to change such configuration files.

However, there's an appropriate use for .htaccess files. For example, when placed in a subdirectory such as /www/html/project, then it can be used to permit access to a group, and such changes would apply only to that directory.

You can improve this by limiting access to all but explicitly allowed users, by adding the following commands to the desired **<Directory>** container:

```
Order deny,allow
Deny from all
```

The next **<Directory>** container example limits access to /var/www/html, which corresponds to the default **DocumentRoot** directive (while these directives are divided by numerous comments, they are all in the same stanza):

```
<Directory /var/www/html>
    Options Indexes FollowSymLinks
    AllowOverride None
    Order allow,deny
    Allow from all
</Directory>
```

The **Options** directive is different; the **Indexes** setting allows readers to see a list of files on the web server if no index.html file is present in the specified directory. The **Order** and **Allow** lines allow all users to access the web pages on this server.

But wait a second! By default, there are no files in the /var/www/html directory. Based on the description, you should navigate to the system in question and see the screen shown in Figure 14-5. As there are no files in the /var/www/html directory, no files are shown in the output.

However, when you navigate to the default web site associated with the Apache server, the page shown in Figure 14-6 appears. For more information on how that worked, see Exercise 14-2.

FIGURE 14-5	
Browse to an index of files	

Index of /

Name	**Last modified**	**Size**	**Description**

Apache/2.2.15 (Red Hat) Server at 192.168.122.50 Port 80

Browse to the
default Apache
test page

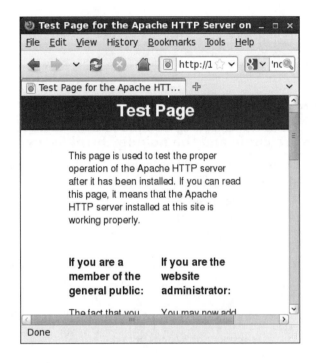

Finally, the **Listen** directive defines the IP address and TCP/IP port for this server. For example, the default shown next means that this server will work with every computer that requests a web page from any of the IP addresses for your computer on the standard TCP/IP port, 80:

```
Listen 80
```

If more than one IP address is available on the local system, the **Listen** directive can be used to limit access to one specific IP address. For example, if a system has two network cards with IP addresses 192.168.0.200 and 192.168.122.1, the following directive can help limit access to systems on the 192.168.122.0 network:

```
Listen 192.168.122.1:80
```

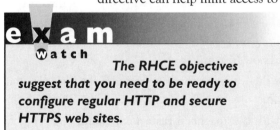

The RHCE objectives suggest that you need to be ready to configure regular HTTP and secure HTTPS web sites.

For secure web sites, there's a second **Listen** directive in the ssl.conf file in the /etc/httpd/conf.d directory. The data from this file is automatically incorporated into the overall Apache configuration, courtesy of a directive described in Exercise 14-2. It includes the following directive, which points to the default secure HTTP (HTTPS) port for TCP/IP, 443:

```
Listen 443
```

EXERCISE 14-2

The Apache Welcome and the noindex.html Story

In this exercise, you'll trace the story behind the standard test page associated with the Apache web server, like that shown in Figure 14-6. This exercise assumes the httpd package is already installed and the Apache service is running. You'll also see what happens when the path to that web page is broken, with an index of a bunch of test files in the /var/www/html directory.

1. Open the httpd.conf file in the /etc/httpd/conf directory. Find the following line:

   ```
   Include conf.d/*.conf
   ```

2. Find the **ServerRoot** directive in the same file. It should read as follows:

   ```
   ServerRoot /etc/httpd
   ```

   In addition, make a note of the **Alias /error/ "/var/www/error/"** line. You'll need that information shortly.

3. Put the effect of the two directives together. In other words, the **Include conf.d/*.conf** directive includes the contents of *.conf files from the /etc/httpd/conf.d directory in the Apache configuration. Exit from the httpd.conf file.

4. Navigate to the /etc/httpd/conf.d directory. Open the welcome.conf file.

5. Note the **ErrorDocument** page. While it points to the /error/noindex.html file, that's based on the aforementioned **Alias** directive. In other words, you should be able to find the noindex.html file in the /var/www/error directory.

6. Take a look at the /var/www/error/noindex.html file. To open it up in the ELinks browser, run the **elinks /var/www/error/noindex.html** command. The web page that appears should now be familiar.

7. Exit from the browser. Move the welcome.conf file from the /etc/httpd/conf.d directory to a backup location.

8. Restart the Apache service with the **apachectl restart** command.

9. Navigate to the localhost system with **elinks http://127.0.0.1** command. What do you see?

10. Open a second terminal, navigate to the /var/www/html directory, and run the **touch test1 test2 test3 test4** command.

11. Reload the browser in the original terminal. In ELinks, CTRL-R reloads the browser. What do you see?

12. Exit from the browser. Restore the welcome.conf file to the /etc/httpd/conf.d directory.

EXERCISE 14-3

Create a List of Files

In this exercise, you'll be setting up a list of files to share with others who access your web server. The process is fairly simple; you'll configure an appropriate firewall, create a subdirectory of **DocumentRoot**, fill it with several files, set up appropriate security contexts, and activate Apache.

1. Make sure the firewall does not block access to port 80. One way to do so is with the Red Hat Firewall Configuration tool, which you can start with the **system-config-firewall** command. In the Trusted Services section, make sure to allow incoming WWW (HTTP) connections. Alternatively, you could use the directions specified earlier for a custom firewall.

2. Create a subdirectory of **DocumentRoot**, which is /var/www/html by default. For this exercise, I've created the /var/www/html/help directory.

3. Copy the files from the /var/www/manual directory:

```
# cp -ar /var/www/manual/* /var/www/html/help/
```

4. Restart the Apache service with the following command:

```
# apachectl restart
```

5. Make sure Apache starts the next time you boot:

```
# chkconfig httpd on
```

6. Use the **ls -Z /var/www/html** and **ls -Z /var/www/html/help** commands to review the security contexts for the /var/www/html/sharing directory and copied files. If it doesn't already correspond to the contexts shown here, set them up with the following commands:

```
# chcon -R -u system_u /var/www/html/sharing/
# chcon -R -t httpd_sys_content_t /var/www/html/sharing/
```

7. Start the ELinks browser on the local server, directed at the help/ subdirectory:

```
# elinks http://127.0.0.1/help
```

8. Go to a remote system and try accessing the same web directory. For example, if the IP address of the local system is 192.168.122.50, navigate to http://192.168.122.50/help. If possible, try this a second time from a conventional GUI browser.

Host-Based Security

You can add the **Order**, **allow**, and **deny** directives to regulate access based on hostnames or IP addresses. This following standard command sequence allows access by default. It reads the **deny** directive first:

```
Order deny,allow
```

You can **deny** or **allow** from various forms of hostnames or IP addresses. For example, the following directive denies access from all computers in the osborne.com domain:

```
Deny from osborne.com
```

*If you set **Order** allow,deny, access is denied by default. Only those hostnames or IP addresses associated with the **allow** directive are allowed access.*

If DNS service is unreliable, you may prefer to use IP addresses. The following example directives use a single IP address; alternatively, you can set up the 192.168.122.0 subnet in partial, netmask, or CIDR (Classless InterDomain Routing) notation, as shown here:

```
Deny from 192.168.122.66
Allow from 192.168.122
Deny from 192.168.122.0/255.255.255.0
Allow from 192.168.122.0/24
```

User-Based Security

You can limit access to web sites configured on the Apache server to authorized users with passwords. As described shortly, these passwords can be different from the regular authentication database.

For example, to configure user-based security for the web site described in Exercise 14-3, you'll need to set up a **<Directory>** container on the /var/www/html/help directory. You'll want several commands in the **<Directory>** container:

- To set up basic authentication, you'll need an **AuthType Basic** directive.
- To describe the site to requesting users, you can include an **AuthName "*some comment*"** directive.
- To refer to a web server password database named /etc/httpd/testpass, you'll need a **AuthUserFile /etc/httpd/testpass** directive.
- To limit the site to a single user named engineer1, you could add a **Require user engineer1** directive.
- Alternatively, to limit the site to a group as defined in /etc/httpd/webgroups, you'd add the **AuthGroupFile /etc/httpd/webgroups** directive. You would also need a directive such as **Require group *Design***, where *Design* is the name of the group specified in webgroups.

Here's an example of code that I've added after the **<Virtual Host>** container:

```
<Directory "/var/www/html/help">
    AuthType Basic
    AuthName "Password Protected Test"
    AuthUserFile /etc/httpd/testpass
    Require user engineer1
</Directory>
```

When properly configured, the next time you try accessing the http://server1.example .com/help web site directory in the Firefox browser, you're prompted for a username and password, as shown in Figure 14-7.

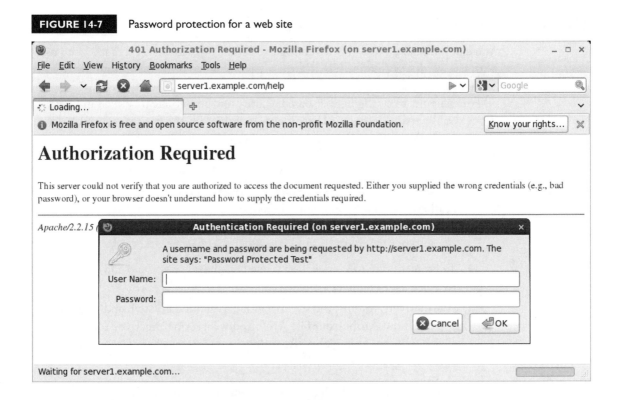

FIGURE 14-7   Password protection for a web site

CERTIFICATION OBJECTIVE 14.03

Specialized Apache Directories

In this section, you'll explore several options for specialized Apache directories. It may be appropriate to set up specialized security for some of these directories with the .htaccess file. As suggested earlier, you can set up password protection based on users and groups, which corresponds to the "private directories" cited in the RHCE objectives. One example appropriate for a private directory is the home directory example included in the httpd.conf file. With the right options, such directories can also be managed by members of a group.

Once any changes are made to Apache configuration files, you may want to test the result. To do so you could run the **apachectl restart** command. Alternatively, to make Apache reload the configuration file without kicking off any currently connected users, run the **apachectl graceful** command. A functionally equivalent alternative command is **/etc/init.d/httpd reload**.

Control Through the .htaccess File

With all of the complexity associated with the httpd.conf file, you might look at the .htaccess file and think, "Great, one more complication." But used correctly, the .htaccess file can simplify the list of directives applied to a directory, or a virtual host, as it can be used to override inherited permissions. To do so, you'll need to include the following command in targeted **<Directory>** containers:

```
AllowOverride Options
```

Then you can configure .htaccess files to override previously set permissions. The .htaccess file can be stored in any web directory, labeled with the httpd_config_t SELinux context.

Password-Protected Access

To configure passwords for a web site, you need to create a separate database of usernames and passwords. Just as the **useradd** and **passwd** commands are used for regular users, the **htpasswd** command is used to set up usernames and passwords for Apache.

For example, to create a database file named webpass in the /etc/httpd directory, start with the following command:

```
# htpasswd -c /etc/httpd/webpass engineer1
```

The **-c** switch creates the specified file, and the first user is engineer1. You're prompted to enter a password for engineer1. Users in the webpass database do not need to have a regular Linux account. Note the use of the **ServerRoot** directory (/etc/httpd). It's also helpful when configuring virtual hosts.

If you want to add more users to this authentication database, leave out the **-c** switch. For example, the following command sets up a second account for user drafter1:

```
# htpasswd /etc/httpd/webpass drafter1
```

To set up access for more than one user, you'll also need a group file. For example, to set up the engineer1 and drafter1 users as a group named design, you could add the following line to the /etc/httpd/grouppass file:

```
design: engineer1 drafter1
```

In this case, the AuthUserFile directive would be associated with the /etc/httpd/webpass authentication database, and the AuthGroupFile directive would be associated with the group database.

Home Directory Access

The default httpd.conf file includes commented suggestions that can enable access to user home directories. One useful option through Apache is access to a user's home directory. You can start to set up access to user home directories by changing the following directives from

```
UserDir disabled
#UserDir public_html
```

to

```
#UserDir disabled
UserDir public_html
```

Then anyone will have access to web pages that a user puts in his or her ~/public_html directory. For example, a user named michael can create a /home/michael/public_html directory and add the web pages of his choice.

However, this requires a bit of a security compromise; you need to make michael's home directory executable for all users. This is also known as *701 permissions*, which can be configured with the following command:

```
# chmod 701 /home/michael
```

You'll also need to make the public_html subdirectory executable by all users in the same way with the following command:

```
# chmod 701 /home/michael/public_html
```

But that entails some security risks. Even though a cracker might not be able to directly read the contents of the noted directories, if he sees a script through the resulting web site, he'd be able to execute that script as any logged-in user.

There's an alternative, if the filesystem with the /home directory has been mounted with the Access Control Lists discussed in Chapter 4. You could create ACLs on the noted directories specifically for the user named apache. For user michael and his home directory, that would work with the following commands:

```
# setfacl -m u:apache:x /home/michael
# setfacl -m u:apache:x /home/michael/public_html
```

Whether permissions are set directly, or through ACLs, the logical next step as a web server is to add an index.html file to this directory. For our purposes, it can be a text file. The commented stanza that follows is one excellent way to help keep home directories so shared a bit more secure.

In addition, SELinux must be configured to "Allow HTTPD To Read Home Directories," associated with the httpd_enable_homedirs boolean. You can activate that option either with the SELinux Administration tool or with the **setsebool -P htttpd_enable_homedirs 1** command.

At that point, a web server that's directed to user michael's directory can read an index.html file in the public.html subdirectory. Figure 14-8 illustrates the result, where the noted text is the only content of index.html.

Of course, additional changes are suggested in the httpd.conf file. If you activate the stanza that starts with the <Directory /home/*/public_html> container, it supports additional levels of access to the public_html subdirectory of all user's home directories.

```
#<Directory /home/*/public_html>
```

FIGURE 14-8

View the index
.html file for user
michael

The AllowOverride directive supports information access by document type (FileInfo), access associated with authorization directives (AuthConfig), and access secured by directives such as Allow, Deny, and Order.

```
#     AllowOverride FileInfo AuthConfig Limit
```

The Options directive configures what can be seen in a specific directory, based on content negotiation (MultiViews), a list of files in the current directory (Indexes), an option that activates symbolic links associated with the same owner (SymLinksIfOwnerMatch), and also activates an option that does not allow scripts (IncludesNoExec). While it may be a bad security practice to allow a script in a user directory, it may be appropriate for users who are developers on test systems, and possibly during a Red Hat exam. In that case, you would remove the IncludesNoExec option.

```
#    Options MultiViews Indexes SymLinksIfOwnerMatch IncludesNoExec
```

The <Limit> container limits access and write options as shown; however, the default is to allow from all users.

```
#     <Limit GET POST OPTIONS>
#         Order allow,deny
#         Allow from all
#     </Limit>
```

In contrast, the <LimitExcept> container shown here denies nothing.

```
#     <LimitExcept GET POST OPTIONS>
#         Order deny,allow
#         Deny from all
#     </LimitExcept>
#</Directory>
```

You could combine these directives with password protection. One straightforward possibility is to require the username and password of the user whose home directory is being shared. But as noted earlier, the authentication database for a shared Apache directory is unrelated to the shadow password suite.

Group-Managed Directories

You can combine the features of group directories discussed in Chapter 8 with the public_html/ subdirectory just described. However, the steps required to set up a group to manage shared web content are somewhat different. Specifically, to set up a group-managed directory, it's best to start that group as a user. The standard Apache configuration directives for a private user can apply to private groups. Conceptually, you'd take the following steps:

1. Create a regular user.
2. Set up that user with a higher UID and GID number, beyond those associated with existing local and network users.
3. Configure the home directory of that user with the user nobody as the owner. Set up the login shell of that user as /sbin/nologin.
4. Create the public_html subdirectory.
5. Change permissions for the group home directory, with associated subdirectories to be consistent with the group requirements described in Chapter 8, along with the requirements of the Apache web server. For example, if the new group directory is /home/design, you'd run the following command:

```
# chmod -R 2771 /home/design
```

Of course, as discussed in Chapter 8, you could substitute an executable ACL for the user named apache for the execute bit for all users. That assumes the filesystem with the /home directory has been mounted with ACLs. In that case, you'd run the following commands:

```
# chmod -R 2770 /home/design
# setfacl -m u:apache:x /home/design
# setfacl -m u:apache:x /home/design/public_html
```

6. Log in as a user member of the new group. Create a new file in the public_html subdirectory. Check the ownership of that file; with the Super Group ID (SGID) bit included in the **chmod** command, the group owner should be the owner of all files created in the public_html subdirectory.
7. Make the changes described earlier in this chapter in the httpd.conf file associated with the **UserDir** directive.
8. Make the Apache web server reread the file.

You will have a chance to set this up in one of the chapter labs, and perhaps more (hint, hint!).

Password Protection for a Web Directory

In this exercise, you'll configure password protection for your regular user account on a subdirectory of **DocumentRoot**. This involves use of the **AuthType Basic**, **AuthName**, and **AuthUserFile** directives. This will be done with the standard Apache web site; virtual hosts are covered in the next major section.

1. Back up the main configuration file, httpd.conf from the /etc/httpd/conf directory. Then open up that file in a text editor.

2. Navigate below the line **<Directory "/var/www/html">**. Create a new stanza for a **DocumentRoot** subdirectory. One option is the /var/www/html/chapter directory. In the default version of httpd.conf, it's just before the commented options for the **UserDir** directive. The first and last directives in the stanza would look like

   ```
   <Directory "/var/www/html/chapter">
   </Directory>
   ```

3. Add the following directives: **AuthType Basic** to set up basic authentication, the **AuthName "Password Protected Test"** directive to configure a comment that you should see shortly, and the **AuthUserFile /etc/httpd/testpass** directive to point to a password file. Substitute your regular username for *testuser* in **Require user *testuser***.

   ```
   <Directory "/var/www/html/chapter">
        AuthType Basic
        AuthName "Password Protected Test"
        AuthUserFile /etc/httpd/testpass
        Require user testuser
   </Directory>
   ```

4. Check the syntax of your changes with either of the following commands.

   ```
   # httpd -t
   # httpd -S
   ```

5. Assuming the syntax checks out, make Apache reread the configuration files:

   ```
   # apachectl restart
   ```

   If you're concerned about currently connected users, make Apache reread the configuration file, without disconnections, with the **service httpd reload** command.

6. Add an appropriate index.html file to the /var/www/html/chapter directory. It's okay to use a text editor to enter a simple line such as "test was successful." No HTML coding is required.

7. Create the /etc/httpd/testpass file with an appropriate password. On my system, I created a web password for user michael in the noted file with the following command:

```
# htpasswd -c /etc/httpd/testpass michael
```

If you're adding another user, leave out the **-c** switch.

8. Test the result, preferably from another system. (In other words, make sure the firewall allows access from at least one remote system.)

9. You should now see a request for a username and password, with the comment associated with the **AuthName** directive. Enter the username and password just added to /etc/httpd/testpass and observe the result.

10. Close the browser, and restore any earlier configuration.

CERTIFICATION OBJECTIVE 14.04

Regular and Secure Virtual Hosts

Perhaps the most useful feature of Apache is its ability to handle multiple web sites on a single IP address. In a world where there are no more new IPv4 addresses available, that can be useful. To do so, you can configure virtual hosts for regular web sites in the main Apache configuration file, /etc/httpd/conf/httpd.conf. In that way, you can configure multiple domain names such as www.example.com and www.mheducation.com on the same IP address on the same Apache server.

on the job

The example.com, example.org, and example.net domain names cannot be registered and are officially reserved by the Internet Engineering Task Force (IETF) for documentation. Many other example.* domains are also reserved by appropriate authorities.

In the same fashion, you can also create multiple secure web sites accessible through the HTTPS protocol in the /etc/httpd/conf.d/ssl.conf configuration file. While the details vary, the basic directives associated with both regular and secure virtual hosts are the same.

If you use the ELinks text-based browser to test the connection to the regular and secure virtual web sites created in this chapter, there are several things to keep in mind.

- Make sure the /etc/hosts file of the client system includes the IP address with the specified fully qualified domain names (FQDNs). Duplicate IP addresses with different FQDNs are normal. (If there's a DNS server for the local network, you can skip this step.)

- Open the /etc/elinks.conf configuration file, and comment out the two standard directives in that file.

- To access a regular web site, make sure to include the protocol in front of the FQDN, such as http://vhost1.example.com or https://vhost2.example.com.

e x a m

ⓦ a t c h
     Be prepared to create multiple web sites on an Apache web server using virtual hosts. It's best to create separate VirtualHost containers for this purpose.

The beauty of **VirtualHost** containers is that you can copy virtually the same stanza to create as many web sites on an Apache server, limited only by the capabilities of the hardware. All that's required is one IP address. The next virtual host can be set up with a copy of the original **VirtualHost** container. All that you absolutely have to change is the **ServerName**. Most administrators will also change the **DocumentRoot**, but even that's not absolutely necessary. You'll see how that works for regular and secure virtual hosts in the following sections.

The Standard Virtual Host

As described earlier, Section 3 of the default httpd.conf includes sample commands that can be used to create one or more virtual hosts. To activate the virtual host feature, the first step is to activate this directive:

```
#NameVirtualHost *:80
```

To use a name-based host, leave the asterisk after this directive. Otherwise, set the IP address for the local network interface. It's often more reliable to substitute the IP address, as it avoids the delays sometimes associated with name resolution through a DNS server. However, you may need to create multiple name-based virtual hosts as well. Normally, I leave the asterisk in place.

You should already know that TCP/IP port 80 is the default for serving web pages. To direct all requests on this server via IP address 192.168.122.50 on port 80, you could substitute **<VirtualHost 192.168.122.50:80>** for the first line. But in most cases, you should leave that directive as is, to support the use of the same IP address for different web sites. (It also makes it possible for DHCP to work on that web server, but that's a more complex issue.)

```
#<VirtualHost *:80>
#      ServerAdmin webmaster@dummy-host.example.com
#      DocumentRoot /www/docs/dummy-host.example.com
#      ServerName dummy-host.example.com
#      ErrorLog logs/dummy-host.example.com-error_log
#      CustomLog logs/dummy-host.example.com-access_log common
#</VirtualHost>
```

If you've read the descriptions of the first two sections of the main part of the httpd.conf file, you should recognize all of these directives. However, each directive points to nonstandard files and directories. To review,

- Error messages are sent to the e-mail address defined by **ServerAdmin**.
- The web pages can be stored in the **DocumentRoot** directory. Make sure the SELinux security contexts of any **DocumentRoot** directory you create is consistent with the contexts of the default /var/www directory (and subdirectories). Apply the **chcon** and **semanage fcontext -a** commands as required to make the security contexts match.
- Clients can call this web site through the **ServerName**.

- The **ErrorLog** and **CustomLog** directives specify a *relative* log directory, relative to the **ServerRoot**. Unless you've created a different **ServerRoot** for this virtual host, these files can be found in the /etc/httpd/logs directory. Normally, that directory is soft linked to /var/logs/httpd.

You can add more directives to each virtual host stanza, to customize the settings for the virtual host relative to the main configuration file. You'll set up a CGI script in a virtual host later in this chapter, with some custom directives.

It's easy to configure a virtual host web site. Substitute the IP domain names, directories, files, and e-mail addresses of your choice. Create the **DocumentRoot** directory if it doesn't already exist. To that end, I've set up two virtual hosts with the following stanzas:

```
<VirtualHost *:80>
    ServerAdmin webmaster@vhost1.example.com
    DocumentRoot /www/docs/vhost1.example.com
    ServerName vhost1.example.com
    ErrorLog logs/vhost1.example.com-error_log
    CustomLog logs/vhost1.example.com-access_log common
</VirtualHost>
<VirtualHost *:80>
    ServerAdmin webmaster@vhost2.example.com
    DocumentRoot /www/docs/vhost2.example.com
    ServerName vhost2.example.com
    ErrorLog logs/vhost2.example.com-error_log
    CustomLog logs/vhost2.example.com-access_log common
</VirtualHost>
```

Make sure the SELinux contexts are appropriate. You can test the syntax of any configuration changes with the following command:

```
# httpd -t
```

Apache will verify your configuration or identify specific problems. When you run this command on the default configuration, you'll get the following message:

```
Syntax OK
```

If you've created multiple virtual hosts, you can check them as well with either of the following commands:

```
# httpd -S
# httpd -D DUMP_VHOSTS
```

The output should list the default and individual virtual hosts. For example, I see the following output from my server1.example.com RHEL 6 system:

```
VirtualHost configuration:
wildcard NameVirtualHosts and _default_ servers:
*:80               is a NameVirtualHost
  default server vhost1.example.com (/etc/httpd/conf/httpd.conf:1010)
  port 80 namevhost vhost1.example.com(/etc/httpd/conf/httpd.conf:1010)
  port 80 namevhost vhost2.example.com(/etc/httpd/conf/httpd.conf:1017)
*:443              is a NameVirtualHost
  default server vhost1.example.com (/etc/httpd/conf.d/ssl.conf:75)
  port 80 namevhost vhost1.example.com(/etc/httpd/conf.d/ssl.conf:75)
  port 80 namevhost vhost2.example.com(/etc/httpd/conf.d/ssl.conf:105)
Syntax OK
```

If a "using 127.0.0.1 for ServerName" error appears, you haven't assigned a value for the **ServerName** directive. In addition, you may want to set up the /etc/hosts file, or a DNS server for the local network, with the IP addresses for domain names like vhost1.example.com and vhost2.example.com.

Secure Virtual Hosts

If you're configuring a secure web server that conforms to the HTTPS protocol, Red Hat provides a different configuration file for this purpose: ssl.conf in the /etc/httpd/conf.d directory. If this file isn't available, you need to install the mod_ssl RPM. Before editing this file, back it up. The first active directive loads the SSL module:

```
LoadModule ssl_module modules/mod_ssl.so
```

Make sure the following **Listen** directive is active:

```
Listen 443
```

As suggested by the title, this configuration file includes a number of passphrase dialogues. Generally, no changes are required to these directives:

```
SSLPassPhraseDialog builtin
SSLSessionCache          shmcb:/var/cache/mod_ssl/scache(512000)
SSLSessionCacheTimeout  300
SSLMutex default
SSLRandomSeed startup file:/dev/urandom  256
SSLRandomSeed connect builtin
SSLCryptoDevice builtin
```

Before the virtual host containers, you'll need to include a **NameVirtualHost** directive for Port 443 before you can configure multiple virtual hosts in this file. It's the same directive used in the main Apache configuration file, just pointed to the standard HTTPS port:

```
NameVirtualHost *:443
```

Now you can set up virtual hosts with the directives that follow. The default ssl.conf file also has a model virtual host container. But it is incomplete and a bit difficult to read with all the comments. So a sample of the revised ssl.conf configuration file, focused on the virtual host container for the vhost1.example.com system, is shown in Figure 14-9.

In the default version of the ssl.conf file, examine the **<VirtualHost _default_:443>** container. Compare it to the **<VirtualHost *:80>** container in httpd.conf. Some changes are required. First, you should replace **_default_** in the **VirtualHost** container with an asterisk (*):

```
<VirtualHost *:443>
```

FIGURE 14-9

Secure virtual host container for vhost1.example .com

```
##
NameVirtualHost *:443

<VirtualHost *:443>
    DocumentRoot /www/securedocs/vhost1.example.com
    ServerName vhost1.example.com
    ErrorLog logs/ssl_error_log
    TransferLog logs/ssl_access_log
    LogLevel warn

    SSLEngine on
    SSLProtocol all -SSLv2
    SSLCipherSuite ALL:!ADH:!EXPORT:!SSLv2:RC4+RSA:+HIGH:+MEDIUM:+LOW
    SSLCertificateFile /etc/pki/tls/certs/localhost.crt
    SSLCertificateKeyFile /etc/pki/tls/private/localhost.key

    <Files ~ "\.(cgi|shtml|phtml|php3?)$">
        SSLOptions +StdEnvVars
    </Files>

    <Directory "/var/www/cgi-bin">
        SSLOptions +StdEnvVars
    </Directory>

    SetEnvIf User-Agent ".*MSIE.*" \
            nokeepalive ssl-unclean-shutdown \
            downgrade-1.0 force-response-1.0

    CustomLog logs/ssl_request_log \
        "%t %h %{SSL_PROTOCOL}x %{SSL_CIPHER}x \"%r\" %b"

</VirtualHost>
```

You should also include **ServerAdmin**, **DocumentRoot**, and **ServerName** directives. Example directives that would be consistent with the virtual hosts created in the preceding section include:

```
ServerAdmin webmaster@vhost1.example.com
DocumentRoot /www/securedocs/vhost1.example.com
ServerName vhost1.example.com
```

While the **DocumentRoot** directive can be set to any directory, it's appropriate if only for organizational purposes, to keep the files associated with each virtual host in a dedicated directory.

The standard error log directives can be changed. In fact, if you want log information for each secure web site to be set up in different files, they should be changed. But for our purposes, you can stick with the default options shown here. Based on the **ServerRoot** directive from the httpd.conf file, these log files can be found in the /var/log/httpd directory.

```
ErrorLog logs/ssl_error_log
TransferLog logs/ssl_access_log
LogLevel warn
CustomLog logs/ssl_request_log \
          "%t %h %{SSL_PROTOCOL}x %{SSL_CIPHER}x \"%r\" %b"
```

The SSL directives in the file are based on the default certificates for the localhost system. Shortly, you'll see how to configure a new SSL certificate. The following five directives, in order, activate SSL, use the more secure SSL version 2, support a variety of encryption ciphers, point to the default SSL certificate, as well as the SSL key file.

```
SSLEngine on
SSLProtocol all -SSLv2
SSLCipherSuite ALL:!ADH:!EXPORT:!SSLv2:RC4+RSA:+HIGH:+MEDIUM:+LOW
SSLCertificateFile /etc/pki/tls/certs/localhost.crt
SSLCertificateKeyFile /etc/pki/tls/private/localhost.key
```

The stanza that follows relates to files with extensions associated with dynamic content. For such files, along with any files in the standard CGI directory, standard SSL environment variables are used:

```
<Files ~ "\.(cgi|shtml|phtml|php3?)$">
    SSLOptions +StdEnvVars
</Files>
<Directory "/var/www/cgi-bin">
    SSLOptions +StdEnvVars
</Directory>
```

The following stanza deals with situations associated with the Microsoft Internet Explorer as a browser client:

```
SetEnvIf User-Agent ".*MSIE.*" \
         nokeepalive ssl-unclean-shutdown \
         downgrade-1.0 force-response-1.0
```

Of course, the virtual host container ends with the following directive:

```
</VirtualHost>
```

When Apache is configured with a secure site, regular GUI clients that access that site get a warning about the secure web host like that seen for so many web sites on the Internet, as shown in Figure 14-10.

Create a New SSL Certificate

While the default SSL certificate listed in the ssl.conf configuration file can work for basic configuration, you may want to either create a specialized local certificate or otherwise use an actual certificate purchased from a certificate authority (CA) such as VeriSign and Thawte.

FIGURE 14-10

A warning about secure hosts

Navigate to the /etc/pki/tls/certs directory. Note the file named Makefile in that directory. The code in that file can be used by the **make** command to create a new certificate for each virtual host. Unless you purchase an actual certificate from a CA, clients will still see screens such as that shown in Figure 14-10.

But you may need to know how to set up a "self-signed certificate." To that end, the following command, when run from the /etc/pki/tls/certs directory, automatically generates a private key and a certificate for the cited FQDN, as shown in Figure 14-11.

```
# genkey vhost2.example.com
```

The **genkey** command is convenient, as when the process is complete, it automatically writes the key to the /etc/pki/tls/private directory and writes the certificate to the /etc/pki/tls/certs directory.

e x a m
ⓦ a t c h   *The published outline for the Red Hat prep course for the RHCE (RH254) specifies the deployment of "an SSL-encapsulated web service." SSL certificates are part of that deployment* *process. If you're asked to create a certificate during an exam, keep the size of the key to the minimum allowed. The process of generating even 512-bit keys can take several minutes.*

| FIGURE 14-11 |

Prompts for a self-signed certificate

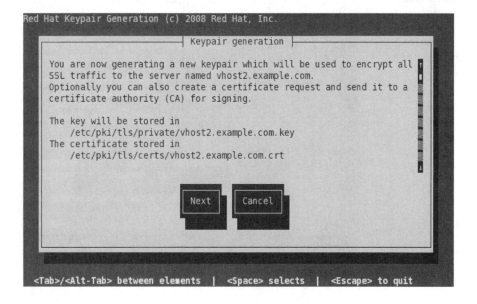

For the purpose of this section, select Next to continue. In the step shown in Figure 14-12, you'd select a key size. What you select depends on the time available and the need for security. The Linux random number generator may require additional activity; this may be an excellent time to put the process aside and do something else.

If you have nothing else to do and need to speed up the process, run some of the scripts in the /etc/cron.daily directory. Run some of the **find** commands described in Chapter 3. Click a bunch of times in an open terminal.

Once a key is generated, you're prompted with a question, whether to generate a Certificate Request (CSR) to send to a CA. Unless you're actually preparing to purchase a valid certificate, select No to continue. You're prompted to encrypt the key with a passphrase, as shown in Figure 14-13.

If security is most important, you should select the Encrypt The Private Key option. If speed is important, avoid the option. Make a choice and select Next to continue. If you did not select the Encrypt The Private Key option, you'll be taken immediately to the certificate details shown in Figure 14-14. Make any appropriate changes and select Next to continue.

If successful, you'll see output similar to that shown in Figure 14-15.

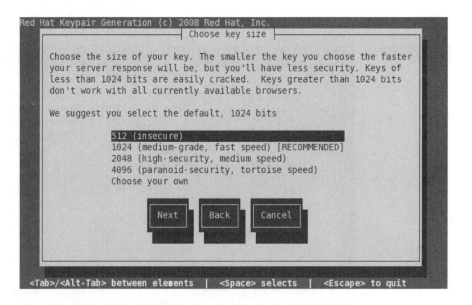

FIGURE 14-12

Select a key size for an SSL certificate.

FIGURE 14-13

Option to
protect with
a passphrase

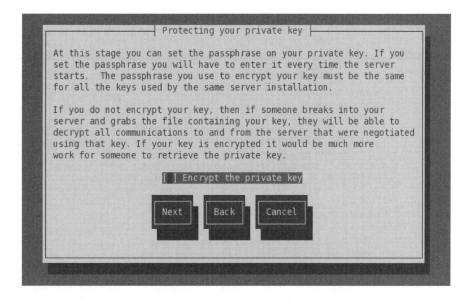

Test Pages

You may need to create some index.html files to test virtual hosts in various
situations, to test various pre-production configurations, or even during an exam.
Fortunately, the Red Hat exams don't test knowledge of HTML. You could use

FIGURE 14-14

SSL certificate
details

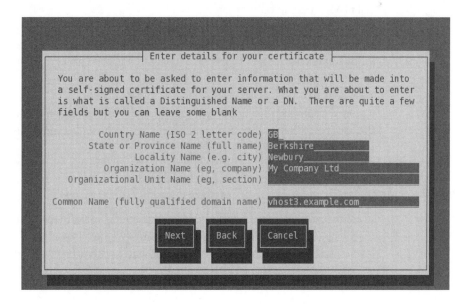

```
[root@server1 certs]# genkey vhost2.example.com
/usr/bin/keyutil -c makecert -g 512 -s "CN=vhost2.example.com, O=My Company Ltd, L=
Newbury, ST=Berkshire, C=GB" -v 1 -a -z /etc/pki/tls/.rand.26412 -o /etc/pki/tls/ce
rts/vhost2.example.com.crt -k /etc/pki/tls/private/vhost2.example.com.key
cmdstr: makecert

cmd_CreateNewCert
command:  makecert
keysize = 512 bits
subject = CN=vhost2.example.com, O=My Company Ltd, L=Newbury, ST=Berkshire, C=GB
valid for 1 months
random seed from /etc/pki/tls/.rand.26412
output will be written to /etc/pki/tls/certs/vhost2.example.com.crt
output key written to /etc/pki/tls/private/vhost2.example.com.key


Generating key. This may take a few moments...

Made a key
Opened tmprequest for writing
(null) Copying the cert pointer
Created a certificate
Wrote 486 bytes of encoded data to /etc/pki/tls/private/vhost2.example.com.key
Wrote the key to:
/etc/pki/tls/private/vhost2.example.com.key
[root@server1 certs]# █
```

Apache's default web page. You can change this or any other web page with a text-
or HTML-specific editor.

You can even save a simple text file as index.html. For the purpose of this chapter,
all I put into the index.html file for the regular vhost1.example.com web site is the
following text:

```
Test web page for Virtual Host 1
```

Once appropriate changes were made to Apache configuration files, I restarted
the service. When I then ran the **elinks http://vhost1.example.com** command, the
screen shown in Figure 14-16 appeared.

Syntax Checkers

In many cases, the **apachectl restart** and the **/etc/init.d/httpd restart** commands will
reveal syntax problems. But that's just in many cases. In some cases, you might try to
restart Apache, proceed to test the result with a client browser, and get frustrated,

FIGURE 14-16

A test web page

only to find that Apache did not start because of a syntax error. To minimize the risk of that issue, the following command checks the work that you've done to edit Apache configuration files:

```
# httpd -S
```

If no problems are found, you should be able to start the local web server and connect from a client with a browser request.

Apache Troubleshooting

When the right Apache packages are installed, the default configuration normally creates a running system. Basic syntax can be checked with the **httpd -t** command. But if you're setting up a real web site, you probably want more than just the test page. Before making changes, back up the httpd.conf Apache configuration file. If something goes wrong, you can always start over.

Some Apache errors fall into the following categories:

■ **Error message about an inability to bind to an address** Another network process may already be using the default http port (80). Alternatively, your computer is running httpd as a normal user (not the user apache) with a port below 1024.

■ **Network addressing or routing errors** Double-check network settings. For more information on network configuration, see Chapter 3's section on network configuration and troubleshooting.

■ **Apache isn't running** Check the error_log in the /var/log/httpd directory.

■ **Apache isn't running after a reboot**   Run **chkconfig --list httpd**. Make sure Apache (httpd) is set to start at appropriate runlevels during the boot process with the command

```
# chkconfig httpd on
```

■ **You need to stop Apache**   Send the parent process a **TERM** signal, based on its PID. By default, this is located in /var/run/httpd.pid. You kill Apache with a command such as

```
#kill -TERM /cat /var/run/httpd.pid'
```

■ Alternatively, you can use the **apachectl stop** command.

Apache administration is a necessary skill for any Linux system administrator. You should develop the ability to install, configure, and troubleshoot Apache quickly. You should also be able to set up and customize virtual web sites.

EXERCISE 14-5

Set Up a Virtual Web Server

In this exercise, you'll set up a web server with a virtual web site. You can use this technique with different directories to set up additional virtual web sites on the same Apache server.

1. Back up the httpd.conf file from the /etc/httpd/conf directory.

2. Add a virtual web site for the fictional company LuvLinex, with a URL of www.example.com. Don't forget to modify the **NameVirtualHost** directive. Use the sample comments at the end of the httpd.conf file for hints as needed.

3. Assign the **DocumentRoot** directive to the /luvlinex directory. (Don't forget to create this directory on your system as well.)

4. Open the /luvlinex/index.html file in a text editor. Add a simple line in text format such as

```
This is the placeholder for the LuvLinex Web site.
```

5. Save this file.

6. If you've enabled SELinux on this system, you'll have to apply the **chcon** command to this directory:

```
# chcon -R -u system_u /luvlinex/
# chcon -R -t httpd_sys_content_t /luvlinex/
```

7. To make sure the changes survive a SELinux relabel, the following command should document the change in the file_contexts.local file in the /etc/selinux/targeted/contexts/files directory.

```
# semanage fcontext -a -s system_u -t httpd_sys_content_t /luvlinux/
```

8. If you've created a DNS service, as discussed in Chapter 11, update the associated database. Otherwise, update /etc/hosts with www.example.com and the appropriate IP address.

9. If you want to check the syntax, run the **httpd -t** and **httpd -D DUMP_VHOSTS** commands.

10. Remember to restart the Apache service; the proper way is with the **apachectl restart** command.

11. Navigate to a remote system. Update the remote /etc/hosts if appropriate. Open the browser of your choice. Test the access to the configured web site (www.example.com).

12. Close the browser on the remote system. Restore the original httpd.conf configuration file.

CERTIFICATION OBJECTIVE 14.05

Deploy a Basic CGI Application

No programming experience is required. When you see the RHCE objective to "Deploy a basic CGI application," the requirement is easier than it looks. In fact, the steps required can be read from the Apache documentation, available from the httpd-manual package. When installed, navigate to http://localhost/manual page. Apache documentation should appear. Select CGI: Dynamic content for detailed directions, explained in the following sections.

Apache Configuration Changes for CGI Files

To allow Apache to read CGI files, the httpd.conf file includes the **LoadModule cgi_module** directive. To make it easier for clients to find CGI files through their browsers, Apache includes the **ScriptAlias** directive. For example, the following **ScriptAlias** directive links the cgi-bin subdirectory to the default /var/www/cgi-bin directory:

```
ScriptAlias /cgi-bin/ "/var/www/cgi-bin"
```

With this **ScriptAlias** directive, if the web site is server1.example.com, scripts can be found in the http://server1.example.com/cgi-bin/ URL.

Alternatively, you can set up CGI scripts in a directory other than /var/www/cgi-bin and change the reference accordingly. However, the associated <Directory> container does not allow executable scripts:

```
<Directory /var/www/cgi-bin>
    AllowOverride None
    Options None
    Order allow,deny
    Allow from all
</Directory>
```

As suggested in the Apache web server documentation available from the httpd-manual package, you'd need to make changes to allow CGI scripts to actually be executable by the Apache server:

```
<Directory /var/www/cgi-bin>
    AllowOverride None
    Options ExecCGI
    AddHandler cgi-script .pl
    Order allow,deny
    Allow from all
</Directory>
```

The **AllowOverride None** command prevents regular users from changing permissions/settings in that directory. Otherwise, smarter users could read the CGI files in the /var/www/cgi-bin directory, a security risk. The **Options ExecCGI** line supports executable scripts in the noted directory. The **AddHandler** directive associates CGI scripts with files with the .pl extension. The **Order allow,deny** command sets up authorization checks; **Allow from all** lets all users run scripts in this directory.

If CGI scripts are required for one of the previously configured virtual hosts, you'll need to set up a different **ScriptAlias** and a corresponding <Directory> container. For the vhost1.example.com site described previously, I add the following directive:

```
ScriptAlias /cgi-bin/ /www/docs/vhost1.example.com/cgi-bin/
```

The Apache documentation continues with instructions on how you can write a simple CGI script.

Set Up a Simple CGI Script

The Apache documentation includes instructions on how to set up a simple CGI script in the Perl programming language. Make sure the httpd-manual package is installed, and the local httpd service is active. In a browser, navigate to http://localhost/manual. Under the How-To / Tutorials section, click CGI: Dynamic Content. Scroll down to the "Writing a CGI Program" section.

In this section, the Apache documentation suggests a simple Perl script, called hello.pl, based on the following code:

```
#!/usr/bin/perl
print "Content-type: text/html\n\n";
print "Hello, World!";
```

The first line is similar to the **#!/bin/bash** found in many scripts; in this case, **perl** is the command interpreter. The content type is declared, followed by two carriage returns (as symbolized by the **\n**). The final line prints the expression commonly used for introductory program scripts. Such scripts need to be executable, with 755 permissions. In other words, once the hello.pl file is saved, you'd apply the noted permissions with the following command:

```
# chmod 755 hello.pl
```

Run the **ls -Z** command on the script. In the /var/www/cgi-bin directory, it should inherit the httpd_sys_script_exec_t SELinux file type associated with the directory. If necessary, you can apply the file type to the file and directory with the **chcon** command, and then make sure the file type stays applied after a SELinux relabel with the **semanage fcontext -a** command. Both commands were described earlier in this chapter and in Chapter 11.

But in most cases, you'll be setting up multiple web sites as virtual hosts in Apache configuration files. If you didn't already add the **Options ExecCGI** and **AddHandler cgi-script .pl** directives described earlier, they should be added to the virtual host container, along with an appropriate **ScriptAlias** directive:

```
Options ExecCGI
AddHandler cgi-script .pl
ScriptAlias /cgi-bin/ /www/docs/vhost1.example.com/cgi-bin/
```

Then you'd copy the hello.pl script to the noted directory and make it executable by all users. Don't forget to make sure the script and directory have the same SELinux contexts (httpd_sys_script_exec_t) as scripts in the /var/www/html/cgi-bin directory. To make sure the change survives a relabel, you also should apply the following command to that directory:

```
# semanage fcontext -a -s system_u -t httpd_sys_script_exec_t
/www/docs/vhost1.example.com/cgi-bin/
```

Connections to a Web Site

Once a CGI script is configured, you should be able to access that script from a client browser. For the purpose of this exercise, assume the hello.pl Perl script has been configured on the server1.example.com system. You should then be able to review the result from a remote system with the **elinks http://vhost1.example.com/cgi-bin/hello.pl** command. If successful, the following words should show up in the body of the browser:

```
Hello, world!
```

On occasion, you may see an error message such as "Internal Server Error." The most likely cause is a Perl script that does not have executable permissions for the user named apache. To repeat, that's normally addressed by giving that Perl script 755 permissions.

SCENARIO & SOLUTION

You need to configure one web site.	Install Apache, configure appropriate files in the /var/www/html directory.
You need to configure multiple web sites.	With Apache, use the <VirtualHost> containers at the end of the httpd.conf file as a template for as many web sites as needed.
You need to configure a secure web site.	Configure a virtual host in the ssl.conf file in the /etc/httpd/conf.d directory.
You need a dedicated SSL certificate for the www.example.org web site.	From the /etc/pki/tls/certs directory, run the **genkey www.example.org** command.
The Apache service is not running after a reboot.	Make sure the httpd service starts in appropriate runlevels with the **chkconfig --list httpd** command. If that's okay, check the contents of the error_log in the /var/log/httpd directory.
CGI scripts in Apache are not running.	In the Apache configuration file, make sure the ExecCGI option is active; the AddHandler directive specifies **cgi-script .pl**, the ScriptAlias is pointed to the appropriate directory; the script is executable by all users and matches default SELinux contexts in the /var/www/cgi-bin directory.

CERTIFICATION SUMMARY

Apache is the most popular web server in use today. Key packages can be installed from the "Web Server" package group. The httpd-manual package includes a locally browsable manual that can help with other Apache configuration tasks, even during an exam. Key configuration files include httpd.conf in the /etc/httpd/conf directory and ssl.conf in the /etc/httpd/conf.d directory. The httpd.conf and ssl.conf files are organized in <VirtualHost> containers. With the help of sample stanzas in both noted configuration files, you can create virtual regular and secure hosts for multiple web sites on one system, even if only one IP address is available. Related log files are stored in the /var/log/httpd directory.

You can allow access to Apache through ports 80 and 443, to some or all systems with **iptables**-command-based firewalls. Apache files and directories are associated with several different SELinux contexts. Different Apache functions may be regulated by a variety of different SELinux boolean settings.

The **Listen** and **NameVirtualHost** directives direct traffic to the Apache web server to ports like 80 and 443, along with specified virtual hosts. Host- and user-based security can also be set up within Apache configuration files with commands like **htpasswd** and directives such as **Allow** and **Deny**.

With the right security options, user- and group-managed directories are possible. In fact, there's a commented stanza that can enable directories in user home directories. Group-managed directories are somewhat more complex, combining aspects of Apache-based user directories and shared group directories discussed in Chapter 8. Also in security, new certificates can be created for a specific host like www.example.org from the /etc/pki/tls/certs directory with a command like **genkey www.example.org**.

The configuration of CGI content on an Apache web site is easier than it looks. In fact, detailed information on the process is included with Apache documentation, including a Perl script that you can use to confirm that the resulting configuration works.

TWO-MINUTE DRILL

Here are some of the key points from the certification objectives in Chapter 14.

The Apache Web Server

❑ Red Hat Enterprise Linux includes the Apache web server, which is currently used by more than twice as many Internet web sites as all other web servers combined.

❑ You can install Apache and associated packages as part of the "Web Server" package group.

❑ Apache configuration files include httpd.conf in the /etc/httpd/conf directory and ssl.conf in the /etc/httpd/conf.d directory.

❑ Log information for Apache is available in the /var/log/httpd directory.

Standard Apache Security Configuration

❑ Apache can be secured through **iptables** rules and various SELinux booleans and contexts.

❑ Apache supports security by specifying active ports through the **Listen** and **NameVirtualHost** directives.

❑ Apache supports host-based security by IP address or domain name.

❑ Apache supports user-based security by password, with the help of the **htpasswd** command.

Specialized Apache Directories

❑ Apache makes it easy to set up access to user home directories in their public_html/ subdirectories.

❑ Group-managed directories can be configured in a fashion similar to user home directories.

Regular and Secure Virtual Hosts

❑ You can configure multiple web sites on your server, even with only one IP address. This is possible through the use of virtual hosts.

❑ The RHEL configuration supports the configuration of virtual hosts for regular web sites at the end of the /etc/httpd/conf/httpd.conf file.

❑ The RHEL configuration supports the configuration of secure virtual hosts for regular web sites at the end of the /etc/httpd/conf.d/ssl.conf file.

❑ SSL certificates can be created with the **genkey** command, when run from the /etc/pki/tls/certs directory.

Deploy a Basic CGI Application

❑ The use of CGI content depends on configuration options like ScriptAlias, ExecCGI, and AddHandler cgi-script.

❑ Standard CGI scripts require 755 permissions. If needed, sample instructions are available in the Apache manual available from the httpd-manual package.

SELF TEST

The following questions will help measure your understanding of the material presented in this chapter. As no multiple-choice questions appear on the Red Hat exams, no multiple-choice questions appear in this book. These questions exclusively test your understanding of the chapter. It is okay if you have another way of performing a task. Getting results, not memorizing trivia, is what counts on the Red Hat exams. There may be more than one answer to many of these questions.

The Apache Web Server

1. What is the Apache directive that specifies the base directory for configuration and log files?

    _____

2. Once you've modified httpd.conf, what command would make Apache reread this file, without kicking off currently connected users?

    _____

3. What directive specifies the TCP/IP port associated with Apache?

    _____

Standard Apache Security Configuration

4. What command creates the /etc/httpd/passwords file and configures a password for user elizabeth?

    _____

5. If you see the following directives limiting access within the stanza for a virtual host, what computers are allowed access?

    ```
    Order Allow,Deny
    Allow from 192.168.0.0/24
    ```

    _____

6. What standard ports do you need to open in a firewall to allow access to a regular web site and a secure one?

    _____

Specialized Apache Directories

7. What regular permissions would work with a home directory that's shared via Apache?

_____

8. What regular permissions would work with a shared group directory that's also shared via Apache?

_____

Regular and Secure Virtual Hosts

9. What file does RHEL provide to help configure a virtual host as a secure server?

_____

10. If you're creating a name-based virtual host, how many IP addresses would be required for three virtual servers?

_____

11. To verify the configuration of one or more virtual hosts, what switch can you use with the **httpd** command?

_____

Deploy a Basic CGI Application

12. What option with the **Options** directive supports dynamic CGI content in an Apache configuration file?

_____

LAB QUESTIONS

Several of these labs involve configuration exercises. You should do these exercises on test machines only. It's assumed that you're running these exercises on virtual machines such as KVM. For this chapter, it's also assumed that you may be changing the configuration of a physical host system for such virtual machines.

Red Hat presents its exams electronically. For that reason, the labs in this and future chapters are available from the CD that accompanies the book, in the Chapter14/ subdirectory. In case you haven't yet set up RHEL 6 on a system, refer to Chapter 1 for installation instructions.

The answers for each lab follow the Self Test answers for the fill-in-the-blank questions.

SELF TEST ANSWERS

The Apache Web Server

1. The **ServerRoot** directive sets the default directory for the Apache server. Any files and directories not otherwise configured—or configured as a relative directory—are set relative to ServerRoot.

2. There are three basic ways to make Apache reread the configuration file without restarting the service. You can keep Apache running and make it reread the file with a command such as **apachectl graceful** or the **/etc/init.d/httpd reload** command. The **service httpd reload** command is also an acceptable answer.

3. The **Listen** directive specifies the TCP port associated with Apache.

Standard Apache Security Configuration

4. The command that creates the /etc/httpd/passwords file and configures a password for user elizabeth is **htpasswd -c /etc/httpd/passwords elizabeth**. If /etc/httpd/passwords already exists, all that's required is **htpasswd elizabeth**.

5. As described in the chapter, the **Order Allow,Deny** directive denies access to all systems by default, except those explicitly allowed access. So access is limited to computers on the 192.168.0.0/24 network.

6. The standard ports you need to open in a firewall to allow access to regular and secure web sites are 80 and 443.

Specialized Apache Directories

7. The associated permissions are 701, executable permissions for other users. As "regular permissions" are specified, ACLs are not an option.

8. The associated permissions are 2771, which combines SGID permissions, standard permissions for a shared group directory, and executable permissions for other users. As "regular permissions" are specified, ACLs are not an option.

Regular and Secure Virtual Hosts

9. The file associated with secure servers for virtual hosts is ssl.conf in the /etc/httpd/conf.d directory.

10. One IP address is required for a name-based virtual server, no matter how many virtual sites are configured.

11. To check your configuration of virtual hosts, you can use one of two switches with the **httpd** command: **httpd -S** checks the configuration file, including virtual host settings. Alternatively, **httpd -D DUMP_VHOSTS** focuses on the virtual host configuration, and is therefore also an acceptable answer.

Deploy a Basic CGI Application

12. The **Options ExecCGI** directive is commonly used in Apache-configured directories that contain CGI scripts such as Perl programs.

LAB ANSWERS

Lab 1

First, make sure the Apache web server is installed. If an **rpm -q httpd** command tells you that it is missing, the Web Server package group has not yet been installed. The most efficient way to do so is with the **yum groupinstall "Web Server"** command. (To find appropriate package group names, run the **yum grouplist** command.) This assumes a proper connection to a repository, as discussed in Chapter 7.

To configure Apache to start, run the **apachectl start** command. To make sure it starts the next time the system is booted, run the **chkconfig httpd on** command.

Once Apache is installed, you should be able to access it from a browser via http://localhost. From the default Apache configuration file, you can verify that the **DocumentRoot** points to the /var/www/html directory. You can then copy the index.html file from the /usr/share/doc/HTML/en-US directory to the /var/www/html directory. Then you can test the result by navigating once again to http://localhost. If you did not copy the other files associated with the default home page, the display will be missing some icons, but that's not an issue for this lab.

Lab 2

This is an informational lab. When complete, you should be able to refer to these Apache configuration hints in situations where this book and the Internet are not available, such as during a Red Hat exam.

Of course, you should study these tips in advance. If you forget the syntax of one or two commands, these files can be a lifesaver.

Lab 3

This lab requires that you create two virtual hosts in the main Apache configuration file, /etc/httpd/conf/httpd.conf. While there are certainly other methods to set up different virtual hosts, the description in this lab answer is one method. And it is important that you know at least one method to create a virtual host. One way to make this happen is with the following steps:

1. The **ServerRoot** directive for the system sets the default directory for the Apache server. Any files and directories not otherwise configured—or configured as a relative directory—are set relative to **ServerRoot**. Don't change this unless you're ready to adjust the SELinux contexts of the new directory accordingly.

2. Set the **NameVirtualHost** directive to the port (80) serving your intended network audience. Don't assign any IP addresses.

3. Add separate **VirtualHost** containers with settings appropriate for the big.example.com and small.example.com systems.

4. Assign the **ServerAdmin** to the e-mail address of this web site's administrator.

5. Configure a unique **DocumentRoot** directory for each virtual host.

6. Set the first **ServerName** to big.example.com.

7. Add **ErrorLog** and **CustomLog** directives, and set them to unique filenames in the /etc/httpd/logs directory (which is linked to the /var/logs/httpd directory). With the default **ServerRoot**, you can use a relative logs directory, such as the following:

```
ErrorLog logs/big.example.com-error_log
```

8. Make sure to close the **VirtualHost** container (with a **</VirtualHost>** directive at the end of the stanza).

9. Repeat the process for the second web site, making sure to set the second **ServerName** to **small.example.com**.

10. Close and save the httpd.conf file with your changes.

11. Create any new directories that you configured with the **DocumentRoot** directives.

12. Create index.html text files in each directory defined by the associated new **DocumentRoot** directives. Don't worry about HTML code; a text file is fine for the purpose of this lab.

13. Make sure these domain names are configured in the authoritative DNS server or in the /etc/hosts file. For example, if the Apache server is on a system with IP address 192.168.122.150 (such as tester1.example.com), you could add the following lines to /etc/hosts:

```
192.168.122.150 big.example.com
192.168.122.150 small.example.com
```

The same data should be included in the /etc/hosts file of a remote client system.

14. Use the Security Level Configuration tool (**system-config-securitylevel**) utility to allow HTTP data through the firewall, as discussed in Chapter 10.

15. You'll need to configure appropriate SELinux file types on the directory associated with the **DocumentRoot**. For example, if that directory is /virt1, one way to do so is with the following commands:

```
# chcon -R -u system_u /virt1/
# chcon -R -t httpd_sys_content_t /virt1
```

In addition, you'll need to set up the file_contexts.local file in /etc/selinux/targeted/contexts/ files directory with a command such as

```
# semanage fcontext -a -s system_u -t httpd_sys_script_exec_t /virt1
```

16. Make sure to run the **apachectl graceful** command (or something similar) to make Apache reread the httpd.conf configuration file, with the changes you've made.

17. Now you can test the results. Navigate to a remote system, and try to access the newly created web sites in the browser of your choice. If it works, the big.example.com and small.example.com domain names should display the index.html files created for each web site.

18. If there are problems, check the syntax with the **httpd -t** and **httpd -S** commands. Check the log files in the /var/log/httpd directory.

Lab 4

This lab should be straightforward; when it is complete, you should find the following two files, which can be used to support a virtual host for a secure version of the big.example.com web site:

```
/etc/pki/tls/certs/big.example.com.crt
/etc/pki/tls/private/big.example.com.key
```

Corresponding files for the small.example.com system should also now exist in these directories. The process is based on standard responses to the questions generated by the **genkey big.example.com** and **genkey small.example.com** commands.

Lab 5

The basics of this lab are straightforward. You'll need to repeat the same basic steps that performed in Lab 3 and use the certificate and key files created in Lab 4. One difference is that secure web sites are generally configured in the /etc/httpd/conf.d/ssl.conf file. In addition, you should be concerned about the following:

1. While not absolutely required, it's a good practice to set up the **DocumentRoot** in a directory different from a regular web server. Otherwise, the same web page will appear for both the regular and secure versions of a web site.

2. It's a good practice to configure the **ErrorLog** and **CustomLog** with appropriate filenames, to help identify that information is from the secure version of a given web site.

3. It's helpful to copy the SSL directives from the template SSL virtual host in the ssl.conf file. All directives can apply to the secure versions of the big.example.com and small.example.com web sites. The only difference is in the SSLCertificateFile and SSLCertificateKeyFile directives:

```
SSLCertificateFile /etc/pki/tls/certs/big.example.com.crt

SSLCertificateKeyFile /etc/pki/tls/private/big.example.com.key
```

Of course, you'd substitute small.example.com for big.example.big for the noted directives in the secure virtual host stanza for that web site.

Lab 6

In the default httpd.conf file, the configuration of user home directories requires that you enable the UserDir directive. You can then customize the commented stanza associated with user home directories. If successful, only one user is allowed access to his home directory through the Apache web server from a client browser. It is understood that the authentication database file for that directory may lead to a different password for that user.

In general, you may see directives such as the following within the container for the given home page:

```
AuthType Basic
AuthName "Just for one user"
AuthUserFile /etc/httpd/oneuser
Require user michael
```

As suggested in the chapter, the home directory should have regular executable permissions for other users, or at least for the user named apache through ACLs. In addition, access won't be allowed unless you've set the httpd_enable_homedirs SELinux boolean. You'll also need to set up user michael in the authentication database for this directory with the **htpasswd -c /etc/httpd/oneuser michael** command.

Lab 7

The process required to set up a group-managed directory is a hybrid. The overall basic steps are as follows:

- Create a regular user and group named techsupport. While not required, it can be helpful to configure that user with a higher UID and GID, to avoid interfering with other future users and groups.

- Make the other users a member of that group named techsupport.

- Set up appropriate permissions to support access by members of the techsupport group, normally 2770 permissions. It should also include either regular executable permissions by other users, or executable permissions by the user named apache.

- Create a public_html/ subdirectory of the new user's home directory.

- Set up an index.html file in that subdirectory. It should already be set with ownership by the techsupport group.

Lab 8

The specified hello.pl script should include something like the following entries:

```
#!/usr/bin/perl
print "Content-type: text/html\n\n";
print "Hello World";
```

That script should be located in the directory specified by a **ScriptAlias /cgi-bin/** directive, in the big.example.com virtual host container. That container should also include the **Options ExecCGI** and **AddHandler cgi-script .pl** directives. While it's normally best to have scripts in the same DirectoryRoot as that configured for a virtual host, it's not required.

In addition, the permissions on the hello.pl file should be set to 755, and the SELinux contexts on the file (and directory) should be of the httpd_sys_script_exec_t file type. Of course, you'll have run an appropriate **semanage fcontext -a** command to make the change permanent, with the SELinux file type documented in the file_contexts.local file in the /etc/selinux/targeted/contexts/files directory. In any case, a successful result is as suggested in the lab question.

15

The Samba File Server

S amba is the Linux implementation of the networking protocols used to connect Microsoft operating systems. Microsoft networking is based on the Common Internet File System (CIFS), which was developed from the Server Message Block (SMB) protocol. Samba was developed as a freely available SMB server for all Unix-related operating systems, including Linux, and has been upgraded to support CIFS.

Samba interacts with CIFS so transparently that Microsoft clients cannot tell your Linux server from a genuine Windows Server, and with Samba on Linux there are no server, client, or client access licenses to purchase. If you can learn to edit the main Samba configuration file from the command line interface, you can configure Samba quickly. In its optional repository, RHEL 6 includes a GUI configuration tool—the Samba Web Administration Tool.

Learn to test network services such as Samba. These are services that you might configure and/or troubleshoot on the Red Hat exams. Take some time to understand the configuration files associated with each of these services, and practice making them work on different Linux systems. In some cases, two or more systems running Linux will be useful to practice what you learn in this chapter.

INSIDE THE EXAM

This chapter directly addresses two RHCE objectives related to Samba File System services. When you're finished with this chapter, you'll know how to

- Provide network shares to specific clients
- Provide network shares suitable for group collaboration

With Samba, communications is seamless with Microsoft clients. But as you won't have access to Microsoft Windows during the Red Hat exams, you'll see how Samba communications are also seamless with other Linux cli-

ents. Shares can be limited to specific clients with Samba and other security options.

Samba also provides support for group collaboration, as does Apache in Chapter 14. The principles are the same as the way group directories were configured on Linux in Chapter 8.

Of course, you can't forget the standard requirements for all network services, discussed in Chapters 10 and 11. To review, you need to install the service, make it work with SELinux, make sure it starts on boot, configure the service for basic operation, and set up user- and host-based security.

CERTIFICATION OBJECTIVE 15.01

Samba Services

Microsoft's CIFS was built on the Server Message Block (SMB) protocol. SMB was developed in the 1980s by IBM, Microsoft, and Intel as a way to share files and printers over a network.

As Microsoft developed SMB into CIFS, the Samba developers have upgraded Samba accordingly. Samba services provide a stable, reliable, fast, and highly compatible file and print sharing service that allows your computer to act as a client, a member server, a Primary Domain Controller (PDC), or a member of an Active Directory (AD) service on Microsoft-based networks. While Samba does not include every feature built into the latest Microsoft networks, I have confidence that it will in the near future.

on the job

I look forward to the final release of Samba 4.0, which will make it possible for Linux to act as an AD controller on a Microsoft-based network. RHEL 6 includes a preliminary version of Samba 4.0 and may include it in the lifetime of RHEL 6.

SMB network communication over a Microsoft-based network is also known as the Network Basic Input/Output System (NetBIOS) over TCP/IP. Through the collective works of Andrew Tridgell and the Samba team, Linux systems provide transparent and reliable SMB support over TCP/IP via a package known as Samba.

Samba emulates many of the advanced network features and functions associated with various Microsoft operating systems through the SMB protocol. Complete information can be found at the official Samba web site at www.samba.org. It is easy to configure Samba to do a number of things on a Microsoft-based network. Here are some examples:

- Participate in a Microsoft Windows Workgroup or a domain as a client, member server, or even a PDC.
- Share user home directories.
- Act as a Windows Internet Name Service (WINS) client or server.
- Link to or manage a workgroup browse service.
- Act as a master browser.

- Provide user/password and share security databases locally, from another Samba server or from a Microsoft NT 4 PDC.
- Configure local directories as shared SMB filesystems.
- Synchronize passwords between Windows and Linux systems.
- Support Microsoft Access Control Lists.

Samba can do more, but you get the idea. Samba features are configured through one very big file, smb.conf, in the /etc/samba directory. As this file may intimidate some users, the Samba Web Administration Tool (SWAT) provides a GUI interface.

Study the /etc/samba/smb. conf configuration file. It includes many useful comments and suggested directives.	**If you use SWAT, back up the Samba configuration file first, as it overwrites the default comments and directives.**

Install Samba Services

The installation of Samba services and packages is somewhat different from other servers. Samba packages are not organized in a single package group. While there is a "CIFS file server" package group, that group includes only the samba RPM package. Although that's the only package required to set up a Samba server, you may find other Samba packages of use. Important Samba packages are described in Table 15-1.

Some Samba Background

Samba services provide interoperability between Microsoft Windows and Linux/Unix computers. Before configuring Samba, you need a basic understanding of how Microsoft Windows networking works with TCP/IP.

The original Microsoft Windows networks were configured with computer hostnames, known as NetBIOS names, limited to 15 characters. These unique hostnames provided a simple, flat hostname system for the computers on a LAN. All computer identification requests were made through broadcasts. This overall network transport system is known as the NetBIOS Extended User Interface (NetBEUI), which is not "routable." In other words, it does not allow communication between two different LANs. As a result, the original Microsoft-based PC networks were limited in size to 255 nodes.

TABLE 15-1	RPM Package	Description
Samba Packages	samba	Includes the basic SMB server software for sharing files and printers.
	samba-client	Provides the utilities needed to connect to shares from Samba and Microsoft servers.
	samba-common	Contains common Samba commands used by both the client and the server.
	samba-doc	Includes Samba documentation in both HTML and PDF formats.
	samba-domainjoin-gui	Supports connections to network workgroups and domains.
	samba-swat	Provides the web-based interface for Samba configuration.
	samba-winbind	Supports Samba as a member server on Microsoft-based domains and supports Windows users on Linux servers.
	samba-winbind-nss	Provides client connections to Winbind via PAM and the Network Switching Service (NSS).

While Microsoft networks could have used the Novell IPX/SPX protocol stack to route messages between networks, that was not good enough. As the Internet grew, so did the dominance of TCP/IP. Microsoft adapted its NetBIOS system to TCP/IP with SMB. Since Microsoft published SMB as an industry-wide standard, anyone could set up their own service to work with SMB. As Microsoft has moved toward CIFS, Samba developers have adapted well. But some fairly recent changes have affected the configuration file as well as the main command line client **mount** command.

One of the nice features of Windows networks is the browser service. All computers register their NetBIOS names with one "elected" master browser, the keeper of the database of network-wide services. In fact, a browse database is maintained by some elected host for every protocol running on the network. For instance, if the NetBEUI, IPX/SPX, and TCP/IP protocols were installed on a host, then three duplicate browse databases were required—one per protocol—as the services available may differ between protocols.

Ports, Firewalls, and Samba

Samba as a service and a client requires access through multiple network protocols. When communications with both Samba clients and servers is enabled through the

Red Hat Firewall Configuration tool, it adds the following rules to the /etc/sysconfig/
iptables configuration file:

```
-A INPUT -m state --state NEW -m udp -p udp --dport 137 -j ACCEPT
-A INPUT -m state --state NEW -m udp -p udp --dport 138 -j ACCEPT
-A INPUT -m state --state NEW -m tcp -p tcp --dport 139 -j ACCEPT
-A INPUT -m state --state NEW -m tcp -p tcp --dport 445 -j ACCEPT
```

In other words, several services are involved, as described in Table 15-2.
You'll note that three of the services use the User Datagram Protocol (UDP), a
connectionless protocol. Collectively, the three associated ports specify NetBIOS
communication over TCP/IP (NBT).

For Samba client systems, only ports 137 and 138 need to be opened.

Configure SELinux Booleans for Samba

There are several directives associated with making a Samba server work with
SELinux in targeted mode, as described in Table 15-3. Only one of these booleans
(qemu_use_cifs) is enabled by default. However, you may have to activate a number
of these booleans to support different Samba functions.

For some readers, this may be getting repetitive. However, SELinux is not well
understood even by many Linux experts. So, for example, if you want to allow
Samba to share local home directories with others on the network, run the following
command:

```
# setsebool -P samba_enable_home_dirs 1
```

The **-P** makes sure the change survives a reboot.

There are cases where it's appropriate to enable the samba_export_all_ro or
samba_export_all_rw booleans, such as on directories that are shared through other
servers. For example, files that are shared via an Apache web server must be labeled
with the httpd_sys_content_t file type.

TABLE 15-2	Port/Protocol	Description
Samba Communication Services	137/UDP	NetBIOS name service
	138/UDP	NetBIOS datagram service
	139/UDP	NetBIOS session service
	445/TCP	Microsoft directory services, also known as Samba over IP

TABLE 15-3	Boolean	Description
Samba Communication Services	allow_smb_anon_write	Supports the writing of files to directories configured with the **public_content_rw_t** SELinux setting.
	cdrecord_read_content	Allows the **cdrecord** command to read shared Samba (and other network) directories.
	qemu_use_cifs	Works with access to CIFS filesystems; enabled by default.
	samba_create_home_dirs	Supports the creation of home directories, normally set up for external users.
	samba_domain_controller	Allows Samba to act as a domain controller for authentication management.
	samba_enable_home_dirs	Enables the sharing of home directories.
	samba_export_all_ro	Sets up read-only access to any directory, even those without the samba_share_t file type label.
	samba_export_all_rw	Sets up read/write access to any directory, even those without the samba_share_t file type label.
	samba_run_unconfined	Supports the execution of unconfined scripts from the /var/lib/samba/scripts directory.
	samba_share_fusefs	Allows Samba to share filesystems mounted to fusefs, a common mount for the Microsoft NTFS filesystem.
	samba_share_nfs	Enables sharing of NFS filesystems.
	use_samba_home_dirs	Supports the use of a remote server for Samba home directories.
	virt_use_samba	Allows a VM to access files mounted to the CIFS filesystem.

Configure SELinux File Types for Samba

Normally, Samba can only share those files and directories labeled with the samba_share_t file type. It is true, the samba_share_t file type is not required if the samba_export_all_ro or samba_export_all_rw booleans are enabled. However, that would be a security risk. So in most cases, you'll want to enable directories (and files therein) with the noted file type with a command like the following:

```
# chcon -R -t samba_share_t /share
```

In addition, to make sure the changes survive a relabel of SELinux, you'll want to set up the file_contexts.local file in /etc/selinux/targeted/contexts/files directory with a command such as the following:

```
# semanage fcontext -a -t samba_share_t /share
```

Samba Daemons

The sharing of directories and printers on a Microsoft-style network requires several daemons and a number of related commands. Working together, the commands can help configure Samba, and the daemons help it communicate through the different communication ports described earlier in this chapter.

Samba includes a substantial number of commands that run the service, as well as aid in configuration. The most important of the commands are the binary files in the /usr/sbin directory that start the various Samba services.

You need two daemons to run Samba: the main Samba service (**smbd**) and the NetBIOS name service (**nmbd**). In addition, most administrators will want to run the Winbind service (**winbindd**) for user and hostname resolution. All three are configured through the /etc/samba/smb.conf configuration file.

If you want to make sure the services are running the next time Linux is booted, the associated scripts in the /etc/init.d directory are **smb**, **nmb**, and **winbind**. They start the associated **smbd**, **nmbd**, and **winbindd** daemons with the following options in the /etc/sysconfig/samba file:

```
SMBDOPTIONS="-D"
NMBDOPTIONS="-D"
WINBINDOPTIONS=""
```

Yes, while no options are included for the **winbind** daemon, they can be included in quotes in the noted file. To confirm the way a daemon is running, the **ps** command can help. For example, the following output to the **ps aux | grep smb** command confirms that the Samba service is running with the **-D** switch:

```
root  12836  0.0  0.2 203612  1648 ?  S  Mar08 0:00 smbd -D
```

Samba Server Global Configuration

You can configure a Samba server through the main Samba configuration file, /etc/samba/smb.conf. This file is long and includes a number of commands that require some understanding of the concepts associated with Microsoft Windows networking. Fortunately, the default version of this file also includes helpful documentation with suggestions and useful options.

Unlike with some other services, the default Samba configuration file includes a number of commented directives other than the default. The default value of such directives can be found in the man page for the smb.conf file.

You can edit this file directly or create directory shares using SWAT. Before using any GUI tool, be brave. Study the original /etc/samba/smb.conf file. Once you see how the file is structured, back it up. Try editing the file directly. Try changing the file with the SWAT tool, described later in this chapter. Test the result by restarting the Samba server with the following command:

```
# service smb restart
```

To help you with this process, I'll analyze the default RHEL 6 version of this file. The code shown next is essentially a complete view of this file. In some cases, I've replaced the comments in the file with my own explanations. You might want to browse your own /etc/samba/smb.conf file as well.

The smb.conf file includes two types of comment lines. The hash symbol (**#**) is used for a general text comment. This is typically verbiage that describes a feature. The second comment symbol is the semicolon (**;**), used to comment out Samba directives (which you may later wish to uncomment to enable the disabled feature).

(Note that the physical dimensions of this book limit the lengths of lines of code. In a few cases, I've modified the code lines slightly to meet this limitation, without changing the intent of any command in this configuration file.)

```
# This is the main Samba configuration file. You should read the
# smb.conf(5) manual page in order to understand the options listed
# here. Samba has a huge number of configurable options (perhaps
# too many!) most of which are not shown in this example.

# NOTE: Whenever you modify this file you should run the command
# "testparm" to check that you have not made any basic syntactic
# errors.
```

exam

ⓦatch   *As stated in the Red Hat Exam Prep guide, RHCEs must be able to configure various services, including Samba,* *for basic operation. Some of the details of the default version of the main Samba configuration go beyond basic operation.*

While you need to know what can be done with different global settings, you should change as little as possible. The less you change, the less can go wrong. Perfect configuration files are not required. Configuration files that meet the specific requirements of an exam or a job are.

In smb.conf, the global settings, which define the overall attributes of a server, follow the first set of comments, including SELinux-related comments covered earlier. The [global] section starts with the following two lines:

```
#======================= Global Settings==========================
[global]
```

Now examine the global settings that follow. First, if you see the line

```
#--authconfig--start-line--
```

this means the configuration file has been modified by the **authconfig** or the **system-config-authentication** tool.

Network-Related Options

Scroll down to the subsection entitled

```
#----------- Network Related Options --------------
```

Examine each of the directives in this part of the Global Settings section. Despite the name, the **workgroup** variable specifies the name of a workgroup or more commonly, a domain. But since peer-to-peer workgroups were developed first, the default Samba **workgroup** is **WORKGROUP**, which happens to be the old name of the default peer-to-peer workgroup. It's now set to the default workgroup for Microsoft Windows 7:

```
workgroup = MYGROUP
```

The **server string** directive that follows becomes the comment shown with the NetBIOS name of the system in the visible browse list, where Samba substitutes the version number for the %v variable:

```
server string = Samba Server Version %v
```

It's a good idea to add a NetBIOS name for the local system to this file. While limited to 15 characters, it can be the same hostname used for the system. This becomes what other clients see in network browse lists such as those shown from a Microsoft **net view** command or a regular Linux **smbclient** command.

```
;    netbios name = MYSERVER
```

If the local system is connected to more than one network, you can specify them with the **interfaces** directive, as shown here. Of course, the devices and network addresses should be changed appropriately.

```
;    interfaces = lo eth0 192.168.12.2/24 192.168.13.2/24
```

If you activate the **hosts allow** directive, that action can limit access to the specified network(s). The following default would limit access to the networks with the 192.168.12.0 and 192.168.13.0 network IP addresses, as well as the local computer (127.):

```
;    hosts allow = 127. 192.168.12. 192.168.13.
```

It's possible to configure a **hosts deny** directive in a similar fashion. With such directives, you can set up host-based security for Samba. In the global section, such security would apply server-wide. You can also use the **hosts allow** and **hosts deny** directives in the definitions for individual shared directories, as described later in this chapter.

Logging Options

The next section sets up logging options, as indicated by the following label:

```
#----------- Logging Options ---------------
```

The **log file** directive, as shown, sets up separate log files for every machine that connects to this Samba server, based on its machine name (%m). By default, the log file is limited to 50KB. As suggested by the comment, log files that exceed the given size are rotated. If logs exceed that size, you'll still see them in the /var/log/samba directory with the .old extension.

```
# logs split per machine
log file = /var/log/samba/%m.log
# max 50KB per log file, then rotate
max log size = 50
```

Standalone Server Options

The following section sets up security options, based on configuration as a standalone server:

```
#----------- Standalone Server Options -------------
```

The **security** directive may be a bit confusing. The standard value of the directive, as shown here, means that connections check the local password database. It is appropriate when configuring this computer as a Domain Controller (DC), specifically a Primary Domain Controller (PDC).

```
security = user
```

Alternatively, to configure this computer as a member server on a domain, use a password database from a DC. Strangely enough, in that case, you would substitute the following command:

```
security = domain
```

To set up a Linux system as a workstation that happens to share directories on a Microsoft domain, you'll need to set up the computer as a member server on that domain.

To configure a system as a member server on an Active Directory network, substitute the following command:

```
security = ads
```

Alternatively, to use a database from another computer that is not a DC, you'd substitute the following command:

```
security = server
```

Finally, to configure a system on a peer-to-peer workgroup that does not require usernames, substitute the following command:

```
security = share
```

To summarize, there are five basic authentication options: **share**, **user**, **server**, **domain**, and **ads**.

Now, refocus this directive on the authentication database. The default is **security = user**; in this case, make sure the Samba usernames and passwords that you create match those on individual Windows NT/2000/XP/Vista systems on the network. If the database is local, it could be either

```
passdb backend = smbpasswd
```

or

```
passdb backend = tdbsam
```

The smbpasswd database is local, stored in the local /etc/samba directory. The tdbsam option, short for the Trivial Database Security Accounts Manager, sets up a local account database in the /var/lib/samba directory.

Alternatively, for a remote database such as LDAP, you could activate the following directive. If the LDAP server is located on a remote system, that Uniform Resource Identifier (URI) address can be included here.

```
passdb backend = ldapsam
```

If you've set up **security = server** or **security = domain**, you'll also want to activate the following directive with the name or IP address of the password server. Alternatively, you could replace <NT-Server-Name> with a * to have Samba search for the password server.

```
;    password server = <NT-Server-Name>
```

If you've set up **security = ads**, you'll also want to activate the following directive to specify the Active Directory (AD) realm, substituting the actual AD realm for MY_REALM:

```
;    realm = MY_REALM
```

Domain Controller Options

The following section supports the configuration of a system as a domain controller, starting with the following comment:

```
#----------- Domain Controller Options --------------
```

Additional configuration is required for a Samba server configured as a domain controller. In brief, these options specify the role of the system as the domain master, as the system that receives requests for logins to the domain:

```
;    domain master = yes
;    domain logins = yes
```

The next command set up Microsoft command line batch files by computer and user. The command afterward stores Microsoft user profiles on the local Samba server. That means these commands can't be tested on the Red Hat exams unless you have access to a Microsoft Windows computer. Since I can't tell you what's on the Red Hat exams, I can only suggest that Red Hat might not want separate Microsoft Windows computers available during their exams. Of course, Microsoft

Windows guest VMs are included in the description for the Red Hat Enterprise Virtualization course.

```
# the login script name depends on the machine name
;   logon script = %m.bat
# the login script name depends on the unix user used
;   logon script = %U.bat
;   logon path = \\%L\Profiles\%U
```

The remaining commands are fairly self-explanatory, as scripts that add and delete users, groups, and machine accounts.

```
;   add user script = /usr/sbin/useradd %u -n -g users
;   add group script = /usr/sbin/groupadd %g
;   add machine script = /usr/sbin/adduser -n -c \
      "Workstation (%u)" -M -d /nohome -s /bin/false %u
;   delete user script = /usr/sbin/userdel %u
;   delete user from group script = /usr/sbin/userdel %u %g
;   delete group script = /usr/sbin/groupdel %g
```

Browse Control Options

The following section controls whether and how a system may be configured as a browse master, which maintains a list of resources on the network. Related directives start with the following comment:

```
#---------- Browser Control Options --------------
```

Unless a Samba server is specifically designated as a local browse master,

```
; local master = no
```

Samba participates in browser elections like any other Microsoft Windows computer, using the specified **os level**.

```
; os level = 33
```

Alternatively, if a Domain Controller isn't already elected as a browse master, you can make it easier for the local computer to win the browser election, with the **preferred master** command:

```
; preferred master = yes
```

Name Resolution

The following section allows you to set up a Samba server with a database of NetBIOS names and IP addresses, starting with the following comment:

```
#----------- Name Resolution --------------
```

The Windows Internet Name Service (WINS) is somewhat functionally equivalent to DNS on Microsoft-based networks such as Samba. If you activate the following command, Samba activates a WINS server on the local computer:

```
;   wins support = yes
```

Alternatively, you can point the local computer to a remote WINS server on the network; of course, you'd have to substitute the IP address for *w.x.y.z*. Do not activate both the **wins support** and **wins server** directives on the same system, as they are incompatible.

```
;   wins server = w.x.y.z
```

Samba servers may not be installed on every Linux system. In that case, you could enable the following directive to allow access from such systems with only Samba client software:

```
;   wins proxy = yes
```

If the answer to a name resolution request is not in a WINS server, the following directive would allow the same search through configured DNS servers:

```
;   dns proxy = yes
```

Printing Options

Printers were included in the RHCT exam objectives for RHEL 5. However, they are not listed in either the RHCSA or the RHCE objectives for RHEL 6. Nevertheless, printing is part of the default Samba server configuration. So you should at least scan the section in the Samba configuration file, starting with the following comment:

```
#----------- Printing Options --------------
```

These default printer settings are required to share printers from this Samba server. The following three directives loads printers as defined by **printcap name = /etc/printcap**.

The **cups options = raw** directive means that print jobs are already processed by a service with print processors, such as the CUPS service.

```
load printers = yes
cups options = raw
printcap name = /etc/printcap
```

Alternatively, it's possible to configure a different print server. The following option obtains information from printers configured on older Linux systems:

```
printcap name = lpstat
```

Filesystem Options

The following section supports the configuration of extended attributes, associated with the Access Control List (ACL) settings for a Microsoft file. With the right options, such attributes can be stored. The comments within the Samba configuration file refer to the Microsoft Disk Operating System (DOS), as shorthand for how permissions and related ACL bits are specified for such shared files. The following would be the default for all shared directories, starting with the following comment:

```
#----------- Filesystem Options --------------
```

First, the **map archive** directive can control whether the DOS file archive attribute is mapped to the local Linux executable bit, if supported by the **create mask** directive.

```
;   map archive = no
```

The **map hidden** directive can control whether DOS hidden files are mapped to the local Linux executable bit.

```
;   map hidden = no
```

The **map read only** directive, also known as **map readonly** in Samba documentation, as shown, is useful for shared mounted media such as DVDs:

```
;   map read only = no
```

The **map system** directive, if set to yes, supports the use of the Linux execute bit for DOS system files:

```
;   map system = no
```

Finally, the **store dos attributes** directive, if active, attempts to store previously configured ACLs of DOS files:

```
;        store dos attributes = yes
```

Shared Samba Directories

The second part of the main Samba configuration file, /etc/samba/smb.conf, is used to set up shared directories and printers via Samba. This section includes an analysis of the default version of the file.

In Samba, settings for shared directories are organized into *stanzas*, which are groups of commands associated with a share name. (*Stanza* doesn't seem like a technical term, but some believe that well-constructed configuration code is like good poetry.)

Shared Home Directories

The first four lines in this section define the **[homes]** share, which automatically shares the home directory of the logged-in user. Every user gets access to his or her own home directory; the **browseable = no** command keeps users away from each other's home directory.

There is no default /homes directory. It's just a label. You don't need to supply a home directory, because Samba will read the user's account record in /etc/passwd to determine the directory to be shared.

By default, this does not allow access to unknown users (**guest ok = no**). In addition, you can limit the systems that can use this share with directives such as **hosts allow** and **hosts deny** described earlier. The effects of the **hosts allow** and **hosts deny** directives are limited to the share stanza where they are used.

```
#============================ Share Definitions =============
[homes]
    comment = Home Directories
    browseable = no
    writable = yes
```

There are a number of variables in smb.conf that are not spelled correctly, such as browseable. *In some cases, the correct spelling (*browsable*) also works. Even if misspelled, they are still accepted Samba variables and generally should be spelled per the Samba defaults, not standard written English.*

Before a shared home directory can actually share files over Samba, **the SELinux samba_enable_home_dirs boolean must be enabled.**

Shared Printers

The **[printers]** stanza normally works as is, to allow access by all users with accounts on a computer or domain. Even though the spool directory (/var/spool/samba) is not browsable, the associated printers are browsable by their NetBIOS names. While changes are straightforward, the standard options mean that guest users aren't allowed to print, related print spools are not writable, and **printable = yes** is a prerequisite for loading associated configuration files, such as for CUPS.

```
# NOTE: If you have a BSD-style print system there is no need to
# specifically define each individual printer
[printers]
   comment = All Printers
   path = /usr/spool/samba
   browseable = no
# Set public = yes to allow user 'guest account' to print
   guest ok = no
   writable = no
   printable = yes
```

Domain Logons

The commands in the following stanza supports the configuration of a **[netlogon]** share for Microsoft Windows workstations. As there are no **[netlogon]** shares even for Samba-enabled Linux workstations, this section requires a Microsoft Windows computer to verify functionality. If you believe that you'll have access to a Microsoft Windows computer during the Red Hat exams, study this section carefully.

```
# Un-comment the following and create the netlogon directory for
# Domain Logons
; [netlogon]
;    comment = Network Logon Service
;    path = /var/lib/samba/netlogon
;    guest ok = yes
;    writable = no
;    share modes = no
```

Workstation Profiles

This next stanza configures profiles for Microsoft Windows workstations. As these profiles become a part of a Microsoft Windows registry when you log on to one of those workstations, you're unlikely to configure this section in a network of Linux-only computers. Make your own judgment on whether this section might apply during an RHCE exam.

```
# Un-comment the following to provide a specific roving profile
# share; the default is to use the user's home directory
;[Profiles]
;       path = /var/lib/samba/profiles
;       browseable = no
;       guest ok = yes
```

Group Directories

The following stanza, as suggested by the comment, configures the /home/samba directory to be shared by the group named staff. You can configure this common group of users to share this directory. To configure special ownership and permissions for /home/samba, you'll need also to configure appropriate permissions. Both processes are described in Chapter 8.

```
# A publicly accessible directory, but read only, except for
# people in the "staff" group
;[public]
;       comment = Public Stuff
;       path = /home/samba
;       public = yes
;       writable = yes
;       printable = no
;       write list = +staff
```

The staff group can be labeled +staff or @staff. To set up appropriate permissions on the shared directory, you may also want to include the following directives for creating files and directories:

```
create mask = 0770
directory mask = 2770
```

One difference with Samba is that Microsoft authentication databases do not allow users and groups to have the same names. Just create a unique group name, preferably with a higher GID number, with the **groupadd** command. Make sure appropriate users in the Samba database are members of that Linux group. In addition, the /home/samba directory, along with any files contained in that directory, normally must have the proper SELinux file type, something made possible with the following command:

```
# chcon -R -t samba_share_t /home/samba
```

Of course, you'll want to make sure such a change survives a SELinux relabel, and that can be configured for the noted directory with the following command:

```
# semanage fcontext -a -t samba_share_t /home/samba
```

Other Sample Stanzas

To learn more about Samba, it may be helpful to examine other stanzas for shared directories. The following examples were included in earlier Red Hat releases of Samba. While they're not included in the comments for Samba, they still can be included in the smb.conf configuration file, and therefore are still useful at least for learning purposes.

For example, the following share of the /tmp directory can share a common location where users share downloaded files. If activated, all users (**public = yes**) get write access (**read only = no**) to this share.

```
# This one is useful for people to share files
;[tmp]
;   comment = Temporary file space
;   path = /tmp
;   read only = no
;   public = yes
```

This stanza configures a directory for Fred's exclusive use. It allows that user exclusive access to his home directory via Samba. A better location for the **path** would be within the /home directory.

```
# A private directory, usable only by fred. Note that fred
# requires write access to the directory.
;[fredsdir]
;   comment = Fred's Service
;   path = /usr/somewhere/private
;   valid users = fred
;   public = no
;   writable = yes
;   printable = no
```

The following stanza is slightly different from the **[tmp]** share. Once connected, the only user that connects is a guest. Unless you've configured a guest user, this defaults to the user named nobody.

```
# A publicly accessible directory, read/write to all users. Note
# that all files created in the directory by users will be owned
# by the default user, so any user with access can delete any
# other user's files. Obviously this directory must be writable
```

```
# by the default user. Another user could of course be specified,
# in which case all files would be owned by that user instead.
;[public]
;    path = /usr/somewhere/else/public
;    public = yes
;    only guest = yes
;    writable = yes
;    printable = no
```

Finally, this is another variation on the User Private Group scheme, which creates a group directory. Unlike the **[public]** stanza, this share is private.

```
# The following two entries demonstrate how to share a directory so
# that two users can place files there that will be owned by the
# specific users. In this setup, the directory should be writable
# by both users and should have the sticky bit set on it to prevent
# abuse. Obviously this could be extended to as many users as required.
;[myshare]
;    comment = Mary's and Fred's stuff
;    path = /usr/somewhere/shared
;    valid users = mary fred
;    public = no
;    writable = yes
;    printable = no
;    create mask = 0765
```

Let Samba Join a Domain

If you've configured a Samba server, and it's not the DC for the network, you may need to configure as a member of the domain. To do so, you can configure an account on the DC for the network. As long as there's one domain on this network, it's easy to do with the following command:

```
# net rpc join -U root
```

If there is more than one domain available, substitute the name of the controller for *DC* in the **net rpc join -S DC -U root** command. This assumes that the user named root is the administrative user on the DC. However, the administrative user on a domain governed by a Microsoft Windows computer is *administrator*. If the command is successful, it prompts for that user's password on the remote DC. The result adds an account for the local computer to the DC's user database in /etc/passwd.

The Samba User Database

You could set up identical usernames and passwords for both the Microsoft Windows and Samba-enabled Linux computers on a network. However, this is not always possible, especially when there are preexisting databases. In that case, you can set up a database of Samba users and passwords that correspond to current Microsoft usernames and passwords on your network. A template is available in /etc/samba/smbusers and is in effect if you add the following entry to the smb.conf file:

```
username map = /etc/samba/smbusers
```

If you're comfortable with the command line interface, the quickest way to set up Samba users is with the **smbpasswd** command. Remember that you can create a new Samba user only from valid accounts on a Linux computer.

However, you can configure such an account without login privileges on the Linux system. For example, the following command adds the noted user without a valid login shell:

```
# useradd winuser1 -s /sbin/nologin
```

You can then configure that user with a Samba password with the **smbpasswd -a winuser1** command. The **smbpasswd** command is powerful; it includes a number of useful switches described in Table 15-4.

TABLE 15-4	smbpasswd Switch	Description
Various smbpasswd Commands	-a *username*	Adds the specified *username* to the database.
	-d *username*	Disables the specified *username*; thus disables that password from Microsoft networking.
	-e *username*	Enables the specified *username*; opposite of **-d**.
	-r *computername*	Allows changes to a Windows or Samba password on a remote computer. Normally goes with **-U**.
	-U *username*	Normally changes the *username* on a remote computer, if specified with the **-r** switch.
	-x *username*	Deletes the specified *username* from the database.

The location of the authentication database depends on the value of the **passdb backend** directive. If it's set to smbpasswd, you'll find it in the /etc/samba/smbpasswd file. If it's set to tdbsam, you'll find it in the passwd.tdb file in the /var/lib/samba/private directory. To read the list of current users, run the following command:

```
# pdbedit -L
```

To configure different usernames and passwords for Linux and Microsoft computers, you'll need to edit them directly into the /etc/samba/smbusers file; alternatively, such users can be configured with SWAT.

Create a Public Share

With this information, you should now know how to create a public access share for use with the entire network. For the purpose of this chapter, create the /home/PublicShare directory. The following sample stanza in the /etc/samba/smb.conf configuration file reflects a directory available to all users.

```
[PublicShare]
    comment= Shared Public Directory
    path = /home/PublicShare
    writeable = yes
    browseable = yes
    guest ok = yes
```

But that kind of security may not be appropriate. For example, assume the following limits are desirable:

- Access to the **[PublicShare]** should be limited to users with a regular local Linux account (or a user who can log in locally based on a remote authentication database such as LDAP).
- Denied access to guest users and others.
- Access to all users in the local example.com domain.
- Denied access to all users from a suspect computer such as outsider1.example.org.

To make this happen, change the last command in this stanza. As **guest ok = no** is the default, you can just erase the **guest ok = yes** directive. To provide access to all users in the given domain, add the following command:

```
hosts allow = .example.com
```

To then deny access to one specific computer on that network, you could add **EXCEPT**; for example, the following line specifically excludes the noted **evil.example. com** system from the list:

```
hosts allow = .example.com EXCEPT evil.example.com
```

Alternatively, if this domain is on the 192.168.122.0 network, either of the following directives supports access to all systems on that network:

```
hosts allow = 192.168.122.
hosts allow = 192.168.122.0/255.255.255.0
```

You could specifically deny access to computers with a command such as the following:

```
hosts deny = evil.example.com
```

Alternatively, you could substitute IP addresses in the same format as with the **hosts allow** directive. You've defined the share attributes in the Samba smb.conf configuration file. But you need to modify the directory associated with the share with the following command:

```
# chmod 1777 /home/PublicShare
```

The digit 1 in front of the 777 directory permission string is known as the "sticky bit." That sticky bit allows any user to do anything in the directory, courtesy of the 777 permission value. But such privileges are limited to files created by the specific user. Otherwise, any user could delete or rename any file in the /home/PublicShare directory, regardless of the file's owner.

Alternatively, a directory with permissions limited to members of a group may have 2770 permissions, with the SGID bit set and full permissions given to members of the group that owns the directory.

EXERCISE 15-1

Configure a Samba Home Directory Share

In this exercise, you'll learn about the basic home directory share. You'll need at least two computers, one of which should be a Samba server. The other can be a Linux or Microsoft Windows workstation. You'll connect to the Samba server from the workstation and access the files in your home directory on the Samba server.

These steps assume that the user account is michael; substitute your regular user account name as appropriate.

1. Install and configure Samba to start using the methods described earlier in this chapter.

2. Open the /etc/samba/smb.conf configuration file. Look for the current value of **workgroup**.

3. Make sure that the computers on the local network have the same value for **workgroup**. If the local network is a Windows-style domain, set **workgroup** to the name of the domain.

4. Test the syntax of the Samba configuration file with the **testparm** command.

5. Read and address any problems that appear in the output from the **testparm** command. Fix any smb.conf syntax problems defined in the output.

6. Activate the samba_enable_home_dirs boolean on the Samba server with the following command:

   ```
   # setsebool -P samba_enable_home_dirs on
   ```

7. Set up a user account on the Samba server in the authentication database with the following command (enter an appropriate password when prompted):

   ```
   # smbpasswd -a michael
   ```

8. Make Samba reread the smb.conf file with the following command:

   ```
   # service smb reload
   ```

9. Go to a remote Linux or Microsoft Windows workstation on the same domain or workgroup.

10. If you can browse the list of computers from the Samba server with the following command, browsing is working. Substitute the name of the configured Samba server host for *sambaserver*.

    ```
    # smbclient -L sambaserver -U michael
    ```

11. Log in as the root user on the remote RHEL 6 Samba client.

12. From that remote RHEL 6 client, use the **mount.cifs** command to configure the remote [homes] directory share on an empty local directory. For example, as the root user, you could mount on the local /share directory (create it if required) with the following command:

    ```
    # mount "//sambaserver/michael" /share -o username=root
    ```

13. Test the result. Can you browse the home directory on the remote computer? Bonus: disable the **samba_enable_home_dirs** boolean and try again. What happens?

The Samba Web Administration Tool

RHEL 6 no longer includes a dedicated Red Hat GUI tool to configure Samba. Instead, Red Hat has included the web-based administration tool created by Samba developers for that purpose, known as SWAT, which you can install from the samba-swat RPM.

SWAT is not available from the standard RHEL 6 DVD. So if that media is all that's available on a Red Hat exam, you won't be able to use SWAT to configure Samba for the RHCE. However, SWAT is such an excellent, well-documented tool, it's worth the trouble to install and activate it. It can help you learn more about Samba.

On a genuine RHEL 6 system, it's available from the RHEL Server Optional repository, which can be activated from a Red Hat Network account at https://rhn .redhat.com. On the Scientific Linux rebuild distribution (and possibly other rebuilds), it's available from standard repositories configured in the /etc/yum.repos.d directory.

on the job

The Red Hat Network web site at https://rhn.redhat.com is now an interface to "Classic Subscription Management." For the latest RHN interface, see the Knowledgebase article at https://access.redhat.com/kb/docs/DOC-47394.

SWAT is installed and run as an Extended Internet Super Server service in the /etc/xinetd.d directory, like those discussed in Chapter 10. Once installed, you can activate it with the following commands:

```
# chkconfig swat on
# /etc/init.d/xinetd restart
```

Next, open a web browser and navigate to http://localhost:901. You'll be prompted for a username and password; the root user account and password should work. When authentication is confirmed, you're taken to a screen similar to that shown in Figure 15-1.

If you want to access SWAT from a remote location, comment out the following directive in the /etc/xinetd.d/swat file and then open up TCP port 901 in any existing local firewall.

```
only_from = 127.0.0.1
```

FIGURE 15-1 The Samba web administration tool

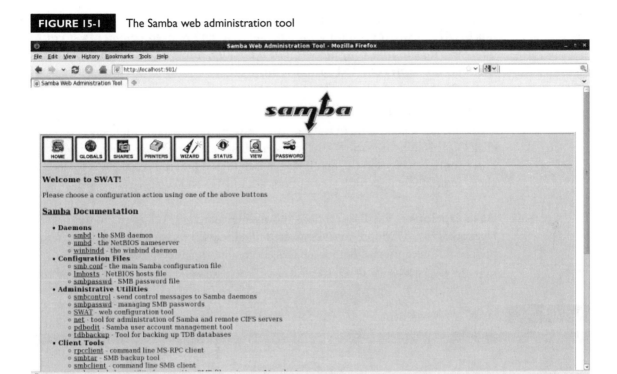

Most of the hyperlinks are associated with the man page for noted commands. At the top of the menu, you should see icons for Home through Password. Figure 15-1 displays the home page for SWAT. The following sections briefly describes the options in each of the other screens.

SWAT provides a comprehensive view of what you can do with Samba. But be careful. Many of the features may be useful for a real network, especially a network mixed with Microsoft systems. However, most go beyond what's necessary for basic operation, and the Red Hat exams. Don't get lost in details. This chapter focuses on Samba directives relevant to the Red Hat exam objectives.

In most cases, in SWAT, there's a Help hyperlink associated with each directive. In most cases, it highlights the relevant portion of the smb.conf man page. Most of the discussion relates to the Global Settings page; many of the security settings on that page may also be used to enhance user- and host-based security for individually shared directories.

The Printers and Wizard options are not covered in this book. If you're interested, try them out. They're not difficult to understand.

*Before making any changes, back up the /etc/samba/smb.conf configuration file. SWAT overwrites not only the file, but also any related comments. If you do overwrite the smb.conf file without a backup, move or delete that file and then run the **yum reinstall samba-common** command.*

Global Settings

To see what SWAT can do to the global settings in the smb.conf configuration file, click Globals from atop the SWAT web-based menu. Changes are straightforward. Enter desired changes in the text boxes that follow. When the process is complete, click Commit Changes. Relevant options fall into several categories.

Base Options   The Base Options shown in Figure 15-2 correspond to the Network Related Options in the smb.conf file discussed earlier in this chapter. With the possible exception of **netbios aliases** and **realm**, the directives may all be important, as described in Table 15-5.

FIGURE 15-2   SWAT global settings

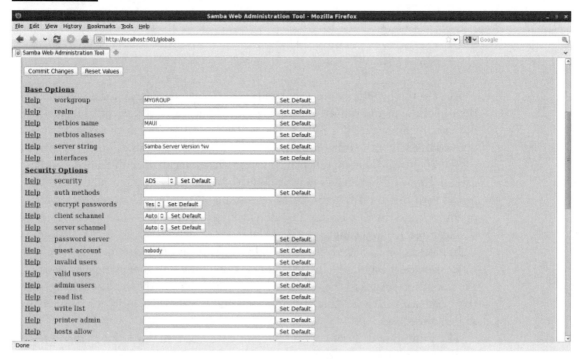

TABLE 15-5	workgroup	The workgroup or domain to which the system belongs.
	realm	The Kerberos realm for the domain, set to the DNS name of the Kerberos server such as server1.example.com. May be used if a system is configured as a Kerberos client, as discussed in Chapter 12.
SWAT Base Options	netbios name	Windows hostname; may be different from the DNS hostname.
	netbios aliases	Additional hostnames for the server.
	server string	Description of the server shown to clients who browse this server.
	interfaces	Devices and IP addresses allowed to connect.

Security Options   A number of security options can be used both globally and for individual shares. Naturally, to use one of these options in a share, you should include it in the stanza associated with the share. The focus of this section is on those directives that can be used to help configure basic user- and host-based security for Samba. While these directives were discussed earlier in this chapter, the different perspective associated with SWAT may help you understand Samba better. As such, the following list is not comprehensive.

- **security**   Basic directive for authentication on Samba systems; may be set to share, user, server, domain, or ads, as discussed earlier in this chapter.
- **password server**   Reference to another system with the authentication database, usually a Samba or a pure Windows server.
- **guest account**   Support for a nonprivileged account for connections.
- **invalid users**   Users not allowed to access a system or share; for example, the following list prohibits users root, michael, and members of the project group:

  ```
  invalid users root michael @project
  ```

- **valid users**   Users allowed to access a system.
- **admin users**   Users allowed administrative access, normally just to a share.
- **read list**   Users given read-only access.
- **write list**   Users given read/write access.
- **hosts allow**   Hosts allowed access to a system (also known as **allow hosts**); for example, the following list supports access from all systems except one. May also use host and domain names.

  ```
  hosts allow 192.168. EXCEPT 192.168.0.100
  ```

- **hosts deny**   Hosts not allowed to access a system (also known as **deny hosts**).

To repeat, this section is focused only on those directives relevant to the RHCE
objectives.

Share Settings

To see what SWAT can do to the share settings in the smb.conf configuration file,
click Shares from atop the SWAT web-based menu. Click the drop-down text box
associated with Choose Share, and then click Homes. Next, to Change View To,
click Advanced to reveal the screen shown in Figure 15-3. Relevant options fall into
several categories.

FIGURE 15-3   SWAT share settings

Options on this page are straightforward. To create a second share, enter a name in the Create Share text box, and then click the Create Share button. You can then configure it in the text boxes that follow. When the process is complete, click Commit Changes. Many of the directives that appear were already explained in the global settings section but apply only to the local share. Those directives are not repeated here.

- **comment** Information included with the share name.
- **path** The path to the directory to be shared.
- **username** Substitute usernames where machine usernames are not available; rarely used.
- **force user** A user account assigned to all who connect to the share.
- **force group** A group account assigned to all who connect to the share.
- **read only** Shares so labeled can only be read.
- **guest only** Only guest user connections are allowed.
- **guest ok** Guest user connections are allowed; no password is required.

You'll note that most of these directives aren't covered here and in fact are rarely used.

Server Status

To see the current status of Samba on the system, click Server Status from atop the SWAT web-based menu. As shown in Figure 15-4, it supports control of the Samba, NetBIOS, and Winbind daemons. If there are active connections, active shared directories, and files in use, they're also listed in this view.

View Configuration

Any changes made with SWAT, once saved are written to the /etc/samba/smb.conf file. Click View. It includes a current read-only view of that file.

User Management

You can manage the Samba user authentication database with SWAT. To do so, click Password from atop the SWAT web-based menu. As shown in Figure 15-5, it supports password changes for current users. In addition, you can use the screen shown to add new users to the local Samba authentication database.

FIGURE 15-4　　Default installed Apache home page

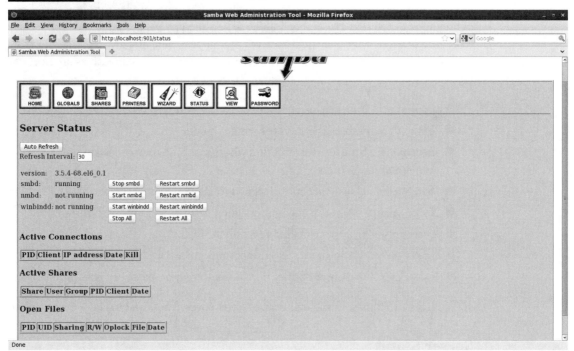

But these are just front ends to the **smbpasswd** command. In either case, the user has to exist in the Linux authentication database. For example, the following command takes the current user michael and prompts for a new password:

```
# smbpasswd michael
```

Alternatively, the following command adds user donna to the Samba authentication database, prompting for a password:

```
# smbpasswd -a donna
```

The **-d**, **-e**, and **-x** options can respectively disable, enable, and delete the given user from the Samba authentication database.

Test Changes to /etc/samba/smb.conf

After making any changes to /etc/samba/smb.conf, you should always test the system before putting it into production. A simple syntax check on the Samba configuration

FIGURE 15-5	SWAT server password management

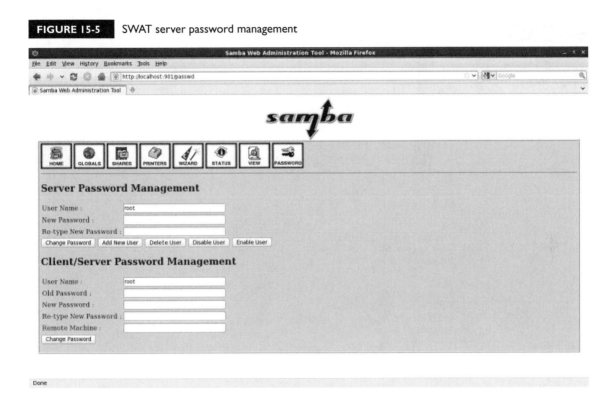

file is possible with the **testparm** utility, as shown in Figure 15-6. This does not actually check to determine whether the service is running or functioning correctly; it checks only basic text syntax and command stanzas.

The directives that are displayed are share stanzas, along with associated directives. For example, the [homes] share is not read only and is not browsable to all clients.

Review User- and Host-Based Samba Security

As suggested in the RHCE objectives, you need to know how to configure "host-based and user-based security for" each service, including Samba. So while this section is repetitive, it's important.

To review, user-based security can be configured within the main Samba configuration file, smb.conf. Users specified in that file are configured in a separate database, normally in the /var/lib/samba directory, managed with the **smbpasswd** command.

FIGURE 15-6

Review the Samba
configuration
with testparm

```
[root@Maui ~]# testparm
Load smb config files from /etc/samba/smb.conf
rlimit_max: rlimit_max (1024) below minimum Windows limit (16384)
Processing section "[homes]"
Processing section "[printers]"
Loaded services file OK.
Server role: ROLE_STANDALONE
Press enter to see a dump of your service definitions

[global]
        workgroup = MYGROUP
        server string = Samba Server Version %v
        log file = /var/log/samba/log.%m
        max log size = 50
        wins server = 127.0.0.1
        cups options = raw

[homes]
        comment = Home Directories
        read only = No
        browseable = No

[printers]
        comment = All Printers
        path = /var/spool/samba
        printable = Yes
        browseable = No
[root@Maui ~]# █
```

User-based security is enabled for the system with the following option:

```
security = user
```

Users can be specified as allowed or denied with the **invalid users** and **valid users**
directives. Those directives can be applied generally in the Global Settings section
or applied per share in the stanza where the shared directory is configured.

Host-based security can be configured in both the Samba configuration file and
any associated **iptables**-based firewalls. Hosts can be allowed or denied with
directives such as **hosts allow** and **hosts deny**. In some configurations, you'll see
synonyms for those directives, such as **allow hosts** and **deny hosts**.

For example, the following **hosts allow** directive can limit access to the specified
network(s):

```
hosts allow = 127. 192.168.122. 192.168.100.
```

The 127. is not required; localhost addresses are always allowed unless specifically
included in a **hosts deny** directive.

Review Basic Samba Shares

Specifically for Samba, the RHCE objectives specify that you need to "provide network shares to specific clients" and to "provide network shares suitable for group collaboration."

To provide network shares to one or more specific clients, you'll need to include directives like **valid users** and **invalid users** in the stanza associated with a shared Samba directory.

To provide network shares suitable for group collaboration, you'll need to remember the following tasks:

- Set up an appropriate group and permissions on the directory to be shared.
- Configure the shared directory and files with the SELinux samba_share_t file type.
- Define a separate share stanza in the Samba configuration file, with appropriate values for **writable**, **create mask**, **directory mask**, and **write list**.

EXERCISE 15-2

Configuring Samba with Shares

In this exercise, you'll configure Samba to share a directory. For this purpose, you'll directly edit the /etc/samba/smb.conf file.

1. Create a /home/ftp/public directory. Change ownership to the ftp user and group, with full permissions for both (770).

2. Make sure to set appropriate SELinux settings for the directory with the following command:

```
# chcon -R -t samba_share_t /home/ftp
```

In addition, to make sure the changes survive a relabel of SELinux, you'll want to set up the file_contexts.local file in the /etc/selinux/targeted/contexts/files directory with a command such as the following:

```
# semanage fcontext -a -t samba_share_t /home/ftp
```

3. Open the /etc/samba/smb.conf file in a text editor.

4. Configure Samba to share as public, in read-only mode, the /home/ftp/pub directory tree. In the Share Definitions section, you could add the following commands:

```
[pub]
        comment = shared FTP directory
        path = /home/ftp/pub
```

5. Allow guest access to all public·shares. In smb.conf, this means adding the following line to the **[pub]** stanza:

```
        guest ok = yes
```

6. To create a guest account, you'll need to add the following command in smb.conf:

```
; guest account = pcguest
```

7. Create a guest account for pcguest, and associate it with an unused UID and GID 600. (If you already have a user with this ID, substitute an unused ID number.) Set the password as "anonymous." While you can do this with the Red Hat User Manager discussed in Chapter 8, the quickest way to do this is with the following commands:

```
# useradd pcguest -u 600
# passwd pcguest
```

8. Create separate log files for each computer host that connects. This is already active by default with the following command:

```
log file = /var/log/samba/%m.log
```

9. Write and save changes to the smb.conf file.

10. You can see if Samba is already running with the **service smb status** command. If it's stopped, you can start it with the **service smb start** command. If it's running, you can make Samba reread your configuration file with the following command:

```
# service smb reload
```

This final option allows you to change your Samba configuration without disconnecting users from the Samba server.

CERTIFICATION OBJECTIVE 15.02

Samba as a Client

You can configure two types of clients through Samba. One connects to directories shared from Microsoft Windows servers or Samba servers on Linux/Unix. The second connects to shared printers from one of the same two types of servers. The Samba client commands are available from the samba-client RPM. With those commands, you should be able to find browse lists and mount shared directories locally.

Command Line Tools

To browse shared directories from a Linux computer, you should know how to use the **smbclient** command. This can test connectivity to any SMB host on a Windows- or Samba-based Linux/Unix computer. Assuming it's allowed by a firewall, you can use **smbclient** to check the shared directories and printers from other systems on at least the local network. For example, the following **smbclient** command checks shared directories and printers:

```
# smbclient -L server1.example.com -U donna
```

I've specified two arguments with the **smbclient** command: the **-L** specifies the name of the Samba server, and the **-U** specifies a username on the remote computer. When the command reaches the Samba server, you're prompted for the appropriate password.

Shares will appear; for example, the following output reveals shares named public and donna, as well as a printer named OfficePrinter on a remote system named Maui.

```
Domain=[MYGROUP] OS=[Unix] Server=[Samba 3.5.4-68.el6_0.2]
    Sharename       Type       Comment
    ---------       ----       -------
    public          Disk       Public Stuff
    IPC$            IPC        IPC Service (Samba Server Version 3.5.4-68.el6_0.2)
    OfficePrinter@Maui Printer   in the office
    donna           Disk       Home Directories
Domain=[MYGROUP] OS=[Unix] Server=[Samba 3.5.4-68.el6_0.2]
```

From the displayed output, there's a share available named public. You can also use the **smbclient** command to make a client connection similar to an FTP connection with the following command:

```
$ smbclient //server1.example.com/public -U michael
```

Of course, most administrators would prefer to mount that share on a local directory. That's where options to the mount command are helpful.

Mount Options

Shares can be mounted by the root administrative user. The standard is with the **mount.cifs** command, functionally equivalent to the **mount -t cifs** command. For example, the following command mounts the share named public on the local /home/shared directory:

```
# mount.cifs //server1.example.com/public /home/shared -o username=donna
```

This command prompts for user donna's password on the remote server. That password should be part of the Samba user authentication database on the server1. example.com system, normally different from the standard Linux authentication database. Of course, that user donna could also mount her remote home directory in a similar fashion, with a command like the following:

```
# mount.cifs //server1.example.com/donna /home/donna/remote -o username=donna
```

While there is no longer a **umount.cifs** command for shared Samba directories, you can still use the **umount** command to unmount such directories.

Automated Samba Mounts

As it certainly takes a few extra steps to set up a shared directory, it would be useful to automate the process. The standard method is through the /etc/fstab configuration file discussed in Chapter 6. To review the essential elements of that chapter, you could set up the public share in /etc/fstab by adding the following line (which can be wrapped in that file):

```
//server1.example.com/public  /home/shared  cifs rw,username=donna,password=pass, 0 0
```

But that can be a risk, as the /etc/fstab file is world-readable. To that end, you can configure a dedicated credentials file with the username and password, as follows:

```
//server/pub  /share  cifs rw,credentials=/etc/smbdonna 0 0
```

As suggested in Chapter 6, you can then set up the username and password in the /etc/smbdonna file:

```
username=donna
password=donnaspassword
```

While the contents of that file must still exist in clear text, you can configure the /etc/donna file as readable only by the root administrative user. It's also possible to configure the automounter with similar information. But as the automounter is a RHCSA skill, you'll have to refer to Chapter 6 for that information.

CERTIFICATION OBJECTIVE 15.03

Samba Troubleshooting

Samba is complex. With a complex service, simple mistakes may be difficult to diagnose. Fortunately, Samba includes excellent tools for troubleshooting. The basic **testparm** command tests syntax. Log files can tell you more. Of course, unless appropriate changes are made in local firewalls, Samba might not even be accessible from remote systems.

Samba Problem Identification

Samba is a forgiving service. It includes synonyms for a number of parameters. Some of the parameters are misspelled; for example, **writable** is a synonym for **writeable**. But beyond those parameters, the **testparm** command can help identify problems. For example, Figure 15-7 illustrates a number of problems. Unrecognized parameters are highlighted with the "unknown parameter" message.

Some parameters don't work with each other. For example, the following message in the testparm output highlights two incompatible directives:

```
ERROR: both 'wins support = true' and 'wins server = <server
list>' cannot be set in the smb.conf file. nmbd will abort with
this setting.
```

Sometimes, troubleshooting commands come in the output to other commands. For example, problems often appear in the output to various commands. Sometimes the output is straightforward, such as the following output to a specific **mount.cifs**

FIGURE 15-7

Review the Samba
Configuration
with testparm

```
[root@Maui ~]# testparm /etc/samba/smb.conf
Load smb config files from /etc/samba/smb.conf
rlimit_max: rlimit_max (1024) below minimum Windows limit (16384)
Unknown parameter encountered: "ecurity"
Ignoring unknown parameter "ecurity"
Unknown parameter encountered: "assdb backend"
Ignoring unknown parameter "assdb backend"
Processing section "[homes]"
Processing section "[printers]"
Processing section "[public]"
Unknown parameter encountered: "rite list"
Ignoring unknown parameter "rite list"
Loaded services file OK.
ERROR: both 'wins support = true' and 'wins server = <server list>' cannot be se
t in the smb.conf file. nmbd will abort with this setting.
Server role: ROLE_STANDALONE
Press enter to see a dump of your service definitions
```

command, associated with an incorrect share name. It also suggests that the case of
share names is less important on networks associated with Microsoft operating systems.

    Retrying with upper case share name

Sometimes, messages may appear to be more straightforward, such as

    mount error(13): Permission denied

But that message could refer to an incorrect password, or a user that has not been
configured in the Samba database.

Sometimes problems may seem more annoying. For example, if you mount a
remote home directory and no files show up in that directory, it could mean that the
SELinux samba_enable_home_dirs boolean has not been enabled. If you mount a
remote directory other than a user home directory, it could mean that the directory
and associated files are not properly labeled with the samba_share_t file type.

Local Log File Checks

Problems associated with Samba may appear in the /var/log/messages file, or they
may appear in different files in the /var/log/samba directory. First, syntax errors
revealed in the output to the **testparm** command may also appear in the /var/log/
messages file. As the Samba services are started, errors in the configuration file are
problems worth reporting in the standard system log file.

In addition, when an attempted mount of a shared Samba directory fails, associated messages also appear in the /var/log/messages file. Sometimes the messages are straightforward such as cifs_mount failed or NT_STATUS_LOGON_FAILURE.

Most Samba log files are located in the /var/log/samba directory. The log files are classified by the host or IP address of the client that connects to the server. In general, fewer messages mean success. For example, a connection to a localhost system, useful for troubleshooting, may include the following message in the log.__ffff_127.0.0.1 log file:

```
__ffff_127.0.0.1 (::ffff:127.0.0.1) connect to service michael
initially as user michael (uid=1000, gid=1000) (pid 23800)
```

The information therein suggests the use of both IPv4 and IPv6 addresses. The connected user is identified by UID, GID, and PID numbers. If an unauthorized user connects, these numbers can help identify a problem user and/or a compromised account, along with an associated process ID number.

Most of the other files in this directory relate to various services as named; for example, the log.smbd, log.nmbd, and log.winbindd files collect messages associated with the daemons named in each respective log file.

Enable Remote Access

Network services aren't much good unless access is allowed from other systems. As with other RHEL 6 systems, each server has a firewall. The ports associated with Samba are closed by default. It's easy to set up access for a Samba server and a Samba client through the Firewall Configuration tool. All you'd need to do is to specify that the server or client is a trusted service.

As discussed in previous chapters, it's possible to limit remote access to certain IP addresses on a firewall. The **-s** switch in an **iptables**-based firewall configures source addresses. For example, the following rule would limit communication to the NetBIOS name service to any system but that on IP address 192.168.122.150:

```
-A INPUT -m state --state NEW -m udp -p udp -s !192.168.122.150 --dport 137 -j
ACCEPT
```

Remember, such specialized **iptables**-command rules can only be configured as a "Custom Rule" as described in Chapter 10.

SCENARIO & SOLUTION

You need to set up sharing on a network with Microsoft computers.	Install Samba, configure shared directories in /etc/samba/smb.conf. Make sure shared directories (except for user home directories) have the appropriate samba_share_t file type.
You want to set up sharing of user home directories via Samba.	Activate the [homes] stanza, set up appropriate users in the Samba authentication database, turn on the samba_enable_home_dirs boolean.
You want to set up host-based security for Samba.	Set up appropriate **hosts allow** and **hosts deny** directives in smb.conf, or configure **iptables**-based firewalls to limit access.
You want to set up user-based security for Samba.	Set up appropriate **valid users** and **invalid users** directives in smb.conf
You need to set up a share for group collaboration.	Set up a share stanza with **valid users** set to a specific group, along with appropriate values for directory mask (2770) and create mask (2770). Set up a shared directory for a group per Chapter 8. Make sure the shared directory is set to samba_share_t.

CERTIFICATION SUMMARY

Samba allows a Linux computer to appear like any other Microsoft computer on a Microsoft Windows–based network. Samba is based on the Server Message Block protocol, which allows Microsoft computers to communicate on a TCP/IP network. It has evolved as Microsoft has adapted SMB to the Common Internet File System. Network communication to Samba works through ports 137, 138, 139, and 445. The key SELinux boolean is samba_enable_home_dirs. Shared directories should be set to the samba_share_t file type.

The main Samba configuration file, /etc/samba/smb.conf, includes separate sections for global settings and share definitions. The **smbpasswd** command can be used to set up existing Linux users in a local Samba authentication database. The Red Hat SWAT tool, with a web-based interface, provides another way to configure smb.conf, as well as a front end to the **smbpasswd** command.

As for troubleshooting, changes to smb.conf can be easily tested with the **testparm** utility. Samba includes a number of synonyms for directives; some proper directives are based on spelling mistakes. While basic Samba service log messages can be found in the /var/log/messages file, most Samba log information can be found in the /var/log/samba directory. Many of the files in that directory include the client name or IP address.

TWO-MINUTE DRILL

Here are some of the key points from the certification objectives in Chapter 15.

Samba Services

❏ Samba allows Microsoft Windows computers to share files and printers across networks, using the Server Message Block (SMB) protocol on the TCP/IP protocol stack.

❏ Samba includes a client and a server. Variations on the **mount -t cifs** or **/sbin/mount.cifs** commands support mounting of a shared Samba or even a shared Microsoft directory.

❏ The main Samba configuration file is /etc/samba/smb.conf. You can configure it in a text editor or a GUI tool such as SWAT.

❏ Samba supports configuration of a Linux computer as a Microsoft Windows server. It can also provide Microsoft browsing, WINS, and Domain Controller services, even on an Active Directory network.

Samba as a Client

❏ The **smbclient** command can display shared directories and printers from specified remote Samba and Microsoft servers.

❏ The **mount.cifs** command can mount directories shared from a Samba or a Microsoft server.

❏ Samba shares can be mounted during the boot process with the help of the /etc/fstab configuration file.

Samba Troubleshooting

❏ The **testparm** command performs a syntax check on the main Samba configuration file, /etc/samba/smb.conf.

❏ Logs of Samba daemons may be written to the /var/log/messages file.

❏ Most Samba log files can be found in the /var/log/samba directory. Different log files can be found by client and by daemon.

SELF TEST

The following questions will help measure your understanding of the material presented in this chapter. As no multiple-choice questions appear on the Red Hat exams, no multiple-choice questions appear in this book. These questions exclusively test your understanding of the chapter. It is okay if you have another way of performing a task. Getting results, not memorizing trivia, is what counts on the Red Hat exams. There may be more than one answer to many of these questions.

Samba Services

1. A group that prefers Microsoft servers has set up a Windows 2008 server to handle file and print sharing services. This server correctly refers to a WINS server on 192.168.55.3 for name resolution and configures all user logins through the DC on 192.168.55.8. If you're configuring the local Linux system as a DC, what directive, at minimum, do you have to configure in the local Samba configuration file?

   _____

2. You've recently revised the Samba configuration file and do not want to disconnect any current users. What command forces the Samba service to reread the configuration file—without having to disconnect Microsoft users or restart the service?

   _____

3. What ports must be open for a Samba server to work with remote systems?

   _____

4. What SELinux setting is appropriate for sharing home directories over Samba?

   _____

5. What SELinux file type is appropriate for shared directories on Samba?

   _____

6. What Samba directive limits access to systems on the example.org network?

   _____

7. What Samba directive limits access to users tim and stephanie?

   _____

8. What Samba directive limits access in a shared stanza to a configured group named ilovelinux?

   _____

9. What Samba directive supports access to all users in a shared stanza?

   _____

10. What command adds user elizabeth to a smbpasswd or a tdbsam Samba authentication database?

    _____

Samba as a Client

11. What command can be used to mount remotely shared Microsoft directories?

    _____

Samba Troubleshooting

12. You made a couple of quick changes to a Samba configuration file and need to test it quickly for syntax errors. What command tests smb.conf for syntax errors?

    _____

LAB QUESTIONS

Several of these labs involve configuration exercises. You should do these exercises on test machines only. It's assumed that you're running these exercises on virtual machines such as KVM. For this chapter, it's also assumed that you may be changing the configuration of a physical host system for such virtual machines.

Red Hat presents its exams electronically. For that reason, the labs in this and future chapters are available from the CD that accompanies the book, in the Chapter15/ subdirectory. In case you haven't yet set up RHEL 6 on a system, refer to Chapter 1 for installation instructions.

The answers for each lab follow the Self Test answers for the fill-in-the-blank questions.

SELF TEST ANSWERS

Samba Services

1. At minimum, to configure a Linux system as a DC, you need to configure the **security = user** directive. If it's on an active directory system, it's better to use the **security = ads** directive.

2. The command that forces the Samba service to reread the configuration file—without disconnecting Microsoft users or restarting the service—is **service smb reload**.

3. Open ports associated with communication to a Samba server are TCP ports 137, 138, 139, and 445.

4. The SELinux boolean associated with the sharing of home directories on Samba is samba_enable_home_dirs.

5. The SELinux file type appropriate for shared Samba directories is samba_share_t.

6. The Samba directive that limits access to systems on the example.org network is

```
hosts allow .example.org
```

The following directive is also an acceptable answer:

```
allow hosts .example.org
```

7. One Samba directive that limits access to the noted users is

```
valid users = tim stephanie
```

8. One Samba directive that limits access to the noted group is

```
valid users = +ilovelinux
```

The **@ilovelinux** group would also be acceptable.

9. One Samba directive that supports access to all users in a shared stanza is

```
guest ok = yes
```

10. The command that adds user elizabeth to either Samba authentication database is

```
# smbpasswd -a elizabeth
```

Samba as a Client

11. The command that can be used to mount remotely shared Microsoft directories is **mount.cifs**. The **mount -t cifs** command is also an acceptable answer.

Samba Troubleshooting

12. The command that can test a Samba configuration file for errors is **testparm**.

LAB ANSWERS

Lab 1: Install and Start Samba

The chapter lab on Samba is designed to be easy to follow. However, you'll need explicit Linux knowledge to complete some specific steps. Answers to these steps can be found in the following:

1. You've installed the "CIFS file server" package group, which includes one RPM, samba. Dependent packages may also be installed.

2. One way to find all related Samba packages is with the **yum search samba | grep samba** command. You can then install noted packages with the **yum install packagename** command. Samba 4 packages are not supported for RHEL 6, at least not yet.

3. The Trusted Services section of the Firewall Configuration tool should make it easy to set up a local firewall to support communication to local Samba servers and clients.

4. You can use the **chkconfig smb on** command, the **ntsysv** tool, or the Service Configuration utility described in Chapter 7 to make sure Samba starts the next time you boot Linux.

5. Use the **service smb start** command to begin the Samba service. The **/etc/init.d/smb start** command is functionally equivalent.

6. One way to verify that Samba is running is to look for the existence of the **smbd** and **nmbd** processes in the process table. Use **ps aux | grep mbd** to see if these processes are present. Another way is with a service command such as **service smb status** command.

Lab 2: Review Samba Documentation

This lab should familiarize you with the available documentation for the Samba File Server. When you run the **man smb.conf** command, it will open the manual for the main Samba configuration file.

You should be able to search through the file with vi-style commands. For example, to search for the **hosts allow** directive, going forward in the file, type in

```
/hosts allow
```

and press **n** to see the next instance of that directive. Alternatively, to search backward, type in the following:

```
?hosts allow
```

and press **n** to see the previous instance of that directive in the man page.

From the browser, you should be able to review Samba documentation. This lab directs you to sample stanzas for shared directories. Of course, you can browse around other Samba documentation. Learn what you need as a reference for the job, or for an exam.

Lab 3: Configure Samba Global Settings

This lab assumes that you've backed up the smb.conf file from the /etc/samba directory.

1. To use SWAT, you'll first need to enable it with the associated Extended Internet Super Server. One way to do so is with the following commands:

    ```
    # /etc/init.d/xinetd.d restart
    # chkconfig swat on
    ```

2. Next, direct a browser to http://localhost:901. SWAT should prompt you for a username and password. By default, the root username and associated password will support access to SWAT.

3. Many administrators stick with the standard Microsoft Windows **workgroup** name of **WORKGROUP**. You can find it in the output from the **smbclient -L //*clientname*** command.

4. To limit access to a Samba server, you can do so in the Globals section, with the **hosts allow** directive. Of course, you can also do so by directly editing the smb.conf file in the /etc/samba directory.

5. To limit access from a specific computer, you can do so in the Globals section, with the **hosts deny** directive. Of course, you can also do so by directly editing the smb.conf file in the /etc/samba directory.

6. Make sure to click the Commit Changes button in SWAT. Then open a command line, and make Samba read the changes with the **service smb reload** command.

7. Before committing the changes, you can test them with the **testparm** command.

8. When testing the connection from another system, use the **smbclient** command. You'll need to allow access through UDP ports 137 and 138 for that purpose, something possible with the Trusted Services section of the Firewall Configuration tool.

9. If you need a fresh version of the smb.conf file, delete or move the existing version of the file from the /etc/samba directory and run the **yum reinstall samba-common** command.

Lab 4: Configure a Share to a Home Directory

If successful, only one remote user will get access to his home directory via Samba, something that can be tested with appropriate **smbclient** and **mount.cifs** commands. One way to implement the requirements of this lab is with the following steps.

1. Open the main Samba configuration file, /etc/samba/smb.conf, in a text editor.

2. Navigate to the **[homes]** share in the last part of this file.

3. Unless there is already an appropriate limitation in the **[global]** section in this file, you can limit the **[homes]** share with the **hosts allow = .example.com**.

4. Add a **guest ok = no** to the **[homes]** stanza.

5. Add a **valid users = *username*** directive with the name of the desired user.

6. Commit the changes. Add the desired user to the Samba authentication database with the **smbpasswd -a *username*** command.

7. Restart or reload the Samba daemon, **smb**, under the Status menu or with the appropriate **service** command.

8. Save the changes made so far.

9. Test the result from a remote system with the **smbclient** command. You should also be able to use the **mount.cifs** command from a client root account, with the **-o username=*username*** switch, to mount the shared user home directory.

Lab 5: Configure a Share to a Public Directory

This lab can be a continuation of Lab 4. You're just adding another stanza to the main Samba configuration file.

1. At the end of the file, start a **[public]** stanza. Add an appropriate comment for the stanza.

2. Set **path = /home/public**.

3. Make sure to set **hosts allow = .example.com**. Save your changes to the smb.conf file.

4. Set permissions for the public share with the following commands:

```
# mkdir /home/public
# chmod 1777 /home/public
```

Create a new directory, /home/public; configure that share and call it public. Set the **hosts allow** setting, and list the domain associated with your network. Deny access to all other systems.

The *777* setting for permissions grants read, write, and execute/search permissions to all users (root, root's group, and everyone else). The *1* at the beginning of the permission value sets the sticky bit. This bit, when set on directories, keeps users from deleting or renaming files they don't own.

5. Commit the changes to the currently running Samba service with the **service smb reload** command.

6. When testing the result from a remote system, any username in the local Samba database should work.

Lab 6: Configure a Shared Network Directory, Limited to a Group

This lab may take a significant amount of work. You'll need to set up a group of users, with group ownership of a dedicated directory. Since that discussion in Chapter 8 was based on an RHCSA requirement, you may have to repeat that process in this lab.

Once complete, you'll want to add the following directives to the stanza for the shared group directory:

```
create mask = 0770
directory mask = 2770
```

Lab 7: Persistency Check

It's important to make sure that the configured service actually runs after a reboot. In fact, it's best to make sure the configured service works after a SELinux relabel, but that process can take several minutes or more. And it's quite possible that you won't have that kind of time during an exam.

1. To complete many Linux configuration changes, you need to make sure that the service will start automatically when you reboot your computer. In general, the key command is **chkconfig**. In this case, the **chkconfig smb on** command sets up the **smbd** daemon to become active when you boot Linux in a standard runlevel.

2. You can use various commands to perform an orderly shutdown, such as **shutdown**, **halt**, **init** 0, and more.

3. After the reboot, you should verify at least one appropriate change to the Samba SELinux settings with the following command:

```
# getsebool samba_enable_home_dirs
```

4. In addition, you should confirm appropriate directories are configured with the samba_share_t file type, not only with the **ls -Z** command in the noted directories, but also in the file_contexts.local file, in the /etc/selinux/targeted/contexts/files directory.

16

More File-Sharing Services

L inux is designed for networking. Besides Samba, covered in Chapter 15, there are two other major services associated with sharing files on a network: NFS and FTP. RHEL 6 does not include GUI tools for these services. Even if Red Hat did as such, it's fastest to learn to configure these services from the command line. If you know these services, you can do more in less time by directly editing key configuration files.

This chapter starts with a description of the Network File System (NFS), a powerful and versatile way of sharing filesystems between servers and workstations. NFS client capabilities are included with a default installation of RHEL 6 and support connections to NFS servers.

The chapter continues with the Very Secure FTP (vsFTP) daemon, which provides both basic and secure FTP server services. With vsFTP, you can secure users, directories, subdirectories, and files with various levels of access control.

These are two more network services that you might configure and/or troubleshoot on the Red Hat exams. Take the time you need to understand the configuration files associated with each of these services, and practice making them work on a Linux computer. In some cases, two or three computers (such as the KVM virtual machines discussed in Chapter 1) running Linux will be useful to practice the lessons of this chapter.

INSIDE THE EXAM

In the RHCE objectives, the requirements for NFS are essentially the same as for Samba. Of course, the requirements associated with the configuration of NFS are quite different from those of Samba. So when you see the following objectives:

- Provide network shares to specific clients

- Provide network shares suitable for group collaboration

You can expect to study different techniques when setting up NFS to achieve those objectives. The process for limiting NFS access to specific clients is straightforward. The process to set up group collaboration for a NFS network share is based more on the shared directories configured on the NFS server.

This chapter also addresses FTP services. It's the same FTP server configured in Chapter 1 for the RHCSA exam, as an installation server for RHEL 6. The RHCE objective is to

- Configure anonymous-only download

The default installation of the vsFTP server already supports anonymous-only downloads. But it actually also supports access from regular users to their own local accounts. That's only stopped by a single SELinux boolean. In addition, the way vsFTP and NFS serves remote clients depends upon the changes made to firewall and SELinux options. And that's related to the standard RHCE objectives that apply to all services, including user- and host-based security.

CERTIFICATION OBJECTIVE 16.01

The Network File System (NFS) Server

NFS is the standard for sharing files and printers on a directory with Linux and Unix computers. It was originally developed by Sun Microsystems in the mid-1980s. Linux has supported NFS (both as a client and a server) for years, and NFS continues to be popular in organizations with Unix- or Linux-based networks.

You can create shared NFS directories directly by editing the /etc/exports configuration file. But it can be helpful to have some information on how NFS works, from the most important of the NFS files, to what you need to do to set up NFS for basic operation. With that information in hand, you'll understand what services to start, and how NFS communicates over a network. NFS communication can be configured over fixed ports with the help of the right settings in the /etc/sysconfig/nfs file. Of course, directories shared via NFS won't work without proper changes to SELinux.

NFS security can be enhanced in a number of ways, not only with the right options in **iptables**-based firewalls, but also with the help of TCP Wrappers.

NFS Options for RHEL 6

While NFS version 4 (NFSv4) is the default for RHEL 6, Linux NFS software also supports NFS versions 2 (NFSv2) and 3 (NFSv3). The differences include the way clients and servers communicate, the supported file sizes, and support for Windows-style access control lists (ACLs)

As NFSv4 is supported by default, you no longer have to set up Remote Procedure Call (RPC) communication with the rpcbind package. Nevertheless, RPC is still available for communications with other NFS clients. If used, you'll need to set up a number of fixed ports for NFS services; one method is based on configuration options available in the /etc/sysconfig/nfs file. NFSv4 supports ACLs.

The primary advantage of NFSv3 is support of 64-bit file sizes, which effectively allows access to more than 2GB of data over a shared directory. NFSv4 retains those advantages.

Basic NFS Installation

The primary group associated with NFS software is the "NFS file server." In other words, if you run the following command, **yum** installs the mandatory packages from that group, nfs-utils and nfs4-acl-tools:

```
# yum groupinstall "NFS file server"
```

But those are not the only packages of interest for NFS, especially for older versions of NFS (versions 2 and 3) that requires RPC support. Three other packages of interest include:

- **portreserve** Supports the portreserve service, the successor to portmap for NFS (and Network Information Service [NIS]) communication. Prevents NFS from taking ports needed by other services.
- **quota** Provides quota support for shared NFS directories; not absolutely required.
- **rpcbind** Includes RPC communication support for different NFS channels.

To make sure all needed packages are installed and operational, run the following commands:

```
# /etc/init.d/rpcbind start
# /etc/init.d/nfs start
# /etc/init.d/nfslock start
```

Depending on previous actions, it may help to substitute restart for start in these commands. After each command, you may want to check the result with the **rpcbind -p** command, as explained later in this chapter. In the next section, you'll examine the scripts relevant to NFS services.

Basic NFS Server Configuration

NFS servers are relatively easy to configure. All you need to do is export a filesystem, either generally or to a specific host, and then mount that filesystem from a remote client. Of course, you'll also need to open up the right ports in the firewall, and modify SELinux options as appropriate. NFS is controlled by a series of scripts, associated with a number of daemons. It also comes with a broad array of control commands.

NFS Service Scripts

Once appropriate packages are installed, they may be controlled by several different service scripts in the /etc/init.d directory:

- **/etc/init.d/nfs**   Control script for NFS; refers to /etc/sysconfig/nfs for basic configuration. Can control NFS services via rpc.nfsd, quotas via rpc.rquotad, the general security services daemon via rpc.svcgssd, and mounts via rpc. mountd.

- **/etc/init.d/nfslock**   Control script for lock files and the statd daemon, which locks and provides status for files currently in use.

- **/etc/init.d/portreserve**   Replacement for the portmap script; used to set up ports for RPC services.

- **/etc/init.d/rpcbind**   RPC program number converter.

- **/etc/init.d/rpcgssd**   Control script for RPC-related general security services.

- **/etc/init.d/rpcidmapd**   Configuration for NFS user ID mapping to LDAP and Kerberos systems.

- **/etc/init.d/rpcsvcgssd**   Control script for the server side of RPC-related general security services.

To configure an NFS server, you'll want to make sure all of these scripts are active in appropriate runlevels. As some of these scripts may not already be active, make sure to apply the following commands to start each of these scripts, and make sure they're active upon reboot:

```
# /etc/init.d/script start
# chkconfig script on
```

NFS Service Daemons

While the basic NFS control script (/etc/init.d/nfs) is fairly simple, that script includes a number of service daemons, each with its own function. These service daemons may be stored either in the /sbin or the /usr/sbin directories. All but **rpc.statd** are controlled by the NFS control script.

- **rpc.idmapd**   Works if /etc/idmapd.conf is configured.
- **rpc.mountd**   Processes mount requests and verifies current exports.
- **rpc.nfsd**   Supports client access with needed kernel threads.
- **rpc.rquotad**   Works with quota information.
- **rpc.statd**   Configures the status monitor, controlled by the /etc/init.d/nfslock script.

NFS Control Commands and Files

NFS includes a wide variety of commands to set up exports, to show what's available, to see what's mounted, to review statistics, and more. Except for specialized **mount** commands, these commands can be found in the /usr/sbin directory.

The NFS mount commands are **mount.nfs**, **mount.nfs4**, **umount.nfs**, and **umount.nfs4**. Functionally, they work like regular **mount** and **umount** commands. As suggested by the extensions, they apply to filesystems shared via NFSv4 and other NFS versions. Like other mount.* commands, they have functional equivalents. For example, the **mount.nfs4** command is functionally equivalent to the **mount -t nfs4** command.

If you're mounting a directory shared via NFSv2 or NFSv3, the **mount.nfs** and **mount -t nfs** commands are available for both systems.

The packages associated with NFS include a substantial number of commands in the /usr/sbin directory. The list of commands shown here are just the ones most commonly used to configure and test NFS.

- **exportfs**   The **exportfs** command can be used to manage directories shared through and configured in the /etc/exports file.
- **nfsiostat**   A statistics command for input/output rates based on an existing mount point. Uses information from the /proc/self/mountstats file.
- **nfsstat**   A statistics command for client/server activity based on an existing mount point. Uses information from the /proc/self/mountstats file.

■ **showmount** The command most closely associated with a display of shared NFS directories, locally and remotely.

Related commands associated with ACLs are available from the nfs4_acl_tools RPM. They work only with filesystems mounted locally with the acl option, as discussed in Chapter 6. The commands themselves are straightforward, as they set (**nfs4_setacl**), edit (**nfs4_editacl**), and list (**nfs4_getacl**) current ACLs of specified files. While these commands go beyond the basic operation of NFS, they are discussed in Chapter 4.

To review, on a /home directory mounted with the ACL option and then shared via NFS, I applied the **nfs4_getacl** command on a file from the remote client and got the following output:

```
A::OWNER@:rwatTcCy
A::GROUP@:tcy
A::EVERYONE@:tcy
```

The ACLs either Allow (A) or Deny (D) the file owner (OWNER, GROUP, or EVERYONE). In this case, the extensive levels of permissions given to the owner of the directory are essentially complete and more fine-grained than regular rwx permissions. For example, write (w) and append (a) are both enabled on a normal Linux file with write permissions.

Perhaps the simplest way to edit these ACLs is with the **nfs4_setacl -e** *filename* command, which opens the current permissions in a text editor. For example, I opened a file mounted via NFSv4 from a remote system with the following command:

```
$ nfs4_setacl -e /test/michael/filename.txt
```

It opened the given NFSv4 ACLs in the default text editor for the user (normally vi). When I deleted the append permissions for the owner of the file and then saved the changes, it actually deleted both append and write permissions for the file, with the following result, the next time the **nfs4_getacl** command was applied to the file:

```
D::OWNER@:wa
A::OWNER@:rtTcCy
A::GROUP@:rwatcy
A::EVERYONE@:rtcy
```

In addition, when the **ls -l** command is applied to the file, it's clear that the file owner no longer has write permissions.

Configure NFS for Basic Operation

The configuration of the basic /etc/exports file is fairly simple. Once it is configured, you can export directories set up in that file with the **exportfs -a** command. Each line in this file lists the directory to be exported, the hosts to which it will be exported, and the options that apply to this export. While multiple conditions can be set, you can export a particular directory only once. Take the following examples from an /etc/exports file:

```
/pub    (ro,sync) tester1.example.com(rw,sync)
/home   *.example.com(rw,sync)
/tftp   nodisk.example.net(rw,no_root_squash,sync)
```

In this example, the /pub directory is exported to all users as read-only. It is also exported to one specific computer with read/write privileges. The /home directory is exported, with read/write privileges, to any computer on the .example.com network. Finally, the /tftp directory is exported with full read/write privileges (even for root users) to the nodisk.example.net computer.

While these options are fairly straightforward, the /etc/exports file is somewhat picky. A space at the end of a line could lead to a syntax error. A space between a hostname and the conditions in parentheses would open access to all hosts.

All of these options include the **sync** flag. This requires all changes to be written to disk before a command such as a file copy is complete. Before NFSv4, many such options included the **insecure** flag, which allows access on ports above 1024. Even though NFSv4 automatically works with port 2049 by default, the **insecure** flag can still be useful to enable access for other ports above 1024, which is discussed later.

Wildcards and Globbing

In Linux network configuration files, you can specify a group of computers with the right wildcard, which in Linux is also known as *globbing*. What can be used as a wildcard depends on the configuration file. The NFS /etc/exports file uses "conventional" wildcards: for example, *.example.net specifies all computers within the example.net domain. In contrast, /etc/hosts.deny is less conventional; .example.net, with the leading dot, specifies all computers in that same domain.

For IPv4 networks, wildcards often require some form of the subnet mask. For example, 192.168.0.0/255.255.255.0 specifies the 192.168.0.0 network of computers with IP addresses that range from 192.168.0.1 to 192.168.0.254. Some services support the use of CIDR (Classless Inter-Domain Routing) notation. In CIDR, since 255.255.255.0 masks 24 bits, CIDR represents this with the number 24. When configuring a network in CIDR notation, you can represent this network as 192.168.0.0/24.

More NFS Server Options

The examples of shared directories shown earlier are just three ways to share a directory. With /etc/exports, it's possible to use a number of different parameters. The parameters described in Tables 16-1 and 16-2 fall into two categories: general and user access.

TABLE 16-1	Parameter	Corresponding /etc/exports Command / Description
NFS /etc/exports General Options	insecure	Supports communications above port 1024, primarily for NFS versions 2 and 3.
	insecure_locks	Allows insecure file locks; suitable for older NFS clients. Does not check user permissions to a file.
	no_subtree_check	Disables subtree checks. If you export a subdirectory such as /mnt/inst, this feature disables checks of higher-level directories for permissions.
	sync	Syncs write operations on request. Active by default.
	no_wdelay	Forces immediate data writes.
	hide	Hide filesystems; if you export a directory and subdirectory such as /mnt and /mnt/inst, shares to /mnt/inst must be explicitly mounted.
	mp	Export only if mounted; requires the export point to also be a mount point on the client.
	fsid	Set explicit filesystem ID; specifies a numeric identifier for the exported filesystem.

Other parameters relate to how users are treated for the purpose of NFS shared directories. As shown in Table 16-2, the options are associated with the root administrative user, anonymous-only users, and other users that may be designated in the parameters.

Activate the List of Exports

It's not enough to configure the /etc/exports file, as it's simply the default set of exported directories. You need to activate them with the **exportfs -a** command. The next time RHEL 6 is booted, if the right services are activated, the **nfs** start script (/etc/init.d/nfs) automatically runs the **exportfs -r** command, which re-exports directories configured in /etc/exports.

However, if you're modifying, moving, or deleting a share, it is safest to temporarily unexport all filesystems first with the **exportfs -ua** command before reexporting the shares with the **exportfs -a** command.

Once exports are active, they're easy to check. Just run the **showmount -e** command on the server. To review the export list for a remote NFS server, just add the name of the NFS server. For example, the **showmount -e server1.example.com** command looks for the list of exported NFS directories from the server1.example.com system. If this command doesn't work, communication may be blocked with a firewall.

Special Requirements for /home Directories

Some systems store user /home directories on a central server. Such directories can be shared via NFS. Administrators can then back up the /home directories on a regular basis, perhaps supplemented by configuration in a RAID array. That works

TABLE 16-2	Parameter	Corresponding /etc/exports Command / Description
NFS Tool User Access Options	no_root_squash	Treat remote root user as local root; remote root users get root privileges on the shared directory.
	all_squash	Treat all client users as anonymous users; all remote users are mapped as an anonymous user.
	anonuid=*userid*	Specify local user ID for anonymous users; supports mapping of remote users to a specific user ID such as guest.
	anonuid=*userid*	Specify local group ID for anonymous groups; supports mapping of remote groups to a specific group ID.

based on a central authentication database of users and passwords, such as LDAP or Kerberos. In some cases, /home directories may be shared on a small network without a shared authentication database.

In either case, you should configure the /etc/idmapd.conf file to set up how the NFS shared /home directories read the authentication database. Otherwise, such home directories may be configured with ownership by the user named nobody, which would be troublesome to regular users.

The /etc/idmapd.conf file is straightforward and well commented. In all cases, you should change the **Domain**, **Nobody-User**, and **Nobody-Group** directives to match the domain of the current network and the nfsnobody user and group to minimize the associated privileges. For the example.com domain, that would be

```
DOMAIN = example.com
Nobody-User = nfsnobody
Nobody-Group = nfsnobody
```

While the nsswitch option shown is supposed to be the default, I've found it useful in my tests to make it explicit:

```
Method = nsswitch
```

As discussed in Chapter 8, LDAP authentication may be incorporated into the associated /etc/nsswitch.conf file. Nevertheless, additional custom options for connections to both LDAP and Kerberos services are shown in the databases.

You'll need to make the same changes to all /etc/idmapd.conf files on each NFS client. Changes are applied when you run the **/etc/init.d/rpcidmapd restart** command on both the NFS server and each client.

Fixed Ports in /etc/sysconfig/nfs

NFSv4 is easier to configure, especially with respect to firewalls. To enable communication with an NFSv4 server, the only ports you absolutely need to open are TCP port 2049 and UDP port 111. Port 2049 is the standard for NFSv4 communications. Port 111 supports RPC communications over a network. However, that does not support full functionality of the commands associated with NFS.

While NFSv4 is the default, RHEL 6 still supports NVSv2 and NFSv3. So given the publicly available information on the RHCE exam, you might also need to know how to handle those versions of NFS. With associated services, NFSv2 and NFSv3 uses dynamic port numbers. Even for NFSv4, you may want to fix some of the associated ports, to support the use of the **showmount** command. With fixed ports, you can configure a firewall with appropriate open ports to support an NFS server.

For that purpose, review the /etc/sysconfig/nfs file. It is already preconfigured with comments suggesting appropriate fixed port numbers. While you don't have to follow the suggested port numbers in the commented version of the file, you can. Generally, such port numbers do not cause trouble, as they do not conflict with any commonly used RHEL 6 services. For convenience, however, many administrators set up a series of consecutive unused ports for this purpose, such as 4000 through 4003.

The port numbers listed in Table 16-3 are listed in the order shown in the default version of the /etc/sysconfig/nfs file. The table does not include now-obsolete references to the **rpc.lockd** daemon, as that's not available for RHEL 6.

Once changes are made and saved to the /etc/sysconfig/nfs file, restart the associated service with the /etc/init.d/nfs restart command. If successful, you'll see the associated ports in the output to the rpcinfo command, which lists all communication channels associated with RPC. The following command is more precise, as it isolates actual port numbers:

```
# rpcinfo -p
```

Sample output is shown in Figure 16-1. At first glance, the lines may appear repetitive; however, every line has a purpose. Unless another RPC-related service such as the Network Information Service (NIS) is running, all of the lines shown here are required for NFS communications, when NFSv2 or NFSv3 is used. Examine the first line shown here:

```
program vers proto   port  service
100000    4   tcp    111  portmapper
```

TABLE 16-3	Port	Parameter	Description
NFS Tool User Access Options	875	RQUOTAD	Remote quota daemon
	892	MOUNTD_PORT	For mount requests
	662	STATD_PORT	For status requests, including locked files (port 662 is assigned to a normally unused FTP protocol)
	2020	STATD_OUTGOING_PORT	Reference to outgoing communications.

FIGURE 16-1

Sample rpcinfo -p
output with NFS-
related ports

```
[root@MinimalRHEL6 ~]# rpcinfo -p
   program vers proto   port  service
    100000    4   tcp    111  portmapper
    100000    3   tcp    111  portmapper
    100000    2   tcp    111  portmapper
    100000    4   udp    111  portmapper
    100000    3   udp    111  portmapper
    100000    2   udp    111  portmapper
    100011    1   udp    875  rquotad
    100011    2   udp    875  rquotad
    100011    1   tcp    875  rquotad
    100011    2   tcp    875  rquotad
    100003    2   tcp   2049  nfs
    100003    3   tcp   2049  nfs
    100003    4   tcp   2049  nfs
    100227    2   tcp   2049  nfs_acl
    100227    3   tcp   2049  nfs_acl
    100003    2   udp   2049  nfs
    100003    3   udp   2049  nfs
    100003    4   udp   2049  nfs
    100227    2   udp   2049  nfs_acl
    100227    3   udp   2049  nfs_acl
    100021    1   udp  32769  nlockmgr
    100021    3   udp  32769  nlockmgr
    100021    4   udp  32769  nlockmgr
    100021    1   tcp  32803  nlockmgr
    100021    3   tcp  32803  nlockmgr
    100021    4   tcp  32803  nlockmgr
    100005    1   udp    892  mountd
    100005    1   tcp    892  mountd
    100005    2   udp    892  mountd
    100005    2   tcp    892  mountd
    100005    3   udp    892  mountd
    100005    3   tcp    892  mountd
[root@MinimalRHEL6 ~]#
```

The first line represents the arbitrary RPC program number, the NFS version, the use of TCP as a communications protocol, over port 111, with the portmapper service. Note the availability of the portmapper service to NFS versions 2, 3, and 4, communicating over the TCP and UDP protocols.

Communication through selected ports should also be allowed through any configured firewall. For example, Figure 16-2 shows the /etc/sysconfig/iptables file for a firewall that supports remote access to a local NFS server.

Of course, you can set up these firewall rules with the Firewall Configuration tool discussed in Chapter 10.

FIGURE 16-2

Firewall rules
for NFS

```
# Firewall configuration written by system-config-firewall
# Manual customization of this file is not recommended.
*filter
:INPUT ACCEPT [0:0]
:FORWARD ACCEPT [0:0]
:OUTPUT ACCEPT [0:0]
-A INPUT -m state --state ESTABLISHED,RELATED -j ACCEPT
-A INPUT -p icmp -j ACCEPT
-A INPUT -i lo -j ACCEPT
-A INPUT -m state --state NEW -m tcp -p tcp --dport 2049 -j ACCEPT
-A INPUT -m state --state NEW -m tcp -p tcp --dport 22 -j ACCEPT
-A INPUT -m state --state NEW -m tcp -p tcp --dport 80 -j ACCEPT
-A INPUT -m state --state NEW -m tcp -p tcp --dport 111 -j ACCEPT
-A INPUT -m state --state NEW -m udp -p udp --dport 111 -j ACCEPT
-A INPUT -j REJECT --reject-with icmp-host-prohibited
-A FORWARD -j REJECT --reject-with icmp-host-prohibited
COMMIT
~
"/etc/sysconfig/iptables" 17L, 740C
```

Make NFS Work with SELinux

Of course, appropriate firewalls are not enough. SELinux is an integral part of the security landscape, with respect to both boolean options and files. First, there are two file types associated with NFS:

- **var_lib_nfs_t**   Associated with dynamic files in the /var/lib/nfs directory. Files in this directory are updated as shares are mounted, as files from shared directories are called and locked.

- **nfsd_exec_t**   Assigned to system executable files such as **rpc.mountd** and **rpc.nfsd** in the /usr/sbin directory. Closely related are the rpcd_exec_t and gssd_exec_t file types, for services associated with RPCs and communications with Kerberos servers.

In general, you won't have to assign a new file type to a shared NFS directory. So for most administrators, these file types are shown for reference.

So for SELinux, the boolean directives are most important. The options are shown in the Booleans section of the SELinux Administration tool, with the nfs filter, as shown in Figure 16-3. The figure reflects the default configuration; in other words, the global modules are all enabled by default.

The following directives are associated with making NFS work with SELinux in targeted mode. While most of these modules were already listed in Chapter 10,

FIGURE 16-3   NFS-related SELinux boolean options

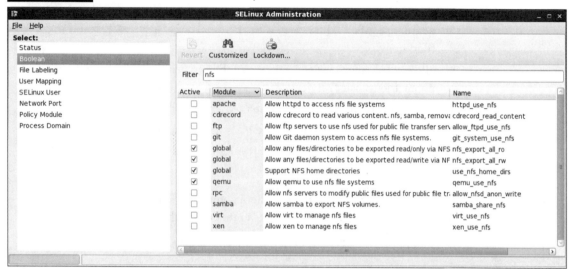

they're worth repeating, if only to help those who fear SELinux. The first module is not shown in Figure 16-3. The remaining modules are described in the order shown in the figure.

- **allow_gssd_read_tmp**   Supports the reading of temporary directories by the General Security Services daemon, **gssd**, which helps protect NFS when systems authenticate through Kerberos 5.
- **httpd_use_nfs**   Supports access by the Apache Web server to shared NFS directories.
- **cd_record_read_content**   Enables access to mounted NFS directories by the cdrecord command.
- **allow_ftpd_use_nfs**   Allows the use of shared NFS directories by FTP servers.
- **git_system_use_nfs**   Supports access of NFS shares by the git revision control system service.
- **nfs_export_all_ro**   Supports read-only access to shared NFS directories.
- **nfs_export_all_rw**   Supports read/write access to shared NFS directories.

- **use_nfs_home_dirs**   Enables the mounting of /home on a remote NFS server.
- **qemu_use_nfs**   Allows access by the quick emulator to NFS-mounted filesystems.
- **allow_nfsd_anon_write**   Supports NFS servers when they modify files on public file transfer services.
- **samba_share_nfs**   Allows Samba to export NFS-mounted directories.
- **virt_use_nfs**   Enables access by VMs to NFS-mounted filesystems.
- **xen_use_nfs**   Allows access by the Xen virtual machine monitor to NFS-mounted filesystems.

To set these directives, use the **setsebool** command. For example, to activate access by an FTP server, in a way that survives a reboot, run the following command:

```
# setsebool -P allow_ftpd_use_nfs 1
```

Quirks and Limitations of NFS

NFS does have its problems. Any administrator who controls shared NFS directories would be wise to take note of these limitations.

Statelessness

NFS is a "stateless" protocol. In other words, you don't need to log in separately to access a shared NFS directory. Instead, the NFS client normally contacts rpc.mountd on the server. The **rpc.mounted** daemon handles mount requests. It checks the request against currently exported filesystems. If the request is valid, **rpc.mounted** provides an *NFS file handle* (a "magic cookie"), which is then used for further client/server communication for this share.

The stateless protocol allows the NFS client to wait if the NFS server ever has to be rebooted. The software waits, and waits, and waits. This can cause the NFS client to hang. The client may even have to reboot or even power-cycle the system.

This can also lead to problems with insecure single-user clients. When a file is opened through a share, it may be "locked out" from other users. When an NFS server is rebooted, handling the locked file can be difficult. The security problems can be so severe that NFS communication is blocked even by the default Red Hat Enterprise Linux firewall.

In theory, the recent change to NFS, setting up sync as the default for file transfers, should help address this problem. In theory, locked-out users should not lose any data that they've written with the appropriate commands.

Absolute and Relative Symbolic Links

If you have any symbolic links on an exported directory, be careful. The client interprets a symbolically linked file from a remotely mounted directory as if it were a local link. Unless the mount point and filesystem structures are identical, the linked file can point to an unexpected location, which may lead to unpredictable consequences.

There are two ways to address this issue. You can take the time to analyze the exported directory, limiting the use of symbolic links. Alternatively, you could use the NFS server-side export option (**link_relative**) that converts absolute links to relative links; however, this can have counterintuitive results if the client mounts a subdirectory of the exported directory.

Root Squash

By default, NFS is set up to **root_squash**, which prevents root users on an NFS client from gaining root access to a share on an NFS server. Specifically, the root user on a client (with a user ID of 0) is mapped to the *nfsnobody* unprivileged account (if in doubt, check the local /etc/passwd file).

This behavior can be disabled via the **no_root_squash** server export option in /etc/exports. For exported directories so disabled, remote root users can use their root privileges on the shared NFS directory. While it can be useful, it is also a security risk, especially from crackers who use their own Linux systems to take advantage of those root privileges.

NFS Hangs

Because NFS is stateless, NFS clients may wait up to several minutes for a server. In some cases, an NFS client may wait indefinitely if a server goes down. During the wait, any process that looks for a file on the mounted NFS share will hang. Once this happens, it is generally difficult or impossible to unmount the offending filesystems. You can do several things to reduce the impact of this problem:

■ Take great care to ensure the reliability of NFS servers and the network.

■ Avoid mounting many different NFS servers at once. If several computers mount each other's NFS directories, this could cause problems throughout the network.

■ Mount infrequently used NFS exports only when needed. NFS clients should unmount these clients after use.

■ Set up NFS shares with the **sync** option, which should at least reduce the incidence of lost files.

■ Avoid configuring a mission-critical computer as an NFS client.

■ Keep NFS mounted directories out of the search path for users, especially that of root.

■ Keep NFS mounted directories out of the root (/) directory; instead, segregate them to a less frequently used filesystem, if possible, on a separate partition.

Inverse DNS Pointers

An NFS server daemon checks mount requests. First, it looks at the current list of exports, based on /etc/exports. Then it looks up the client's IP address to find its host name. This requires a reverse DNS lookup.

This hostname is then finally checked against the list of exports. If NFS can't find a hostname, **rpc.mountd** will deny access to that client. For security reasons, it also adds a "request from unknown host" entry in /var/log/messages.

File Locking

Multiple NFS clients can be set up to mount the same exported directory from the same server. It's quite possible that people on different computers end up trying to use the same shared file. This is addressed by the file-locking daemon service.

While mandatory locks can now be configured with NFSv4, NFS has historically had serious problems with file locks. If you have an application that depends on file locking over NFS, test it thoroughly before putting it into production.

Performance Tips

You can do several things to keep NFS running in a stable and reliable manner. As you gain experience with NFS, you might monitor or even experiment with the following factors:

- Eight kernel NFS daemons, which is the default, is generally sufficient for good performance, even under fairly heavy loads. To increase the capacity of the service, you can add additional NFS daemons through the **RPCNFSDCOUNT** directive in the /etc/sysconfig/nfs configuration file. Just keep in mind that the extra kernel processes consume valuable kernel resources.

- NFS write performance can be extremely slow, particularly with NFS v2 clients, as the client waits for each block of data to be written to disk.

- You may try specialized hardware with nonvolatile RAM. Data that is stored on such RAM isn't lost if you have trouble with network connectivity or a power failure.

- In applications where data loss is not a big concern, you may try the **async** option. This makes NFS faster because **async** NFS mounts do not write files to disk until other operations are complete. However, a loss of power or network connectivity can result in a loss of data.

- Hostname lookups are performed frequently by the NFS server; you can start the Name Switch Cache Daemon (**nscd**) to speed lookup performance.

on the **job**

NFS is a powerful file-sharing system. But there are risks with NFS. If an NFS server is down, it could affect the entire network. In my personal opinion, it's also not sufficiently secure to use on the Internet. NFS is primarily used on secure networks.

NFS Security Directives

NFS includes a number of serious security problems and should never be used in hostile environments (such as on a server directly exposed to the Internet), at least not without strong precautions.

Shortcomings and Risks

NFS is an easy-to-use yet powerful file-sharing system. However, it is not without its problems. The following are a few security issues to keep in mind:

- **Authentication** NFS relies on the host to report user and group IDs. However, this can be a security risk if root users on other computers access your NFS shares. In other words, data that is accessible via NFS to *any user* can potentially be accessed by *any other* user. This risk is addressed in part by NFSv4, if the system is configured as a Kerberos client.

■ **Privacy**   Before NFSv4, such network connections were not encrypted. NFSv4 connections with the support of a Kerberos server are encrypted.

■ **portmap infrastructure**   Both the NFS client and server depend on the RPC portmap daemon. The portmap daemon has historically had a number of serious security holes. For this reason, RHEL 6 has replaced it with the portmapper service.

Security Tips

If NFS *must* be used in or near a hostile environment, you can reduce the security risks:

■ Educate yourself in detail about NFS security. If possible, set up encrypted NFSv4 communications with the help of Kerberos. Otherwise, restrict NFS to friendly, internal networks protected with a good firewall.

■ Export as little data as possible, and export filesystems as read-only if possible.

■ Unless absolutely necessary, don't supersede the **root_squash** option. Otherwise, crackers on allowed clients may have root-level access to exported filesystems.

■ If an NFS client has a direct connection to the Internet, use separate network adapters for the Internet connection and the LAN. Then limit use of NFS to the network adapter connected to the internal network.

■ Use appropriate firewall settings to deny access to the portmapper and nfsd ports, except from explicitly trusted hosts or networks. If you're using NFSv4, it's good enough to open the following ports:

```
111     TCP/UDP     portmapper     (server and client)
2049    TCP/UDP     nfsd           (server)
```

■ Set fixed port numbers for the services associated with NFS. As discussed earlier, it's possible in /etc/sysconfig/nfs. If you prefer a continuous group of port numbers, one option is 4000:4003:

```
LOCKD_TCPPORT=4000
LOCKD_UDPPORT=4000
MOUNTD_PORT=4001
STATD_PORT=4002
RQUOTAD_PORT=4003
```

■ Use a port scanner such as **nmap** to verify that these ports are blocked for untrusted network(s).

Options for Host-Based Security

To review, host-based security on NFS systems is based primarily on the systems allowed to access a share in the /etc/exports file. Of course, host-based security can also include limits based on **iptables** firewall rules.

Options for User-Based Security

As NFS mounts should reflect the security associated with a common user database, the standard user-based security options should apply. That includes the configuration of a common group, as discussed in Chapter 8.

watch   *As long as there's a common user database, such as LDAP, the permissions associated with a common*   *group directory carry over to a mount shared via NFS.*

EXERCISE 16-1

NFS

This exercise requires two systems: one set up as an NFS server, the other as an NFS client. Then, on the NFS server, take the following steps:

1. Set up a group named IT for the Information Technology group in /etc/group.
2. Create the /MIS directory. Assign ownership to the MIS group with the **chgrp** command.
3. Set the SGID bit on this directory to enforce group ownership.
4. Update the /etc/exports file to allow read and write permissions to the share for the local network. Run the following command to set it up under NFS:

```
# exportfs -a
```

5. Make sure the SELinux booleans are compatible; specifically, make sure the nfs_export_all_ro and nfs_export_all_rw booleans are both still set. You can do so either with the **getsebool** command or the SELinux Management tool.

6. Set fixed ports for the parameters described in the /etc/sysconfig/nfs file.

7. Open those ports in the firewall. Restart the firewall with the **/etc/init.d/iptables restart** command.

8. Restart the NFS service with the **/etc/init.d/nfs restart** command.

Then, on an NFS client, take the following steps:

9. Create a directory for the server share called /mnt/MIS.

10. Mount the shared NFS directory on /mnt/MIS.

11. List all exported shares from the server and save this output in the shares.list file in the /mnt/MIS directory.

12. Make this service a permanent connection in the /etc/fstab file. Assume that the connection might be troublesome and add the appropriate options, such as soft mounting.

13. Run the **mount -a** command to reread /etc/fstab. Check to see if the share is properly remounted.

14. Test the NFS connection. Stop the NFS service on the server, and then try copying a file to the /mnt/MIS directory. While the attempt to copy will fail, it should not hang the client.

15. Restart the NFS service on the server.

16. Edit /etc/fstab again. This time, assume that NFS is reliable, and remove the special options added in Step 12.

17. Now shut down the server and test what happens. The mounted NFS directory on the client should hang when you try to access the service.

18. The client computer may lock. If so you can boot into single-user mode, as described in Chapter 5, to avoid the pain of a reboot. Restore the original configuration.

Test an NFS Client

Now you can mount a shared NFS directory from a client computer. The commands and configuration files are similar to those used for any local filesystem. In the preceding section, you configured an NFS server. For now, stay on the NFS server system, as the first client test can be run directly from the server system.

NFS Mount Options

Before doing anything elaborate, you should check for the list of shared NFS directories. Then you can test the shared NFS directory from a second Linux system, presumably a RHEL 6 system (or equivalent). To that end, the **showmount** command displays available shared directories.

The two options of significance are **-d** and **-e**; when coupled with the hostname or IP address of the NFS server, the command displays the shared directories, possibly including the host limits of the share. For example, given a simple share of the /mnt and /home directories on a given NFS server, the **showmount -d server1.example.com** command provides the following result:

```
Directories on server1.example.com:
/home
/mnt
```

As suggested, the **showmount -e server1.example.com** command provides more information:

```
Export list for server1.example.com:
/mnt   192.168.100.0/24
/home  192.168.122.0/24
```

If you don't see a list of shared directories, log in to the NFS server system. Repeat the **showmount** command, substituting localhost or 127.0.0.1 for the hostname or IP address. If there's still no output, review the steps described earlier in this chapter. Make sure the /etc/exports file is configured properly. Remember to export the shared directories. Use the command

```
# /etc/init.d/nfs status
```

to see if the nfsd, rpc.mountd, and rpc.rquotad services are running. Unless the system is a Kerberos client, don't be concerned by the following message in the **nfs status** command output:

```
rpc.svcgssd is stopped
```

The advertising of shared NFS directories depends on RPC. And that starts with the rpc.statd service, controlled by the /etc/init.d/rpcbind script. If all such services are in operation, one more thing to check is the output to the **rpcinfo -p** command. As shown back in Figure 16-1, it lists a number of services and ports.

For NFSv2 and NFSv3, if the ports are not fixed per /etc/sysconfig/nfs, it won't be possible to set up an iptables-based firewall to support communication through those ports. If not all of the services shown in Figure 16-1 show up on the local system, something may be missing.

Now to mount this directory locally, you'll need an empty local directory. Create a directory such as /remotemnt. You can then mount the shared directory from a system like 192.168.122.50 with the following command:

```
# mount.nfs4 192.168.122.50:/mnt /remotemnt
```

This command mounts the NFS shared /mnt directory from the computer on the noted IP address. If desired, you could substitute the **mount -t nfs4** command for **mount.nfs4**. When it works, you'll be able to access files from the remote /mnt directory as if it were a local directory. If the local mount works, but the remote mount does not, the most likely cause of the problem is the firewall.

Configure NFS in /etc/fstab

You can also configure an NFS client to mount a remote NFS directory during the boot process, as defined in /etc/fstab. For example, the following entry in a client /etc/fstab mounts the /homenfs share from the computer named nfsserv, based on NFSv4, on the local /nfs/home directory:

```
nfsserv:/homenfs   /nfs/home  nfs4   soft,timeo=100  0  0
```

w a t c h

NFS-specific options to the mount command that can also be used in /etc/fstab can be found in the nfs man page.

The **soft** and **timeo** options are part of a variety of specialized NFS mount options. Such options as shown here can also be used to customize how mounts are done during the boot process in the /etc/fstab file. For more information on these and related options, see the nfs man page, available with the **man nfs** command.

Alternatively, an automounter can be used to mount NFS filesystems dynamically as required by the client computer. The automounter can also unmount these remote filesystems after a period of inactivity. For more information on the governing autofs service, see Chapter 6.

Without a timeout, NFS mounts through /etc/fstab can be troublesome. For example, if the network or the NFS server is down, the lack of a timeout can hang the client. (I discussed this issue in more detail earlier in this chapter.) A hang is a big problem if it happens during the boot process, because the boot may never complete, and you would have to restore your system by booting into some runlevel where networking is not started, such as runlevel 1.

Diskless Clients

NFS supports diskless clients, which are computers that do not store the operating system locally. A diskless client may use a boot floppy or a boot programmable read-only memory (PROM) chip to get started. Then embedded commands can mount the appropriate root (/) directory, set up swap space, set the /usr directory as read-only, and configure other shared directories such as /home in read/write mode. If your computer uses a boot PROM, you'll also need access to DHCP and TFTP servers for network and kernel information.

Red Hat Enterprise Linux includes features that support diskless clients. While they are not listed as part of the current Red Hat exam requirements or related course outlines, I would not be surprised to see such requirements in the future. For more information on an open-source Red Hat project on the topic, see the Cobbler project at https://fedorahosted.org/cobbler/.

Soft Mounting

Consider using the **soft** option when mounting NFS filesystems. When an NFS server fails, a soft-mounted NFS filesystem will fail rather than hang. However, this risks the failure of long-running processes due to temporary network outages.

In addition, you can use the **timeo** option to set a timeout interval, in tenths of a second. For example, the following command would mount /nfs/home with a timeout of 30 seconds (**timeo** uses tenths of a second):

```
# mount -o soft,timeo=300 myserver:/home /nfs/home
```

Current NFS Status

The current status of NFS services, mostly, is documented in two directories: /var/lib/nfs and /proc/fs/nfsd. If there's a problem with NFS, look at some of the files in these directories. Take these directories one at a time. First, there are two key files in the /var/lib/nfs directory:

- **etab**   Includes a full description of exported directories, including default options.
- **rmtab**   Specifies the state of shared directories currently mounted.

Take a look at the contents of the /proc/fs/nfsd directory. As a virtual directory, files in the /proc directory tree have a size of zero. However, as dynamic files, they can contain valuable information. Perhaps the key option for basic operation is the file named versions. The contents of that file specifies the currently recognized versions of NFS.

The normal content of this file is just a little cryptic, which suggests that the current NFS server can communicate using NFSv2, NFSv3, and NFSv4, but not NFS version 4.1.

```
+2 +3 +4 -4.1
```

So when I accidentally activated the **#RPCNFSDARGS="-N 4"** option in the /etc/sysconfig/nfs file, the contents of the versions file changed to

```
+2 +3 -4 -4.1
```

The difference is subtle, but tells me that the local NFS server does not currently recognize NFSv4 connections. Of course, with the advantages associated with NFSv4, you should not activate the **RPCNFSDARGS="-N 4"** option.

CERTIFICATION OBJECTIVE 16.03

The Very Secure FTP Server

The File Transfer Protocol is one of the original network applications developed with the TCP/IP protocol suite. It follows the standard model for network services, as FTP requires a client and a server. The **lftp** command line client is easy to install from a package of the same name. The FTP Server package group includes the default Red Hat FTP Server, the very secure FTP (vsFTP) daemon.

This section is focused on the configuration of the FTP server. You'll test the result with the **lftp** client, described in Chapter 2. While there are many other excellent FTP servers for Linux, vsFTP is the only one supported on RHEL 6.

Basic vsFTP Configuration

The simplest way to install vsFTP with dependencies is with the following command:

```
# yum install vsftpd
```

Of course, if you're installing vsFTP in production or during an exam, it's important to run commands such as the following:

```
# /etc/init.d/vsftpd start
# chkconfig vsftpd on
```

As noted in Chapter 11, these commands start the noted service and make sure the service starts the next time the system is rebooted. Once installed, associated configuration files can be found in the /etc/vsftpd directory. There's one additional configuration file, vsftpd, in the /etc/pam.d directory. A check with the **ldd** and **strings** commands, applied to the vsftpd daemon in the /usr/sbin directory, confirms that vsFTP can be protected with the TCP Wrappers files described in Chapter 10. However, before vsFTP can be protected with TCP Wrappers, you need to make sure to keep a key option at the end of the vsftpd.conf configuration file.

The man page for the vsftpd.conf configuration file has a full list of available directives, split into three categories:

- **boolean**   Like SELinux options, may be set to yes or no.
- **numeric**   Can be set to a specific numeric value.
- **string**   Associated with values such as filenames.

The Main vsFTP Configuration File

The main vsFTP configuration file is vsftpd.conf, in the /etc/vsftpd directory. Normally, it's pretty secure. But if it is configured incorrectly, you could end up providing access to the top-level root directory for users who connect with regular user accounts. To start securing a vsFTP server, you can configure vsFTP to disable logins from regular users. You can configure vsFTP through the vsftpd.conf configuration file in the /etc/vsftpd directory.

Many standard settings in the vsftpd.conf file are different from the actual default value of a directive listed in the file. In this section, I refer to the original version of the vsftpd.conf file, as installed, as the "standard" version of the file. Before starting, there's one critical directive not listed in the file:

```
ftp_username
```

It's the default user for anonymous connections. In other words, when a remote user connects with username anonymous, that user connects on the server as a user named ftp. In the /etc/passwd file, that user is listed with the following settings:

```
ftp:x:14:50:FTP User:/var/ftp:/sbin/nologin
```

In other words, users can't log in directly as the user named ftp. However, anonymous users on the vsFTP server are taken to that user's home directory, /var/ftp. So if you want to change the default directory associated with anonymous logins, change the home directory associated with the local user named ftp.

The following is an analysis of the default RHEL 6 version of this file. Some of it may be reformatted for clarity, some for desirable options. In a couple of cases, directives are analyzed in an order different from that shown in the file. First note the following comment:

```
# The default compiled in settings are fairly paranoid. This sample
# file loosens things up a bit, to make the ftp daemon more usable.
```

The vsFTP service is designed for anonymous access. The following comment emphasizes it. To disable anonymous access, you'll have to set this to **NO**.

```
# Allow anonymous FTP? (Beware - allowed by default if you comment
# this out).
anonymous_enable=YES
```

The standard vsftpd.conf file supports access by users configured in the local authentication database. The RHCE objectives suggests "anonymous-only download." To set up the server for anonymous-only access, change this option to **local_enable=NO**. Since that's the default, it's sufficient to comment out the directive as shown here:

```
# local_enable=YES
```

If there's actually a need to enable local users, you'll also have to enable the SELinux ftp_home_dir boolean. By default, such users are also able to access the top-level root directory, unless you include the following directive:

```
chroot_local_user=YES
```

While the standard version of the vsftpd.conf file supports write commands by users, the default value of the write_enable directive is no. As the relevant RHCE objective requires support only for anonymous downloads, be prepared to comment out or change this directive:

```
# write_enable = yes
```

The target directory also needs a special SELabel: public_content_rw_t. Changes are also required to activate either the allow_ftpd_anon_write or the ftp_home_dir boolean, depending on the users who are allowed to write files through the FTP server.

If writes are enabled, files are written with some permissions. New files on a local system are given permissions based on the value of umask, as discussed in Chapter 4. The umask associated with writes is set with the following directive:

```
local_umask=022
```

While support for anonymous-only downloads is listed in the RHCE objectives, there are circumstances where you might allow anonymous users to upload files. Yes, allowing anonymous users to write anything to a server can be a security risk.

As suggested by the associated comment, it also requires an appropriate directory, writable by the FTP user, and configured with the public_content_rw_t SELinux file type.

```
# Uncomment this to allow the anonymous FTP user to upload files.
# This only has an effect if the above global write enable is
# activated. Also, you will

# obviously need to create a directory
# writable by the FTP user.
#anon_upload_enable=YES
```

In a similar fashion, you could set up the server to go one step further and allow anonymous users to actually create directories:

```
#anon_mkdir_write_enable=YES
```

Further down in the file, a couple of directives can be set to change ownership of uploaded files. The default user owner for files uploaded by anonymous users is root. And that's an additional security risk. What if a cracker were able to upload and run a script on a server with root privileges? So if you do enable anonymous uploads, make sure to set the chown_username directive to a nonprivileged user such as nobody.

```
#chown_uploads=YES
#chown_username=whoever
```

A couple of useful features for users help welcome them to the vsFTP server on a successful login. Skipping down in the file, the following command provides a message for users who are logging in to the local vsFTP server:

```
ftpd_banner=Welcome to blah FTP service
```

This next message looks for a .message file in each directory and sends it to the client:

```
dirmessage_enable=YES
```

Unfortunately, these messages don't work for users who log in to using a client such as **lftp**.

The following option enables logging of both uploads and downloads:

```
xferlog_enable=YES
```

By itself, it enables logging to the /var/log/vsftpd.log file. But there are a couple of related directives a few lines down. First, the following directive sets the actual log file:

```
#xferlog_file=/var/log/vsftpd.log
```

And then the next xferlog directive configures a standard format for logging, including a date, a time, an IP address, the file in question, the user, and more. Unless superseded, it also directs logging to the /var/log/xferlog file.

```
xferlog_std_format=YES
```

While there is no requirement to open port 20 in a firewall for the standard **lftp** client, some other FTP clients may require the use of that port. So while the following directive enables such communication over port 20, in most cases, you need not be concerned with that port:

```
connect_from_port_20=YES
```

One standard security measure automatically logs out a user after a period of inactivity. The default is 300 seconds. The following commented directive suggests 600 seconds:

```
idle_session_timeout=600
```

Sometimes data transfers can stall for various reasons, such as an overloaded server. While the default timeout is 300 seconds, the following commented directive suggests a shorter period:

```
#data_connection_timeout=120
```

The default nonprivileged user is named nobody, which does exist in the standard user authentication database. If you change the directive as suggested here, make sure the noted user actually exists in the authentication database.

```
#nopriv_user=ftpsecure
```

Some FTP clients may require the use of this feature to abort requests such as big file transfers. It's disabled by default:

```
#async_abor_enable=YES
```

Further down in the file is one other option associated with certain FTP clients, associated with recursive file lists. If you're configuring an FTP server for such clients, consider enabling the following directive:

```
#ls_recurse_enable=YES
```

As ASCII transfers to FTP servers are a known security risk, they are disabled by default. The following commented directives make it possible to enable such transfers:

```
#ascii_upload_enable=YES
#ascii_download_enable=YES
```

The first FTP servers were developed in a world where most Internet users could be trusted. Users who logged in anonymously were asked to supply their e-mail addresses as the password. An early security measure denied access to users who supplied e-mail addresses listed in the associated banned_email_file:

```
#deny_email_enable=YES
#banned_email_file=/etc/vsftpd/banned_emails
```

The following two directives are important for vsFTP, especially on a network where both IPv4 and IPv6 networks have been enabled. First, one of these directives should be enabled to allow the control of vsFTP from the vsftpd script in the /etc/init.d directory. Second, both parameters can't be activated on the same vsFTP server. In other words, vsFTP can't communicate on both IPv4 and IPv6 networks simultaneously.

```
listen=YES
#listen_ipv6=YES
```

The final three directives in the standard vsftpd.conf file have been added by Red Hat. First, RHEL 6 includes user lists associated with Pluggable Authentication Modules (PAM) described in Chapter 10.

```
pam_service_name=vsftpd
```

If you allow something more than anonymous-only access, it's important to keep out certain users such as root, as well as any other users with privileges. By default, vsFTP is configured to disable logins from sensitive users such as root, bin, and mail. The following directive implicitly refers to the user_list file in the /etc/vsftpd directory, through the userlist_deny directive.

```
userlist_enable=YES
```

While vsFTP has been compiled with TCP Wrappers libraries, you can't use the associated /etc/hosts.allow and/or the /etc/hosts.deny files unless this final directive is kept active:

```
tcp_wrappers=YES
```

As vsFTP also uses PAM for security, it also disables the users in /etc/vsftpd/ftpusers. The lists of users in the default versions of these files are identical.

Other vsFTP Configuration Files

The contents of the user_list and the ftpusers files in the /etc/vsftpd directory are identical. They include a standard list of service users, including the root administrative user. In general, you don't want to give any such users login privileges, under any circumstances. The aforementioned **userlist_enable=YES** directive activates the **userlist_deny=YES** directive, which denies all listed in the user_list file.

The ftpusers file is used by the /etc/pam.d/vsftpd configuration file. Chapter 10, Lab 6, gave you an opportunity to explore and reconfigure that file. To review, the appropriate PAM directive in that file is

```
auth required pam_listfile.so item=user sense=deny
file=/etc/vsftpd/ftpusers onerr=succeed
```

The directive denies all users in the ftpusers file. There's one other file in the directory, vsftpd_conf_migrate.sh, which links configuration files created in previous versions of the vsFTP server.

Configure SELinux Support for vsFTP

There are a variety of SELinux settings available for vsFTP. The major settings are related to file types and boolean options. If you've run Linux without SELinux before, note that some of these options are required to make vsFTP work in ways otherwise expected.

Of course, appropriate firewalls are not enough. SELinux is an integral part of the security landscape, with respect to boolean options as well as files. First, there are four major file types associated with FTP servers:

- **ftpd_exec_t**   Used for the executable daemon, vsftpd, in the /usr/sbin directory.
- **xferlog_t**   Assigned to the xferlog file for vsFTP logs, in the /var/log directory.
- **public_content_t**   Required for files shared via an FTP server, unless associated with a user home directory.
- **public_content_rw_t**   Required for directories where users can write files when logged in via an FTP server, unless associated with a user home directory.

Of course, there are also boolean options associated with the vsFTP server. All options associated with FTP are shown in the Booleans section of the SELinux Administration tool, with the ftp filter, as shown in Figure 16-4. The figure reflects the default configuration; in other words, no module directly related to FTP services is normally enabled.

Most of these directives were covered in general terms in Chapter 11. For the vsFTP server, you may use the following boolean options under certain circumstances. For example,

- To set up directories where anonymous users can write files, you'll need to activate the **allow_ftpd_anon_write** boolean and configure those directories with the **public_content_rw_t** file type.
- To allow regular users access to all files on a system with an FTP server, set the **allow_ftpd_full_access** boolean.
- To let regular users full access their home directories, protected by their usernames and passwords, set the **ftp_home_dir** boolean.

FIGURE 16-4 FTP-related SELinux boolean options

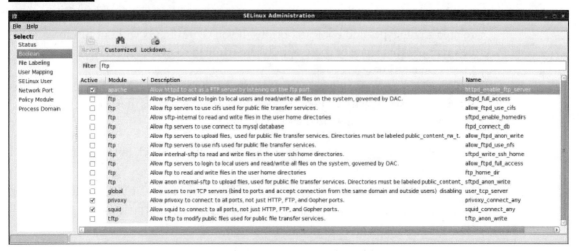

To set these directives, use the **setsebool** command. For example, to go beyond the RHCE requirement for anonymous-only download, by activating read/write access from FTP on user home directories, run the following command:

```
# setsebool -P ftp_home_dir 1
```

Ports, Firewalls, and vsFTP

The configuration of a firewall for an FTP server is a relatively simple process. In most cases, communication requires access to just one TCP port, 21. The standard firewall rule for that purpose, as may be configured in the /etc/sysconfig/iptables file, is

```
-A INPUT -m state --state NEW -m tcp -p tcp --dport 21 -j ACCEPT
```

If desired, you can also limit access to one or more IP addresses. For example, the following variation on the **iptables** rule limits access to systems on the 192.168.122.0/255.255.255.0 network:

```
-A INPUT -m state --state NEW -m tcp -p tcp -s 192.168.122.0/24 --dport 80 -j
ACCEPT
```

Some rare FTP clients may also need access to TCP port 20. To configure vsFTP to allow connections from such clients, you should apply any firewall changes made for port 21 also to port 20.

Assuming you retain the **tcp_wrappers=YES** option in the vsftpd.conf configuration file, you can further protect this service with the files associated with TCP Wrappers, /etc/hosts.allow and /etc/hosts.deny. To review and cite an example, the following entry in /etc/hosts.allow would permit access from user donna on system tester1.example.com:

```
vsftpd : donna@tester1.example.com
```

That limit would work if coupled with the following entry in /etc/hosts.deny:

```
vsftpd : ALL
```

EXERCISE 16-2

Configure a Basic vsFTP Server

In this exercise, you'll install and activate a basic vsFTP server on a RHEL system. This exercise assumes that you've configured an open port 21 through a local firewall. If you've enabled SELinux and want to support an FTP server just for downloads, you'll also need to modify SELinux policies to "Allow Ftpd To Read/Write Files In The User Home Directories," which corresponds to the boolean **ftp_home_dir** option described earlier.

1. Make sure the vsFTP server is installed. The easiest way is with the following command:

   ```
   # rpm -q vsftpd
   ```

2. If it isn't already installed, use the techniques discussed earlier to install the vsFTP RPM package.

3. Activate the vsFTP server with the **service vsftpd start** command.

4. Make sure this server is automatically activated the next time the local system boots with the following command:

   ```
   # chkconfig vsftpd on
   ```

5. Log in to the vsFTP server as a regular user, from a remote system.

6. Once logged in, run the **cd ..** command twice (remember the space between the command and the two dots). Explore the local directory. You should see a danger here, as this is the root directory for the FTP server computer.

7. Close the FTP client session.

8. If you're concerned about the security issues, deactivate the **ftp_home_dir** SELinux boolean.

Anonymous-Only Download Configuration

While you've just seen a lot can be done with the vsftpd.conf file, the configuration of an anonymous-only download configuration for the vsFTP service is relatively simple. To sum up, all you need to do is disable the following directive, which allows locally configured users to log in with their regular accounts:

```
#local_enable=yes
```

If you're asked to set up anonymous only downloads elsewhere than the /var/ftp tree, a few additional steps are required:

■ Create the target directory.

■ Populate the new target directory with files to be downloaded.

■ Set the target directory (and files therein) with the public_content_t file type.

■ Change the home directory for the ftp user to match the new target.

SCENARIO & SOLUTION	
You're having trouble configuring a firewall for NFS.	Fix the ports associated with various NFS services. Open firewall ports for those services. Also open port 111 for the portmapper.
You want to prohibit read/write access to shared NFS directories.	Make sure shares are configured with the **ro** parameter in /etc/exports. Disable the nfs_export_all_rw SELinux boolean.
You need to set up automatic mounts of a shared NFS directory.	Configure the shared directory in /etc/fstab, with options such as **soft** and **timeo**.
You want to disable user-based access to a vsFTP server.	Set the **local_enable=no** directive in the vsftpd.conf file in the /etc/vsftpd directory. Don't activate the ftp_home_dir boolean.
You need to set up a nonstandard directory for anonymous-only vsFTP downloads.	Configure the new directory as the home directory for the ftp user, and assign it the SELinux public_content_t file type.

CERTIFICATION SUMMARY

NFS allows you to share filesystems between Linux and Unix computers. It is an efficient way to share files between such systems, but there are many security concerns involved with its use. Be careful when setting up an NFS share on an unprotected network.

While RHEL 6 supports NFSv4, it also supports access by NFSv2 and NFSv3 clients. It depends on the portreserve service to keep NFS from taking ports needed by other services. It depends on the rpcbind service to set up RPC support. It can even set up quota support for shared NFS directories. It's controlled by a group of scripts in the /etc/init.d directory (nfs, nfslock, portreserve, rpcbind, rpcidmapd). If it's supported by Kerberos-based user authentication, it's also controlled by the rpcgssd and rpcsvcgssd scripts in the same directory. Each of these scripts is associated with daemons in the /sbin and /usr/sbin directories. Configuration of these scripts is configured primarily in the /etc/sysconfig/nfs file. Related commands include **exportfs** and **showmount**. It even supports ACLs with the **nfs4_setfacl**, **nfs4_getfacl**, and the **nfs4_editfacl** commands.

In most cases, basic configuration of NFS is accomplished by relatively simple directives in the /etc/exports file. Once the NFS service is running, such exports are activated through the **exportfs** command. Firewalls should be configured based on the ports fixed in the /etc/sysconfig/nfs file. Appropriate active ports and services can be confirmed with the **rpcinfo -p** command.

Generally, for basic NFS operation, no SELinux changes are required. As mounted NFS directories may appear local, user security, as well as directories configured for group collaboration, can be set up as if the filesystem were local. It works if the systems use the same or matching authentication databases. NFS mounts can be automated in /etc/fstab or through the automounter. The current status of NFS is documented in various files in the /var/lib/nfs and /proc/fs/nfsd directories.

Red Hat includes one FTP server, the very secure FTP service. You can configure it in detail through the /etc/vsftpd/vsftpd.conf configuration file. Anonymous users are configured through the default ftp user's home directory, /var/ftp. Other vsftpd.conf directives can be used to set up access by regular users, various forms of anonymous access, and more. It also supports standard options for PAM and TCP Wrappers security.

Generally, vsFTP requires access only through TCP port 21. Unless it involves access to home directories, access requires labeling with the public_content_t or public_content_rw_t file types. Home directory access requires an active ftp_home_dir boolean. In general, to set up the anonymous-only download access specified in the RHCE objectives, you need to set **local_enable=no** and keep the ftp_home_dir boolean off. If it's a nonstandard directory, you'll need to set the public_content_t file type on that directory.

TWO-MINUTE DRILL

Here are some of the key points from the certification objectives in Chapter 16.

The Network File System (NFS) Server

❑ NFS is the standard for sharing files and printers between Linux and Unix computers. RHEL 6 supports NFS versions 2, 3, and 4.

❑ Key NFS processes are **rpc.mountd** for mount requests, **rpc.rquotad** for quota requests, and **nfsd** for each network share.

❑ Configuration options for these processes, as well as parameters to fix key ports can be found in the /etc/sysconfig/nfs file.

❑ NFS shares are configured in /etc/exports and activated with the **exportfs -a** command.

❑ Firewalls can be set based on ports fixed in /etc/sysconfig/nfs as well as port 111 for the portmapper and 2049 for NFSv4.

❑ In most cases, required booleans for SELinux are already active. In fact, to disallow read/write access, you may choose to disable the nfs_export_all_rw boolean.

❑ When NFS directories are mounted, they should appear seamless. User authentication works with a common or matching authentication database.

Test an NFS Client

❑ Clients can make permanent connections for NFS shares through /etc/fstab.

❑ Clients can review shared directories with the **showmount** command.

❑ The **mount.nfs4** command is designed to mount directories shared via NFSv4. The **mount.nfs** command works with NFSv2 and NFSv3.

❑ If an NFS server fails, it can "hang" an NFS client. The **soft** and **timeo** options to the **mount** command can help prevent such hangs, which could otherwise force users to reboot a system.

❑ NFS and portmap have security problems. Limit their use when possible to secure internal networks protected by an appropriate firewall.

The Very Secure FTP Server

❑ RHEL includes the vsFTP server. The default configuration allows anonymous and real user access.

❑ To configure anonymous-only download access, you'll need to disable the **local_enable** directive.

❑ To set up anonymous-only access on a nonstandard directory, you'll have to change the home directory of the default user named ftp and set up that directory with the public_content_t SELinux file type.

❑ You can customize vsFTP through the /etc/vsftpd/vsftpd.conf configuration file. It also uses authentication files in the /etc/vsftpd/ directory: ftpusers and user_list.

❑ The ftpusers file is cited by a PAM configuration file, /etc/pam.d/vsftpd, to disallow access from cited system users. That can be used as a model to limit or allow user access in other ways.

SELF TEST

The following questions will help you measure your understanding of the material presented in this chapter. As no multiple-choice questions appear on the Red Hat exams, no multiple-choice questions appear in this book. These questions exclusively test your understanding of the chapter. It is okay if you have another way of performing a task. Getting results, not memorizing trivia, is what counts on the Red Hat exams. There may be more than one answer to many of these questions.

The Network File System (NFS) Server

1. In the /etc/exports file, to export the /data directory as read-only to all hosts and grant read and write permission to the hostname superv in the example.com domain, what directive would you enter in that file?

   _____

2. Once you've configured /etc/exports, what command exports these shares?

   _____

3. What port number is associated with the port mapper?

   _____

4. What port number is associated with NFSv4?

   _____

5. What is the NFS configuration option that supports access by the root administrative user?

   _____

Test an NFS Client

6. You're experiencing problems with NFS clients for various reasons, including frequent downtime on the NFS server and network outages between NFS clients and servers. What type of mounting can prevent problems on NFS clients?

   _____

7. What is the command that can display NFS shared directories from the outsider1.example.org system?

   _____

The Very Secure FTP Server

8. What default directive in /etc/vsftpd/vsftpd.conf should you disable to prevent users from logging in to their accounts through the vsFTP server?

_____

9. What directive should you include to keep regular users from getting to the top-level root directory (/) on a vsFTP server?

_____

10. Based on the default RHEL 6 configuration, what file includes a list of users not allowed to log in to the vsFTP server?

_____

11. What user account determines the default directory for anonymous users who connect to the vsFTP server?

_____

12. What additional directives do you need to add to the default vsFTP configuration file to allow security using PAM and TCP wrappers?

_____

LAB QUESTIONS

Several of these labs involve configuration exercises. You should do these exercises on test machines only. It's assumed that you're running these exercises on virtual machines such as KVM. For this chapter, it's also assumed that you may be changing the configuration of a physical host system for such virtual machines.

Red Hat presents its exams electronically. For that reason, the labs in this and future chapters are available from the CD that accompanies the book, in the Chapter16/ subdirectory. In case you haven't yet set up RHEL 6 on a system, refer to Chapter 1 for installation instructions.

The answers for each lab follow the Self Test answers for the fill-in-the-blank questions.

SELF TEST ANSWERS

The Network File System (NFS) Server

1. The following entry in /etc/exports would export the /data directory as read-only to all hosts and grant read and write permission to the host superv in the example.com domain:

   ```
   /data (ro,sync)  superv.example.com(rw,sync)
   ```

2. Once you've revised /etc/exports, the **exportfs -a** command exports all filesystems. Yes, you can re-export filesystems with the **exportfs -r** command. But there's no indication that NFS shares have yet been exported.

3. The port number associated with the portmapper is 111.

4. The port number associated with NFSv4 is 2049.

5. The NFS configuration option that supports access by the root administrative user is no_root_squash.

Test an NFS Client

6. Soft mounting and time-outs associated with the **soft** and **timeo** options can prevent problems such as lockups with NFS clients.

7. The command that can display NFS shared directories from the named remote system is **showmount -e outsider1.example.org**.

The Very Secure FTP Server

8. The default directive in /etc/vsftpd/vsftpd.conf that you should disable to prevent users from logging into their accounts through the vsFTP server is **local_enable=YES**.

9. The directive that prevents regular users from getting to the top-level root directory (/) after logging into a vsFTP server is **chroot_local_user=YES**.

10. Based on the default RHEL 6 configuration, both ftpusers and user_list in the /etc/vsftpd directory include a list of users not allowed to log in to the vsFTP server. Strictly speaking, the user_list file is the right answer, as it's associated with the userlist_enable directive. But the active contents of the standard ftpusers file are identical.

11. The default directory for anonymous access is the home directory of the user named ftp.

12. The additional directives to add to the default vsFTP configuration file to allow security using PAM and TCP wrappers are **pam_service_name=vsftpd** and **tcp_wrappers=YES**.

LAB ANSWERS

Lab 1: Basic NFS Configuration

When this lab is complete, you'll see the following features on the system with the NFS server:

- Installed NFS packages, including related packages such as portreserve and rpcbind. Without these packages, communication won't be possible with NFS clients.
- An active NFSv4 service, which can be confirmed in the output to the **rpcinfo -p** command.
- A firewall that supports access through the noted ports. It should also be limited by IP address network.

  In addition, you'll be able to perform the following tasks from the NFS client:

- Run the **showmount -e server1.example.com** command, where server1.example.com is the name of the NFS server system (substitute if and as needed).
- Mount the shared directory as the root user with the **mount.nfs4 server1.example.com:/shared /testing** command.
- The first time the share is mounted, you should be able to copy local files as the root user to the /testing directory.
- The second time the share is mounted, with the no_root_squash directive in effect, such copying should not work, at least from the client root user account.

Lab 2: Standard NFS Configuration

This lab is the first step toward creating a single /home directory for your network. Once you get it working on a single client/server combination, you can set it up on all clients and servers. You can then use the LDAP server described in Chapter 8 to set up a single Linux/Unix database of usernames and passwords for the network. Alternatively, matching usernames (with matching UID and GID numbers) on different local systems should also work. On the NFS server, take the following steps:

1. Set up a couple of users and identifying files such as user1 and user1.txt on the system being used as the NFS server.

2. Configure the /etc/idmapd.conf file for the current domain, appropriate users, and the translation method for authentication. As discussed in the chapter, that refers to

   ```
   Domain = example.com
   Nobody-User = nfsnobody
   ```

```
Nobody-Group = nfsnobody
Method = nsswitch
```

3. Make the system reread the modified configuration file, using the /etc/init.d/rpcidmapd script.

4. Share the /home directory in /etc/exports on the server1.example.com client. You can do this in this file with the following command:

```
/home nfsclient(rw,sync)
```

5. Export this directory with the following command:

```
# exportfs -a
```

6. Restart the NFS service:

```
# service nfs restart
```

7. Make sure that the exported /home directory shows in the export list. On the local server, you can do this with the following command:

```
# showmount -e server1.example.com
```

8. If problems appear during this process, check the /etc/exports file carefully. Make sure there aren't extra spaces in /etc/exports, even at the end of a code line. Make sure the NFS service is actually running with the **service nfs status** command.

9. You may also want to check your firewall and make sure the appropriate services described in this chapter are running with the **rpcinfo -p** command.

10. Remember to make sure that the NFS server starts automatically the next time that system is booted. One way to do so is with the following command:

```
# chkconfig nfs on
```

Now on the NFS client, take the following steps to connect to the shared /home directory:

1. First, make the same changes to the /etc/idmapd.conf file as was done on the server, and restart the rpcidmapd service script available from the /etc/init.d directory.

2. Make sure that you can see the shared /home directory. If there is no DNS server or the /etc/hosts file does not include the IP address of the server1.example.com system, substitute the IP address:

```
# showmount -e server1.example.com
```

3. Now **mount** the share that is offered on the local /remote directory:

```
# mount.nfs4 server1.example.com:/home /remote
```

4. Check to see that the mounting has worked. If it did, you'll see the NFS mount in the output to the **mount** command.

5. Now look through the mounted /home directory for the special files that created in Step 1. If found, you've succeeded in creating and connecting to the /home directory share.

6. To make the mount permanent, add it to the /etc/fstab file on the client. Once you've added a line such as the following to that file, the Linux client automatically mounts the shared /home directory from the NFS server the next time that client is booted.

```
server1.example.com:/home    /remote nfs4 soft,timeout=100  0  0
```

Lab 3: NFS and SELinux

The reference to SELinux is deliberate and should provide an important hint. If you have to modify every directory shared and configured in the /etc/exports file on each NFS server, that can be time consuming. Perhaps the simplest way to prevent writes to shared NFS directories is to deactivate the associated SELinux boolean setting. While there are other methods, the quickest way to do so on a permanent basis is with the following command:

```
# setsebool -P nfs_export_all_rw off
```

You should then be able to test the result with the next mounting of a shared NFS directory.

Lab 4: Configure a vsFTP Server with Messages

The vsFTP server can be installed from one RPM package. So if you have not installed this server earlier, you could install it with the following command:

```
# yum install vsftpd
```

This also installs configuration files in the /etc and /etc/vsftpd directories. The main configuration file is /etc/vsftpd/vsftpd.conf. Based on the RHEL default version of this file, you can make a couple of changes to enable messages. But by default, messages are already enabled for directory access on an FTP server, courtesy of the following command:

```
dirmessage_enable=yes
```

The actual configuration of a message is a matter of creating a text file and saving it as .message in the desired directories, /var/ftp and /var/ftp/pub. You could add a simple line such as "root directory for the FTP server" or "main download directory."

Finally, to configure the Red Hat FTP server to start, run the **service vsftpd start** command. To make sure it starts the next time you boot your computer, run the **chkconfig vsftpd on** command.

Lab 5: Configure a vsFTP Server for Anonymous-Only Downloads

This lab can be run as a continuation of Lab 4. To allow only anonymous access, comment out or change the following line in the /etc/vsftpd/vsftpd.conf file:

```
local_enable=yes
```

Anonymous users are already prevented from uploading files in the standard vsFTP server configuration. You could enable uploads by activating the **anon_upload_enable=yes** command, and by setting the upload directory to the public_content_rw_t SELinux file type.

Lab 6: Configure a vsFTP Server on a Special Directory

This lab is more complex than it sounds. The following highlights the required changes:

- Change the home directory of the user ftp to the /ftp directory; make sure the change is shown in /etc/passwd.
- Create the /ftp directory.
- Make sure the /ftp directory is set to the public_content_r SELinux file type.
- Make sure the public_content_r SELinux file type is documented in the file_contexts.local file in the /etc/selinux/targeted/contexts/files directory. As discussed in several previous chapters, that's possible with the **semanage** command; in this case, the command would be

```
# semanage fcontext -a -s system_u -t public_content_t /ftp/
```

17

Administrative Services: DNS, FTP, and Logging

T his chapter examines four administrative services: the Domain Name System (DNS), system activity reports, system logging services, and the Network Time Protocol (NTP) service. That's less complex than it sounds. As for DNS, the RHCE objectives require only the configuration of a caching-only nameserver hat may forward queries. So this book does not cover the configuration of a master or secondary DNS server.

Linux system utilization reports are associated with the **sar** command, which is relatively easy to configure as a cron job. While basic logging on a local system was described in Chapter 9, this chapter covers the configuration of a central logging server. Finally, while NTP clients were described in Chapter 5, this chapter covers the configuration of an NTP server.

INSIDE THE EXAM

While this chapter addresses several RHCE objectives, the steps required to meet each of these objectives are fairly simple, relative to the tasks associated with the configuration of file sharing services such as Samba, NFS, and vsFTP.

Domain Name Service

Examine the RHCE objectives associated with DNS:

■ Configure a caching-only name server

■ Configure a caching-only name server to forward DNS queries

This is less than was required in previous versions of the RHCE objectives, which specified the configuration of a slave (or secondary) name server. Red Hat has addressed

that change in the latest objectives, with the following statement:

"Note: Candidates are not expected to configure master or slave name servers."

As the only SELinux targeted setting relates to the overwriting of master zone files, it is not an issue for RHCE-related DNS configuration.

System Utilization Reports

While system utilization reporting is a new requirement for the RHCE, it's an important skill for all computer professionals. As an RHCE, you'll be expected to have the answers for a variety of computer-related questions. Since RHEL 6 includes the sysstat package for such reports, the related objective, as follows, makes sense:

- Produce and deliver reports on system utilization (processor, memory, disk, and network)

As this is not a network objective, there is no need to configure a firewall. There are no current SELinux-related system utilization options. However, as with other services, it's hard to see how you'd get credit for any configuration made for system utilization reports unless such services are booted automatically.

System Logging Server

Nominally, the standard RHEL 6 system logging service is a network server, like other network servers discussed in the second half of this book. But based on the way the RHCE objectives are written, system logging is an element of "System Configuration and Management." System logging information that's transmitted over a network should be configured on the client, to send logging in-formation to a remote system, and the logging server should be configured to accept logging information from remote systems.

The system logging server normally uses TCP or UDP port 514. However, there are no current SELinux-related options. As system logging is the province of the root administrative user, there are no other real user limitations, unless you configure users in the /etc/sudoers file to administer the rsyslog service using the techniques discussed in Chapter 8. However, host limits are possible based on **iptables**-based firewalls.

The Network Time Service

Finally, the last service covered in the RHCE objectives is based on NTP. The requirement suggests that you need to know how to take advantage of the cooperative nature of NTP servers:

- Synchronize time using other NTP peers

Basic Domain Service Organization

DNS is a service that translates human-readable domain names such as www .mheducation.com to IP addresses such as 12.163.148.101, and vice versa. DNS is a distributed database; each server has its own delegated zone of authority for one or more domains. The DNS service associated with RHEL is the Berkeley Internet Name Domain (BIND). As no individual DNS server is large enough to keep a database for the entire Internet, each server is configured by default to refer requests to other DNS servers.

Basic Parameters

DNS on RHEL 6 is based on the **named** daemon, built on the BIND package developed through the Internet Software Consortium. RHEL 6 includes BIND version 9.7. You can use the **rndc** command to manage DNS operation; it's functionally similar to how you can use the **apachectl** command to manage the Apache web server.

DNS Package Options

To configure a system as a DNS server, you should be interested in the packages associated with the Network Infrastructure Server package group. As all packages in that group are options, you'll need to specify packages individually. With that in mind, you should know something about the RPM packages associated with DNS:

- **bind**   Includes the basic name server software and extensive documentation.
- **bind-chroot**   Adds directories that isolate BIND in a so-called "chroot jail," which limits access if DNS is compromised.
- **bind-devel**   Includes development libraries for BIND.
- **bind-dyndb-ldap**   Supports dynamic updates to LDAP.
- **bind-libs**   Adds library files used by the bind and bind-utils RPMs.
- **bind-sdb**   Supports alternative databases, such as LDAP.
- **bind-utils**   Contains tools such as **dig** and **host** that provide information about a specific network host in some DNS database.

By now, you should be comfortable installing these packages with commands like **yum** from installation databases as discussed in Chapter 7.

on the job   *RHEL 6 also supports the dnsmasq package, which can also be used to set up a forwarding DNS server.*

Different Types of DNS Servers

While additional options are available, there are four basic types of DNS servers:

- A master DNS server, authoritative for one or more domains, includes host records for that domain.
- A slave DNS server, which relies on a master DNS server for data, can be used in place of that master DNS server.
- A caching-only DNS server stores recent requests like a proxy server. If configured with forwarding features, it refers to other DNS servers for requests not in its current cache.
- A forwarding-only DNS server refers all requests to other DNS servers.

Each of these servers can be configured with access limited to internal networks, or even just a local system. Alternatively, they can be configured as public DNS servers, accessible to the entire Internet. But such access comes with risks, as successful attacks against an authoritative corporate DNS server could easily keep their web sites hidden from customer's web browsers, a different form of denial of service.

CERTIFICATION OBJECTIVE 17.02

Minimal DNS Server Configurations

You can configure DNS servers by directly editing the associated configuration files. In this section, you'll briefly review the configuration files installed with the BIND software. You'll then learn how to configure a caching-only nameserver, as well as a nameserver that includes forwarding to specified DNS servers.

BIND Configuration Files

DNS configuration files can help you configure a Linux system as a database of hostnames and IP addresses. That database can be cached, listed in a local database, or the request can be forwarded to a different system. The configuration files that support the use of DNS as a server are described in Table 17-1. While the table includes references to standard /var/named database files, changes to such files are not required to configure a caching-only or forwarding DNS server.

	DNS Configuration File	Description
TABLE 17-1 DNS Server Configuration Files	/etc/sysconfig/named	Specifies nonstandard configuration and data file directories.
	/etc/named.conf	Notes the standard location for the main DNS configuration file. Can incorporate data from other files, normally in the /etc/named directory, with the include directive.
	/etc/named.iscdlv.key	Specifies the standard DNS encryption key.
	/etc/named.rfc1912.zones	Adds appropriate zones for localhost names and addresses.
	/etc/rndc.key	Lists the authentication key required to support requests to the DNS server.
	/var/named/named.empty	Includes a template zone file.
	/var/named/named.localhost	Lists the zone file for the localhost computer.
	/var/named/named.loopback	Lists the zone file for the loopback address.

If you've installed the bind-chroot package and have started the **named** service, a hard link to these files will also be available in the /var/named/chroot directory. That directory is configured through the ROOTDIR directive in the /etc/sysconfig/named file.

In the following sections, you'll experiment with the /etc/named.conf file. You should back it up in some fashion. Just be aware of the ownership and yes, the SELinux contexts of the file, as shown in this output:

```
# ls -Z /etc/named.conf
-rw-r-----. root named system_u:object_r:named_conf_t:s0 /etc/named.conf
```

If backups are restored haphazardly, even by the root user, the group ownership and/or the SELinux contexts may be lost. So if there's ever a failure in starting or restarting the named service, check the ownership and SELinux contexts of the /etc/named.conf file. If necessary, apply the following commands to that file:

```
# chgrp named /etc/named.conf
# chcon -u system_u -t named_conf_t /etc/named.conf
```

In addition, after testing a DNS configuration, some information may remain in a cache. That's the nature of a caching DNS server. If that cache still exists after a change to DNS configuration files, that could affect the results. Therefore, it's wise to flush the DNS cache after each configuration change with the following command:

```
# rndc flush
```

A Caching-Only Name Server

When you request a web page such as www.mcgraw-hill.com, the request is sent to the configured DNS server. The response is the associated IP address. The request is also known as a *name query*. For requests to external DNS servers, responses can take time. That's where a caching-only name server can help, as repeated requests are stored locally.

---

e x a m

ⓦ a t c h   *The default version of /etc/named.conf is set up for a caching-only nameserver, limited to the localhost system.*   *Minor changes are required to open that server up to a local network.*

When configuring a caching-only name server, the first step is to look at the default version of the /etc/named.conf configuration file. The directives in the default version of this file are organized to set up a caching-only nameserver. One view of this file is shown in Figure 17-1.

■ The **options** directive encompasses several basic DNS directives, including the following:

    ■ The **listen-on port** (and **listen-on-v6 port**) directives specify the TCP/IP port number (for IPv4 and IPv6).

    To extend this to a local network, you'll need to include the IP address of the local network card. For example, for an IPv4 address of 192.168.122.50, you'd change the directive to read (don't forget the semicolon followed by a space after each IP address)

```
listen-on port 53 { 127.0.0.1; 192.168.122.50; }
```

    If IPv6 networking is active on the local network, you would need to configure similar IPv6 addresses for the **listen-on-v6** directive. If IPv6 networking is not active, the default **listen-on-v6** directive is sufficient.

    ■ The **directory** directive specifies where the DNS server looks for data files. Be aware, if the bind-chroot RPM is installed, these files are hard-linked to files in /var/named/chroot subdirectories.

FIGURE 17-1

/etc/named.conf
for a caching-only
nameserver

```
//
// named.conf
//
// Provided by Red Hat bind package to configure the ISC BIND named(8) DNS
// server as a caching only nameserver (as a localhost DNS resolver only).
//
// See /usr/share/doc/bind*/sample/ for example named configuration files.
//

options {
        listen-on port 53 { 127.0.0.1; };
        listen-on-v6 port 53 { ::1; };
        directory       "/var/named";
        dump-file       "/var/named/data/cache_dump.db";
        statistics-file "/var/named/data/named_stats.txt";
        memstatistics-file "/var/named/data/named_mem_stats.txt";
        allow-query     { localhost; };
        recursion yes;

        dnssec-enable yes;
        dnssec-validation yes;
        dnssec-lookaside auto;

        /* Path to ISC DLV key */
        bindkeys-file "/etc/named.iscdlv.key";
};

logging {
        channel default_debug {
                file "data/named.run";
                severity dynamic;
        };
};

zone "." IN {
        type hint;
        file "named.ca";
};

include "/etc/named.rfc1912.zones";
```

- The **dump-file** specifies the cache for the current DNS database and the output from the **rndc flush** command.

- The **statistics-file** specifies the cache for the current DNS database and the output from the **rndc stats** command.

- The **memstatistics-file** specifies the location for memory usage statistics.

- The **allow-query** lists the IP addresses allowed to get information from this server. By default, it's limited to the local system. To extend this to another network such as 192.168.122.0/24, you'd change the directive to this:

```
allow-query { 127.0.0.1; 192.168.122.0/24; }
```

■ Since BIND version 9.5, the software has included references to DNS security, in **dnssec-*** directives. The following directives enable DNS security, validation (to check authenticity), and querying, with the noted bindkeys-file:

```
dnssec-enable yes;
dnssec-validation yes;
dnssec-lookaside auto;
bindkeys-file "/etc/named.iscdlv.key";
```

■ The **logging** directive specifies several more parameters; the **channel** directive specifies output methods, in this case to **default_debug**, activated in the named.run file in the /var/named/data, logging only **dynamic** issues.

■ But wait, the **zone "."** directive specifies the root zone for the Internet, along with the root DNS servers as specified in the /var/named/named.ca file.

■ Finally, the **include** directive includes the localhost settings described in the /etc/named.rfc1912.zones file.

No changes are required to create a caching DNS server, all you need to do is install the aforementioned **bind-*** packages, start the **named** service with the following command:

```
# /etc/init.d/named start
```

Next, run the **rndc status** command. If successful, you'll see output similar to that shown in Figure 17-2. The **rndc** command is the name server control utility.

Starting named

Make sure your computer is connected to a network. Now you can start the DNS server with the **/etc/init.d/named start** command. View the syslog message file with the **tail -f /var/log/messages** command. If there are problems, you'll see error messages in that file. As needed, the **named** daemon will display the file with the error. You can then stop the service with the **rndc stop** or **/etc/init.d/named stop** command and then check the applicable configuration files.

FIGURE 17-2

FIGURE 17-2	

```
[root@Maui michael]# rndc status
version: 9.7.0-P2-RedHat-9.7.0-5.P2.el6_0.1
CPUs found: 4
worker threads: 4
number of zones: 16
debug level: 0
xfers running: 0
xfers deferred: 0
soa queries in progress: 0
query logging is OFF
recursive clients: 0/0/1000
tcp clients: 0/100
server is up and running
[root@Maui michael]# █
```

The status of an operational DNS server

Once satisfied with the new configuration, make sure that DNS starts the next time you reboot Linux. As noted in other chapters, the following command makes sure that the **named** daemon starts the next time you boot Linux in the standard login runlevels:

```
# chkconfig named on
```

A Forwarding Name Server

This type of DNS server is simple. It requires a single command in the /etc/named.conf configuration file. As you can see, it's straightforward; I've set it to refer to a couple of other DNS servers on my home network:

```
options {
    listen-on port 53 { 127.0.0.1; };
    listen-on-v6 port 53 { ::1; }
    directory "/var/named";
    forward only;
    forwarders {
        192.168.122.1;
        192.168.0.1;
    };
};
```

With this configuration, any computer that looks to the local DNS server is forwarded to DNS servers on the IP addresses shown.

If you want to open up this server to external queries, a couple more changes are required. The changes are the same as made earlier to the caching-only nameserver configuration. In other words, for an IPv4 network, where the local network card has an address of 192.168.122.50, you'd change the **listen-on** directive to

```
listen-on port 53 { 127.0.0.1; 192.168.122.50; };
```

You should also include the **allow-query** directive described earlier, with references to the localhost system and the local network address:

```
allow-query     { localhost; 192.168.122.0/24; };
```

Forwarding from a Caching-Only Name Server

As suggested earlier, the caching-only name server configured in the default version of the /etc/named.conf file has forwarding features. Otherwise, it would not be able to return any results from DNS requests.

But you can combine aspects of the caching-only and forwarding name servers just described. Requests not in the local cache would be forwarded to the name servers specified with the **forwarders** directive. Figure 17-3 displays the relevant excerpt of a /etc/named.conf file where the forwarding directives have been included.

FIGURE 17-3

A caching
nameserver
that forwards
to specific DNS
servers

```
//
// named.conf
//
// Provided by Red Hat bind package to configure the ISC BIND named(8) DNS
// server as a caching only nameserver (as a localhost DNS resolver only).
//
// See /usr/share/doc/bind*/sample/ for example named configuration files.
//

options {
        listen-on port 53 { 127.0.0.1; 192.168.122.50; };
        listen-on-v6 port 53 { ::1; };
        directory       "/var/named";
     forwarders {
         192.168.122.1;
         192.168.0.1;
     };
        dump-file       "/var/named/data/cache_dump.db";
        statistics-file "/var/named/data/named_stats.txt";
        memstatistics-file "/var/named/data/named_mem_stats.txt";
        allow-query     { localhost; 192.168.122.0/24; };
        recursion yes;
```

BIND Troubleshooting Commands

There are four commands associated with the BIND service: **named**, **rndc**, **host**, and **dig**. The **named** command is the daemon in the /usr/sbin directory. It can be controlled by **named** script in the /etc/init.d directory. The preferred way to start DNS on a system is with the **/etc/init.d/named start** command. In contrast, the **dig** and **host** commands are successors to **nslookup**.

The **rndc** commands are straightforward. Try **rndc** by itself. The output guides you through the available options. The options I use are straightforward: **rndc status**, **rndc flush**, **rndc reload**, and **rndc stop**. If the DNS server is running correctly, the **rndc status** command should display the results shown back in Figure 17-2. The **rndc flush** command may help after changing a configuration file, as parts of the existing configuration may still reside in local memory. The **rndc reload** command rereads any changes made to the configuration or DNS database files. Finally, the **rndc stop** command stops the operation of the DNS server.

After you configure DNS and make it reread the configuration files with the **rndc reload** command, examine the results with the **host mheducation.com localhost** command. The output confirms the use of the local system as a DNS server and then provides a straightforward view of the IP address of the host and the hostname of the mail server:

```
Using domain server:
Name: localhost
Address: 127.0.0.1#53
Aliases:

mheducation.com has address 12.163.148.101
mheducation.com mail is handled by 0 mail.eppg.com.
```

Now test the setup. Use the **dig** command to examine your work. For example, with the command **dig @127.0.0.1 www.mcgraw-hill.com**, you'll see something like the output shown in Figure 17-4.

The **dig** command as shown asks the local DNS server to look for the www .mcgraw-hill.com server. Assuming IP address information for www.mcgraw-hill.com isn't stored locally, it then contacts one of the DNS systems listed in the named.conf file. If those systems are down or otherwise inaccessible, the local DNS server proceeds to forward the request to one of the name servers listed in the named.ca file. As though those are the root name servers for the Internet, the request will probably be passed on to other DNS servers. Therefore, it may take a number of seconds before you see an answer.

FIGURE 17-4

Test a local DNS
server with the
dig command

```
; <<>> DiG 9.7.0-P2-RedHat-9.7.0-5.P2.el6 <<>> @127.0.0.1 mcgraw-hill.com
; (1 server found)
;; global options: +cmd
;; Got answer:
;; ->>HEADER<<- opcode: QUERY, status: NOERROR, id: 24220
;; flags: qr rd ra; QUERY: 1, ANSWER: 2, AUTHORITY: 13, ADDITIONAL: 12

;; QUESTION SECTION:
;mcgraw-hill.com.                 IN     A

;; ANSWER SECTION:
mcgraw-hill.com.        1660     IN     A        204.8.135.3
mcgraw-hill.com.        1660     IN     A        198.45.24.143

;; AUTHORITY SECTION:
.                       518195   IN     NS       e.root-servers.net.
.                       518195   IN     NS       j.root-servers.net.
.                       518195   IN     NS       a.root-servers.net.
.                       518195   IN     NS       h.root-servers.net.
:
```

EXERCISE 17-1

Set Up Your Own DNS Server

Following the example files shown previously, set up one local caching DNS server.
Access can be limited to the local system.

1. Install the bind package.

2. Review the contents of the /etc/named.conf file, based on the discussion so
   far in this chapter. Do not make any changes.

3. Start the DNS server with the following command:

   ```
   # /etc/init.d/named start
   ```

4. To make sure the DNS server is running, run the **rndc status** command. The
   output should be similar to that shown in Figure 17-2.

5. Flush the current cache with the **rndc flush** command.

6. Test the DNS server. Try the **dig @127.0.0.1 www.osborne.com** command.

7. If desired, you can now set up the local system as the DNS server. One
   method would be with the help of the network configuration tools described
   in Chapter 5.

CERTIFICATION OBJECTIVE 17.03

Set Up System Utilization Reports

As an administrator, it's helpful to know when a system is being overloaded. To that end, RHEL 6 includes the sysstat package. In addition, there are other commands related to measuring system utilization, specifically **top**. Of course, you can identify current disk usage with commands like **df** and **fdisk**. Once system utilization reports are collected, you can review the results, to help identify times when a system is in heavier use.

Of course, to paraphrase the relevant RHCE objective, there are other important commands that can help you "prepare and deliver reports" on the load on the CPU, RAM, hard drives, and the network. While they collect data similar to commands like **top**, **df**, and **fdisk**, the commands associated with the **sysstat** service collects such data on each of the noted components. It's configured to set up such data in log files. Then, the **sadf** command is designed to actually use that log data to prepare such reports. When written to an appropriate text or database file, such reports can then be delivered for evaluation and processing.

System Utilization Commands

Basic system utilization commands are already available for Linux. For example, the **top** command provides a current view of three important items: CPU, RAM, and processes. Take a look at the output of the **top** command, shown in Figure 17-5. Current CPU, RAM, and swap space use is shown atop the display; currently running processes are shown below the bar. Processes that take a lot of CPU and RAM are shown first. By default, the view is refreshed every three seconds.

Alternatively, there's the **dstat** command, part of the dstat package. As shown in Figure 17-6, it lists of a variety of statistics, refreshed every second. The one item added here relative to the **top** command is network traffic, which can help you view current network usage.

Of course, these are real-time statistics, and something that you can't stare at all the time. That's the reason behind the tools that I will call the system status service.

FIGURE 17-5

```
top - 17:50:53 up  3:09,  2 users,  load average: 0.00, 0.00, 0.00
Tasks: 151 total,   1 running, 150 sleeping,   0 stopped,   0 zombie
Cpu(s):  0.0%us,  0.0%sy,  0.0%ni,100.0%id,  0.0%wa,  0.0%hi,  0.0%si,  0.0%st
Mem:    761264k total,    390932k used,    370332k free,     22188k buffers
Swap:  1023992k total,         0k used,   1023992k free,    142580k cached

  PID USER      PR  NI  VIRT  RES  SHR S %CPU %MEM    TIME+  COMMAND
 3523 root      20   0 14940 1180  872 R  0.3  0.2   0:00.04 top
    1 root      20   0 19244 1404 1132 S  0.0  0.2   0:00.67 init
    2 root      20   0     0    0    0 S  0.0  0.0   0:00.01 kthreadd
    3 root      RT   0     0    0    0 S  0.0  0.0   0:00.01 migration/0
    4 root      20   0     0    0    0 S  0.0  0.0   0:00.00 ksoftirqd/0
    5 root      RT   0     0    0    0 S  0.0  0.0   0:00.00 watchdog/0
    6 root      RT   0     0    0    0 S  0.0  0.0   0:00.01 migration/1
    7 root      20   0     0    0    0 S  0.0  0.0   0:00.00 ksoftirqd/1
    8 root      RT   0     0    0    0 S  0.0  0.0   0:00.00 watchdog/1
    9 root      20   0     0    0    0 S  0.0  0.0   0:00.02 events/0
   10 root      20   0     0    0    0 S  0.0  0.0   0:00.48 events/1
   11 root      20   0     0    0    0 S  0.0  0.0   0:00.00 cpuset
   12 root      20   0     0    0    0 S  0.0  0.0   0:00.00 khelper
   13 root      20   0     0    0    0 S  0.0  0.0   0:00.00 netns
```

The top command displays system utilization.

The System Status Service

To set up the system status service, install the sysstat package. It's a regular server service, with its own daemon in the /etc/init.d directory. It's a cron job, run on a regular basis, as defined in the /etc/cron.d directory. It's a series of related commands, which are covered here.

FIGURE 17-6

```
[root@server1 etc]# man dstat
[root@server1 etc]# dstat
----total-cpu-usage---- -dsk/total- -net/total- ---paging-- ---system--
usr sys idl wai hiq siq| read  writ| recv  send|  in   out | int   csw
  0   0 100   0   0   0|  35k 2279B|   0     0 |   0     0 |  45    39
  0   0 100   0   0   0|   0     0 |  66B  114B|   0     0 |  42    35
  0   0 100   0   0   0|   0    16k|  66B  834B|   0     0 |  50    46
  0   0 100   0   0   0|   0     0 |  66B  354B|   0     0 |  39    31
  1   0 100   0   0   0|   0     0 |  66B  354B|   0     0 |  45    34
  0   0 100   0   0   0|   0     0 |  66B  354B|   0     0 |  46    34
  0   0 100   0   0   0|   0     0 |  66B  354B|   0     0 |  48    38
  0   0  97   3   0   0|   0    88k| 132B  468B|   0     0 |  49    45
  1   0  99   0   0   0|   0     0 |  66B  354B|   0     0 |  34    33
  0   0 100   0   0   0|   0     0 |  66B  354B|   0     0 |  47    36
  0   0 100   0   0   0|   0     0 |  66B  354B|   0     0 |  34    31
  0   0 100   0   0   0|   0     0 |  66B  354B|   0     0 |  35    33
  0   0 100   0   0   0|   0     0 |  66B  354B|   0     0 |  36    38
  0   0 100   0   0   0|   0     0 |  66B  354B|   0     0 |  38    36
  0   0 100   0   0   0|   0     0 |  66B  354B|   0     0 |  44    34
  0   0 100   0   0   0|   0     0 |  66B  354B|   0     0 |  35    31
  0   0 100   0   0   0|   0     0 |  66B  354B|   0     0 |  55    41
```

The dstat command displays system utilization

When the **sysstat** service is started, it uses parameters shown in the sysstat and sysstat.ioconf files, in the /etc/sysconfig directory. The sysstat file is relatively simple; the following directive specifies that log files should be kept for seven days:

```
HISTORY=7
```

And this directive specifies that log files that are more than ten days old should be compressed:

```
COMPRESSAFTER=10
```

Of course, that means system status log files are erased before they can be compressed. Naturally, you can change either variable as needed. The meaty /etc/sysconfig file is sysstat.ioconf, as it helps collect activity data from a variety of storage devices. It guides the **sysstat** service, to help it collect data from devices detected and listed in the /proc directory, in files named partitions and diskstats. While the sysstat.ioconf file is large, changes should not be required to that file unless there's new disk storage hardware. And the Red Hat exams are not hardware exams.

Collect System Status into Logs

The sysstat package includes a regular cron job. Available in the /etc/cron.d directory, that job collects information on system utilization and sends it to log files in the /var/log/sa directory. Examine the sysstat file in the /etc/cron.d directory. The first line suggests a job that's run every ten minutes by the root administrative user.

```
*/10 * * * * root /usr/lib64/sa/sa1 -S DISK 1 1
```

The **sa1** command, with the 1 and 1 at the end, specifies that the job should be written once, one second after the job is started. The **-S DISK** option is associated with the **sar** command and collects utilization statistics on swap space. Information from this command is collected in the file named s*dd* in the /var/log/sa directory, where *dd* represents the day of the month.

The next line is more powerful than it looks. On a daily basis, at seven minutes before midnight, with the privileges of the root administrative user, the **sa2** command writes a daily report on most system activity.

```
53 23 * * * root /usr/lib64/sa/sa2 -A
```

As before, the **-A** switch is associated with the **sar** command. As suggested by the following excerpt from the **sar** man page, that essentially collects every reasonable bit on system utilization:

```
-A      This is equivalent to specifying -bBdqrRSuvwWy
-I SUM -I XALL -n ALL -u ALL -P ALL.
```

Information from this command is collected in the file named sar*dd* in the /var/log/sa directory, where *dd* represents the day of the month. The sar*dd* files in that directory have already been processed into text files.

Prepare a System Status Report

This section will not prepare a report for a presentation. It's simply an analysis of the **sadf** command, and how it can be used to specify information to filter from the log files in the /var/log/sa directory. The binary log files with names like sa10 (for the tenth day of the month) can be processed in a number of ways by the **sadf** command. Some of the more important **sadf** switches are listed in Table 17-2.

For example, the following command sets up a report with data between the start and end of the tenth of the month:

```
# sadf -s 00:00:01 -e 23:59:59 /var/log/sa/sa10 > activity10
```

The data is redirected to the activity10 file, for later processing. But the power of the sysstat package comes from the way it interacts with other command, **sar**. But only some of the switches to the **sar** command work with **sadf**. As suggested in the **sadf** man page, the following command prepares a report based on "memory, swap space, and network statistics" from the /var/log/sa/sa21 file:

```
# sadf -d /var/log/sa/sa21 -- -r -n DEV
```

TABLE 17-2	Switch	Description
Switches for the sadf Command	-d	Display contents in a format usable by a database.
	-D	Same as **-d**, except time is noted in number of seconds since 1/1/1970.
	-e hh:mm:ss	List end time of report, in 24-hour format.
	-p	Display contents in a format usable by the **awk** command; do not use with **-d**, **-D**, or **-x**.
	-s hh:mm:ss	List start time of report, in 24-hour format.
	-x	Display contents in XML format; do not use with **-d**, **-D**, or **-p**.

I cite the man page, as it's an excellent reference for the command required to create a report, while on the job, or even during a Red Hat exam. As with many other commands, this can be found in the EXAMPLES section. While the **-d** is associated with the **sadf** command, the double-dash (--) points to options associated with the **sar** command. So the **-r** reports memory usage, and the **-n DEV** reports statistics from network devices.

Of course, there are other important **sar** command switches. Those which may be relevant when you prepare a report on "processor, memory, disk, and network" utilization are described in Table 17-3.

With the switches listed in Table 17-3, you might modify the previous **sadf** command to meet all four of the items listed in the related RHCE objective:

```
# sadf -d /var/log/sa/sa21 -- -u -r -dp -n DEV
```

In other words, the **sadf** command specifies output usable by a database (**-d**) from the database file in the /var/log/sa directory associated with the twenty-first of the month. The double dash (--) points to **sar** command switches, with CPU utilization (**-u**); RAM utilization (**-r**); activity by block device; presented in more familiar block files such as sda (**-p**); with statistics from network devices (**-n DEV**).

TABLE 17-3	Switch	Description
System Utilization Switches for the sar Command	-d	Lists activity by block device, normally used with **-p** to specify common drive device filenames such as sda and sdb.
	-n DEV	Reports statistics from network devices.
	-P cpu	Lists statistics on a per-processor (or core) basis; e.g., **-P cpu 0** specifies the first CPU.
	-r	Reports memory utilization statistics.
	-S	Collects swap space utilization statistics.
	-u	Sets up a CPU utilization report, including categories related to applications executed at the user and system levels, idle time, and more.
	-W	Reports swap statistics.

CERTIFICATION OBJECTIVE 17.04

Configure a System Logging Server

Briefly, while local logging is an RHCSA objective, remote logging is an RHCE objective. In other words, this section addresses the configuration of a system as a logging client, and a second system to receive associated data as a logging server. The rsyslog package, which should be installed by default even in minimal RHEL 6 configurations, represents the remote system logging server. With the proliferation of VMs, a central logging server is even more useful.

Chapter 9 describes the local logging aspects of the rsyslog package. If you're familiar with older Linux distributions, including RHEL 5, you should recognize that the local logging commands have not changed significantly. What has changed with the rsyslog package is the inclusion of modules, which can enable the transmission and receipt of log files over a given TCP/IP port; the default port for logs is 514.

The rsyslog package includes extensive documentation in HTML format, in the /usr/share/doc/rsyslog-4.6.2 directory (the version number may vary). If Internet access is not available in certain circumstances, such as during a Red Hat exam, critical files such as rsyslog_conf.html should be available in the noted directory. If you're familiar with the older syslog system, the rsyslog system should be easy. The configuration of a local log is identical for both systems.

<table>
<tr><td>

e x a m

ⓦ a t c h   *In general, SELinux booleans do not directly affect log files. The SELinux booleans that affect individual services that may affect log messages are covered in other chapters.*

</td></tr>
</table>

System Logging Modules

Modules associated with the rsyslog service fall into three categories: input, output, and library. For the purposes of this chapter, you only need be concerned with input modules, and only those input modules already implemented or suggested in comments in the default /etc/rsyslog.conf file. Output modules are associated with sending data to other applications. Shortly, you'll examine those commands that send logging data from a client.

Enable Logging Clients

In this section, you'll look at those input modules listed in the standard rsyslog.conf configuration file. Some comments are already included in the default version of the file. The first command loads the imuxsock.so module with the **ModLoad** directive. The comment suggests that the module supports local system logging:

```
$ModLoad imuxsock.so    # provides support for local system
# logging (e.g. via logger command)
```

The next directive (**$ModLoad imklog.so**) loads the module associated with logging kernel-based information. The commented immark.so module, if active, would activate the **--MARK--** message periodically, if there is no other log activity.

The next two directives are important if you're configuring the system as a logging server. The module names (and associated comments) are descriptive, as imudp.so and imtcp.so refer to UDP and TCP communications, respectively.

```
# Provides UDP syslog reception
#$ModLoad imudp.so
# Provides TCP syslog reception
#$ModLoad imtcp.so
```

As noted in the commented directives described in the next section, UDP and TCP rsyslog communication is associated with port 514. For a logging server, the protocol you select depends on the importance of the information. UDP is associated with "best effort" delivery. While UDP is faster, it does not tell you if there's a transmission problem. But for many administrators, the occasional loss of data is trivial, given the large amounts of data often associated with log files.

If all of the data associated with log files are important, you should select the TCP module and directive. Of course, if you change the port number, you should also change the port number of any logging clients, as well as associated open firewall ports.

Configure Logging Servers

A logging server is a system set up to receive log information from clients. To review, such servers should have an open UDP or TCP port 514 to receive such information. On a real logging server, the disk space available on that server may be a concern. For example, some web servers create gigabytes of logging information every day. With that in mind, terabyte hard drives on logging servers may fill up quickly.

The default rsyslog.conf file includes suggested information for both UDP and TCP directives. Other directives can be added to further customize a logging server.

For more information, see www.rsyslog.com/doc/imudp.html and www.rsyslog.com /doc/imtcp.html.

UDP Directives

The standard suggested UDP directive specifies the port number where the server listens for logging clients:

```
$UDPServerRun 514
```

If there are multiple network cards on the local system, the following directive limits the logging server to the network card with the noted IP address:

```
$UDPServerAddress 192.168.122.50
```

TCP Directives

As with UDP, the standard suggested TCP directive specifies the port number where the server listens for logging clients. Multiple port numbers are supported, for configurations where you want to set up support for multiple clients.

```
$InputTCPServerRun 514
```

You can configure rsyslog to send a message if a logging client closes a connection:

```
$InputTCPServerNotifyOnConnectionClose on
```

If this server is working with a number of clients on different ports, you can use the **$InputTCPMaxListeners** directive to increase the number of such ports beyond the default of 20. This can work with the following directive, which sets the maximum number of supported sesssions (the default is 200):

```
$InputTCPMaxSessions
```

If you set a nondefault value of $InputTCPMaxSessions, that directive must be set before directives such as **$InputTCPServerRun 514**.

Configure Logging Clients

One of the features of the default rsyslog.conf file is the group of comments shown in Figure 17-7.

FIGURE 17-7

Draft logging
client commands
from /etc/rsyslog
.conf

```
# ### begin forwarding rule ###
# The statement between the begin ... end define a SINGLE forwarding
# rule. They belong together, do NOT split them. If you create multiple
# forwarding rules, duplicate the whole block!
# Remote Logging (we use TCP for reliable delivery)
#
# An on-disk queue is created for this action. If the remote host is
# down, messages are spooled to disk and sent when it is up again.
#$WorkDirectory /var/spppl/rsyslog # where to place spool files
#$ActionQueueFileName fwdRule1 # unique name prefix for spool files
#$ActionQueueMaxDiskSpace 1g    # 1gb space limit (use as much as possible)
#$ActionQueueSaveOnShutdown on # save messages to disk on shutdown
#$ActionQueueType LinkedList   # run asynchronously
#$ActionResumeRetryCount -1    # infinite retries if host is down
# remote host is: name/ip:port, e.g. 192.168.0.1:514, port optional
#*.* @@remote-host:514
# ### end of the forwarding rule ###
```

As suggested in the comments, most of the directives are based on the use of TCP communication. All but the last commented directive define what happens on a logging client if it can't connect the network logging server.

The last commented directive applies to both TCP and UDP communications from a server. To configure the local system to send all logging messages, over TCP port 514, to a remote host on IP address 192.168.122.1, you'd add the following command:

```
*.* @@192.168.122.1:514
```

Alternatively, to configure just mail messages to be sent over UDP port 514 to a remote host on IP address 192.168.100.1, you'd add the following command:

```
mail.* @192.168.100.1:514
```

The *.* sends all logging messages. You can substitute options like authpriv, kern, and cron for the first asterisk. You can substitute log severity options such as debug, info, notice, warn, and so on for the second asterisk. A single @ represents UDP communication. A double @@ represents TCP communication.

Limit Access to Specified Systems

To limit access to a logging server, you'll need to configure an appropriate rule in an **iptables**-based firewall. For example, the following rule listed in the /etc/sysconfig/iptables file would allow communications from the noted IP address over TCP port 514.

```
-A INPUT -m state --state NEW -m tcp -p tcp -s 192.168.122.50 --dport 514 -j
ACCEPT
```

As noted in earlier chapters, if you use the Firewall Configuration tool, it's best to set this up as a custom rule. Otherwise, future changes in the Firewall Configuration tool may overwrite this custom rule.

CERTIFICATION OBJECTIVE 17.05

The Network Time Server Service

While NTP is no longer part of the RHCSA objectives, NTP as a client is implicitly covered in Red Hat's introductory RH124 course, a prep course for that exam. The configuration of NTP as a client is therefore covered in Chapter 5. In contrast, the configuration of NTP as a server is an RHCE objective covered here. NTP is classified as an RHCE-level network service. In other words, you need to know how to secure NTP just as you secure other network services such as Samba and NFS.

To allow NTP to work as a server, you need to allow access through UDP port 123. NTP uses the UDP protocol, because it's faster.

The NTP Server Configuration File

As discussed in Chapter 5, the configuration of an NTP client depends on the time zone documented in the /etc/sysconfig/clock file, as well as the servers configured in the /etc/ntp.conf file. Now it's time to configure one of those NTP servers, with the help of other settings in that ntp.conf file. Now you'll examine the default version of this file.

It starts with the **driftfile** directive, which monitors the error in the local system clock:

```
driftfile /var/lib/ntp/drift
```

There are also **restrict** directives that can help protect an NTP server. While a plain **restrict** directive works with IPv4 networking, a **restrict -6** directive works with IPv6 networking, Nevertheless, the same options are used with each **restrict** directive.

```
restrict default kod nomodify notrap nopeer noquery
restrict -6 default kod nomodify notrap nopeer noquery
```

The options to the **restrict** directive can be described as follows:

- **default**   Refers to default connections from other systems; may be further limited by other **restrict** directives.
- **kod**   Sends a "kiss of death" packet to systems that violate access restrictions; but it works only if there's a **limited** flag in the **restrict** line. So unless there's a security breach in the NTP server (always possible), the **kod** option can be removed.
- **nomodify**   Denies queries that attempt to change the local NTP server.
- **notrap**   Denies the control message trap service; you might remove this option to enable remote logging.
- **nopeer**   Stops access from potential peer NTP servers. To configure a server that "synchronizes time using other NTP peers," as suggested in the RHCE objectives, you'd need to remove this option.
- **noquery**   Ignores information and configuration requests.

But these restrictions, when combined, are good only for an NTP client. To set up an NTP server, specifically one that "synchronizes time using other NTP peers," you should remove at least the **nopeer** directive from this list. Some NTP servers may need to synchronize with yours, which is possible if you remove the noquery from the list as well.

The next two restrict directives limit access to the local NTP server to the local system. You should recognize the default IPv4 and IPv6 loopback addresses here:

```
restrict 127.0.0.1
restrict -6 ::1
```

Of course, when setting up an NTP server for other clients, you'll want to loosen that restriction. The comment that follows includes a network address in the required format. So to set up an NTP server for the 192.168.122.0/24 network, you'd change the **restrict** directive to

```
restrict 192.168.122.0 mask 255.255.255.0 notrap nomodify
```

For basic configuration, no additional changes should be required. Of course, the local NTP server should also be configured as a client to master NTP servers. And to repeat the reference from the RHCE objectives, the reference is to peers. The relevant directive is **peer**.

To test the directive on one NTP server, you could change the **server** in each of the default directives to **peer**, as shown here:

```
peer 0.rhel.pool.ntp.org
peer 1.rhel.pool.ntp.org
peer 2.rhel.pool.ntp.org
```

Alternatively, you could be given the URI to an NTP peer server, perhaps on a corporate network, perhaps on a network that's been configured during the exam.

Security Limits on NTP

As just described, the **restrict** directive from the /etc/ntp.conf configuration file can be used to limit access to a local NTP server. But that assumes an open port 123. Security limits can also refer to configured firewalls. Just be aware that an appropriate firewall rule for NTP opens up UDP (not TCP) port 123.

To test a connection to an NTP server, the **ntpq -p** *hostname* command can help. That command looks for the peers listed in the /etc/ntp.conf file. If the server is operational, you'll see something similar to the following output to the **ntpq -p localhost** command shown in Figure 17-8.

watch   *Since NTP is a UDP-based service, the telnet and nmap commands won't verify the operation of that service. You'll need a command like ntpq -p hostname for that purpose.*

Of course, if that command works from a remote system, using the local hostname or IP address, you've verified that the remote NTP server is operational.

FIGURE 17-8

NTP server peers, verified with the ntpq -p command

```
[root@Maui michael]# ntpq -p localhost
     remote           refid      st t when poll reach   delay   offset  jitter
==============================================================================
 ntp.pbx.org      192.5.41.40       2 u   30   64    17  103.586 462.252  10.857
 ntp1.Housing.Be 169.229.128.214   3 u   22   64    17   38.452 462.901  12.111
 ntp.sunflower.c 132.236.56.250    3 u   23   64    17   74.502 536.253   5.584
[root@Maui michael]#
```

SCENARIO & SOLUTION

You need to configure a caching-only DNS server for the local network.	Use the default named.conf file; modify the **listen-on** and **allow-query** directives
You need to configure a caching-only DNS server to forward requests elsewhere.	Use the named.conf file, modified for the caching-only directive; add a **forwarders** directive to point to a desired DNS server.
You need to set up a system utilization report for various hardware components.	Start with the man page for the **sadf** command; use options associated with the **sar** command for desired components.
You want to configure a system logging server.	Modify the rsyslog.conf file to activate a TCP or UDP module, and accept input over a port number.
You want to configure a system logging client.	Modify the rsyslog.conf file. Use the commented options at the bottom of the file to point to a system logging server.
You need to set up an NTP server as a peer.	Modify the ntp.conf file, to specify the host or IP address of a peer NTP server with the **peer** directive. Change the **restrict** directive of the server to remove the **nopeer** option and allow access to desired systems server.

CERTIFICATION SUMMARY

DNS provides a database of domain names and IP addresses that help web browsers, FTP clients, NTP clients, and more find sites on various networks, including the Internet. The default DNS server uses the **named** daemon, based on the Berkeley Internet Name Domain (BIND). It's a distributed database where each administrator is responsible for his or her own zone of authority, such as mcgraw-hill.com.

There are four basic types of DNS servers: master, slave (or secondary), caching-only, and forwarding-only. The RHCE objectives specifically exclude master and slave name servers. The default /etc/named.conf file is built in a caching-only DNS server configuration. A forwarding-only name server uses the **forward only** and **forwarders** directives in the named.conf file. In either case, you should configure the

listen-on and **allow-query** directives to support access from the local system and desired network(s). To test a DNS server, use commands like **rndc status**, **dig**, and **host**.

As an RHCE, you need to be able to monitor the performance of administered systems. That's the province of the sysstat service. While commands like **df**, **top**, and **dstat** can display CPU, RAM, disk, and network utilization data, actual reports can be prepared with the help of the sysstat service. That service is configured with the help of the sysstat and sysstat.ioconf files, with data collected on a periodic basis. Such data is collected into log files in the /var/log/sa directory with the help of a sysstat cron job in the /etc/cron.d directory. System status reports can be prepared from these log files with the help of the **sadf** command. An example of how this collects RAM and network data is available in the **sadf** man page; you can then add CPU and disk use data from related **sar** command switches.

With the proliferation of VMs, a central logging server can be more convenient. RHEL 6 includes the rsyslog package for that purpose. Administrators who are familiar with syslog should have no problem with rsyslog. Just be sure to activate TCP or UDP port 514 on the server, open up the associated port in the firewall, and add appropriate modules. The rsyslog.conf file even includes suggested directives for both logging clients and servers.

Finally, to configure an NTP server for a network, you need to do more to the associated configuration file, /etc/ntp.conf. As suggested in a file comment, the **restrict** directive should be changed to specify the network address. To support the peers suggested in the RHCE objectives, you also need a **restrict** directive without the **kod**, **noquery**, and (most important) **nopeer** options. Then to set up other systems as peers, you'd use the **peer** *hostname* format.

✓ TWO-MINUTE DRILL

Here are some of the key points from the certification objectives in Chapter 17.

Basic Domain Service Organization

❑ DNS is based on the Berkeley Internet Name Domain (BIND), using the **named** daemon.

❑ Key packages include bind-chroot, which adds security by supporting DNS in a chroot jail, and bind-utils, which includes command utilities such as **dig** and **host**.

❑ Four basic types of DNS servers are: master, slave (secondary), caching-only, and forwarding-only. The RHCE objectives specifically exclude coverage of master and secondary DNS services.

Minimal DNS Server Configurations

❑ Critical DNS configuration files include /etc/sysconfig/named, /etc/named.conf, and the files in the /var/named directory.

❑ The default /etc/named.conf is set up for a caching-only nameserver, limited to the local system. Changes to the **listen-on** and **allow-query** directives can enable access from DNS clients on a network.

❑ A forwarding name server requires a **forward only** or a **forwarders** directive that specifies the IP addresses of the remote DNS servers.

❑ The **forwarders** directive, with the IP address of the remote DNS servers, can be combined with the caching-only named.conf configuration.

Set Up System Utilization Reports

❑ System utilization reports are made possible in RHEL 6 with the help of the sysstat service.

❑ The sysstat service collects data regularly based on a job in the /etc/cron.d directory, in day-labeled files in the /var/log/sa directory.

❑ System status reports can be created with the **sadf** command, with an assist from **sar** command switches.

❑ A prime example of a system status report command is shown in the **sadf** man page, but it needs additional **sar** command switches to support the collection of CPU and disk performance information.

Configure a System Logging Server

❑ The RHEL 6 rsyslog service, for local clients, is essentially the same as the older syslog service.

❑ The rsyslog.conf file includes commented directives for the modules associated with the configuration of a system logging server.

❑ Default communications to a remote system logging server work over TCP or UDP port 514.

❑ Logging clients can be configured to send logs of all types and levels with a *.*, or the information that is sent can be customized. Information can be sent via TCP (@@) or UDP (@).

The Network Time Server Service

❑ The default NTP configuration file, /etc/ntp.conf, sets up a client with access limited to the local system.

❑ A standard **restrict** directive in the default ntp.conf file is available that opens access over UDP port 123 to systems on a specified network.

❑ The RHCE objectives suggest connections to peers; such connections can be configured by substituting **peer** for **server**. In addition, you'd substitute the hostname or IP address of the remote peer servers for the default NTP servers such as 0.rhel.pool.ntp.org.

❑ Standard network test tools such as **nmap** and **telnet** don't work with the UDP communication associated with NTP networking.

SELF TEST

The following questions will help measure your understanding of the material presented in this chapter. As no multiple-choice questions appear on the Red Hat exams, no multiple-choice questions appear in this book. These questions exclusively test your understanding of the chapter. It is okay if you have another way of performing a task. Getting results, not memorizing trivia, is what counts on the Red Hat exams. There may be more than one answer to many of these questions.

Basic Domain Service Organization

1. What is the name of the RPM package that helps hide DNS files in a chroot jail? Do not include the version number.

   _____

2. Name two types of DNS servers referenced in the RHCE objectives.

   _____

   _____

Minimal DNS Server Configurations

3. To configure DNS communication on port 53, what changes would you make to a firewall to support access by other clients to the local DNS server?

   _____

4. What file includes a basic template for a DNS caching-only nameserver?

   _____

5. What command can display the current operational status of the standard RHEL 6 DNS server?

   _____

6. What command makes sure that the DNS service starts the next time you boot Linux in a normal runlevel?

   _____

Set Up System Utilization Reports

7. What directory includes the job that creates standard system utilization reports? Assume the appropriate package is installed.

_____

8. On a RHEL 6 system, where can you find an example command to create a system utilization report? Where can you find additional switches for that report?

_____

Configure a System Logging Server

9. What module is associated with TCP reception for a system logging server?

_____

10. What command in /etc/rsyslog.conf sends all log information, using TCP, to a system on IP address 192.168.100.100, on port 514?

_____

The Network Time Server Service

11. Enter a directive, suitable for /etc/ntp.conf, that limits access to the 192.168.0.0/24 network. Hint: additional restrictions such as kod may be included in a different directive.

_____

12. What directive in /etc/ntp.conf is suited for connections to remote NTP peer servers?

_____

LAB QUESTIONS

Several of these labs involve configuration exercises. You should do these exercises on test machines only. It's assumed that you're running these exercises on virtual machines such as KVM. For this chapter, it's also assumed that you may be changing the configuration of a physical host system for such virtual machines.

Red Hat presents its exams electronically. For that reason, the labs in this and future chapters are available from the CD that accompanies the book, in the Chapter17/ subdirectory. In case you haven't yet set up RHEL 6 on a system, refer to Chapter 1 for installation instructions.

The answers for each lab follow the Self Test answers for the fill-in-the-blank questions.

SELF TEST ANSWERS

Basic Domain Name Service Organization

1. The package that supports additional security for a DNS name server based on BIND through a special chroot directory is bind-chroot.

2. Two types of DNS servers specified in the RHCE objectives are caching-only and forwarding.

Minimal DNS Server Configurations

3. To support access by other clients to the local DNS server, make sure TCP and UDP traffic is supported through the firewall on port 53.

4. The default /etc/named.conf file includes a basic template for a DNS caching nameserver.

5. Several answers work here, such as **/etc/init.d/bind status**, **rndc status**, and **service bind status**.

6. The command that makes sure that the DNS service starts the next time you boot Linux is

   ```
   # chkconfig named on
   ```

   Similar commands such as **chkconfig named --level 35 on** are also acceptable answers.

Set Up System Utilization Reports

7. The directory with the standard sysstat job is /etc/cron.d.

8. On a RHEL 6 system, one place where you can find a command example of a system utilization report is the **sadf** man page. Additional switches can be found in the **sar** man page.

Configure a System Logging Server

9. The module associated with TCP reception for a system logging server is imtcp.so.

10. The command in /etc/rsyslog.conf that sends all log information, using TCP, to a system on IP address 192.168.100.100, on port 514 is

    ```
    *.* @@192.168.100.100:514
    ```

The Network Time Server Service

11. One directive in the /etc/ntp.conf file that limits access based on the noted conditions is

```
restrict 192.168.122.0 mask 255.255.255.0
```

Of course, there are other ways to meet the same requirement. It's acceptable if the **restrict** directive includes options such as **kod, nomodify,** or **notrap.**

12. The directive in /etc/ntp.conf is suited for connections to remote NTP peer servers is

```
peer
```

LAB ANSWERS

Lab 1: Caching-only DNS Server

In this lab, you have the benefit of the /etc/named.conf configuration file. All you need to do is

1. Modify the **listen-on port 53** directive to include the local IP address; for example, if the local IP address is 192.168.122.150, the directive will look like

```
listen-on port 53 { 127.0.0.1; 192.168.122.150; };
```

2. Modify the **allow-query** directive to include the local IP network address:

```
allow-query { localhost; 192.168.122.0/24; };
```

3. Save your changes to /etc/named.conf.

4. Start the **named** service (other methods are available):

```
# service named start
```

5. Change the local client to point to the local DNS caching name server; replace any **nameserver** directives in /etc/resolv.conf with the IP address of the local system. For example, if the local computer is on 192.168.122.150, the directive is

```
nameserver 192.168.122.50
```

6. Test out the new local DNS server. Try commands such as **dig www.mheducation.com**. You should see the following near the end of the output:

```
;; SERVER: 192.168.122.50#53(192.168.122.50)
```

7. Point client systems points to the DNS server. Add the aforementioned **nameserver** directive to /etc/resolv.conf on those remote client systems:

   ```
   nameserver 192.168.122.50
   ```

   To review the various methods to make the change permanent, see Chapter 3. One method is to set up **DNS1=192.168.122.50** in the configuration file for the network card, such as ifcfg-eth0 in the /etc/sysconfig/network-scripts directory.

8. To make sure the DNS service starts the next time Linux is booted, run the following command:

   ```
   # chkconfig named on
   ```

9. Open up TCP and UDP ports 53 in the firewall on the local system. The simplest method is with the Firewall Configuration tool, which would include the following directives in the /etc/sysconfig/iptables file:

   ```
   -A INPUT -m state --state NEW -m tcp -p tcp --dport 53 -j ACCEPT
   -A INPUT -m state --state NEW -m udp -p udp --dport 53 -j ACCEPT
   ```

Lab 2: Caching and Forwarding DNS Server

As with Lab 1, the focus is on the configuration of the /etc/named.conf file. Nominally, the default caching-only DNS server already includes forwarding features, courtesy of the named.ca file listed near the end of the file. But to set up a specific forwarding server, you should add a forwarders entry such as the following in the **options** stanza.

```
forwarders { 192.168.122.1; };
```

Don't forget to configure a firewall, with an open UDP port 53. If necessary, you can set up host restrictions on the **iptables** rule that opens up that port, as discussed in the answer to Lab 1. You'll also need the rules to limit access to the local network. For example, the following output to the **iptables -L** command shows TCP and UDP port 53 (listed as domain in /etc/services) available to the 192.168.122.0/24 network:

```
ACCEPT  tcp  --  192.168.122.0/24  anywhere   state NEW udp dpt:domain
ACCEPT  tcp  --  192.168.122.0/24  anywhere   state NEW tcp dpt:domain
```

In general, it's best to set up such a change as a custom rule in the Firewall Configuration tool, if you want to use that tool in the future. As for the other requirements of the lab, you can clear the current cache with the **rndc flush** command and reload the configuration file with the **rndc reload** command.

Lab 3: Create a System Utilization Report

If you understand this lab, the answer should be easy. While there are other methods, one appropriate command that meets the given requirements is available on the man page for the **sadf** command:

```
# sadf -d /var/log/sa/sa21 -- -r -n DEV
```

Of course, to get that information into the noted file, the output must be redirected:

```
# sadf -d /var/log/sa/sa21 -- -r -n DEV > sysstat_report.txt
```

Lab 4: Create a Detailed System Utilization Report

This lab builds upon what you did in Lab 3. If you haven't memorized the additional switches that specify information on CPU and disk usage, the appropriate switches are available in the man page for the **sar** command, for switches that apply after the double dash (--). As suggested in the man page, the **-u** can be used to report CPU usage, the **-d** reports activity by block device. It can help users read the output if the **-p** is combined with the **-d**.

But there's one more requirement: the **-p** next to the **sadf** command leads to output in a format usable by the **awk** command utility. The following way is one method to meet the requirements of the lab:

```
# sadf -p /var/log/sa/sa21 -- -u -r -dp -n DEV > morestat_report.txt
```

Lab 5: Configure a System Logging Server

Just a few changes are required to configure a system logging server. For example, to set up TCP communications, you can activate the following directives:

```
$ModLoad imtcp.so
$InputTCPServerRun 514
```

Of course, access requires an open port 514 in a local firewall. You could set up a custom rule with the Firewall Configuration tool such as the following:

```
-A INPUT -m state --state NEW -m tcp -p tcp --dport 514 -j ACCEPT
```

If you've selected UDP instead of TCP communication in the /etc/rsyslog.conf file, the associated custom firewall rule would change accordingly.

As a system logging server is not a regular network server in the RHCE objectives, this rule opens access to all systems. Of course, if needed, you can add such limits in a fashion similar to Lab 2. Don't forget to make sure the rsyslog service is running and set to start at appropriate runlevels upon reboot with a command like **chkconfig rsyslog on**.

Lab 6: Configure a System Logging Client

The default version of the /etc/rsyslog.conf file includes proposed directives that can be used to help configure a system as a logging client. While most of the directives aren't absolutely necessary, they can help save log data after a network break. So it's acceptable to activate one or more of these directives. Of course, for the final line, you'd want to substitute the IP address of the rsyslog server for the IP address shown here.

```
$WorkDirectory /var/spppl/rsyslog # where to place spool files
$ActionQueueFileName fwdRule1 # unique name prefix for spool files
$ActionQueueMaxDiskSpace 1g   # 1gb space limit (use as much as pos-
sible)
$ActionQueueSaveOnShutdown on # save messages to disk on shutdown
$ActionQueueType LinkedList   # run asynchronously
$ActionResumeRetryCount -1    # infinite retries if host is down
*.* @@192.168.122.50:514
```

Lab 7: Configure a NTP Server

In this lab, you'll set up one NTP server as a peer to another. That's possible with the **peer** directive, configured in the /etc/ntp.conf configuration file. For example, if a regular NTP server is configured on IP address 192.168.122.50, you can set up a peer on the 192.168.122.150 server with the following directive:

```
peer 192.168.122.50
```

Just remember, an NTP peer doesn't work unless the **nopeer** option has been removed from the **restrict** directive in the ntp.conf file.

A

Prepare a System for the Sample Exams

Randy Russell, Red Hat's Director of Certification, stated in a 2009 blog entry that the Red Hat exams no longer require "a bare-metal installation." In other words, when you sit down for a Red Hat exam today, a preinstalled system will be provided for you. In this appendix, you'll set up a preinstalled system that will work for the sample exams included in electronic format on the CD in the Exams/ subdirectory. Each exam is described on the first page of Appendixes B through E and the answers follow.

If you're just studying for the RHCSA, read the following section. If you're also studying for the RHCE, read the section after that as well.

Basic Sample Exam System Requirements

A test system for RHEL 6 requires more. There is no requirement for a *physical* "bare-metal" installation in the objectives for either the RHCSA or the RHCE exam. However, for the RHCSA, you do need to "configure a physical machine to host virtual guests." As the default RHEL 6 virtual machine solution (KVM) can only be installed from its 64-bit release, you should have 64-bit hardware. (Scientific Linux 6 does include 32-bit packages for KVM.)

You can expect to "install Red Hat Enterprise Linux systems as virtual guests." That's an implicit requirement for a *virtual* "bare-metal" installation. With those objectives in mind, you can set up a test system based on the following criteria:

- Installation on physical 64-bit hardware
  - A dual-boot configuration with another operating system is acceptable.
  - Red Hat does not support Intel Itanium CPUs.
- Sufficient hard drive space
  - 50GB total should be sufficient (though more would be helpful).
  - While you could live with less, figure on 15GB for the physical system.
  - And 15GB each for two or three virtual machine systems should be sufficient.

In most cases, it's not possible to install a virtual machine within a virtual machine. While I did not test such a configuration for this book, virtual machine solutions that run on bare-metal systems reportedly can in turn host other virtual machines. If this is too expensive or complex, just install RHEL 6 on a physical 64-bit system.

Since one of the objectives is to "configure a physical machine to host virtual guests," you'll need to set up a 64-bit physical system without installing KVM software. (Of course, you should be prepared to install KVM during an exam.) As discussed in Chapter 1, it's ideal if you have a genuine release of RHEL 6 for this purpose. Rebuild distributions such as Scientific Linux 6, CentOS 6, or even Oracle Linux 6 should work equally well, as they are based on the publicly available RHEL 6 source code.

However, you should not use Fedora Linux to study for the Red Hat exams. While RHEL 6 is based on Fedora Linux, RHEL 6 has a modestly different look and feel. In some cases, it has a different functionality from the most similar Fedora releases, Fedora 12 and Fedora 13.

With those provisos in mind, you should prepare a 64-bit physical test system per the requirements described in Chapter 1. As suggested in that chapter, you should configure a Basic Server installation, and make sure to select Customize Now as shown in Figure A-1.

FIGURE A-1

RHEL 6 installation, Basic Server, Customize Now

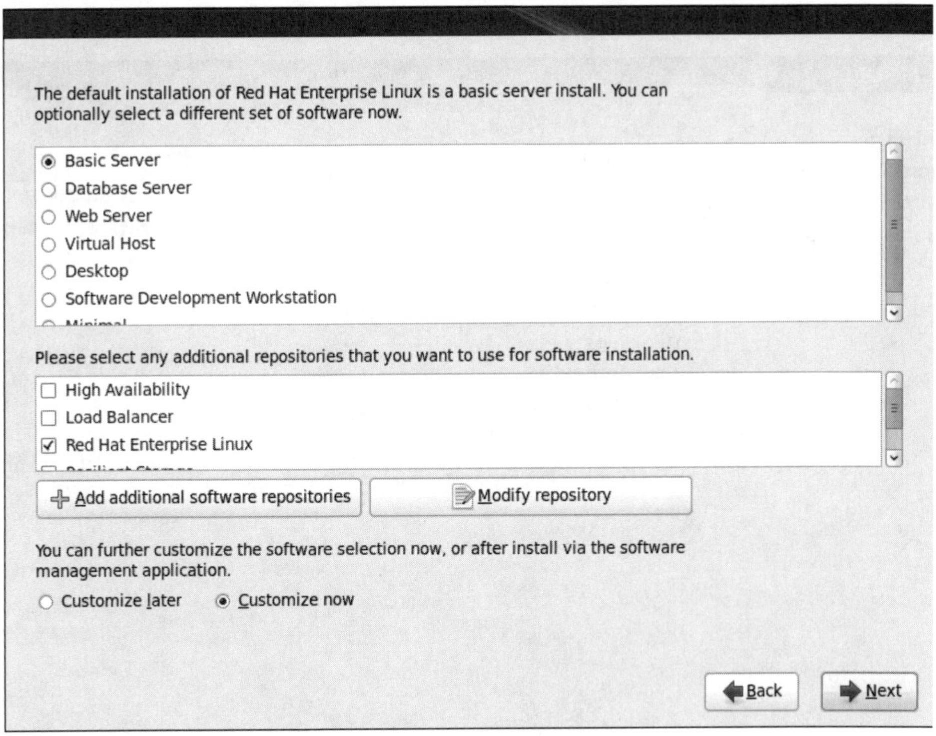

The default installation of Red Hat Enterprise Linux is a basic server install. You can optionally select a different set of software now.

- ● Basic Server
- ○ Database Server
- ○ Web Server
- ○ Virtual Host
- ○ Desktop
- ○ Software Development Workstation
- ○ Minimal

Please select any additional repositories that you want to use for software installation.

- ☐ High Availability
- ☐ Load Balancer
- ☑ Red Hat Enterprise Linux

➕ Add additional software repositories   📝 Modify repository

You can further customize the software selection now, or after install via the software management application.

- ○ Customize later   ● Customize now

⬅ Back   ➡ Next

You may also set up a GUI, as also discussed in Chapter 1. To review, you should select the following package groups during the installation process:

- **Desktops – Desktop**   Includes the basic GNOME Desktop Environment.
- **Desktops – Fonts**   Installs fonts that improve system readability in the GUI.
- **Desktops – X Window System**   Adds the server packages associated with the GUI.
- **Applications – Internet Browser**   Includes the Firefox web browser.

But to meet the implied requirements of a test system for the RHCSA, you'll need to make sure that virtual machine software is not installed during the installation process, as shown in Figure A-2.

Once installation is complete, the system will be ready for the RHCSA exam. But there are a couple more steps required. You'll need to set up an installation repository for the local network. It's okay to do so on the physical host system. One method is

---

FIGURE A-2

RHEL 6 installation, no virtual machine software

Base System	☑ **Virtualization**
Servers	☐ **Virtualization Client**
Web Services	☐ **Virtualization Platform**
Databases	☐ **Virtualization Tools**
System Management	
Virtualization	
Desktops	
Applications	
Development	

Provides an environment for hosting virtualized guests.

Optional packages

Back   Next

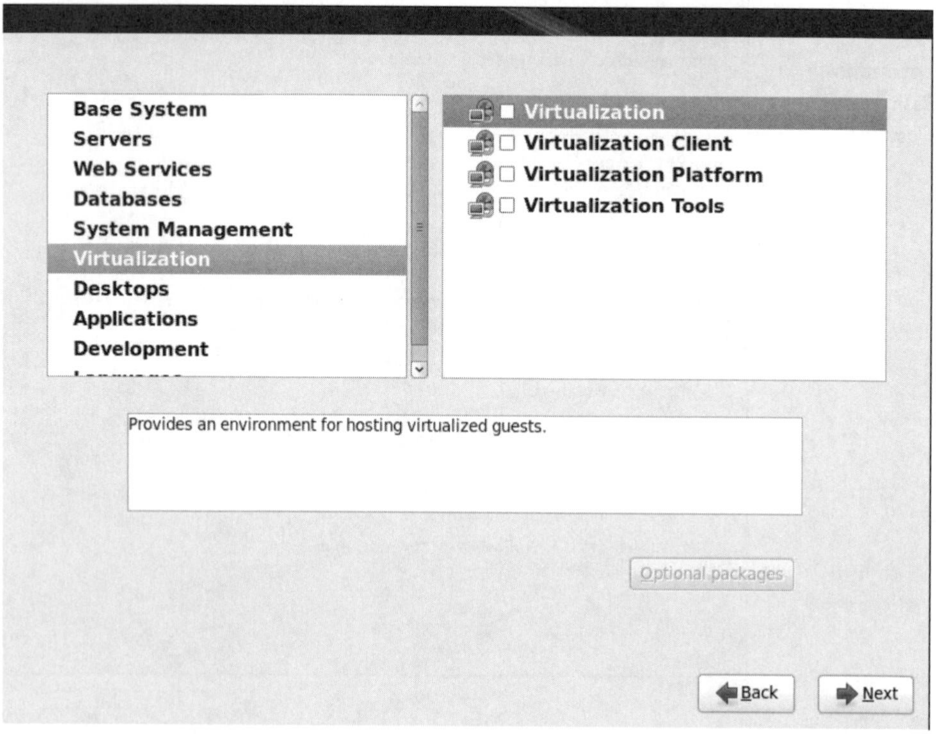

described in Chapter 1, Lab 2. Next, download the package for the latest available kernel. If the yum-utils package is available, run the following command:

```
# yumdownloader kernel kernel-firmware
```

Otherwise, use the kernel and kernel-firmware RPM packages available on the CD, in the Chapter7/ subdirectory.

Additional Sample Exam System Requirements for the RHCE

To be ready for the RHCE exam, you'll need to do more. Specifically, you'll want at least two virtual machine systems on the physical host system. Each of those systems should be configured on different networks, as discussed in Chapter 1.

If you're just studying for the RHCE, you can choose to include virtual machine software in the installation process for the physical host system, as shown in Figure A-2. You should set up the virtual systems per the requirements discussed in Chapters 1 and 2. Kickstart files ks.cfg, ks1.cfg, and ks2.cfg are available on the CD, in the Exams/ subdirectory, to help create those virtual systems.

B

Sample Exam 1: RHCSA

T

he following questions will help measure your understanding of the material presented in this book. As discussed in the introduction, you should be prepared to complete the RHCSA exam in 2.5 hours.

The RHCSA exam is "closed book." However, you are allowed to use any documentation that can be found on the Red Hat Enterprise Linux computer. While test facilities allow you to make notes, you won't be allowed to take these notes from the testing room.

The RHCSA is entirely separate from the RHCE. While both exams cover some of the same services, the objectives for those services are different.

In most cases, there is no one solution, no single method to solve a problem or install a service. There are a nearly infinite number of options with Linux, so I can't cover all possible scenarios.

Even for these exercises, *do not use a production computer*. A small error in some or all of these exercises may make Linux unbootable. If you're unable to recover from the steps documented in these exercises, you may need to reinstall Red Hat Enterprise Linux. Saving any data that you have on the local system may then not be possible.

Red Hat presents its exams electronically. For that reason, the exams in this book are available from the companion CD, in the Exams/ subdirectory. This exam is in the file named RHCSAsampleexam1, and is available in .txt, .doc, and .html formats. For details on how to set up RHEL 6 as a system suitable for a practice exam, refer to Appendix A. Be very sure to set up the repository configured in Chapter 1, Lab 2.

Don't turn the page until you're finished with the sample exam!

RHCSA Sample Exam I Discussion

In this discussion, I'll describe one way to check your work to meet the requirements listed for the Sample 1 RHCSA exam.

1. One way to see if SELinux is set in enforcing mode is to run the **sestatus** command.

2. If VM software is installed on the local system, you'll have access to the Virtual Machine Manager in the GUI, or at least the **virt-install** and **virsh** commands from the command line.

3. If successful, you should be able to access the new server2.example.com system, either via ssh or with the Virtual Machine Manager.

4. One way to set the noted system to start automatically the next time the host is booted is with the **virsh autostart server2.example.com** command. One way to confirm is in the output to the **virsh dominfo server2.example.com** command.

5. To review current logical volumes, run the **lvs** command.

6. Make sure the volume is encrypted. Did you run the **cryptsetup** command on the volume?

7. To make sure that volume is automatically mounted the next time the system is booted, it should be configured in /etc/fstab to the appropriate format, with the UUID associated with the encrypted volume, as defined by the **blkid** command.

8. The /home/angels directory should be owned by the group angels. As long as users donna and mike are not part of that group, and other users don't have permissions (or ACLs) on that directory, access should be limited to members of the angels group. The directory should also have SGID permissions.

9. If you've modified user mike's account to make his account expire in seven days, the right expiration date should appear in the output to the **chage -l mike** command.

10. There are a number of ways to set up a cron job; it could be configured in the /etc/cron.monthly directory or as a cron job for the user root or mike in the /var/spool/cron directory. In any of these cases, the delete command would be associated with an appropriate time stamp, with a line such as:

```
50 3 2 * * /bin/rm /home/mike/*
```

11. Permanently configured ACLs are associated with the acl option on the appropriate volume in the /etc/fstab configuration file. Volumes mounted with the acl option should be revealed in the output to the **mount** command.

12. Run the **getfacl /home/mike/project.test** command. If user donna has read permissions in the ACLs, you'll see it in the output to that command.

13. For a GRUB stanza to point to runlevel 1, that number must be included in the command associated with the **kernel** directive.

14. A change to the root password, where that password isn't already known, is intended to make you boot into single-user mode.

15. The process for installing an Apache Web server is straightforward. It can be verified with the **rpm -q httpd** command.

16. But you need to make sure the server starts automatically the next time the system is booted, something that can be checked with the **chkconfig --list httpd** command.

17. To make that server accessible to all systems over a network, at least port 80 should be open in the **iptables**-based firewall. If a local system is on IP address 192.168.122.51, that can be confirmed from a remote system with the **nmap 192.168.122.51** command.

C

Sample Exam 2: RHCSA

T he following questions will help measure your understanding of the material presented in this book. As discussed in the introduction, you should be prepared to complete the RHCSA exam in 2.5 hours.

The RHCSA exam is "closed book." However, you are allowed to use any documentation that can be found on the Red Hat Enterprise Linux computer. While test facilities allow you to make notes, you won't be allowed to take these notes from the testing room.

The RHCSA is entirely separate from the RHCE. While both exams cover some of the same services, the objectives for those services are different.

In most cases, there is no one solution, no single method to solve a problem or install a service. There are a nearly infinite number of options with Linux, so I can't cover all possible scenarios.

Even for these exercises, *do not use a production computer*. A small error in some or all of these exercises may make Linux unbootable. If you're unable to recover from the steps documented in these exercises, you may need to reinstall Red Hat Enterprise Linux. Saving any data that you have on the local system may then not be possible.

Red Hat presents its exams electronically. For that reason, the exams in this book are available from the companion CD, in the Exams/ subdirectory. This exam is in the file named RHCSAsampleexam2, and is available in .txt, .doc, and .html formats. For details on how to set up RHEL 6 as a system suitable for a practice exam, refer to Appendix A. Be very sure to set up the repository configured in Chapter 1, Lab 2.

Don't turn the page until you're finished with the sample exam!

RHCSA Sample Exam 2 Discussion

In this discussion, I'll describe one way to check your work to meet the requirements listed for the Sample 1 RHCSA exam.

1. If VM software is installed on the local system, you'll have access to the Virtual Machine Manager in the GUI, or at least the **virt-install** and **virsh** commands from the command line

2. If the newly Kickstarted installation is successful, you should be able to access the new outsider2.example.org system, either via ssh or with the Virtual Machine Manager.

3. Anyone with access to the administrative account on the VM can review ssh-based logins in the /var/log/secure file. It's an easy way to verify that you've used the **ssh** command to connect to the new system.

4. All partitions (the new 500MB partition, additional swap space) should be shown in the output to the **fdisk -l** command.

5. When properly configured, the ext4 format should be shown in the output to the **mount** command, and permanent settings (including the acl option, the /cooks directory, and corresponding UUIDs) shown in the /etc/fstab file.

6. When additional swap space is implemented, it should be shown in the contents of the /proc/swaps file. Alternatively, the total amount of swap space should be shown in the output to the **top** command. Run the **blkid** command. Use the UUID of the new swap volume in /etc/fstab.

7. New local users should be documented in /etc/passwd and /etc/shadow.

8. To specifically deny regular users access to a directory, it's easiest to use ACLs. You should be able to confirm that users bill and richard don't have access to the /cooks directory with the **getfacl /cooks** command.

9. To confirm, you should be able to insert a DVD into the appropriate drive. (Alternatively, you can set up an ISO file on a virtual machine.) Then when you run the **ls /misc/dvd** command, the automounter will mount the DVD and provide file information on that drive. This should be an easy configuration, based on a slight change to the default /etc/auto.misc file. Of course, you'll need to make sure the autofs service runs after a reboot, which can be confirmed with an **chkconfig --list autofs** command.

10. When new kernels are installed, they should include a new stanza in the bootloader configuration file, /boot/grub/grub.conf. The default stanza is based on the **default** directive; just remember, **default=0** points to the first stanza, **default=1** points to the second stanza, and so on.

11. Default runlevels are still configured in the /etc/inittab file.

12. If successful the home directory of the FTP user in /etc/passwd should be /ftp. You should be able to retain (or restore) the same SELinux contexts as /var/ftp with the **restorecon /ftp** command. That requires appropriate entries in the file_contexts.local file, in the /etc/selinux/targeted/contexts/files directory, based on the appropriate **semanage fcontext** command.

13. On an NTP client configured to point to another system, look at the /etc/ntp.conf file. The **server** directive in that file should point to the desired system, in this case, the physical host. Of course, a test on that system with the **ntpq -p** command won't work unless the physical host is also an NTP server. In real-world configuration, that second host would be an actual NTP server. Once again, you'll need to make sure the ntpd service runs after a reboot, which can be confirmed with an **chkconfig --list ntpd** command.

14. To make sure SELinux is set in permissive mode, run the **sestatus** command.

D

Sample Exam 3: RHCE Sample Exam 1

T he following questions will help measure your understanding of the material presented in this book. As discussed in the introduction, you should be prepared to complete the RHCE exam in 2.0 hours.

Like the RHCSA, the RHCE exam is "closed book." However, you are allowed to use any documentation that can be found on the Red Hat Enterprise Linux computer. While test facilities allow you to make notes, you won't be allowed to take these notes from the testing room.

While the RHCE exam is entirely separate from the RHCSA, you need to pass both exams to receive the RHCE certificate. Nevertheless, you can take the RHCE exam first. While both exams cover some of the same services, the objectives for those services are different.

In most cases, there is no one solution, no single method to solve a problem or install a service. There are a nearly infinite number of options with Linux, so I can't cover all possible scenarios.

Even for these exercises, *do not use a production computer.* A small error in some or all of these exercises may make Linux unbootable. If you're unable to recover from the steps documented in these exercises, you may need to reinstall Red Hat Enterprise Linux. Saving any data that you have on the local system may then not be possible.

Red Hat presents its exams electronically. For that reason, the exams in this book are available from the companion CD, in the Exams/ subdirectory. This exam is in the file named RHCEsampleexam1, and is available in .txt, .doc, and .html formats. For details on how to set up RHEL 6 as a system suitable for a practice exam, refer to Appendix A. Be very sure to set up the repository configured in Chapter 1, Lab 2.

In most cases, there is no one solution, no single method to solve a problem or install a service. There are a nearly infinite number of options with Linux, so I can't cover all possible scenarios.

Don't turn the page until you're finished with the sample exam!

RHCE Sample Exam I Discussion

In this discussion, I'll describe one way to check your work to meet the requirements listed for the Sample 1 RHCE exam. Since there is no one way to set up a Red Hat Enterprise Linux configuration, there is no one right answer for the listed requirements. But there are some general things to remember. You need to make sure your changes work after a reboot. For the RHCE, you'll need to make sure that the services that you set up are active at the appropriate runlevels. For example, if you're configuring Apache, it should be active for at least runlevels 3 and 5.

1. The first task should be straightforward. Users katie and dickens should have accounts on the SSH server (or possibly an LDAP server for the network). While it's possible to limit user access to SSH via TCP Wrappers, the most straightforward way to do so is with the following directive in the main SSH server configuration file:

   ```
   AllowUsers katie
   ```

   Of course, the "proof of the pudding" is the ability for user katie to log in from a remote system on the local network, and for user dickens to be refused such access. In addition, limited access to the local network requires an appropriate limit via an **iptables**-based firewall rule, or an appropriate line in the TCP Wrappers configuration files, /etc/hosts.allow and /etc/hosts.deny.

2. The Samba server will be configured with two different shared directories. The system can be configured with the samba_export_all_rw SELinux boolean, or the directories can be set with the samba_share_t type label. In addition, the most straightforward way to limit access to the given users is with the **allow users** directive in the smb.conf configuration file in appropriate stanzas. The given users should exist in the separate Samba password database. Of course, success is based on the ability of users dickens, tim, and stephanie to access the given directories from a remote system.

3. Since there are no host limits in the vsFTP configuration file, access limits require appropriate rules in iptables-based firewalls and/or TCP Wrappers configuration files. Success is based on anonymous access from the given server1.example.com and physical host systems (along with access prohibited from other systems).

4. NTP servers are limited to the local system by default. Expanding access to the local network requires a change to the /etc/ntp.conf file, in the **restrict**

directive, as well as appropriate open ports in the firewall. You can test the connection remotely with the **ntpq -p ntpserver** command. (Of course, you're welcome to substitute the IP address for the hostname of the NTP server.) Remember, NTP communicates over UDP port 123.

5. While other methods are available, the straightforward way to limit access in the main NFS configuration file (/etc/exports) can be limited to a single host, with a directive such as the following:

```
/home maui.example.com(rw)
```

You should substitute the hostname or IP address of your physical exam system. In addition, you may run into different requirements, such as read-only (ro), no root access (root_squash), and more. Access should be confirmed from the physical host system by mounting the shared NFS directory.

6. The most straightforward way to configure a secure virtual web site is with the help of the standard configuration defined in the ssl.conf file in the /etc/httpd/conf directory. If successful, you'll be able to access the secure web sites https://shost1.example.com and https://shost2.example.com. Since these certificates aren't from an official authority, the "invalid security certificate" message that appears in a browser should not be a problem, assuming the SSL key names are shown in the message.

7. Since a test system is not supposed to have Internet access, you should check access to the caching-only DNS server a bit indirectly with a command like **telnet server1.example.com 53** or **nmap server1.example.com**. Substitute the name or IP address of the DNS server if needed.

8. A daily script can be stored either in the /etc/cron.daily directory or in a user account–based cron configuration file in the /var/spool/cron directory.

9. Success in this step is most straightforward; copy the RPM that you've created to a second system. Install it. If successful, you'll see the README file in the /opt/tcpwrap directory.

10. To configure IP forwarding for both IPv4 and IPv6 addressing, you'll need to add the following directives in /etc/sysctl.conf:

```
net.ipv4.ip_forward=1
net.ipv6.conf.all.forwarding=1
```

11. The time period when the system accounting tool is run is ten minutes, as shown in the default /etc/cron.d/sysstat file. It's easy to change that to five minutes in the noted file.

E

Sample Exam 4: RHCE Sample Exam 2

Тhe following questions will help measure your understanding of the material presented in this book. As discussed in the introduction, you should be prepared to complete the RHCE exam in 2.0 hours.

Like the RHCSA, the RHCE exam is "closed book." However, you are allowed to use any documentation that can be found on the Red Hat Enterprise Linux computer. While test facilities allow you to make notes, you won't be allowed to take these notes from the testing room.

While the RHCE exam is entirely separate from the RHCSA, you need to pass both exams to receive the RHCE certificate. Nevertheless, you can take the RHCE exam first. While both exams cover some of the same services, the objectives for those services are different.

In most cases, there is no one solution, no single method to solve a problem or install a service. There are a nearly infinite number of options with Linux, so I can't cover all possible scenarios.

Even for these exercises, *do not use a production computer*. A small error in some or all of these exercises may make Linux unbootable. If you're unable to recover from the steps documented in these exercises, you may need to reinstall Red Hat Enterprise Linux. Saving any data that you have on the local system may then not be possible.

Red Hat presents its exams electronically. For that reason, the exams in this book are available from the companion CD, in the Exams/ subdirectory. This exam is in the file named RHCEsampleexam2, and is available in .txt, .doc, and .html formats. For details on how to set up RHEL 6 as a system suitable for a practice exam, refer to Appendix A. Be very sure to set up the repository configured in Chapter 1, Lab 2.

In most cases, there is no one solution, no single method to solve a problem or install a service. There are a nearly infinite number of options with Linux, so I can't cover all possible scenarios.

Don't turn the page until you're finished with the sample exam!

RHCE Sample Exam 2 Discussion

In this discussion, I'll describe one way to check your work to meet the requirements listed for the Sample 2 RHCE exam. Since there is no one way to set up a Red Hat Enterprise Linux configuration, there is no one right answer for the listed requirements. But there are some general things to remember. You need to make sure your changes work after a reboot. For the RHCE, you'll need to make sure that the services that you set up are active at the appropriate runlevels. For example, if you're configuring Apache, it should be active for at least runlevels 3 and 5.

1. System logging servers require access through either the TCP or UDP protocols. For our purposes, either is acceptable. In general, if the logging data is mission critical, use TCP. Otherwise, UDP is faster. Options for both are shown in comments in the default /etc/rsyslog.conf file.

   As for the logging client, the last commented directive provides a template. To review, the following directive sends all log messages over TCP port 514, to the logging server named server1.example.com.

   ```
   *.*  @@server1.example.com:514
   ```

2. Since there is no exam requirement to create a Kerberos server, you may not be able to verify the Kerberos client directly. So to verify, review the Kerberos client. For example, based on the question, it should include the following directives in /etc/krb5.conf:

   ```
   default_realm = EXAMPLE.COM
   ```

   In addition, the kdc and admin_server directives in the /etc/krb5.con file should be set to the FQDN of the physical host system. When complete, the /etc/nsswitch.conf file should include

   ```
   passwd:    files sss
   shadow:    files sss
   group:     files sss
   ```

   In addition, the sssd service should be running—now and upon reboot. That can be verified with the **chkconfig --list sssd** command.

3. If successful, you should see the contents of the noted index.html files for each web site.

The httpd.conf file in the /etc/httpd/conf directory includes a commented sample virtual host stanza. You can use it as a template for both virtual hosts. You should also use the SELinux contexts of the /var/www/html directory as a template as well for the /web subdirectory.

4. If you are successful, users elizabeth and fred, and no others, will have access to the cubs subdirectory of the main directory. Both users will have access only from systems on the local network. In the Apache httpd.conf file, there is a template for single home directories. It can be modified to accommodate a group of users.

5. The CGI application should be accessible from the following URL: http://test1.example.com/cgi-bin/good.pl. When you navigate to that URL, the browser should tell you "Good Job!"

6. Given the presumed change to the SELinux ftp_home_dir boolean, you need to pay attention to the vsftpd.conf configuration file in the /etc/vsftpd directory. And in that directory, you'll see that logins by regular users are enabled by default.

7. The default named.conf configuration file is itself sufficient for a caching-only DNS server. To that file, you'll need to add a **forwarders** directive, with the IP address of the physical host system, which presumably has a DNS server.

8. In principle, it should not matter whether you configure Postfix or sendmail as the SMTP server. You should be able to check access with commands like **telnet server1.example.com 25**, only from systems within the local network. The response should reveal the name of the SMTP server. Of course, you can go further with an e-mail client like mutt.

9. When user mike attempts to connect from a given client, the system should prompt for and accept the passphrase defined in the exam question. ("Linux rocks, Windows does not." with the comma and period, but without the quote marks.)

10. When masquerading is configured, connections from internal systems such as server1.example.com appear as if they come from the physical host system. That can be confirmed in log messages associated with user connections. In an **iptables**-based configuration, it adds forwarding rules.

11. Users with an account on the Samba server should be able to connect to their home directories on that server. But the files on that directory won't be accessible unless the samba_enable_home_dirs boolean is enabled.

12. Peers on an NTP server can be enabled in the /etc/ntp.conf file, in place of the **server** directive. Just remember, NTP communicates over UDP port 123. Accordingly, you can't use the **telnet** command to verify the open connection. One way to check if UDP port 123 is open is with the following command: **nmap -sU server1 -p 123**.

13. To avoid responding to the **ping** command, which works over IPv4, the icmp_echo_ignore_all option must be active. You can set that up permanently in the /etc/sysctl.conf file with the **net.ipv4.icmp_echo_ignore_all = 1** directive.

F

About the CD

The CD-ROM included with this book comes complete with the lab files as explained in each chapter and also includes a digital copy of the book. To access the lab files and e-book, insert the CD. Unless you're running a GUI where automounting has been enabled, you'll have to mount the CD with a command such as the following:

```
# mount /dev/cdrom /media
```

System Requirements

The Electronic book requires Adobe Reader, or an equivalent Linux PDF reader such as Evince. As discussed in Chapter 1, the RHCSA exam includes KVM, which Red Hat supports only on 64-bit systems.

Electronic Book

The contents of the Study Guide are provided in PDF format. If you've mounted the CD as suggested earlier, you'll find everything except most of the chapter labs and sample exams in PDF files in the /media directory. When the CD is mounted in that way, you can access files for each chapter in the /media/Chapter1, /media/Chapter2, /media/Chapter3 directories, and so on. Besides the PDF files for individual chapters, you'll also find different files for chapter labs, some scripts, and sample exams, as explained in the body of the book. You'll also find the Glossary in the /media/Glossary directory.

There are many excellent PDF readers available for Linux. Adobe Reader is just one of the options. If you're running RHEL 6, Adobe Reader is available from the RHEL 6 supplementary repository. If you activate that repository, you'll be able to install Adobe Reader with the following command:

```
# yum install acroread
```

Once it is installed, you'll be able to start Adobe Reader from the GUI command line with the **acroread** command.

Alternatively, you can connect to Adobe's Linux repository with the following command, which works with 32-bit and 64-bit systems and may be suitable for RHEL 6 rebuild distributions such as Scientific Linux 6 and CentOS-6:

```
# rpm -ivh http://linuxdownload.adobe.com/adobe-release/adobe-release-i386-
1.0-1.noarch.rpm
```

You can then install Acrobat Reader with the following command:

```
# yum install AdobeReader_enu
```

You'll be prompted with a message similar to the following, where you should accept the Adobe GPG key:

```
Importing GPG key 0xF6777C67 "Adobe Systems Incorporated
(Linux RPM Signing Key) <secure@adobe.com>" from
/etc/pki/rpm-gpg/RPM-GPG-KEY-adobe-linux

Is this ok [y/N]: y
```

The installation of Adobe Reader proceeds, installing dependencies from Red Hat or related repositories. When you first run the **acroread** command based on this installation, you're prompted to accept the license.

Alternatively, you can download an RPM or related archive package from the web site http://get.adobe.com/reader/otherversions/. One possible problem with this download is that there may be dependencies as discussed in Chapter 7. If you choose to download a Linux package from Adobe in that manner, the process may be more difficult. Refer to Chapter 7 for guidance.

Technical Support

For questions regarding the content of the electronic book, please visit www.mhprofessional.com or e-mail customer.service@mcgraw-hill.com. For customers outside the 50 United States, e-mail international_cs@mcgraw-hill.com.

INDEX

G